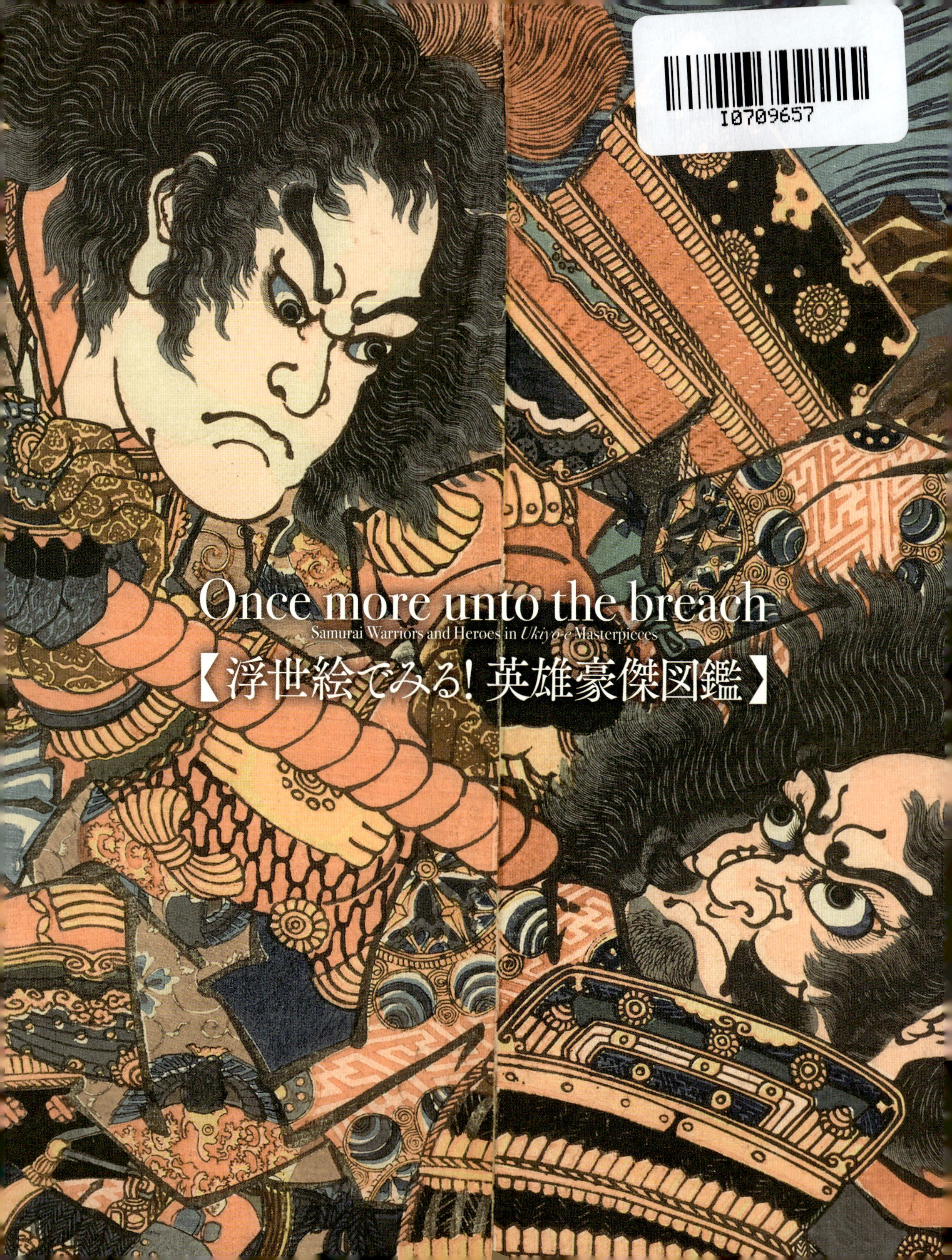

Once more unto the breach
Samurai Warriors and Heroes in *Ukiyo-e* Masterpieces
【浮世絵でみる！英雄豪傑図鑑】

| 目次 | | Contents |

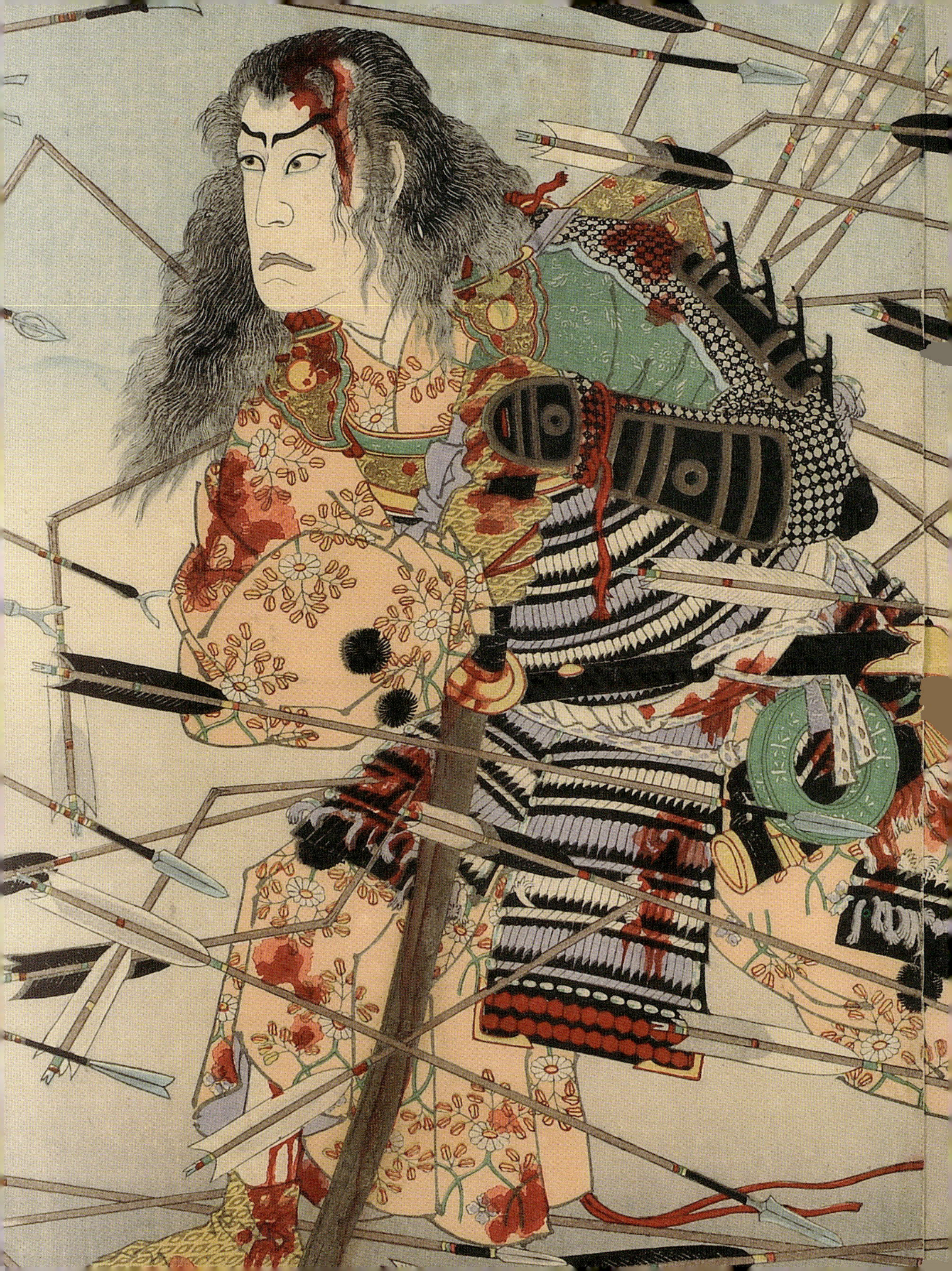

はじめに

伝奇ロマンのスーパー・ヒーローたち

中右 瑛（国際浮世絵学会常任理事）

浮世絵の武者絵には、強き者、美しき者たちへの憧れ、英雄崇拝のこころなど、乱世に生きる男のロマンが息づいている。伝奇ロマンの英雄、豪傑、戦乱時代の武将たちサムライが数多く登場する。

剣豪・宮本武蔵の武勇伝は講談や小説に登場し多くの人々に語りつがれてきた。

源為朝は馬琴の冒険小説に登場し波瀾万丈の活躍をした。

武将・源義経（牛若丸）は知略にたけ武勲をたてるが兄・頼朝に疎まれ悲劇の武将として判官びいきの精神が日本人の心に印象づけられた。老若男女の誰もがその破天荒でスリリングな冒険譚、ドラマチックな活躍にハラハラドキドキ胸を踊らされてきた。ときにはゴジラもどきの巨大な怪獣と対峙する。

源頼光や弁慶（鬼若丸）ら豪傑、天下統一をかけた平清盛、源頼朝ら源平一族、戦国の上杉謙信、武田信玄、織田信長、立身出世を願った豊臣秀吉、徳川家康らの武将たちの国取り合戦は歴史を彩った。そして、子供たちのアイドル・金太郎、桃太郎らヒーローたちの登場に、胸のすく痛快さを覚える。

当時の徳川幕政の時代、秀吉の立身出世などの物語は敵対者を美化するとしてご法度となり、明治になって日の目を見た。楠木正成の父と子の話も教科書で蘇る。

歌舞伎芝居の世界に人気者が多く登場する。天下の大泥棒・石川五右衛門や毛剃九右衛門、蝦蟇の忍者・天竺徳兵衛、哀話・平敦盛と熊谷直実、男伊達・野晒悟助、忠臣蔵の大石内蔵助など人気者は多い。

浮世絵は、史実、伝奇、読本、講談、歌舞伎芝居の世界を美しく具現化している。

ショッキングで奇想天外な発想、強烈なフォルム、カラフルな色彩美、ドラマチックな冒険ロマンの劇画の世界が広がる。映画やテレビがなかった時代の娯楽のひとつである。

サムライ、ヒーローたちよ！ 豪傑、人気者たちよ！ 集え！ 浮世絵の武者絵に喝采を惜しまない。

The Superheroes of Romantic Legend

Nakau Ei (Permanent Board Member of the International Ukiyo-e Society)

Ukiyo-e woodblock prints featuring Japanese warriors pulse with romantic passion for men who struggled through turbulent times, with longing for strength and beauty, and with worship of heroism. Legendary heroes, gallant men, and the "samurai" generals of the eras of civil war fill our romantic legends.

Heroic tales about the master swordsman Miyamoto Musashi, for example, are known far and wide through oral storytelling and novels. Minamoto no Tametomo's dramatic and lively adventures are narrated in Takizawa Bakin's *Strange Tales of the Crescent Moon*. The brilliance of the great commander Minamoto no Yoshitsune (known as Ushiwakamaru in his youth) gained him many battlefield glories, while the tragedies that befell him as a magistrate after being betrayed by his brother Yoritomo have permanently left their mark on the Japanese soul. Young and old, men and women – few amongst us have not felt our heats race with these warriors' singular and thrilling adventures and their breathtaking physical feats. Even giant monsters on the scale of Godzilla fail to intimidate them.

General Minamoto no Yorimitsu and Benkei (also known as Oniwakamaru), men who aimed to unify Japan like Taira no Kiyomori and Minamoto no Yoritomo of the Genpei clans, Uesugi Kenshin, Takeda Shingen, and Oda Nobunaga of the Sengoku Period, Toyotomi Hideyoshi who rose to the greatest

heights from the humblest of origins, and Tokugawa Ieyasu – all great military leaders to whom we owe a colorful national history of coups, wars, and power struggles. And how heroes like Kintarō and Momotarō, idols of Japanese childhood, delight the heart!

Under the Tokugawa Shogunate, the story of Hideyoshi's rise from obscurity was banned as a glorification of a Tokugawa enemy. It was finally popularized in the Meiji period, when it stood next to Kusunoki Masashige and his son Masatsura's acts of loyalty as a model of behavior in national textbooks.

Warriors were also popular on the kabuki stage, including the great thief Ishikawa Goemon, the pirate Kezori Kuemon, ninja Tenjiku Tokubee with his giant toad, the tragic story of Taira no Atsumori and Kumagai Naozane, the chivalrous Nozarashi Gosuke, and Ōishi Kuranosuke of the Forty-Seven Rōnin.

Enriched by history, legends, popular novels, oral storytelling, and the kabuki stage, ukiyo-e prints offer a world of shocking and fantastic imagination, intense visual forms, beautiful colors, and dramatic romantic adventures. Imagine how much more brilliant these images must have appeared in an age before movies and television.

Hear ye, heroic samurai! Famed and gallant men of the sword! Come hither, and show our dear readers that warrior woodblock prints are second to none.

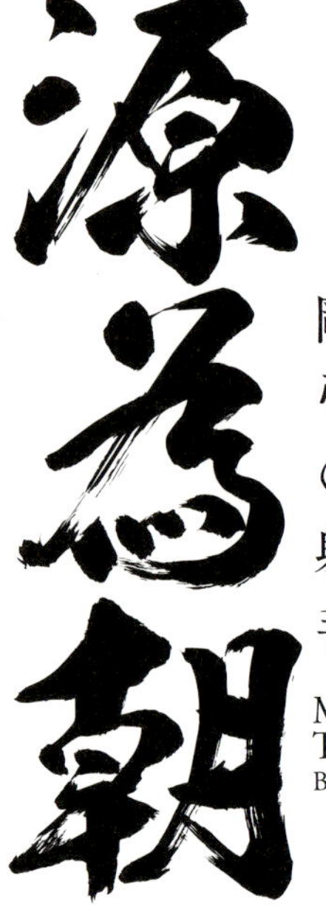

源為朝

蛮勇極めし
剛弓の射手

Minamoto no
Tametomo

Brave Heroes and Gallant Men

6

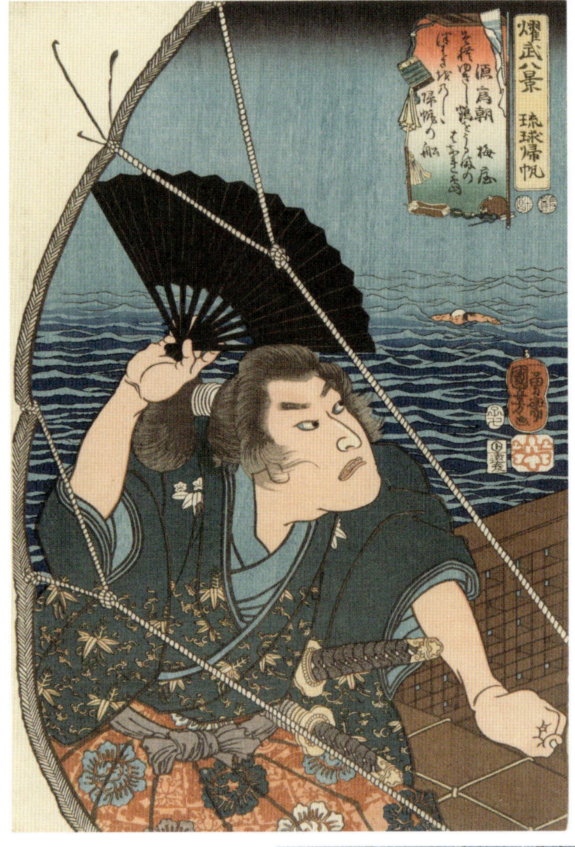

平安時代の武将で、曲亭馬琴の読本『椿説弓張月』の主人公。為義の第八
男、母は摂津国江口の遊女。九州に勢力を張り、鎮西八郎と呼ばれる。保元
の乱で崇徳上皇について敗れ、伊豆に流罪。のちに自害した不遇の英雄。琉
球に渡り、初代琉球王の舜天の父となったという伝説が残る。

Minamoto no Tametomo was a general during the Heian period (794-1185) and
the hero of Takizawa Bakin's *Strange Tales of the Crescent Moon* (*Chinsetsu
yumiharizuki*, 1807-11). He was the eighth son of Minamoto no Tameyoshi, and
his mother is said to be a woman of the pleasure quarters in Eguchi, in Settsu
Province, modern-day Osaka. He was also known as Chinzei Hachirō (Eighth Son
Who Quells the West) for the influence he wielded in the western island of
Kyushu. Defeated while fighting for Emperor Sutoku during the Hōgen Rebellion
(1156), Tametomo was banished to the Izu Islands. His life ended unhappily in
seppuku, ritual suicide. Legends also exist claiming that he sailed for the Ryūkyū
Islands (Okinawa) and fathered Shunten, the first Ryūkyū King.

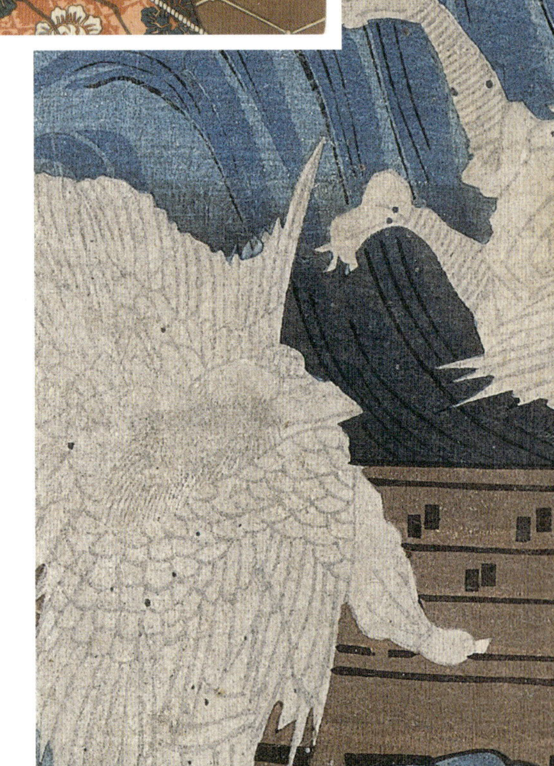

【燿武八景 琉球帰帆 源為朝】歌川国芳 嘉永5年（1852）
琉球から帰る船に乗り込んだ為朝。家来の喜平治が後を追う。

"Eight Scenes of Military Brilliance: Ship Bound for Ryūkyū,
Minamoto no Tametomo" by Utagawa Kuniyoshi

This print shows Tametomo aboard a ship bound for the Ryūkyū Islands.
His loyal retainer Kiheiji swims after him in the background.

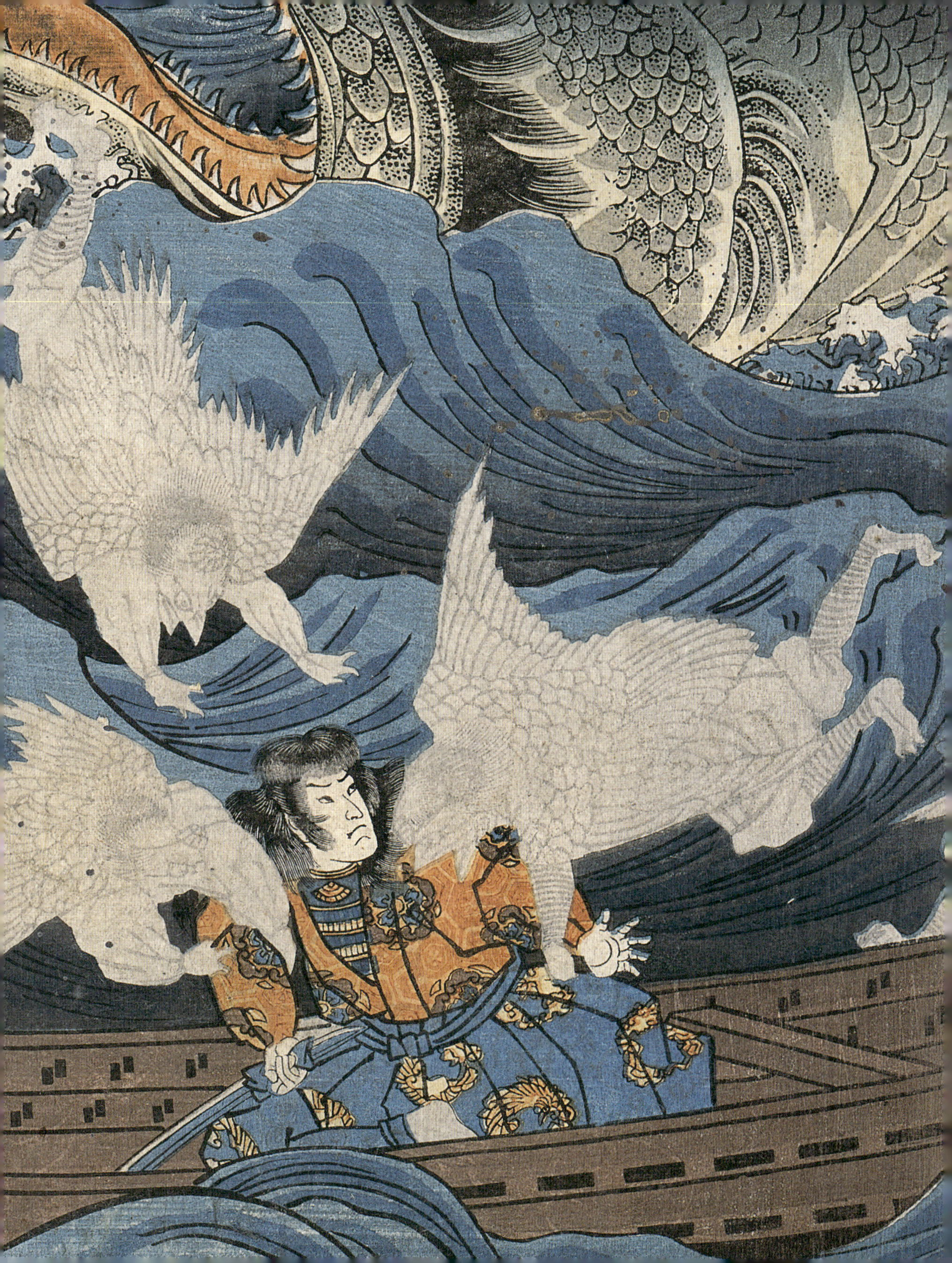

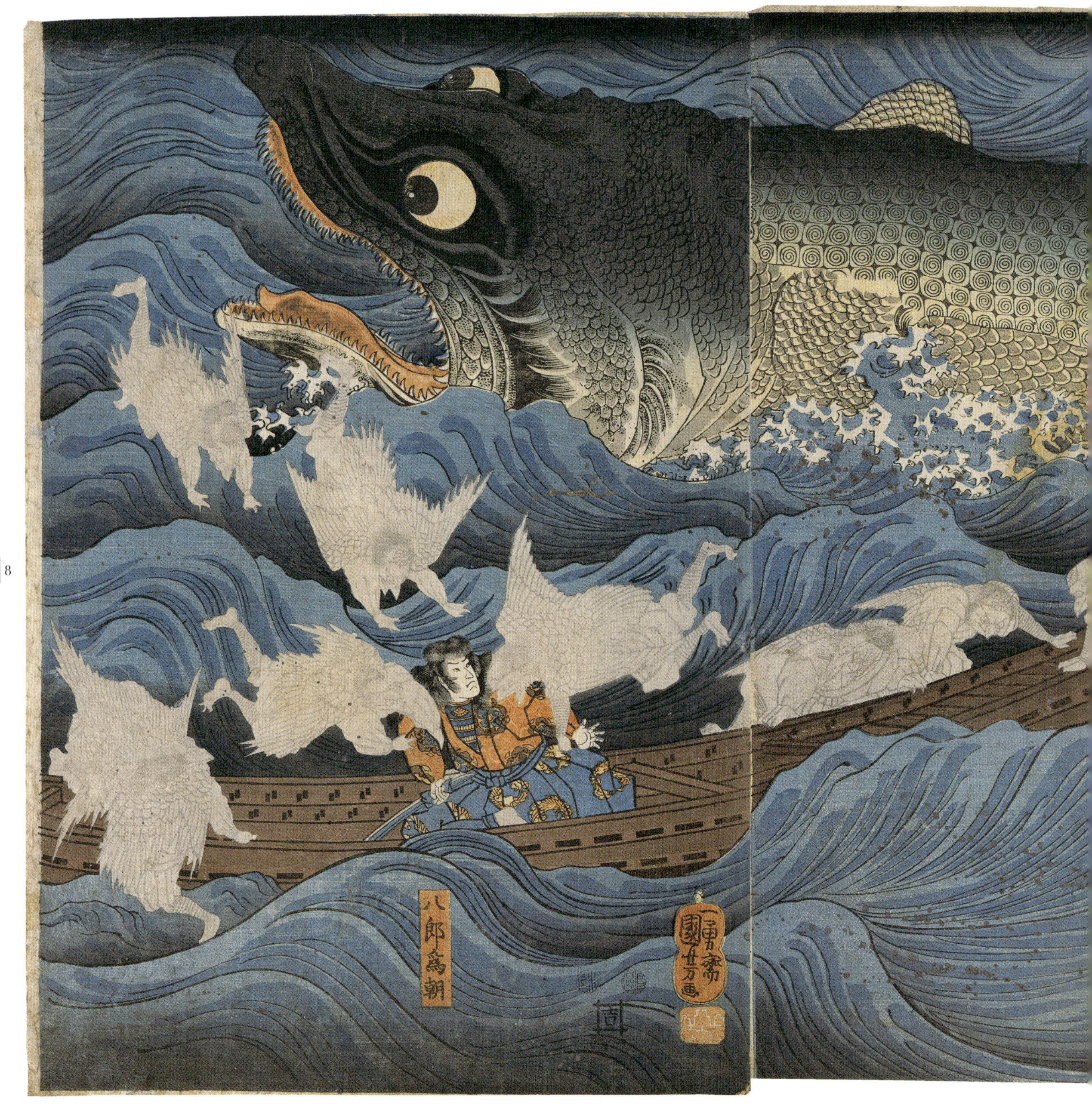

8

【讃岐院眷属をして為朝をすくふ図】歌川国芳　嘉永4年（1851）

為朝一門を乗せた船を大嵐が襲う。妻白縫姫は海神の怒りを鎮めるため入水し、為朝は讃岐院（崇徳上皇）が遣わした天狗に救い出される。家来の高間夫婦が憑依した巨大な鰐鮫が子舜天丸と喜平治を背中に乗せる。

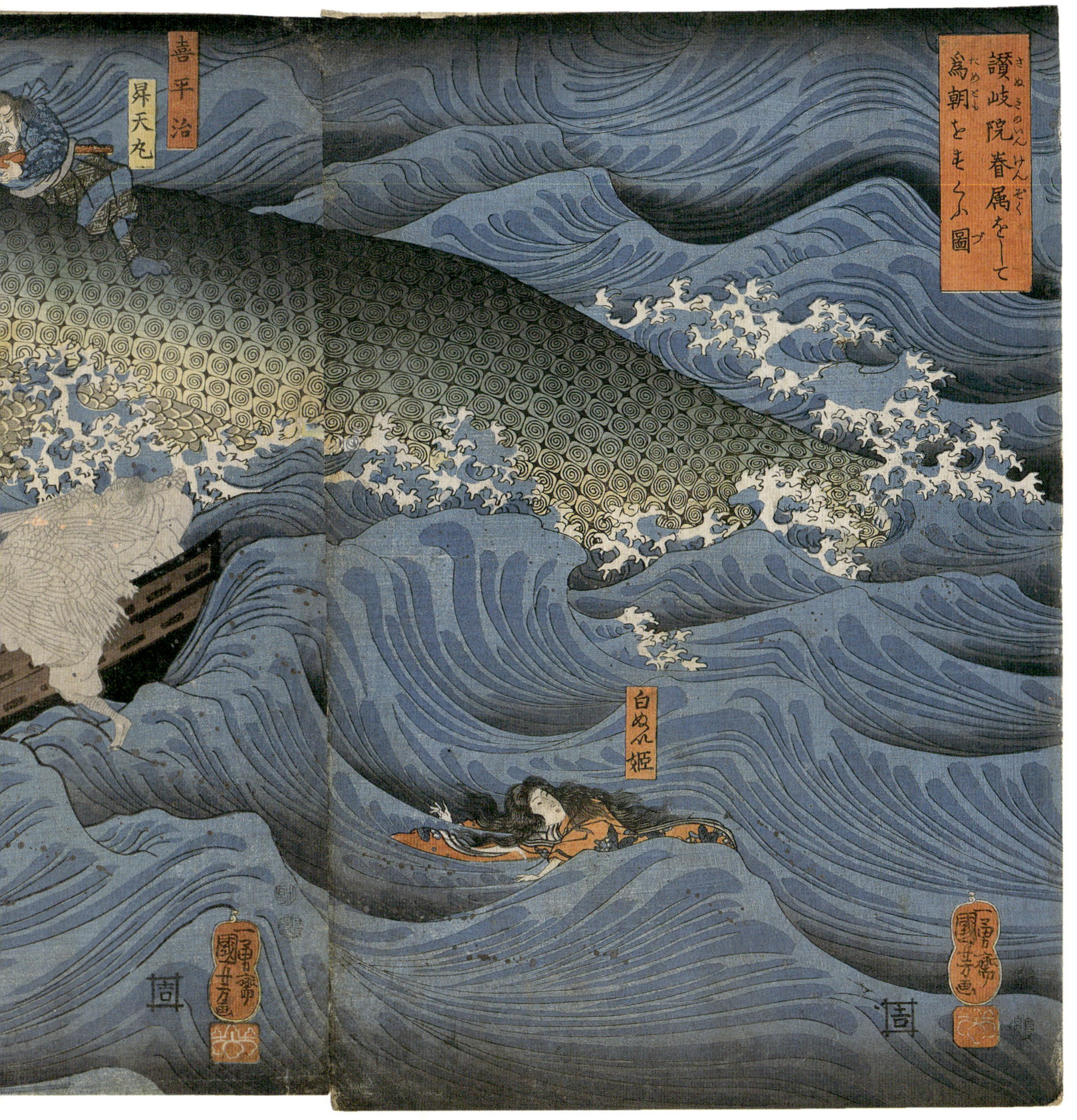

"Retired Emperor Sanuki Sends Allies to Rescue Tametomo" by Utagawa Kuniyoshi

Tametomo's boat is assailed by a raging storm. His wife, Princess Shiranui, leaps into the water to pacify the angry water god.
Tametomo is saved by tengu goblins dispatched by Retired Emperor Sanuki (Sutoku).
The loyal Takama no Tarō and his wife transform into a giant "crocodile shark." Tametomo's son Sutemaru and his retainer Kiheiji ride on the beast's back to safety.

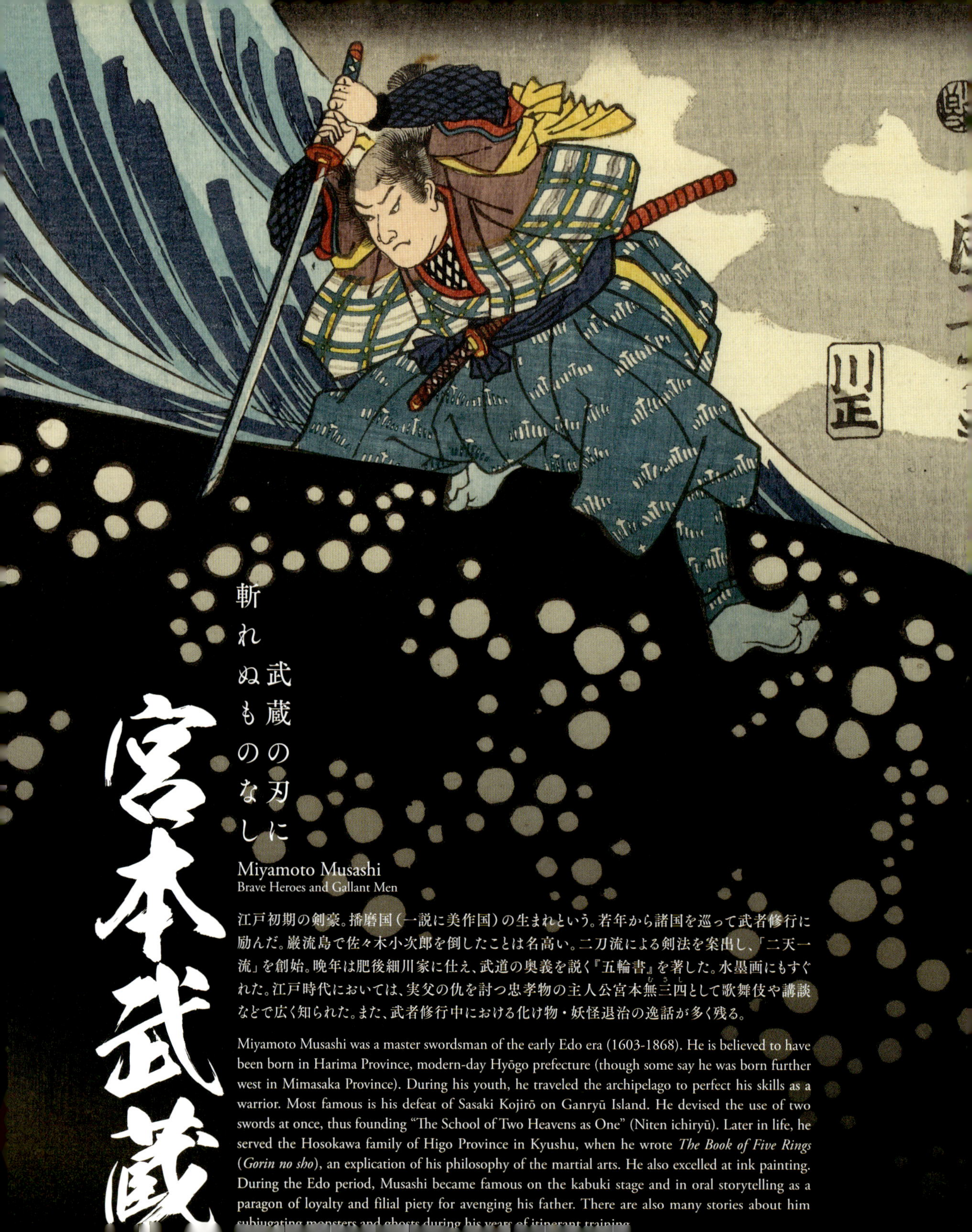

宮本武蔵

Miyamoto Musashi
Brave Heroes and Gallant Men

江戸初期の剣豪。播磨国（一説に美作国）の生まれという。若年から諸国を巡って武者修行に励んだ。巌流島で佐々木小次郎を倒したことは名高い。二刀流による剣法を案出し、「二天一流」を創始。晩年は肥後細川家に仕え、武道の奥義を説く『五輪書』を著した。水墨画にもすぐれた。江戸時代においては、実父の仇を討つ忠孝物の主人公宮本無三四として歌舞伎や講談などで広く知られた。また、武者修行中における化け物・妖怪退治の逸話が多く残る。

Miyamoto Musashi was a master swordsman of the early Edo era (1603-1868). He is believed to have been born in Harima Province, modern-day Hyōgo prefecture (though some say he was born further west in Mimasaka Province). During his youth, he traveled the archipelago to perfect his skills as a warrior. Most famous is his defeat of Sasaki Kojirō on Ganryū Island. He devised the use of two swords at once, thus founding "The School of Two Heavens as One" (Niten ichiryū). Later in life, he served the Hosokawa family of Higo Province in Kyushu, when he wrote *The Book of Five Rings* (*Gorin no sho*), an explication of his philosophy of the martial arts. He also excelled at ink painting. During the Edo period, Musashi became famous on the kabuki stage and in oral storytelling as a paragon of loyalty and filial piety for avenging his father. There are also many stories about him subjugating monsters and ghosts during his years of itinerant training.

宮本武蔵ハ肥後の産ゆして
後豊前小倉に来つて奉仕をます
諸国をめぐつて劔術を修行せし
ある時肥前の国の海上ゆて
大ひなる背美鯨をさ〜と〜

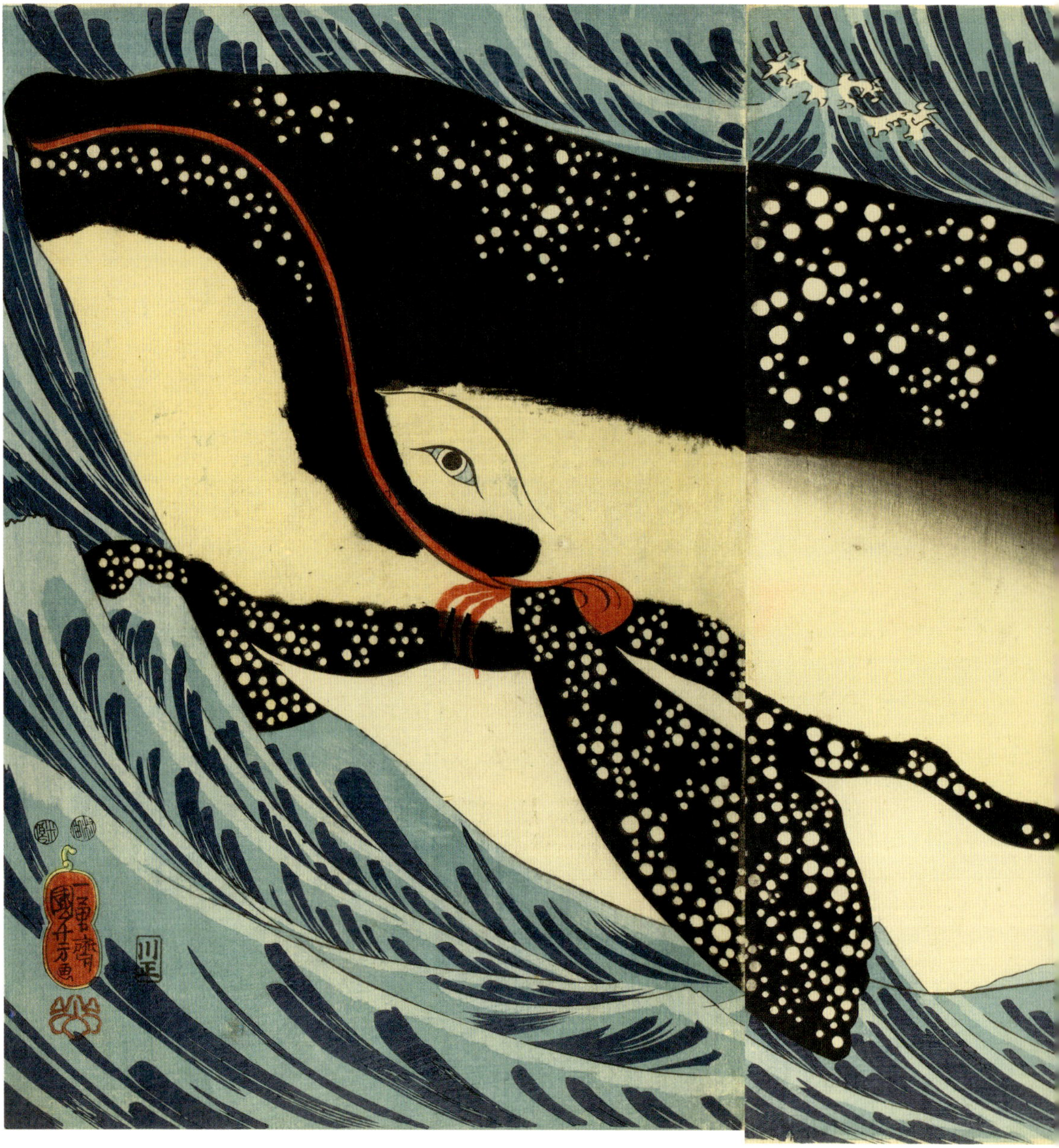

12

【宮本武蔵の鯨退治】 歌川国芳　弘化4年〜嘉永3年（1847-51）頃　ギャラリー紅屋収蔵
武者修行しながら実父の仇を追う武蔵。ある時、船に乗ると、海上に巨大な背美鯨が現れる。
武蔵はこれに飛び乗り、刀を突きたてる。

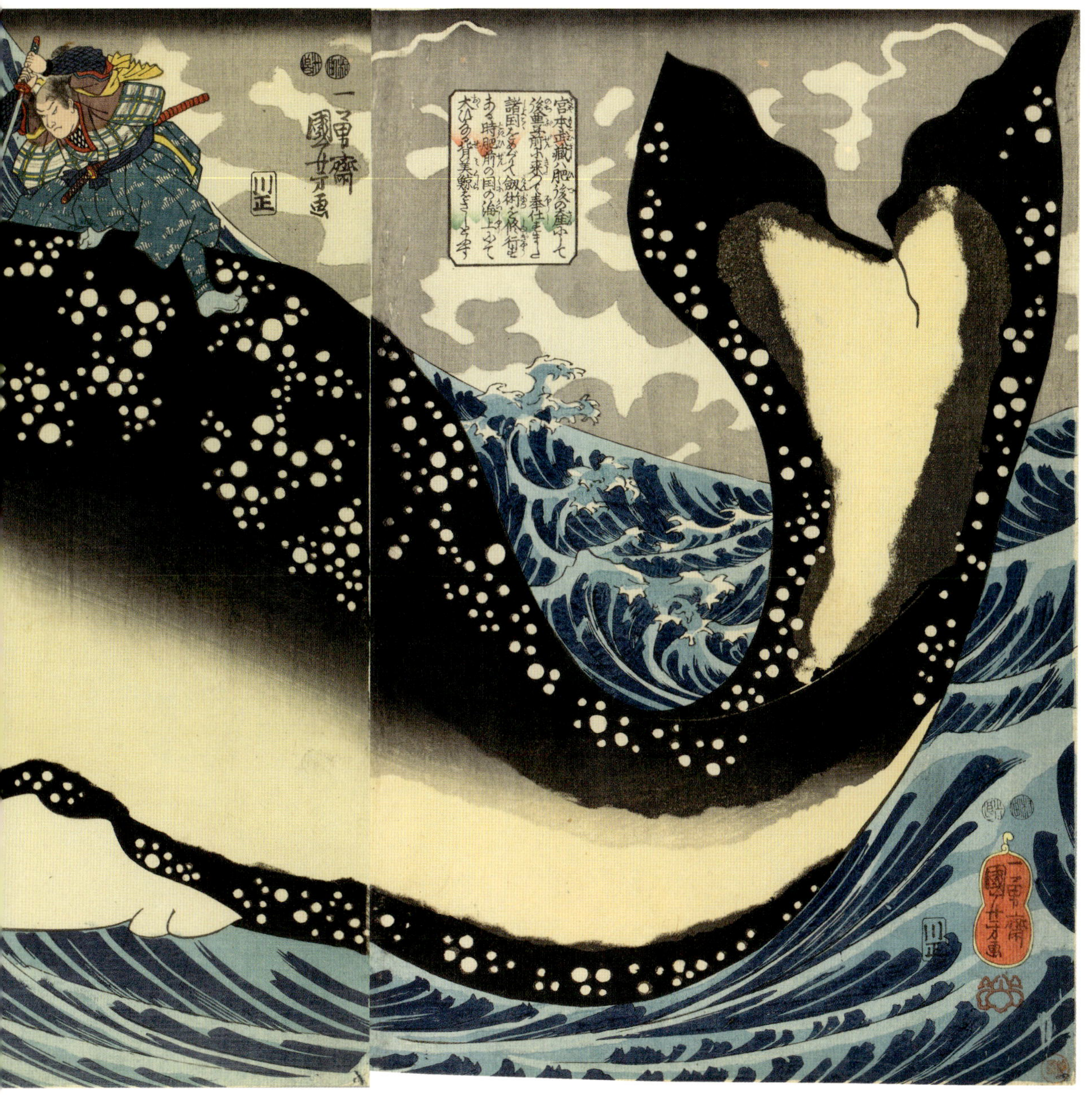

"Miyamoto Musashi Vanquishes the Whale" by Utagawa Kuniyoshi, Gallery Beniya Collection

While traveling the country in training, Musashi seeks to avenge his father.
A giant baleen whale appears beside his ship. Musashi leaps upon him and sinks his sword into his back.

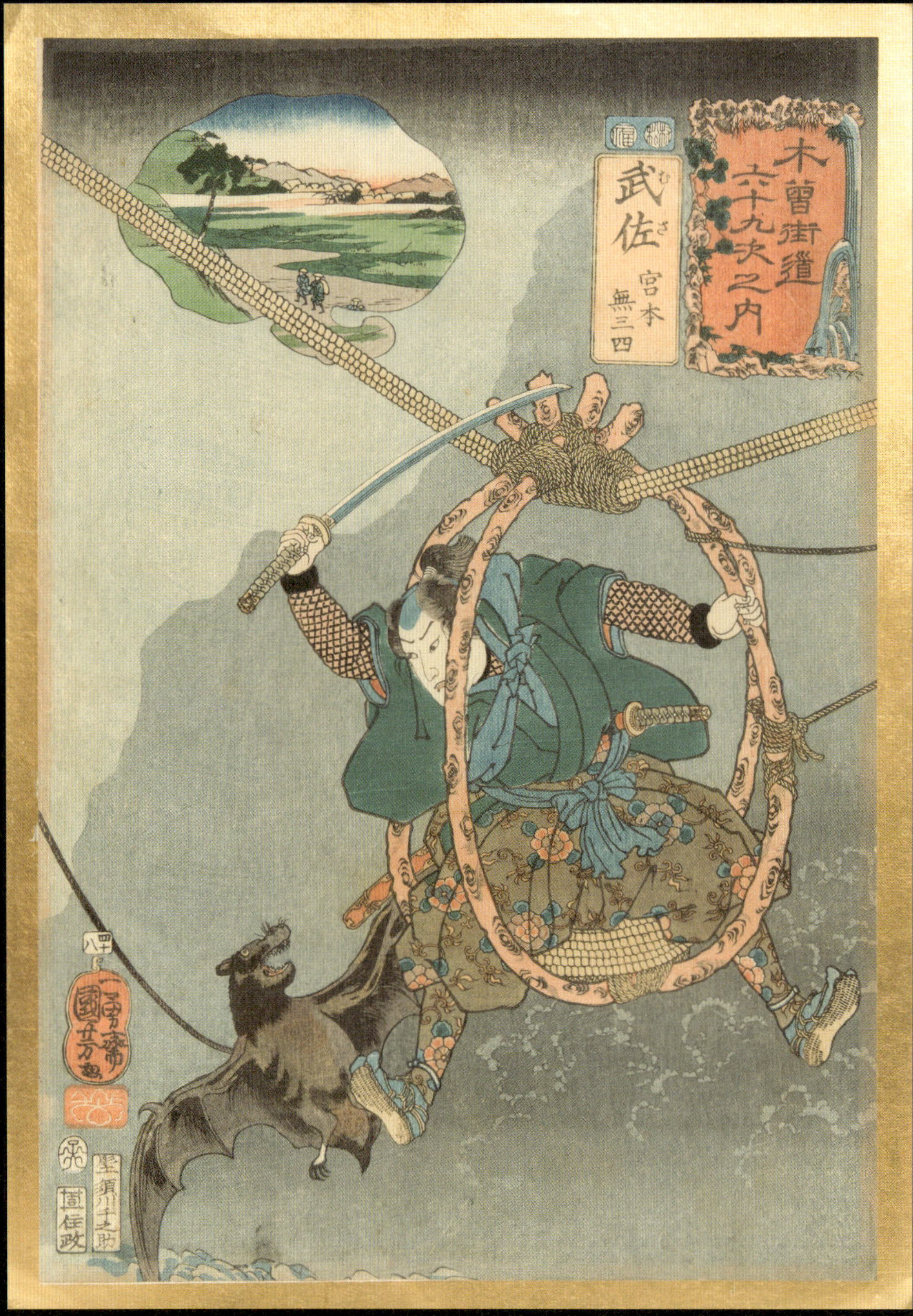

【木曽街道六十九次之内 武佐 宮本無三四】歌川国芳　嘉永5年（1852）

諸国修行の途中、空飛ぶ妖怪野衾（のぶすま）に出逢った武蔵は、籠渡しに乗ってこれを斬りつけ退治する。
野衾とはムササビのお化けで、長い年月を生きた蝙蝠が化けるといわれている。

"Sixty-Nine Stations of the Kiso Kaidō: Musa, Miyamoto Musashi" by Utagawa Kuniyoshi

While traveling during his youth, Musashi confronts a yōkai known as the nobusuma, leaping into a rope basket to cut the monster down. Resembling a flying squirrel, the nobusuma is said to be a bat that turned into a monster due to old age.

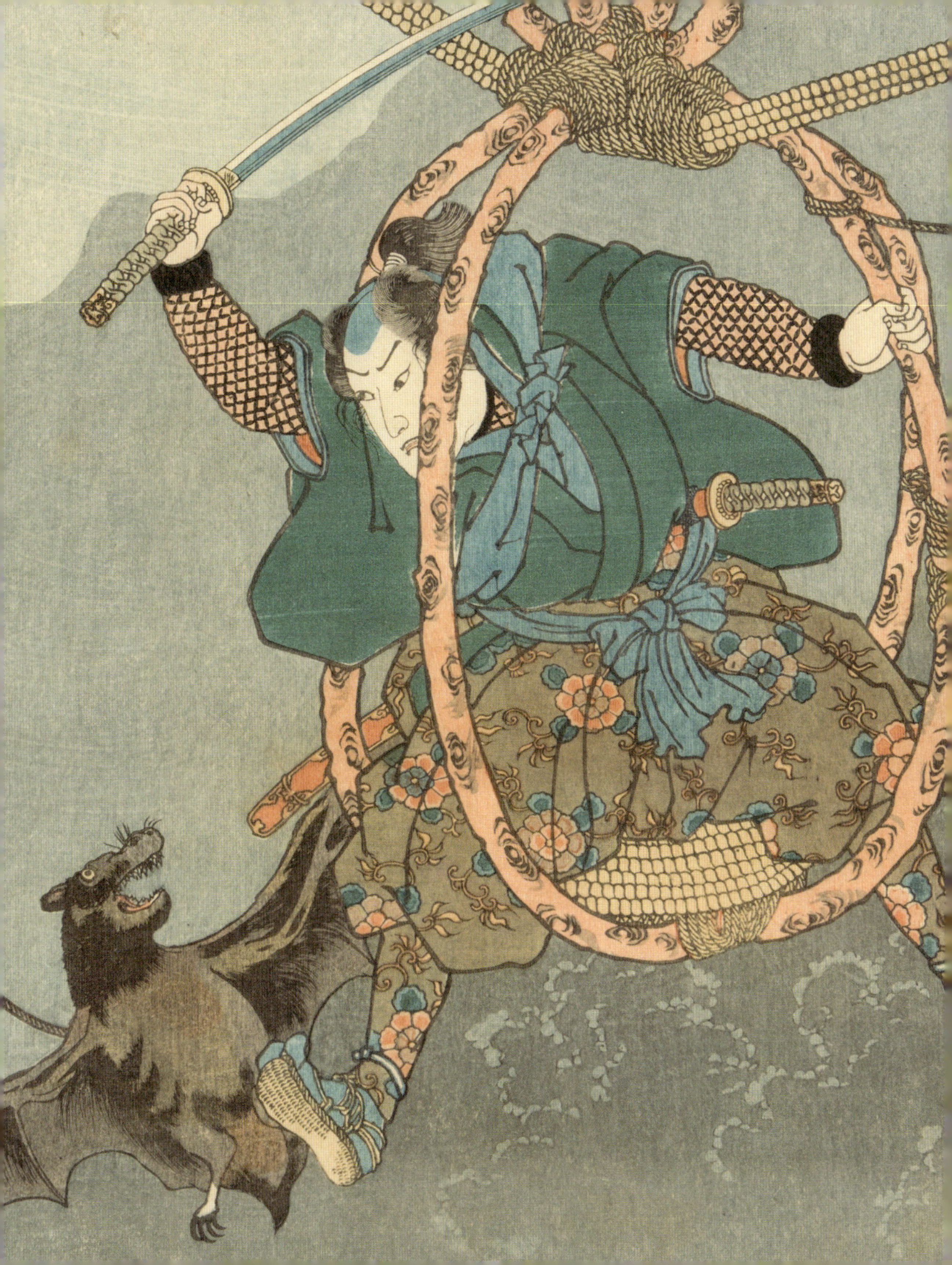

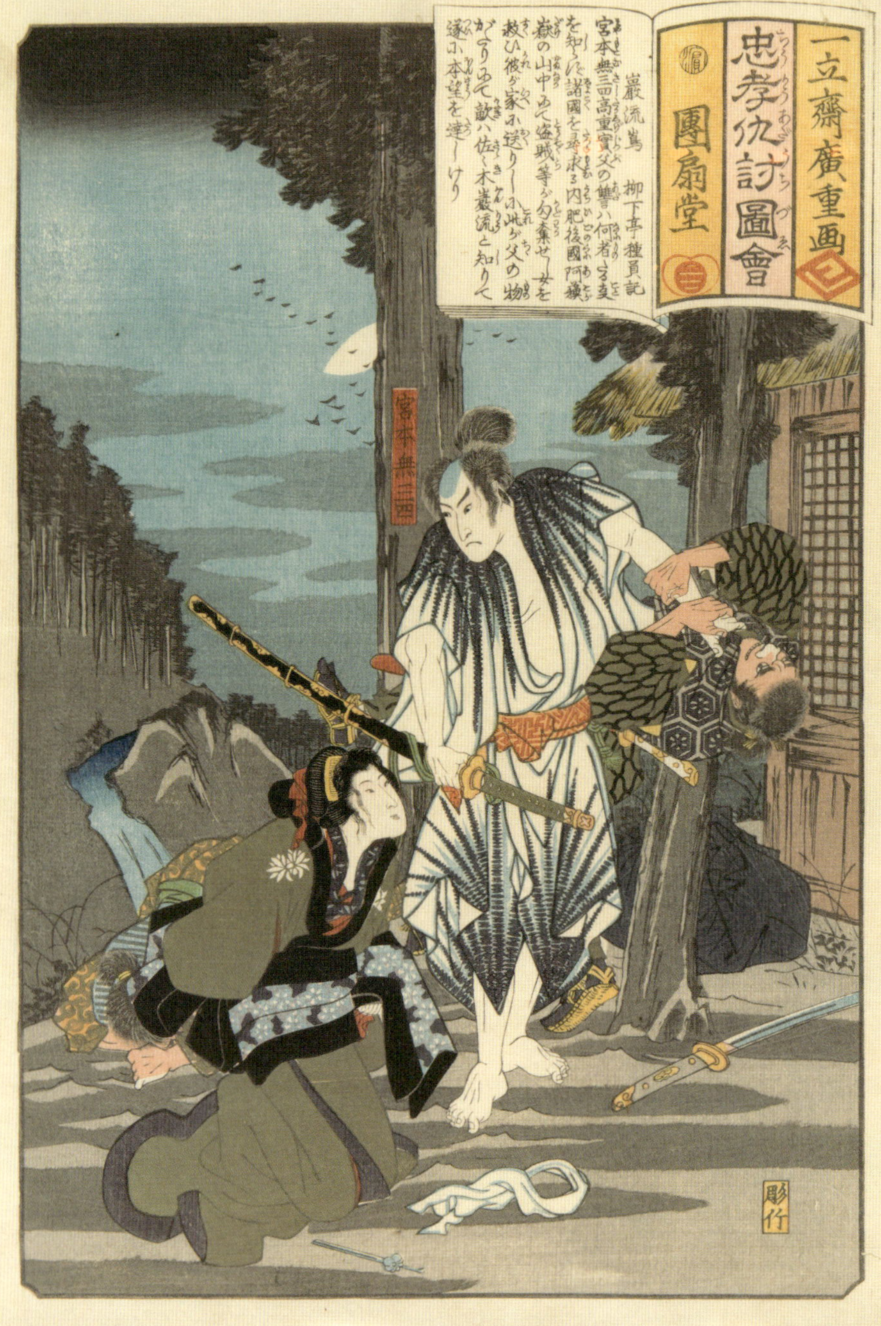

【忠孝仇討図会 巌流島】歌川広重 天保14〜弘化3年（1843-46）頃

阿蘇の山中で盗賊に誘拐された娘を助ける武蔵。
娘の父の話から、仇敵が佐々木巌流（小次郎）であることを知る。

"Pictures of Loyalty and Filial Piety , Ganryū Island" by Utagawa Hiroshige

Deep in the mountains of Aso in Kyushu, Musashi saves a young woman after she was kidnapped by a bandit.
In talking with the girl's father, Musashi learns who killed his father: Sasaki Kojirō.

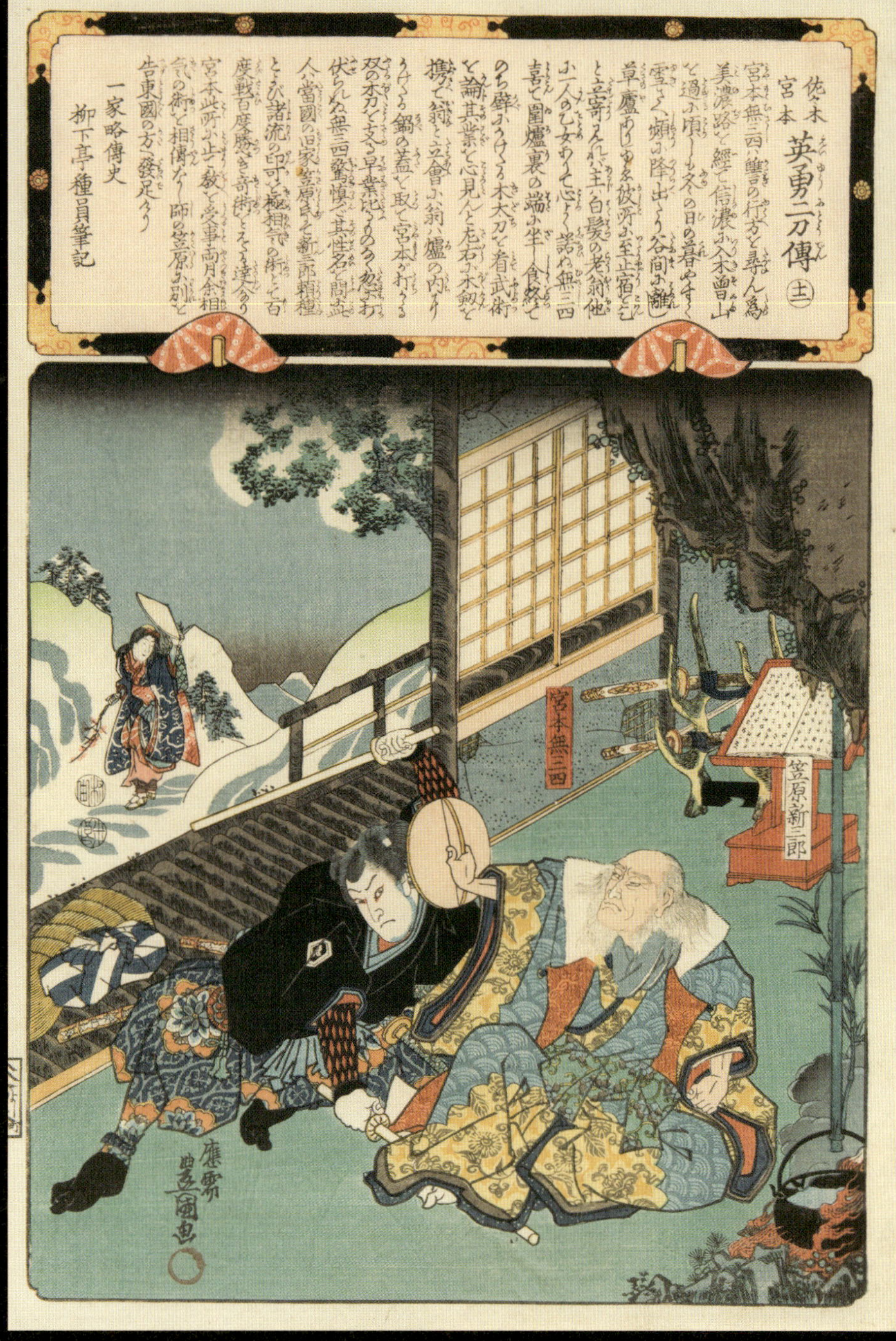

【佐々木宮本英雄二刀伝 十二】歌川国貞（三代豊国）弘化4年～嘉永3年（1847-51）

信濃国の山中に住む老人笠原新三郎の武芸論に感銘を受け、武蔵は手合わせを願う。
二本の木刀で武蔵が仕掛けると、相気の術を用いて鍋蓋であざやかにかわした。

Tale of Two Swords: The Heroes Sasaki Kojirō and Miyamoto Musashi, No. 12" by Utagawa Kunisada (Toyokuni III)

In the mountains of Shinano Province (present-day Nagano) lived an old man named Kasahara Shinzaburō. Impressed by the man's theories of the martial arts, Musashi requests a duel. Musashi attacks him with double wooden swords, but the man easily parries with the wooden lid of a cauldron.

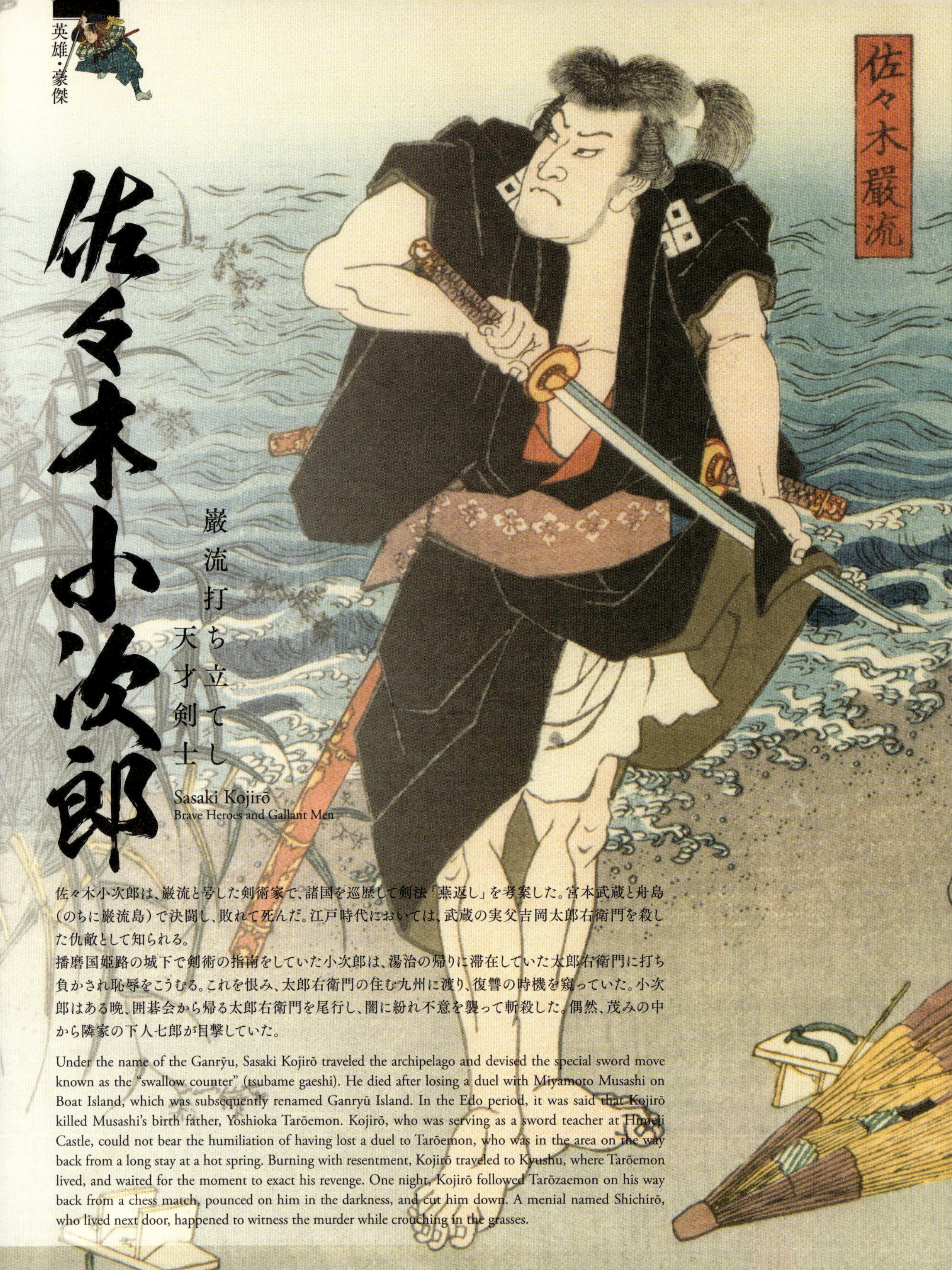

佐々木小次郎

巖流打ち立てし
天才剣士

Sasaki Kojirō
Brave Heroes and Gallant Men

佐々木小次郎は、巖流と号した剣術家で、諸国を巡歴して剣法「燕返し」を考案した。宮本武蔵と舟島（のちに巖流島）で決闘し、敗れて死んだ。江戸時代においては、武蔵の実父吉岡太郎右衛門を殺した仇敵として知られる。

播磨国姫路の城下で剣術の指南をしていた小次郎は、湯治の帰りに滞在していた太郎右衛門に打ち負かされ恥辱をこうむる。これを恨み、太郎右衛門の住む九州に渡り、復讐の時機を窺っていた。小次郎はある晩、囲碁会から帰る太郎右衛門を尾行し、闇に紛れ不意を襲って斬殺した。偶然、茂みの中から隣家の下人七郎が目撃していた。

Under the name of the Ganrȳu, Sasaki Kojirō traveled the archipelago and devised the special sword move known as the "swallow counter" (tsubame gaeshi). He died after losing a duel with Miyamoto Musashi on Boat Island, which was subsequently renamed Ganryū Island. In the Edo period, it was said that Kojirō killed Musashi's birth father, Yoshioka Tarōemon. Kojirō, who was serving as a sword teacher at Himeji Castle, could not bear the humiliation of having lost a duel to Tarōemon, who was in the area on the way back from a long stay at a hot spring. Burning with resentment, Kojirō traveled to Kyushu, where Tarōemon lived, and waited for the moment to exact his revenge. One night, Kojirō followed Tarōzaemon on his way back from a chess match, pounced on him in the darkness, and cut him down. A menial named Shichirō, who lived next door, happened to witness the murder while crouching in the grasses.

【佐々木宮本英雄二刀伝 二】歌川国貞（三代豊国）弘化4年〜嘉永3年（1847-51）頃
"A Tale of Two Swords: The Heroes Sasaki Kojirō and Miyamoto Musashi, No. 2" by Utagawa Kunisada (Toyokuni III)

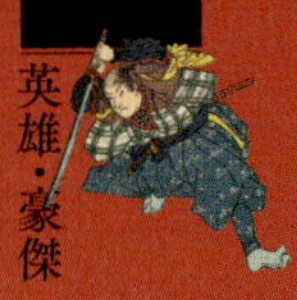

犬塚信乃　犬飼見八

珠が導く運命の徒

【八犬伝】

Inuzuka Shino
and Inukai Genpachi

 Brave Heroes and Gallant Men

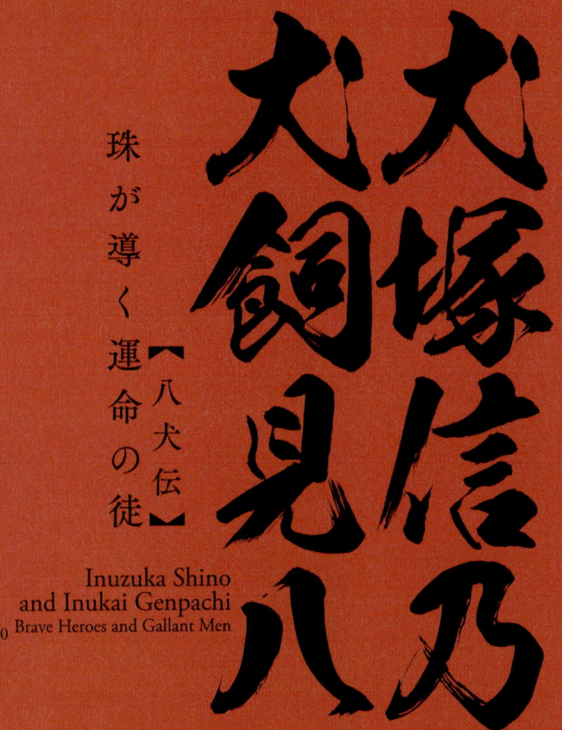

曲亭馬琴の読本『南総里見八犬伝』は、室町時代の下総国の豪族里見家の興亡を背景に、仁・義・礼・智・忠・信・孝・悌の珠を持つ八犬士の活躍を描いた物語である。

八犬士の一人犬塚信乃は父から託された足利家の宝刀村雨丸をすり替えられ、嫌疑をかけられる。同じく八犬士の犬飼見八は足利成氏の命を受け、信乃を捕えようとする。

Set against the rise and fall of the powerful Satomi Clan of Shimōsa Province (modern-day Chiba prefecture) during the Muromachi period (1336-1573), Takizawa Bakin's epic novel *The Chronicles of the Eight Dog Heroes of the Satomi Clan of Nansō Hakkenden* (1814-1842) features the adventures of eight "dog" samurai. Each carries a crystal ball representing an attribute: benevolence, justice, propriety, wisdom, loyalty, faith, filial piety, and respect for one's elders. One of the eight, Inuzuka Shino, has been entrusted by his father with a famous sword that belongs to the Ashikaga clan, and is suspected of wrongdoing when it is stolen. Another of the eight, Inukai Genpachi, has been ordered by Ashikaga Shigeuji to capture Shino.

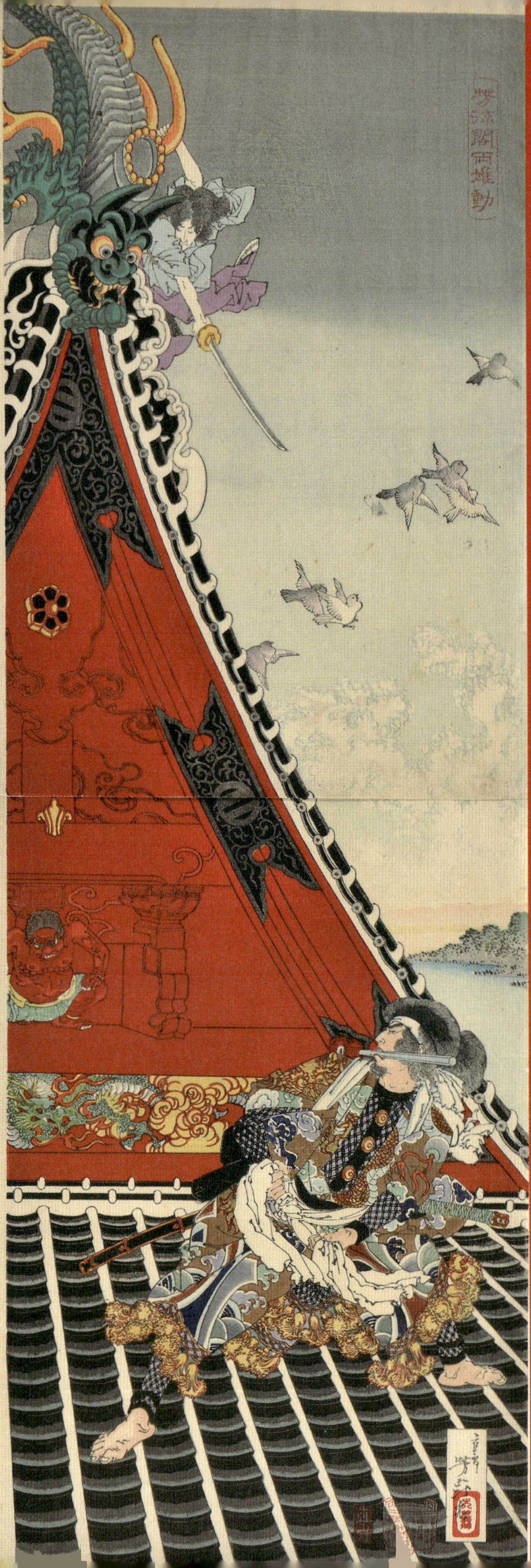

【芳涼閣両雄動】月岡芳年

明治18年（1885）西井コレクション収蔵

"Two Brave Men on the Roof of the Hōryūkaku,"
by Tsukioka Yoshitoshi, Nishii Collection

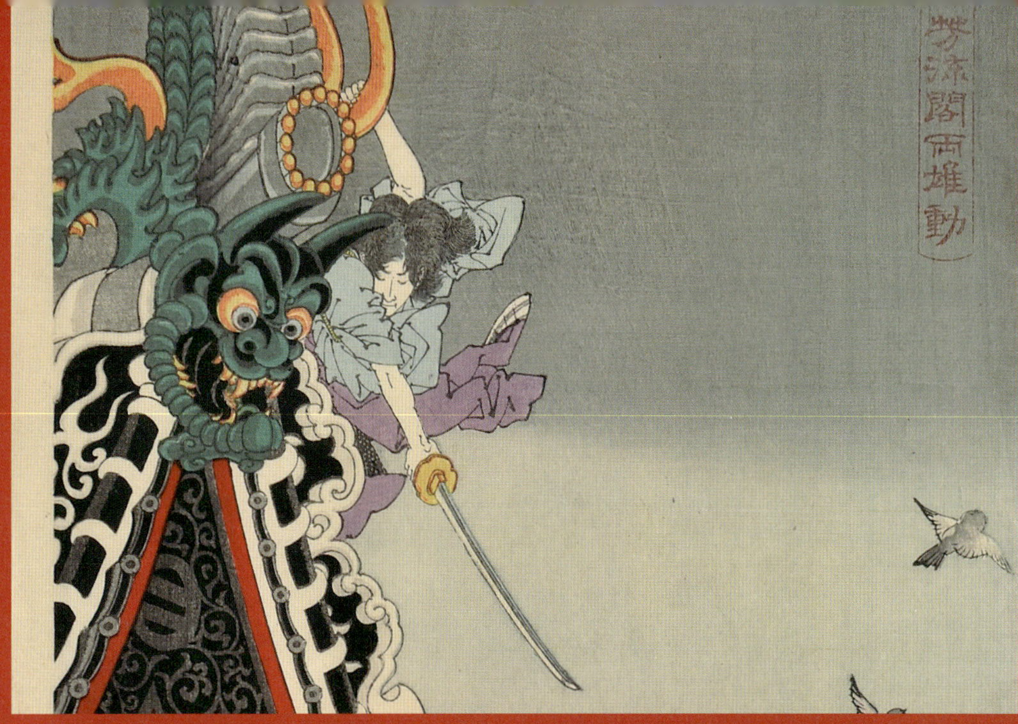
芳流閣両雄動

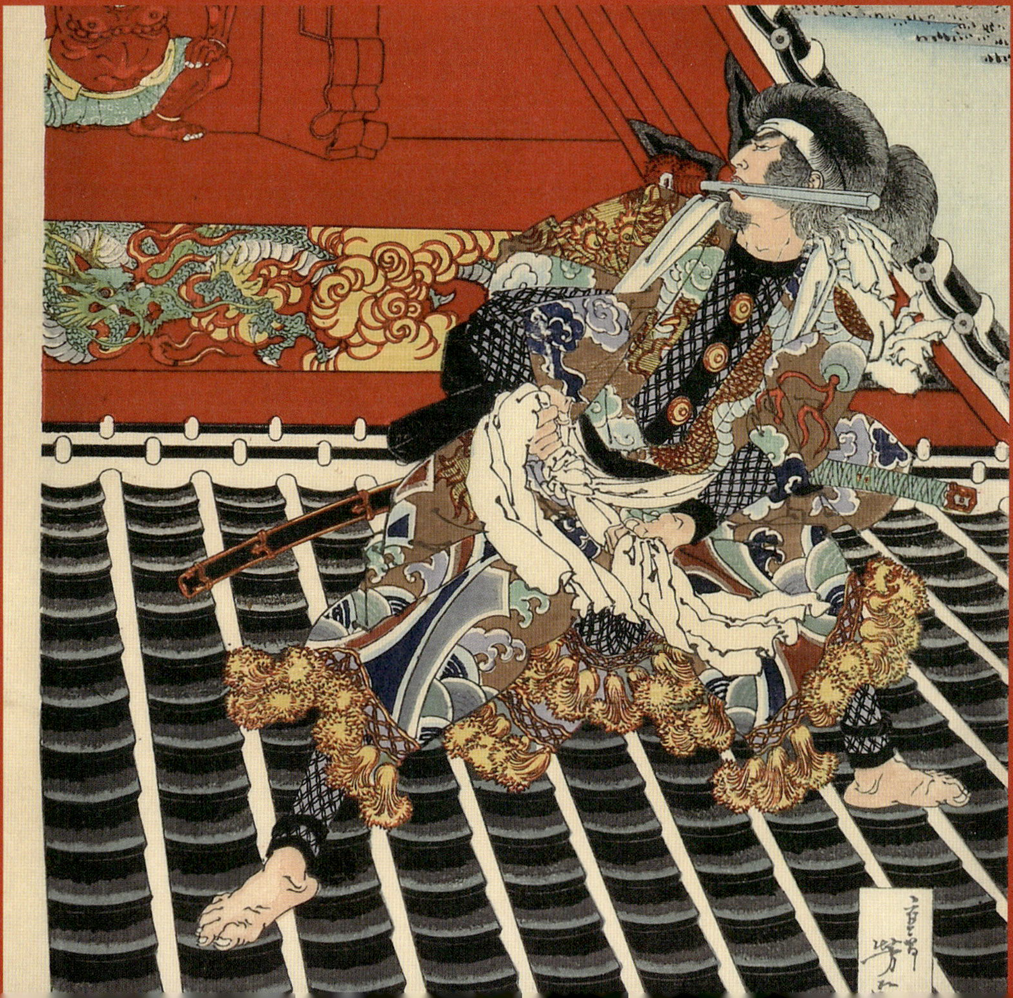

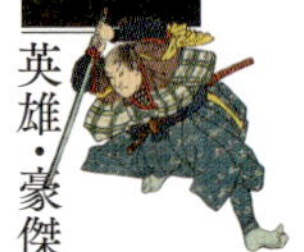

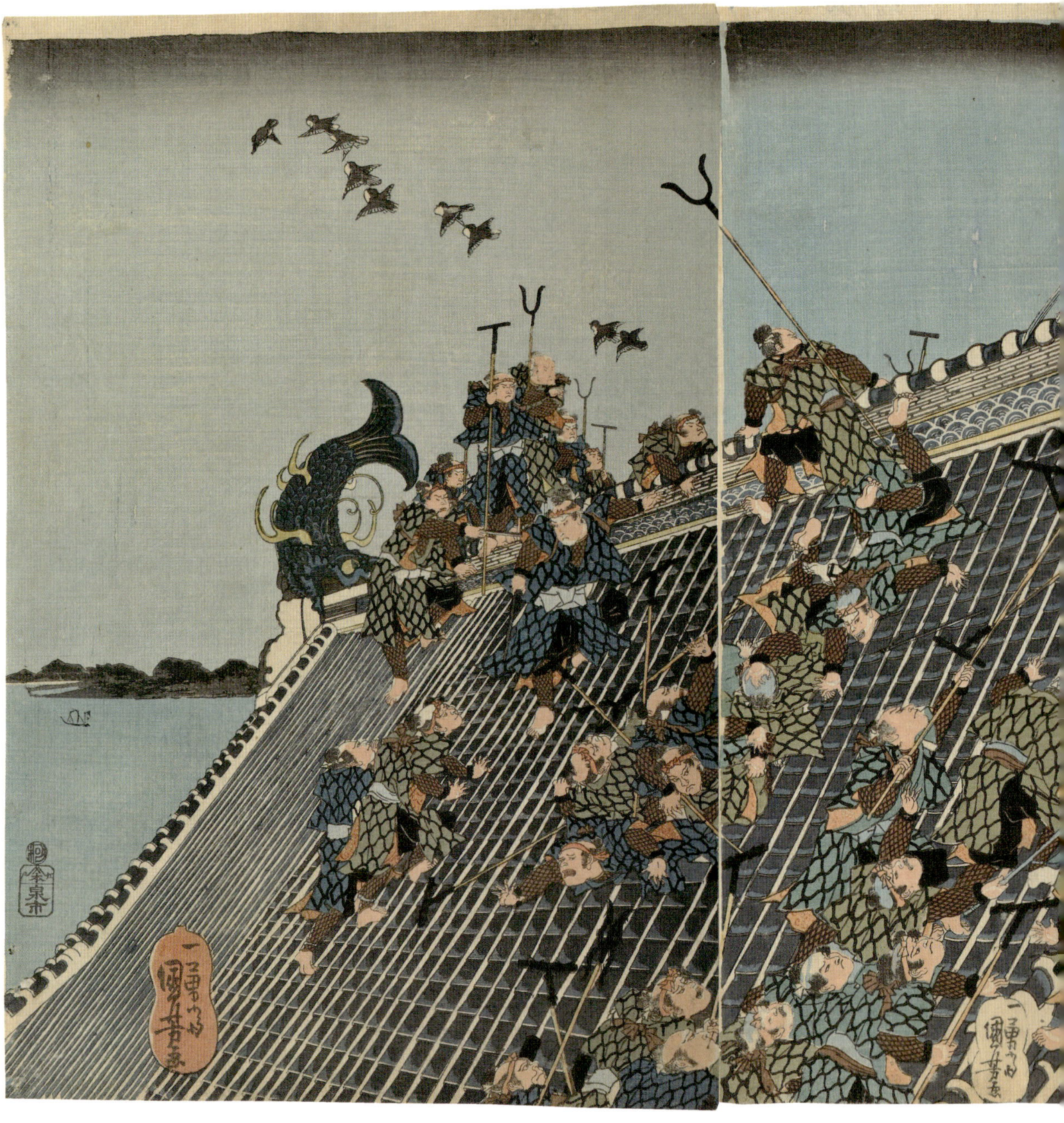

22

【八犬伝之内芳流閣】歌川国芳　天保7年（1836）頃

芳流閣の屋根によじ登り捕手を蹴散らす信乃。十手を咥えて睨みつける見八。
眼下に流れるのは大河坂東太郎（利根川）。二人は後に珠を持つ者同士と知り、義兄弟の誓いを結ぶ。

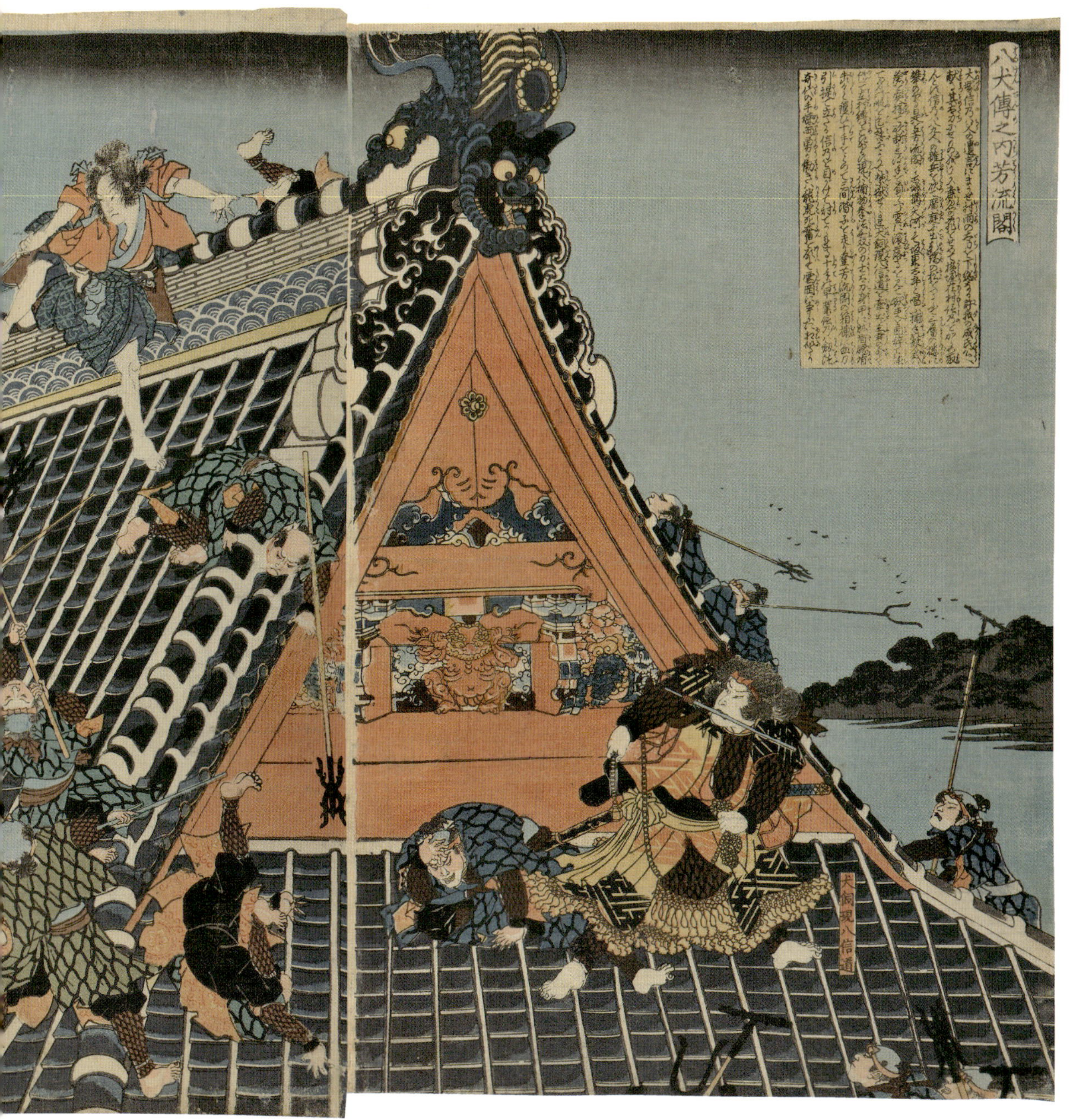

"Chronicles of the Eight Dog Heroes: Hōryūkaku" by Utagawa Kuniyoshi
Inuzuka Shino escapes capture by climbing up the roof of the Hōryūkaku.
Inukai Genpachi stares him down, clenching a metal truncheon in his mouth. In the background is the Tonegawa River.
The two men later discover that they both carry the special crystal balls, thus realizing that they are half-brothers and vowing allegiance to one another.

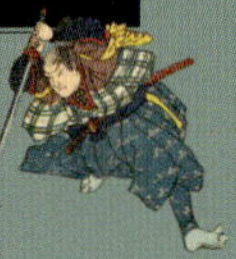

平維茂

鬼女紅葉を狩る

Taira no Koremochi
Brave Heroes and Gallant Men

平安時代中期の武将。ある時、維茂が従者を連れて戸隠山へ入ると、山中で紅葉狩りをしていた高貴な美女の一行に酒宴に誘われる。勧められるままに盃を重ね、酔い伏してしまったところ、夢で神のお告げを受け、神剣を授かる。女は実は鬼女で、目を覚ました維茂に襲い掛かるが、これを討って退治した。この逸話は能「紅葉狩」で知られる。

A general of the middle Heian period, Taira no Koremochi one day found himself invited to a drinking party by a beautiful noblewoman while out viewing the autumn foliage in the company of his servant on Togakushi Mountain. One drink followed another, and soon Koremochi was drunk. Just then, a god appeared to him in his dream with a warning and the gift of a divine sword. The woman, who is in fact a demon, attacks Koremochi just as he awakes, but Koremochi strikes her down. This story is known through the Noh play, *Autumn Foliage Hunting*.

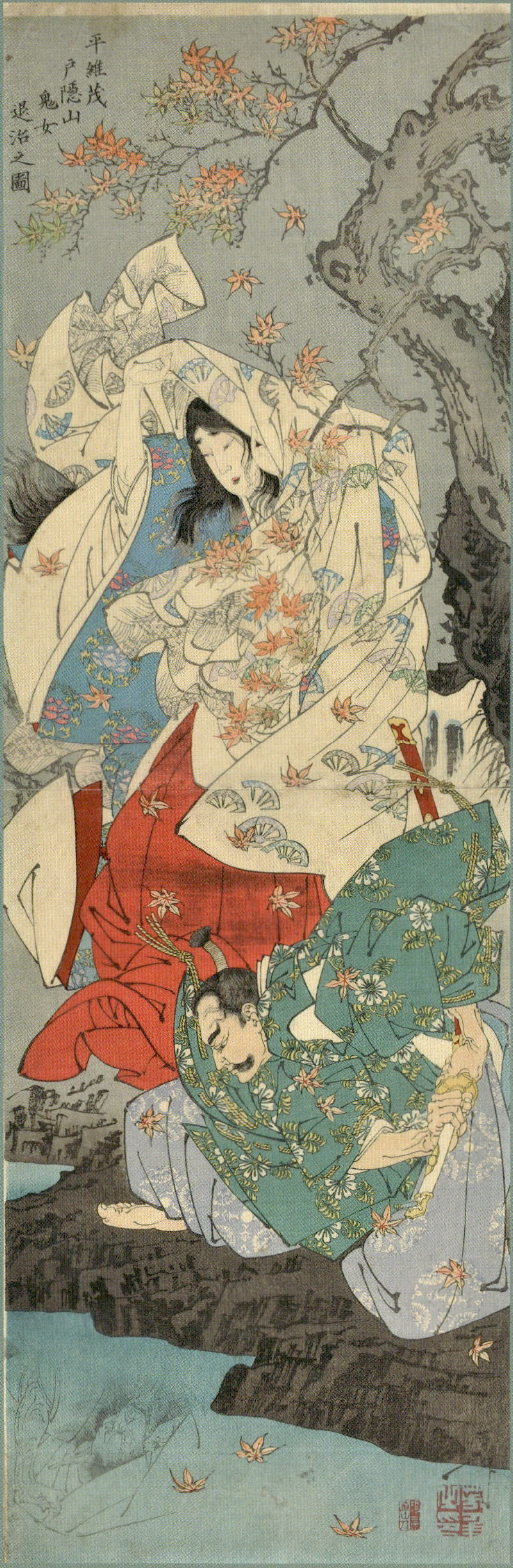

【平維茂戸隠山鬼女退治之図】
月岡芳年 明治20年（1887）西井コレクション収蔵
"Taira no Koremochi Vanquishes a Female Demon at Togakushi Mountain" by Tsukioka Yoshitoshi,
Nishii Collection

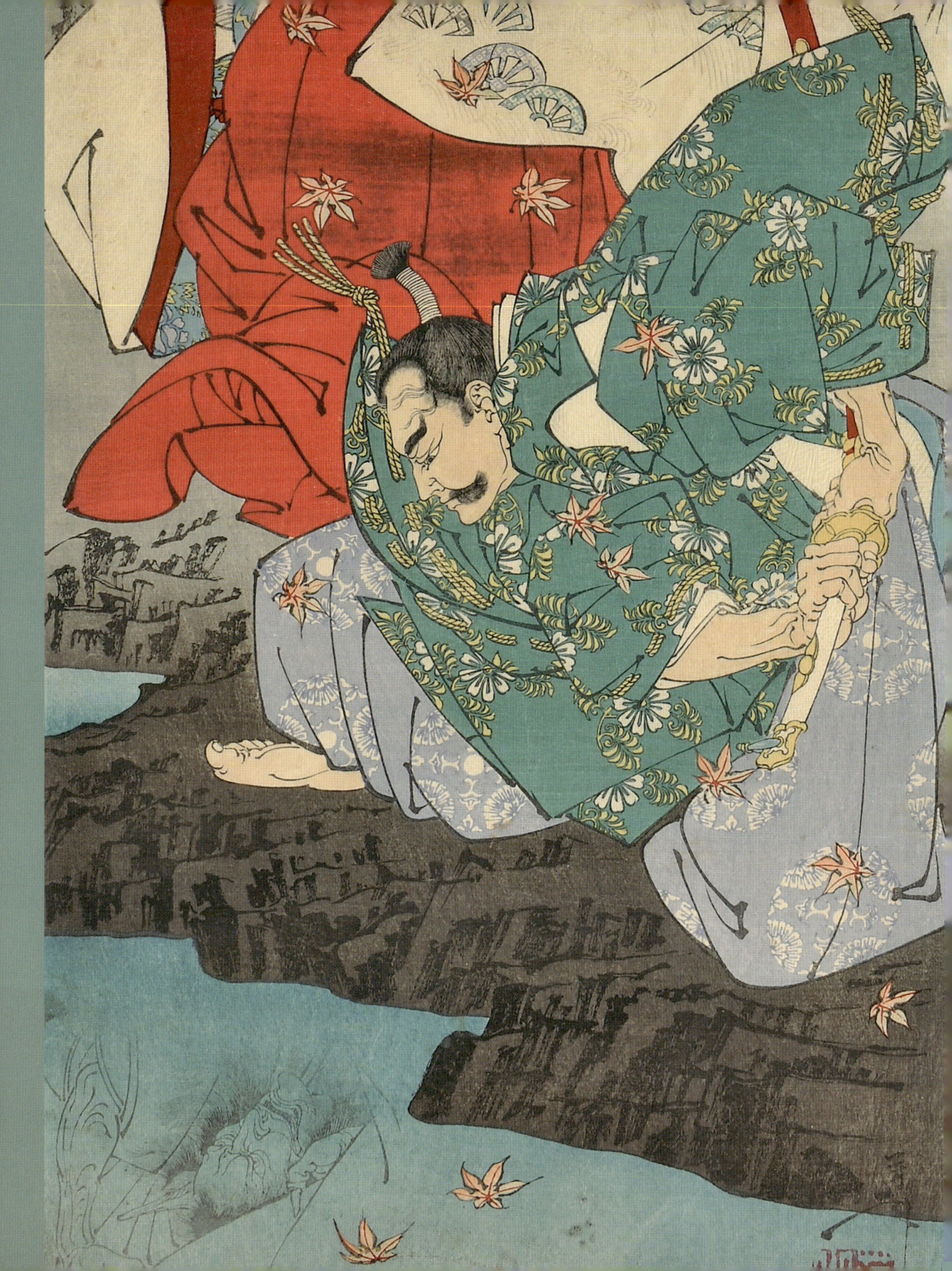

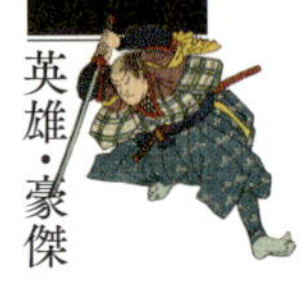

樋口兼光

木曽義仲の忠臣

Higuchi Kanemitsu
Brave Heroes and Gallant Men

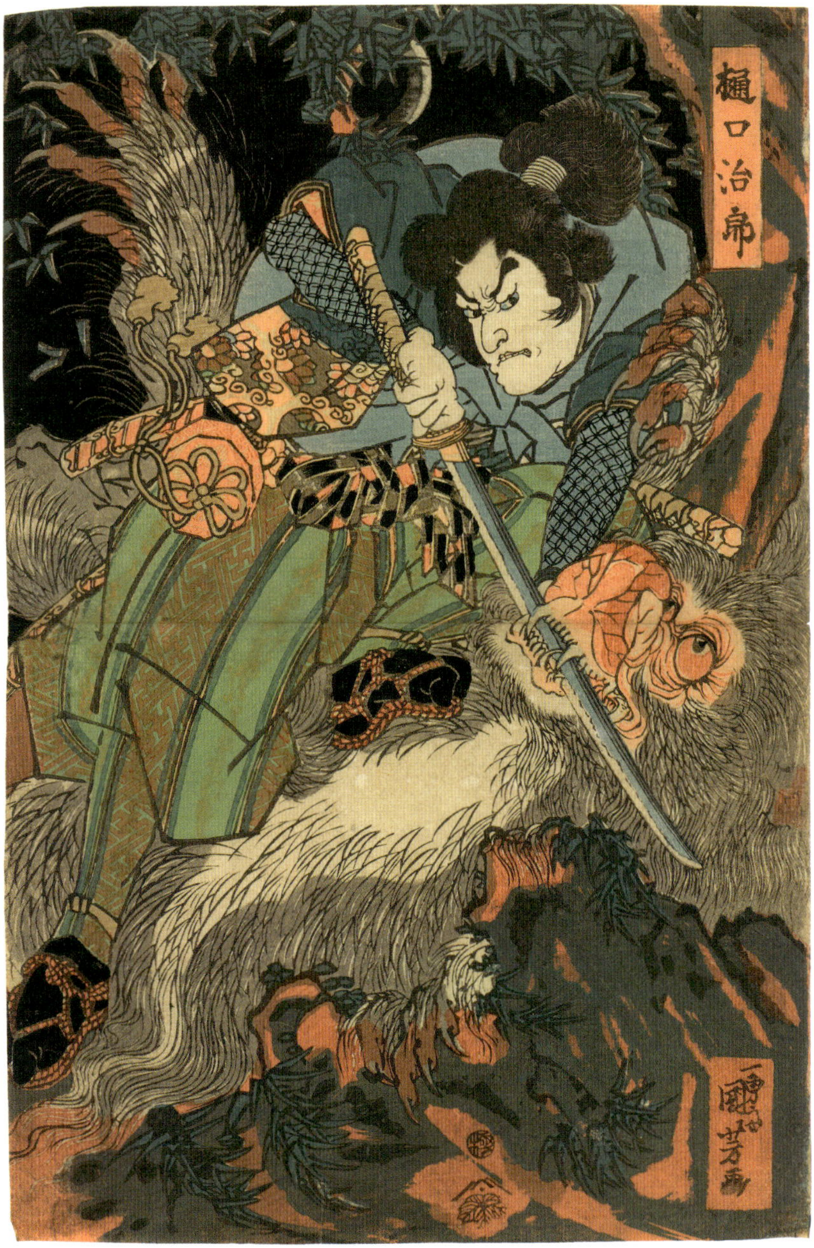

平安時代末期の武将。木曽義仲の乳
兄弟で巴御前の兄。義仲四天王の一
人とうたわれ、倶利伽羅峠の戦いなどで
活躍し平氏を破り、義仲とともに入京を
果たす。河内国石川城に出陣の際、義
仲が粟津の戦いで戦死したと知り降伏
を決意するも、朝議はこれを許さず、処
刑された。

Higuchi Kanemitsu was a general in the
late Heian period. He was Kiso Yoshinaka's
milk brother, and his younger sister was
the female warrior Tomoe Gozen. As one
of Yoshinaka's so-called Four Guardian
Kings, Kanemitsu helped defeat the Taira
clans at the Battle of Kurikara Pass (1183)
and march into the capital of Kyoto. En
route to Ishikawa Castle in Kawachi
Province (Osaka area), Kanemitsu learned
that Yoshinaka had been killed at the
Battle of Awazu and decided to surrender.
The Imperial Council would not permit
this, however, and instead sentenced
Kanemitsu to death.

【樋口治郎】歌川国芳　文政9～10年（1826-27）頃
木曽山中で大猿を退治する兼光。

"Higuchi Jirō" by Utagawa Kuniyoshi
Kanemitsu subjugating a giant monkey in the Kiso mountains.

【新形三十六怪撰
藤原秀郷竜宮城蜈蚣を射るの図】
月岡芳年 明治23年（1890）

稲妻とともに比良山の方からやってきた
大百足に矢を向ける秀郷。

"New Forms of Thirty-Six Ghosts:
Fujiwara no Hidesato Shooting
the Giant Centipede at the Dragon King's Palace"
by Tsukioka Yoshitoshi

Hidesato aims his arrow at the giant centipede,
which has arrived with claps of thunder
from over the Hira Mountains.

平安時代中期の下野の豪族。弓術に優れ、平将門の乱
では平貞盛について将門を討った。俗に俵（田原）藤太
と呼ばれ、百足退治の伝説で知られる。琵琶湖の竜神
が遣わした大蛇に頼まれ、竜宮城で百足の化け物に矢
を射って退治した。龍神がお礼として与えた釣鐘を、三
井寺に寄進したという。

Member of a powerful warrior family in Shimotsuke
Province (Tochigi), Fujiwara no Hidesato was an
exceptional archer and fought alongside Taira no Sadamori
in suppressing the revolt of Taira no Masakado in 940.
Nicknamed Tawara no Tōta, he is famed in legend for
subjugating a giant centipede that threatened the Dragon
Palace at Lake Biwa. After destroying the monster with an
arrow, Hidesato was rewarded by the Dragon God with a
bronze bell, which he purportedly donated to Miidera
Temple.

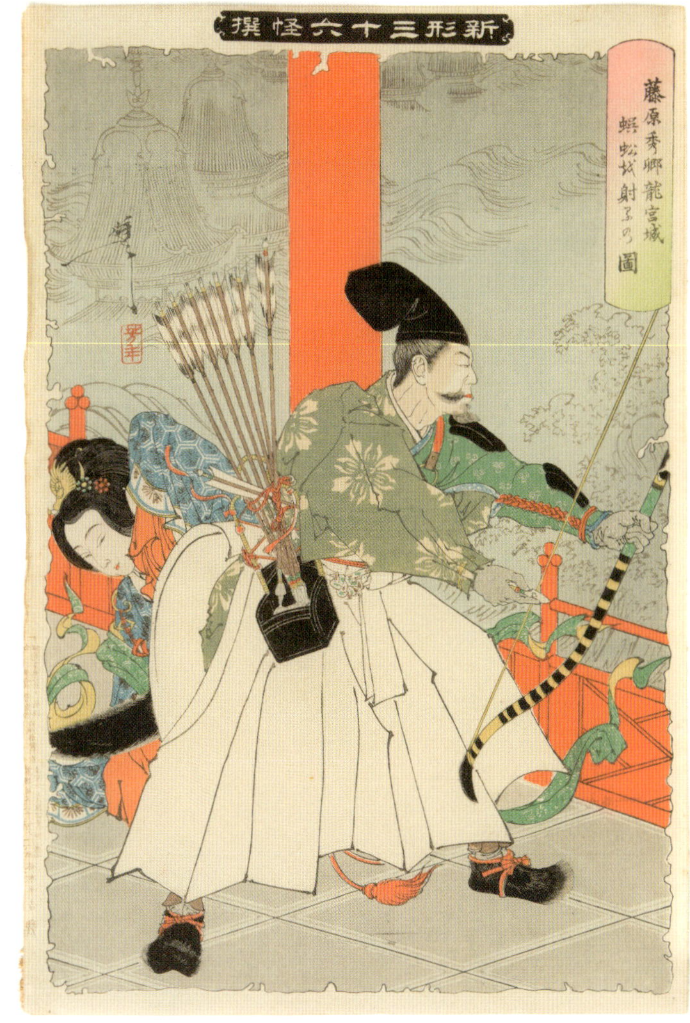

藤原秀郷

百足退治の武人

Fujiwara no
Hidesato
Brave Heroes
and Gallant Men

【秀郷近江国瀬田のはしにて大百足を退治す龍じんよろこび給ふ】歌川芳員 慶応3年（1867）

"Hidesato Kills the Giant Centipede at Seta Bridge in Omi Province,
Pleasing the Dragon God" by Utagawa Yoshikazu

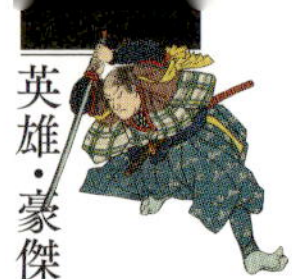

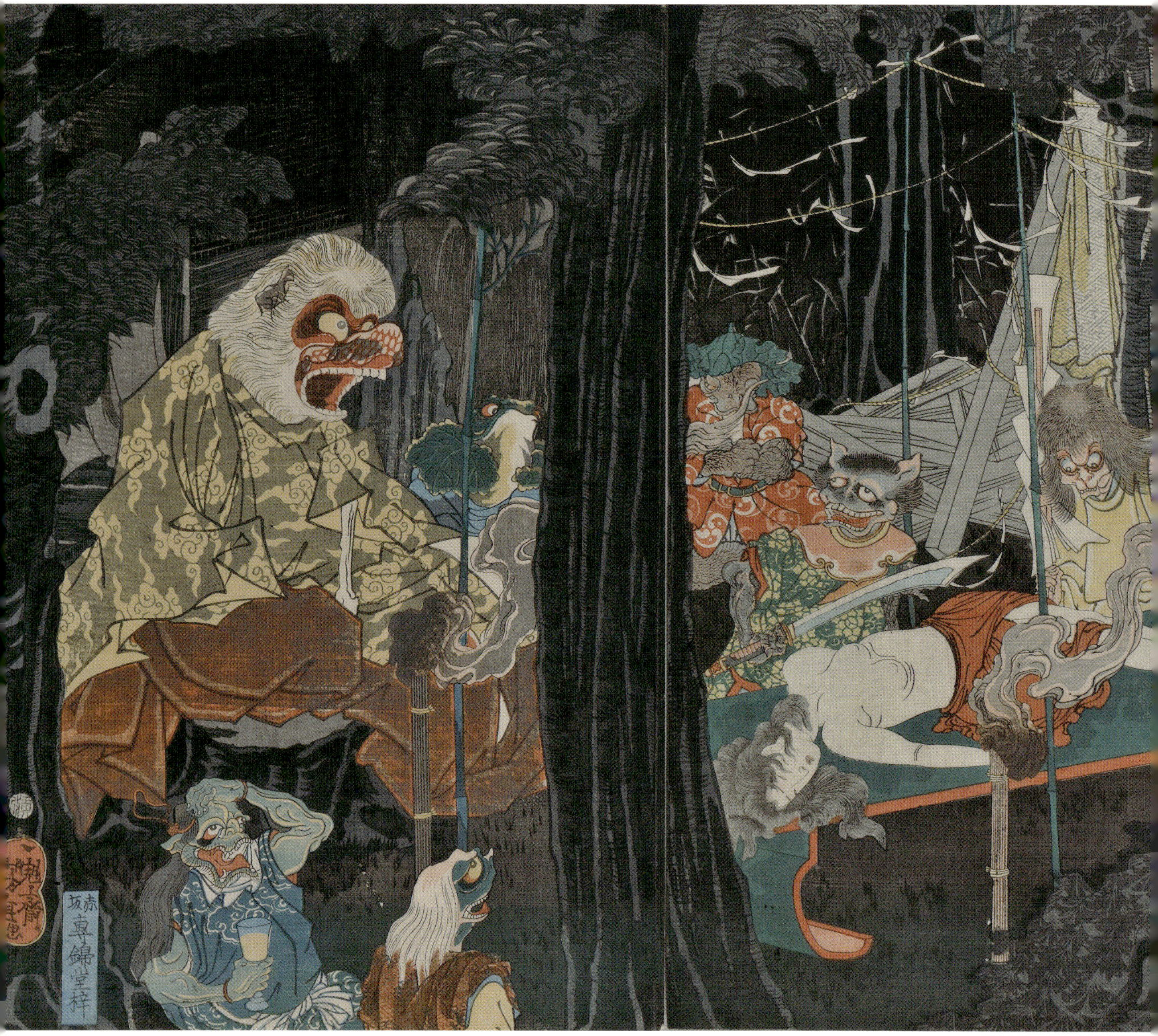

【岩見重太郎の狒々退治】月岡芳年 慶応元年（1865）
邪神の生贄として捧げられた生娘を救う重太郎。邪神は狒々の化け物であった。

"Iwami Jūtarō Routs the Hihi" by Tsukioka Yoshitoshi
Jūtarō is shown here saving a young woman offered as a living sacrifice to an evil deity, which has taken the form of a giant monkey yōkai known as the hihi.

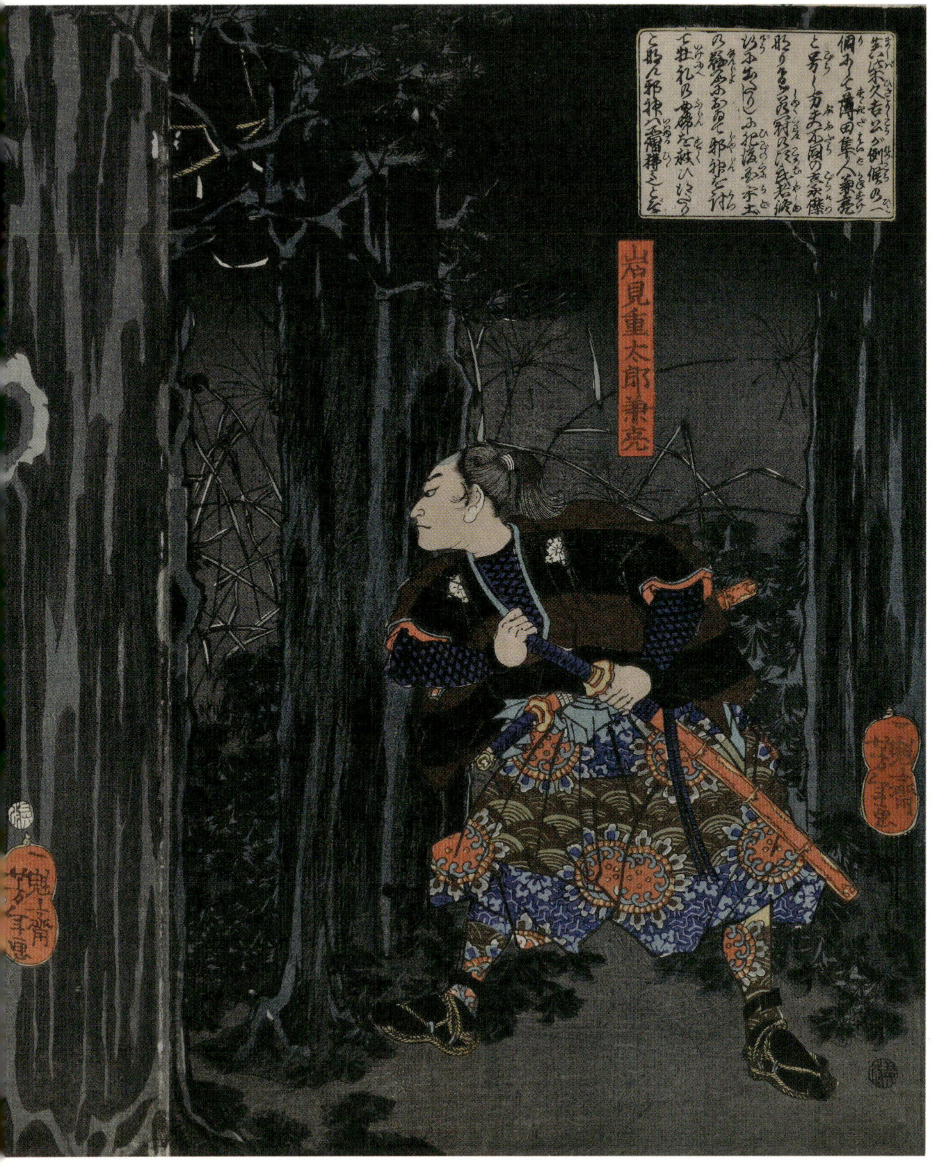

岩見重太郎【狒々退治】

Iwami Jūtarō
Brave Heroes
and Gallant Men

諸国巡りて化け物退治

読本、講談、歌舞伎などで有名な桃山時代の伝説的豪傑。筑前小早川家に仕え、諸国を周遊し、狒々や大蛇などの化け物退治で勇名をとどろかせた。天橋立で父の仇を討ったのち、豊臣秀吉に仕えて大坂の陣で戦死したといわれている。

A legendary warrior of the Momoyama period (1573-1600), Iwami Jūtarō is widely known through novels, oral tales, and kabuki plays. While serving the Kobayakawa family in Chikuzen Province (northern Kyushu), Jūtarō's reputation as a warrior grew as the traveled across the archipelago quelling giant monkeys, serpents, and other monsters. After avenging his father in Amanohashidate, he served under Toyotomi Hideyoshi during the unsuccessful defense of Osaka Castle, where he is believed to have died in battle.

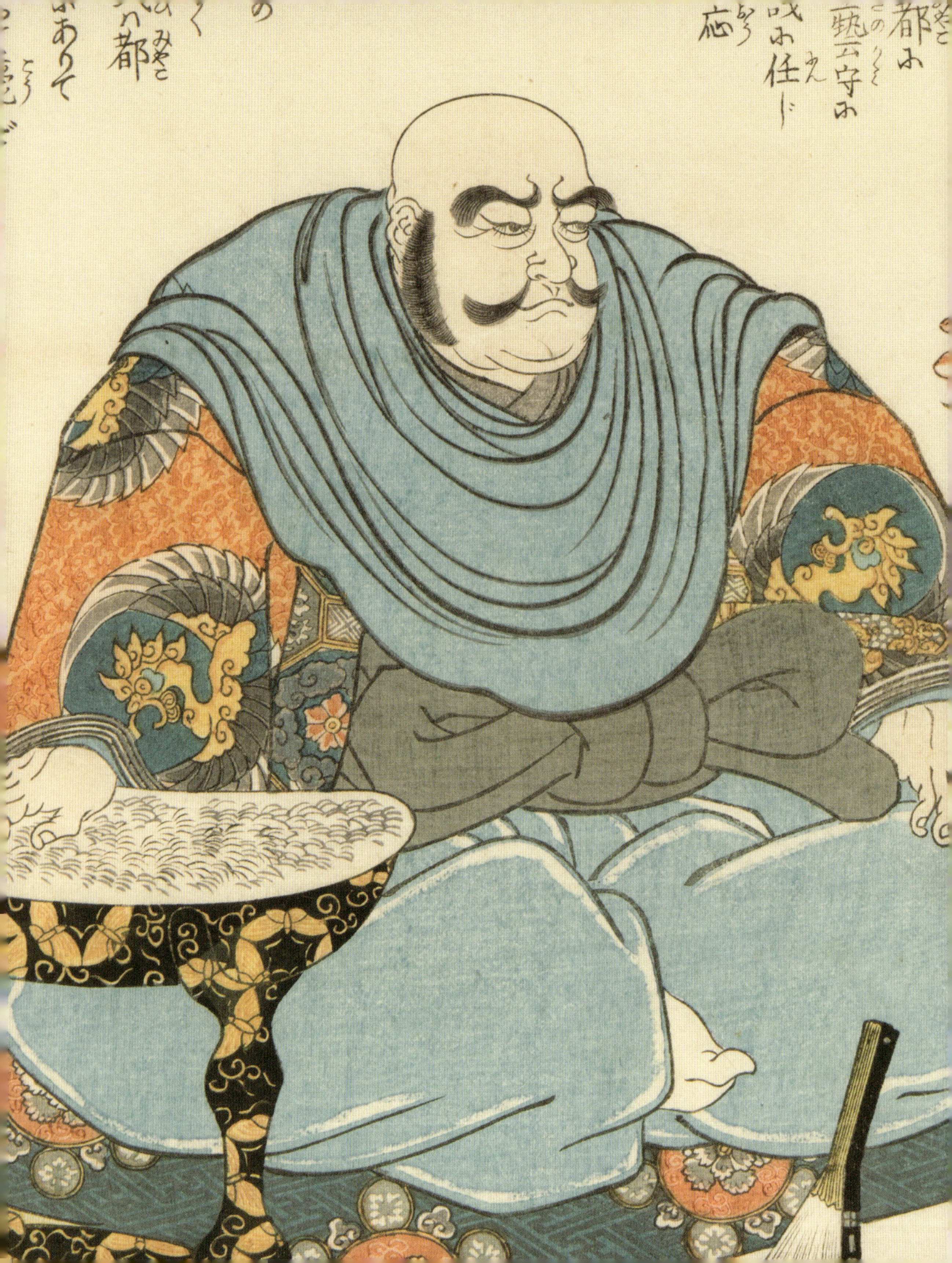

都
みやこ
くにの
応

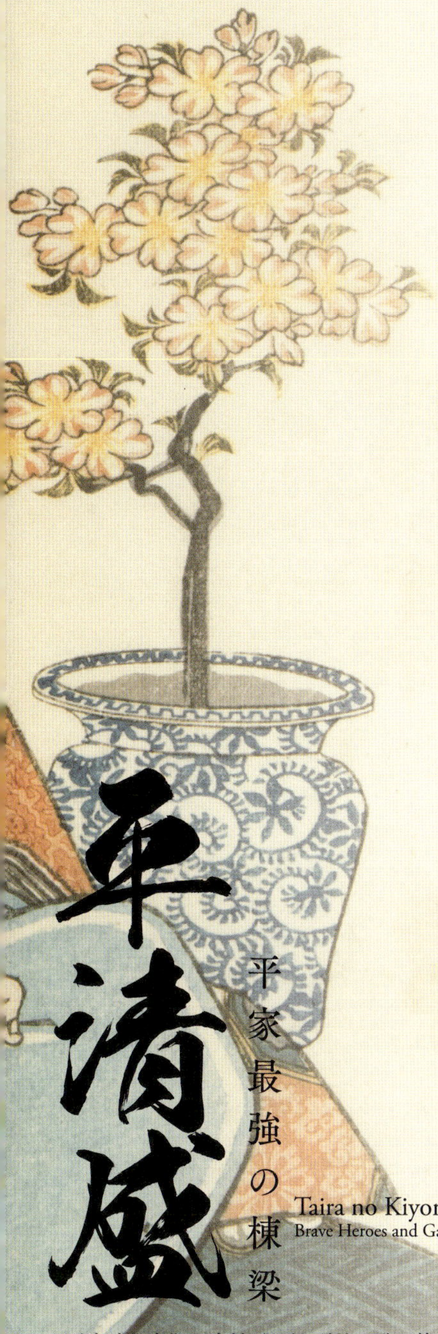

平清盛

平家最強の棟梁

Taira no Kiyomori
Brave Heroes and Gallant Men

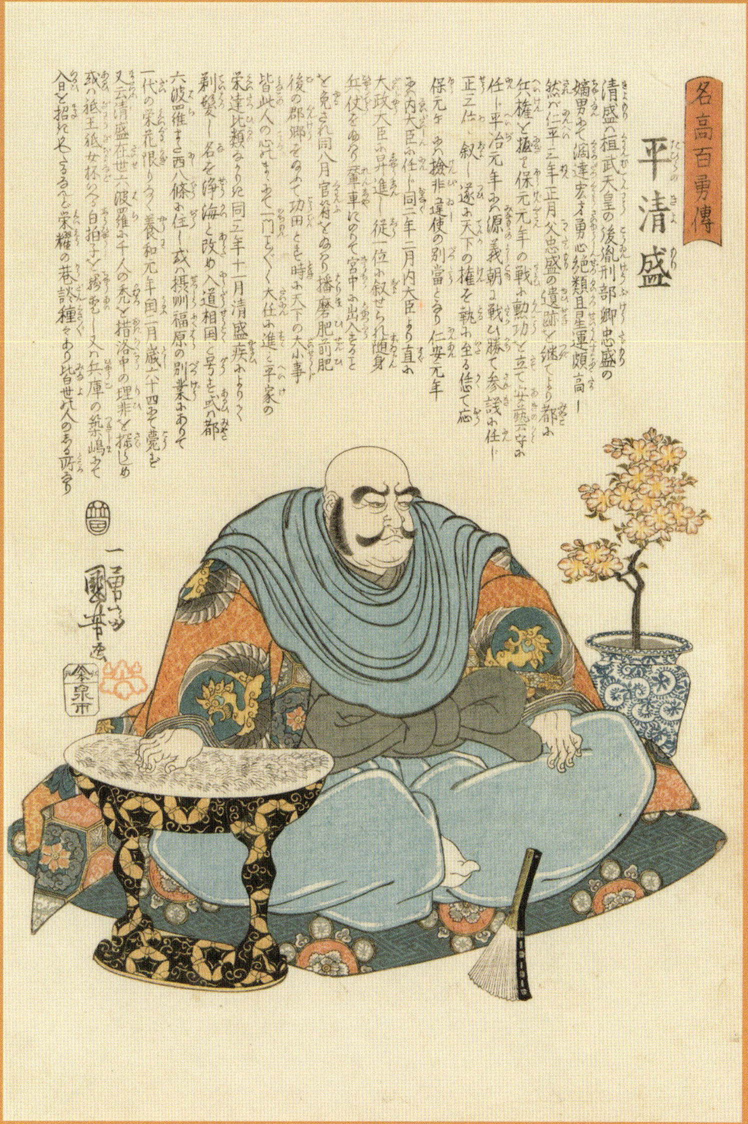

【名高百勇伝 平清盛】歌川国芳 天保14年〜弘化3年（1843-46）頃
"One Hundred Heroes of Great Courage:
Taira no Kiyomori" by Utagawa Kuniyoshi

平安時代末期の武将。保元・平治の乱で勢力を伸ばし、太政大臣となって平氏政権を樹立。娘徳子を高倉天皇の中宮に入れ、その子安徳天皇を即位させ、外戚として権勢をふるう。一門はみな公卿や殿上人となって全盛期を築いた。晩年、諸国源氏の挙兵にあい、熱病のため失意のうちに死去する。

Taira no Kiyomori was a military commander active during the late Heian period. Having expanded his influence during the Hōgen and Heiji Rebellions in 1156 and 1159, he became Chancellor of the Realm and established the political authority of the Taira clan. After marrying his daughter Tokuko to Emperor Takakura, Kiyomori exercised power through their son Antoku, who was made Emperor when he was still a toddler. With his family and allies dominating the ranks of kugyō, tenjōbito, and other of the highest positions in the Emperor's court, Kiyomori was responsible for the glory days of the Taira clan. At the end of his life, Kiyomori lay conscious with a fatal fever, as provincial Minamoto leaders began to raise armies against the Taira.

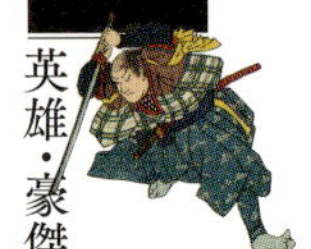

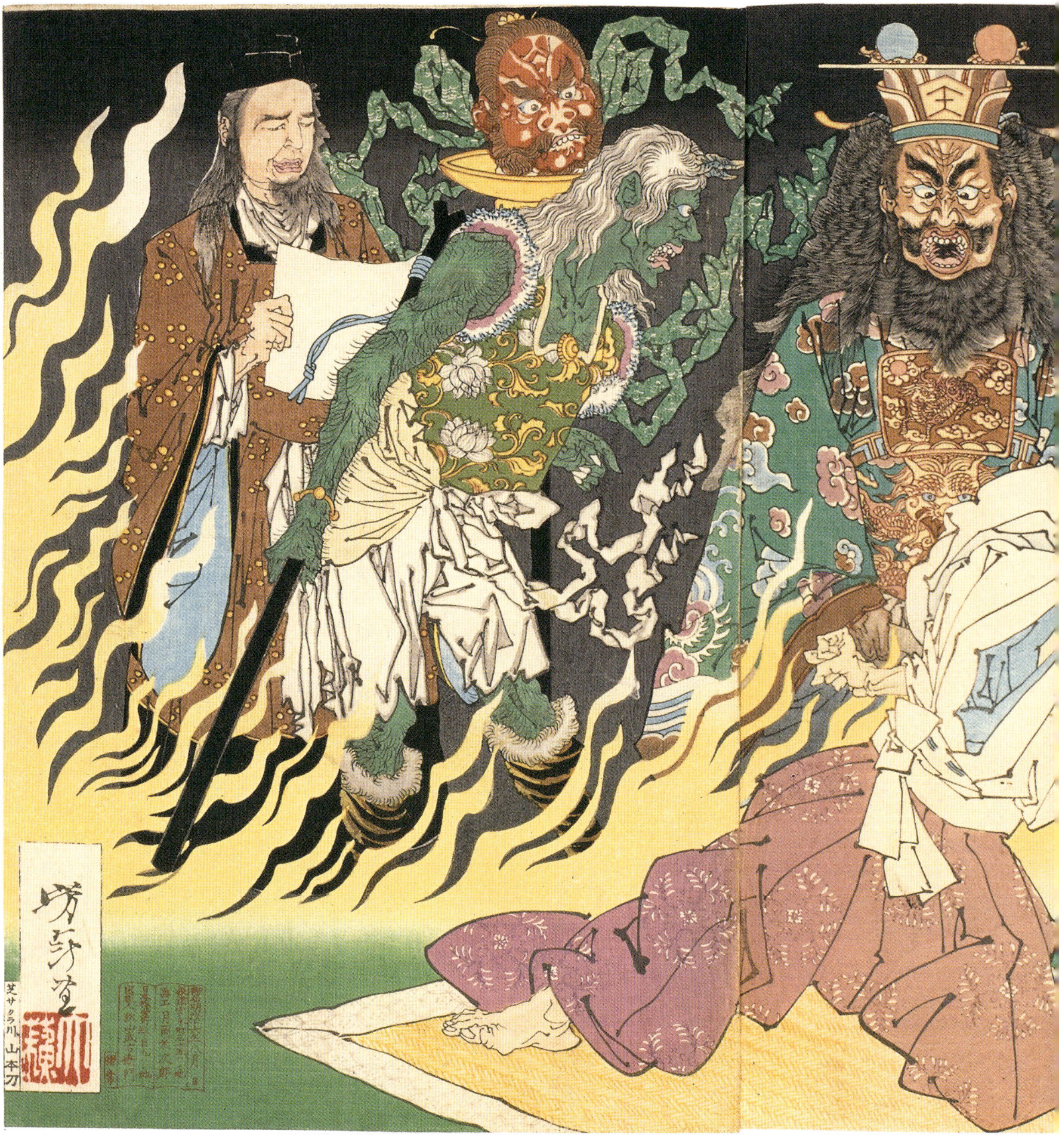

【平清盛炎焼病之図】月岡芳年 明治16年(1883)

熱病でもだえ苦しむ清盛を、地獄の閻魔大王とその眷属たちが責め立てる。
傍らでは、妻の時子と三男宗盛がひたすらに祈る。

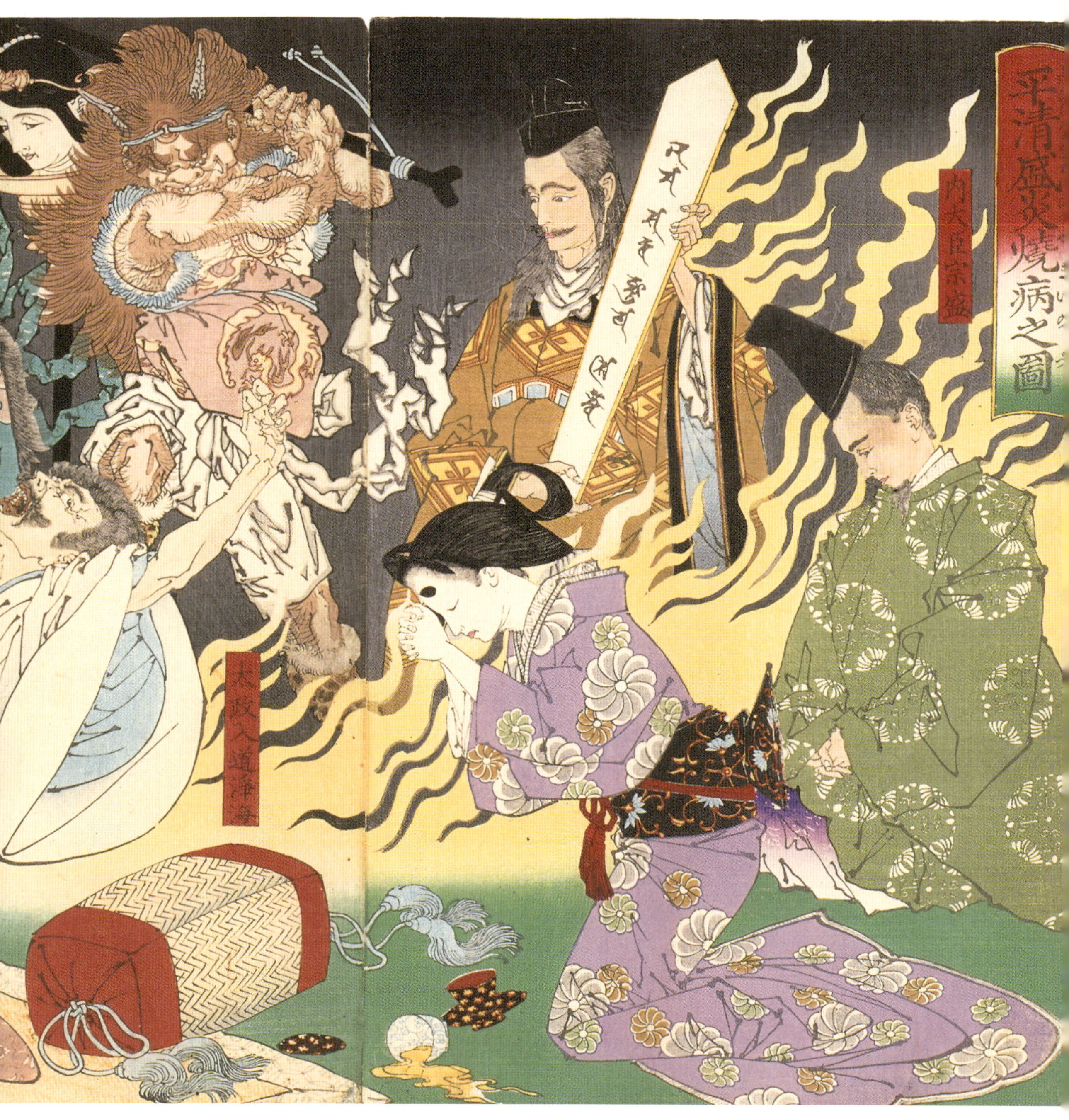

The Fever of Taira no Kiyomori by Tsukioka Yoshitoshi

Afflicted with intense fever, Kiyomori is shown here being assailed by Enma, the King of Hell, and his followers.
To the side, his wife Tokiko and his third son Munemori pray for his soul.

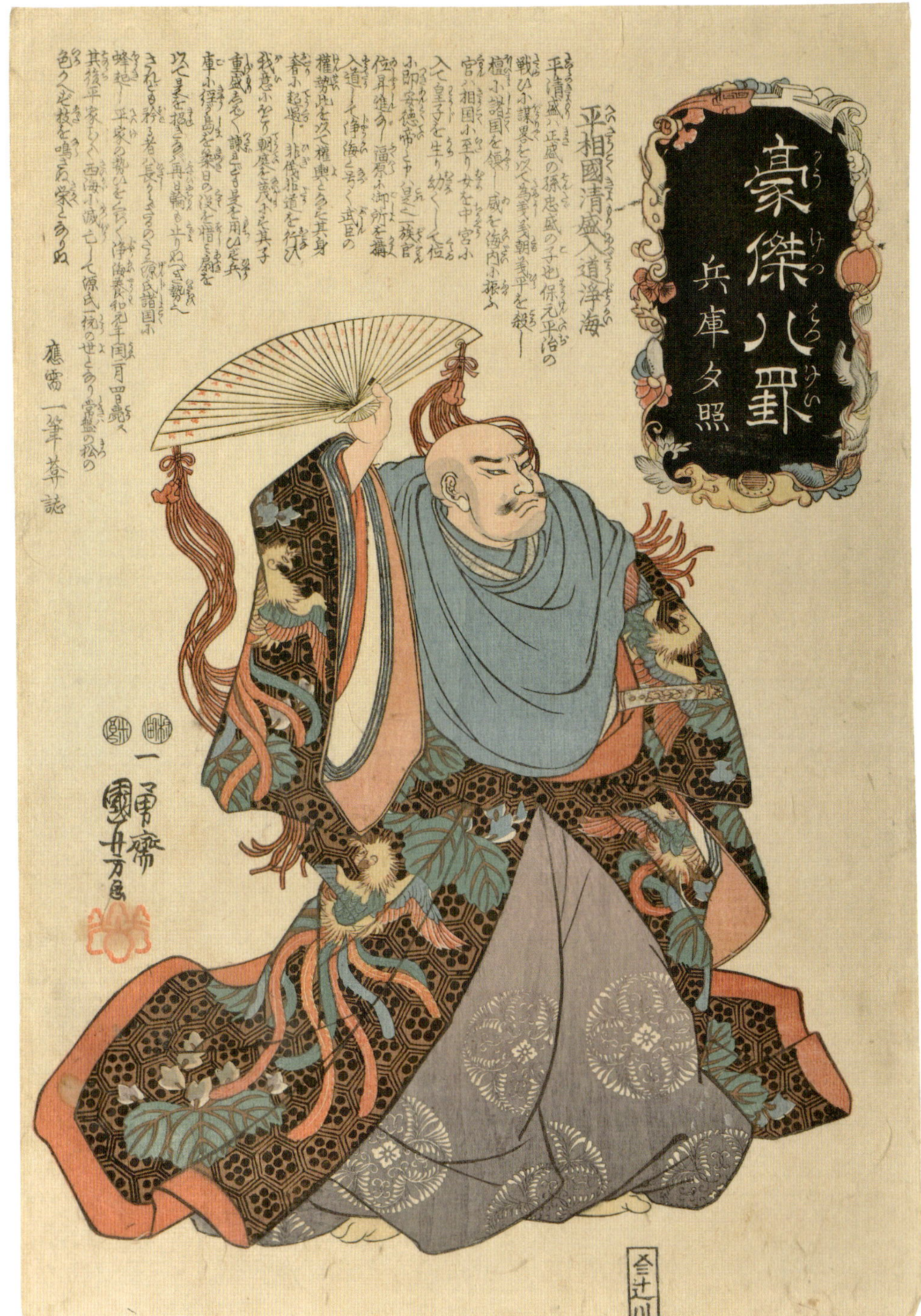

【豪傑八犭 兵庫夕照】歌川国芳　弘化4年〜嘉永3年（1847-51）頃
清盛は剃髪して入道相国と呼ばれ、摂津国福原の別荘に移り住んだのち、なおも実権を握った。

"Heroes of the Eight Views: Evening Glow at Hyōgo" by Utagawa Kuniyoshi

Though having shaved his head and technically become a Buddhist priest by the name of Nyūdō Shōkoku, Kiyomori continued to wield power from his villa in Fukuhara, in Settsu Province, present-day Kōbe.

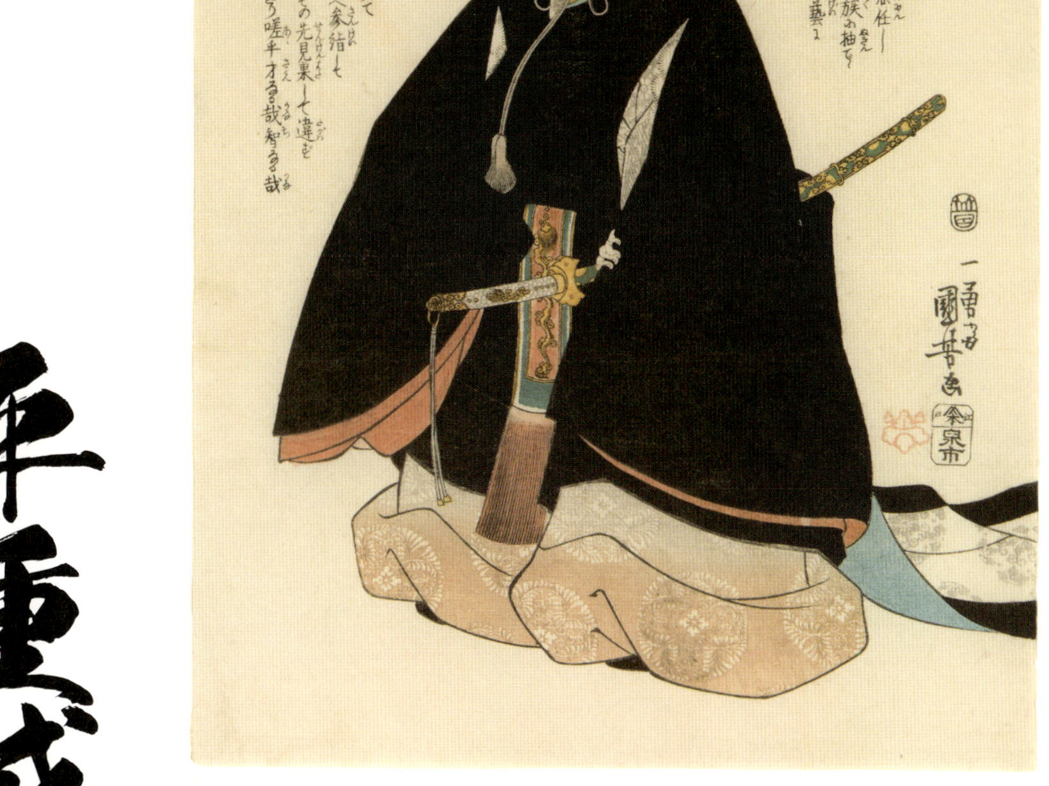

平重盛
文武二道の兵（つわもの）

Taira no Shigemori
Brave Heroes and Gallant Men

【名高百勇伝 平重盛】歌川国芳　天保14年〜弘化3年（1843-46）頃

"One Hundred Heroes of Great Courage:
Taira no Shigemori" by Utagawa Kuniyoshi

平安時代末期の武将で、平清盛の長男。保元・平治の乱で父に従い活躍し、平氏の全盛とともに内大臣に進んだが、父に先立ち病死した。鹿ケ谷事件の際に、父が後白河法皇を幽閉しようとするのを諫止し、清盛、朝廷間の対立の和解に努めた。我意驕慢な父とは異なり、謹直・温厚・忠孝の人として名高い。

Taira no Kiyomori's eldest son, Shigemori was a general during the late Heian period. After supporting his father in the Hōgen and Heiji Rebellions, Shigemori served as Inner Minister during the Taira's glory days. Due to illness, however, he preceded his father in death. After the Shishigatani Incident of 1177, a failed coup, he dissuaded his father from banishing Retired Emperor Goshirakawa and advocated for the reconciliation of Kiyomori and the Imperial court. In contrast to his self-centered and arrogant father, Shigemori was respected for being mild and conscientious with a strong sense of filial piety.

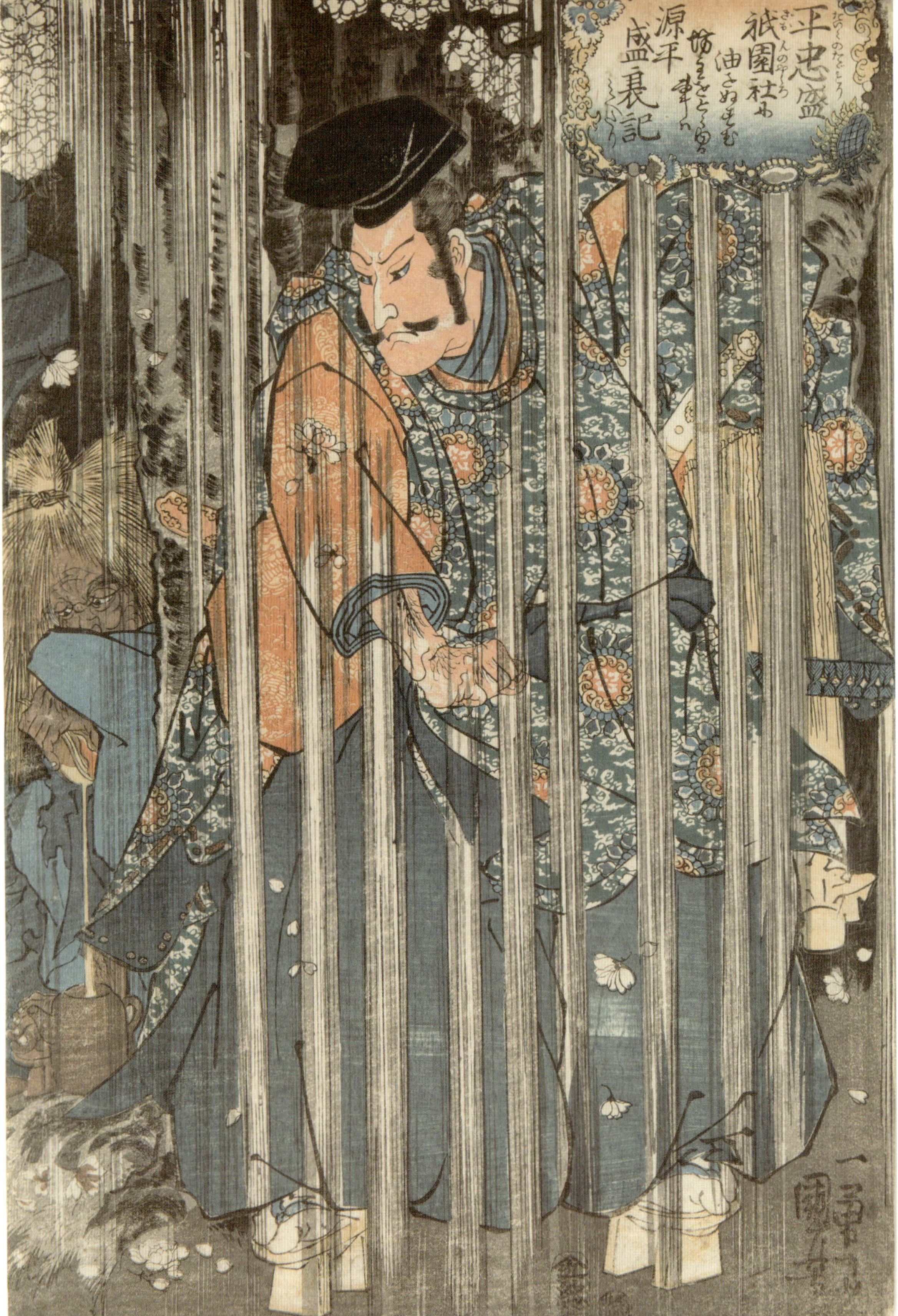

平忠盛
祇園社の
油さぬまむ
源平
盛裏記
一勇斎國芳画

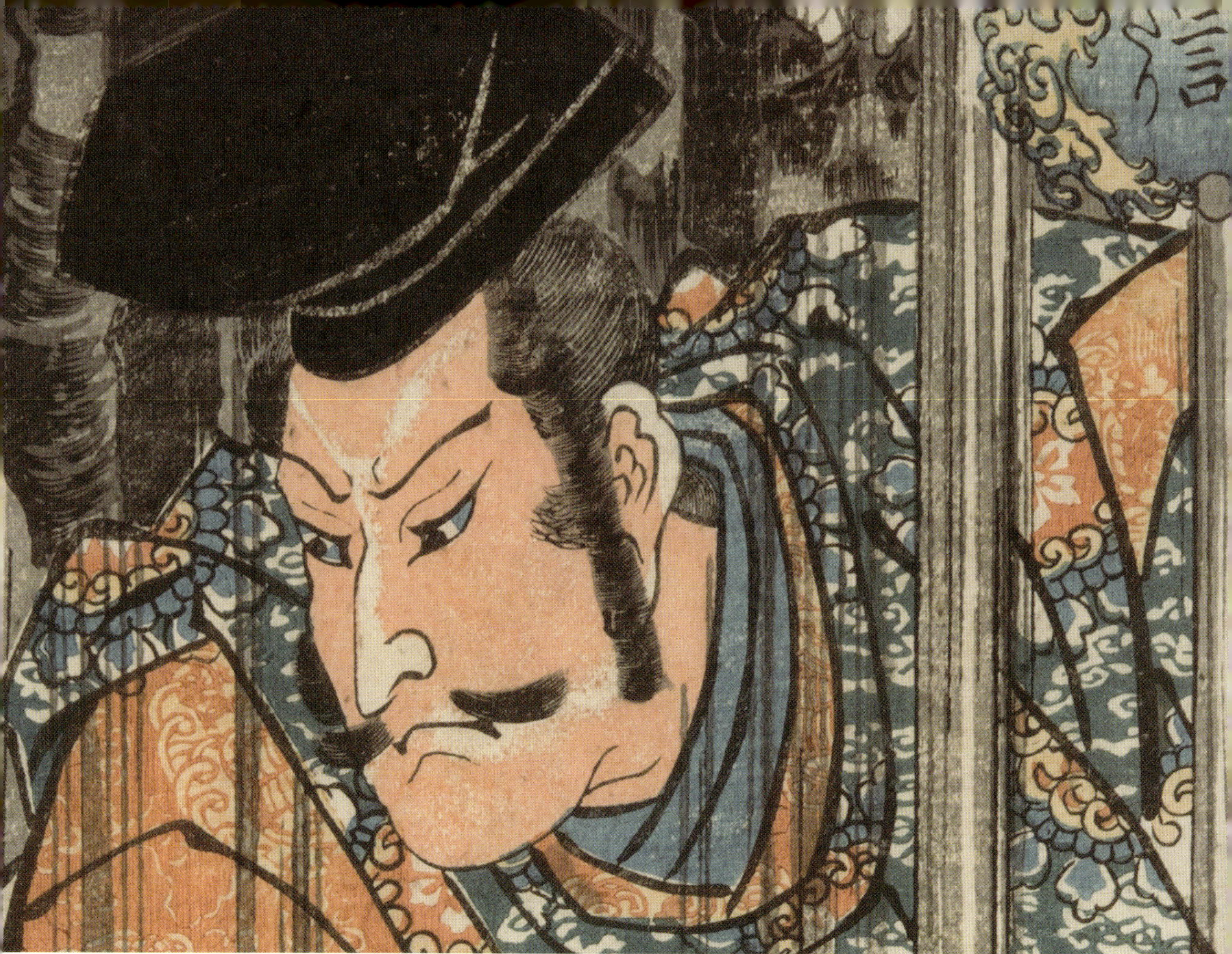

平忠盛

灯篭に刻まれた剛毅
【清盛の父】

Taira no Tadamori
Brave Heroes and Gallant Men

平安末期の武将。平清盛の父。ある雨の夜、白河法皇が寵愛する祇園女御（ぎおんのにょうご）に会いに出かけると、近所の御堂から怪しげな物が出てきた。頭は針のように尖り、片手に槌のようなもの、片手に光るものを持っていた。この化け物を退治するよう命じられた忠盛が近づくと、それは化け物ではなく人間であった。老坊主が灯明をあげるため、油差しと灯明皿を持ち、雨に濡れないよう頭から藁を被っていたのである。忠盛の冷静な振舞いに感心した法皇は、褒美として祇園女御を賜ったが、このときすでに法皇の子を宿していたという。このことから、清盛は白河法皇の落胤とする説がある。

A military leader of the late Heian period, Tadamori was the father of Taira no Kiyomori. One rainy night, when Emperor Shirakawa paid a visit to his beloved wife, Gion no Nyōgo, a frightening beast manifested from a nearby temple hall. Its head was as sharp as a needle, and held a hammer-like object in one hand and something glowing in the other. Ordered to subdue the monster, Tadamori approached to find that it was nothing more than a man, an old monk, who was holding an oil jug in one hand and a candle plate in the other, in order to light the stone lanterns. He was wearing a cone of straw on his head to shield himself from the rain. Impressed by Tadamori's sober calm, the Emperor offered Gion no Nyōgo to Tadamori as a reward, but she was already pregnant with the emperor's child. Some say that Tadamori was in fact Shirakawa's illegitimate son.

【平忠盛】歌川国芳　天保（1830-44）後期
"Taira no Tadamori" by Utagawa Kuniyoshi

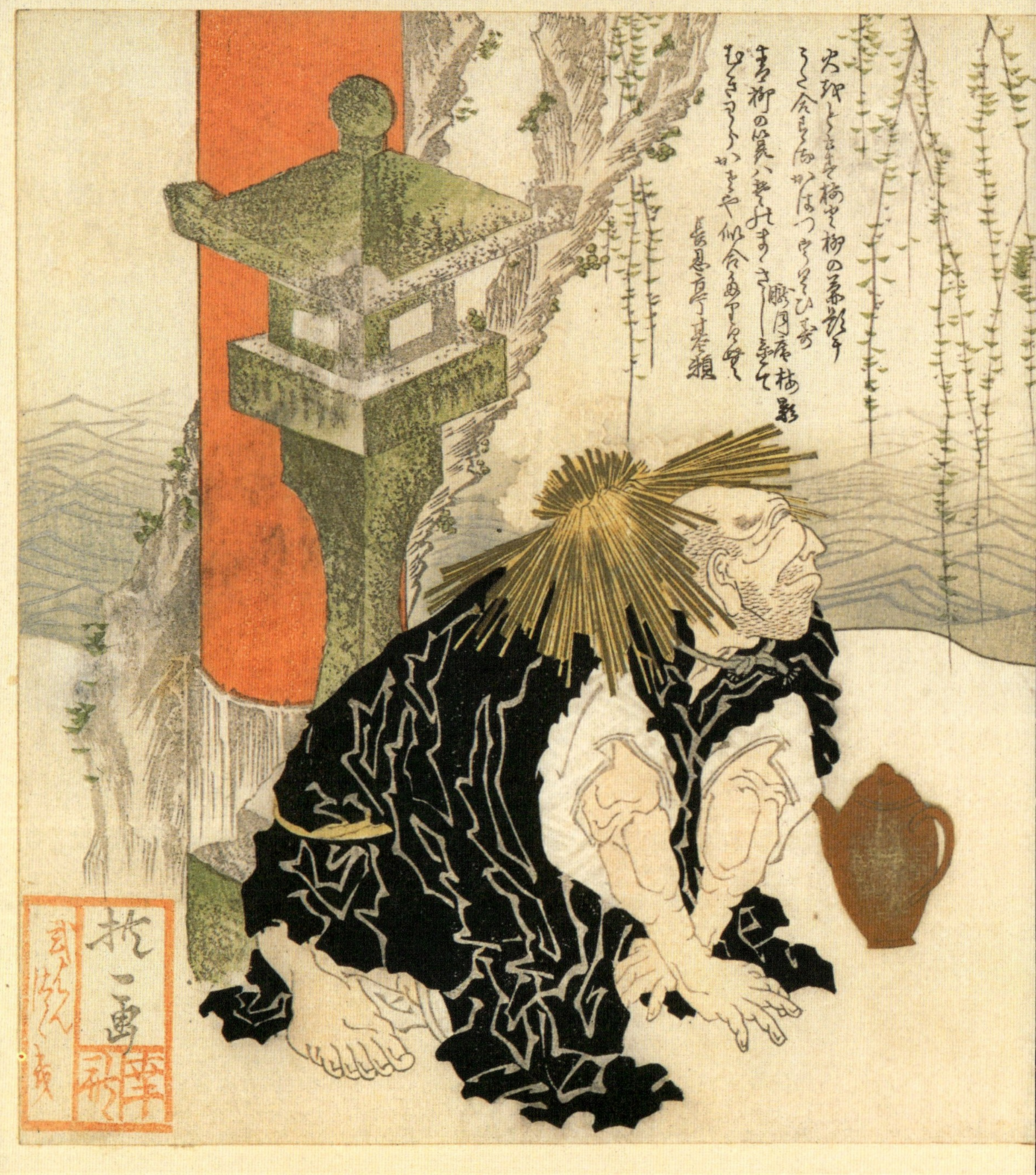

火ともして橋や柳の薄曙
うつくしうらかけはつらゆき
青柳の實は老みませさ朧月庵梅影
ひきつくしたるや似合あるらめや
長恩亭守其頼

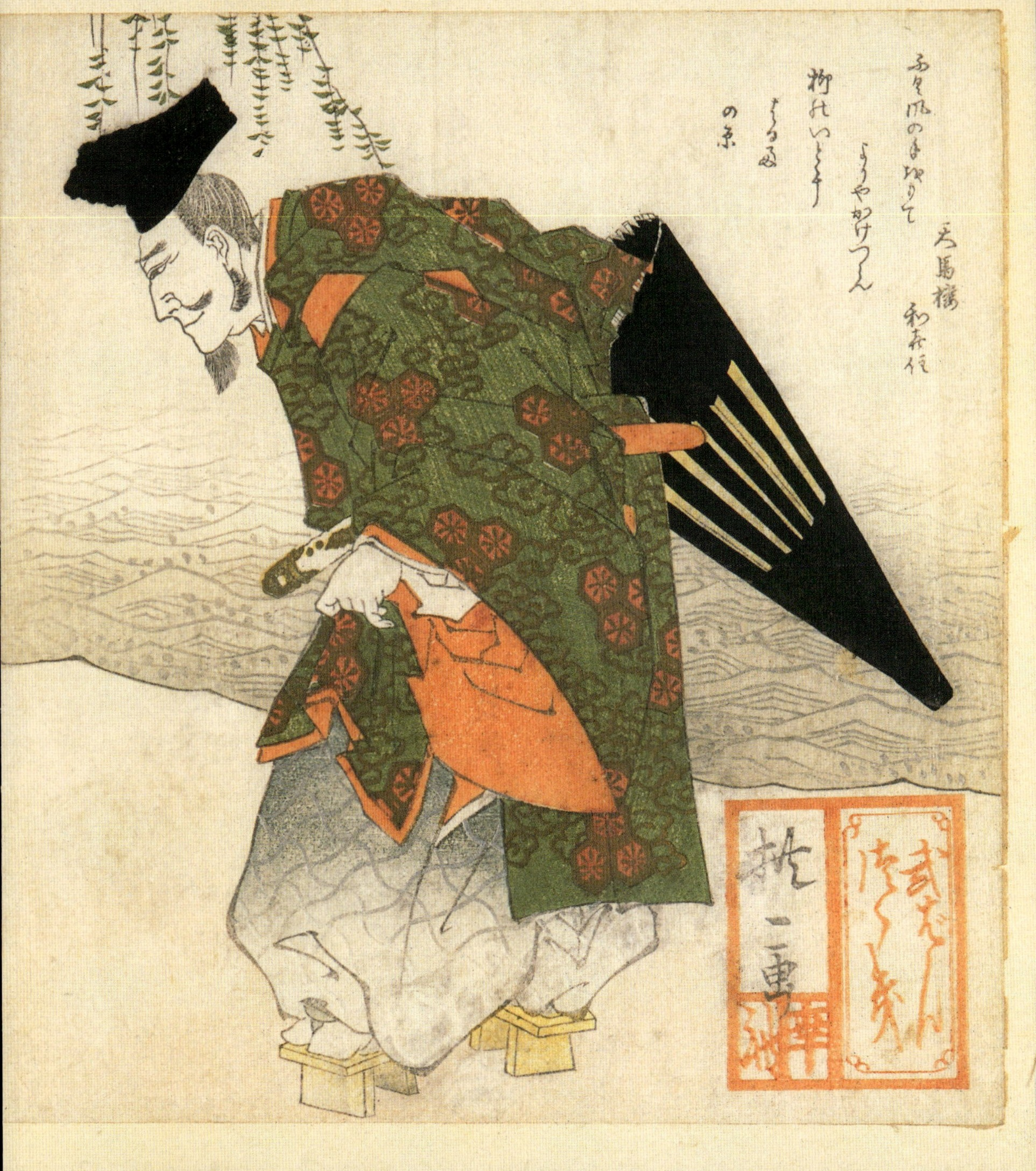
ふゆ風のほゆりて
ものれいとゝ
うゝやかけつん
するゝ
の糸
天馬橋
和春信

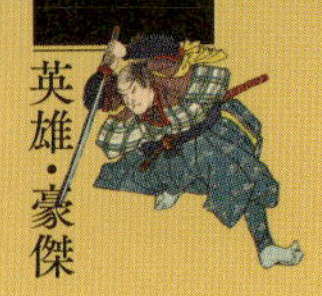

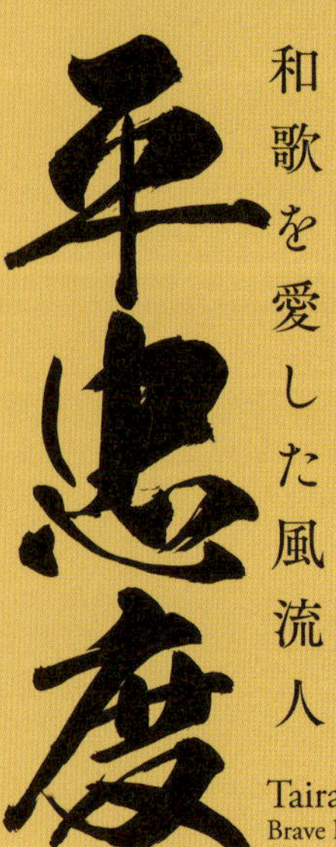

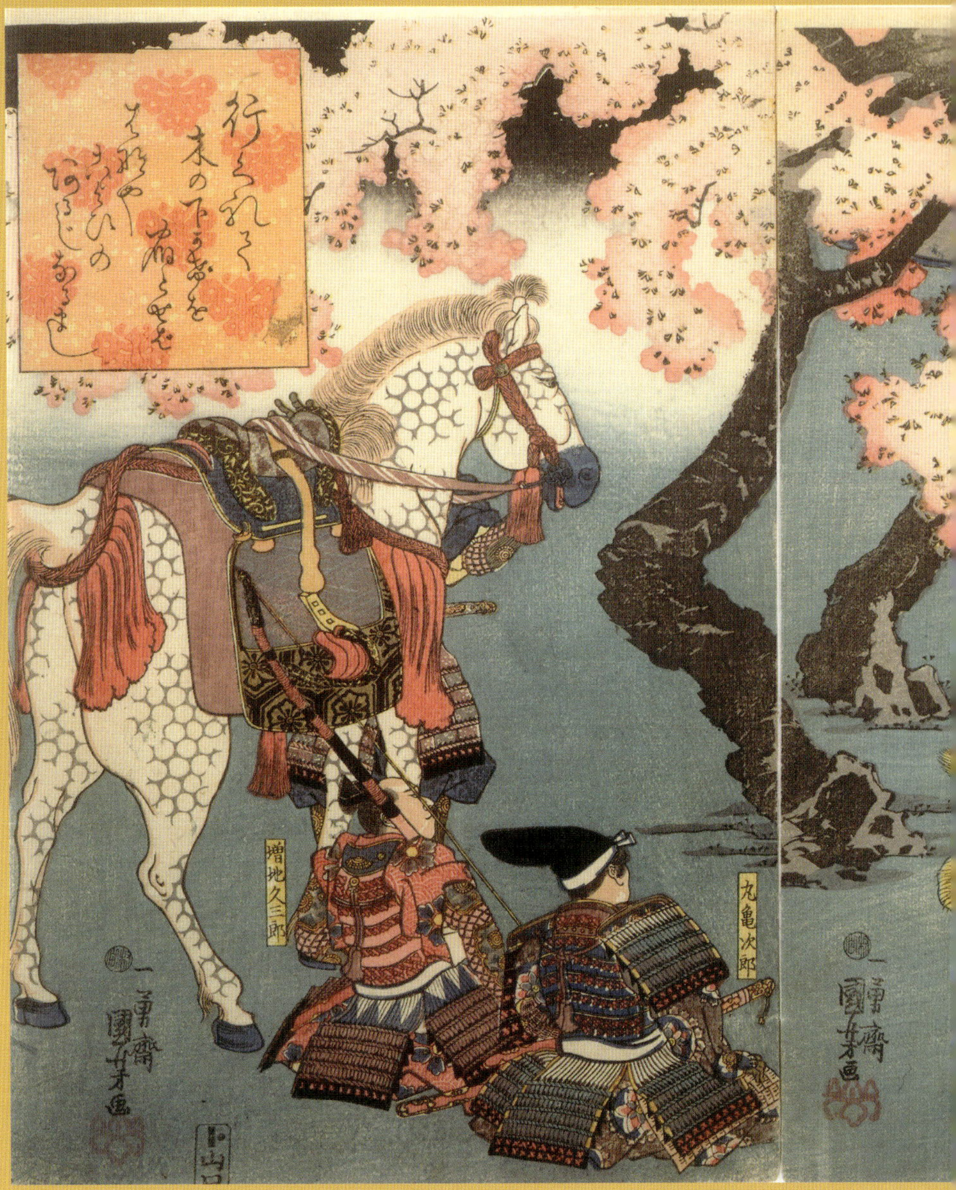

増地久三郎

丸亀次郎

一勇齋
國芳画

一勇齋
國芳画

平忠度

和歌を愛した風流人

Taira no Tadanori
Brave Heroes and Gallant Men

平安時代末期の武将。平忠盛の子で、清盛の弟。歌人としても優れ、藤原俊成に師事した。平氏都落ちの途中、わざわざ京都に引き返して師に詠草を託し、自分の和歌を勅撰集へ選び入れてほしいと頼んだ話は有名。一ノ谷の戦いで戦死した際には、「行き暮れて木の下陰を宿とせば　花や今宵の主ならまし（日が暮れて、桜の木の下を宿とするならば、花が今宵の主人となってもてなしてくれるだろう）」の一首を身につけていたという。

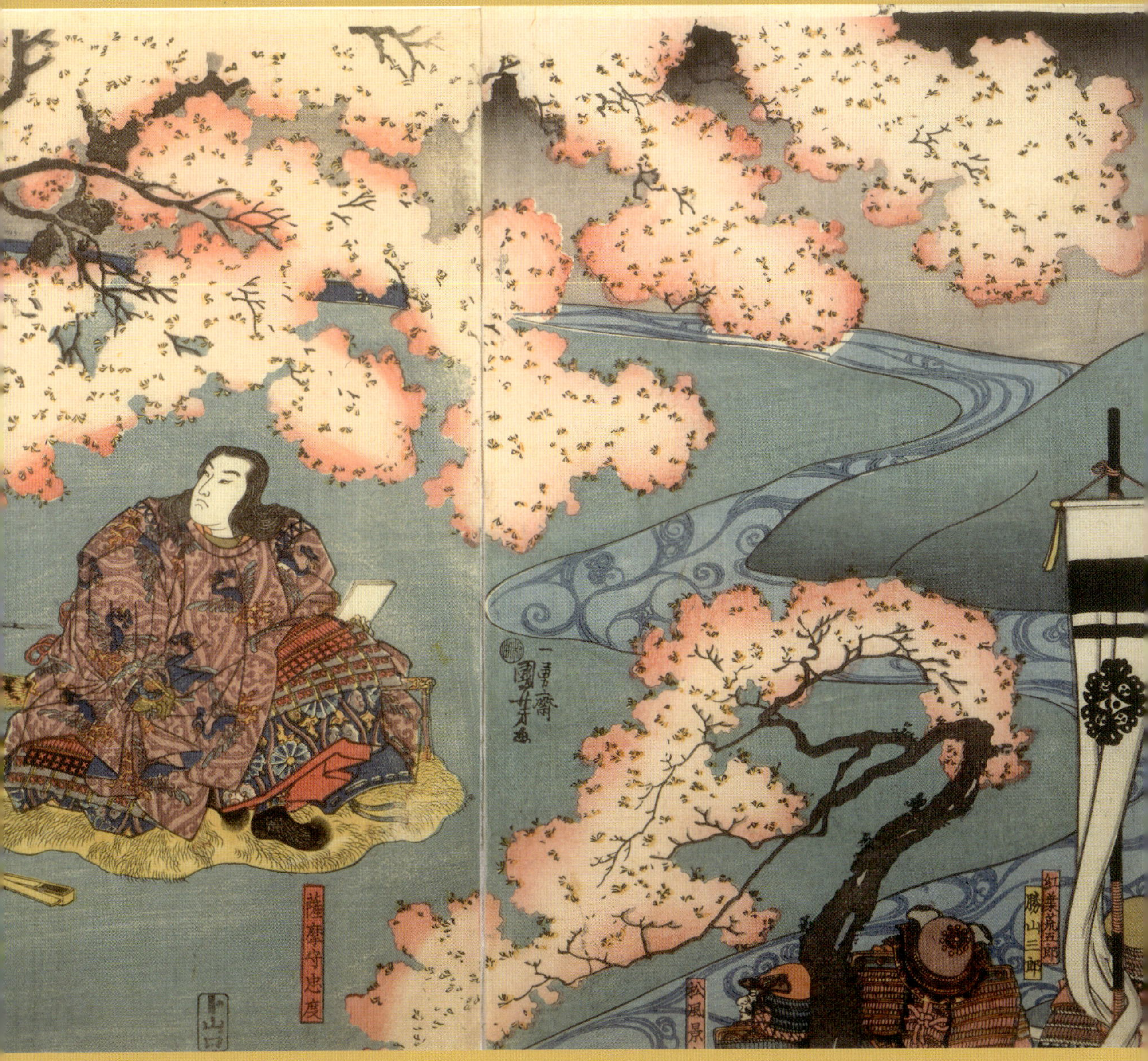

【行きくれて…】歌川国芳 弘化3年（1846）頃
"Were I, still traveling . . ." by Utagawa Kuniyoshi

A military leader of the late Heian period, Tadanori was the son of Taira no Tadamori and the younger brother of Kiyomori. As a student of Fujiwara no Toshinari, he also excelled in poetry. One of the most famous stories about him occurred during the collapse of the Taira's control over Kyoto, when Tadanori dared returned to the capital to give his teacher a group of verses and ask that some be included in one of the Imperial collections of poetry. After the Battle of Ichinotani in 1184, it is said the following verse was found upon his corpse: "Were I, still traveling as night falls, to make a sheltering tree my inn, then would my host tonight be the blossoms themselves?"

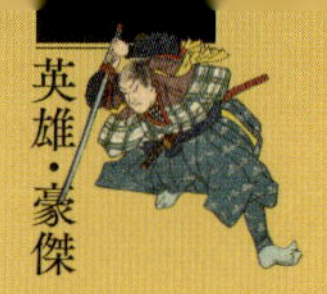

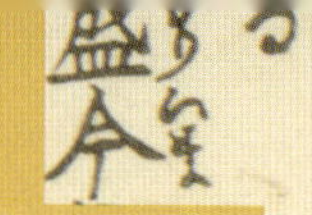

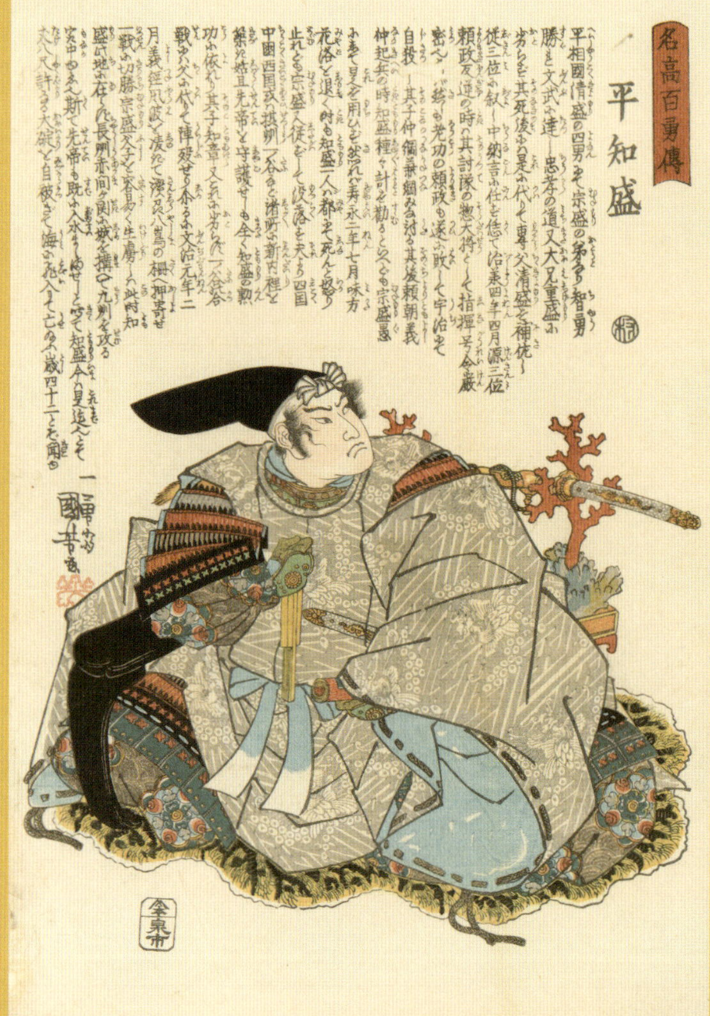

42

平家、滅びの美学

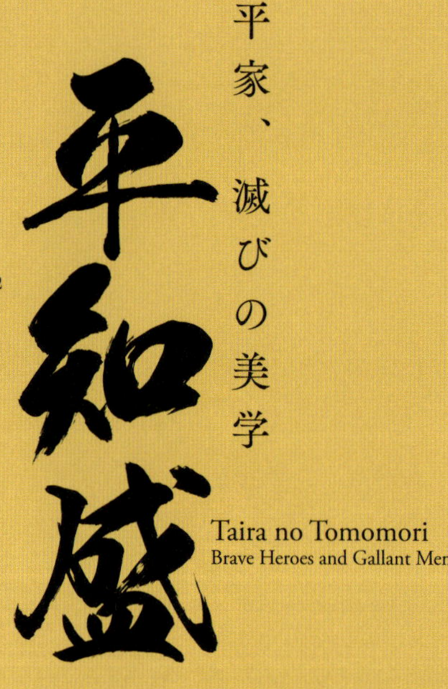

平知盛

Taira no Tomomori
Brave Heroes and Gallant Men

平安末期の武将。平清盛の四男。平氏随一の勇将として源平合戦で活躍したが、一ノ谷の戦いで敗れて屋島に逃れ、次いで壇ノ浦の戦いでも敗れた。奮戦の末、安徳天皇をはじめとする一門の女性が入水するのを見届け、「見るべき程のことは見つ」と言い残し、大碇を担いで入水した。能「舟弁慶」や歌舞伎「大物浦（義経千本桜）」の主人公として知られる。

A military leader of the late Heian period, Tomomori was the fourth son of Taira no Kiyomori. Though he proved to be the bravest of the Taira generals during the Genpei Wars, he was defeated during the Battle of Ichinotani and fled to Yashima in Shikoku, before being defeated again at the decisive Battle of Dan-no-ura. He watched as Emperor Antoku and the Taira women drowned themselves in the sea, leaving behind the words "I supervised what I had to," before following them by sinking himself upon a large anchor. He is famed as the protagonist of the Noh play *Benkei and the Boat* and the kabuki play *Daimotsu-no-ura* (*Yoshitsune and the Thousand Cherry Trees*).

【名高百勇伝 平知盛】歌川国芳
天保14年〜弘化3年（1843-46）頃
"One Hundred Heroes
of Great Courage:
Taira no Tomomori"
by Utagawa Kuniyoshi

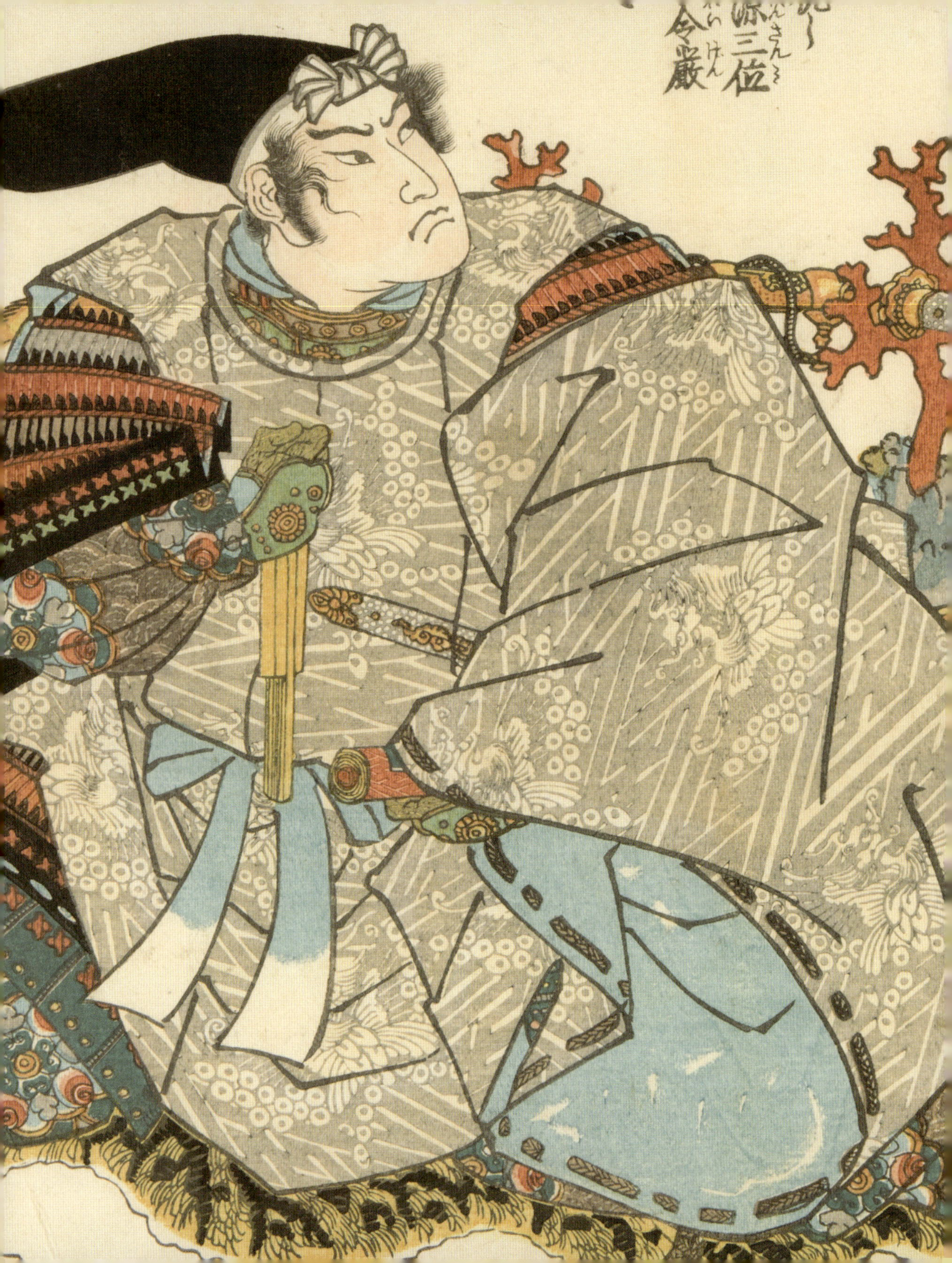
源三位
令巌

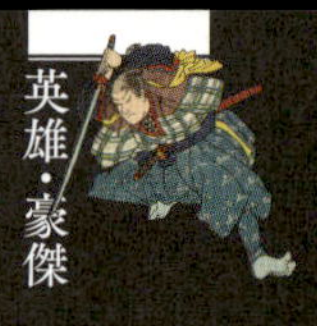

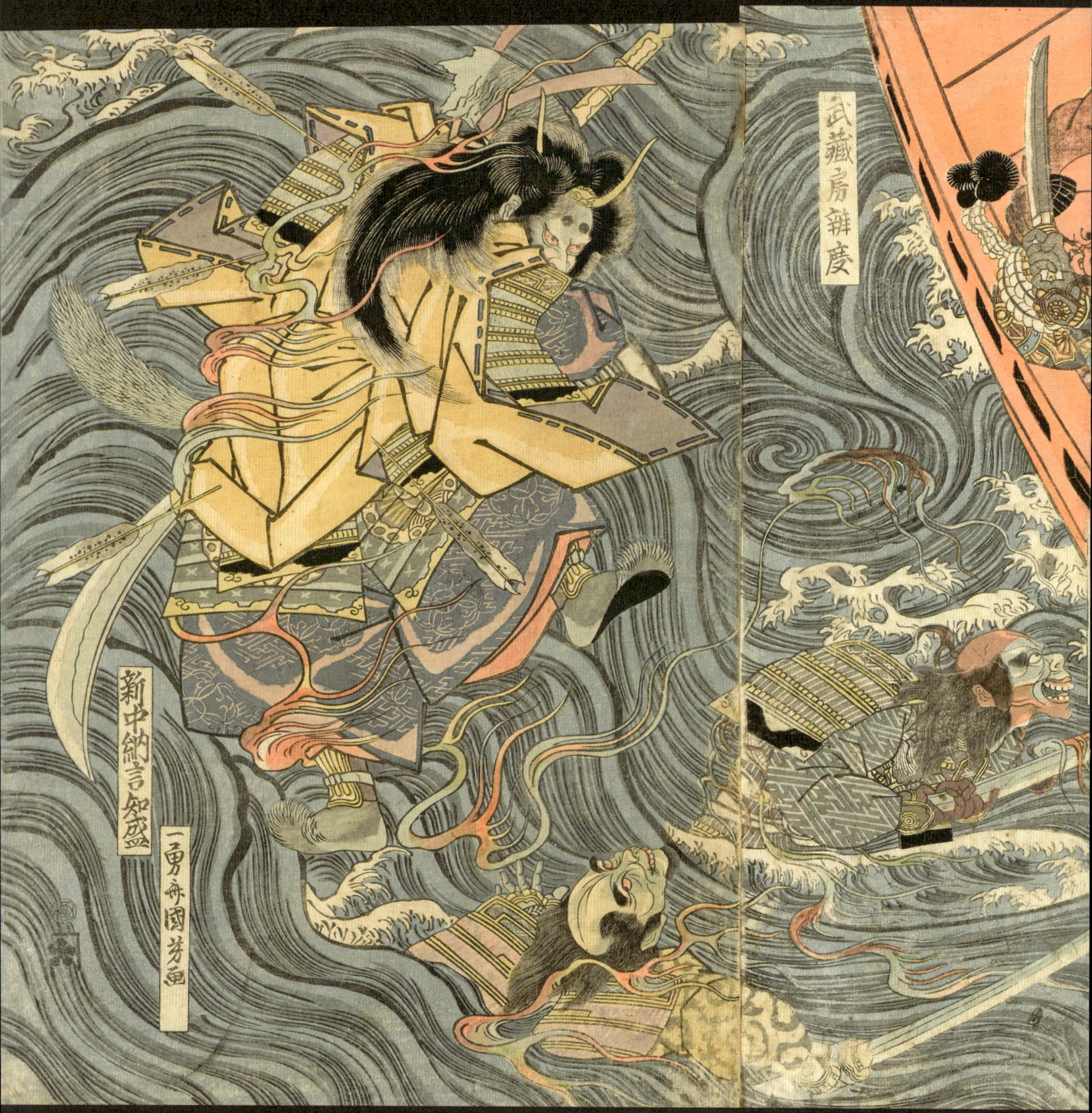

【大物之浦 知盛の亡霊】歌川国芳 文政元〜3年（1818-20）頃

海中から知盛の亡霊が現れ、壇ノ浦で敗れた平氏の恨みを晴らすため、大物浦で源義経一行が乗る船を襲う。

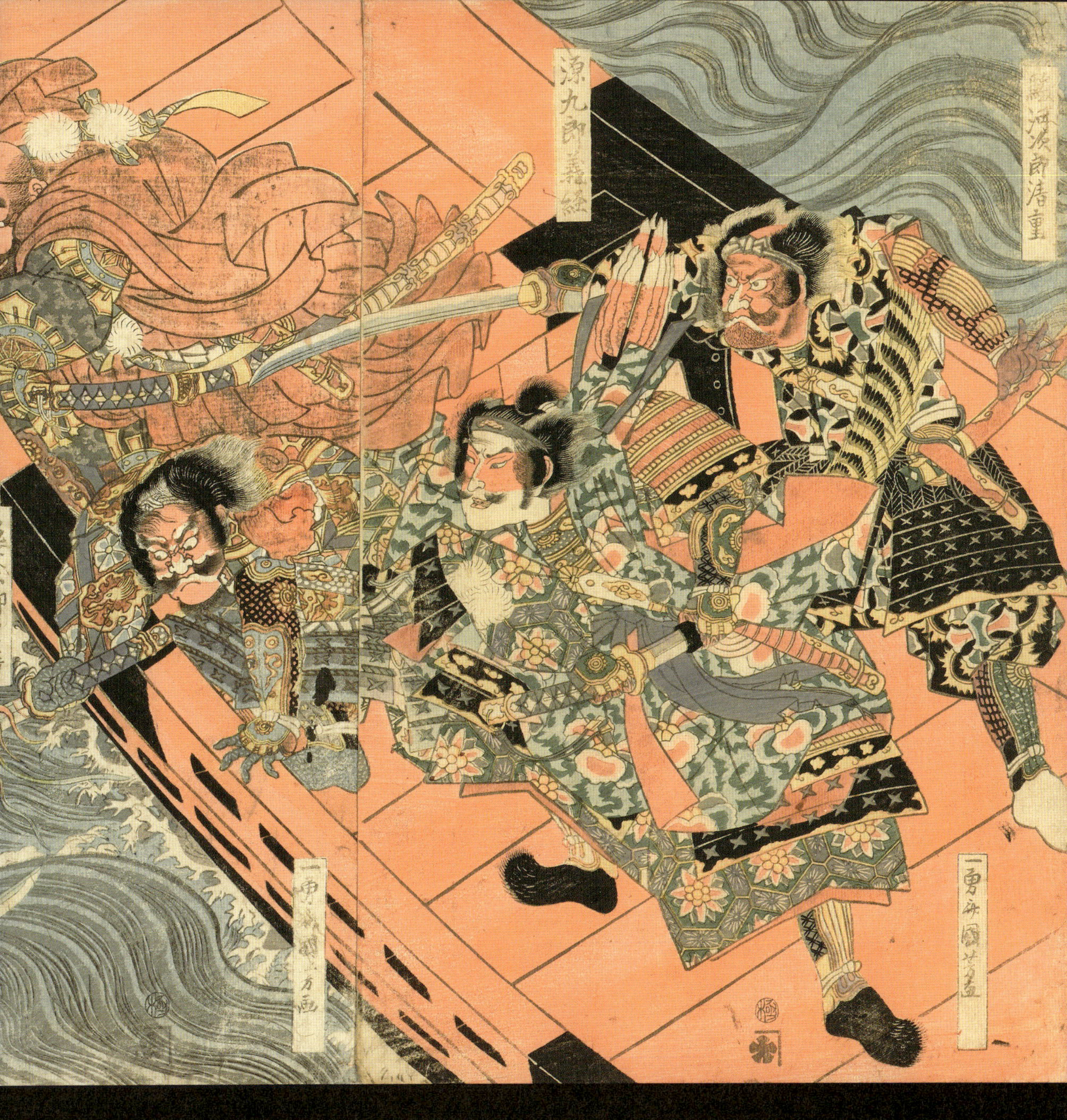

"Daimotsu-no-ura and the Ghost of Taira no Tomomori" by Utagawa Kuniyoshi

Tomomori's ghost rises from the sea and attacks the ship of Minamoto no Yoshitsune and his entourage at Daimotsu-no-ura in order to appease the vengeful spirits of the Taira clan who perished at the Battle of Dan-no-ura.

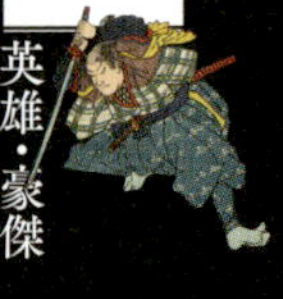

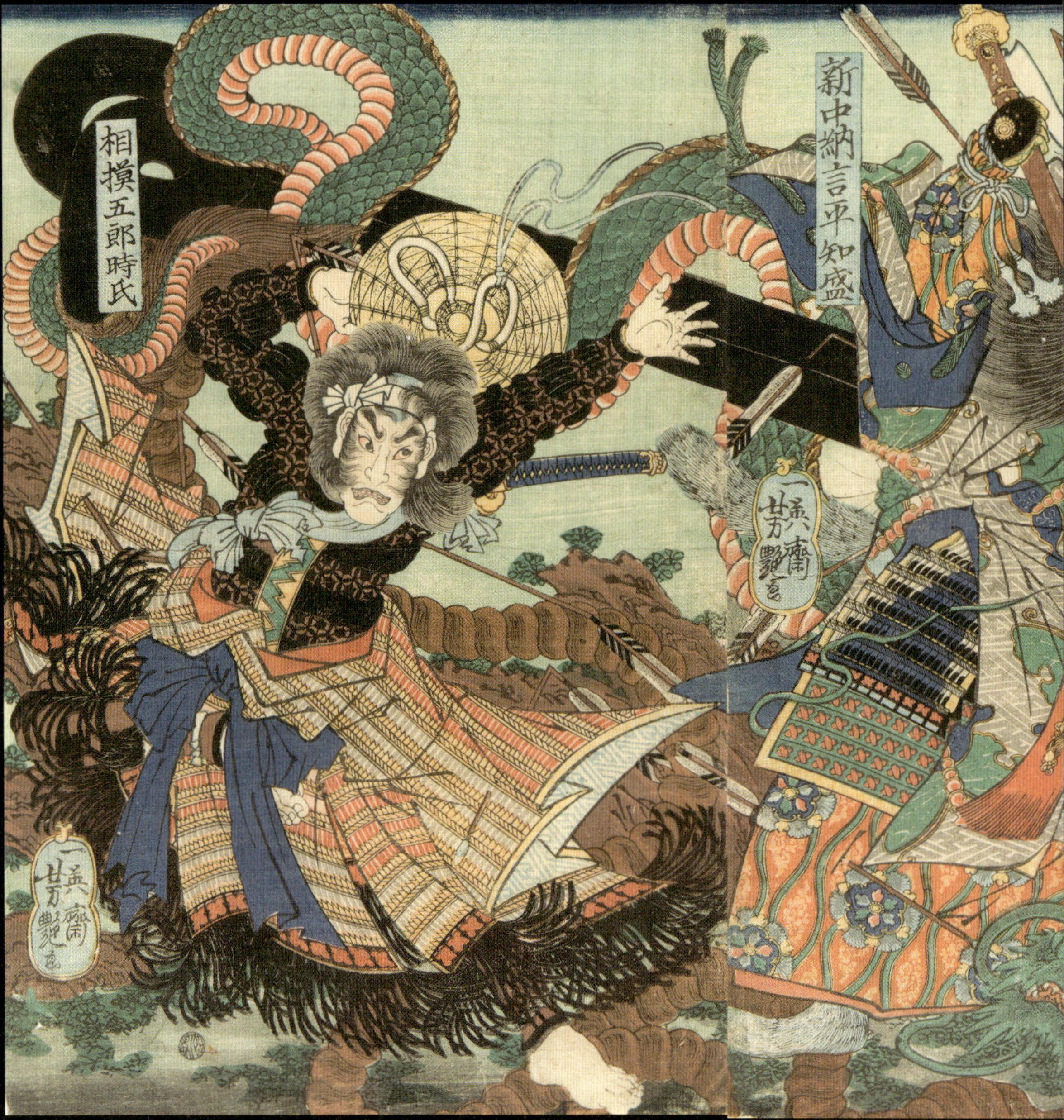

【矢島海底図】歌川芳艶　文久元年（1861）

海底で復讐の機を窺う知盛の亡霊のもとへ、義経一行の動向を伝えに相模五郎がやってきた。背後の大碇には龍神が絡みつく。

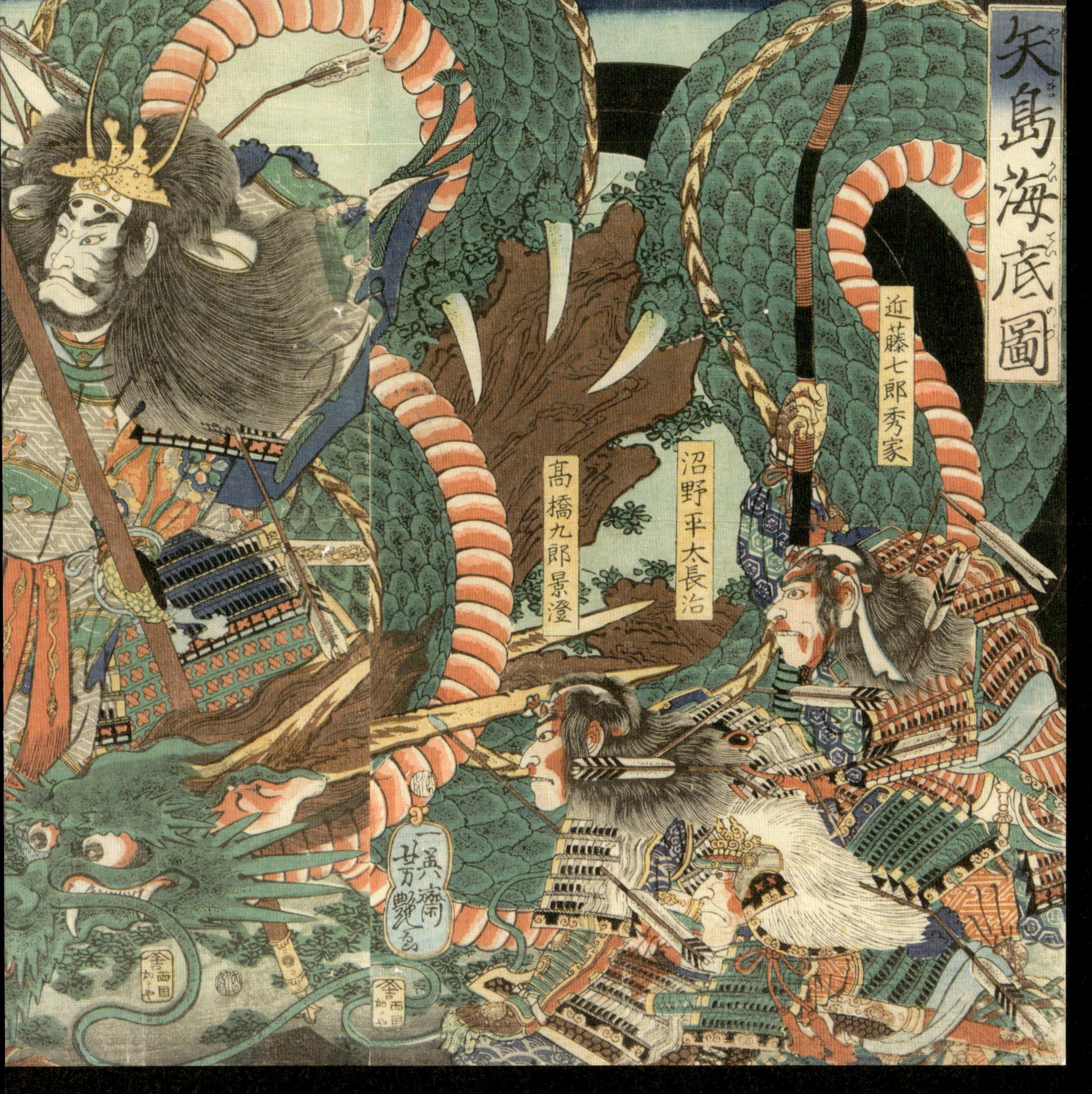

"The Bottom of the Sea at Yashima" by Utagawa Yoshitsuya

Tomomori's ghost waits on the bottom of the sea for the opportunity to exact revenge against the Minamoto, when Sagami Gorō arrives to tell him about the movements of Yoshitsune's entourage. The Dragon God wraps himself around the anchor in the background.

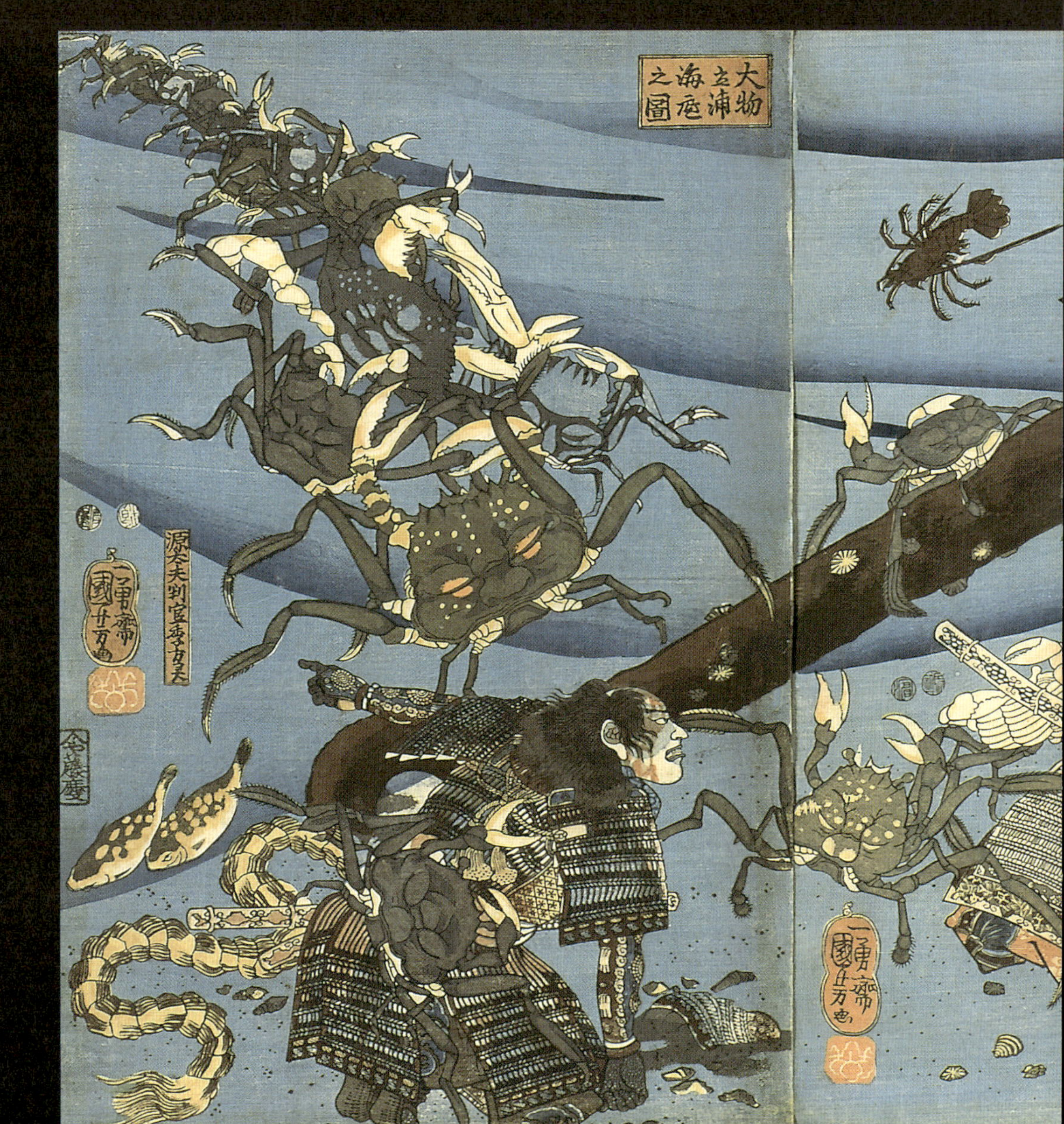
大物立浦海底之圖
源三天判宣平方天
一勇齋國芳画
一勇齋國芳画

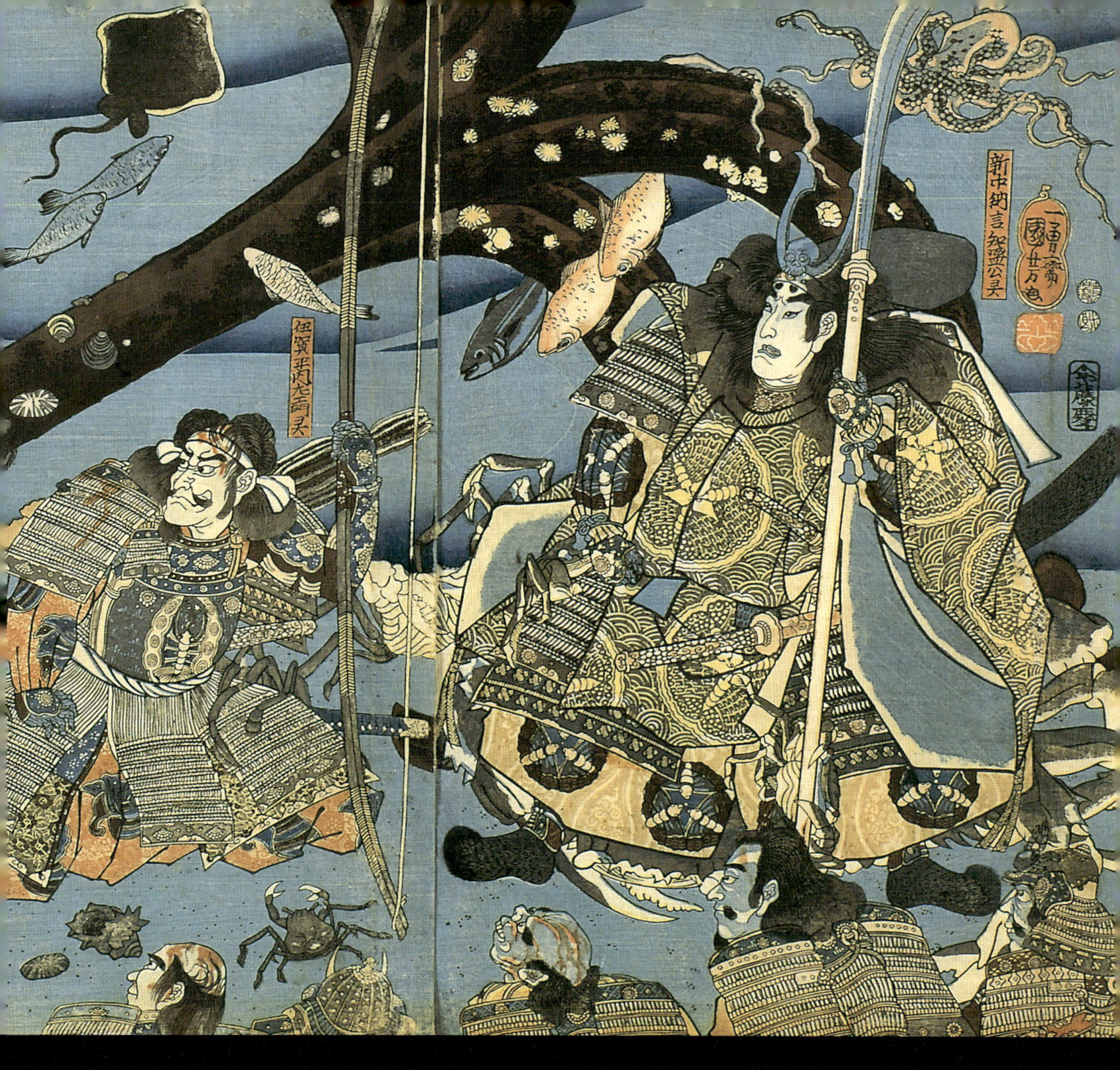

"The Bottom of the Sea at Daimotsu-no-ura" by Utagawa Kuniyoshi

At far right is Taira no Tomomori, who sank to the bottom of the sea on a giant anchor. Next to him is Iga no Heinaizaemon, his milk brother, who leapt into the sea with him. The souls of the rest of the Taira clan have turned into crabs, floating back and forth with the waves.

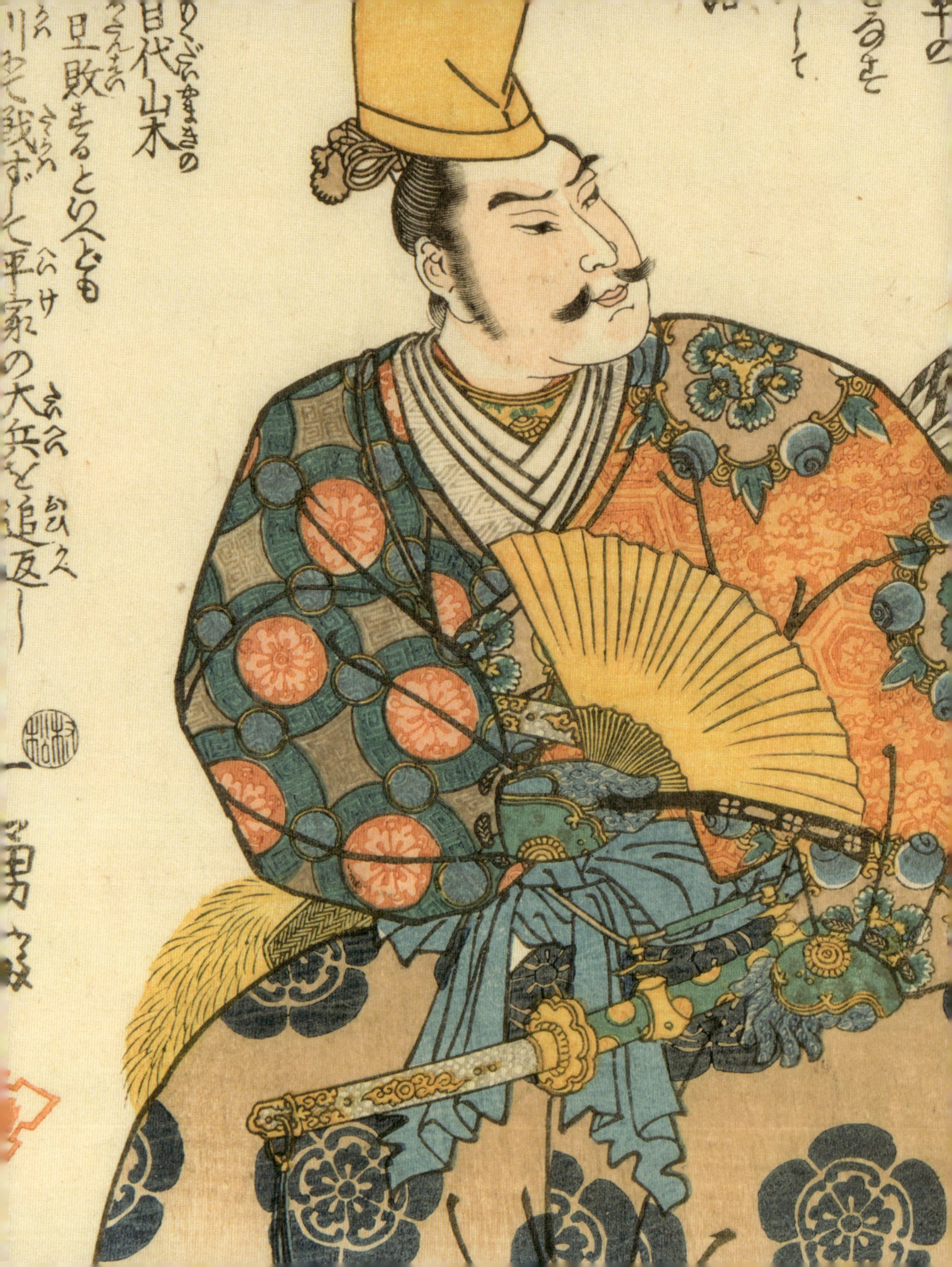

日代山木
旦敗きるとりへども
我すして平家の大兵を追返し

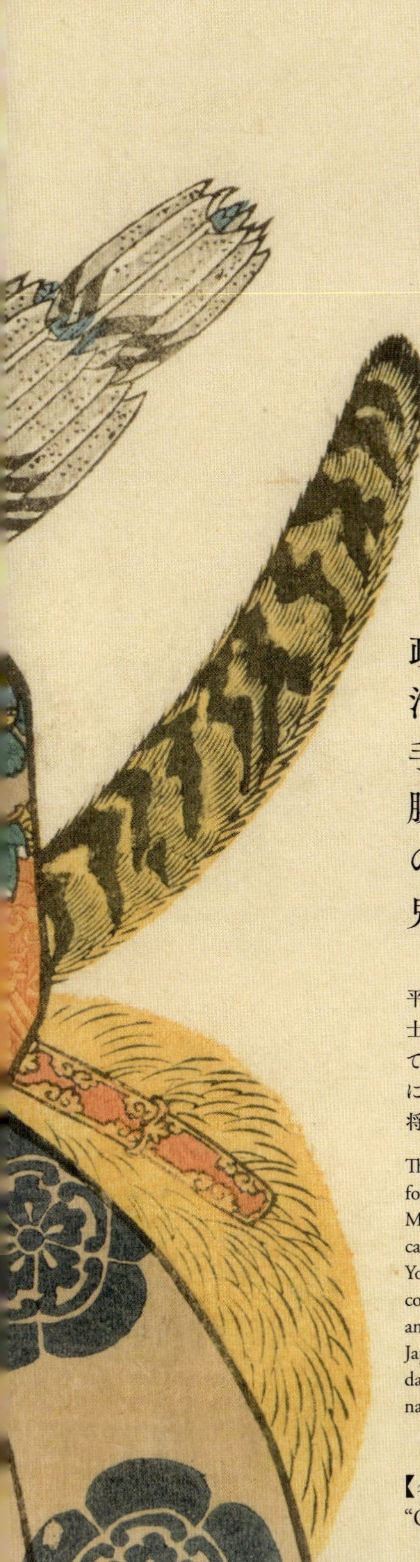

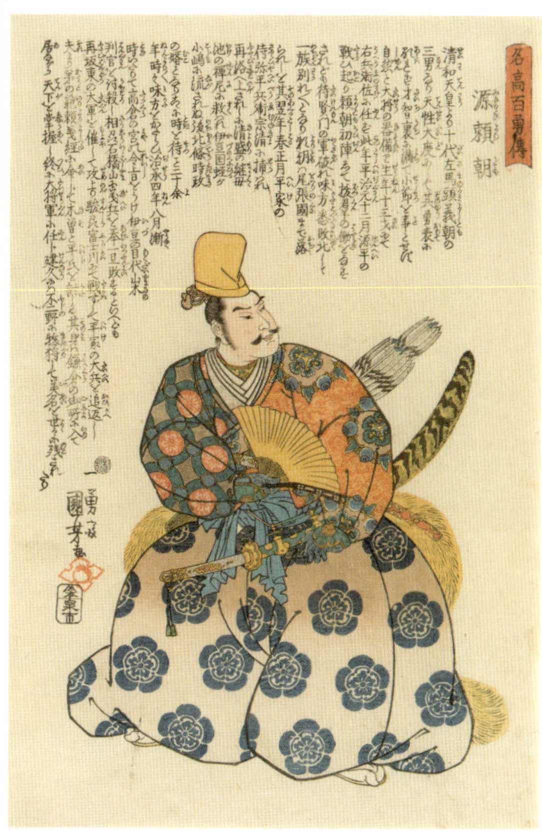

源頼朝

政治手腕の鬼

Minamoto no Yoritomo
Brave Heroes and Gallant Men

平治の乱で伊豆に流されたが、以仁王の命を受けて平氏追討の兵をあげた。石橋山で敗れたあと富士川の戦いに大勝、鎌倉を本拠に東国軍事政権を確立する。弟の範頼・義経に命じて源義仲、続いて平氏を壇ノ浦で滅亡させた。この間、後白河法皇に接近した義経と対立、その追補を口実に諸国に守護・地頭を置き、武家政治の基礎を固める。建久元年（1190）、上洛して権大納言、右近衛大将に任じられ、翌々年、征夷大将軍を拝した。

Though exiled to the Izu Islands after the Heiji Rebellion of 1160, Yoritomo returned to organize military forces against the Taira at the request of Prince Mochihito. He was defeated by the Taira at the Battle of Mount Ishibashi in 1180, then routed them at the Battle of Fujikawa, which he waged from Kamakura, the capital of his military government in the east. With the help of his younger brothers Noriyori and Yoshitsune, Yoritomo eliminated his rival cousin Yoshinaka before destroying the Taira at Dan-no-ura. Meanwhile, countering Yoshitsune's alliance with Retired Emperor Goshirakawa, Yoritomo appointed constables (shugo) and stewards (jito) to provinces across the archipelago, thus reinforcing the foundations of warrior rule in Japan. In 1190, Yoritomo returned to Kyoto, where he was officially appointed Grand Councilor (Gondainagon) and Captain of the Right Imperial Guard (U-konoe-daishō). The following year, he was also named Commander-in-Chief of the Expeditionary Force Against the Barbarians (Sei-i taishōgun).

【名高百勇伝 源頼朝】歌川国芳　天保14年〜弘化3年（1843-46）頃
"One Hundred Heroes of Great Courage: Minamoto no Yoritomo" by Utagawa Kuniyoshi

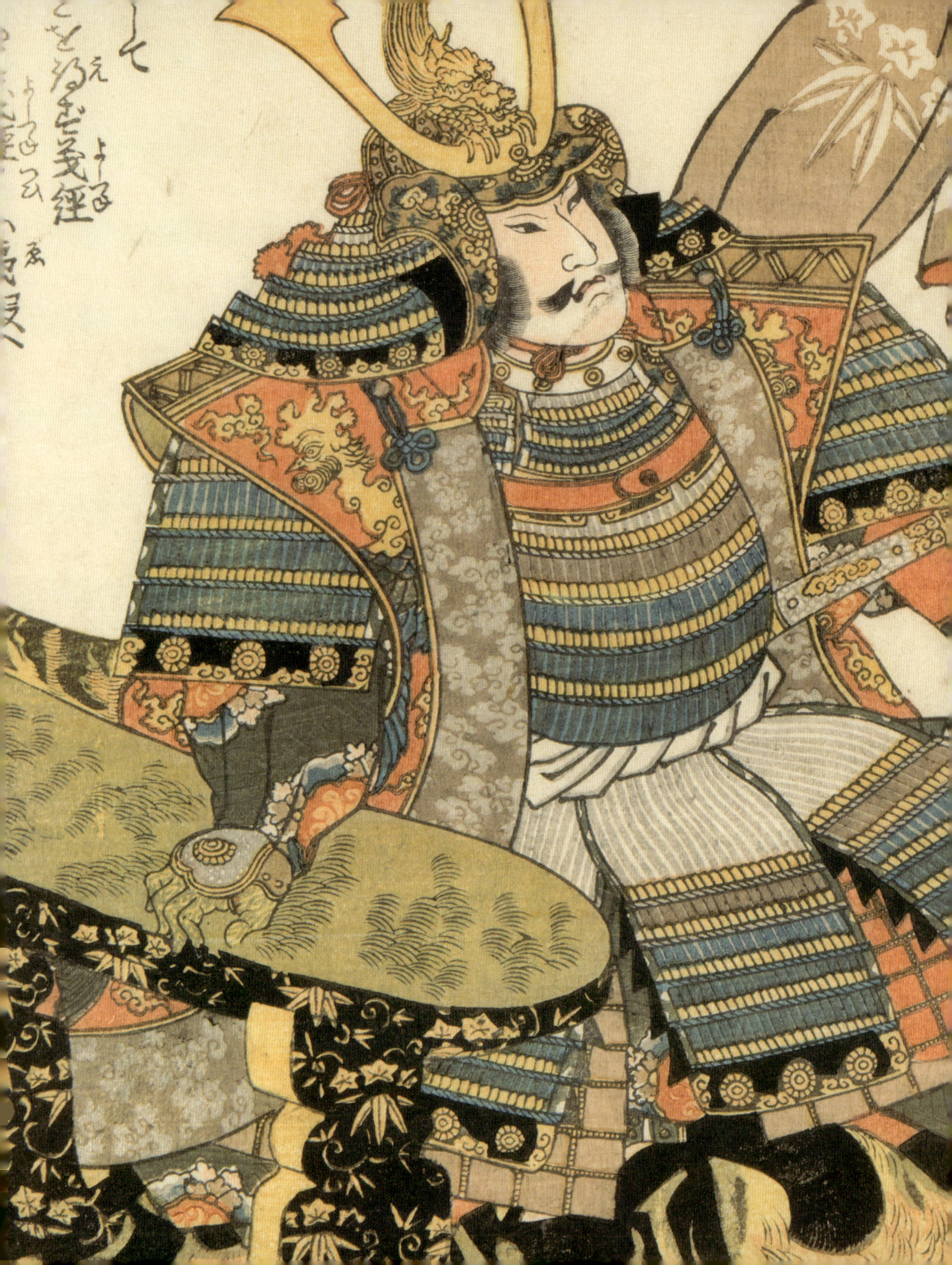
義經

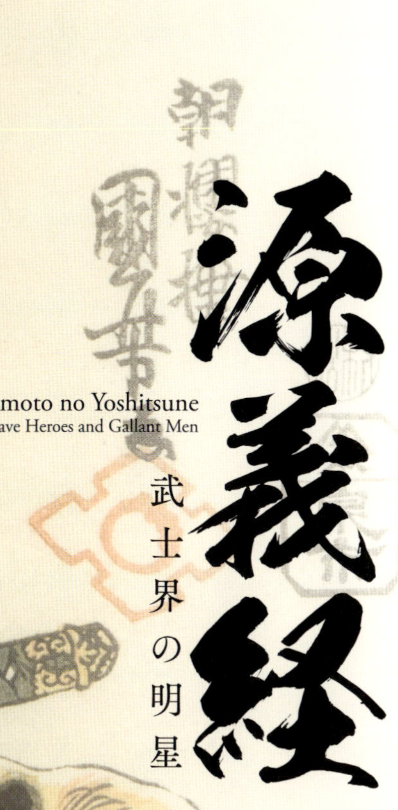

源義経

Minamoto no Yoshitsune
Brave Heroes and Gallant Men

武士界の明星

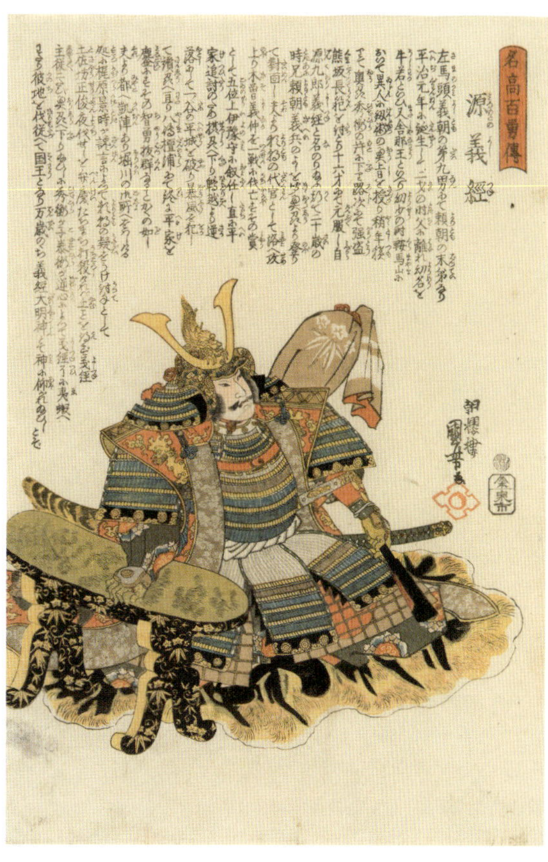

平安時代末期の武将で源頼朝の異母弟。幼名は牛若丸。俗に九郎判官とも呼ばれる。平治の乱で平氏に捕らえられ鞍馬寺に入れられたが、のちに陸奥の藤原秀衡のもとに身を寄せた。兄頼朝の挙兵に参じ、源義仲の追討や平氏の滅亡に活躍した。のち頼朝と不和となり、諸国を潜行。再び秀衡を頼って奥州へ赴くが、秀衡の死後、子の泰衡に急襲され、衣川の館で自殺した。その不遇な生涯は、いわゆる「判官贔屓」の風潮を生み、後世多くの文芸作品の題材となった。

A military leader of the late Heian period, Minamoto Yoshitsune was the younger half-brother of Yoritomo, with whom he shared a father. During his youth, he was known as Ushiwakamaru. He was also called Magistrate Kurō Hōgan. As a boy, he was captured by the Taira during the Heiji Rebellion in 1160 and placed in the care of Kurama-dera Temple. He was subsequently relocated north to Hiraizumi, where he was put under the protection of Fujiwara no Hidehira, head of the northern Ōshū Fujiwara clan. He joined his brother Yoritomo's call to arms and participated in the ousting of Yoshinaka and the crushing of the Taira. Due to conflicts with Yoritomo, however, he was later forced to lay low in the provinces and returned to Hiraizumi. Following Hidehira's death, he was attacked by Hidehira's son Fujiwara no Yasuhira and committed suicide at his residence on the Koromogawa River. The story of Yoshitsune's life seeded affection for tragic, underdog heroes in Japanese culture, known as "hōgan biiki" ("sympathy for Magistrate Yoshitsune"), and served as the theme of countless works of literature over the years.

【名高百勇伝 源義経】歌川国芳　天保14年〜弘化3年（1843-46）頃
"One Hundred Heroes of Great Courage: Minamoto no Yoshitsune" by Utagawa Kuniyoshi

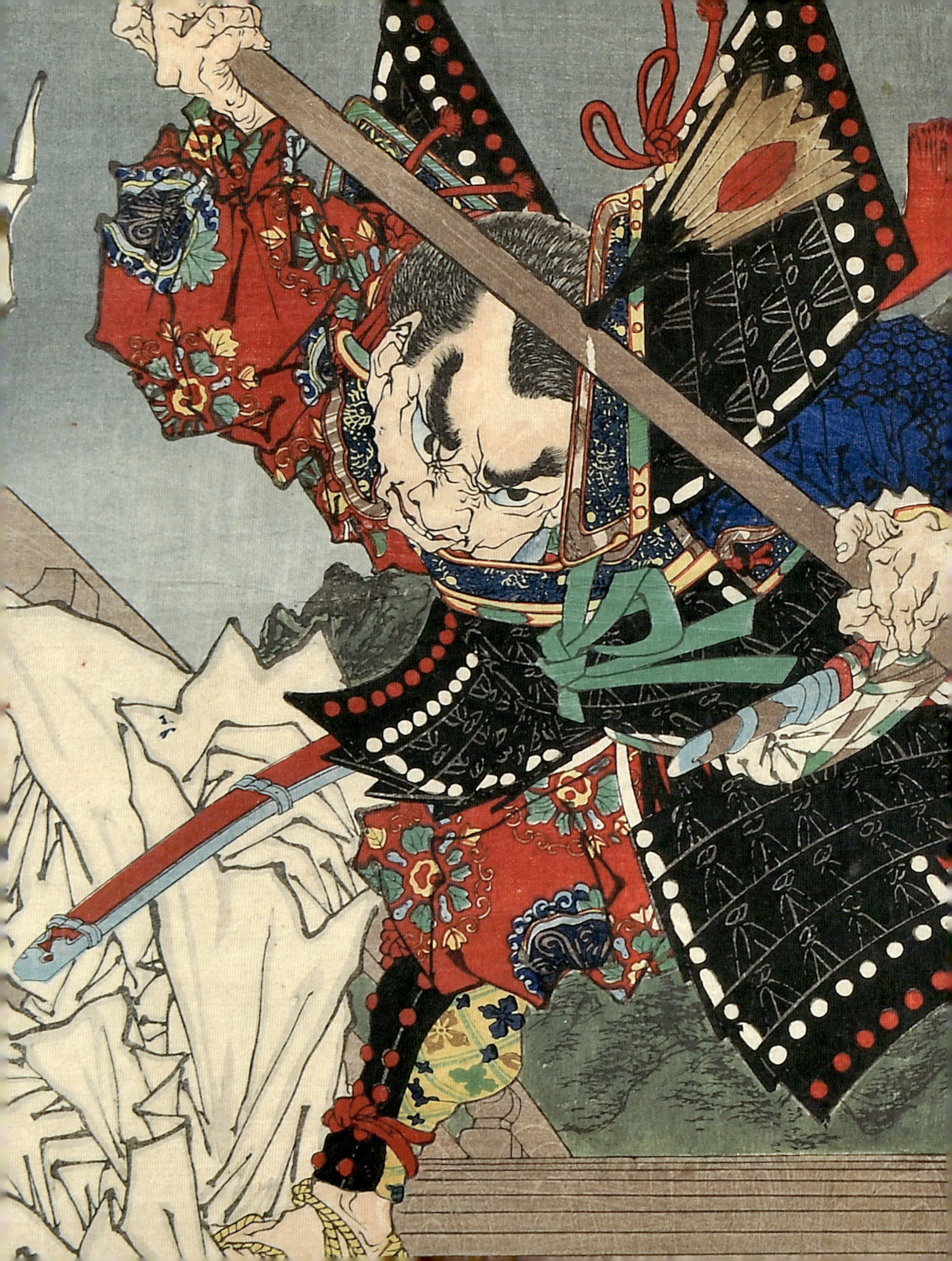

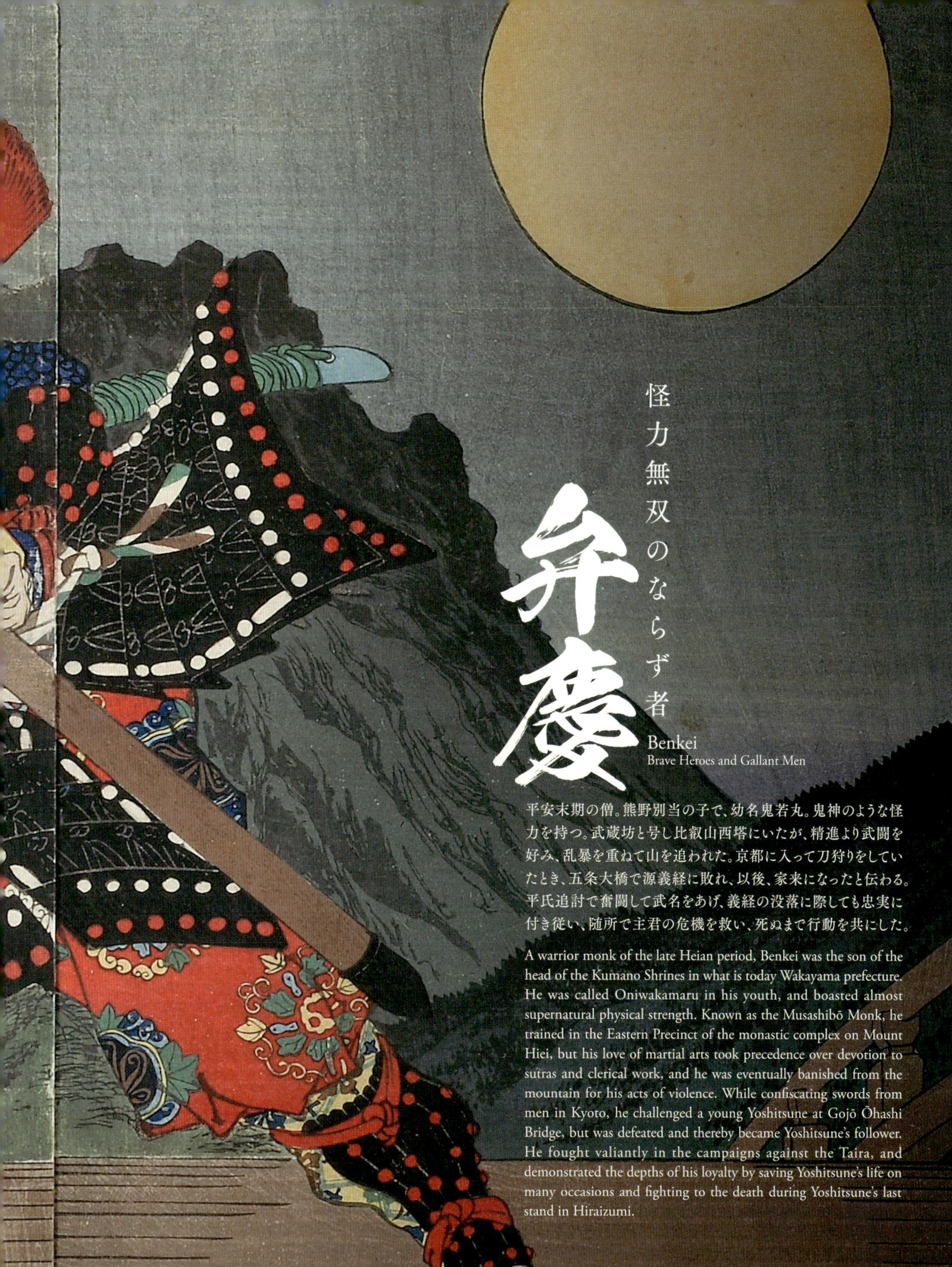

平安末期の僧。熊野別当の子で、幼名鬼若丸。鬼神のような怪力を持つ。武蔵坊と号し比叡山西塔にいたが、精進より武闘を好み、乱暴を重ねて山を追われた。京都に入って刀狩りをしていたとき、五条大橋で源義経に敗れ、以後、家来になったと伝わる。平氏追討で奮闘して武名をあげ、義経の没落に際しても忠実に付き従い、随所で主君の危機を救い、死ぬまで行動を共にした。

A warrior monk of the late Heian period, Benkei was the son of the head of the Kumano Shrines in what is today Wakayama prefecture. He was called Oniwakamaru in his youth, and boasted almost supernatural physical strength. Known as the Musashibō Monk, he trained in the Eastern Precinct of the monastic complex on Mount Hiei, but his love of martial arts took precedence over devotion to sutras and clerical work, and he was eventually banished from the mountain for his acts of violence. While confiscating swords from men in Kyoto, he challenged a young Yoshitsune at Gojō Ōhashi Bridge, but was defeated and thereby became Yoshitsune's follower. He fought valiantly in the campaigns against the Taira, and demonstrated the depths of his loyalty by saving Yoshitsune's life on many occasions and fighting to the death during Yoshitsune's last stand in Hiraizumi.

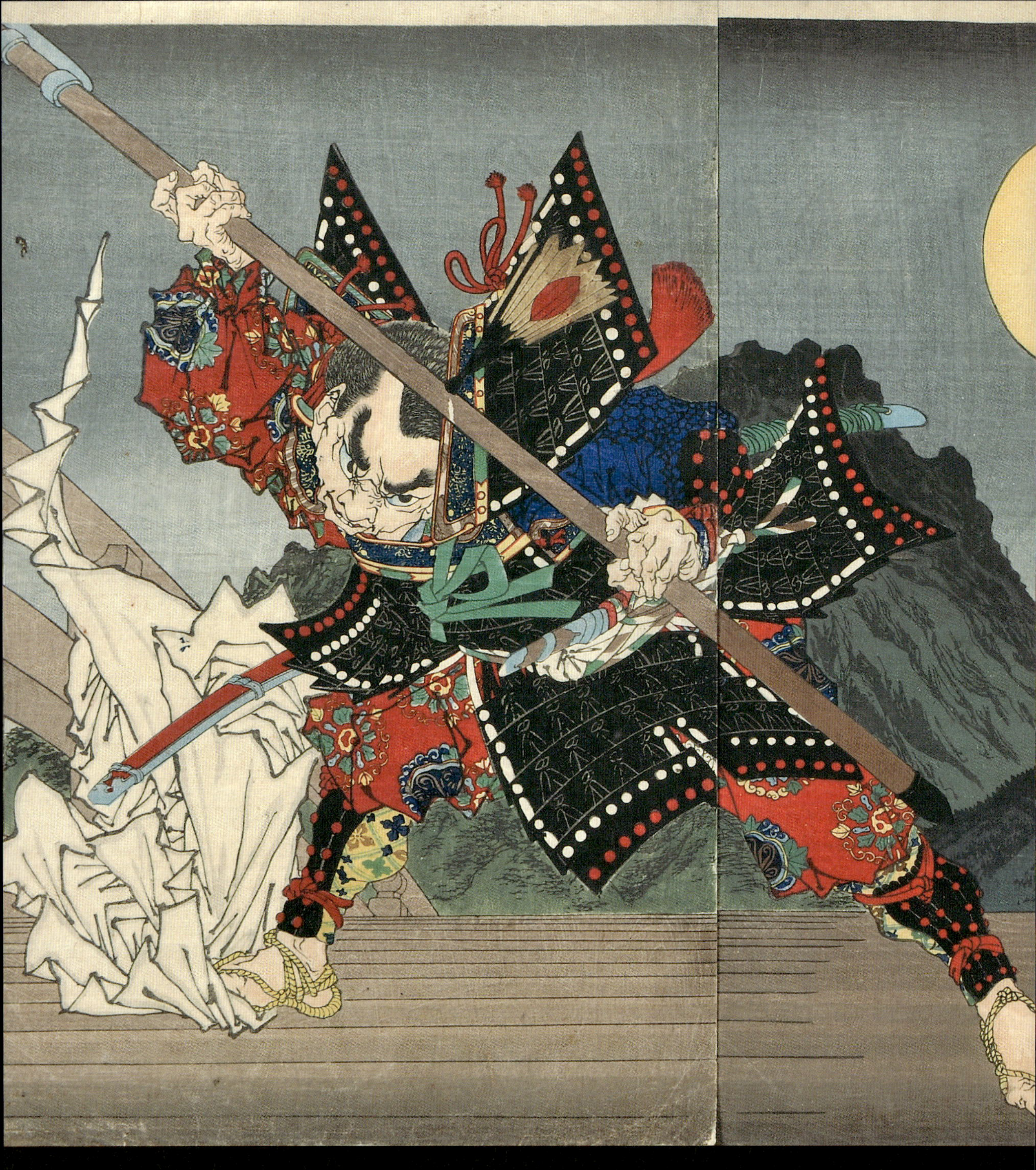

【義経記五条橋之図】月岡芳年　明治14年（1881）西井コレクション収蔵
夜な夜な五条大橋で、道行く人を襲って刀を奪う弁慶。女物の白い衣被きをかぶり、笛を吹きながら通りすがる牛若丸。
弁慶が打ち込む長刀を、牛若丸はひらりとかわす。

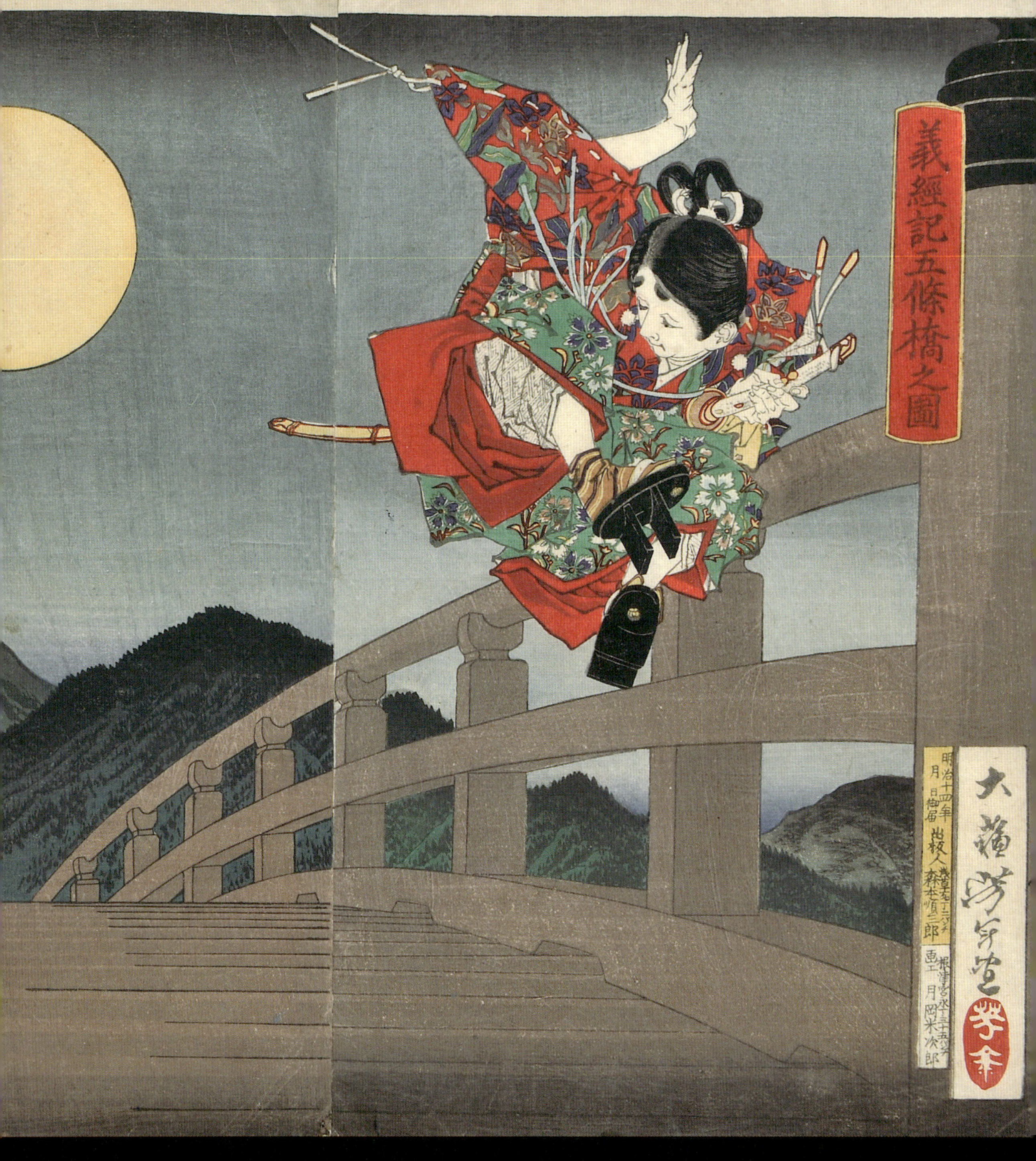

"Yoshitsune and Benkei on Gojō Ōhashi Bridge" by Tsukioka Yoshitoshi, Nishii Collection

It is night on the Gojō Ōhashi Bridge in Kyoto, and Benkei has been forcibly taking swords from men walking the capital's streets.

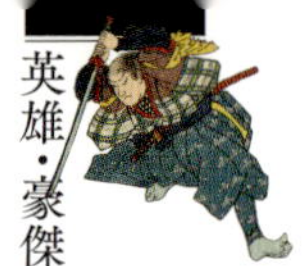

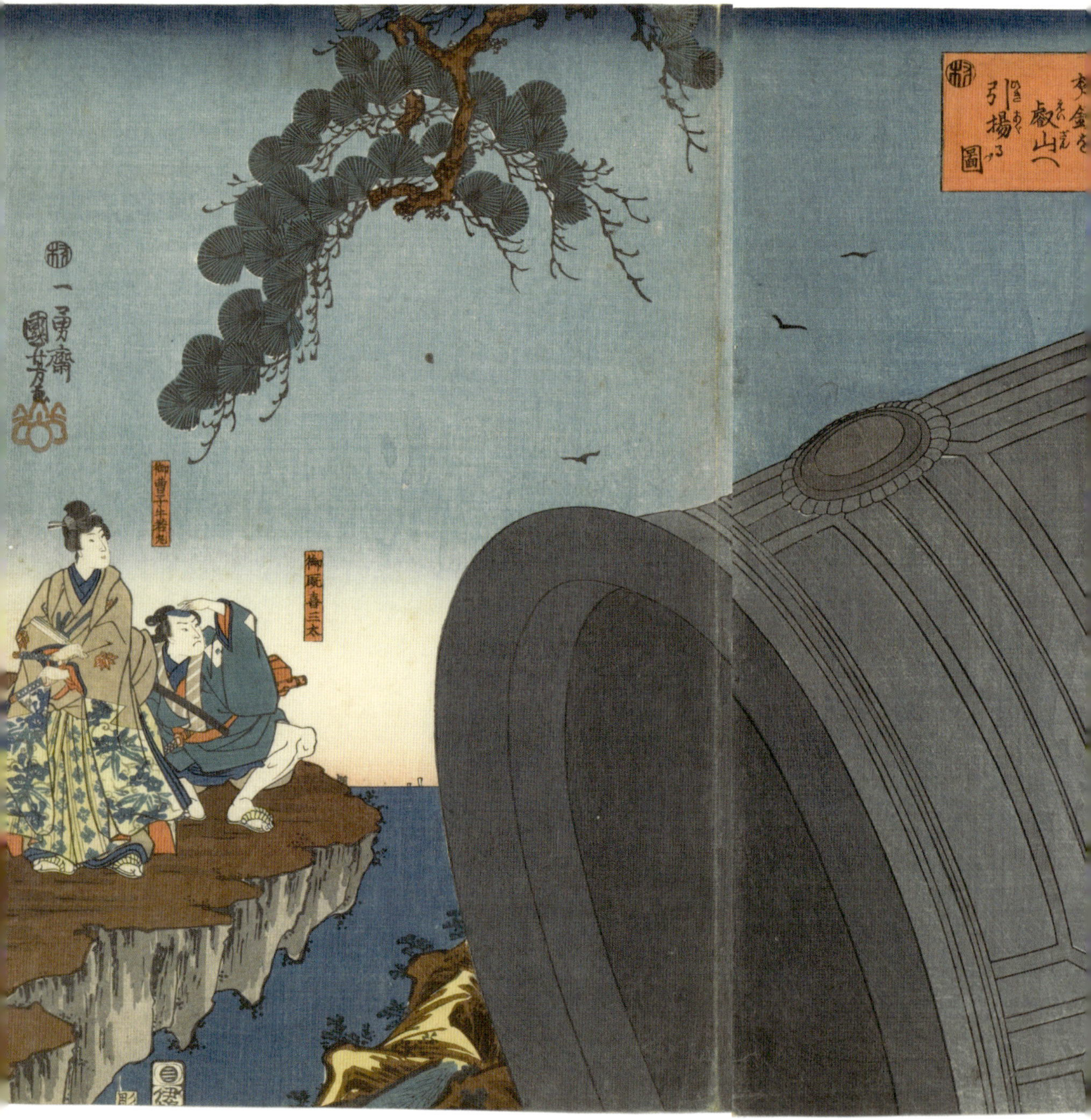

【弁慶が勇力戯に三井寺の梵鐘を叡山へ引揚る図】歌川国芳　弘化2～3年（1845-46）頃　ギャラリー紅屋収蔵

藤原秀郷（俵藤太）が龍神より賜った三井寺の釣鐘を、山門との争いで弁慶が奪い、引きずりながら比叡山へ持って帰った。
鐘を撞いてみると、「イノー、イノー（帰りたいの意）」と響いたので、弁慶は怒って谷底へ投げ捨ててしまった。

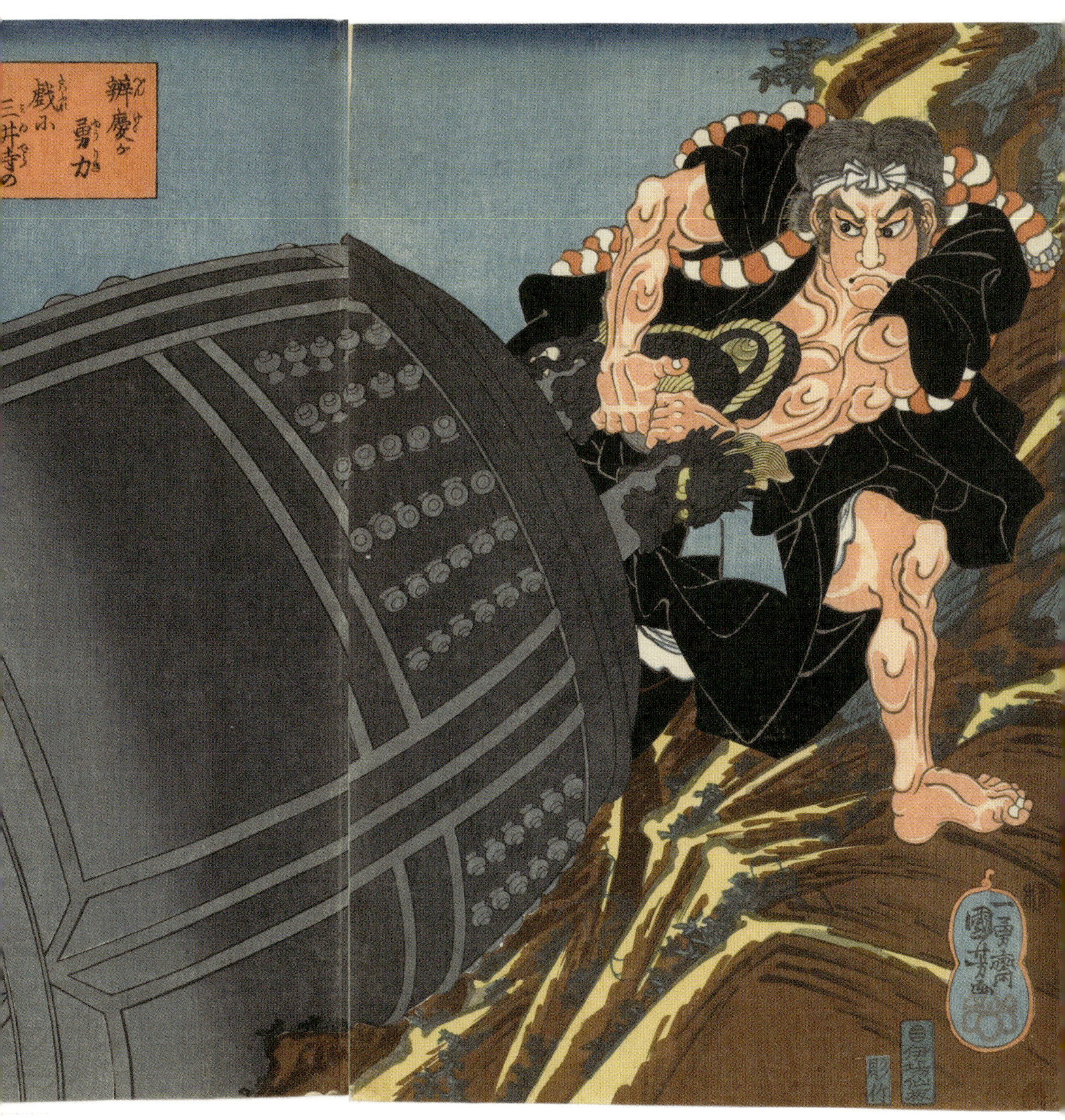

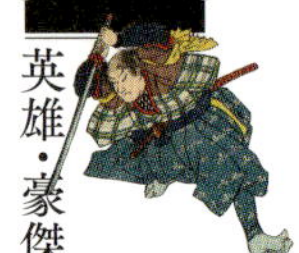

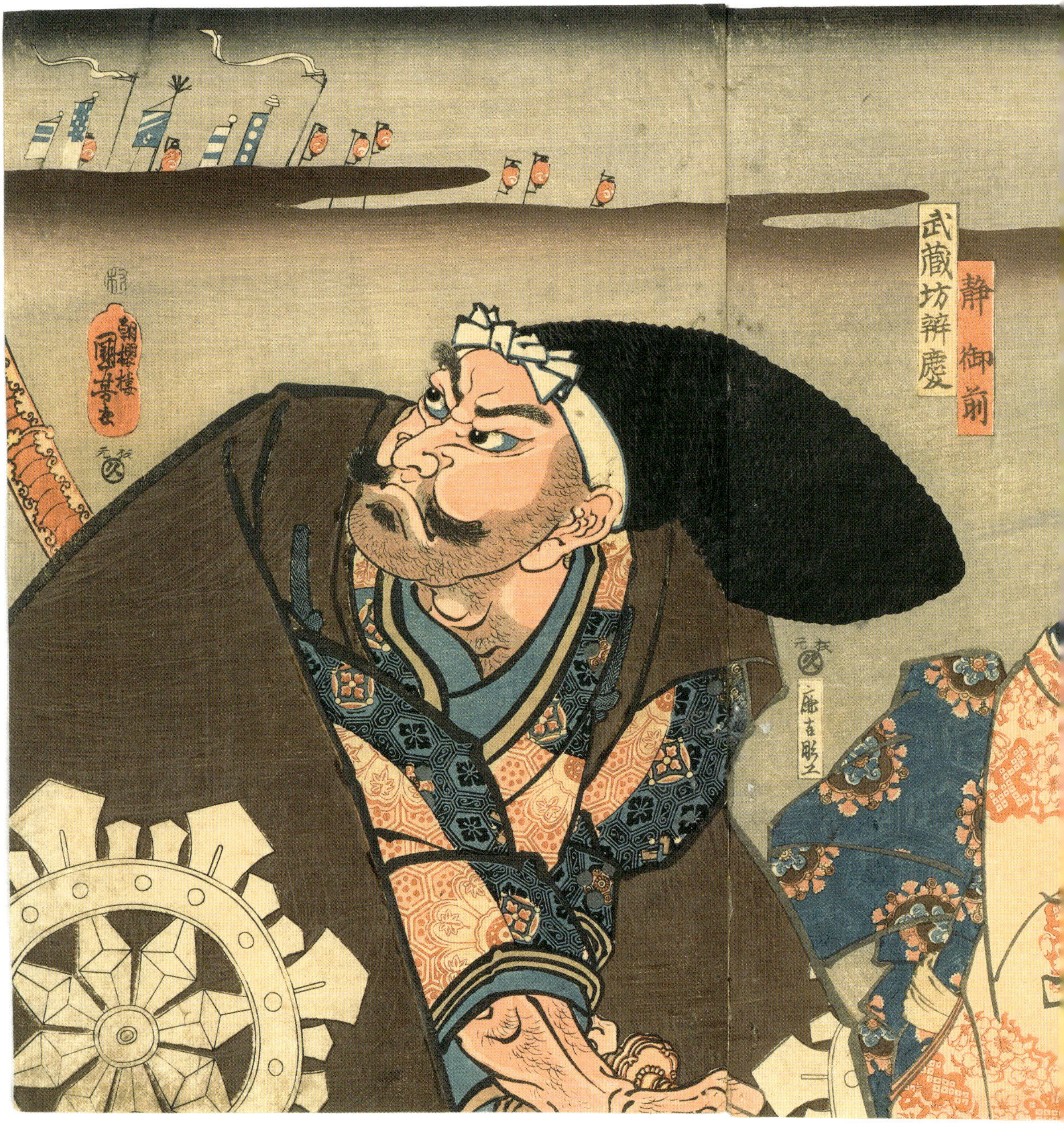

【堀川夜討土佐坊昌俊遠寄之図】歌川国芳　天保14年〜弘化3年（1843-46）頃
頼朝命を受け、土佐坊昌俊の軍勢が京都六条堀川の義経館を取り巻く。この強襲ののち、義経一行は都落ちを余儀なくされる。

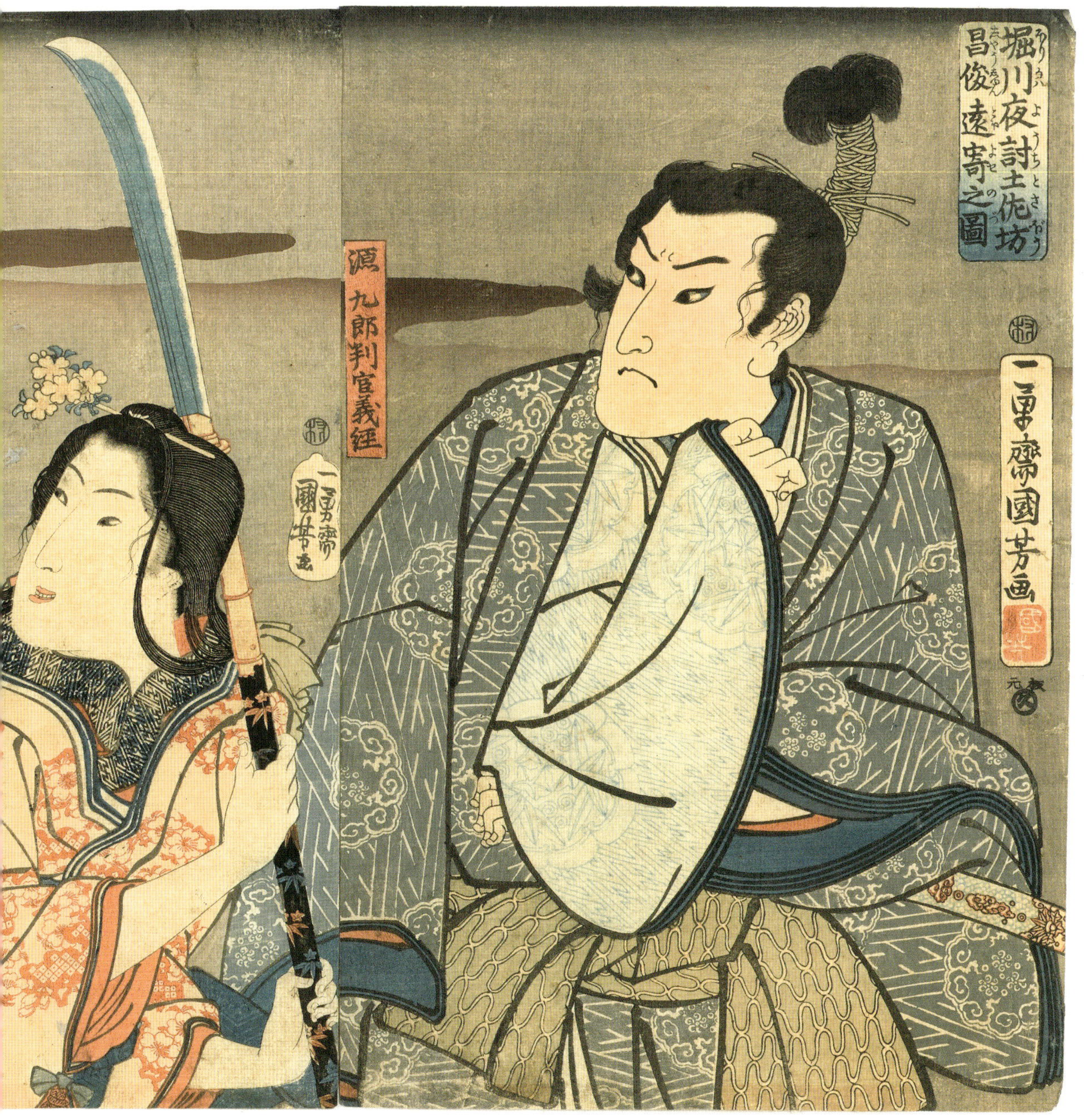

"Night Attack on Horikawa Palace: Tosanobō Shōshun Approaches in the Distance" by Utagawa Kuniyoshi

Acting on orders from Yoritomo, the forces of Tosanobō Shōshun surrounds Yoshitsune's palace on the Horikawa River in Kyoto.
Due to the size of the attacking army, Yoshitsune and his loyal retainers have no choice but to quit the capital.

佐々木高綱　梶原景季

宇治川の先陣争い

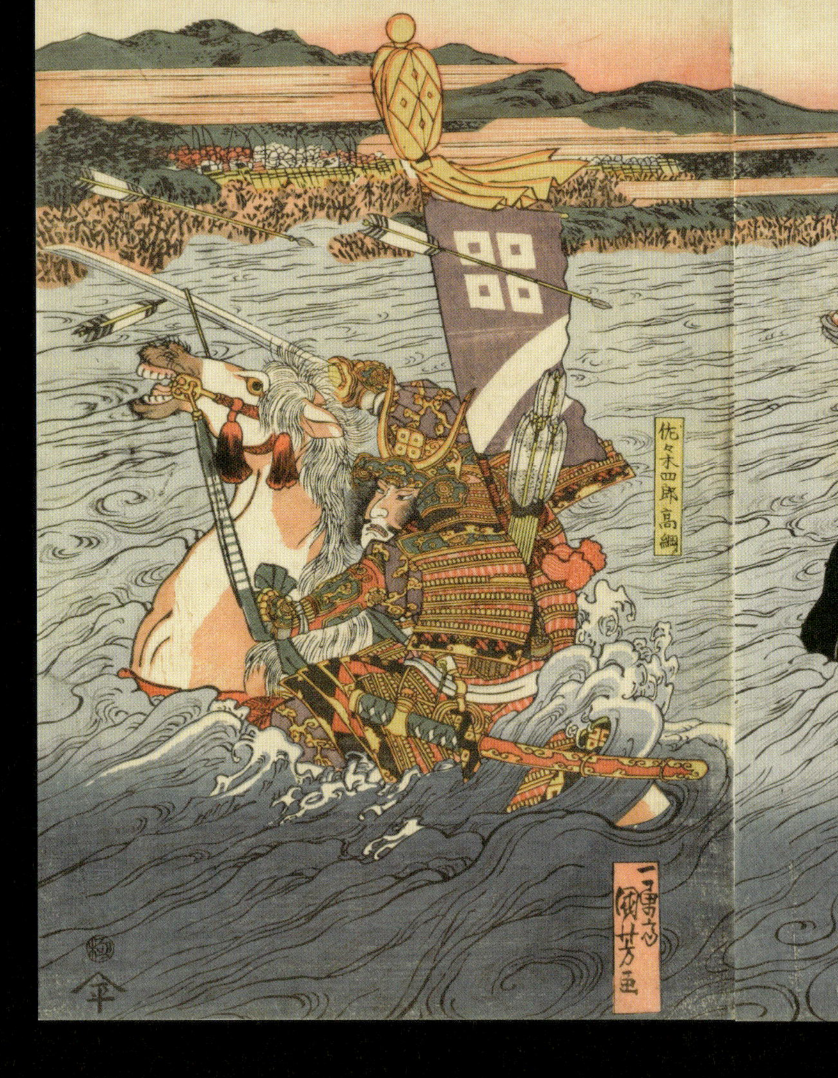

Sasaki Takatsuna and Kajiwara Kagesue
Brave Heroes and Gallant Men

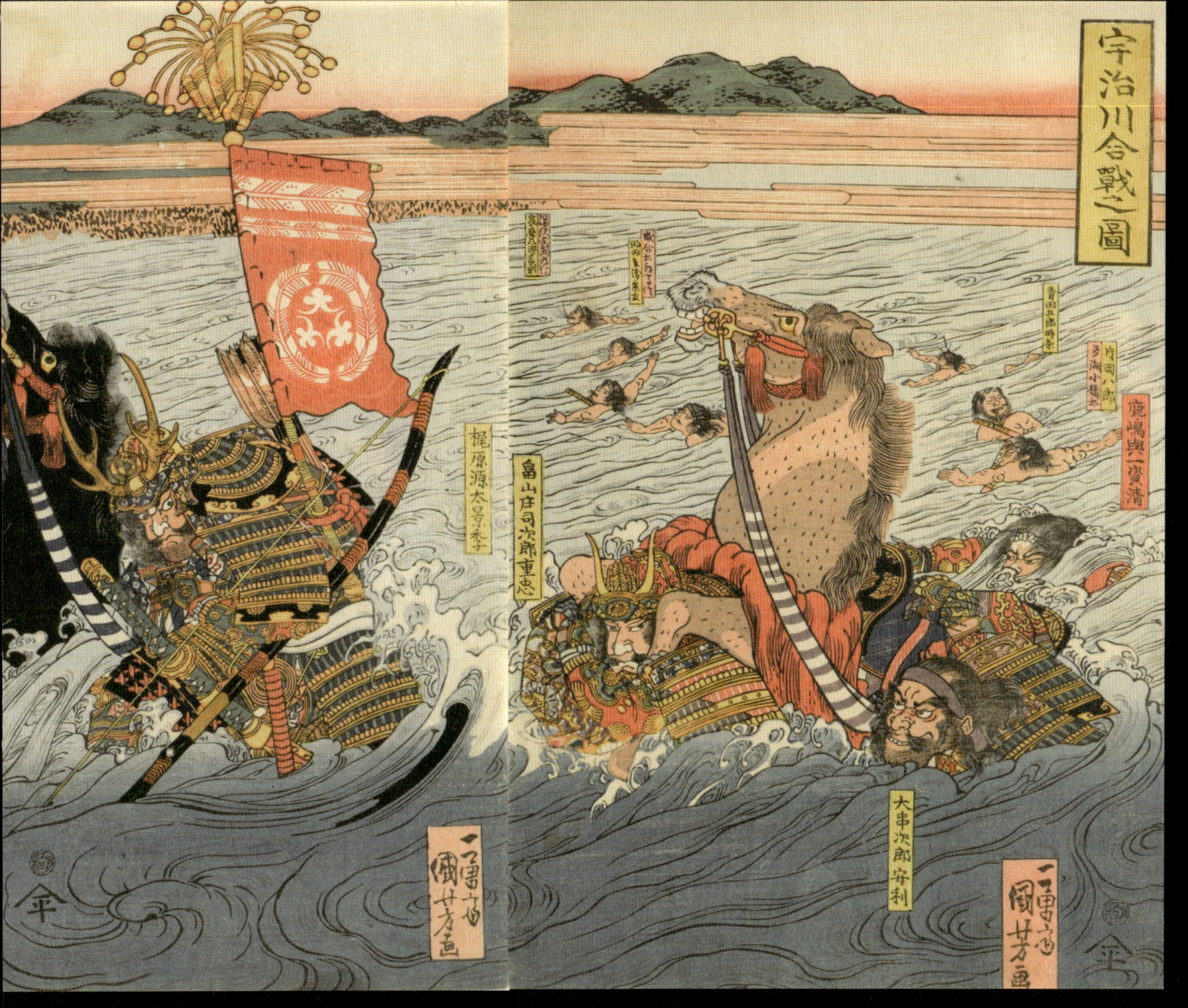

【宇治川合戦之図】歌川国芳 天保2〜3年（1831-32）頃 ギャラリー紅屋収蔵

"Competing to the Take the Lead at Uji River"by Utagawa Kuniyoshi, Gallery Beniya Collection

Both men were military leaders in the early Kamakura Shogunate under the Minamoto clan. On their way to crush the rival Yoshinaka in Kyoto, Yoshitsune's forces were halted by the defenses at Uji River. It is early spring, and the melting snows have made the river's current fast and dangerous. Should they go around, or wait until the waters subside? As Yoshitsune and his retainers debate what to do, two warriors on horseback stride forth. It is Kajiwara Kagesue and Sasaki Takatsuna, each riding one of Yoshitsune's best horses, Ikezuki and Surusumi respectively. They ride into the river, vying with one another to be the first to make it to the other side, with Takatsuna ultimately winning. The rest of Yoshitsune's forces follows suit, and smash through Yoshinaka's army.

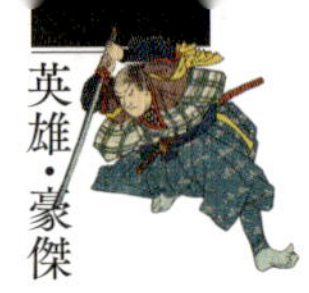

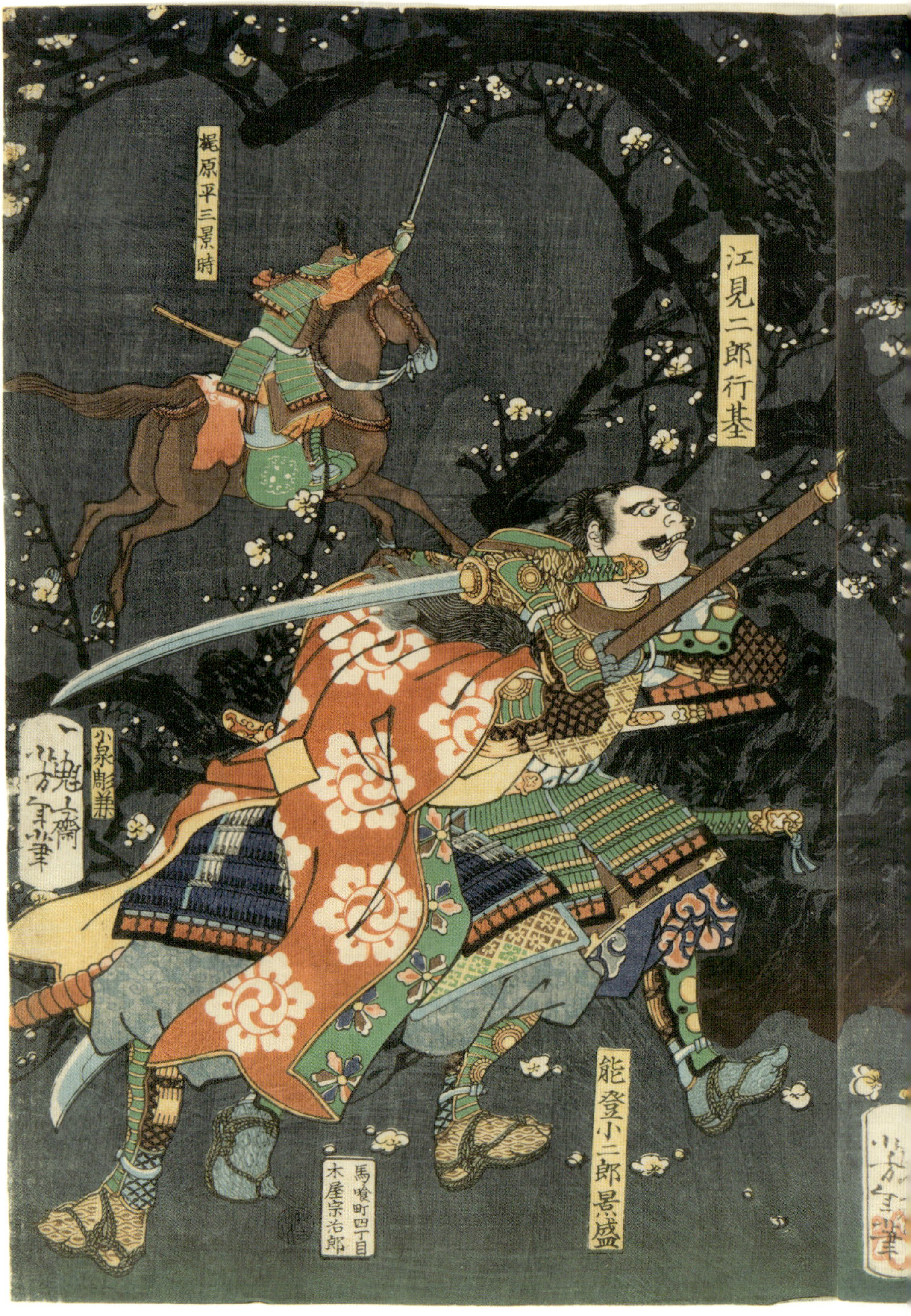

64

【武勇雪月花之内 生田森ゑびらの梅】月岡芳年 慶応3年（1867）（三枚続の中・左図）

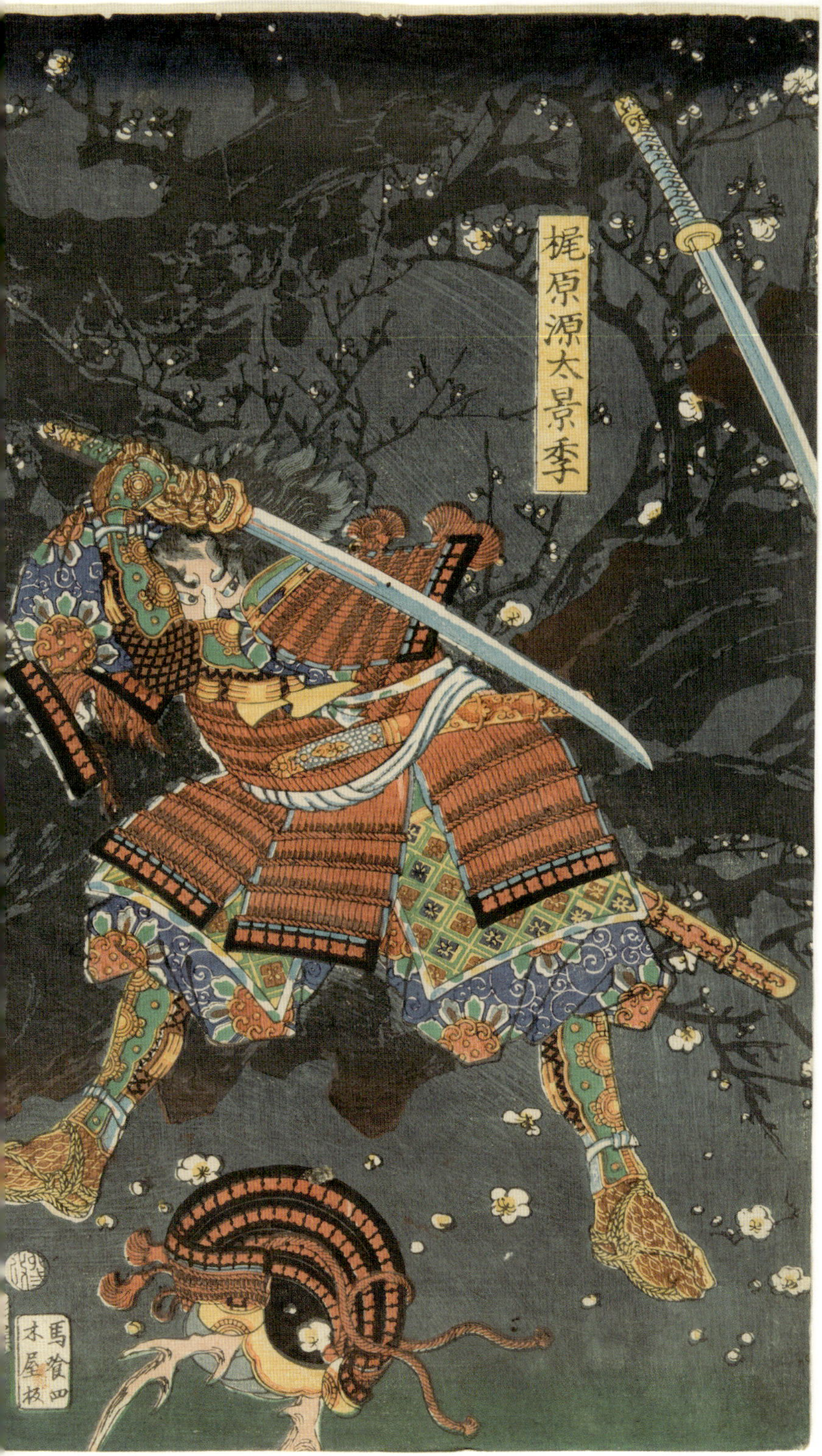

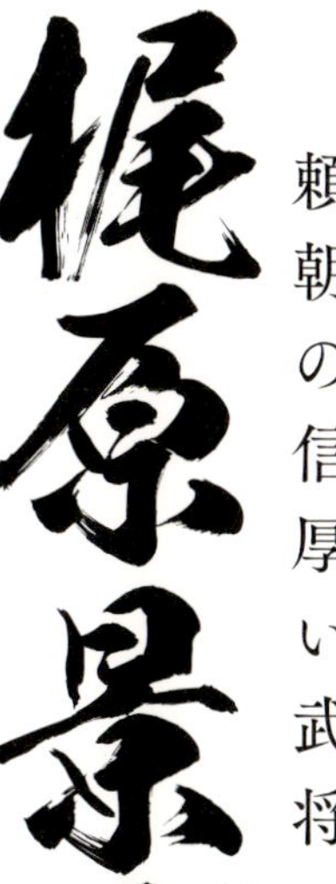

梶原景季

頼朝の信厚い武将

Kajiwara Kagesue
Brave Heroes and Gallant Men

鎌倉時代初期の武将。父景時とともに頼朝に仕え、義仲および平氏の追討で戦功をあげた。一ノ谷の戦いの際、味方とはぐれ生田の森で平氏の軍勢に囲まれたとき、そこに生えていた美しい梅を一枝折って箙に差し、「花は散っても香は袖にのこるだろう」と言って戦い、敵方を感心させたという。一方、父景時は我が子を探しに生田の森へと舞い戻り、ともに戦い敵を倒した。

A general of the early Kamakura period, Kajiwara Kagesue, like his father Kagetoki, served under Yoritomo. He participated in the battles against Yoshinaka and the Taira. During the Battle of Ichinotani, Kagesue was separated from his allies and surrounded by the Taira forces in Ikuta Wood. He broke off a branch from beautiful plum tree and slid it into his quiver, moving his foes by saying "Even if the petals fall, surely their fragrance will cling to my clothes," before launching himself into battle. In search of his son, his father Kagetoki rushed into the woods and helped his son defeat their enemies.

"Bravery in the Four Seasons: Plum Blossoms in Ikuta Wood" by Tsukioka Yoshitoshi (showing two sheets in a triptych)

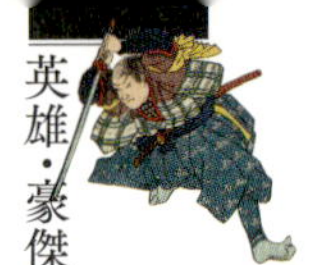

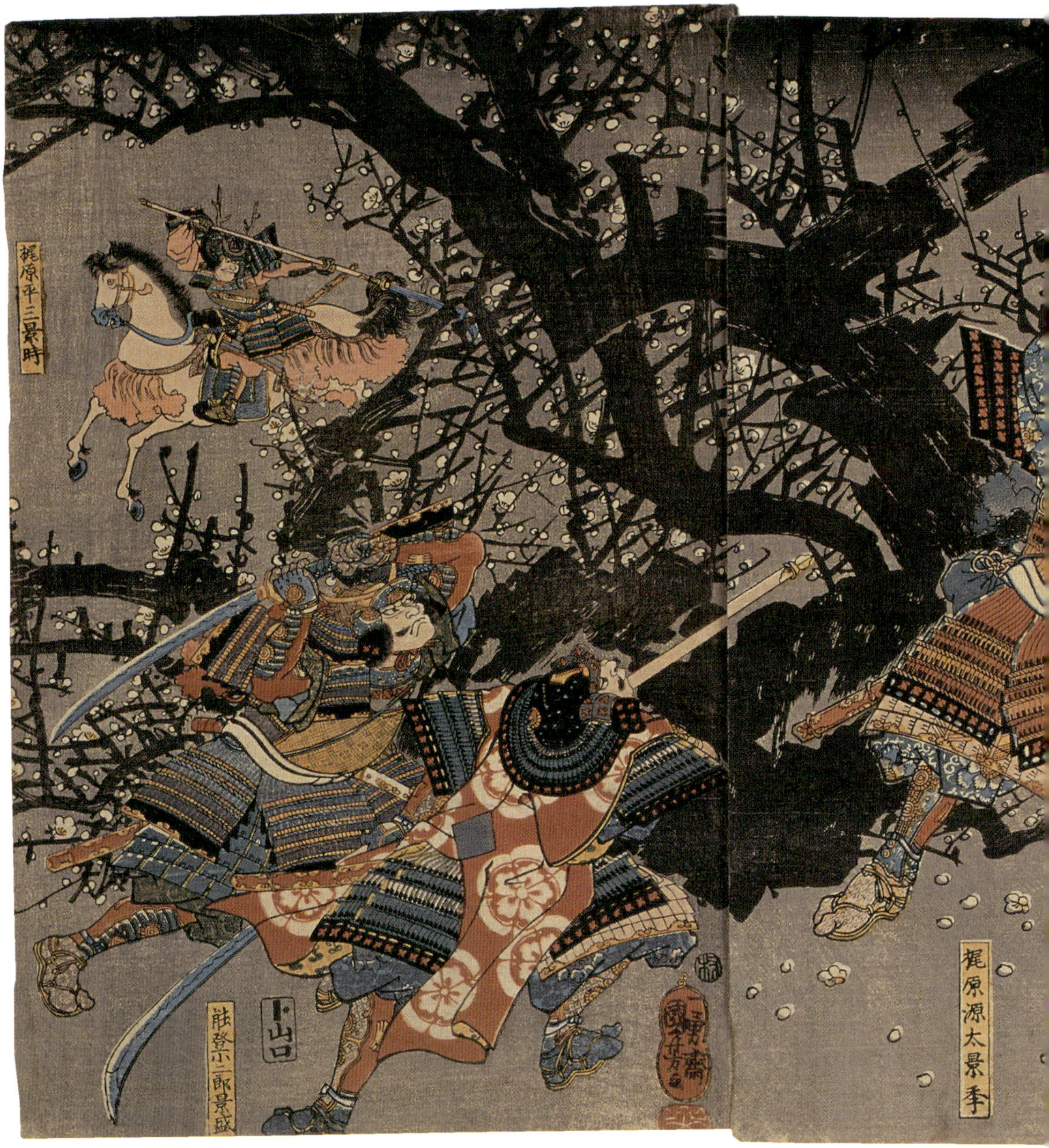

【生田森追手源平大合戦】歌川国芳　天保14年〜弘化3年（1843-46）頃

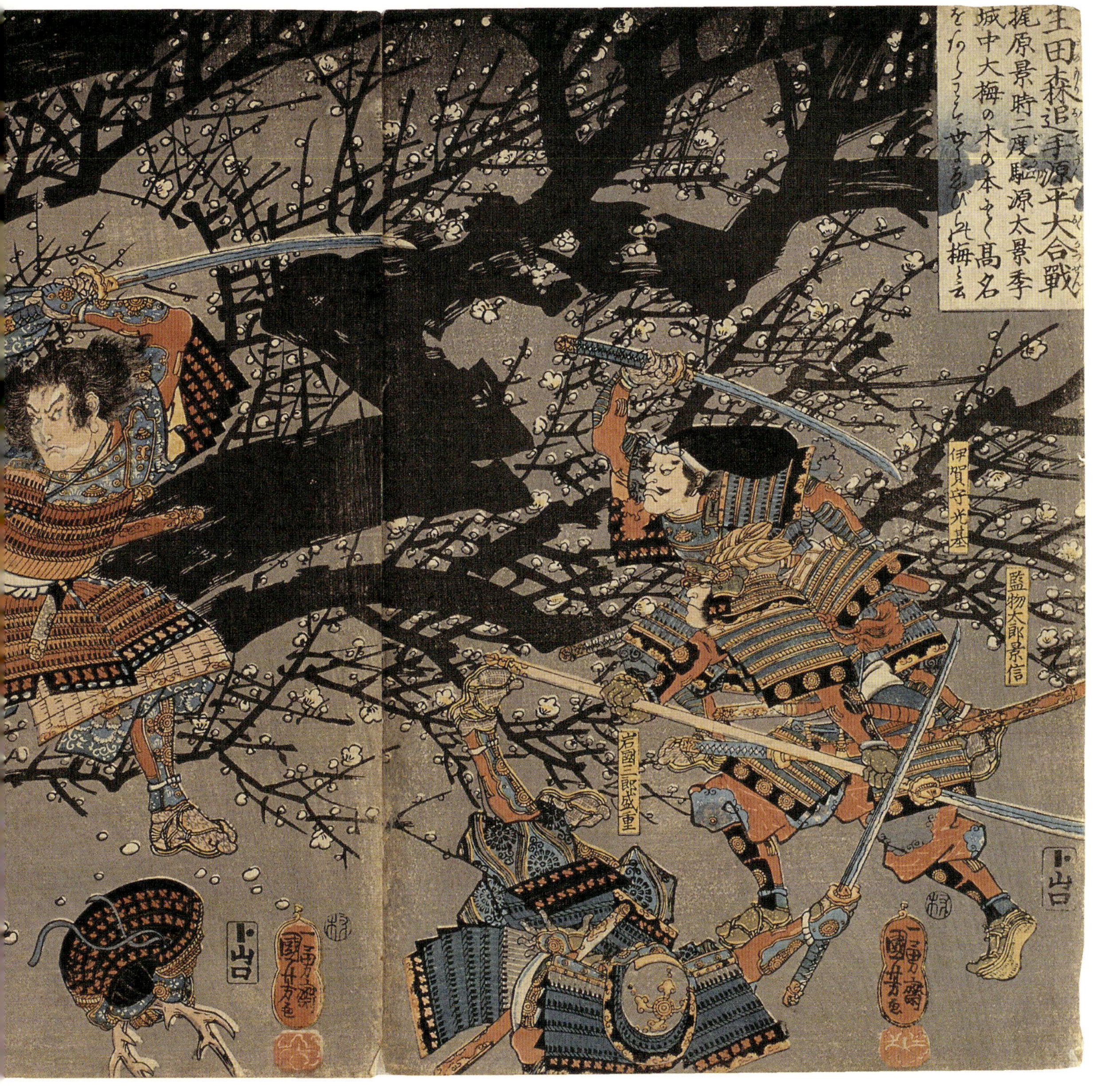

"The Genpei War: Skirmish in Ikuta Wood" by Utagawa Kuniyoshi

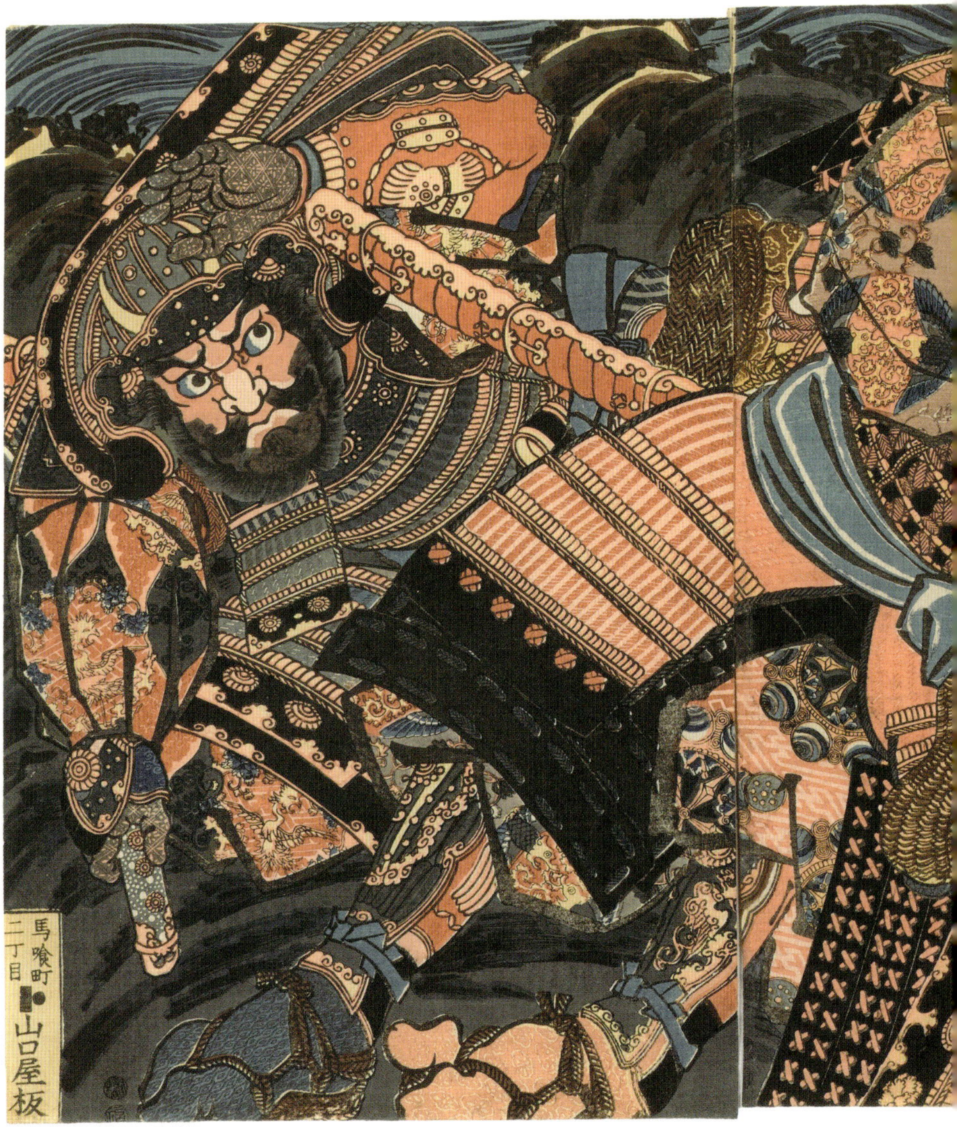

石橋山の死闘

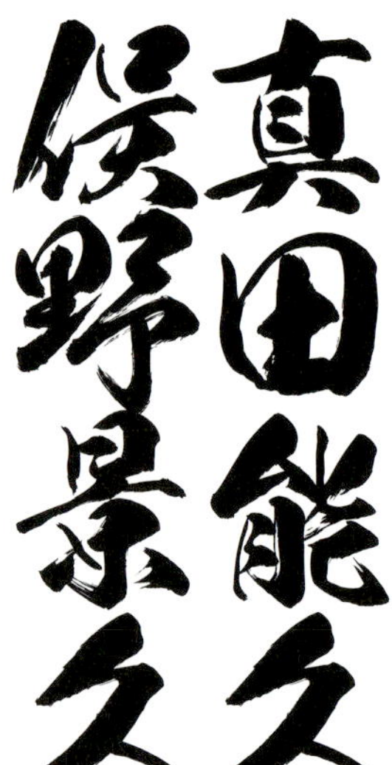

真田能久 俣野景久

Sanada Yoshihisa and Matano Kagehisa
Brave Heroes and Gallant Men

ともに平安時代末期の武将。真田能久は、頼朝挙兵後初の合戦である石橋山の戦いで先陣を命じられ、勇戦した若武者。平家方の俣野景久に出会い、組打ちとなった。能久は脇差で景久の首を掻こうとしたが、別の敵を討ったときの血で錆びついてしまって鞘から抜けない。そうこうするうちに、景久の家来長尾定景が背後から組みかかり、能久の首を掻いて打ち取った。

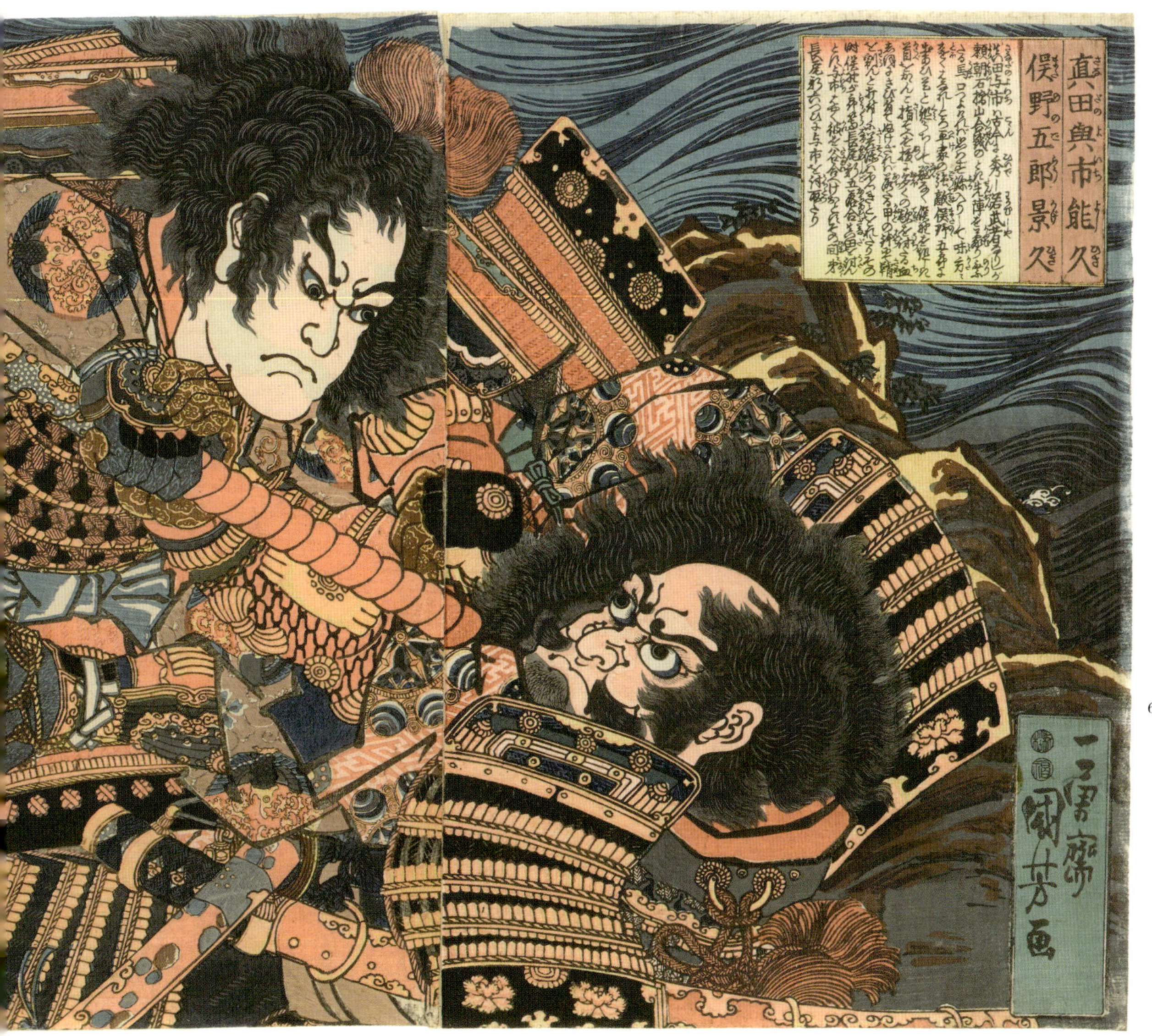

【真田与市能久 俣野五郎景久】歌川国芳 嘉永2〜4年(1849-51)頃
"Sanada Yoshihisa and Matano Kagehisa" by Utagawa Kuniyoshi

Both men were generals during the late Heian period. Sanada Yoshihisa was ordered to lead the attack at Mount Ishibashi in 1180, the first battle under Yoritomo as leader of the Minamoto clan. Though young, Yoshihisa demonstrated great bravery, particularly in close quarters combat with Matano Kagehisa of the Taira. Hoping to behead Yoshihisa, Kagehisa reached for his wakizashi (short sword), but was unable to withdraw it from its scabbard as it had rusted shut from a previous victim's blood. This gave Kagehisa's retainer, Nagao Sadakage, time to sneak up from behind and behead the fumbling Yoshihisa.

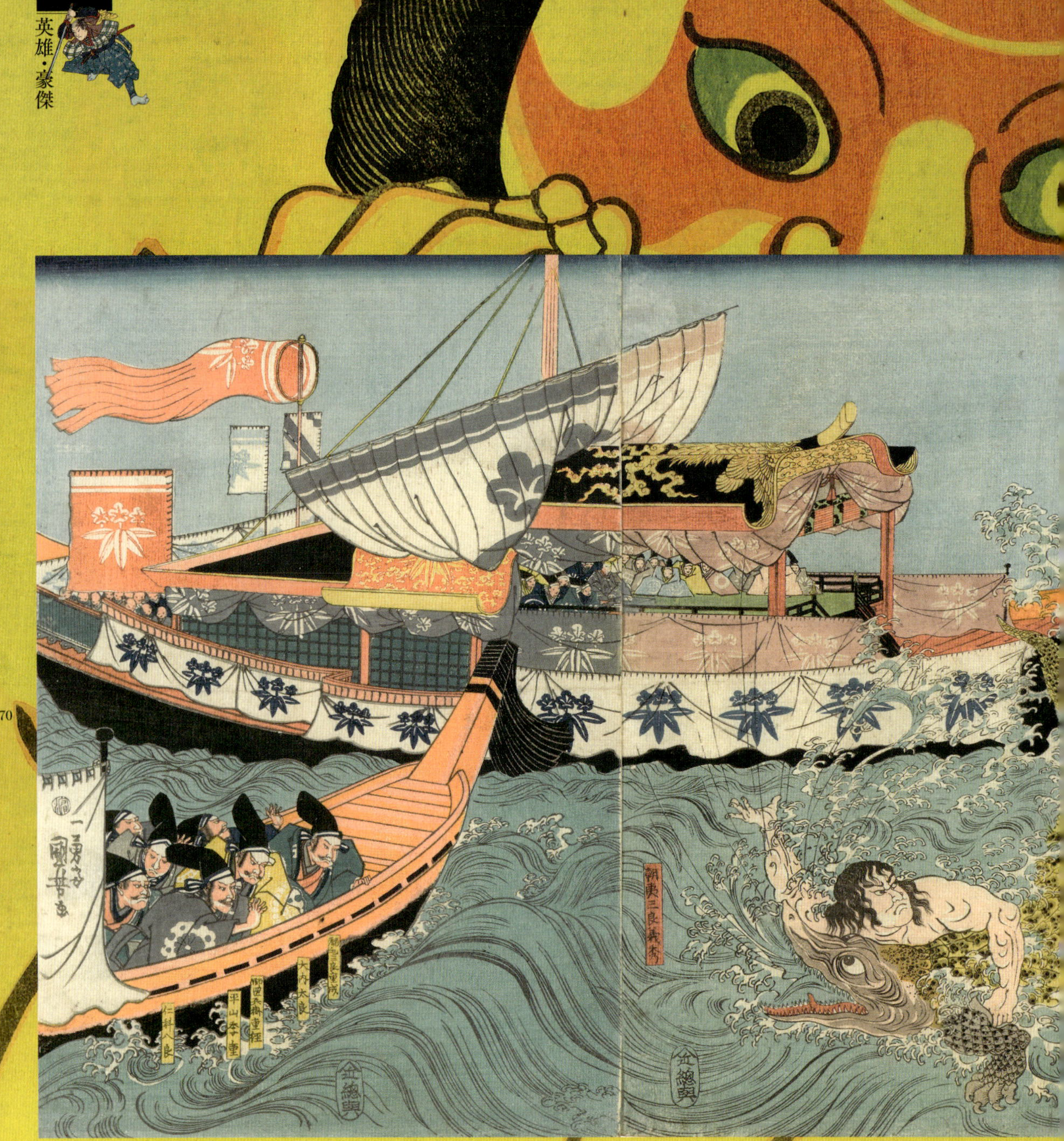

【源頼家公鎌倉小壺海遊覧 朝夷義秀雌雄鰐を捕ふ図】歌川国芳 天保14年（1843）頃
"Asahina Yoshihide Wrestling Male and Female Alligators" by Utagawa Kuniyoshi

A warrior of the early Kamakura period, Asahina Yoshide was raised in the Asai district of Awa Province, on the Bōsō Peninsula in present-day Chiba prefecture. He is also known as Asahina Saburō. He had unrivaled physical strength, and was also an excellent swimmer. While playing on the beach with future shogun Minamoto no Yoriie, the latter challenged him to a display of his swimming skills: Yoshihide dove deep into the sea and reemerged with a shark in each hand. Yoshihide fought alongside the Wada clan during the Wada Conflict of 1213, striking fear into his enemies with his ferocious fighting. Legends claim that Yoshihide traveled to various fantastical lands, including ones populated with miniature and one-eyed people. He starred in many comic novellas and woodblock prints during the Edo period.

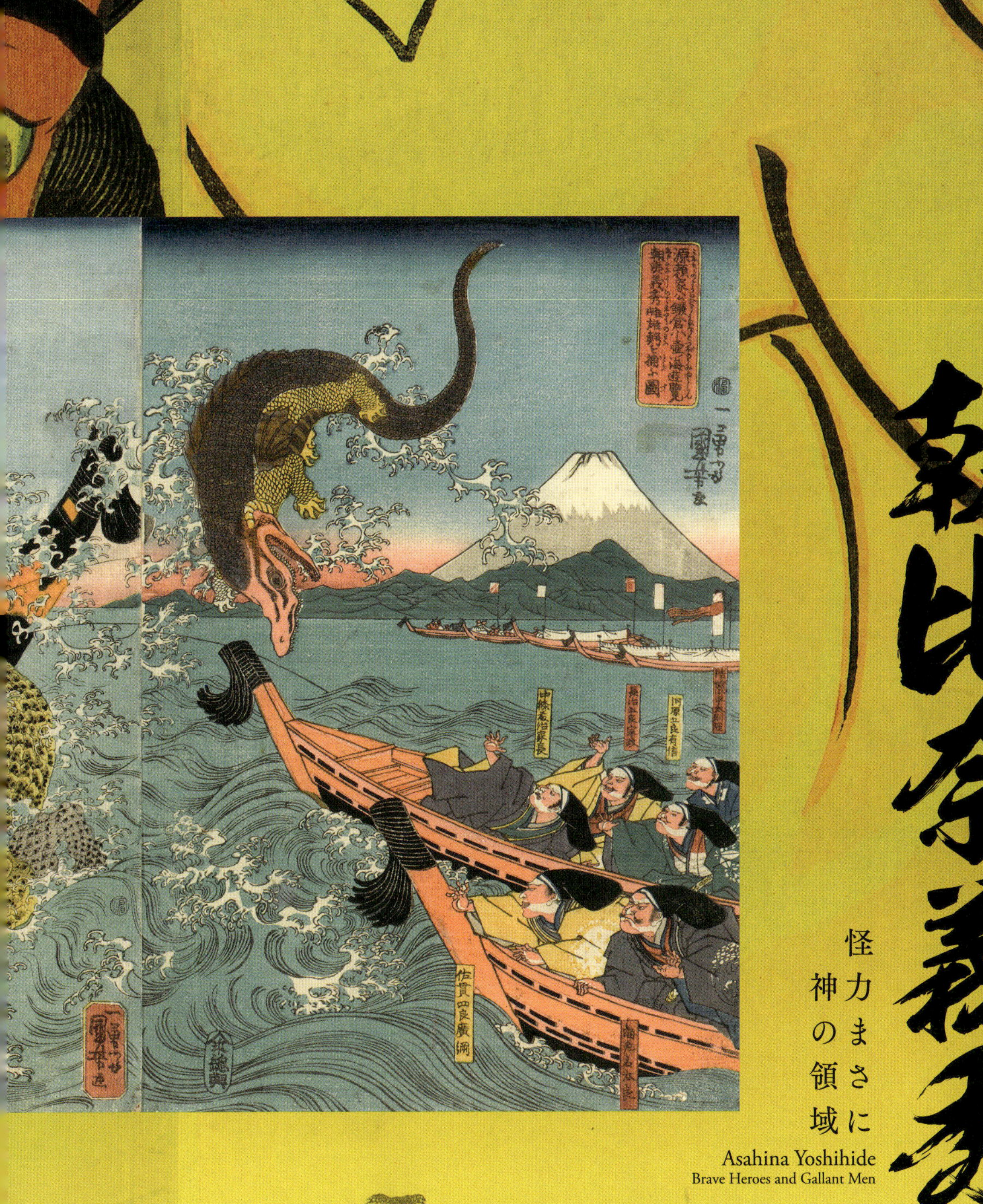

朝比奈義秀

怪力まさに神の領域

Asahina Yoshihide
Brave Heroes and Gallant Men

鎌倉時代初期の武士。安房国朝夷群で育ち、朝比奈三郎とも称した。剛力無双で、泳ぎにも長じた。将軍源頼家が海辺遊覧の際、水練の技を披露せよと命じられると、水中深く潜って鮫を素手で捕らえ、人々を感嘆させたという。和田合戦では一族とともに戦い、勇猛な戦いぶりで敵を恐れさせた。なお、義秀が小人国や一つ目国などを次々と巡るという朝比奈島巡り伝説があり、江戸時代においては滑稽本や浮世絵の題材となった。

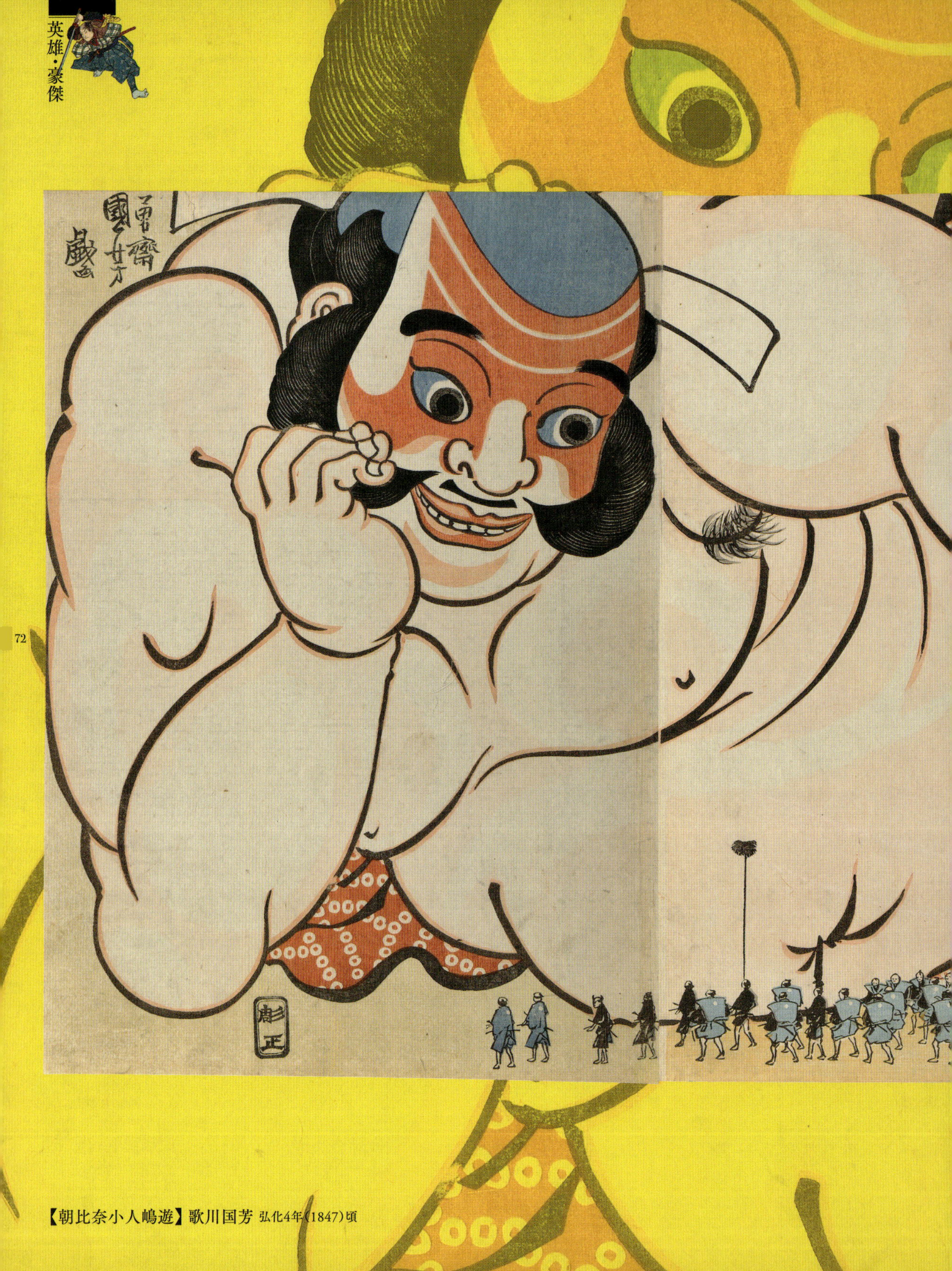

72

【朝比奈小人嶋遊】 歌川国芳　弘化4年（1847）頃

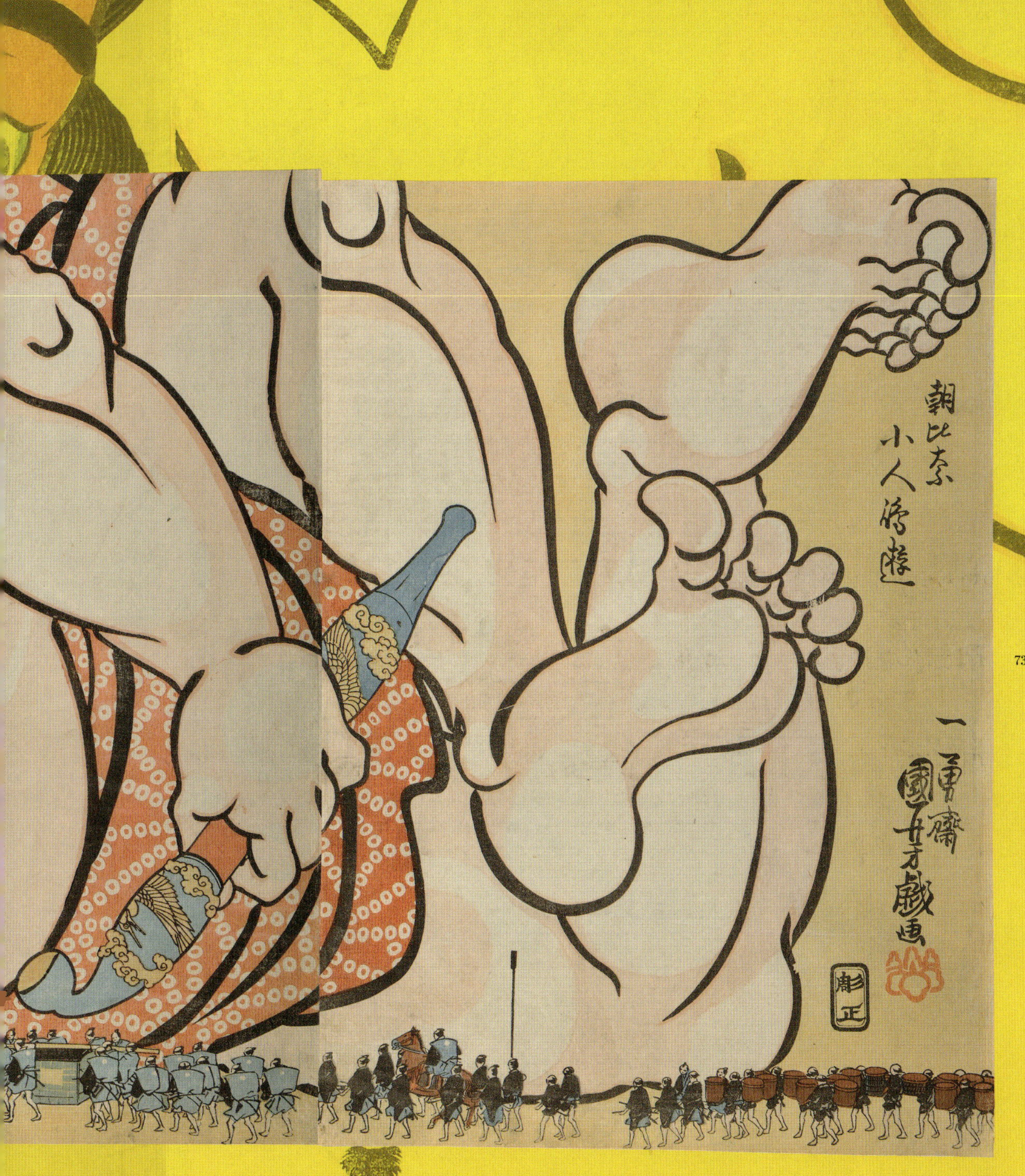

"Asahina Yoshihide Visits the Land of Small People" by Utagawa Kuniyoshi

74

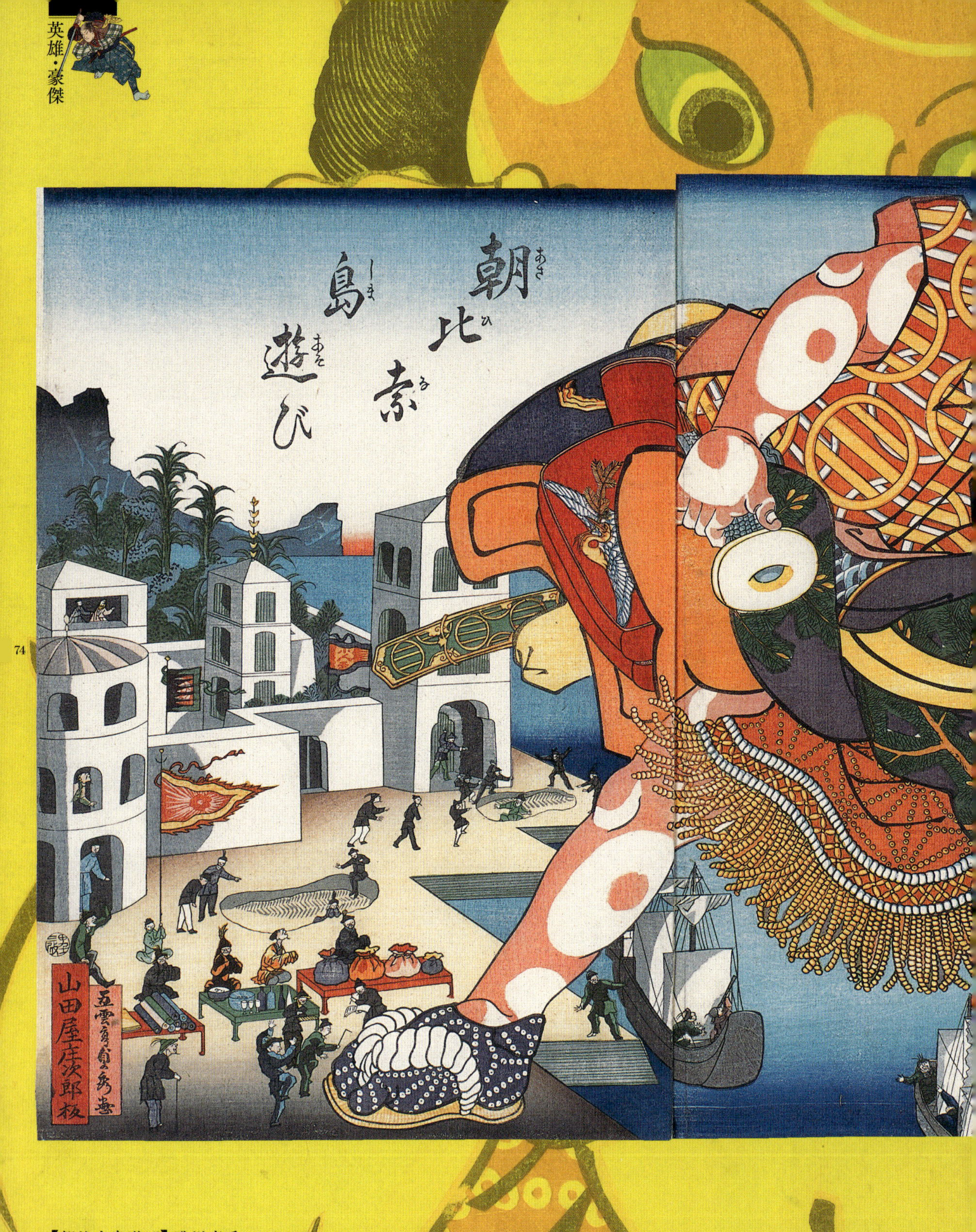

【朝比奈島遊び】歌川貞秀　万延元年(1860)

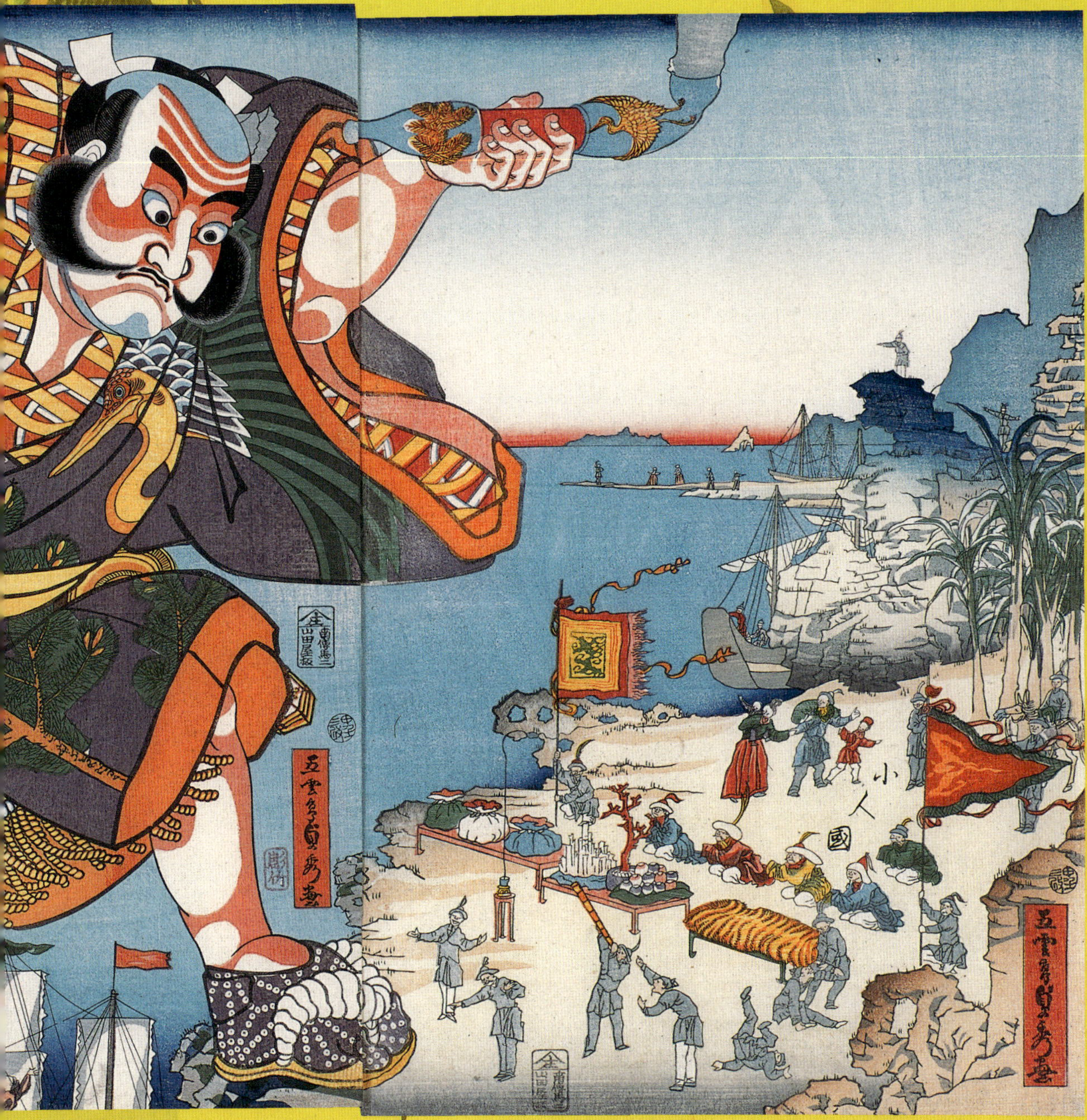

"Asahina Yoshihide's Island Adventures" by Utagawa Sadahide

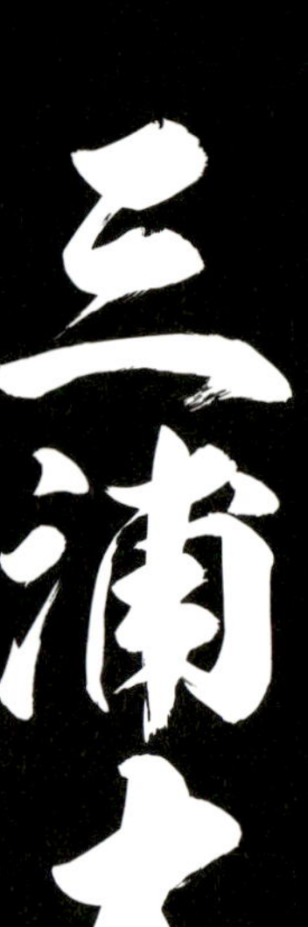

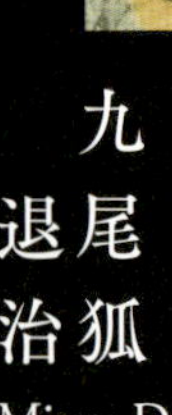

九尾退治狐

Miura Daisuke
Brave Heroes and Gallant Men

平安時代末期の武将。相模国三浦の人。金毛九尾の狐を下野国那須野原で上総介広常とともに退治した。金毛九尾の狐は絶世の美女に化け、天竺・唐土・日本で時の権力者をたぶらかした妖狐である。日本では玉藻前に化けて鳥羽法皇の寵愛を受けたが、陰陽師に見破られて那須野原に飛んで逃げる。苦戦の末、三浦大介の矢が見事命中し、広常がとどめを刺した。石と化してもなお毒気を吐いたので殺生石と呼ばれたが、玄翁和尚によって解脱した。

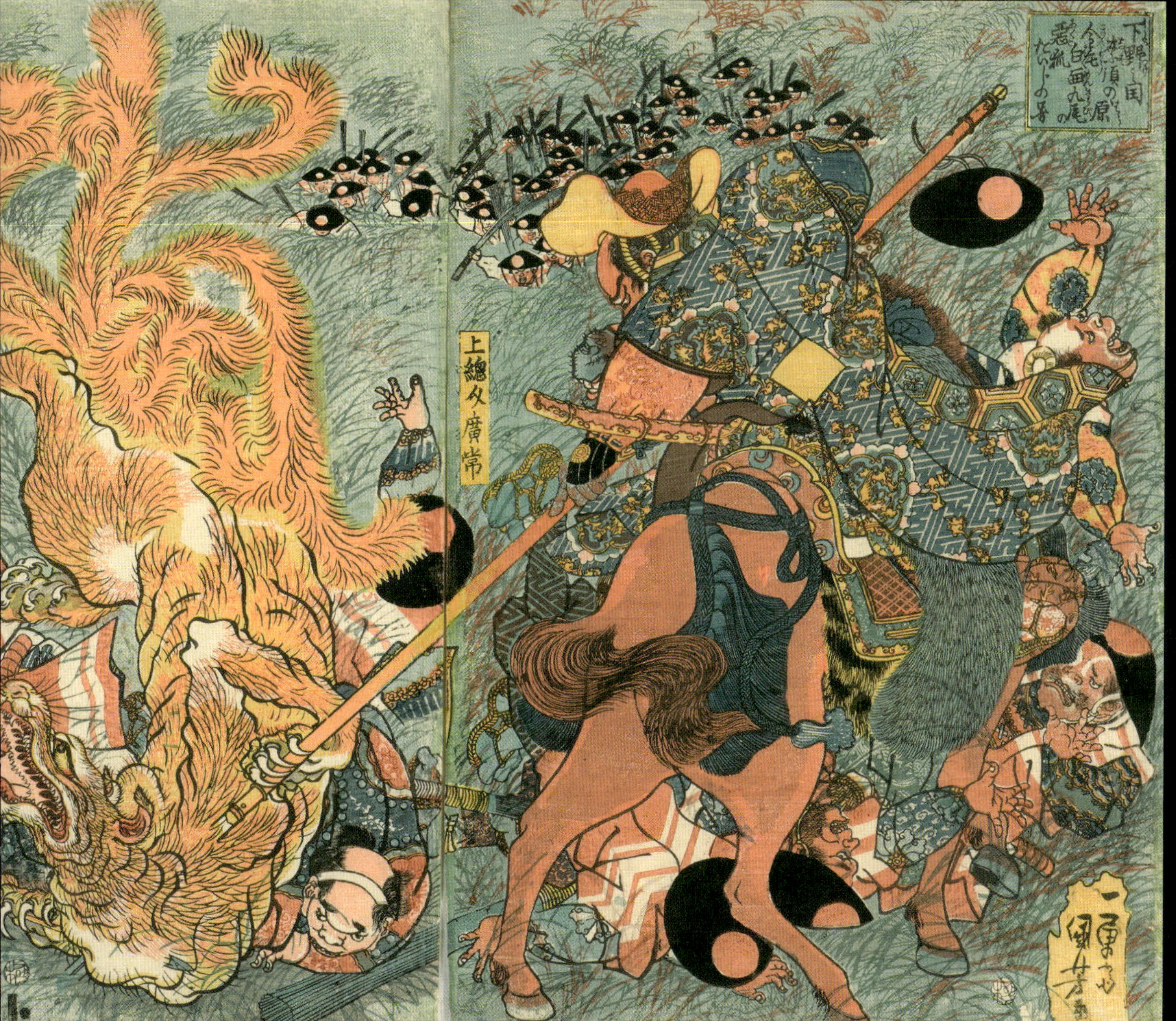

【下野之国奈須の原金毛白面九尾の悪狐たいじの図】歌川国芳 天保（1830-44）前期
"Miura-no-suke and Kazusa-no-suke Defeat the Nine-tailed Fox on Nasuno Moor" by Utagawa Kuniyoshi

A military leader of the late Heian period, Miura Daisuke was from Miura Peninsula in Sagami Province, present-day Kanagawa. With Kazusa Hirotsune, he subjugated the gold-haired nine-tailed fox upon the Nasuno Moor, in Shimotsuke Province (Tochigi). This female fox was famed for its ability to transform into a human woman of unparalleled beauty, over the years tricking male rulers in India, China, and Japan. In Japan, she seduced Emperor Toba while in the guise of Tamamo-no-mae, but fled to Nasuno Moor after being exposed by an astrologer. Following a long battle, Miura Daisuke's arrow pierced the fox's heart while Hirotsune delivered the finishing blow. Upon her death, the fox turned into a poisonous "killing stone." Her spirit finally left the stone after rituals were performed by an old priest named Gennō.

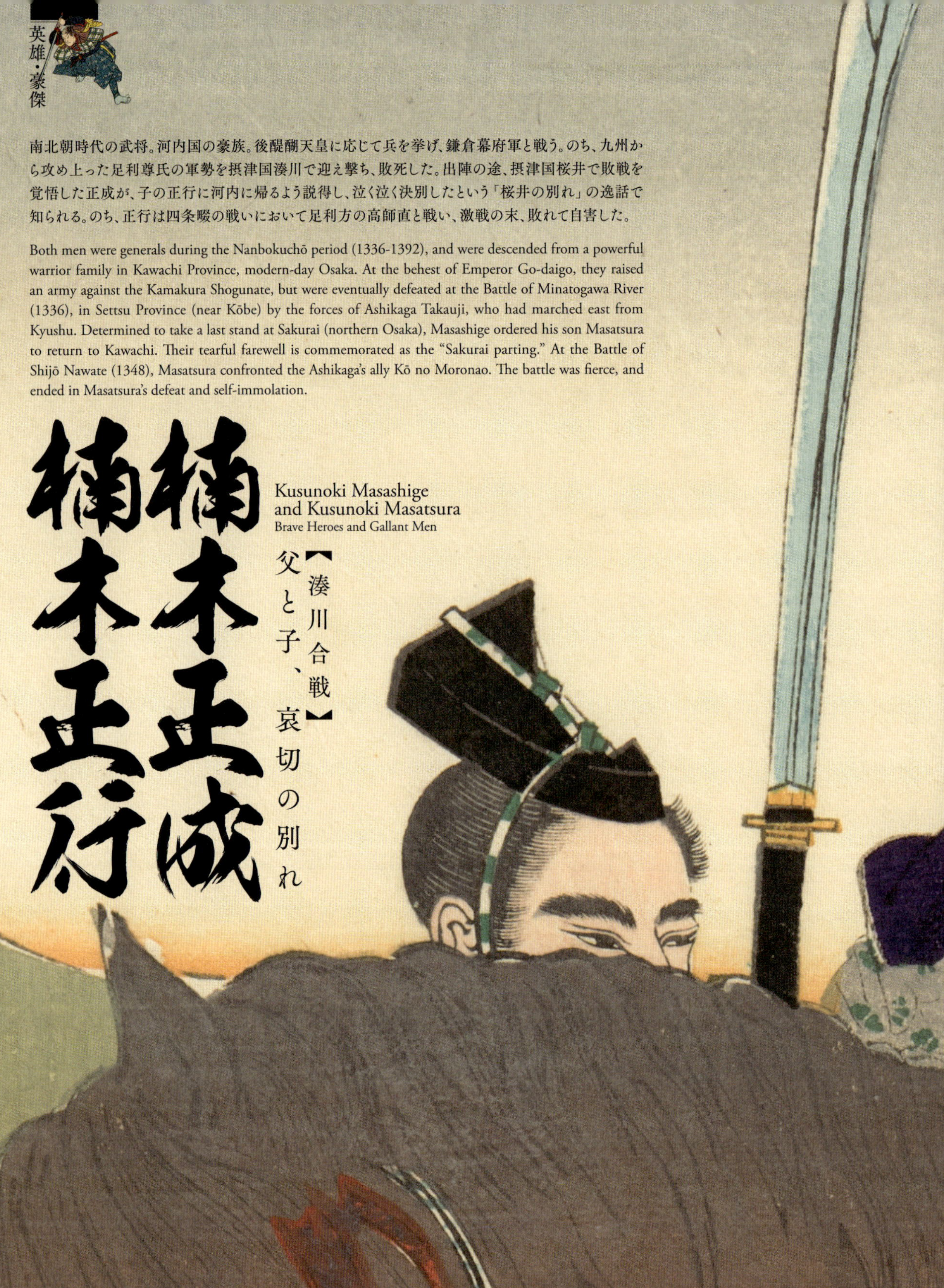

南北朝時代の武将。河内国の豪族。後醍醐天皇に応じて兵を挙げ、鎌倉幕府軍と戦う。のち、九州から攻め上った足利尊氏の軍勢を摂津国湊川で迎え撃ち、敗死した。出陣の途、摂津国桜井で敗戦を覚悟した正成が、子の正行に河内に帰るよう説得し、泣く泣く決別したという「桜井の別れ」の逸話で知られる。のち、正行は四条畷の戦いにおいて足利方の高師直と戦い、激戦の末、敗れて自害した。

Both men were generals during the Nanbokuchō period (1336-1392), and were descended from a powerful warrior family in Kawachi Province, modern-day Osaka. At the behest of Emperor Go-daigo, they raised an army against the Kamakura Shogunate, but were eventually defeated at the Battle of Minatogawa River (1336), in Settsu Province (near Kōbe) by the forces of Ashikaga Takauji, who had marched east from Kyushu. Determined to take a last stand at Sakurai (northern Osaka), Masashige ordered his son Masatsura to return to Kawachi. Their tearful farewell is commemorated as the "Sakurai parting." At the Battle of Shijō Nawate (1348), Masatsura confronted the Ashikaga's ally Kō no Moronao. The battle was fierce, and ended in Masatsura's defeat and self-immolation.

楠木正成 楠木正行

Kusunoki Masashige
and Kusunoki Masatsura
Brave Heroes and Gallant Men

【湊川合戦】父と子、哀切の別れ

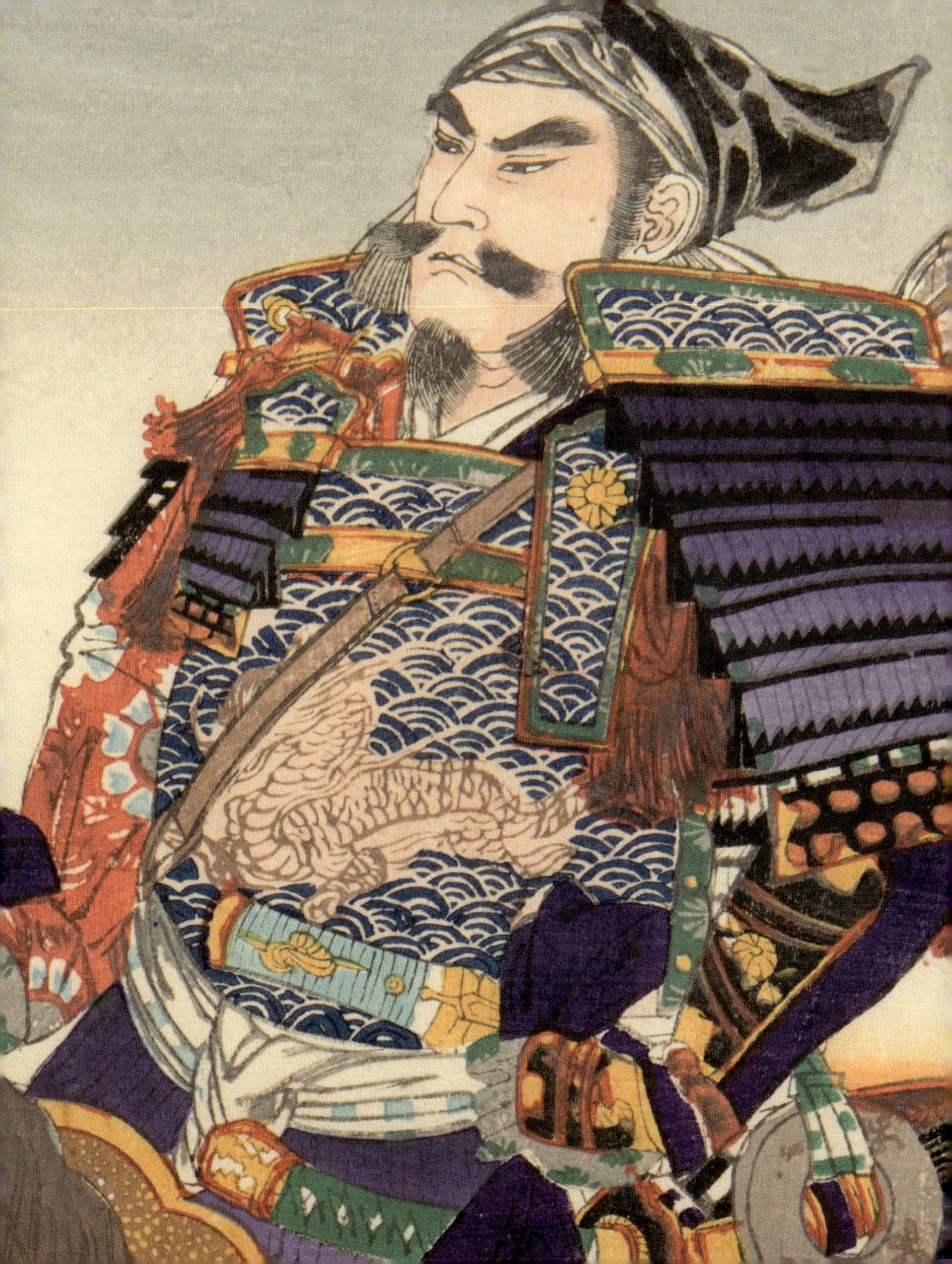

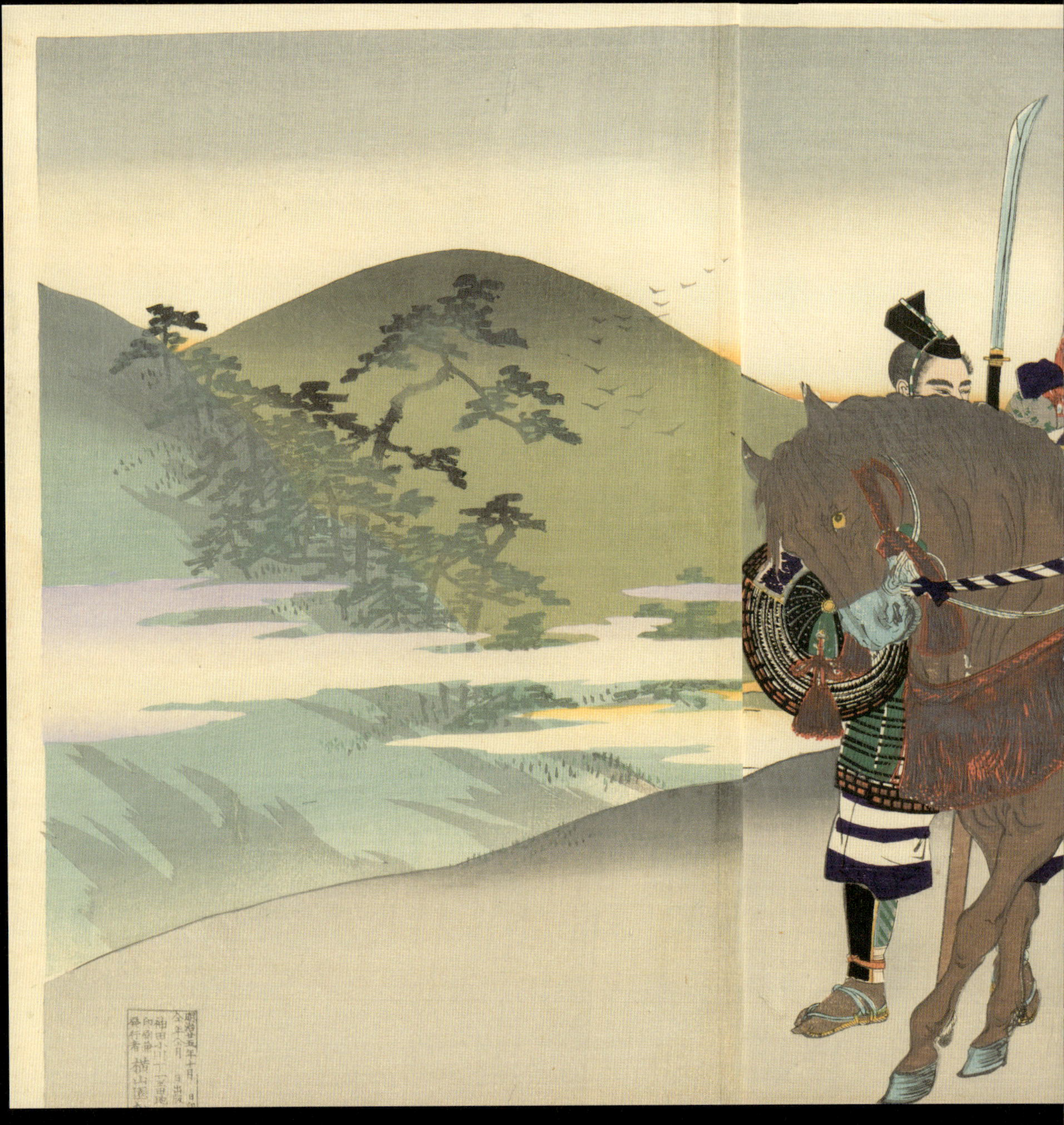

【正成正行桜井宿ニ別ヲ告ル図】楊斎延一　明治25年（1892）

正成は今年11歳になる正行に、天皇より賜った宝刀を形見として手渡した。

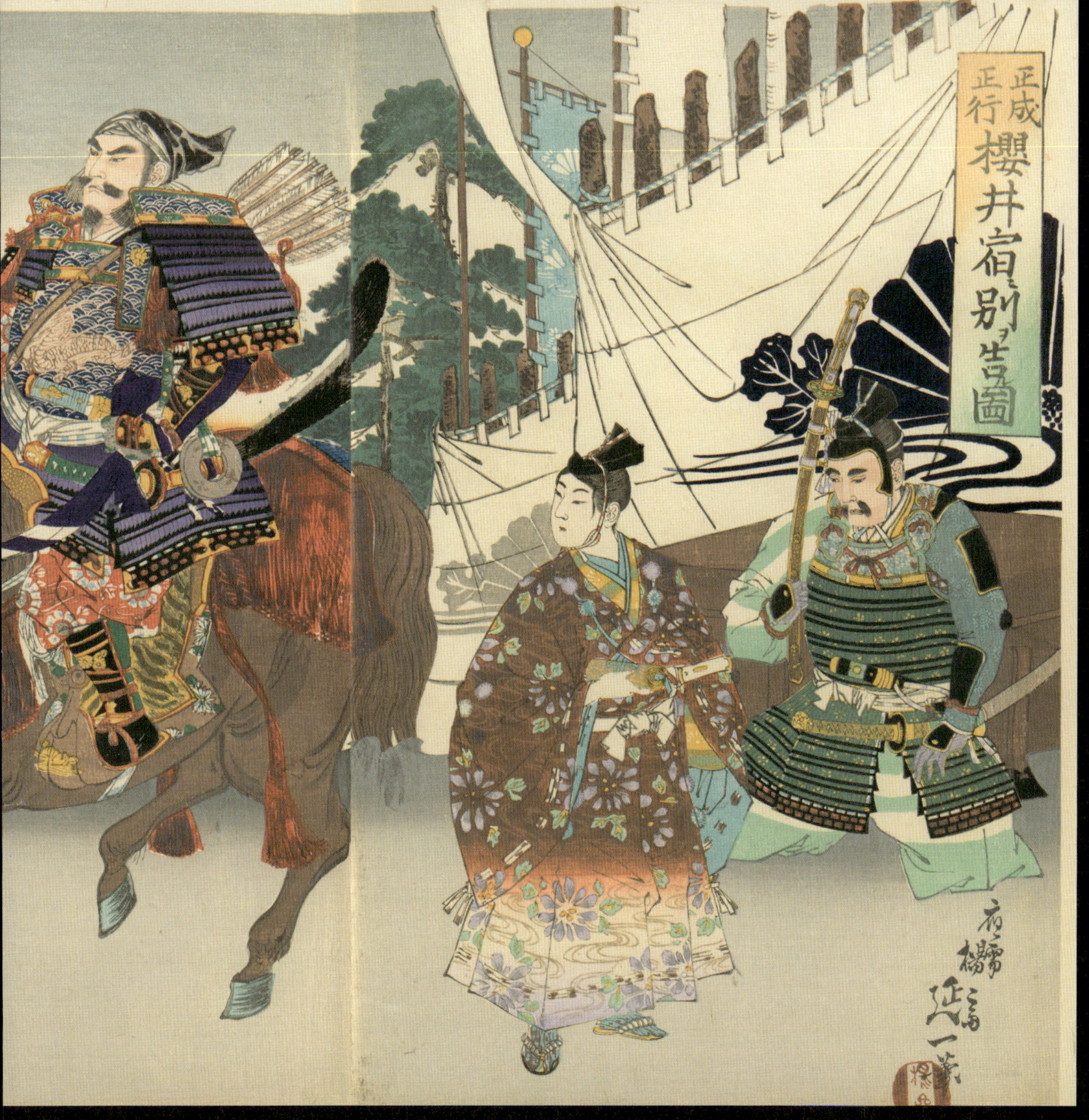

"The Parting of Masashige and Masatsura at Sakurai" by Yōsai Nobukazu

Masashige bids farewell to his son Masatsura, who was just 11 years old, imparting to him as a keepsake a sword from the Emperor.

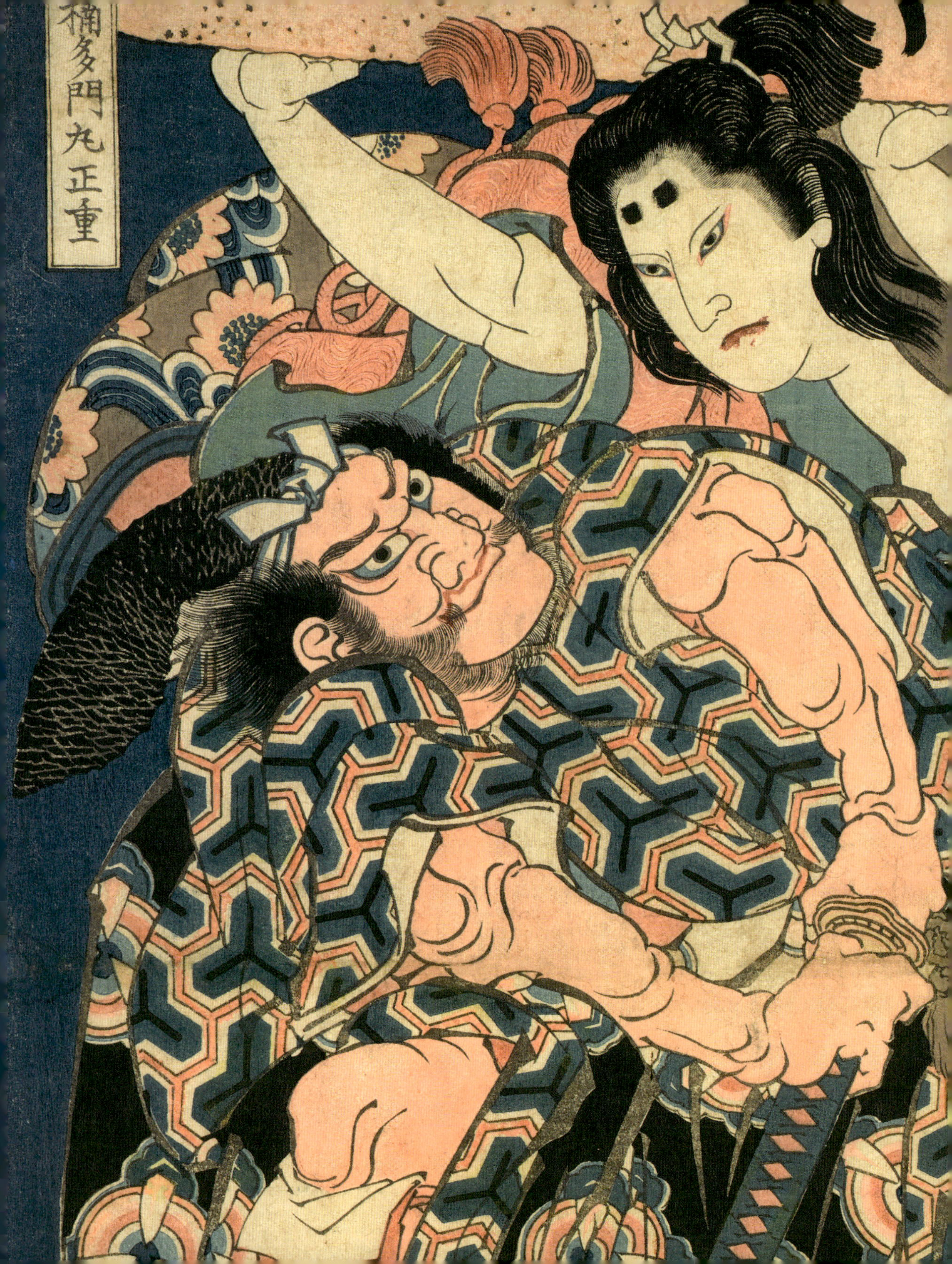
楠多門丸正重

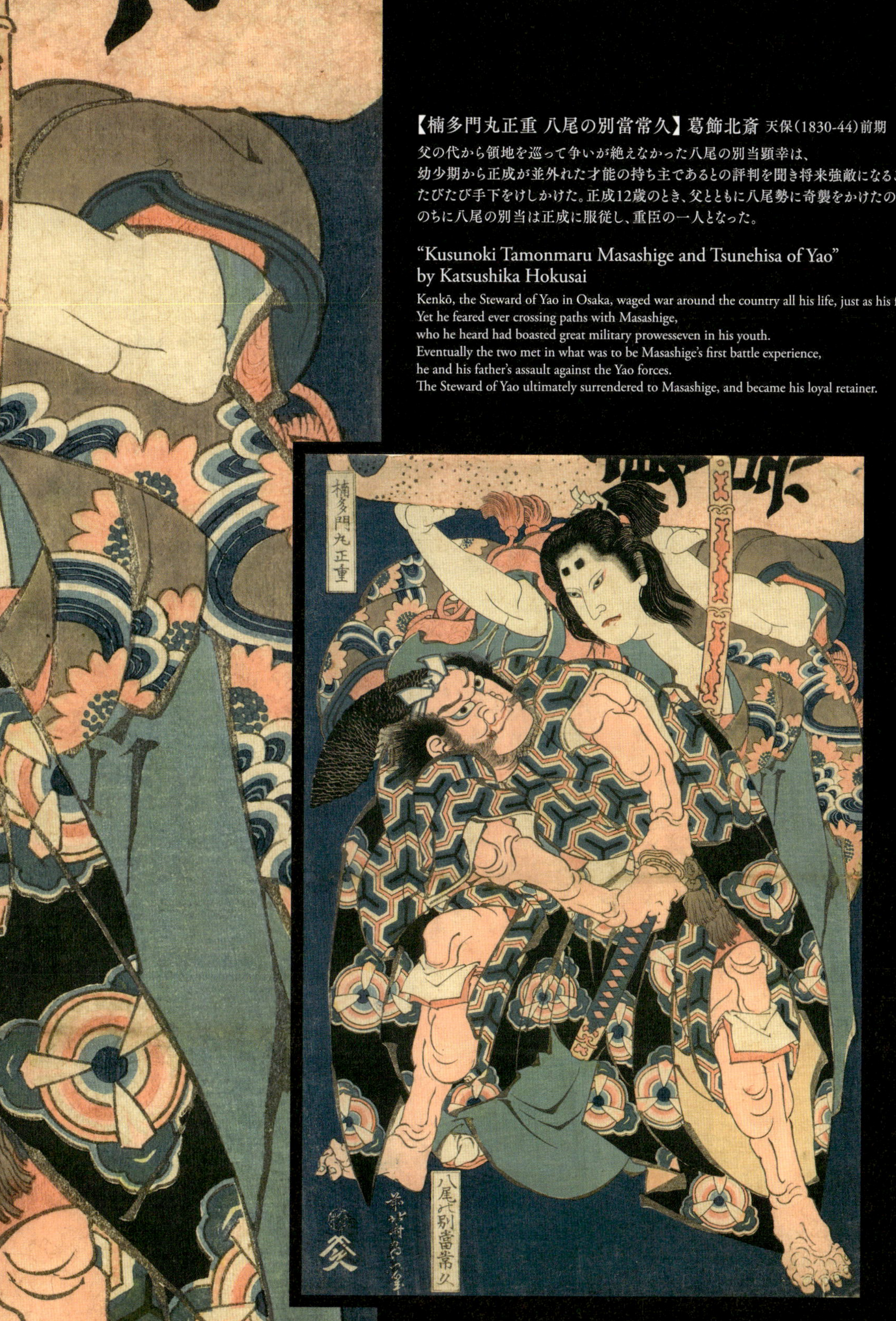

【楠多門丸正重 八尾の別當常久】葛飾北斎 天保(1830-44)前期

父の代から領地を巡って争いが絶えなかった八尾の別当顕幸は、
幼少期から正成が並外れた才能の持ち主であるとの評判を聞き将来強敵になることを恐れ、
たびたび手下をけしかけた。正成12歳のとき、父とともに八尾勢に奇襲をかけたのが初陣である。
のちに八尾の別当は正成に服従し、重臣の一人となった。

"Kusunoki Tamonmaru Masashige and Tsunehisa of Yao"
by Katsushika Hokusai

Kenkō, the Steward of Yao in Osaka, waged war around the country all his life, just as his father had.
Yet he feared ever crossing paths with Masashige,
who he heard had boasted great military prowesseven in his youth.
Eventually the two met in what was to be Masashige's first battle experience,
he and his father's assault against the Yao forces.
The Steward of Yao ultimately surrendered to Masashige, and became his loyal retainer.

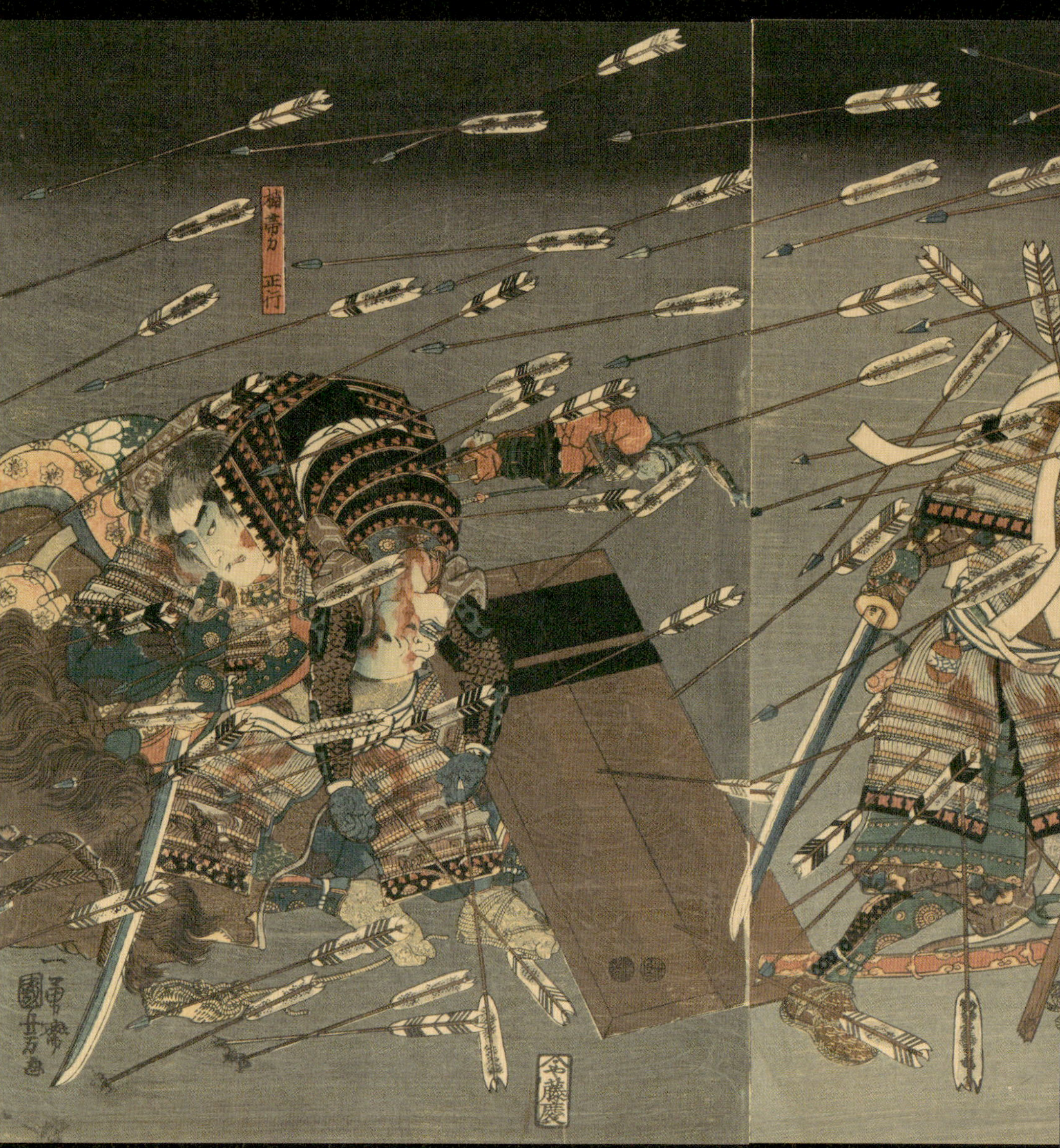

【楠家勇士四條縄手にて討死】歌川国芳　嘉永4年（1851）頃

四条畷の戦で、一族の和田源秀・正朝兄弟は正行と行動を共にし、無数の矢を浴びながら敵の本陣に迫った。

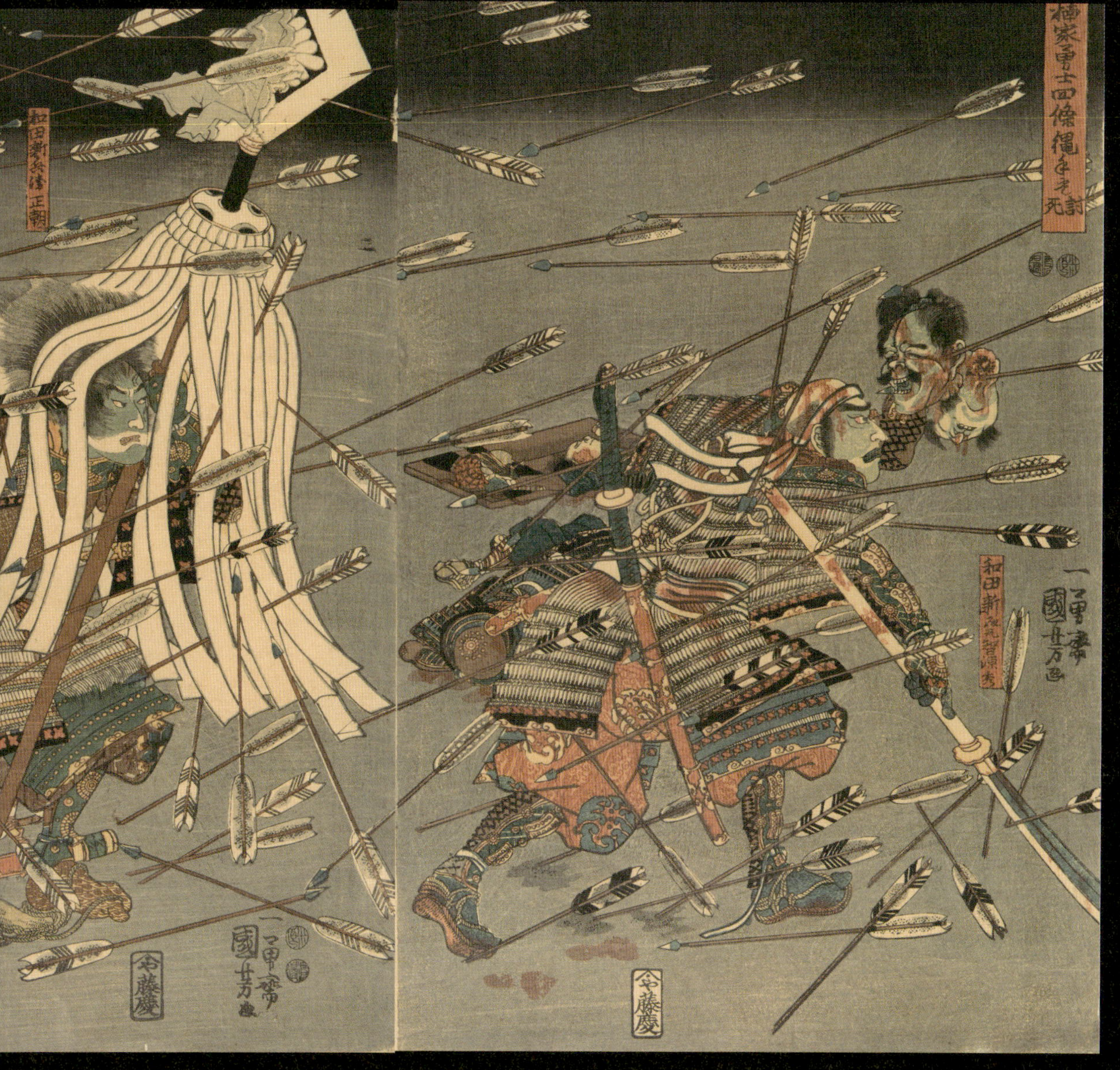

"Last Stand of the Brave Kusunoki Warriors at Shijō Nawate" by Utagawa Kuniyoshi

At the Battle of Shijō Nawate, Masatsura with his relatives and allies, the brothers Wada Genshū and Wada Masatomo, march on their enemies' stronghold despite being pummeled with arrows.

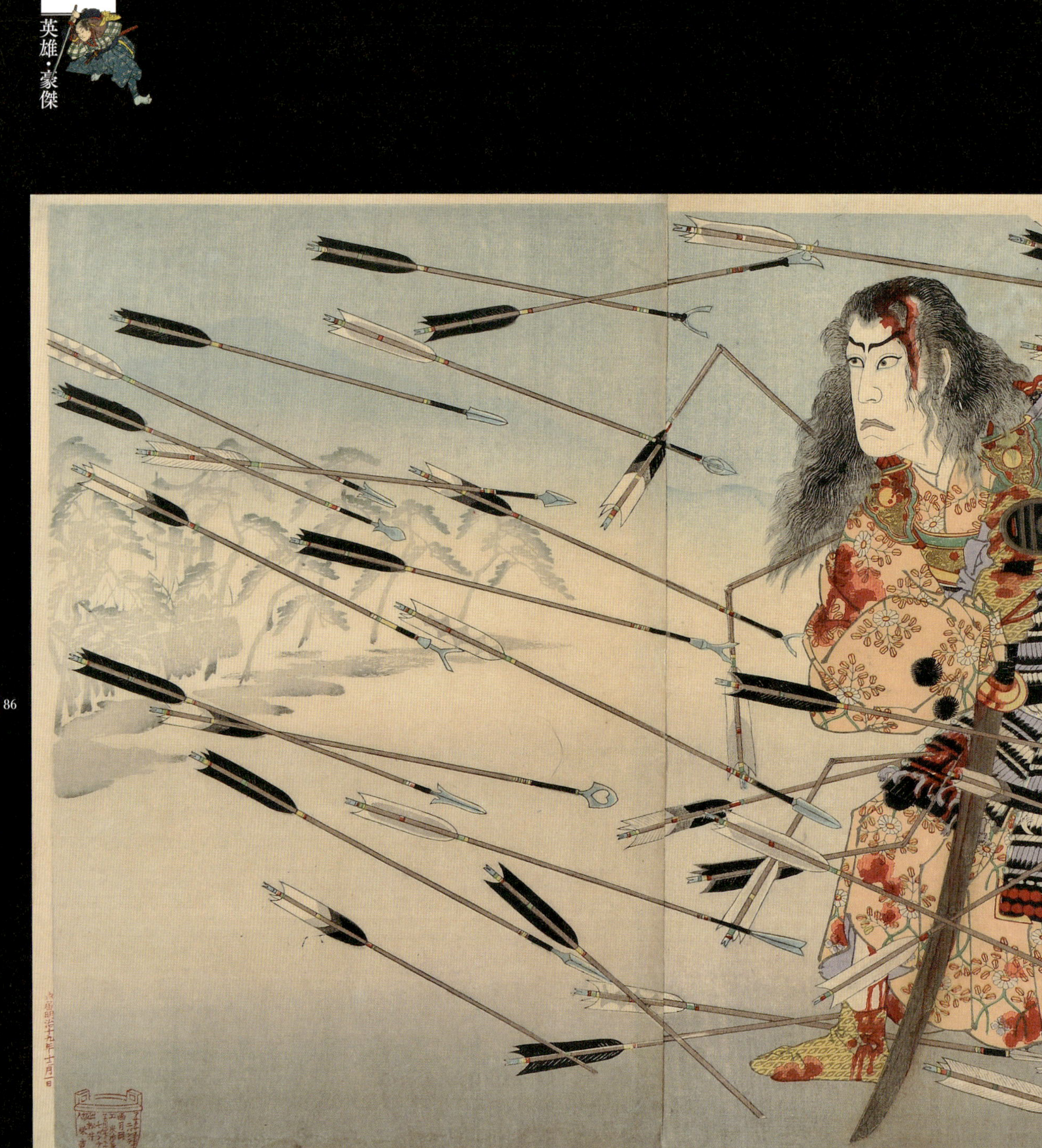

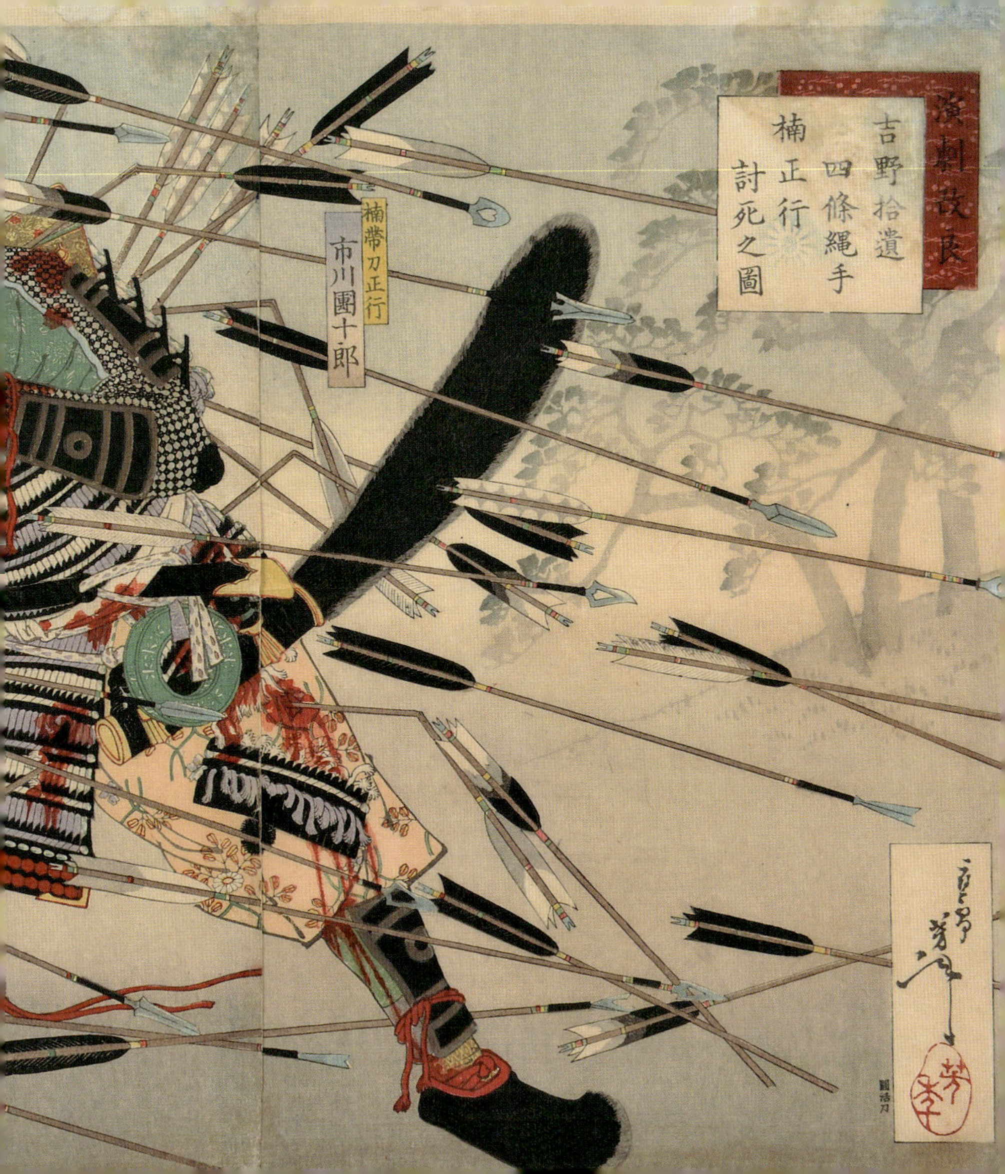
演劇改良

吉野拾遺
四條繩手
楠正行
討死之圖

楠帶刀正行
市川團十郎

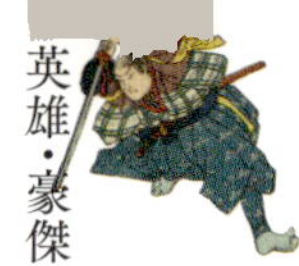

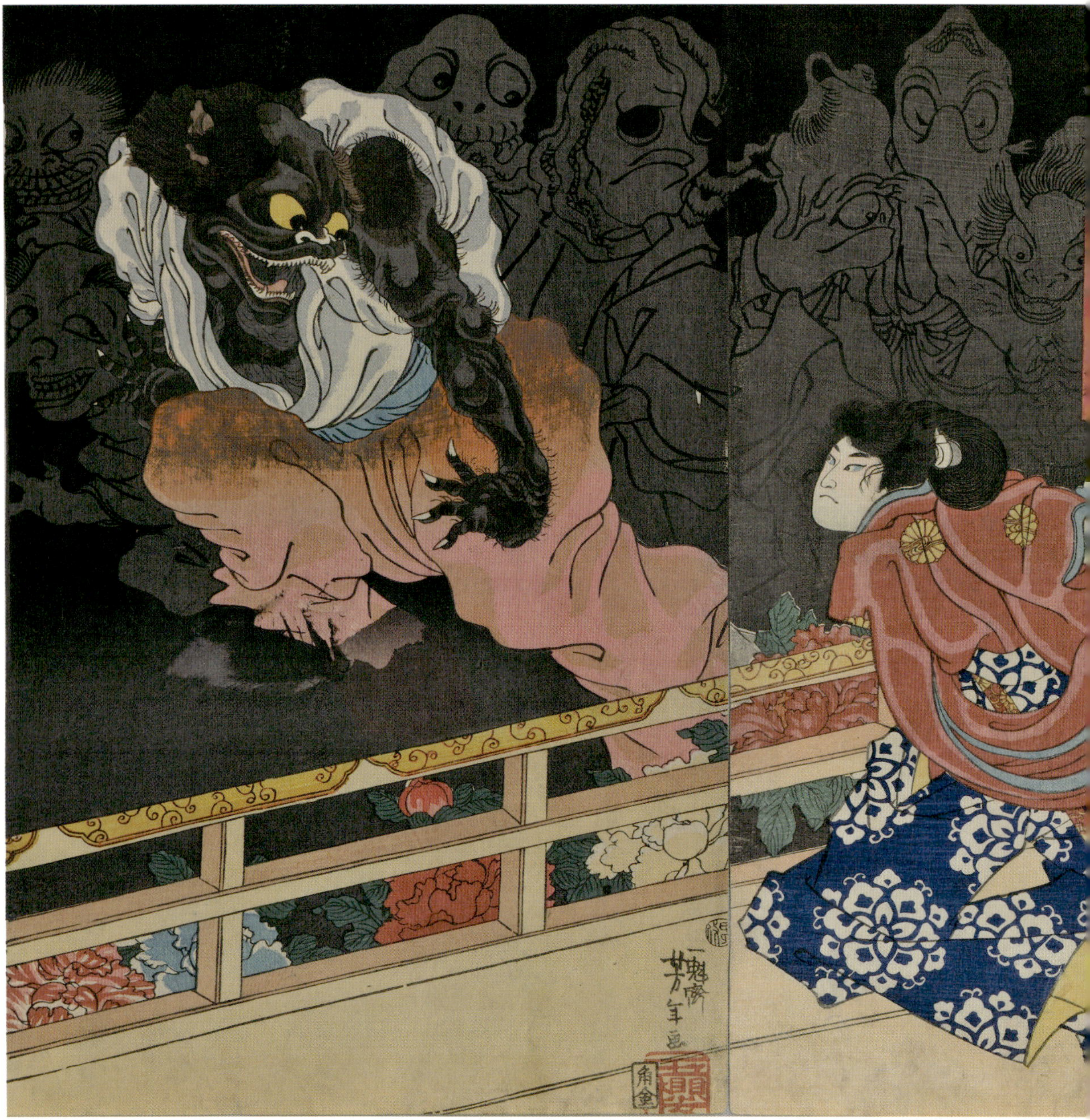

【楠多門丸古狸退治之図】月岡芳年　万延元年（1860）
正行は幼少の頃より武勇に優れた。ある晩庭に現れた古狸の妖怪を、臆することなく斬りつけた。

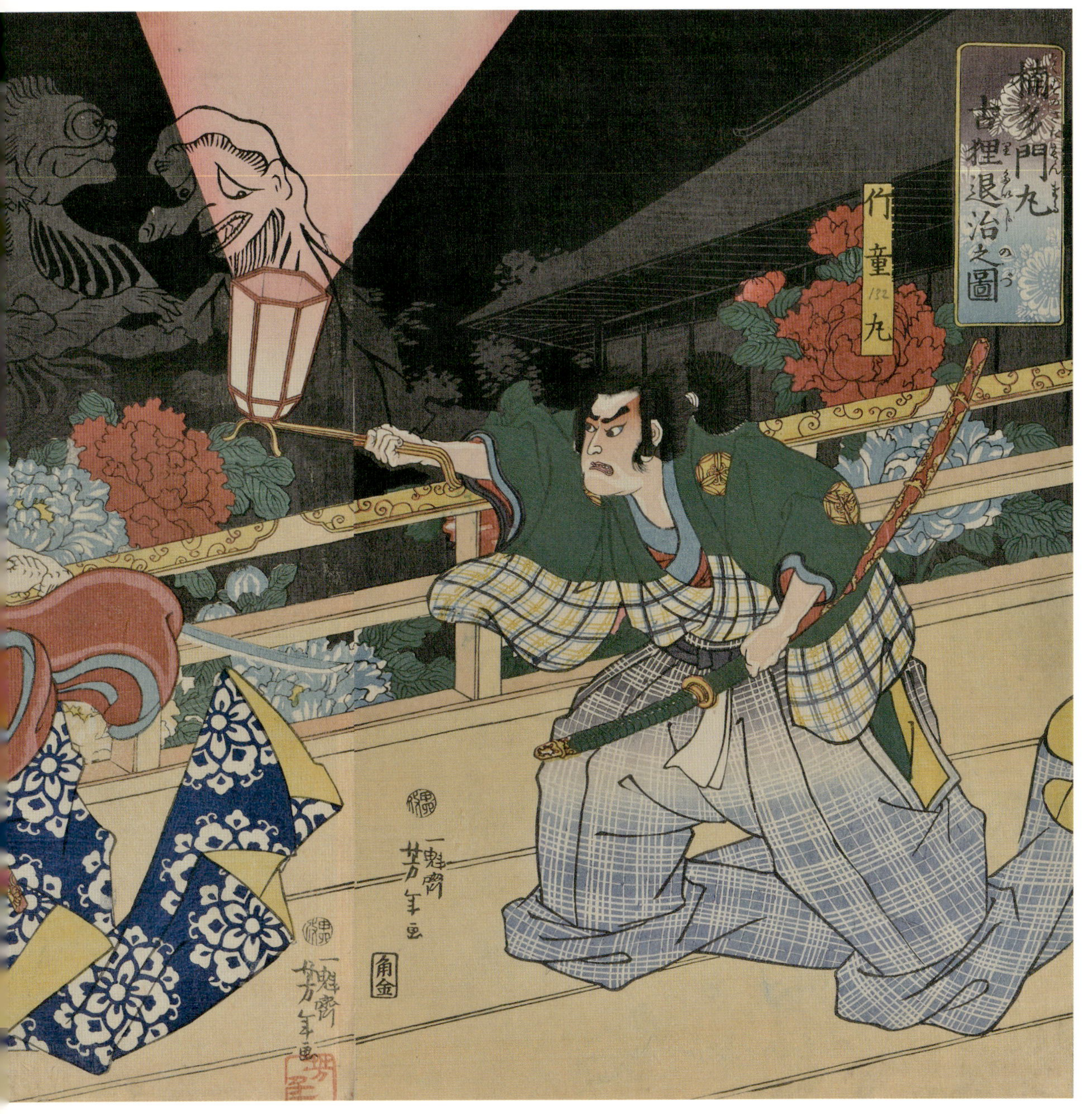

Kusunoki Tamonmaru Conquers the Old Tanuki by Tsukioka Yoshitoshi

Even when he was young, Masatsura excelled in the martial arts. One evening, an old tanuki, having transformed into a yōkai, appeared in his garden. Feeling no fear whatsoever, Masatsura dispatched with him with his sword.

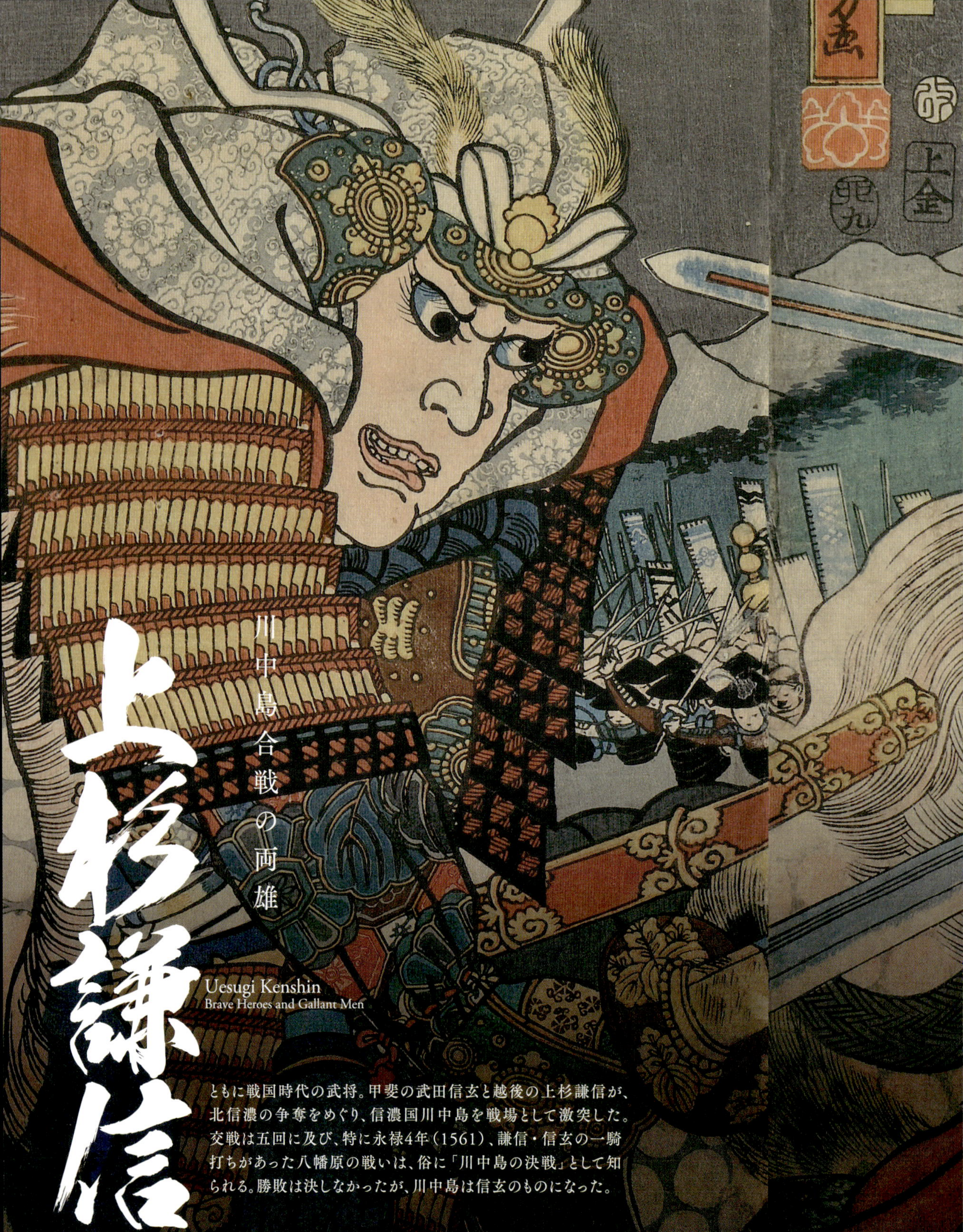
川中島合戦の両雄
上杉謙信
Uesugi Kenshin
Brave Heroes and Gallant Men
ともに戦国時代の武将。甲斐の武田信玄と越後の上杉謙信が、
北信濃の争奪をめぐり、信濃国川中島を戦場として激突した。
交戦は五回に及び、特に永禄4年（1561）、謙信・信玄の一騎
打ちがあった八幡原の戦いは、俗に「川中島の決戦」として知
られる。勝敗は決しなかったが、川中島は信玄のものになった。

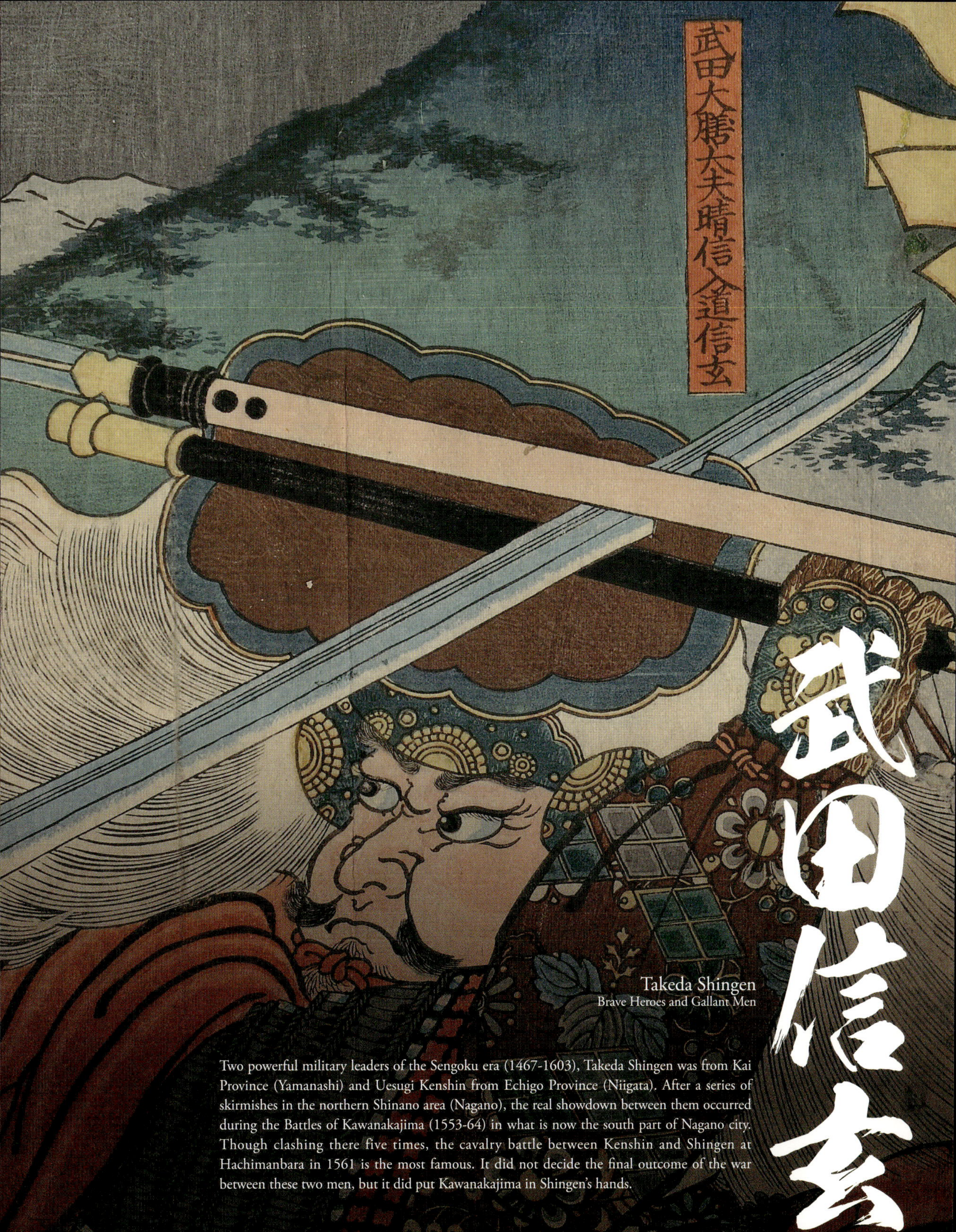

Takeda Shingen
Brave Heroes and Gallant Men

Two powerful military leaders of the Sengoku era (1467-1603), Takeda Shingen was from Kai Province (Yamanashi) and Uesugi Kenshin from Echigo Province (Niigata). After a series of skirmishes in the northern Shinano area (Nagano), the real showdown between them occurred during the Battles of Kawanakajima (1553-64) in what is now the south part of Nagano city. Though clashing there five times, the cavalry battle between Kenshin and Shingen at Hachimanbara in 1561 is the most famous. It did not decide the final outcome of the war between these two men, but it did put Kawanakajima in Shingen's hands.

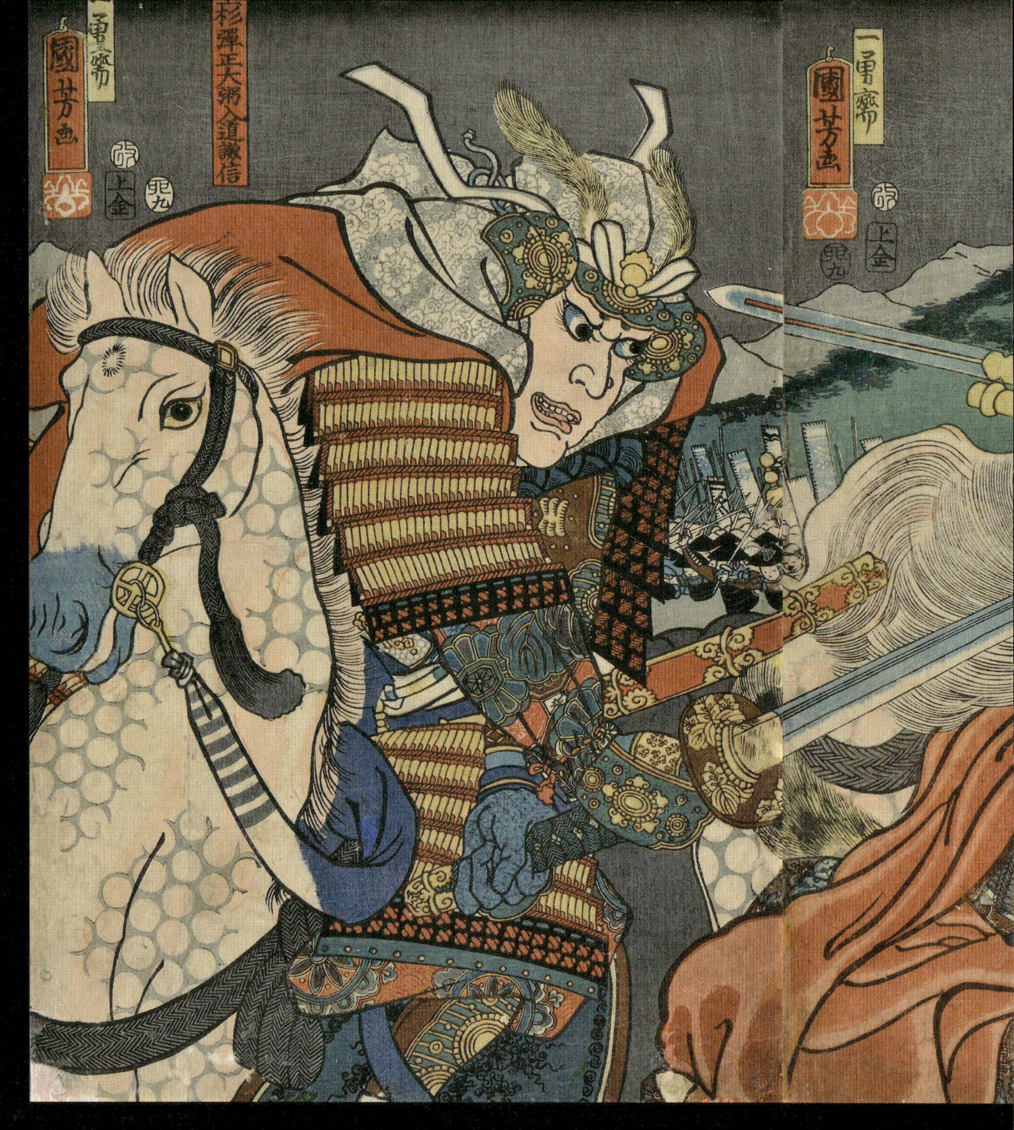

【川中島合戦】歌川国芳 安政2年（1855）

杉謙信が馬上から武田信玄に斬りかかるが、信玄は軍配で受け止める。

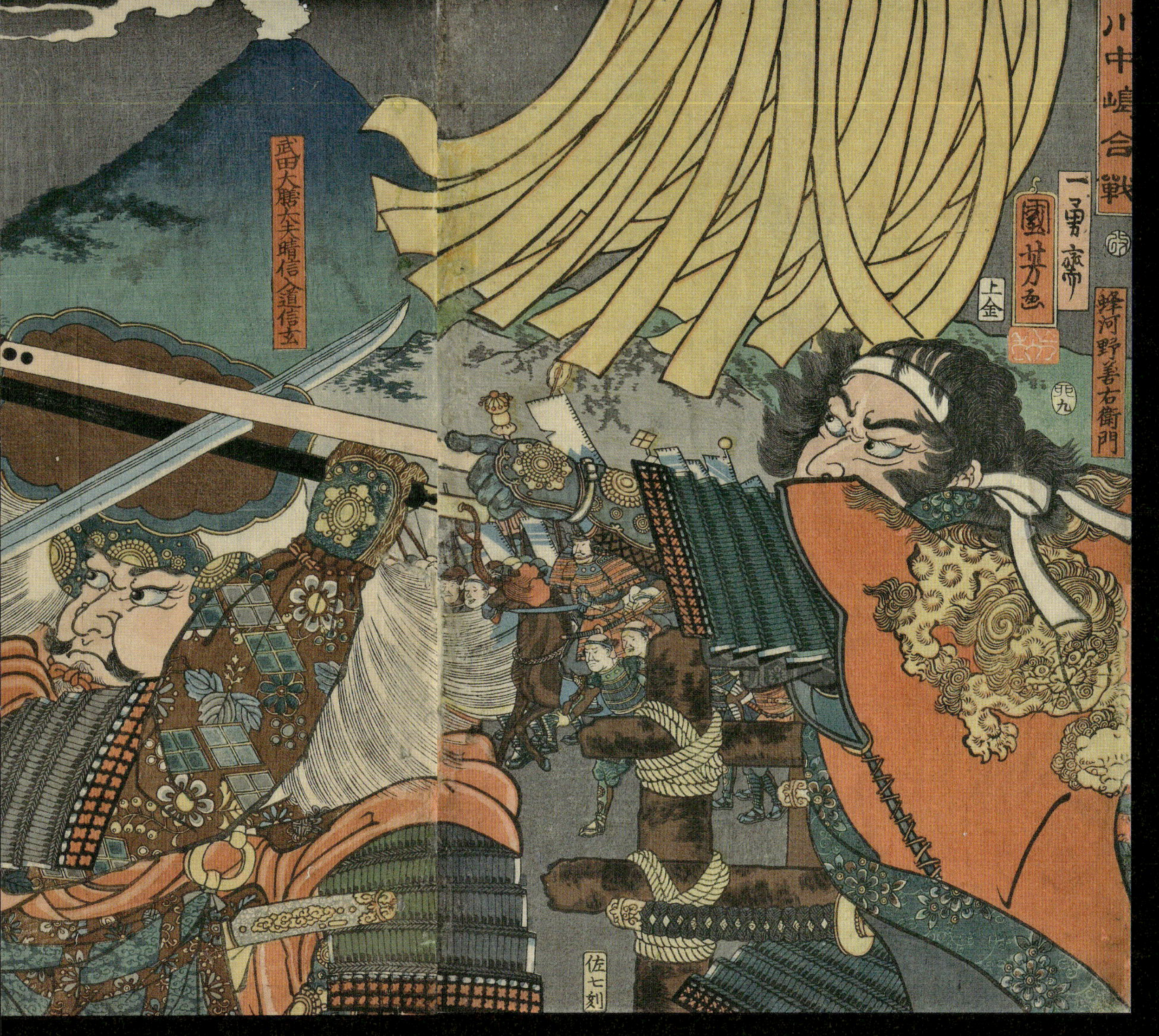

"The Battle of Kawanakajima" by Utagawa Kuniyoshi

Uesugi Kenshin attempts to cut down Takeda Shingen from atop his horse, but Shingen successfully parries the blow with his gunbai (war fan).

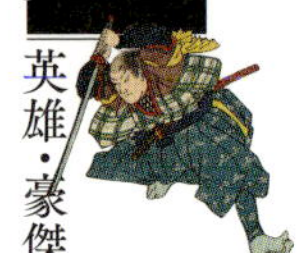

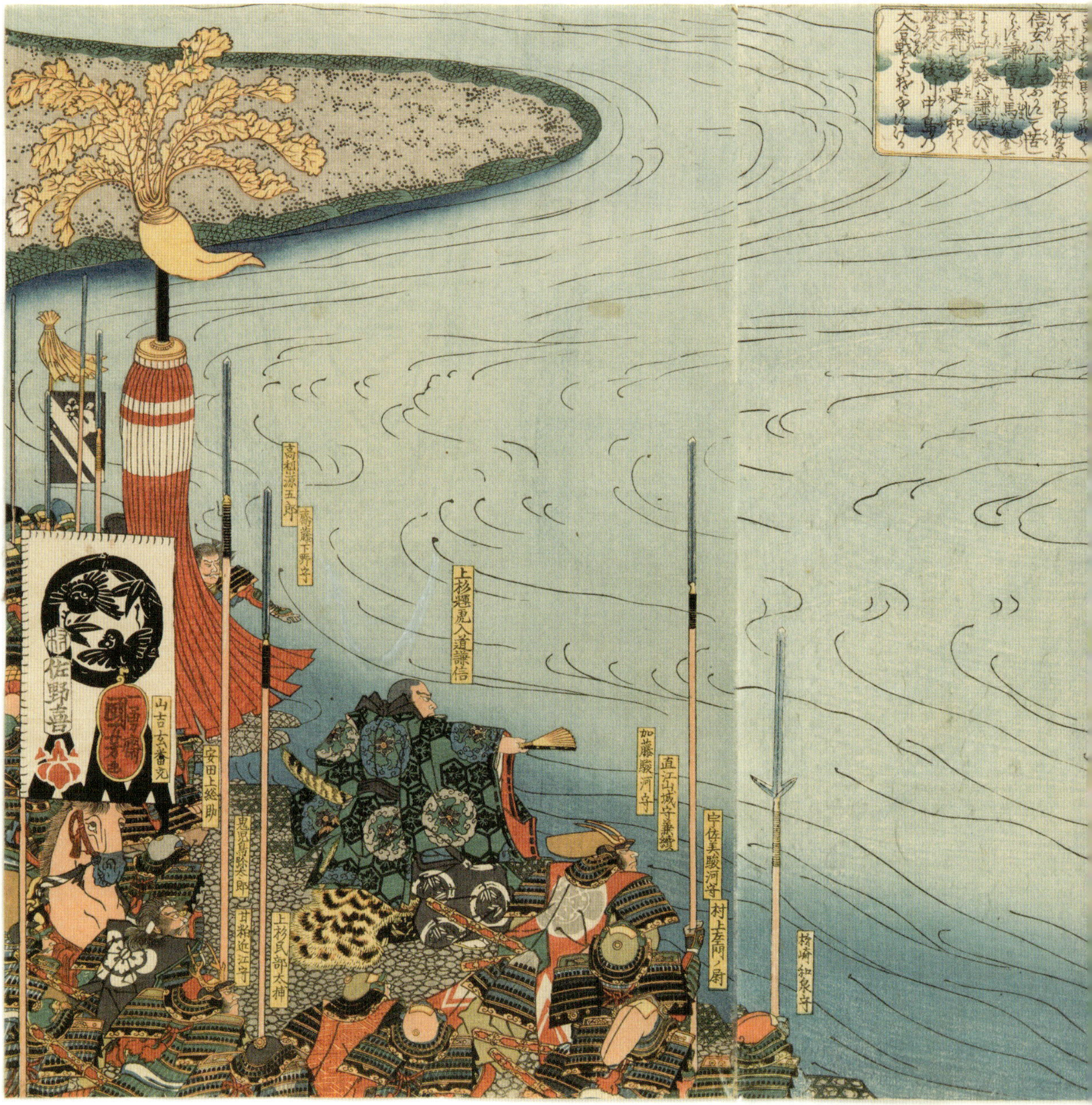

94

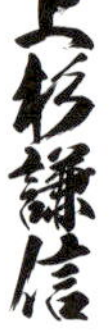

【五月十五日両将和睦対面図】歌川国芳 天保14年～弘化3年（1843-46）頃

両軍が千曲川を挟んで和睦の儀を取り行った際、事前の約束通り謙信は馬から下り床几に座ったが、信玄は降りようとしない。
謙信はこの無礼に腹を立て、和睦は撤回となった。

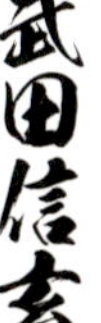

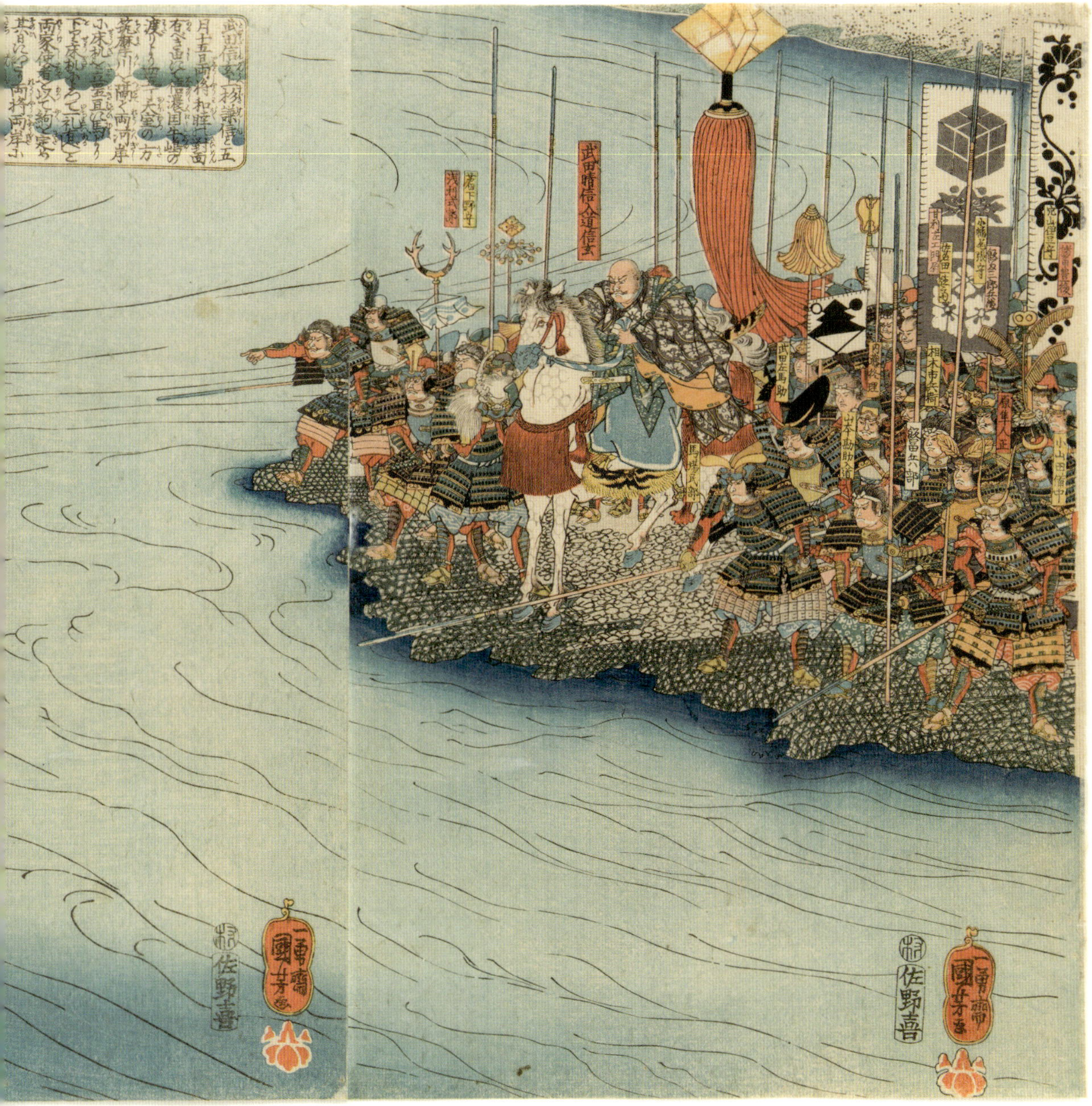

"The Failed Truce of May 15th" by Utagawa Kuniyoshi

Shingen and Kenshin's forces stand on either side of the Chikumagawa River to meet over a possible truce.
As decided beforehand, Kenshin has dismounted his horse and sits on a stool, but Shingen refuses to do the same,
insulting and angering Kenshin and making any peace impossible.

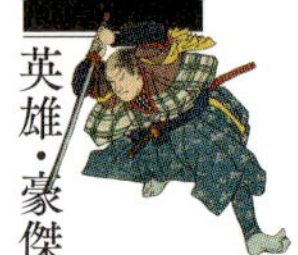

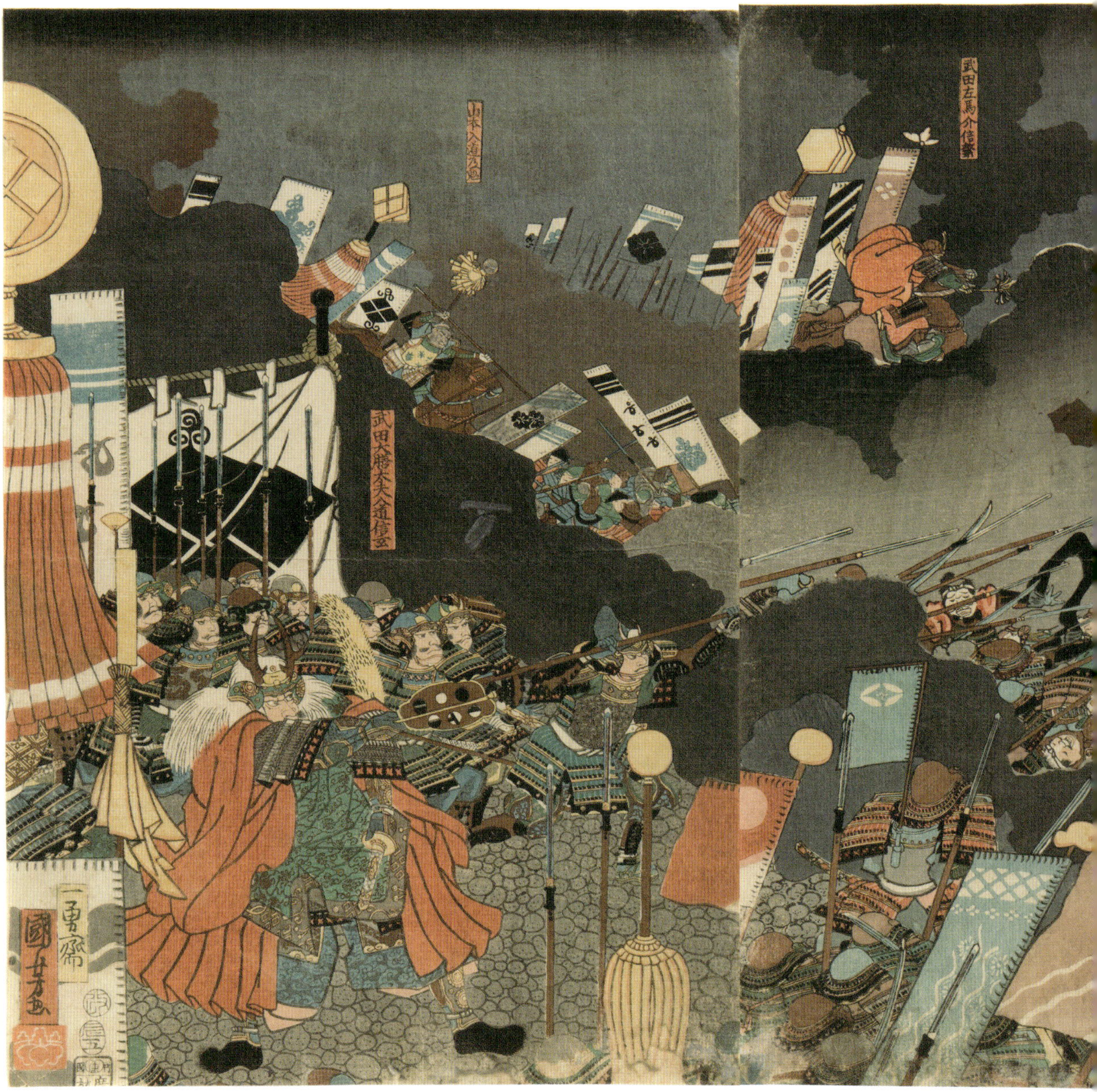

【川中島両将直戦図】歌川国芳 安政3年（1856）
白頭巾を被った謙信は、刀を振り上げながら本陣の信玄に向かって馬を走らせる。迎え撃つ信玄が頭に被るのは、家宝の諏訪法性の兜。

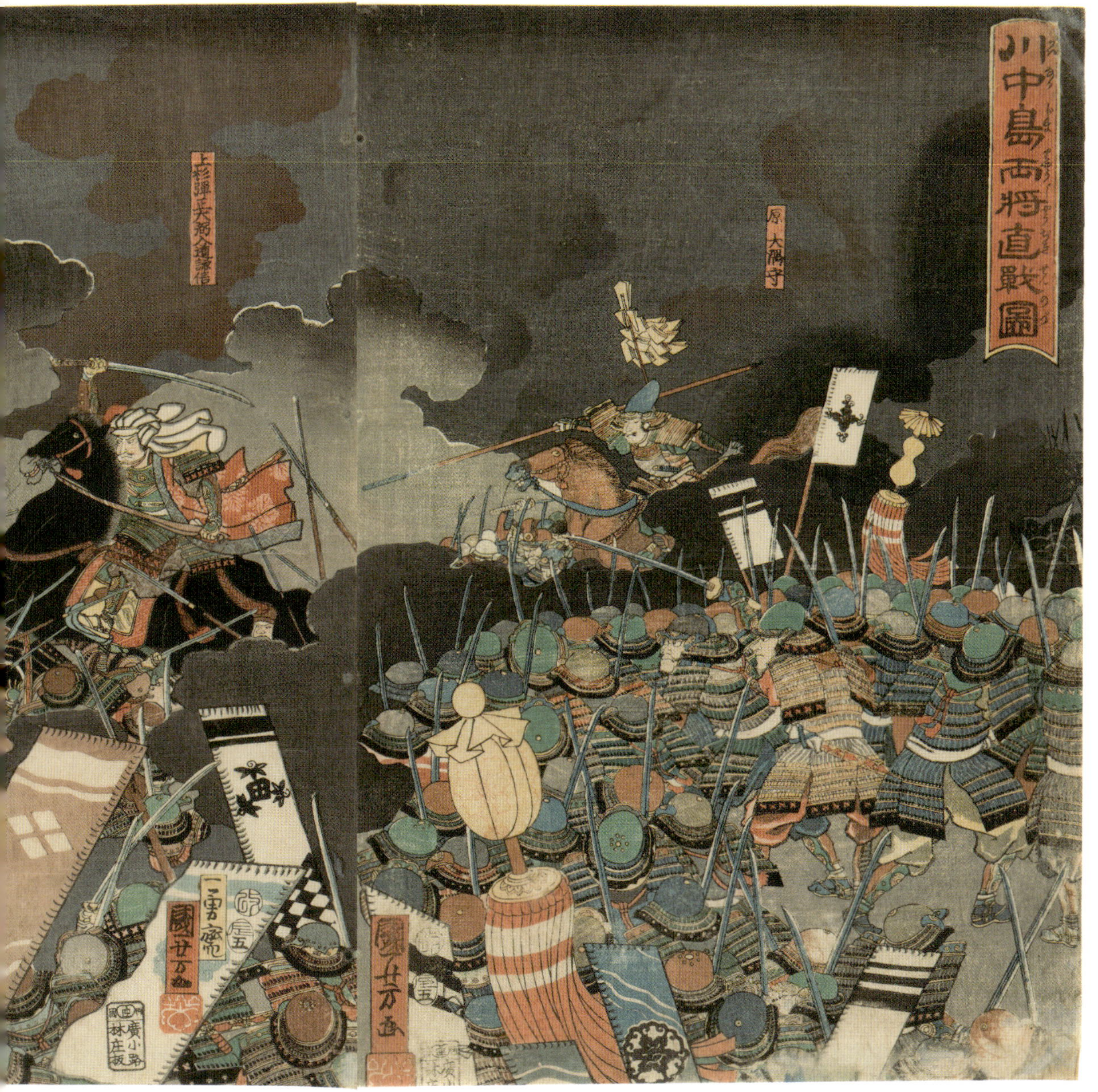

"Kenshin and Shingen Meet Face to Face at Kawanakajima" by Utagawa Kuniyoshi
Wearing a white cowl, Kenshin brandishes his sword and charges toward Shingen's base camp.
Ordering a defensive attack, Shingen wears on his head a treasured family heirloom, a helmet known as the Suwa Hosshō.

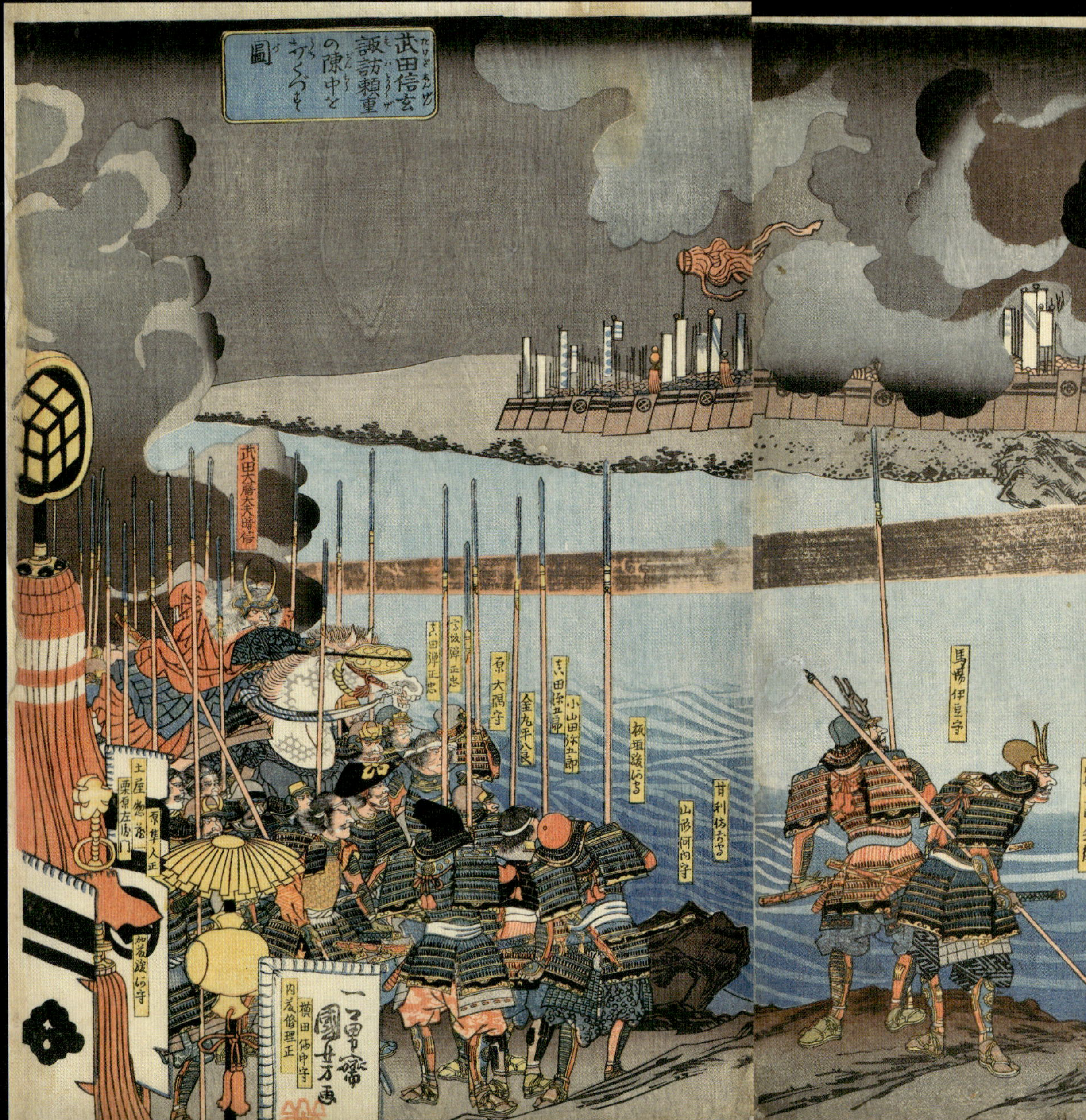
武田信玄諏訪頼重の陳中をさぐるの圖
武田六郎太夫晴信
一勇齋國芳画
横田伊豆守中守
内藤修理正
馬場伊豆守

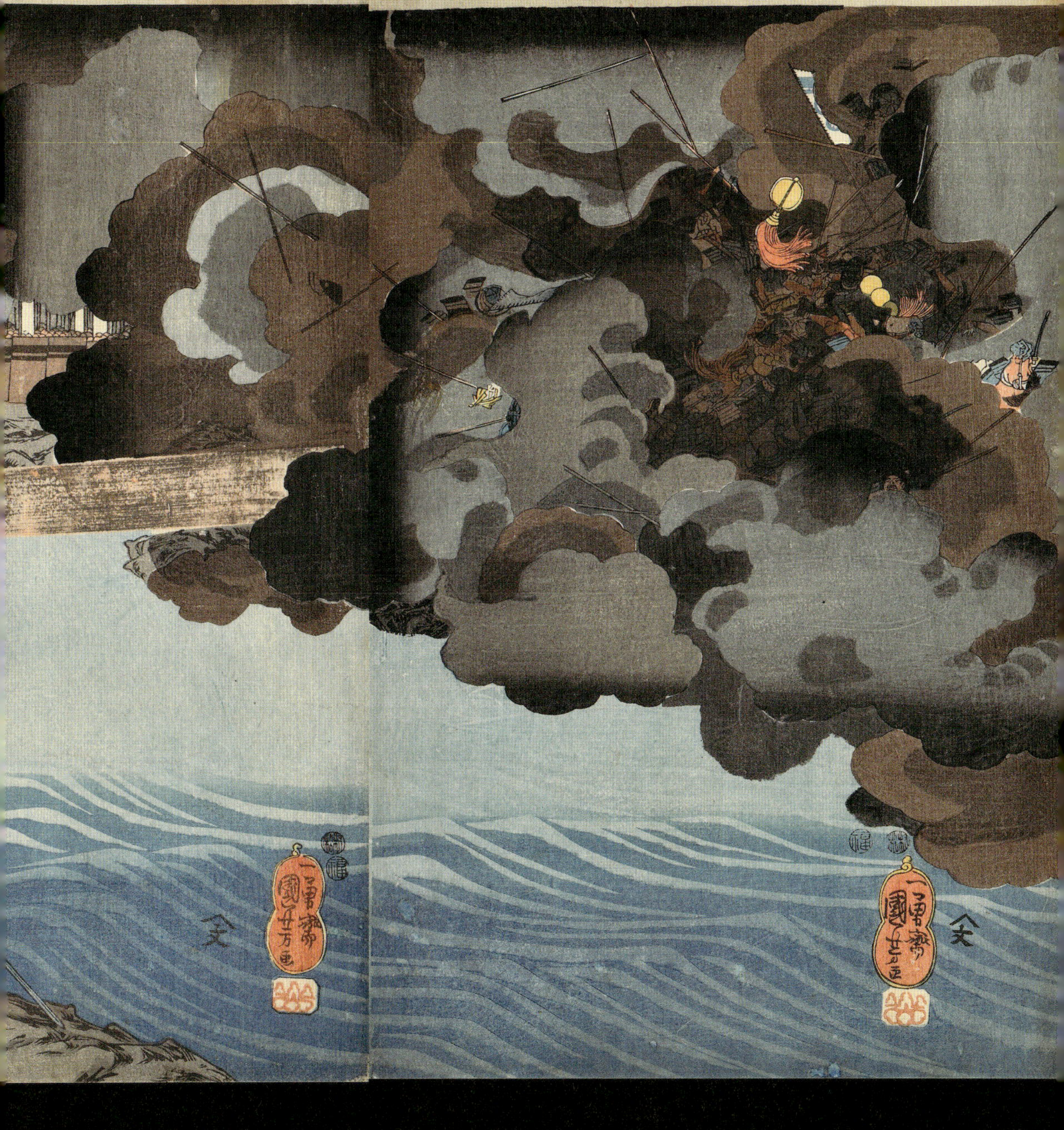

"Takeda Shingen Pummels Suwa Yorishige's Stronghold" by Utagawa Kuniyoshi
Soon after becoming the head of Kai Province, Shingen invaded Shinano and in 1542 defeated Suwa Yorishige, head of the Suwa domain, at Kuwabara Castle.

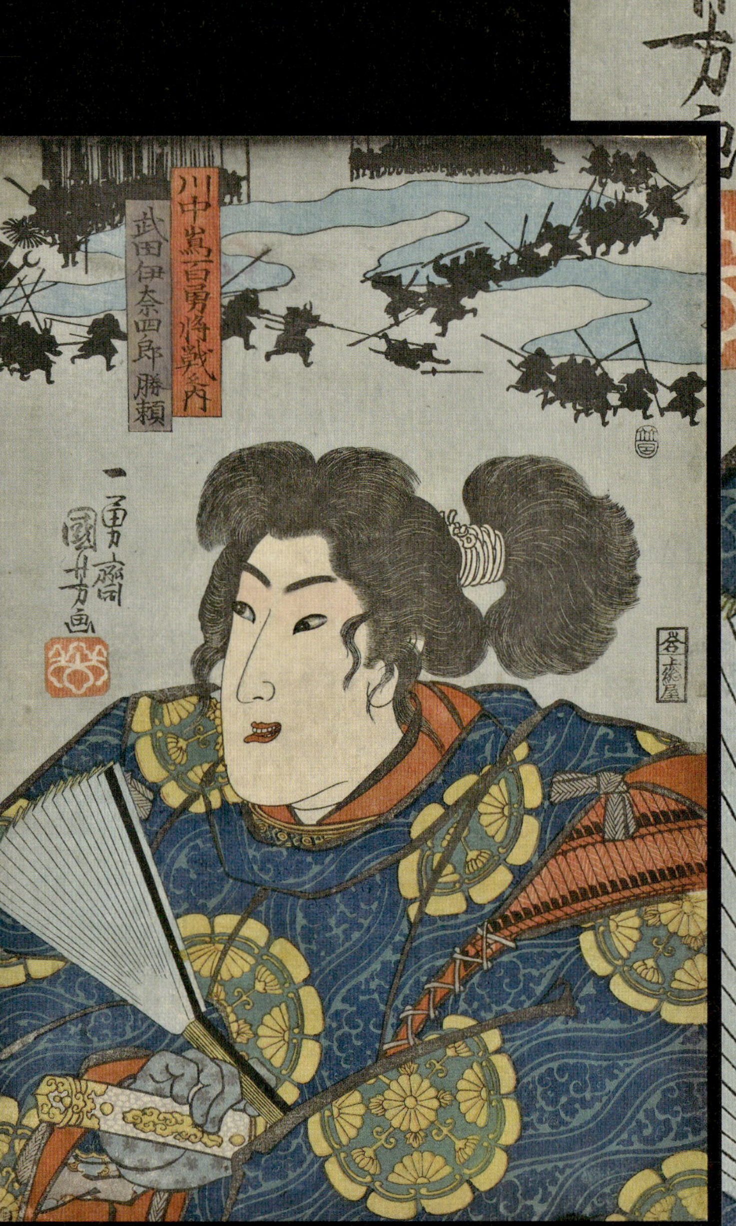

【川中嶋百勇将戦之内 武田伊那四郎勝頼】
歌川国芳 弘化2年（1845）頃
"One Hundred Brave Warriors of Kawanakajima:
Takeda Ina Shirō Katsuyori" by Utagawa Kuniyoshi

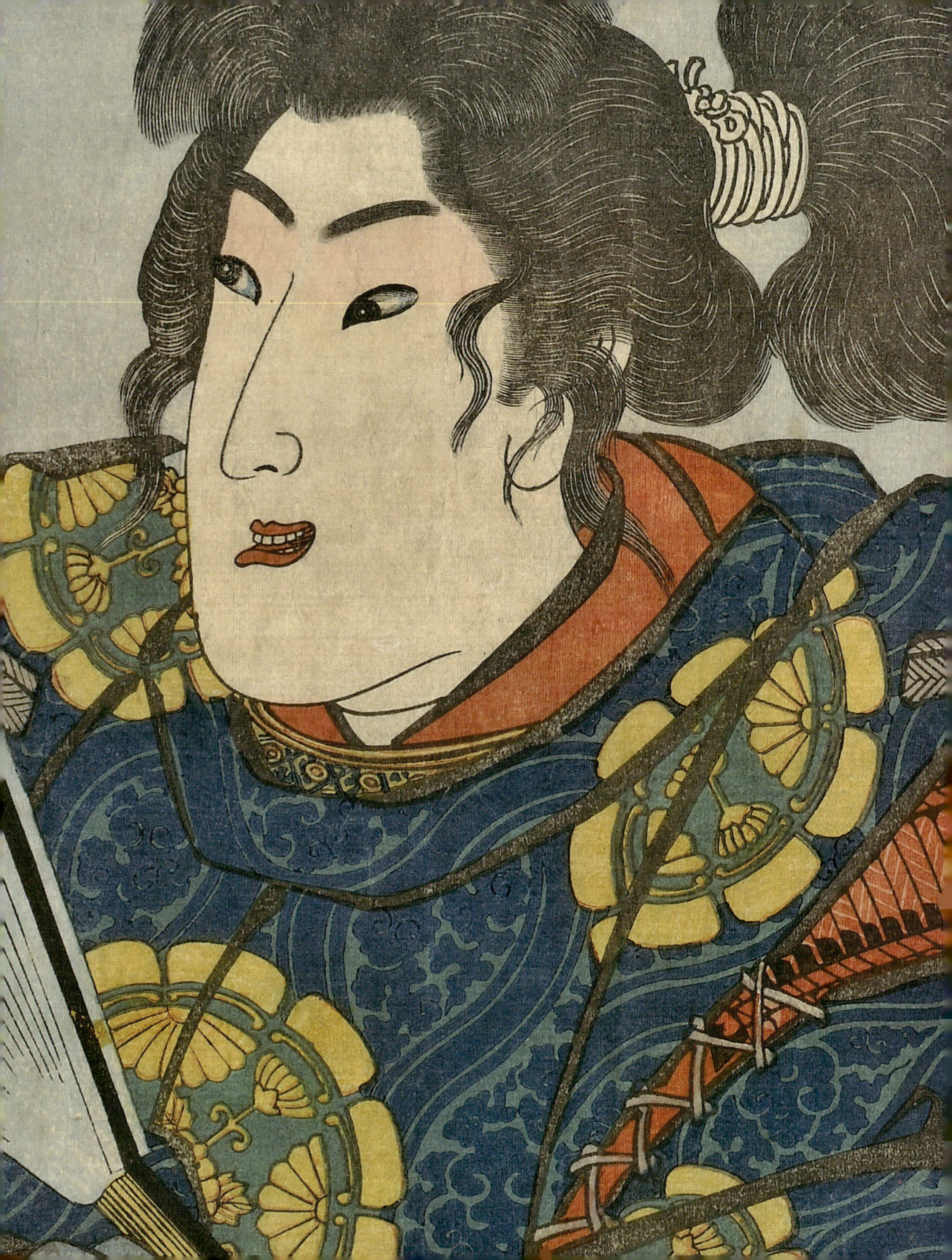

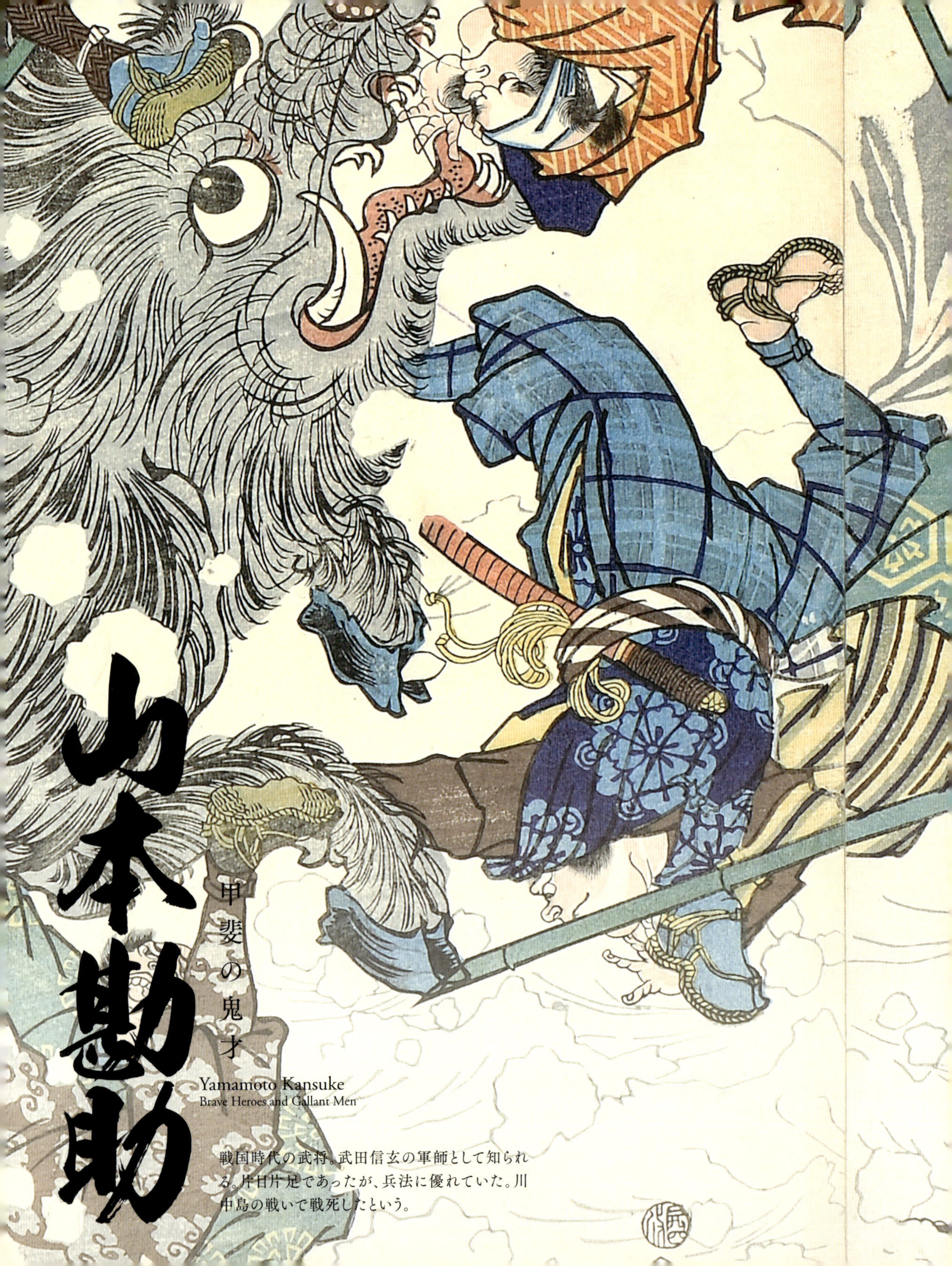

山本勘助

甲斐の鬼才

Yamamoto Kansuke
Brave Heroes and Gallant Men

戦国時代の武将。武田信玄の軍師として知られ
る。片目片足であったが、兵法に優れていた。川
中島の戦いで戦死したという。

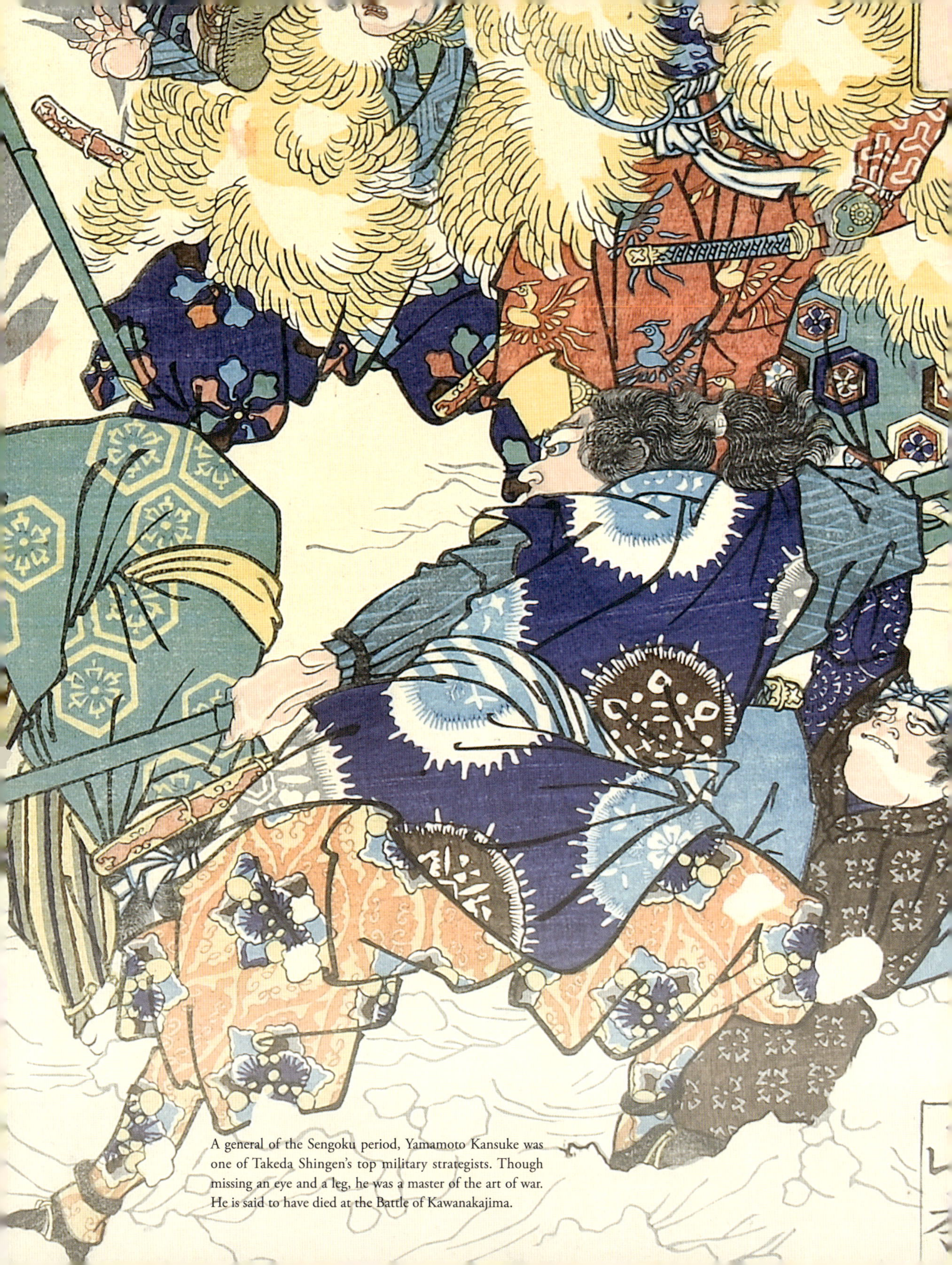

A general of the Sengoku period, Yamamoto Kansuke was one of Takeda Shingen's top military strategists. Though missing an eye and a leg, he was a master of the art of war. He is said to have died at the Battle of Kawanakajima.

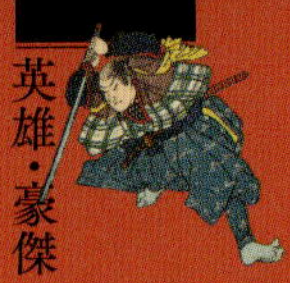

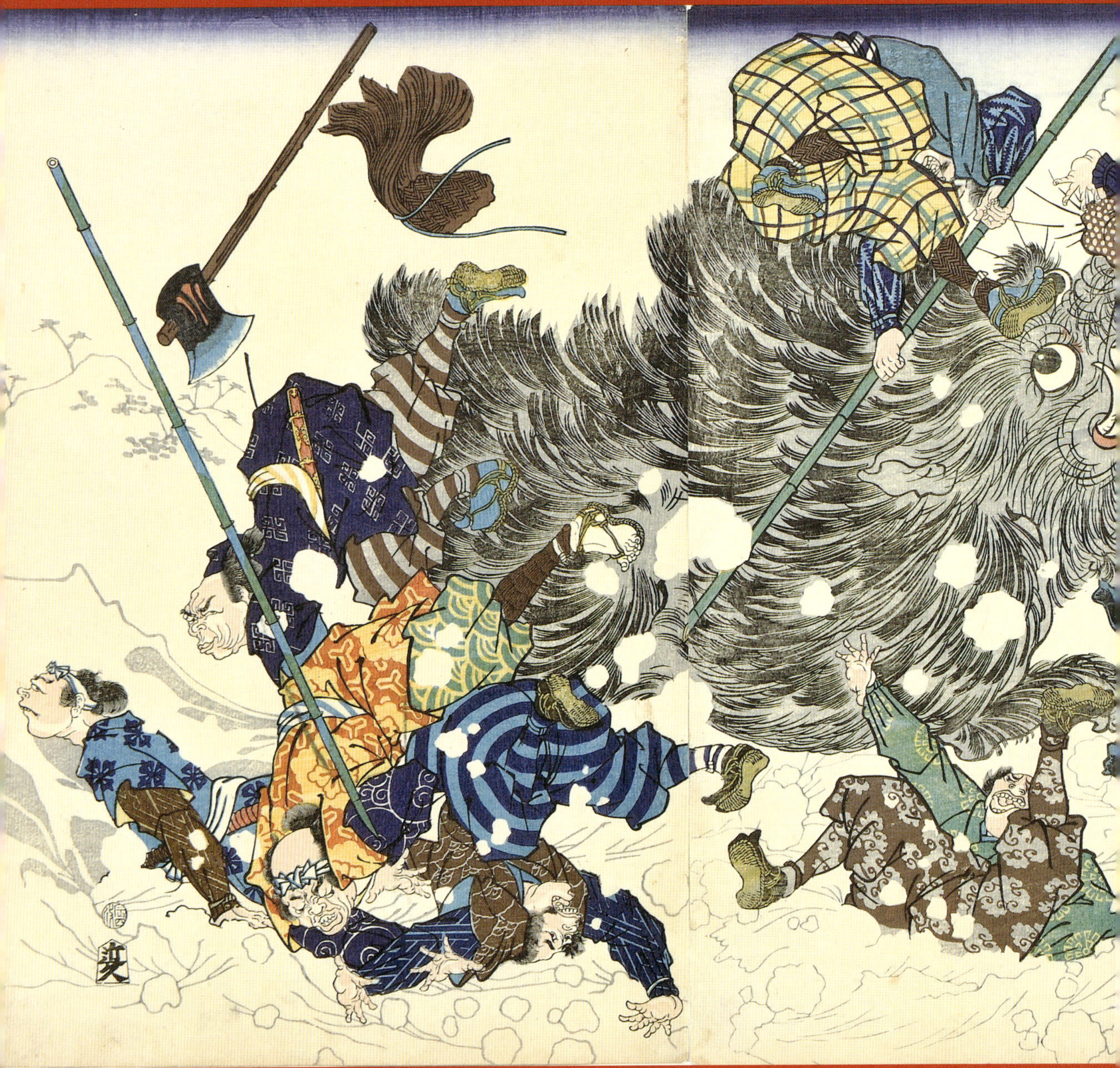

【山本勘助、武田勝千代丸、大猪成敗の場】月岡芳年　明治元年（1968）
一説によると、手負いの猪と戦った際に負傷して片目片足になったという。

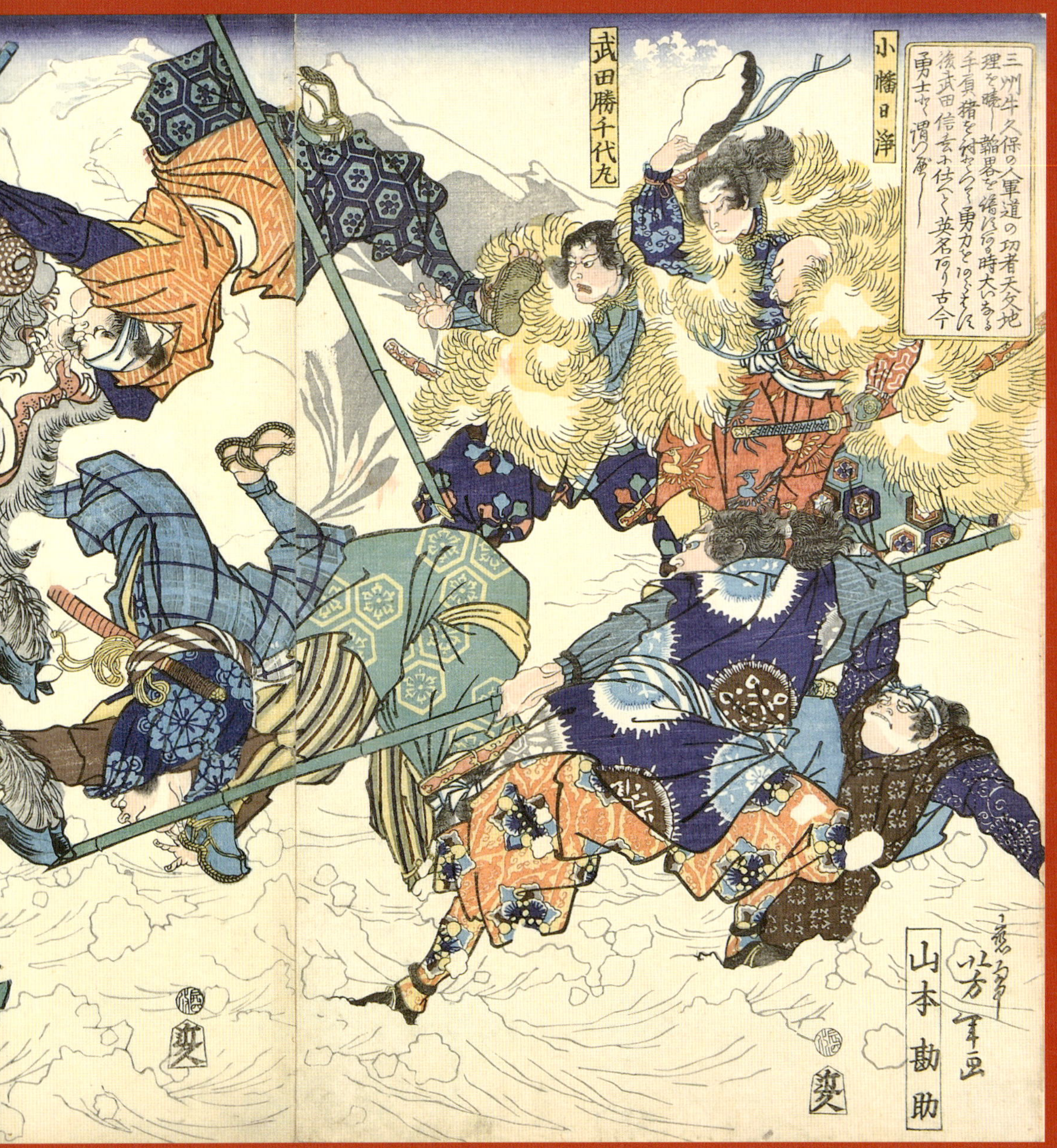

"Yamamoto Kansuke and Takeda Katsuchiyomaru Defeating a Giant Wild Boar" by Tsukioka Yoshitoshi

According to one legend, Kansuke lost his eye and leg in a battle with a large, injured wild boar.

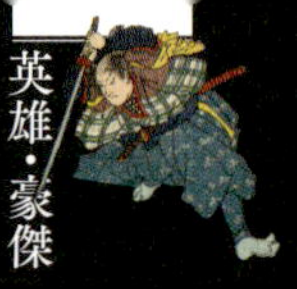

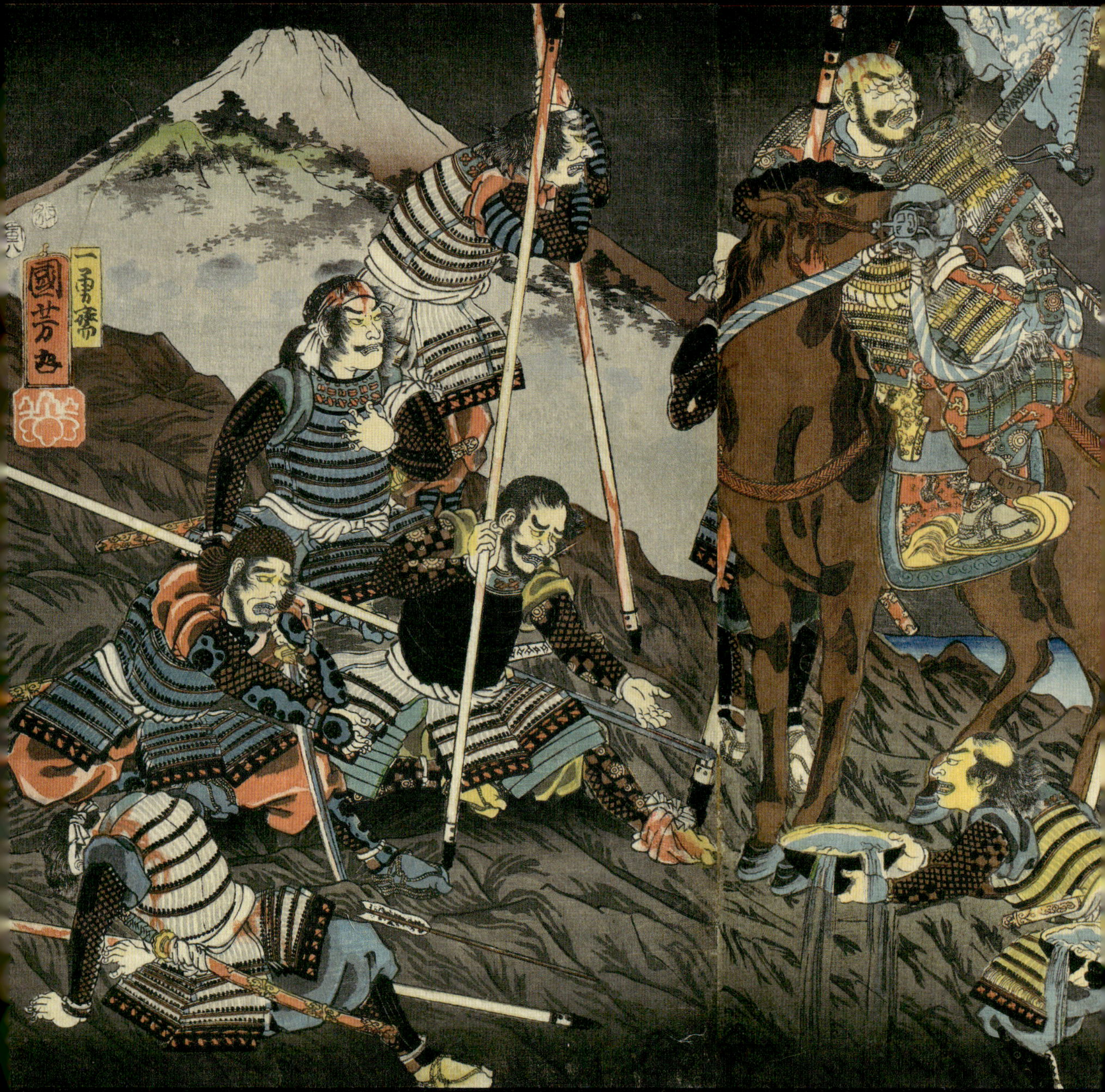

【永禄四年九月 川中嶋大合戦】歌川国芳 安政元年（1854）

数度にわたる川中島の戦いのうち、激戦で知られる永禄4年（1561）の八幡原での戦い。奇襲を受け、勘助はこの地で討ち死にする。

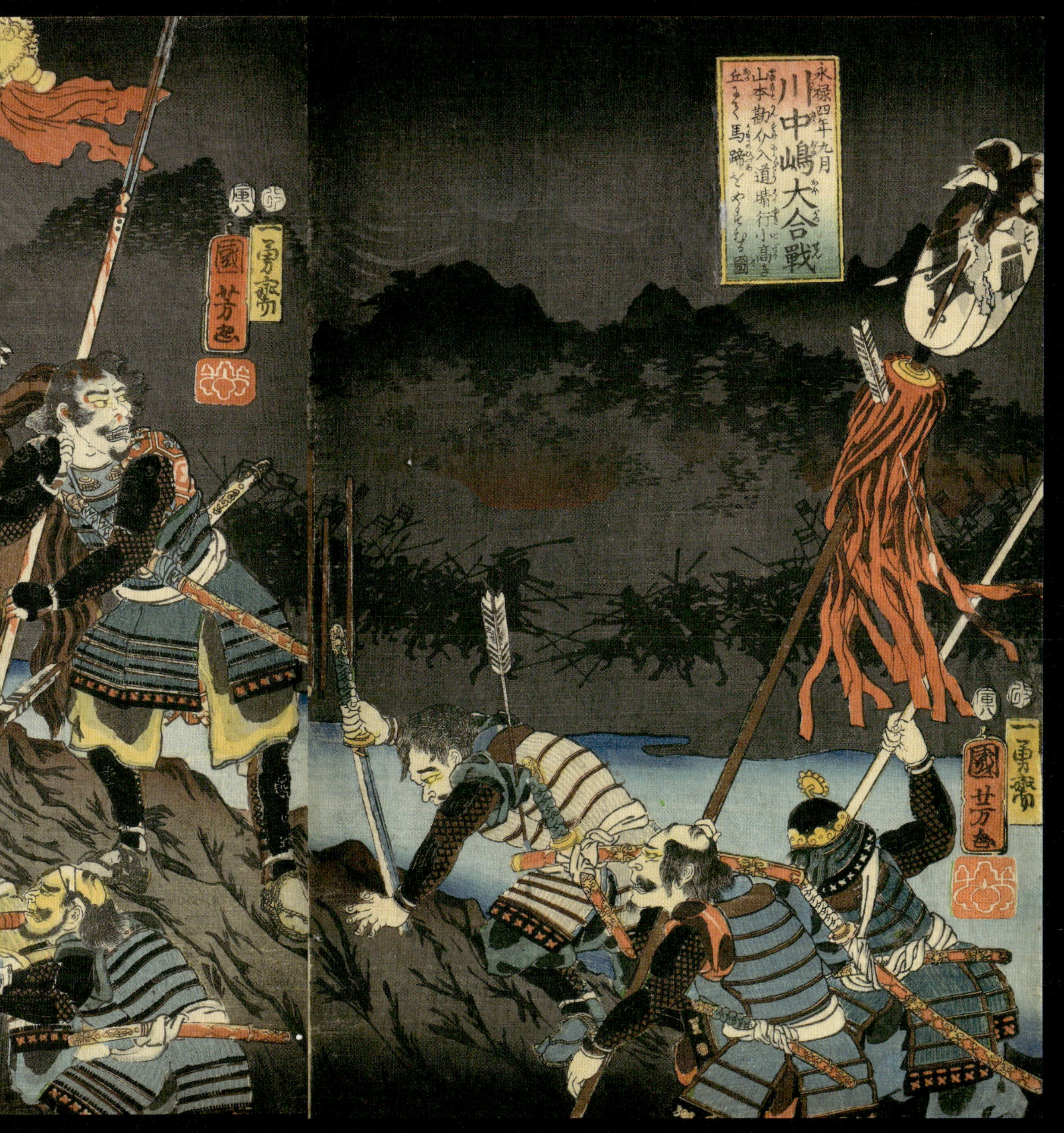

"The Battle of Kawanakajima, 1561" by Utagawa Kuniyoshi

Among the many battles in Kawanakajima, the most famous and ferocious was that at Hachimanbara in 1561.
This is where Kansuke died, after charging into his enemies' ranks.

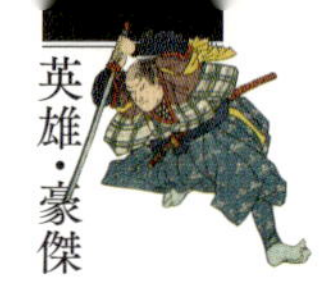

長尾政景

謙信麾下の武将

Nagao Masakage
Brave Heroes
and Gallant Men

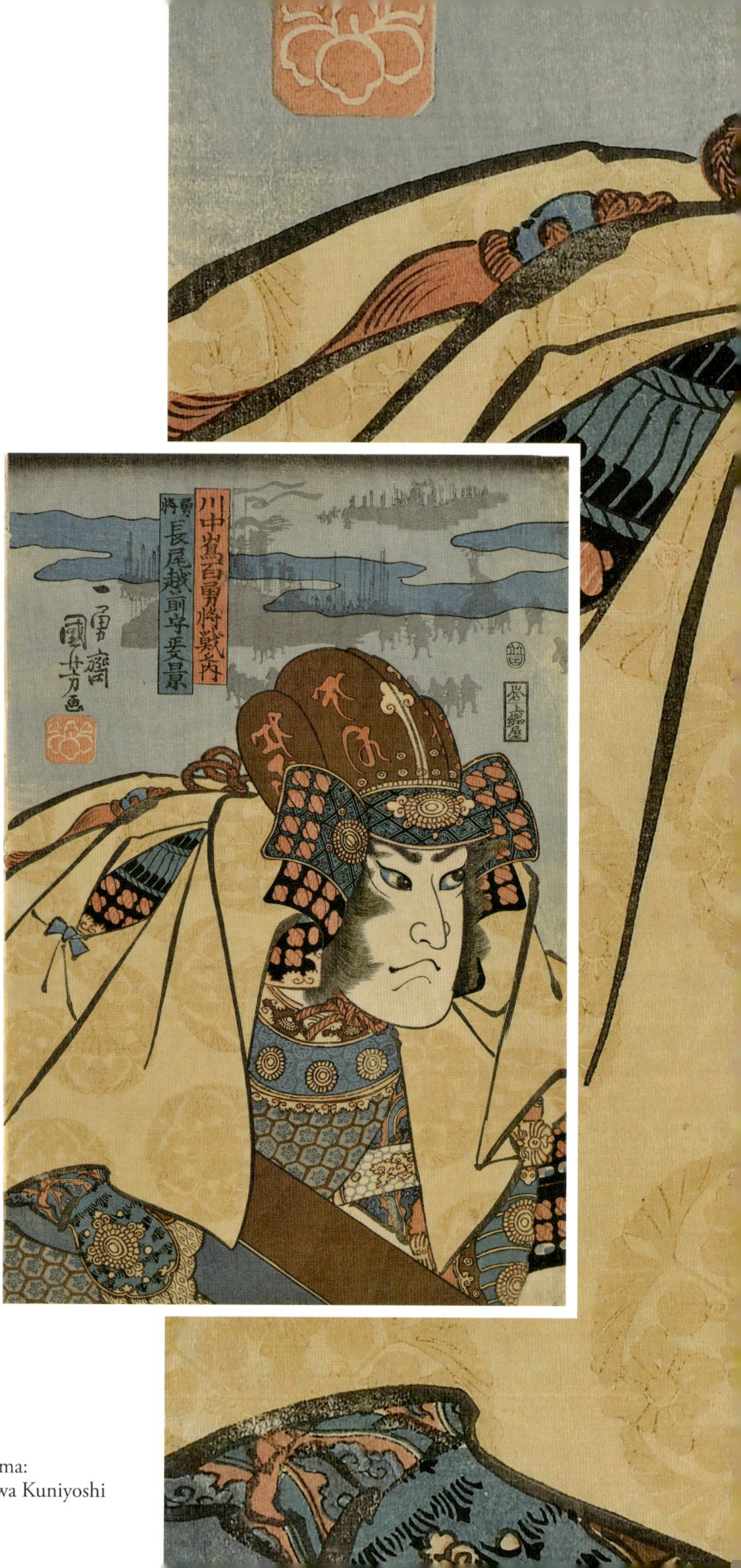

戦国時代の武将。長尾景虎（のちの上杉
謙信）と兄晴景の間で抗争が起こった際、
晴景側につき景虎に抵抗するものちに和
睦し、また、景虎の姉仙洞院を妻とした。
出家した景虎を説得して復帰させるなど、
景虎の重臣として活躍した。しかしながら、
野尻池で舟遊びの際に溺死し、一説には
景虎による謀殺ではないかといわれている。

A military leader of the Sengoku period,
Masakage mediated the conflicts between Nagao
Kagetora (later known as Uesugi Kenshin), his
brother-in-law, and Kagetora's elder brother,
Nagao Harukage. He was married to Kagetora's
sister, Sentōin. When Kagetora attempted to
abandon his leadership of the clan in 1556,
Masakage successfully talked him out of it.
Though he was a loyal retainer, some suspect
that his death by drowning while drinking on a
boat on Lake Nojiri in 1564 was actually an act
of assassination ordered by Kagetora.

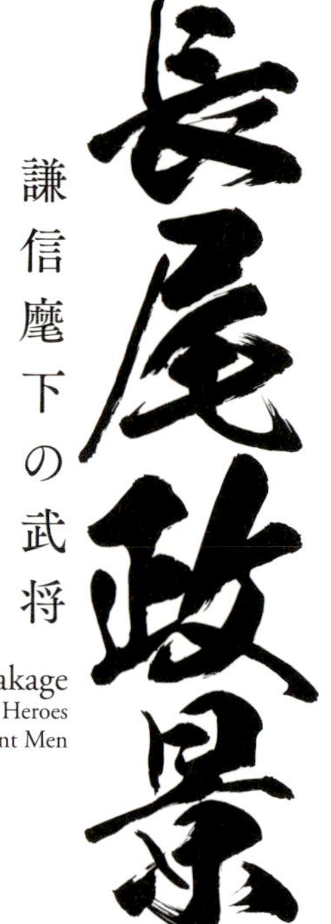

【川中嶋勇将戦之内 勇将長尾越前守政景】
歌川国芳 弘化2年（1845）頃

"One Hundred Brave Warriors of Kawanakajima:
Nagao Echizen-no-kami Masakage" by Utagawa Kuniyoshi

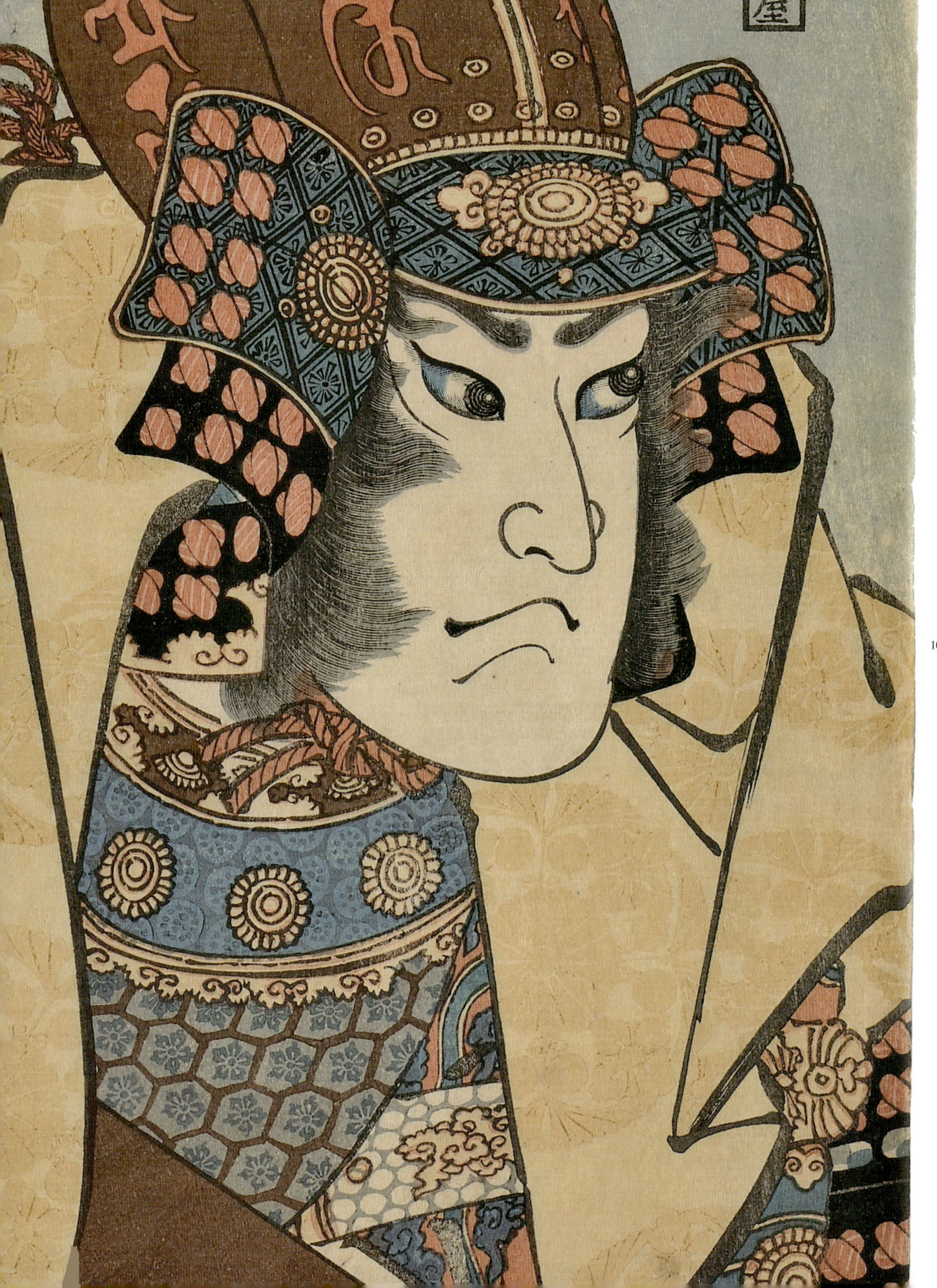

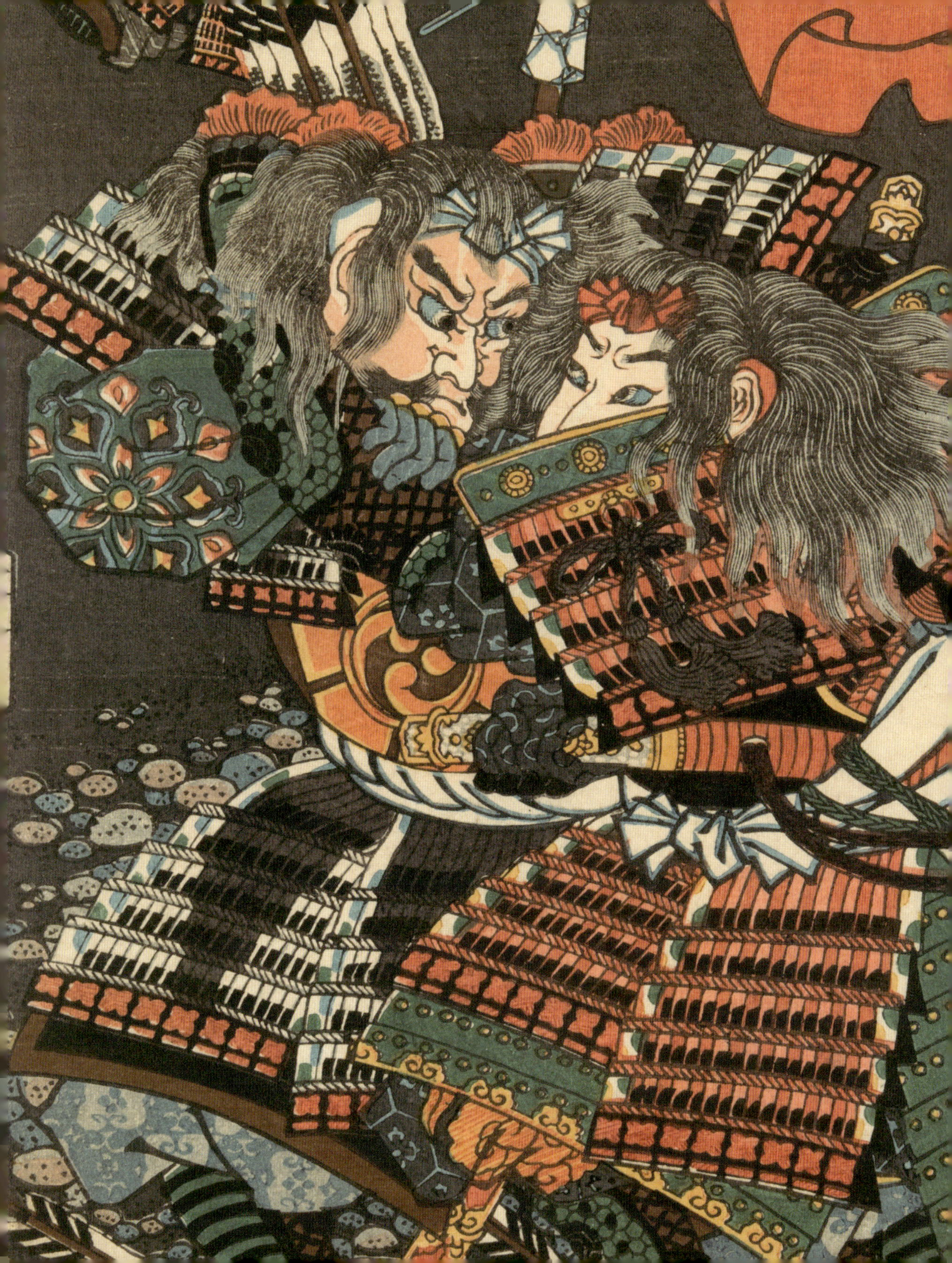

馬場美濃守

武田家最強の守護神

Baba Mino-no-kami
Brave Heroes and Gallant Men

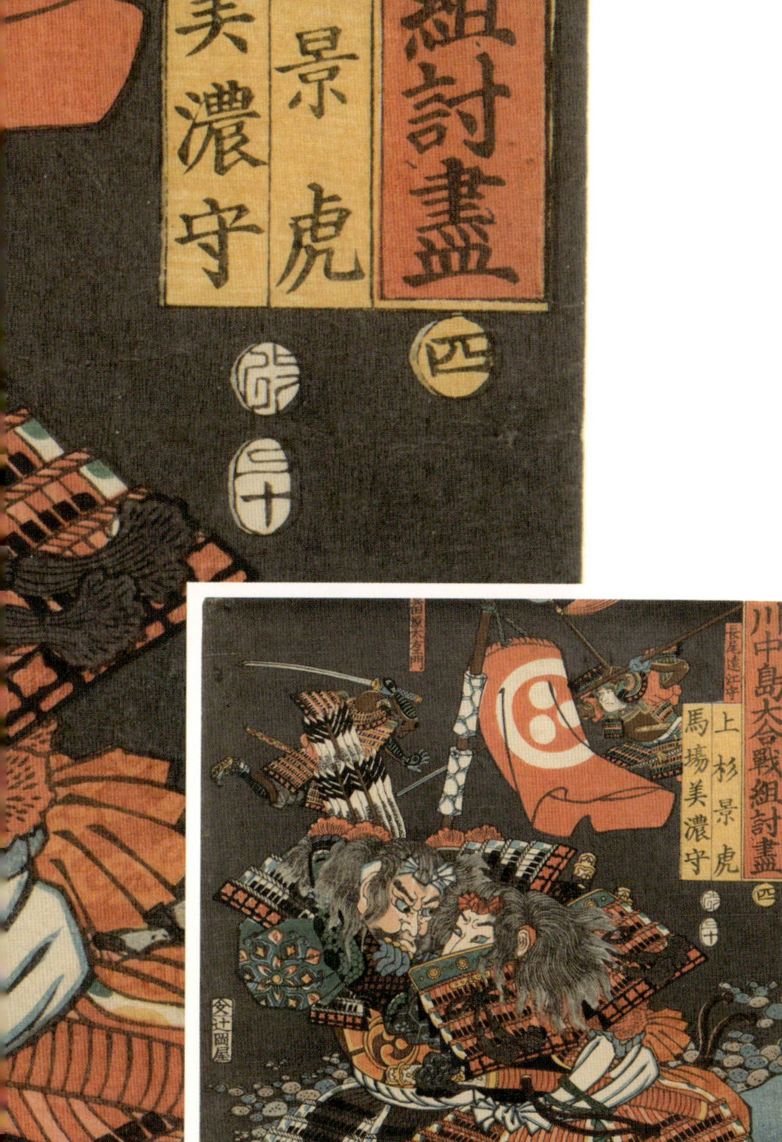

戦国時代の武将。馬場信房、あるいは馬場信春とも称す。武田信玄の右腕として活躍し、武田四天王の一人に数えられる。川中島の戦いでは山本勘助とともに、いわゆる啄木鳥戦法を実行したが、上杉軍に見破られた。馬場美濃守はまた、山本勘助から築城法を教授され、築城の名手としても知られる。信玄亡き後は父の志を継いだ勝頼に仕え、長篠の戦いにて討ち死にした。

A military leader of the Sengoku era, Mino-no-kami (the Governor of Mino) also went by the names Baba Nobufusa and Baba Nobuharu. He was Takeda Shingen's righthand man, and is counted as one of the Four Guardian Kings of the Takeda clan. At the Battle of Kawanakajima, he and Yamamoto Kansuke devised the famous "woodpecker attack," which was alas foiled by Uesugi Kenshin's army. He also learned from Kansuke how to build castles, and gained fame for his expertise in that field as well. After Shingen's death, he served under Takeda Katsuyori and was killed at the Battle of Nagashino in 1575.

【川中島大合戦組討尽 四 上杉景虎 馬場美濃守】
歌川芳艶 安政4年（1857）
"Combat at the Battle of Kawanakajima:
Uesugi Kagetora versus Baba Mino-no-kami" by Utagawa Yoshitsuya

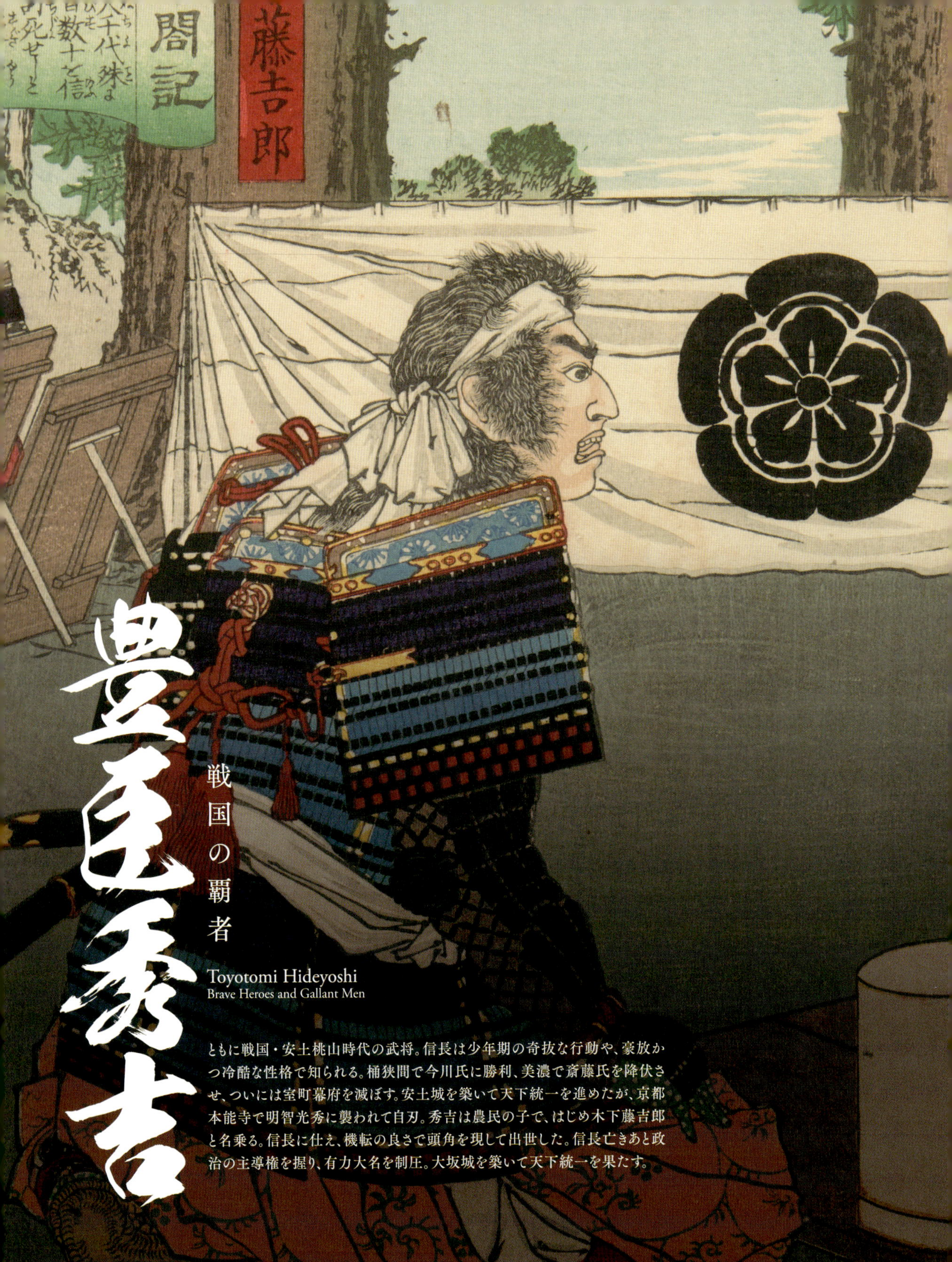

豊臣秀吉

戦国の覇者

Toyotomi Hideyoshi
Brave Heroes and Gallant Men

ともに戦国・安土桃山時代の武将。信長は少年期の奇抜な行動や、豪放かつ冷酷な性格で知られる。桶狭間で今川氏に勝利、美濃で斎藤氏を降伏させ、ついには室町幕府を滅ぼす。安土城を築いて天下統一を進めたが、京都本能寺で明智光秀に襲われて自刃。秀吉は農民の子で、はじめ木下藤吉郎と名乗る。信長に仕え、機転の良さで頭角を現して出世した。信長亡きあと政治の主導権を握り、有力大名を制圧。大坂城を築いて天下統一を果たす。

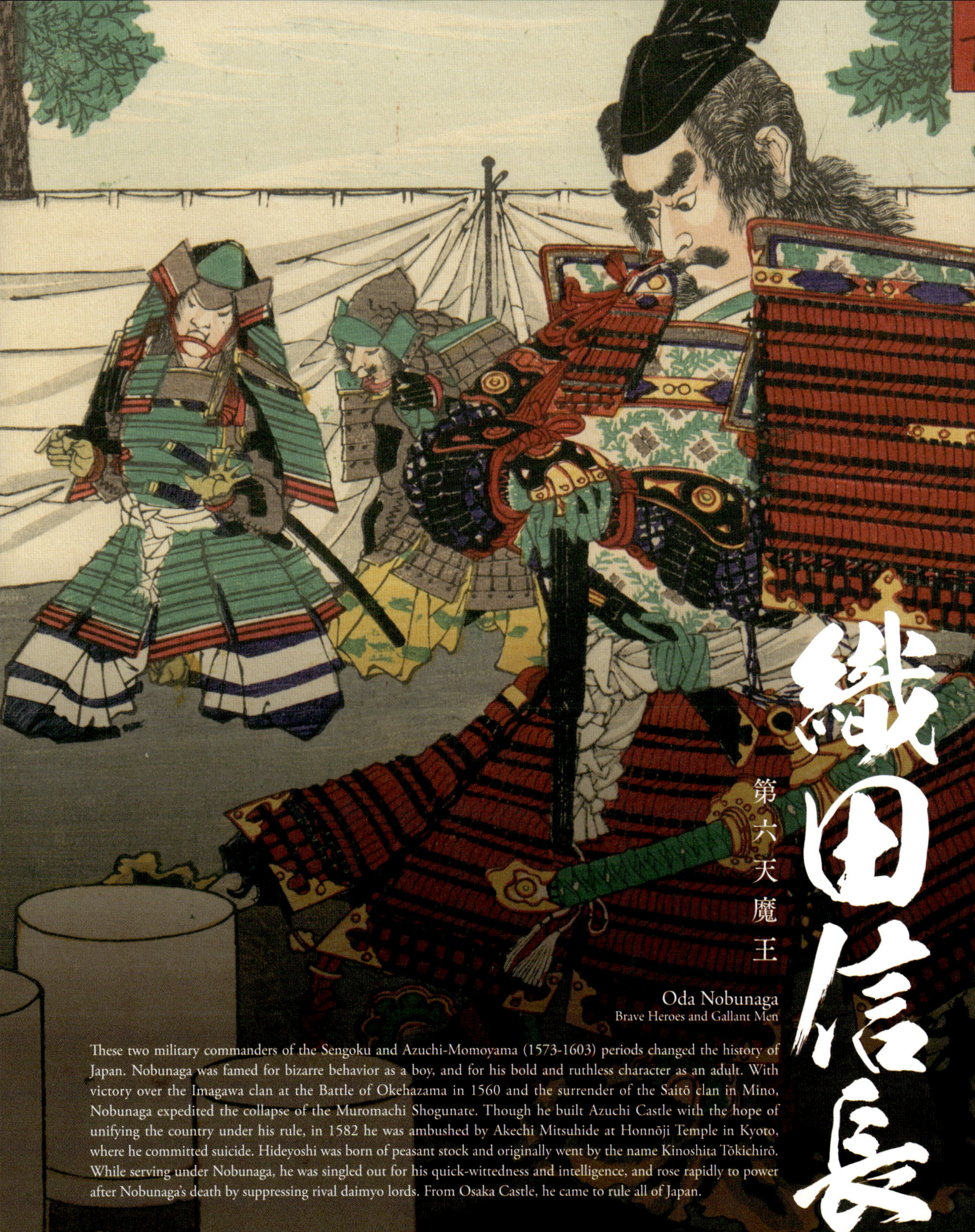

Oda Nobunaga
Brave Heroes and Gallant Men

These two military commanders of the Sengoku and Azuchi-Momoyama (1573-1603) periods changed the history of Japan. Nobunaga was famed for bizarre behavior as a boy, and for his bold and ruthless character as an adult. With victory over the Imagawa clan at the Battle of Okehazama in 1560 and the surrender of the Saitō clan in Mino, Nobunaga expedited the collapse of the Muromachi Shogunate. Though he built Azuchi Castle with the hope of unifying the country under his rule, in 1582 he was ambushed by Akechi Mitsuhide at Honnōji Temple in Kyoto, where he committed suicide. Hideyoshi was born of peasant stock and originally went by the name Kinoshita Tōkichirō. While serving under Nobunaga, he was singled out for his quick-wittedness and intelligence, and rose rapidly to power after Nobunaga's death by suppressing rival daimyo lords. From Osaka Castle, he came to rule all of Japan.

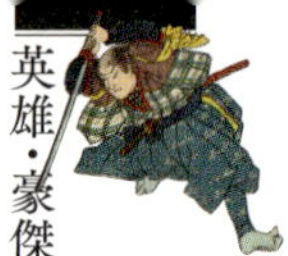

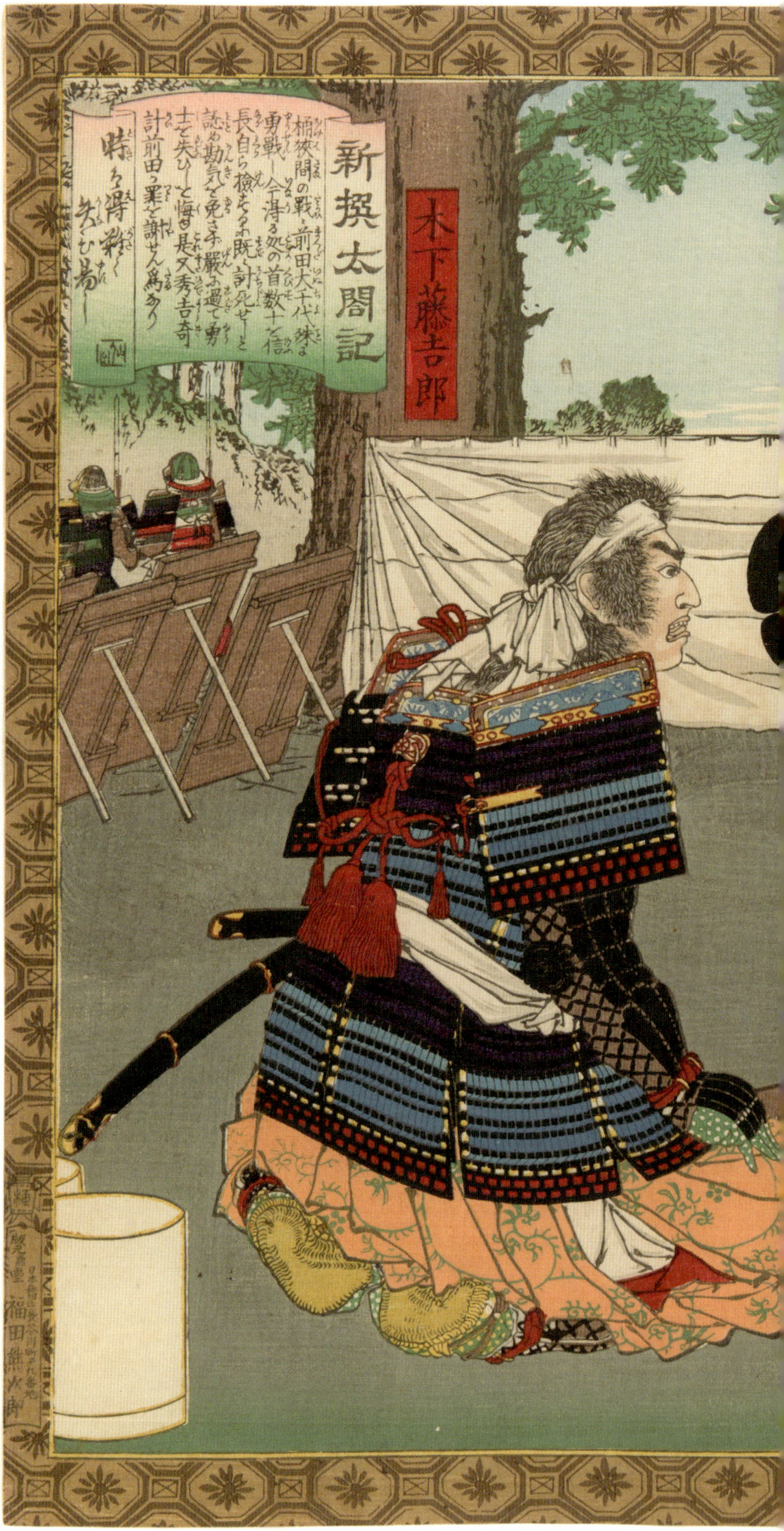

114

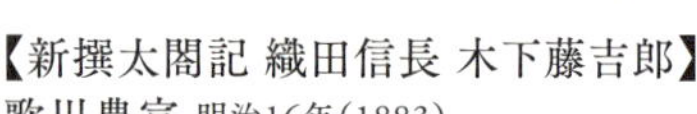

【新撰太閤記 織田信長 木下藤吉郎】
歌川豊宣　明治16年（1883）

秀吉は、信長の怒りに触れた友の前田利家のため、
桶狭間の戦いで利家が取った首を信長に見せ、
許してもらえるよう仲立ちをした。

"Newly Selected Scenes from the *Taikōki*: Oda Nobunaga and Kinoshita Tōkichirō" by Utagawa Toyonobu

Nobunaga was angry with Maeda Toshiie,
one of his generals and Hideyoshi's childhood friend.
In order to pacify Nobunaga, Hideyoshi brought
before his lord trophy heads that Toshiie had culled
at the Battle of Okehazama.

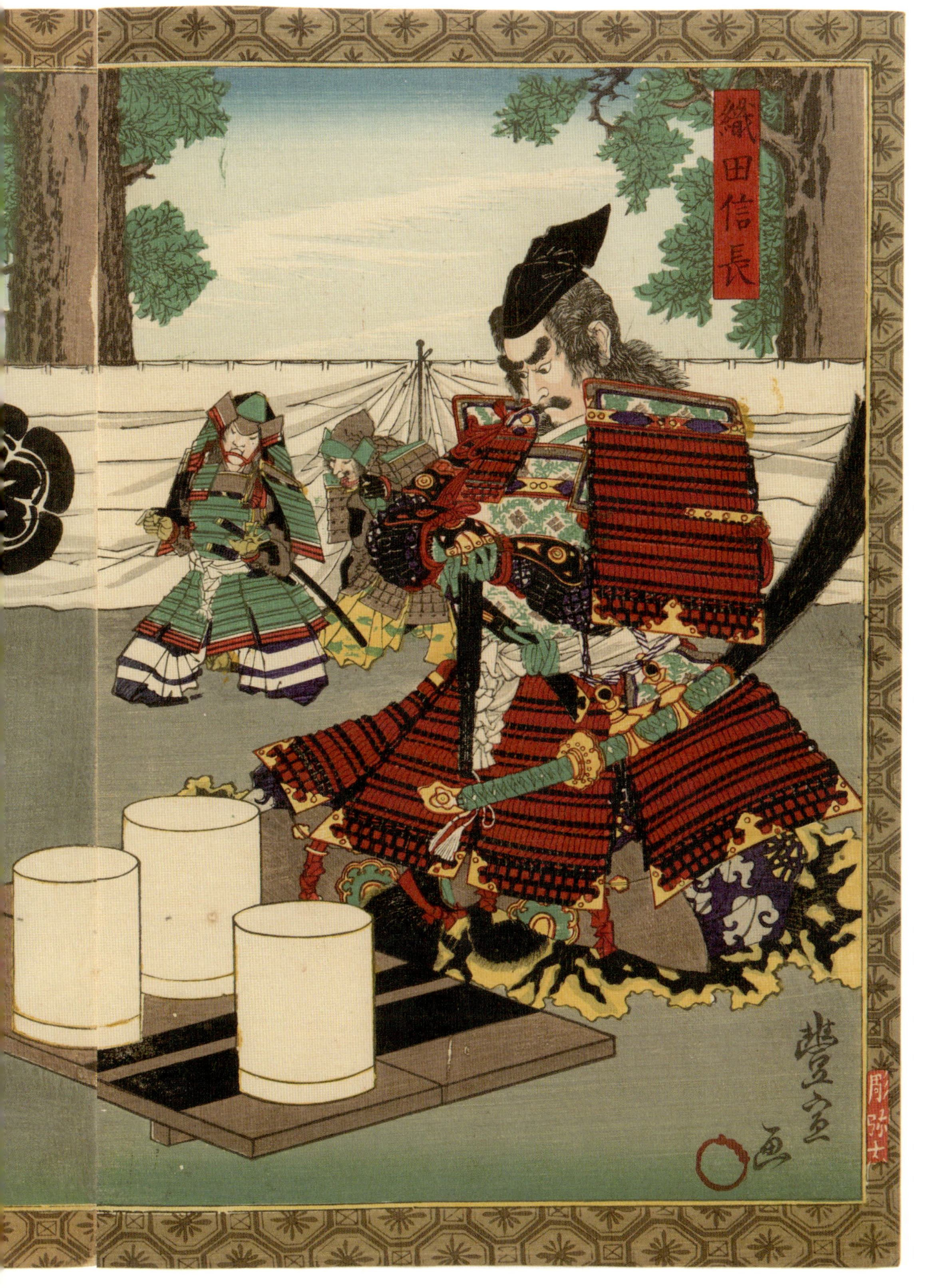

織田信長

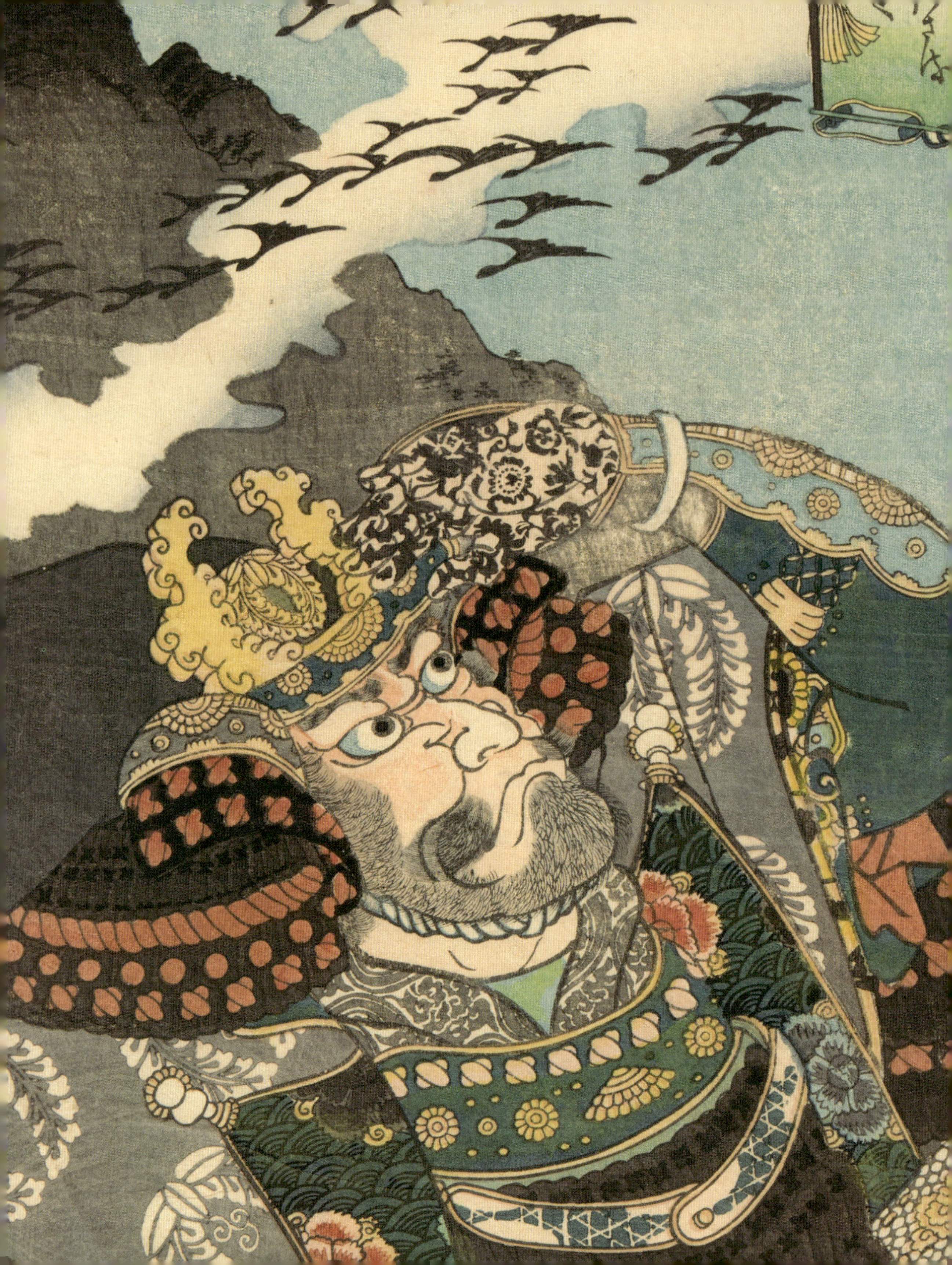
はな

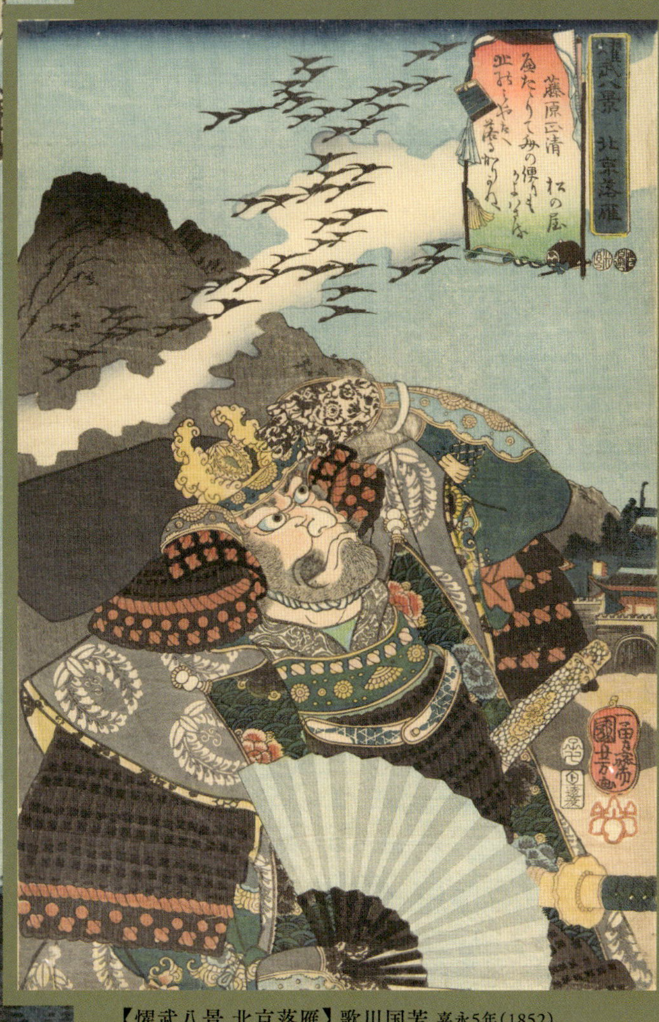

【煌武八景 北京落雁】歌川国芳　嘉永5年（1852）

"Eight Scenes of Military Brilliance:
Katō Kiyomasa Watching Geese Flying Towards Kyoto
from Korea" by Utagawa Kuniyoshi

Katō Kiyomasa
Brave Heroes and Gallant Men

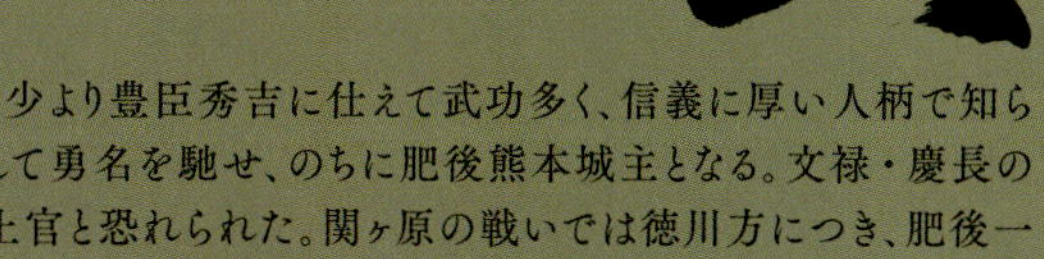

加藤清正

猛勇なる賤ヶ岳の七本槍

安土桃山時代の武将。尾張国の人。幼少より豊臣秀吉に仕えて武功多く、信義に厚い人柄で知られる。賤ヶ岳の戦いで七本槍の一人として勇名を馳せ、のちに肥後熊本城主となる。文禄・慶長の役では先陣を務め、蔚山城で奮戦、鬼上官と恐れられた。関ヶ原の戦いでは徳川方につき、肥後一国を与えられたが、戦後、豊臣家の安泰を図って恩に報いた。

A military leader of the Azuchi-Momoyama period, Katō Kiyomasa was from Owari Province, present-day Nagoya. In the service of Toyotomi Hideyoshi from a young age, Kiyomasa amassed many honors on the battlefield and was known as a man who could be trusted in any situation. Achieving fame as one of the Seven Spears for his service at the Battle of Shizugatake in 1583, Kiyomasa was later appointed head of Kumamoto Castle in Higo Province, Kyushu. In the 1590s, Kiyomasa helped lead Hideyoshi's invasion of Korea, and defended Ulsan Castle against Ming and Joseon Forces. He was feared in Korea as the "Demon Lieutenant." For his support of Tokugawa Ieyasu during the Battle of Sekigahara in 1600, Kiyomasa was rewarded all of Higo. He also repaid his obligation to the Toyotomi by advocating on the clan's behalf after they were defeated in that watershed battle.

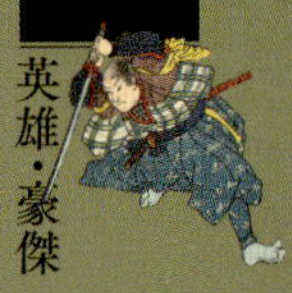

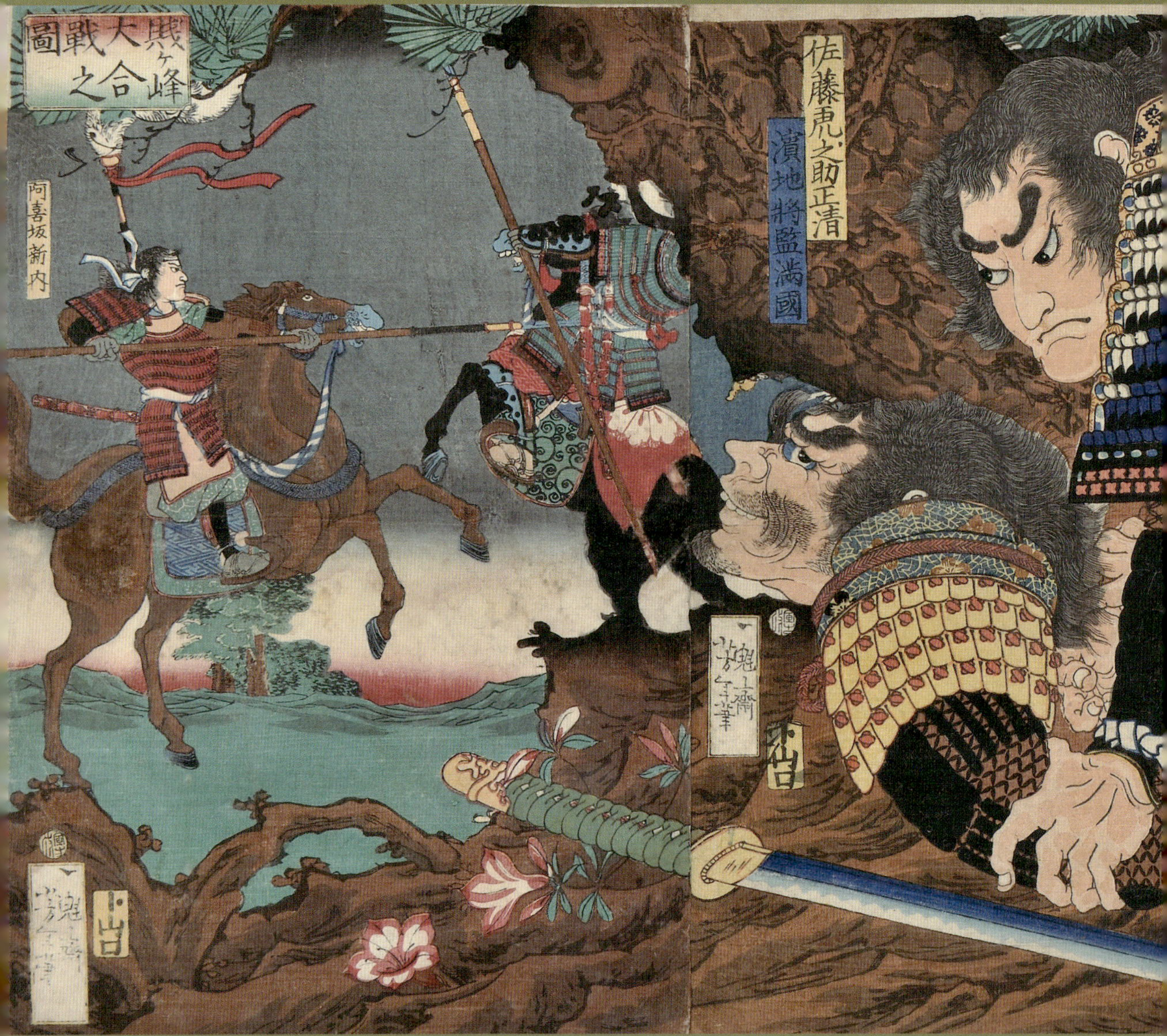

【賤ヶ峰大合戦之図】月岡芳年 慶応2年（1866）
賤ヶ岳の戦いで、清正は柴田勝家側に寝返った山路正国、通称 将監を討ち取った。

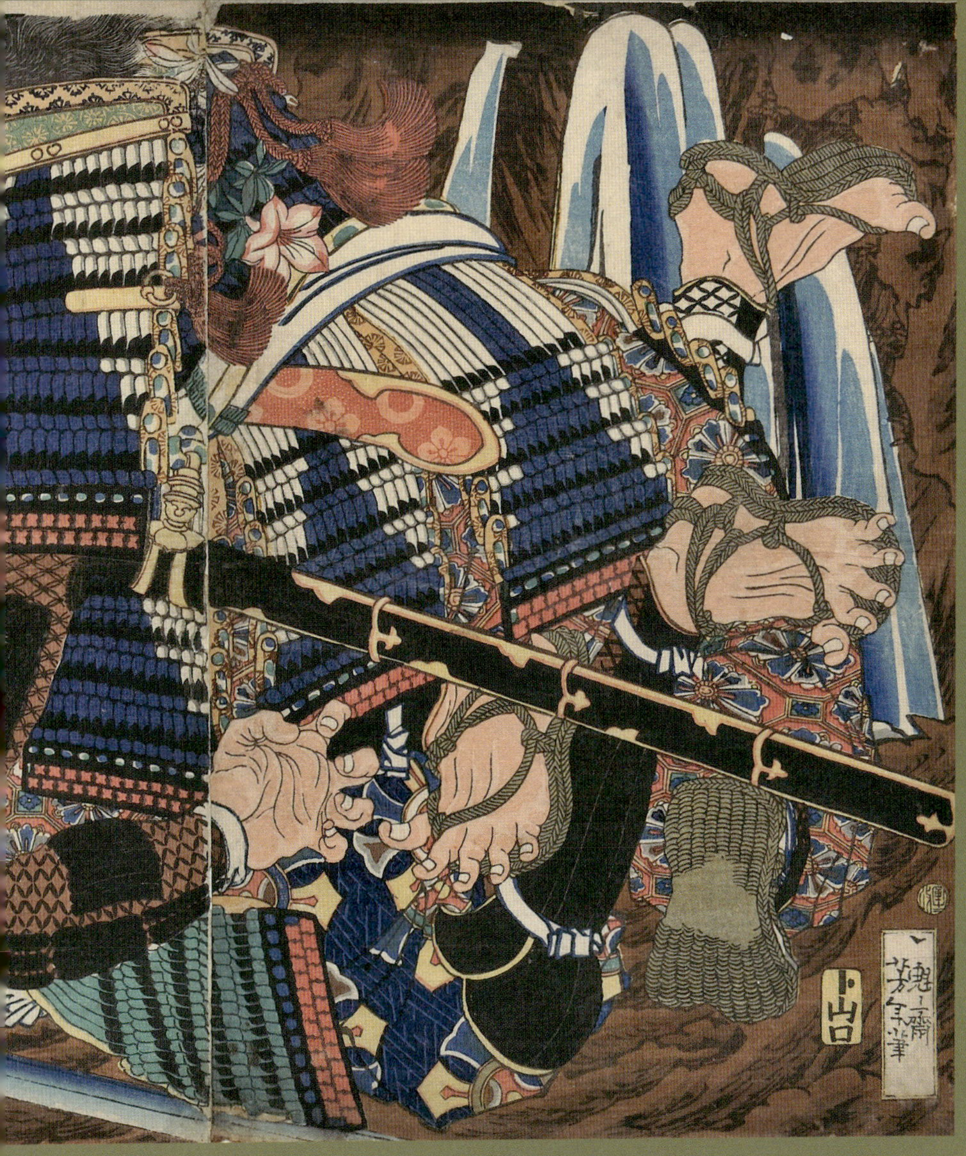

"The Battle of Shizugatake" by Tsukioka Yoshitoshi

Set during the Battle of Shizugatake, this print shows Kiyomasa subduing Yamaji Shōgen Masakuni, who betrayed Hideyoshi by joining Shibata Katsuie.

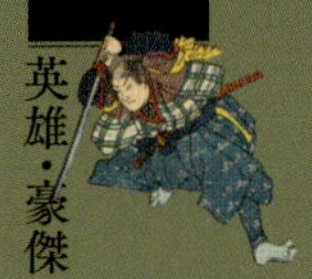

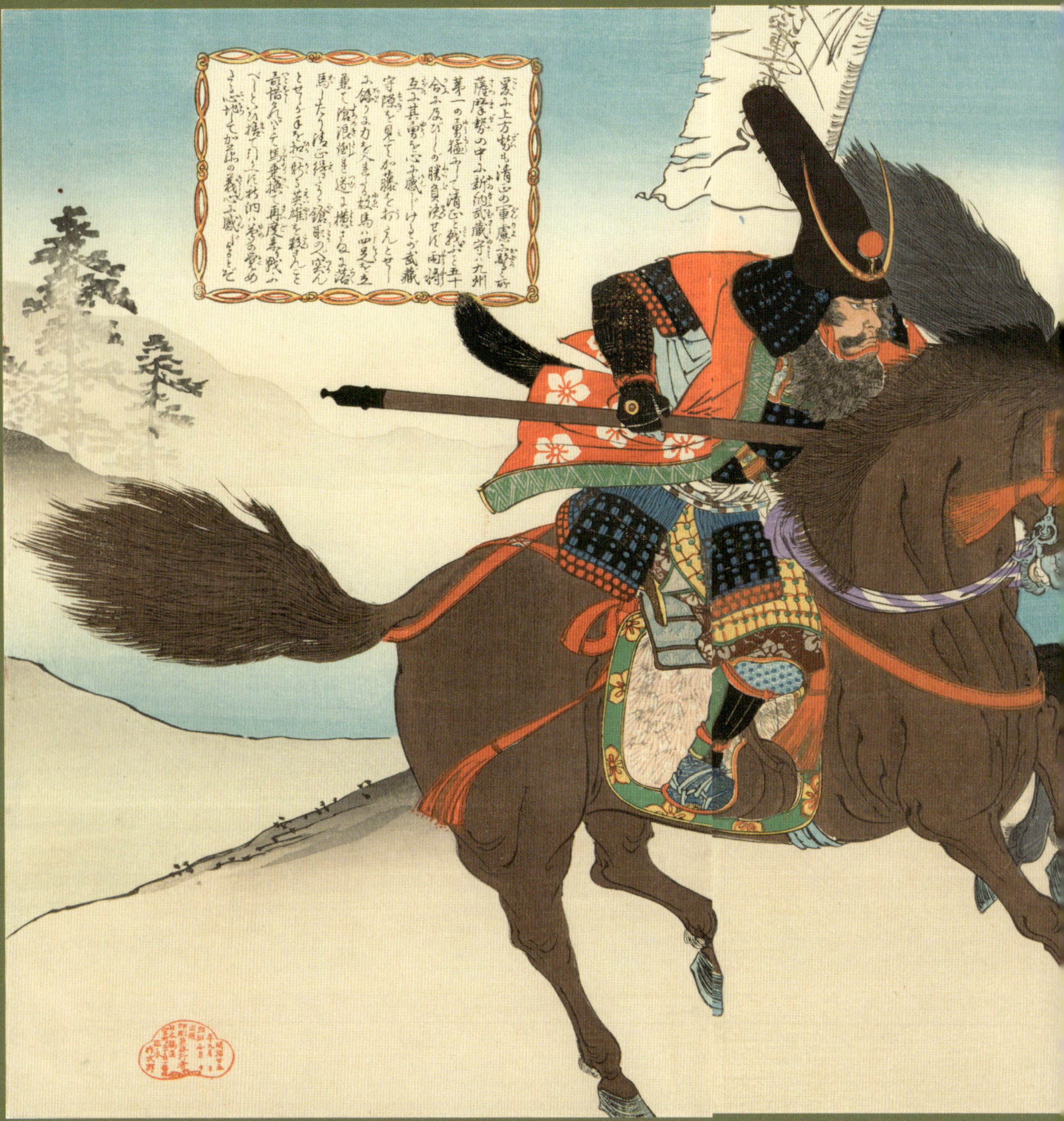

【加藤清正 新納武蔵守 千代川大勇戦之図】楊斎延一 明治25年（1892）
新納忠元と一騎打ちの際、鉄棒を振りかざした反動で忠元は落馬してしまう。
清正は槍を持つ手を止めて、「馬を乗り換えたら再度戦おう」と言って引き返したという。

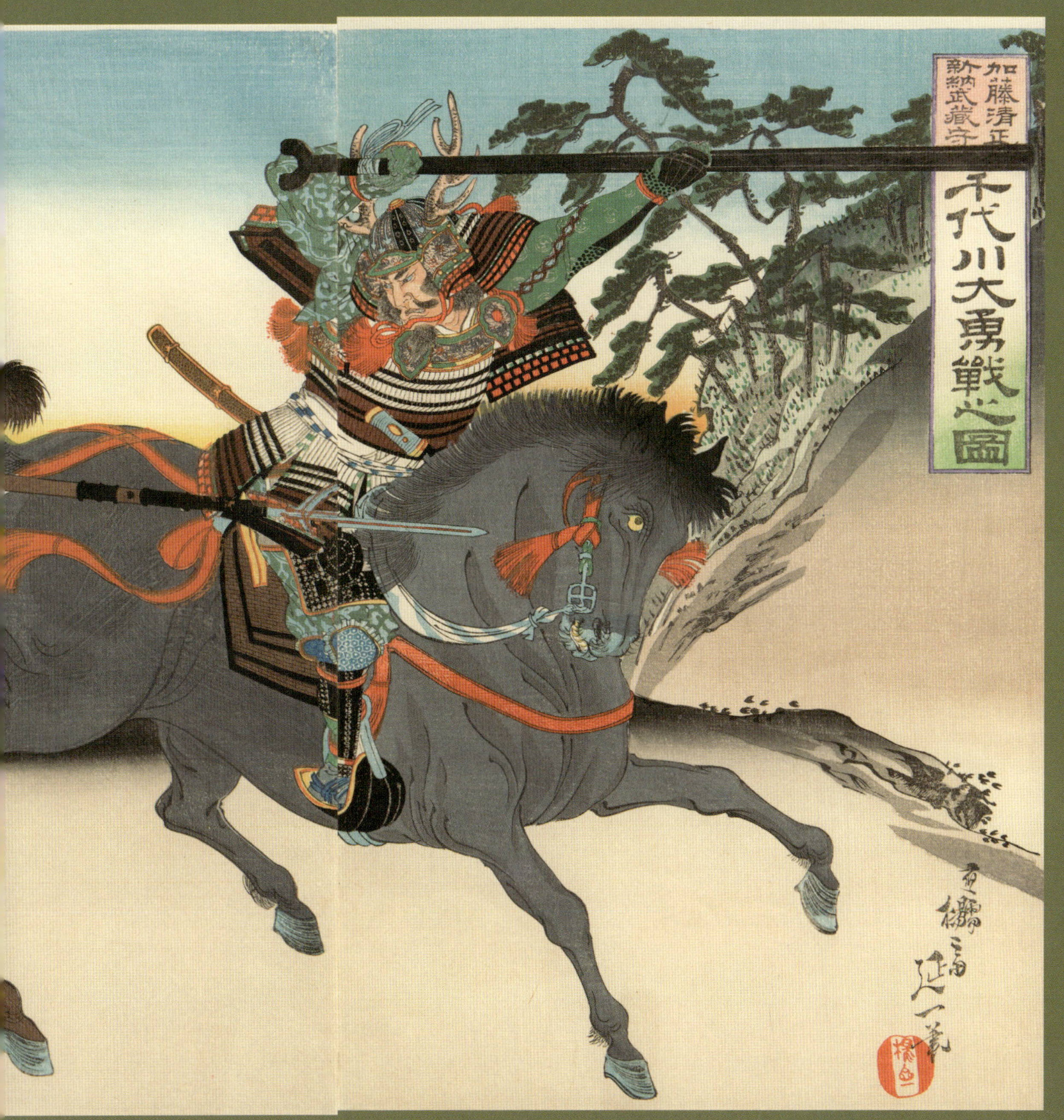

"Kato Kiyomasa and Niiro Tadamoto Fighting at Sendaigawa" by Yōsai Nobukazu
Fighting on horseback, Kiyomasa swung his iron club at Niiro Tadamoto, causing the latter to fall from his horse while dodging the blow.
Rather than spearing the fallen Tadamoto, Kiyomasa graciously said, "May we continue this duel when you get back on your horse," and rode off.

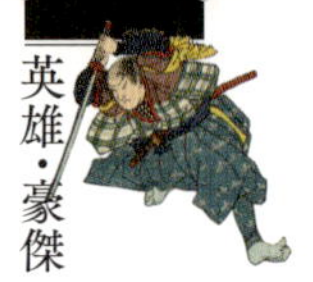

山中鹿之助

山陰の麒麟児　忠義貫く

Yamanaka Shikanosuke
Brave Heroes and Gallant Men

戦国時代の武将。本名幸盛。出雲尼子氏の
重臣。尼子氏が毛利氏に降伏した後も主家
の再興を図り、京都にあった遺児の尼子勝
久を豊臣秀吉の中国方面征伐に擁す。これ
に従い播磨上月城に籠ったが、毛利氏に攻
略されて落城、捕らえられて備中高梁川で殺
されたといわれる。

A warrior general of the Sengoku period,
Yamanaka Shikanosuke actual given name was
Yukimori. He was a loyal retainer of the Amago
clan in Izumo. Even after they fell to the Mōri
clan in 1566, Yukimori labored for the Amago's
revival, succeeding in having Amago Katsuhisa
(an orphan in Kyoto) accepted into the service
of Hideyoshi's march across the western
provinces. Katsuhisa was thus entrusted with
Kōzuki Castle, in Harima Province (Hyōgo).
However, the castle fell to the Mōri in 1578,
and Yukimori was captured and later killed at
the Takahashigawa River in Bitchū (Okayama).

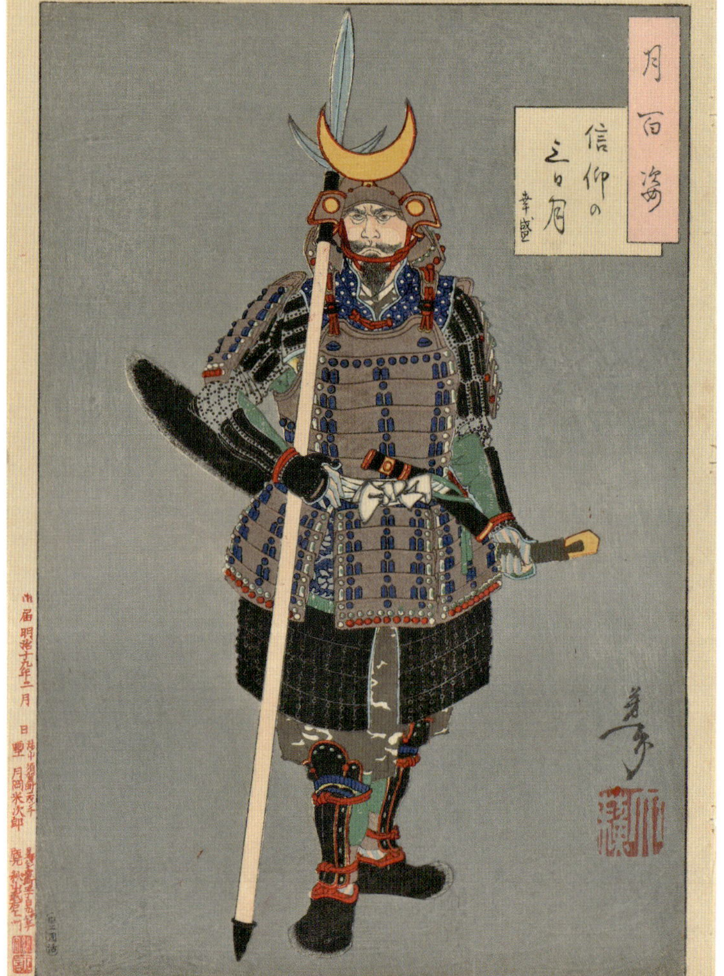

【月百姿 信仰の三日月 幸盛】月岡芳年　明治19年（1886）

"One Hundred Aspects of the Moon:
Faith Under the Crescent Moon, Yamanaka Yukimori"
by Tsukioka Yoshitoshi

122

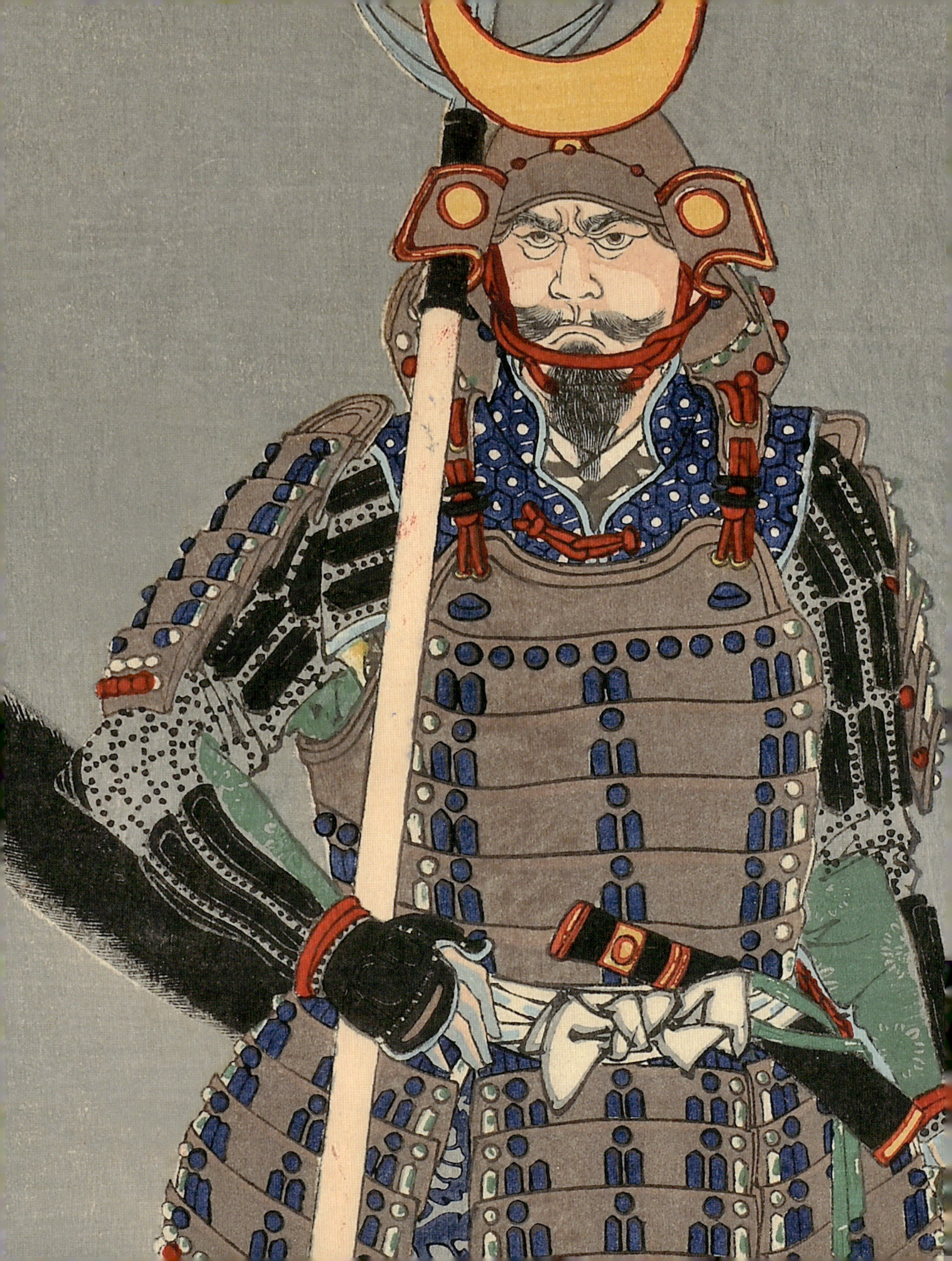

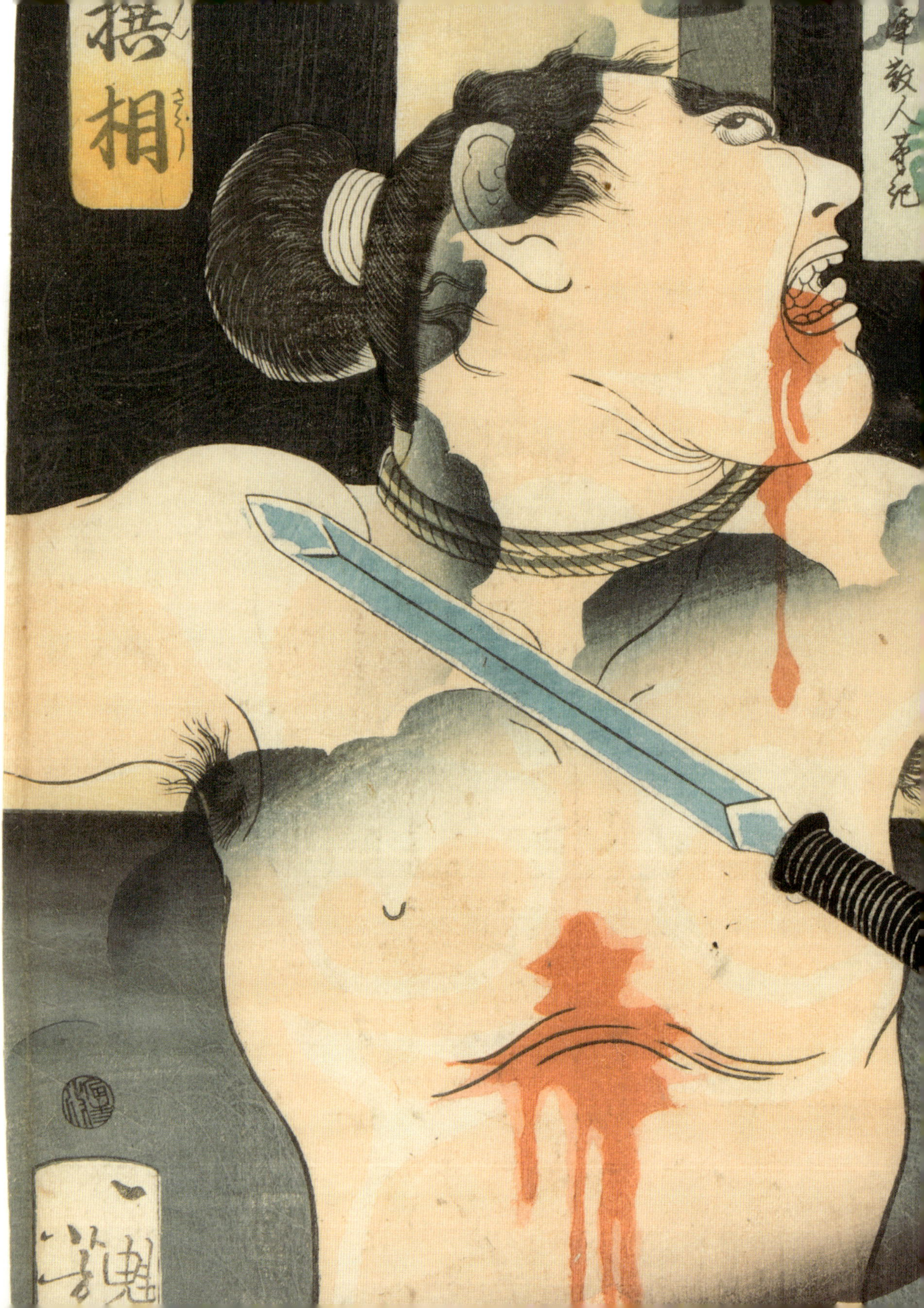

相揃

坤教人妾多記

一魁

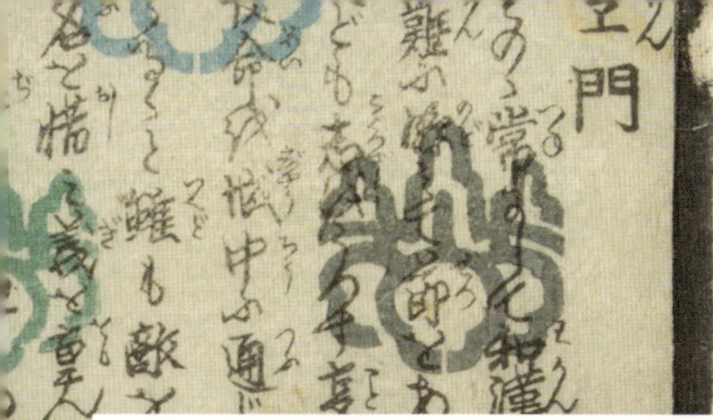

魁題百撰相

【魁題百撰相 堀井恒右エ門】月岡芳年 明治元年（1868）

"One Hundred Stalwarts: Horii Tsuneemon"
by Tsukioka Yoshitoshi

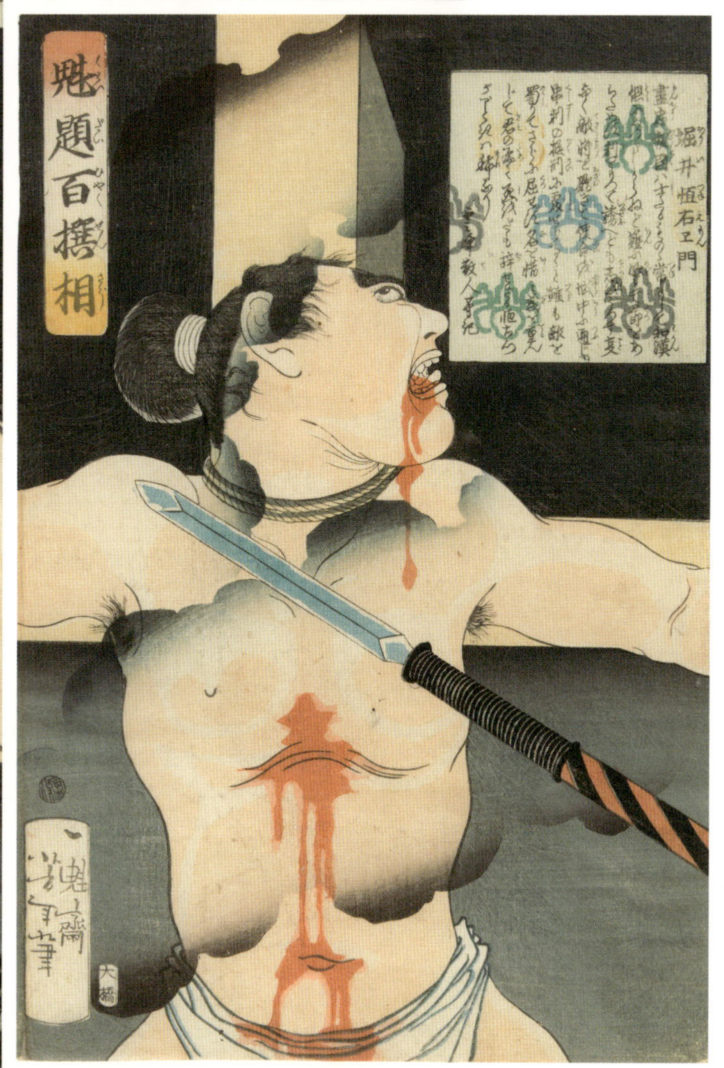

鳥居強右衛門

忠臣命賭して
勝利を導く

Torii Suneemon
Brave Heroes and Gallant Men

戦国時代の足軽。三河長篠城主奥平貞昌の家臣。長篠城が武田勝頼の大軍に包囲された際、城を脱出し岡崎城に赴いて徳川家康に援軍を求めた。これを味方に伝えるため城中に戻る途中、武田方に捕らえられ、城門で「援軍は来ない」と告げるよう命じられた。しかし、強右衛門は敵を欺き、「援軍は来る」と城中に向かって叫んだため、その場で磔にされた。強右衛門の決死の行動は城兵たちの士気を鼓舞し、援軍が来るまで城を守り抜いた。

Torii Suneemon was a low-class footman (ashigaru) of the Sengoku period. He served Okudaira Sadamasa, the lord of Nagashino Castle in Mikawa (Aichi). When Takeda Katsuyori attacked and surrounded Nagashino Castle in 1575, Suneemon snuck out and proceeded to Okazaki Castle to ask Tokugawa Ieyasu for military support. On his way back to Nagashino, Suneemon was captured by the Takeda and ordered to yell to his comrades, from the castle's gates, that no help would be coming. Instead, he shouted loudly that they would be, and was crucified on the spot. His message and fearlessness of death gave his comrades the confidence they needed to defend the castle until reinforcements arrived.

袴垂保輔 鬼童丸

盗賊と鬼の化かし合い

Hakamadare Yasusuke and Kidōmaru
Wizards and Ninja

126

袴垂は平安時代の伝説上の盗賊。藤原保昌の弟保輔ともいわれ、のちに同一視された。鬼童丸は岩窟に住む妖怪で、酒呑童子の子ともいわれる。あるとき、二人は妖術競べをした。鬼童丸が毒蛇を出すと、保輔が大鷲を出して引っ掴む。互角の戦いの末、互いの弱点を言い合うことになった。鬼童丸が人の唾と言うと、保輔は良馬と嘘を言った。保輔は、馬に変身した鬼童丸のたてがみに唾をかけまわし、これに乗って都まで馳せたという。

Hakamadare is a legendary bandit from the Heian period. Sometimes he has been regarded as the same person as Fujiwara no Yasusuke, the younger brother of the distinguished aristocrat Yasumasa. Kidōmaru is a yōkai who lived in a cave, and is sometimes seen as the son of the ogre Shuten Dōji. During a contest of their sorcery, Kidōmaru turned into a poisonous snake and Yasusuke into a giant eagle. Deadlocked, the two asked each other their respective weaknesses. Kidōmaru reveals that if someone spits on him while he is transformed, he will not be able to change back. Yasusuke lies and says he is afraid of fine horses. Kidōmaru promptly turns into a horse, while Yasusuke stays himself, hops on Kidōmaru's back, spits on his mane, and rides him into Kyoto.

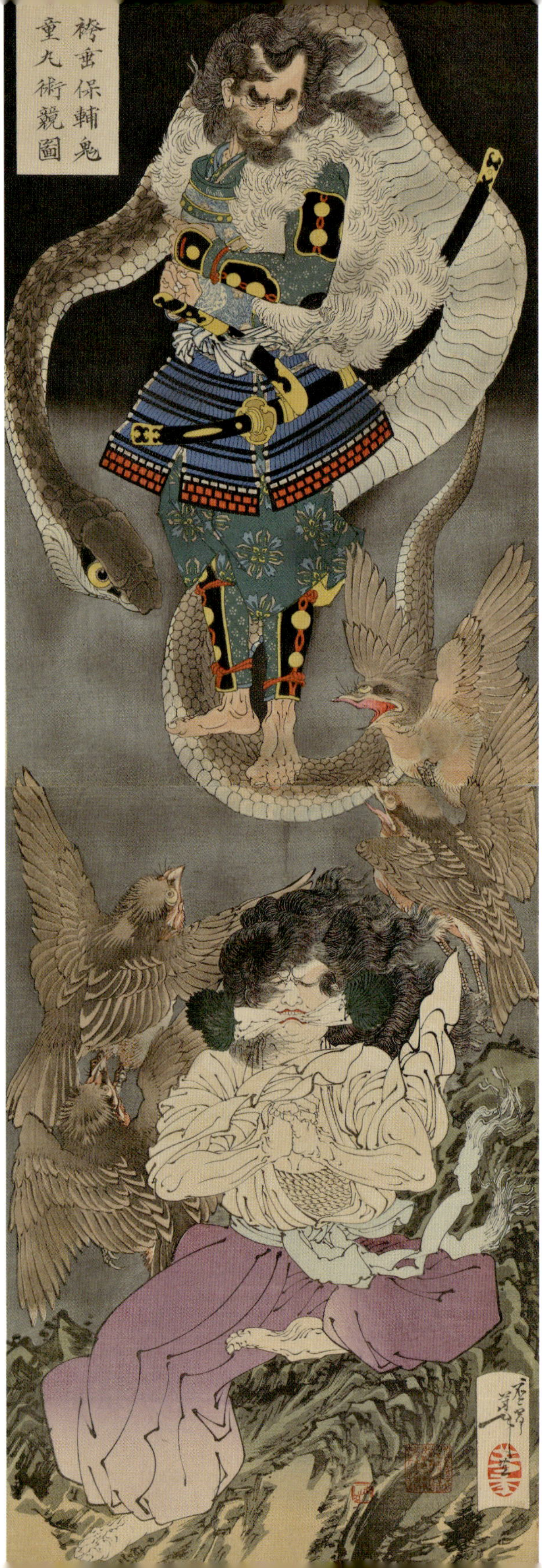

【袴垂保輔鬼童丸術競図】月岡芳年
明治20年（1887）

"Hakamadare Yasusuke and Kidōmaru Fighting with Magic" by Tsukioka Yoshitoshi

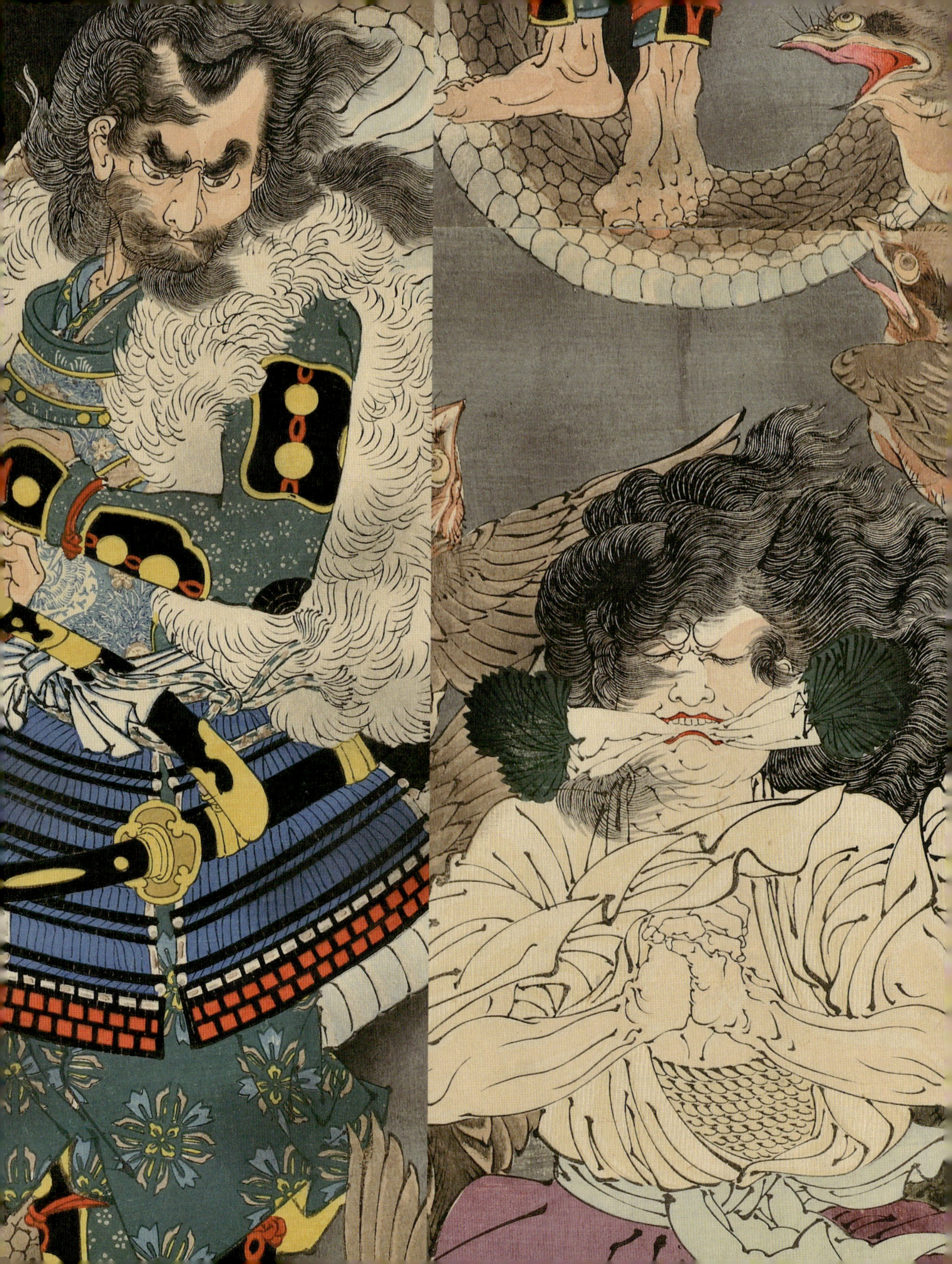

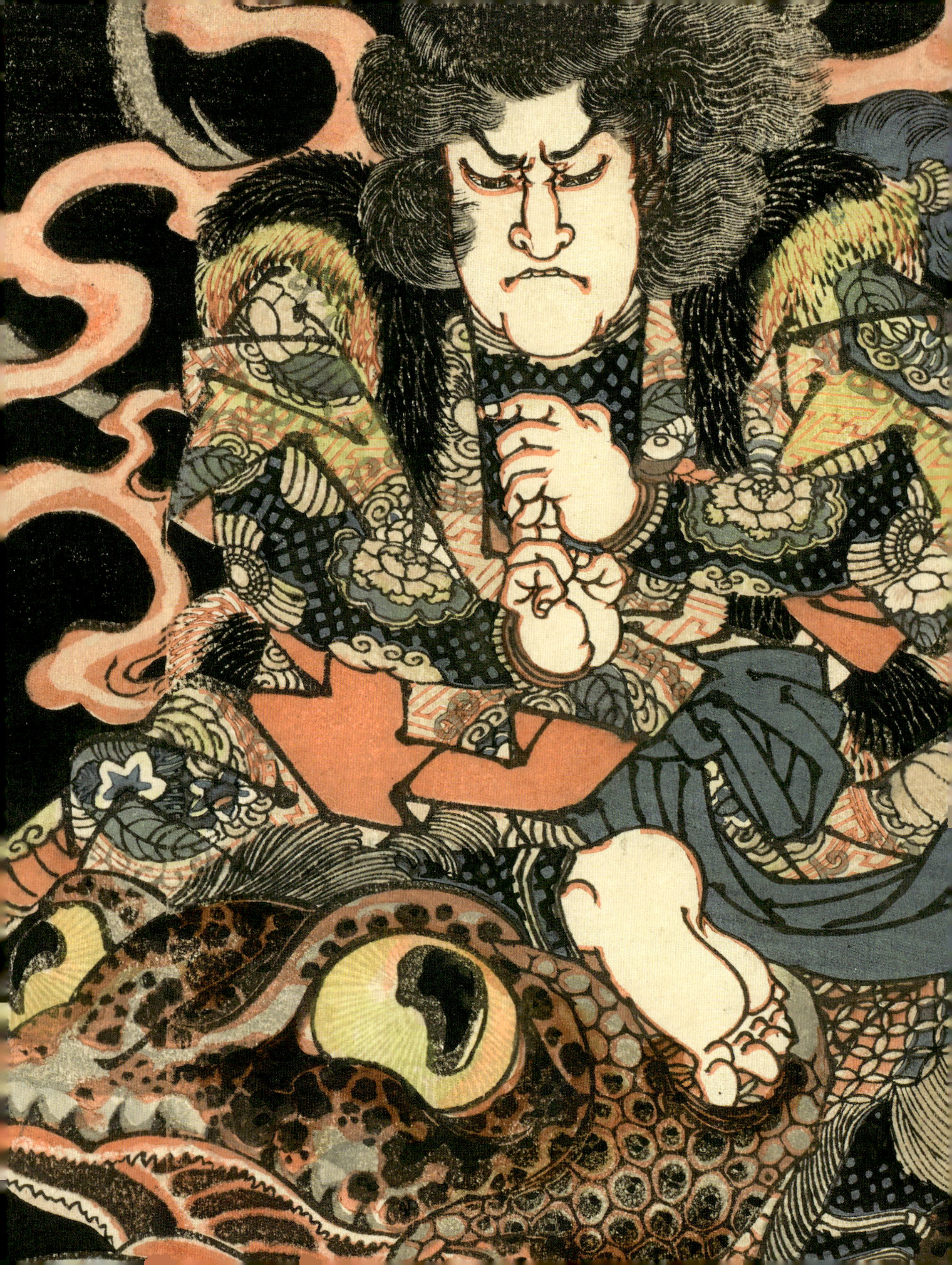

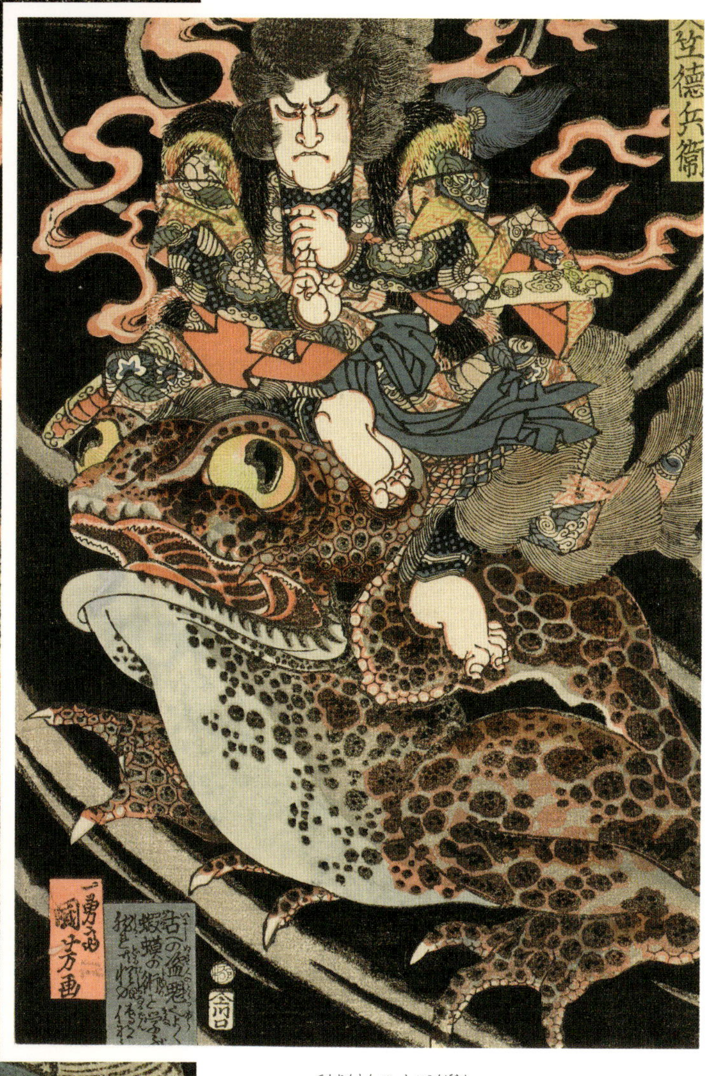

天竺徳兵衛

【ガマの妖術】

天竺帰りの妖術師

Tenjiku
Tokubee
Wizards and Ninja

129

歌舞伎「天竺徳兵衛 韓 噺」の主人公。播磨国高砂生まれの船頭で、天竺帰り。自分の素性を
吉岡宗観（実は大明国王の臣下・木曾官）の子大日丸であると知る。父譲りの蝦蟇の妖術を操
り、遺志を継いで日本転覆を謀る。しかし、巳年巳月巳日巳刻生まれの女の生き血によって術を
破られてしまう。歌舞伎などで知られた徳兵衛の物語は、江戸時代初期、天竺に渡航して貿易を
した実在の商人の見聞記がモデルになっている。

The eponymous hero of the kabuki play *Tenjiku Tokubee's Adventures in Foreign Lands* (1804),
Tokubee was born in Takasago, Harima Province, present-day Hyōgo. Upon returning from India
(formerly called "Tenjiku" in Japanese) while working as a boatman, he discovers that he is the son of
Yoshioka Sōkan (who is in fact the Korean warrior Moku Sokan) and that his name is Dainichimaru.
Like his father, he is capable of magically calling forth giant toads and control them at will, and vows
to carry out his father's dying wish of overthrowing Japan. His sorcery is thwarted, however, by the
blood of a living girl born in the year of the dragon, in the month of the dragon, on the day of the
dragon, at the hour of the dragon. Though much embellished on the kabuki stage, Tokubee's story
was inspired by the travelogues of an actual merchant who had sailed to India for trade.

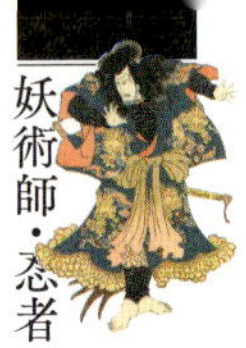

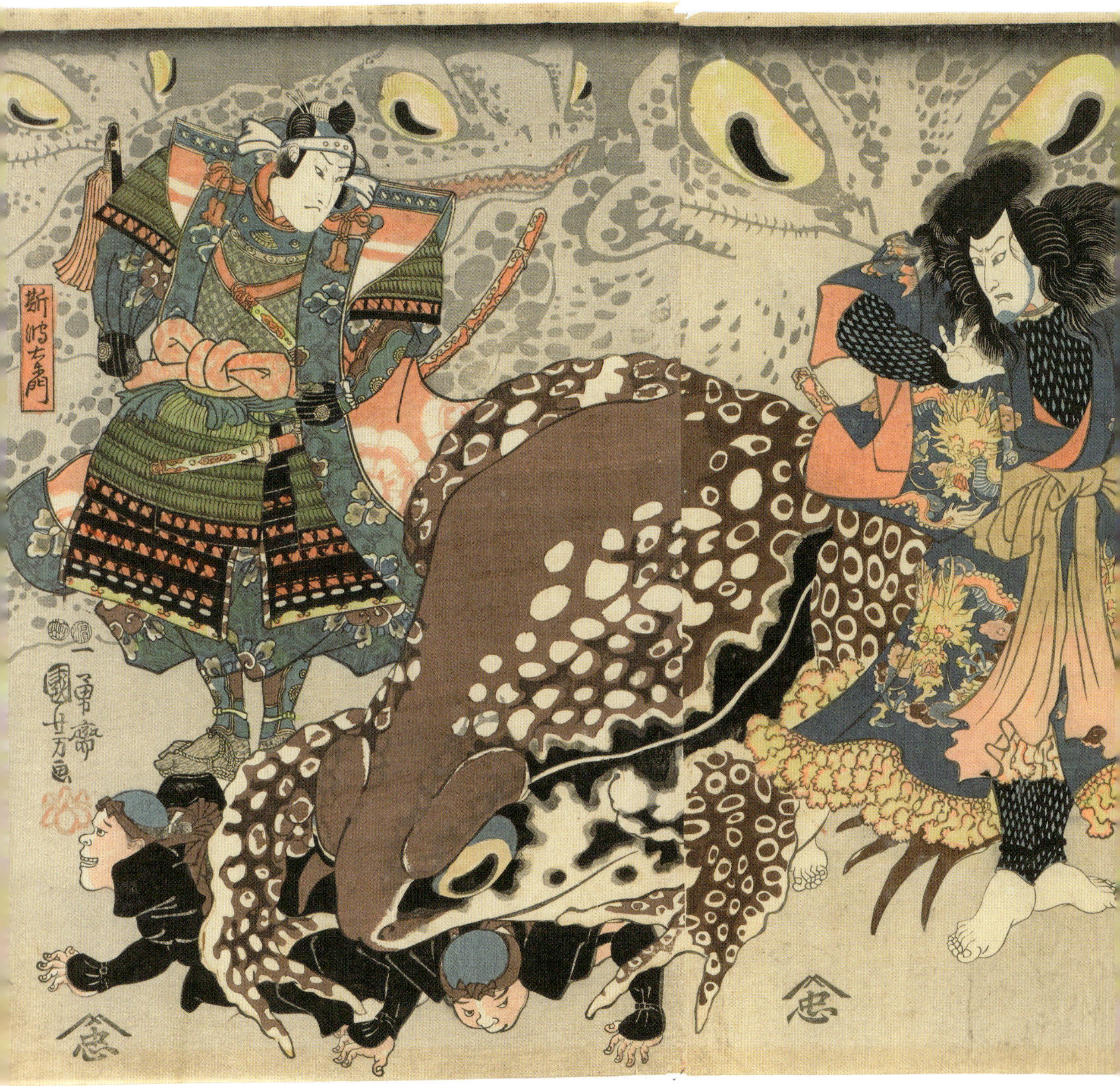

【天竺冠者】歌川国芳 弘化4年（1847）
妖術で現れた巨大な蝦蟇の妖怪が、捕手たちを押しつぶす。

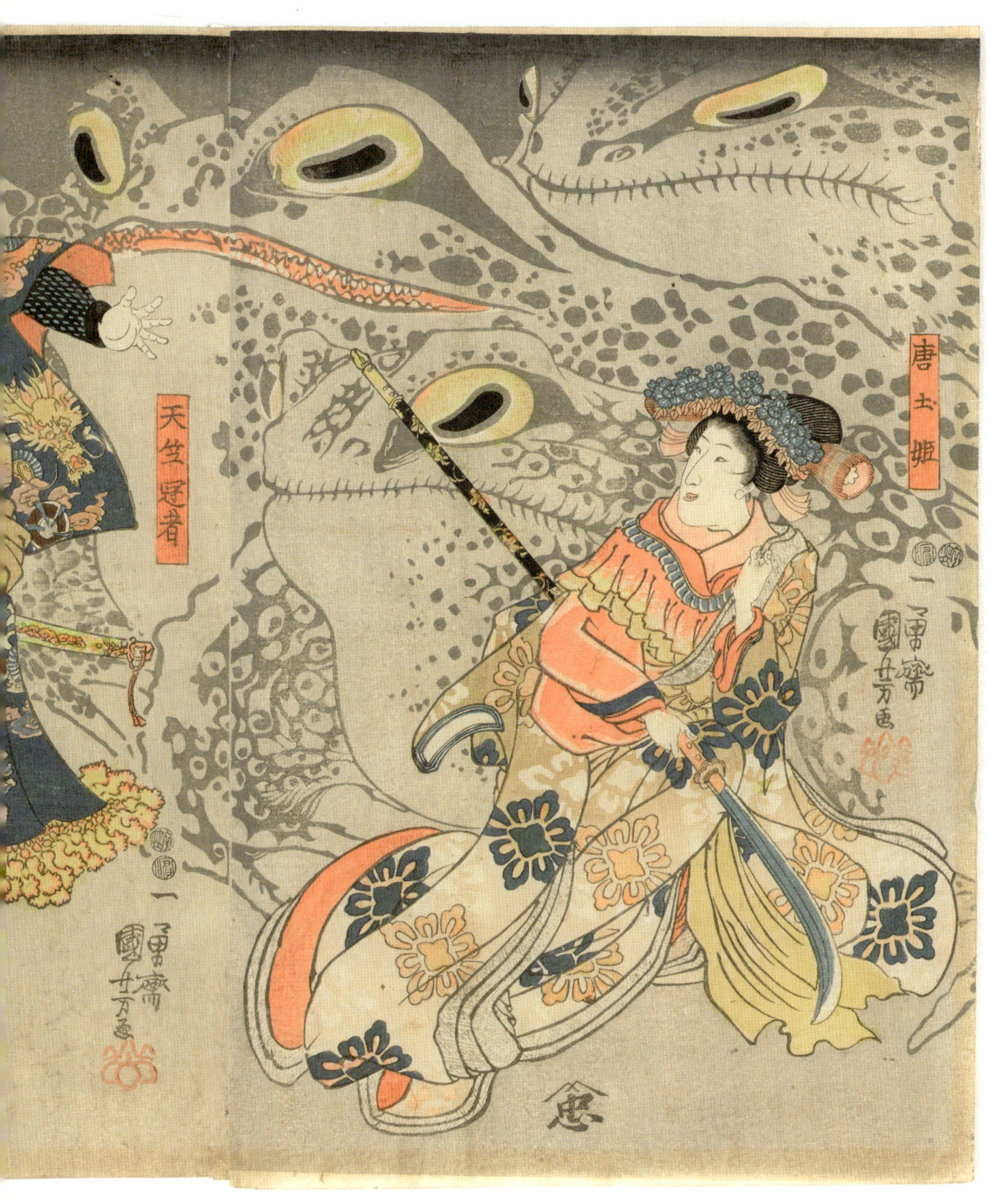

"The Man from Tenjiku" by Utagawa Kuniyoshi
Tokubee magically calls forth the giant toad and has him crush the police.

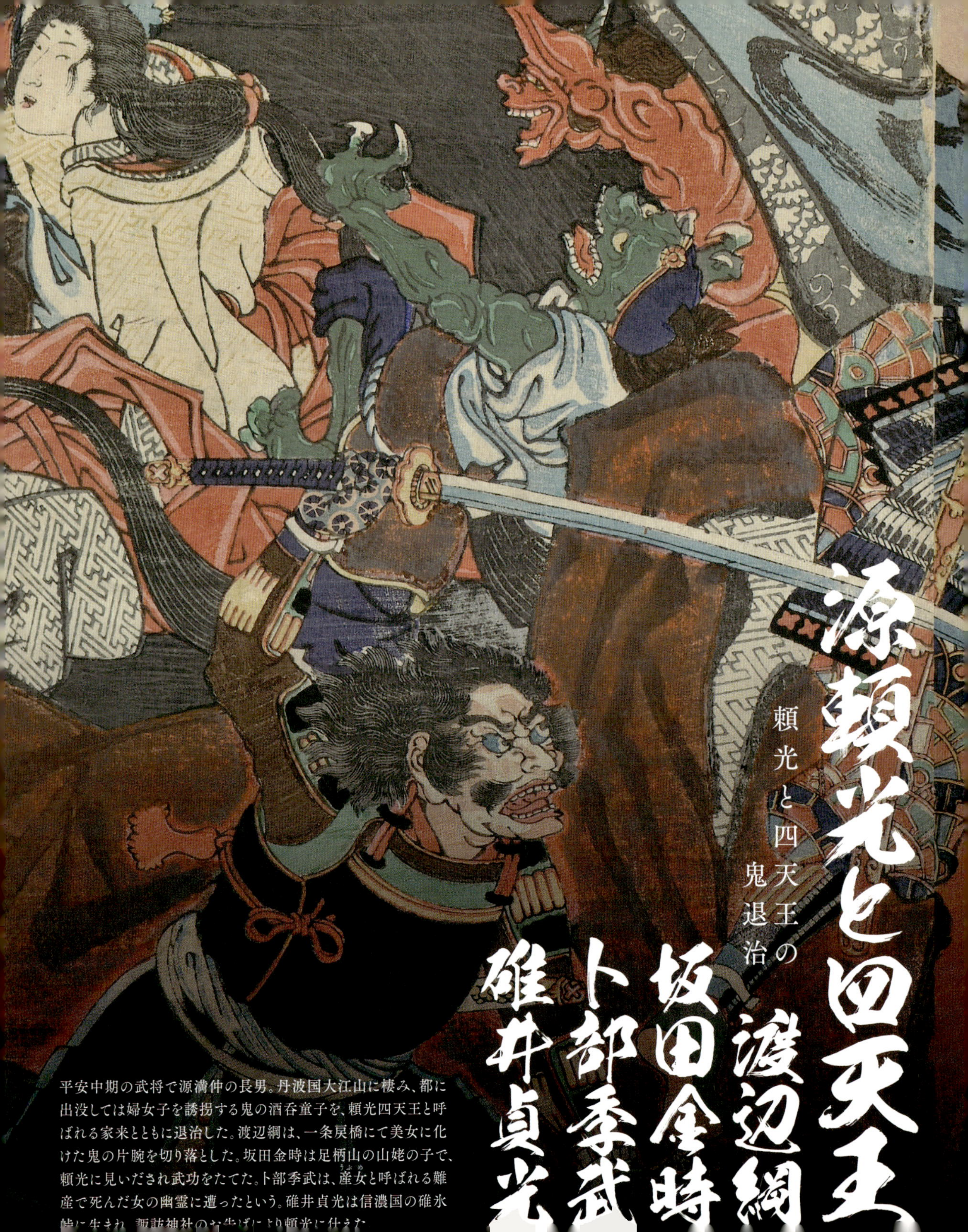

平安中期の武将で源満仲の長男。丹波国大江山に棲み、都に出没しては婦女子を誘拐する鬼の酒呑童子を、頼光四天王と呼ばれる家来とともに退治した。渡辺綱は、一条戻橋にて美女に化けた鬼の片腕を切り落とした。坂田金時は足柄山の山姥の子で、頼光に見いだされ武功をたてた。卜部季武は、産女と呼ばれる難産で死んだ女の幽霊に遭ったという。碓井貞光は信濃国の碓氷峠に生まれ、諏訪神社のお告げにより頼光に仕えた。

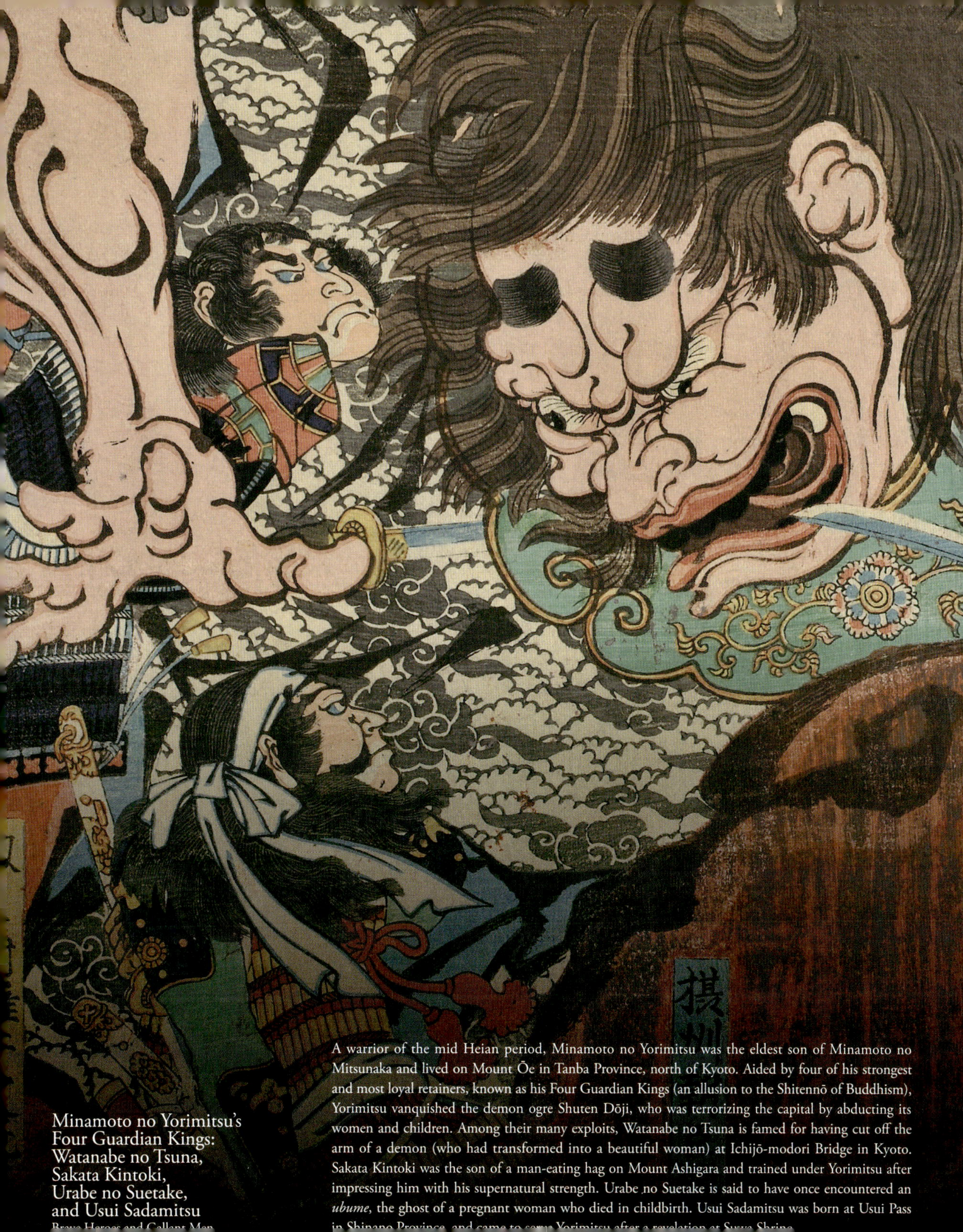

Minamoto no Yorimitsu's Four Guardian Kings: Watanabe no Tsuna, Sakata Kintoki, Urabe no Suetake, and Usui Sadamitsu

Brave Heroes and Gallant Men

A warrior of the mid Heian period, Minamoto no Yorimitsu was the eldest son of Minamoto no Mitsunaka and lived on Mount Ōe in Tanba Province, north of Kyoto. Aided by four of his strongest and most loyal retainers, known as his Four Guardian Kings (an allusion to the Shitennō of Buddhism), Yorimitsu vanquished the demon ogre Shuten Dōji, who was terrorizing the capital by abducting its women and children. Among their many exploits, Watanabe no Tsuna is famed for having cut off the arm of a demon (who had transformed into a beautiful woman) at Ichijō-modori Bridge in Kyoto. Sakata Kintoki was the son of a man-eating hag on Mount Ashigara and trained under Yorimitsu after impressing him with his supernatural strength. Urabe no Suetake is said to have once encountered an *ubume*, the ghost of a pregnant woman who died in childbirth. Usui Sadamitsu was born at Usui Pass in Shinano Province, and came to serve Yorimitsu after a revelation at Suwa Shrine.

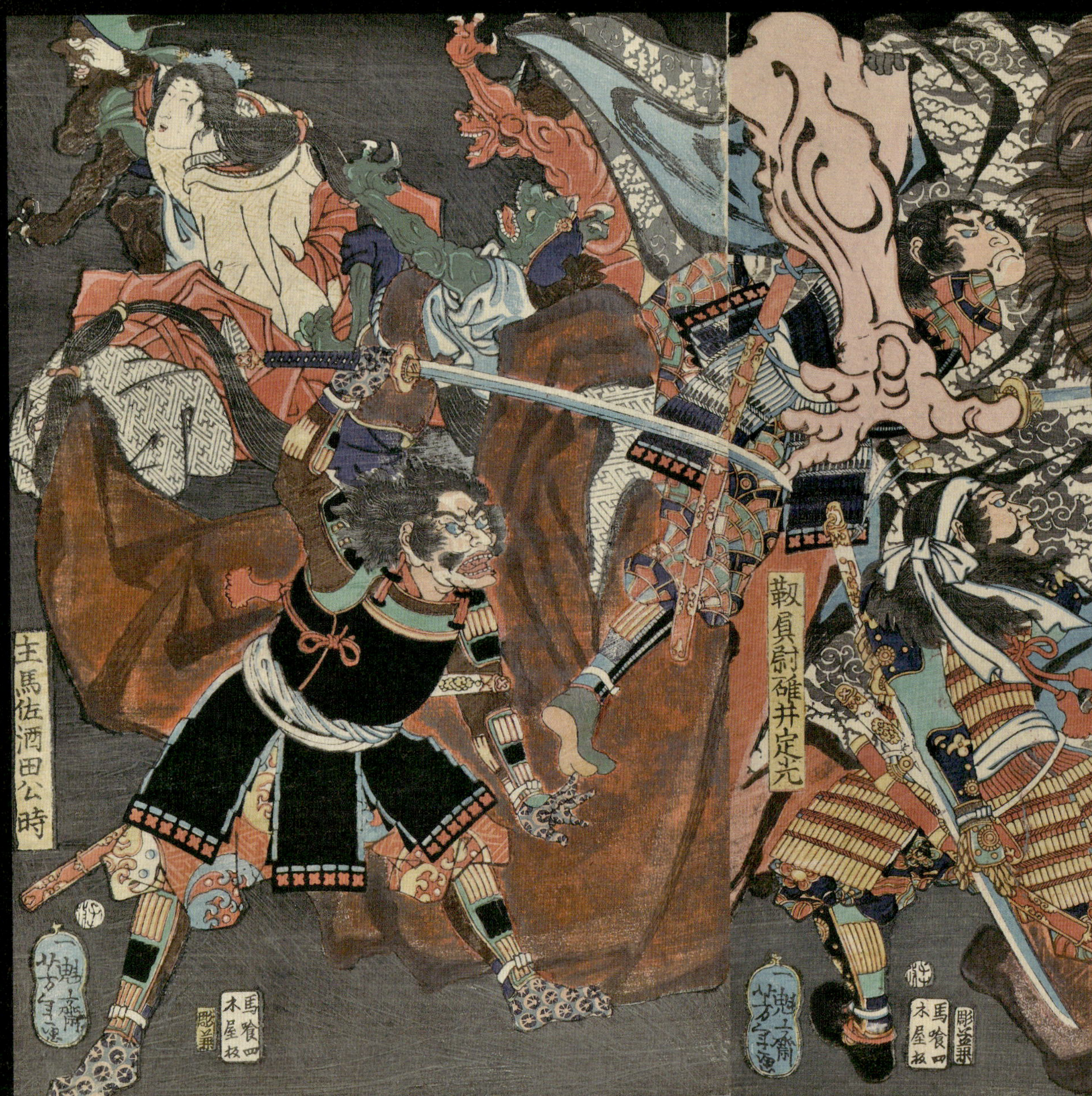

【頼光四天王大江山鬼神退治之図】月岡芳年　元治元年（1864）

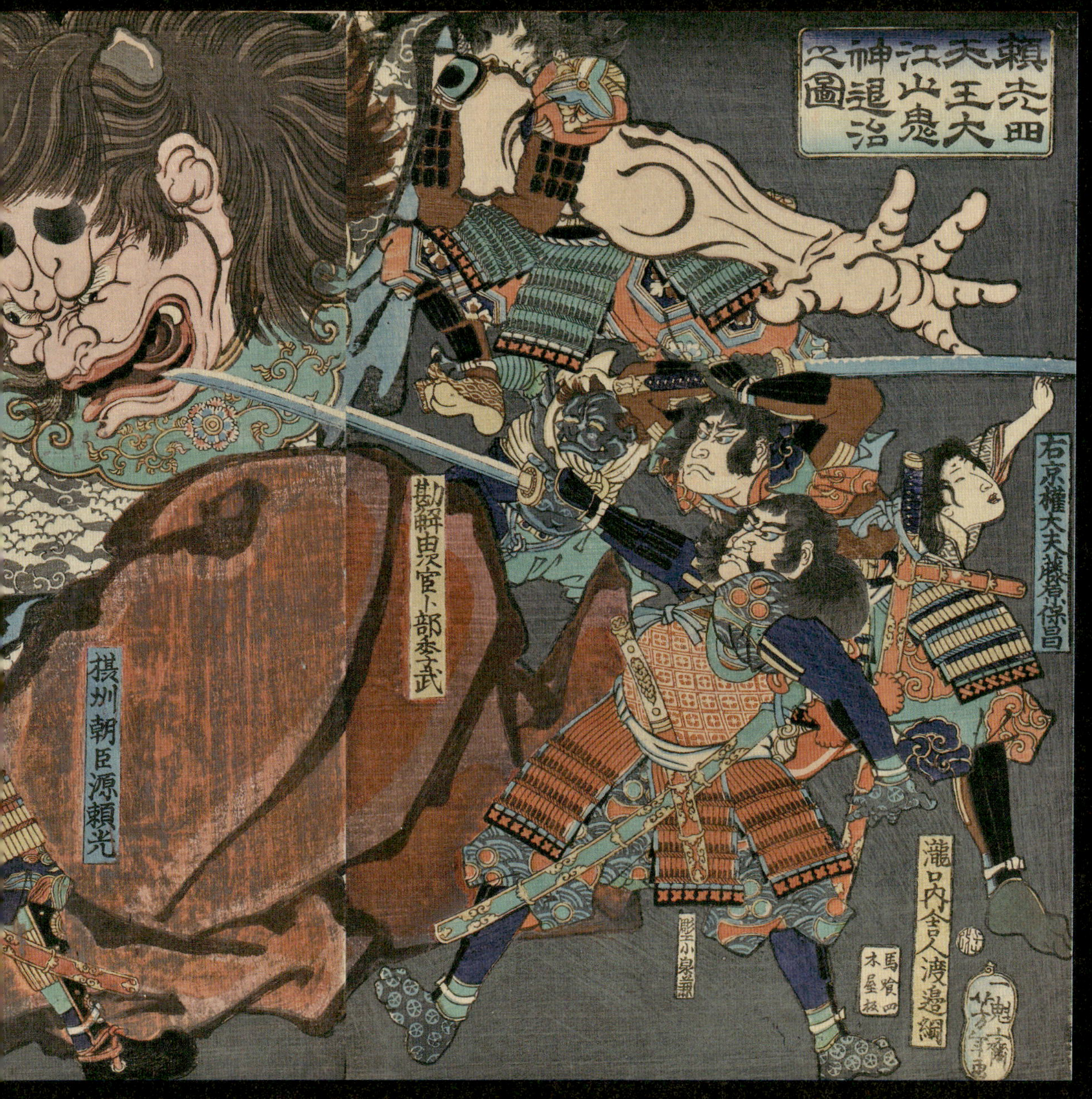

"The Four Guardian Kings of Yorimitsu Defeat the Demon Gods at Mount Ōe" by Tsukioka Yoshitoshi

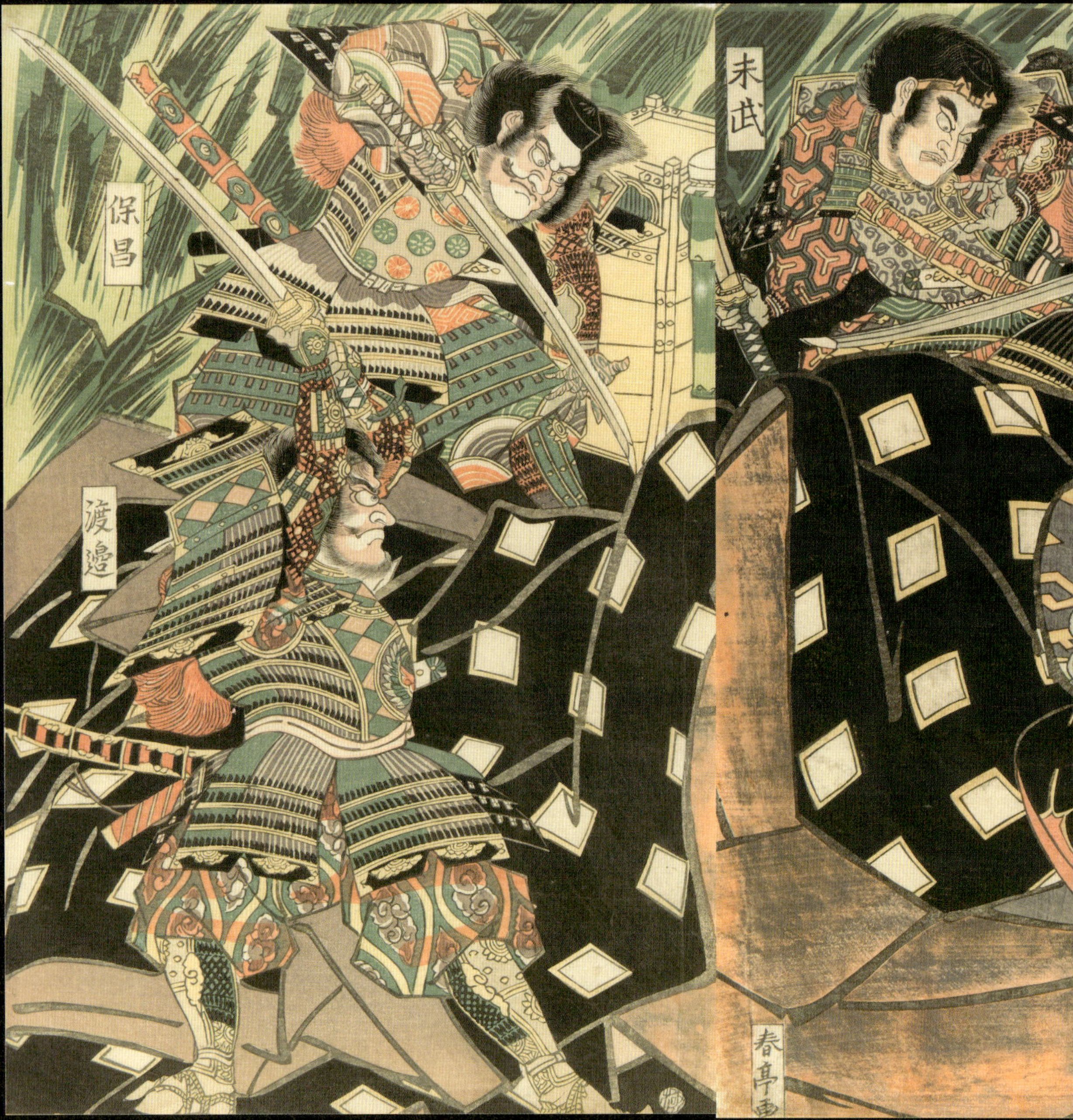

【大江山酒呑童子退治】勝川春亭　文政(1818-30)初期

勅命を受けた頼光らは、神から授かった毒酒を酒呑童子に飲ませ、酔いつぶして首を斬り落とした。
その首が頼光に襲いかかるも、これまた神から授かった星兜の威力で撃退した。

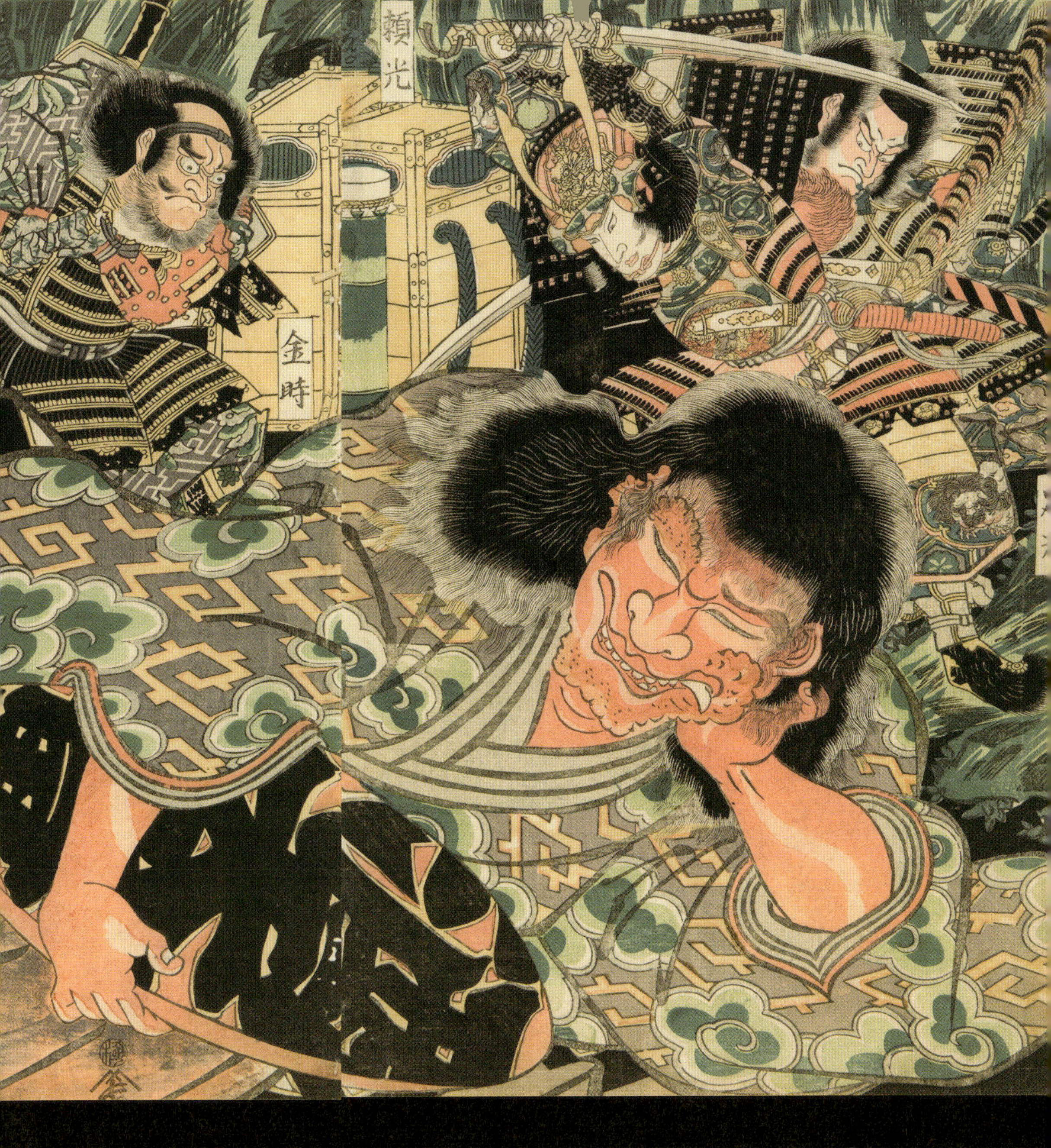

"The Subjugation of the Ogre Shuten Dōji at Mount Ōe" by Katsukawa Shunte

On orders from the Emperor to kill Shuten Dōji, Yorimitsu and his men went to Mount Ōe
got the demon drunk with poisoned liquor obtained from the gods, then cut off his head

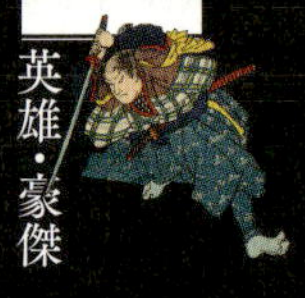

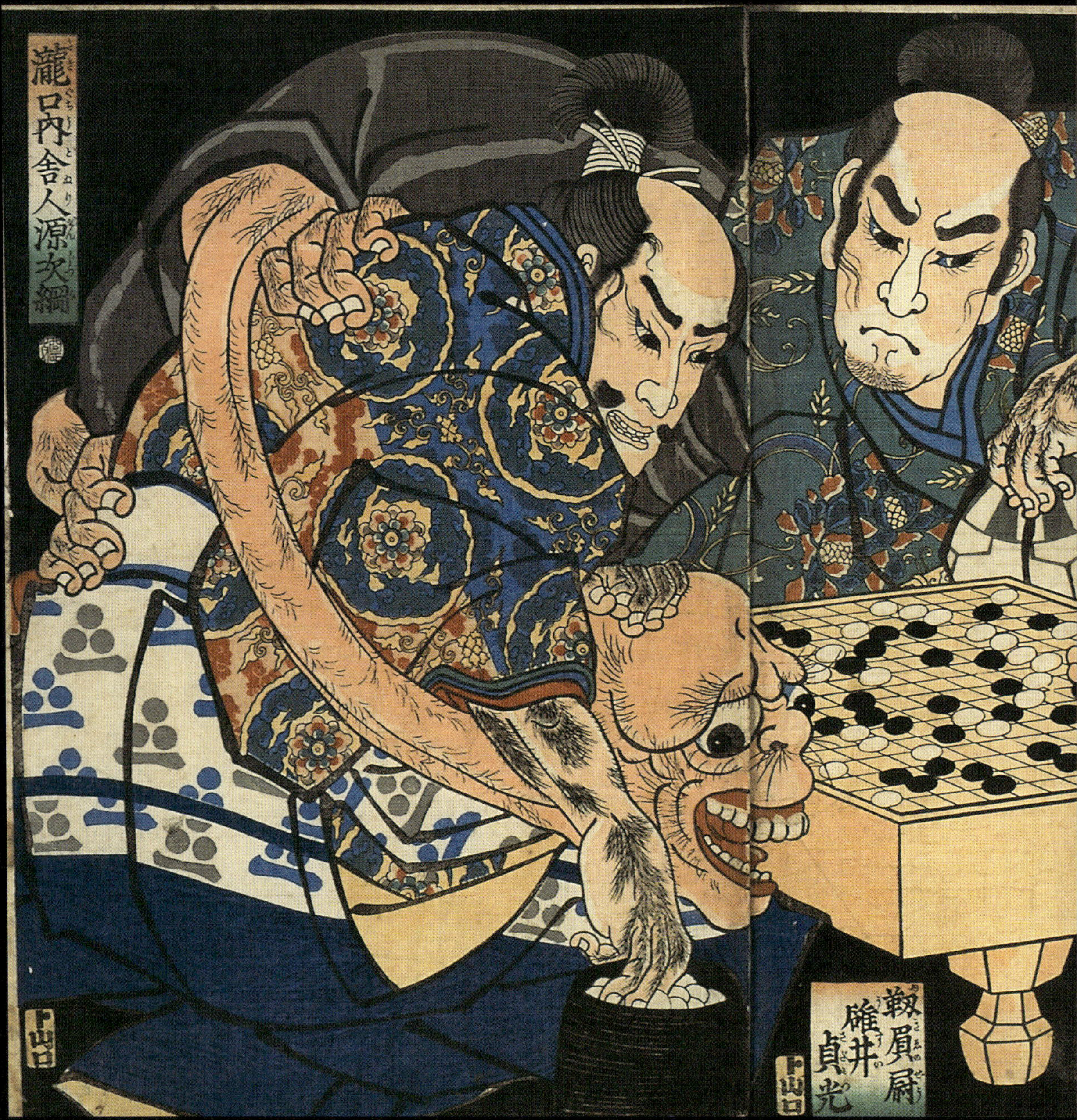

【主馬佐酒田公時 靭負尉碓井貞光 瀧口内舎人源次綱と妖怪】歌川国芳 文久元年（1861）

土蜘蛛の妖怪の仕業で熱病に苦しめられる頼光のため、宿直の番をする金時、貞光、綱。次々と妖怪が現れるが、物怖じせずに囲碁を打ち続けた。

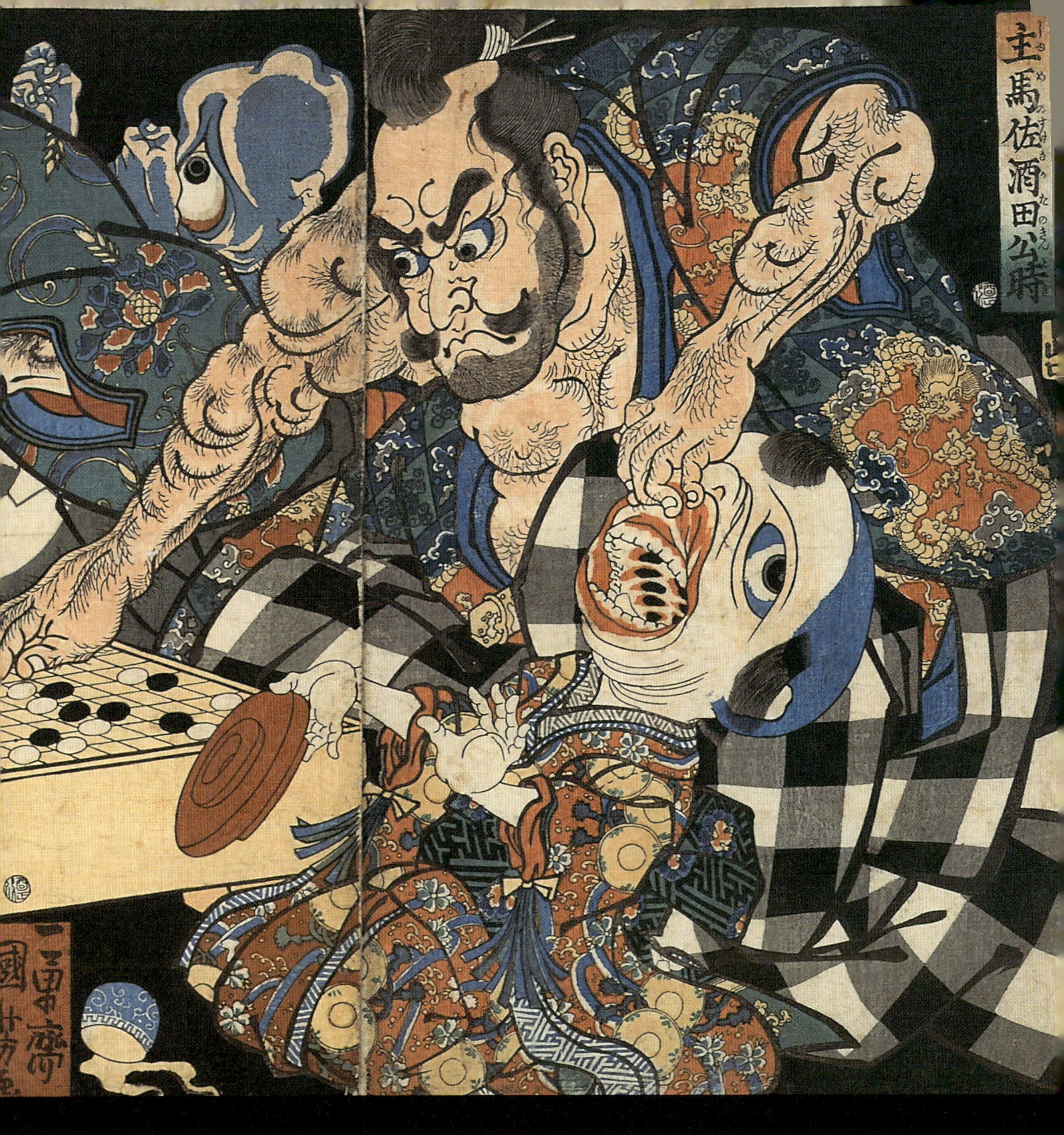

"Sakata no Kintoki, Usui Sadamitsu, Genji no Tsuna, and Demonic Creatures" by Utagawa Kuniyoshi

Three of Yorimitsu's men stay up through the night while Yorimitsu suffers from a fever that is the result of a spell cast by a tsuchigumo spider yōkai. Demon spirits appear one after another, but the heroes dispatch them handily without taking their eyes off their game of go.

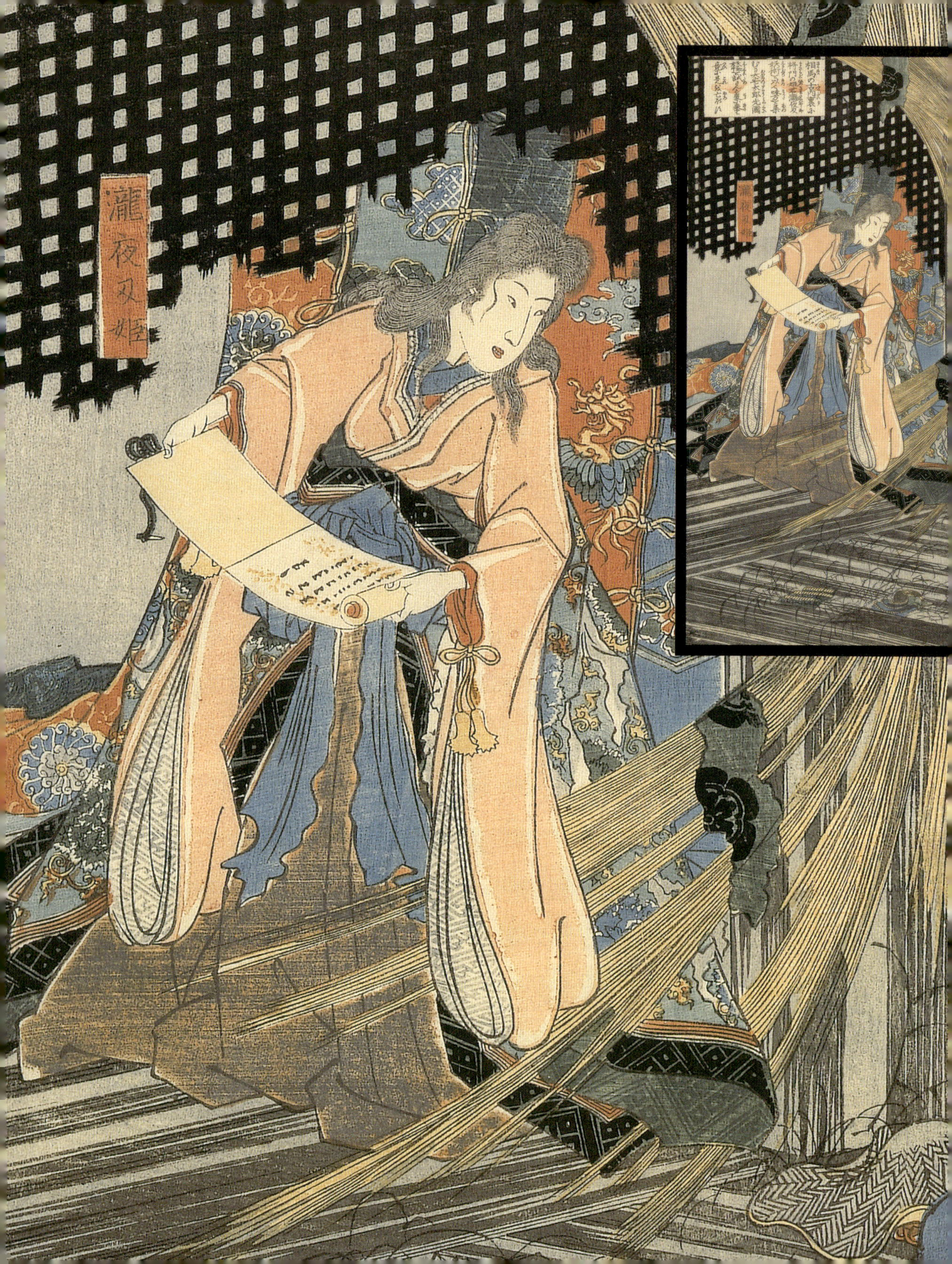
瀧夜叉姫

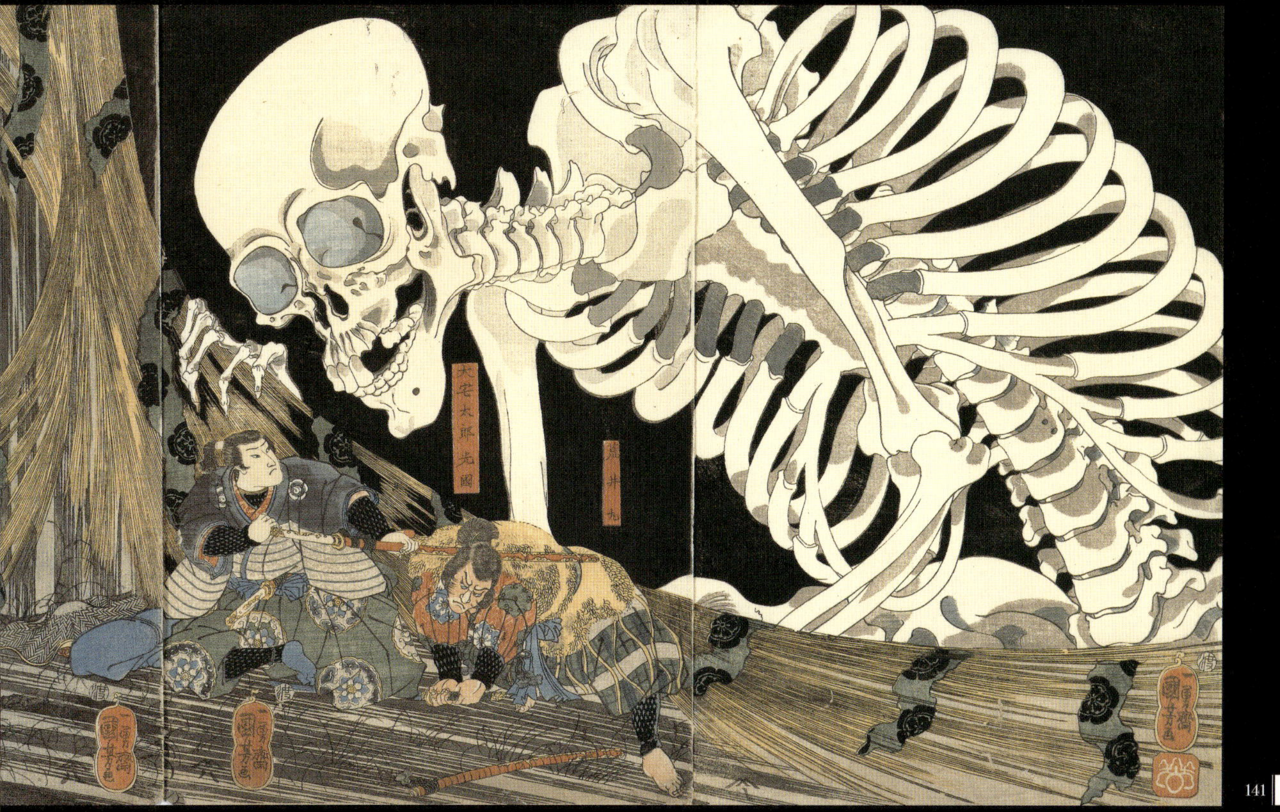

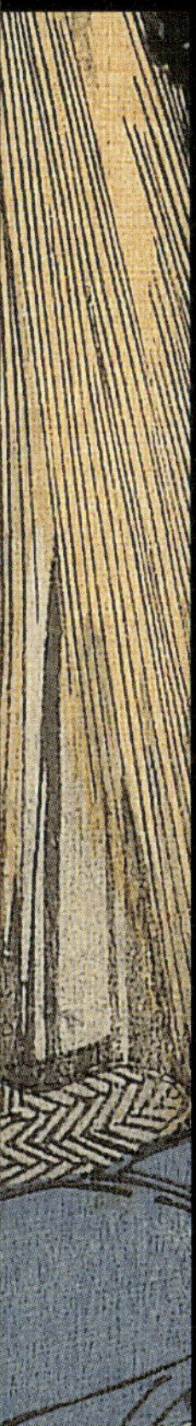

【相馬の古内裏】歌川国芳 弘化2〜3年(1845-46)頃

光国に連判状への血判を迫る滝夜叉姫。
破れた御簾の中から大髑髏が現れ、家来の荒猪丸が光国を襲う。

The Old Palace at Sōma: Princess Takiyasha and the Huge Skeleton by Utagawa Kuniyoshi

Princess Takiyasha pressures Mitsukuni to sign a blood oath at her father's former palace.
As a giant skeleton rises from behind broken bamboo blinds,
Mitsukuni subdues Araimaru, one of Takiyasha's henchmen, below.

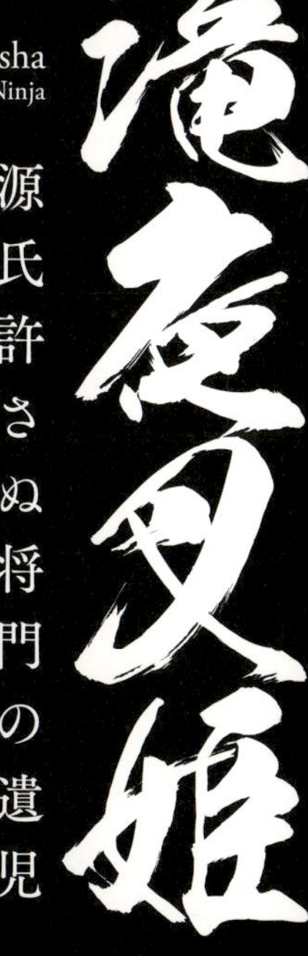

Princess Takiyasha
Wizards and Ninja

滝夜叉姫

源氏許さぬ将門の遺児

山東京伝の読本『善知鳥安方忠義伝』の登場人物。謀反を起こして朝敵となった平将門の遺児。尼となり仏門に入っていたが、弟の平良門が肉芝仙人から授かった妖術によって豹変し、ともに源氏への復讐を企てる。相馬の古内裏に潜伏し、自身も妖術を使って妖怪を操る。武者修行で訪れた浪人大宅太郎光国が妖怪に動じないのを見て、仲間にしようとするが失敗。最期は朝命を受けた源氏の征伐軍に攻め込まれ自刃した。

A character in Santō Kyōden's *Account of the Loyal Vassal Utō Yasukata* (1806), Princess Takiyasha is the orphaned child of Taira no Masakado, who led a rebellion against the Heian court. Though she originally served as a Buddhist nun, her personality is transformed by a spell from her brother Taira no Yoshikado, who learned sorcery from the immortal hermit Nikushi. Joining Yoshikado in his plot of vengeance against the Minamoto clan, they live secretly in Masakado's ruined palace in Sōma. Takiyasha also learns how to summon and control monsters. A rōnin traveling the country named Ōya Tarō Mitsukuni visits the palace. Seeing that he is unmoved by the monsters, they unsuccessfully invite him to join them. A punitive expedition, led by the Minamoto, is sent by the Imperial court to defeat them, leading Takiyasha to commit suicide.

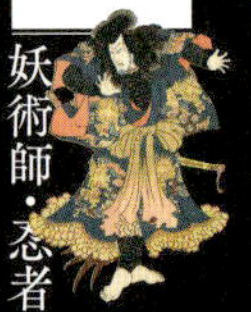

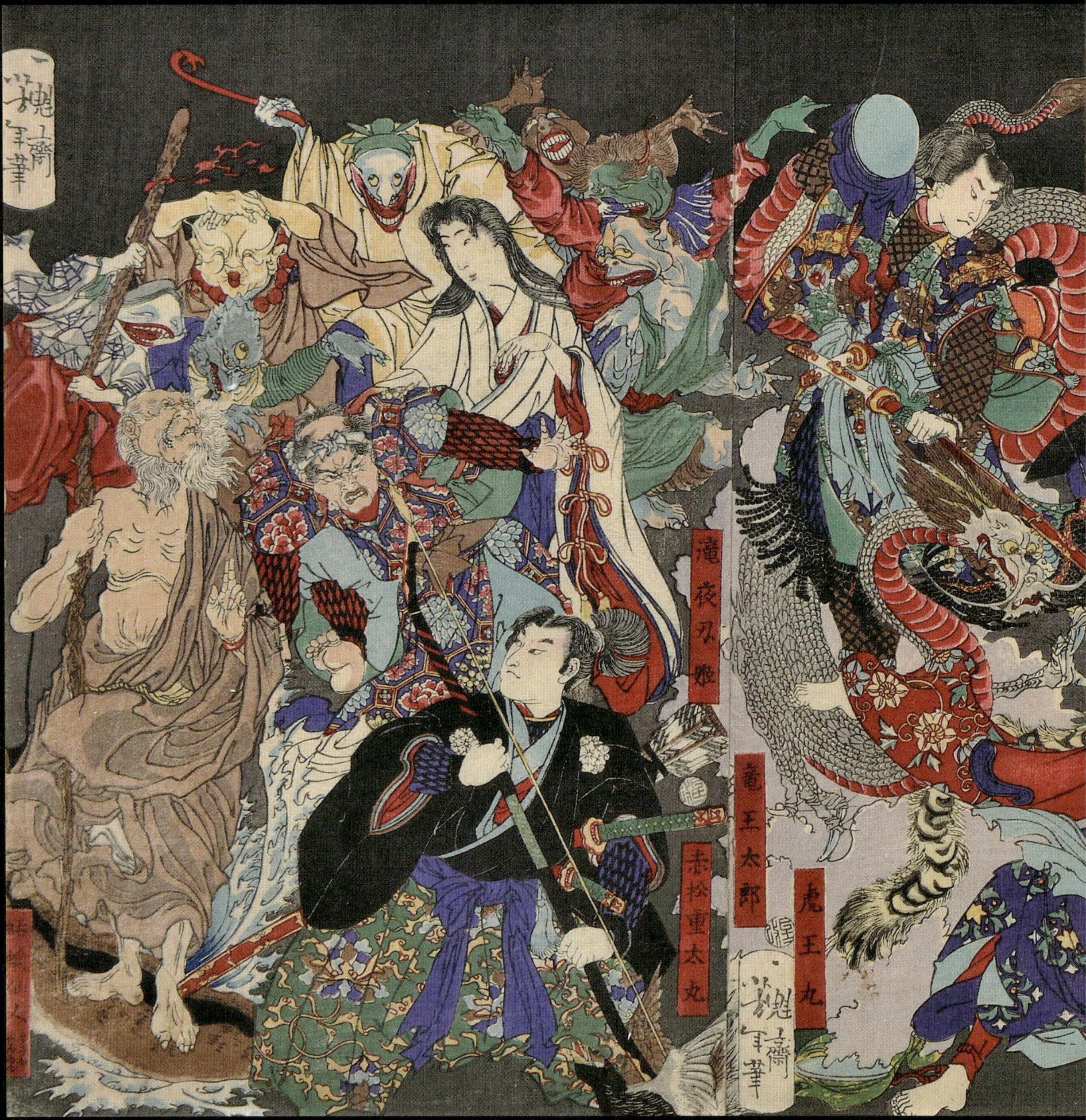

【豪傑奇術競】月岡芳年　明治2年（1869）

右から、火遁の術の寂寞道人、古狸の幻術使い妙椿尼、蝦蟇遣いの天竺徳兵衛、大盗賊で飛行の術の暁星五郎、
絵から虎を出す虎王丸、竜使いの竜王太郎、妖怪を操る滝夜叉姫、変身術の赤松重太丸、なめくじ使いの蛞蝓仙人。

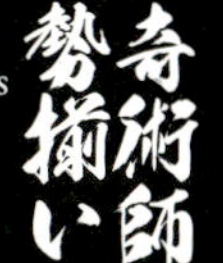

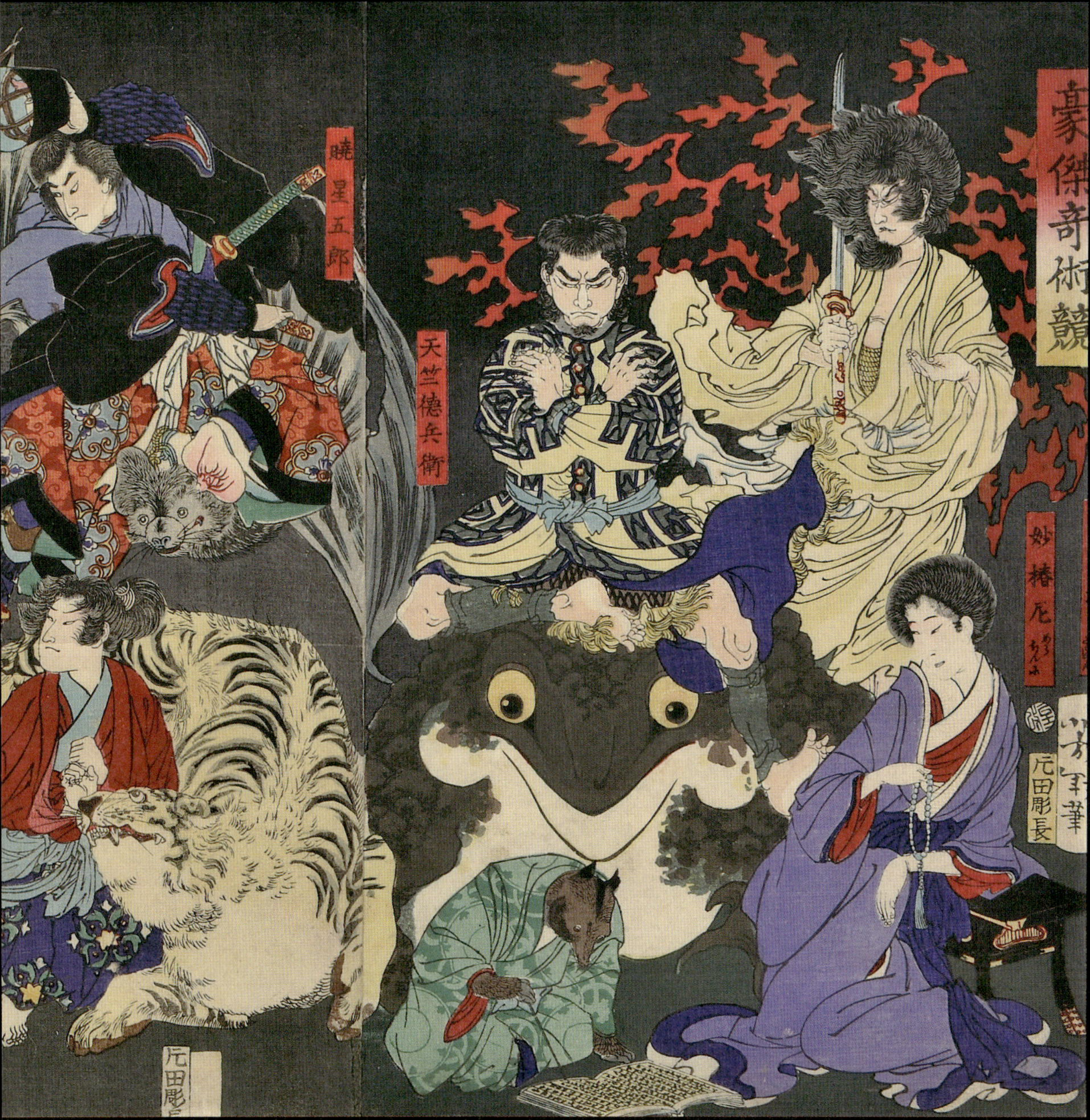

143

"A Contest of Master Sorcerers" by Tsukioka Yoshitoshi
From right to left: fire magician Jyakumaku Dōjin; Myōchinni, the magical old raccoon; Tenjiku Tokubee, master of giant toads;
the flying bandit Akatsuki Hoshigorō; Tora-ō-maru, who can make painted tigers come alive;
dragoneer Ryu-ō-tarō; yokai master Prince Takiyasha; shape-shifter Akamatsu Jūtamaru; the immortal hermit Katsuyu, master of slugs.

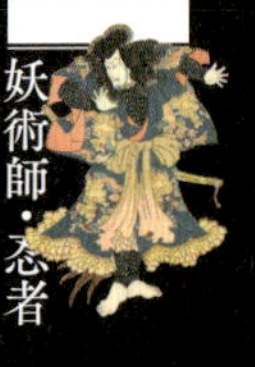

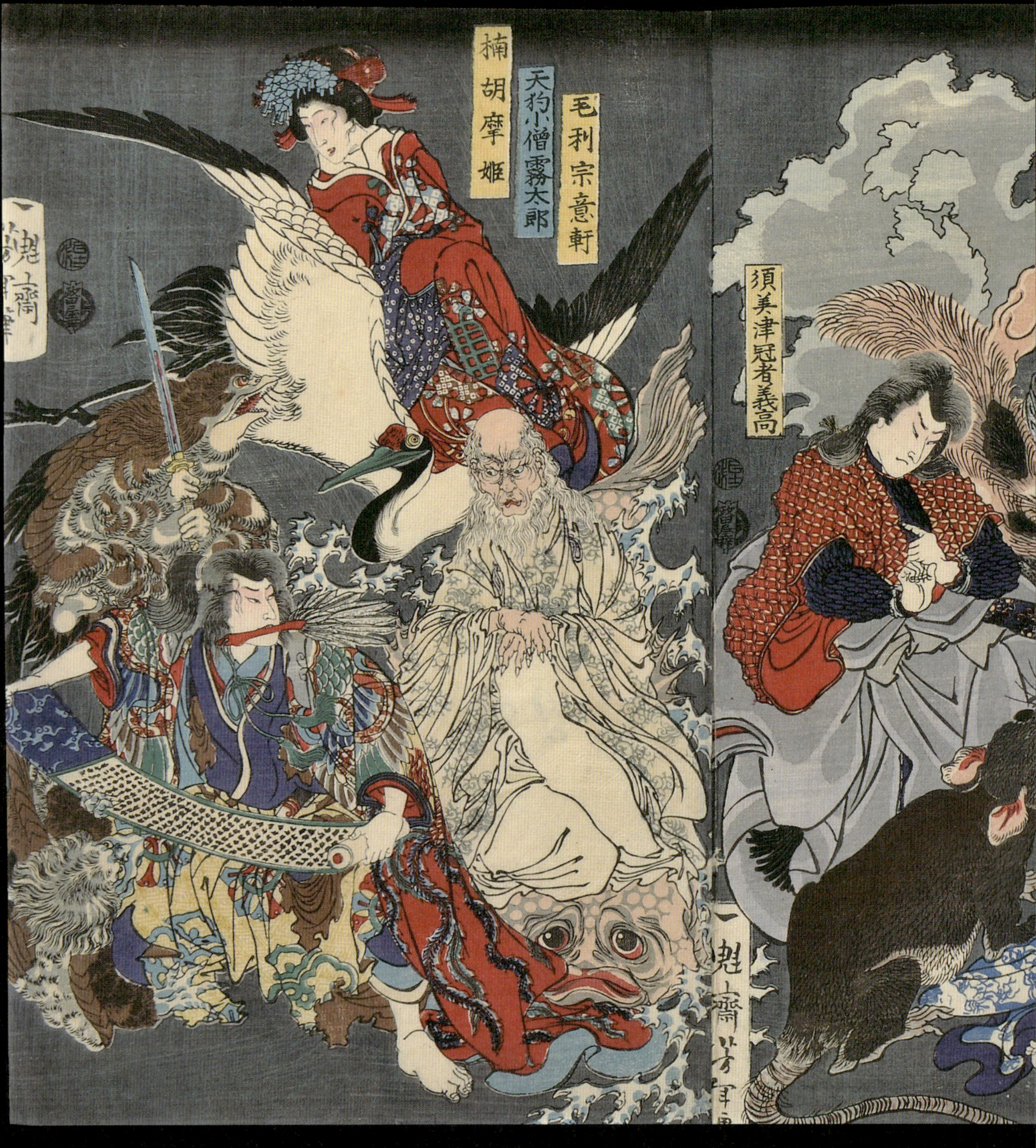

楠胡摩姫
天狗小僧霧太郎
毛利宗意軒
須美津冠者義高

【豪傑奇術競】月岡芳年　明治2年（1869）

右より、蝶に乗って飛ぶ岩藤 局、仙術で大鷲に乗る仙冠者義虎、大蛇を操る大蛇丸、蜘蛛の妖術使い大友若菜姫、猫の妖術の魔陀羅丸、鼠使いの須美津冠者義高、魚を操る切支丹の残党毛利宗意軒、天狗の妖術の盗賊天狗小僧霧太郎、鶴を操って飛ぶ 楠 胡摩姫。

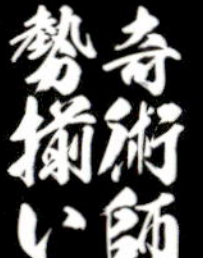

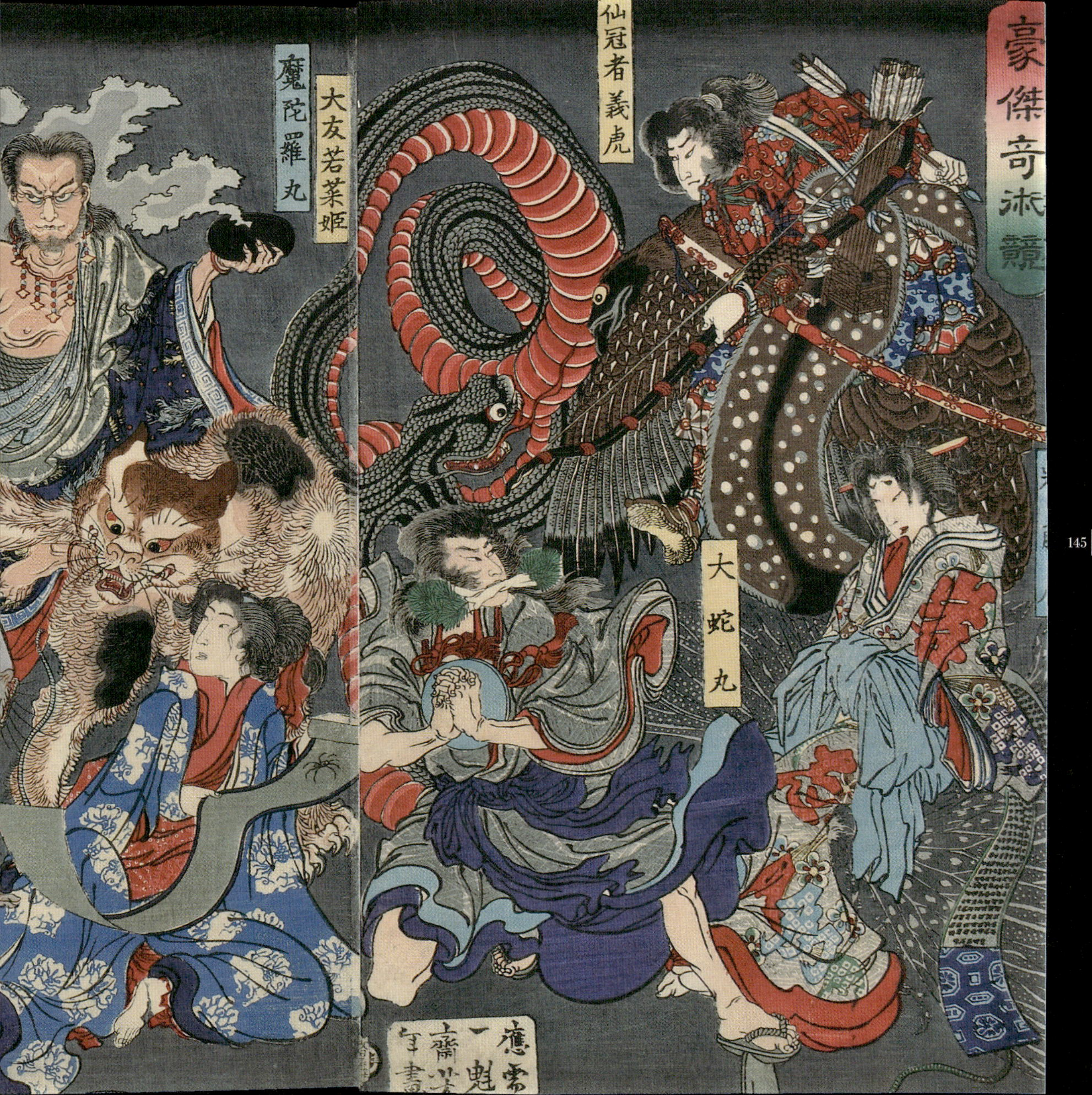

"A Contest of Master Sorcerers" by Tsukioka Yoshitoshi

From right to left: butterfly-rider Iwafuji no Tsubone; Senkanja Yoshitora, who uses his hermit wizardry to ride giant eagles; Orochimaru, master of giant serpents; spider magician Princess Ōtomo Wakana; cat magician Madaramaru; Shimizu Kanja Yoshitaka, master of rats; exiled Christian Mōri Sōiken, master of fishes; bandit Tengu Kozō Kiritarō, mountain goblin magician; crane-rider Princess Kusunoki Komahime.

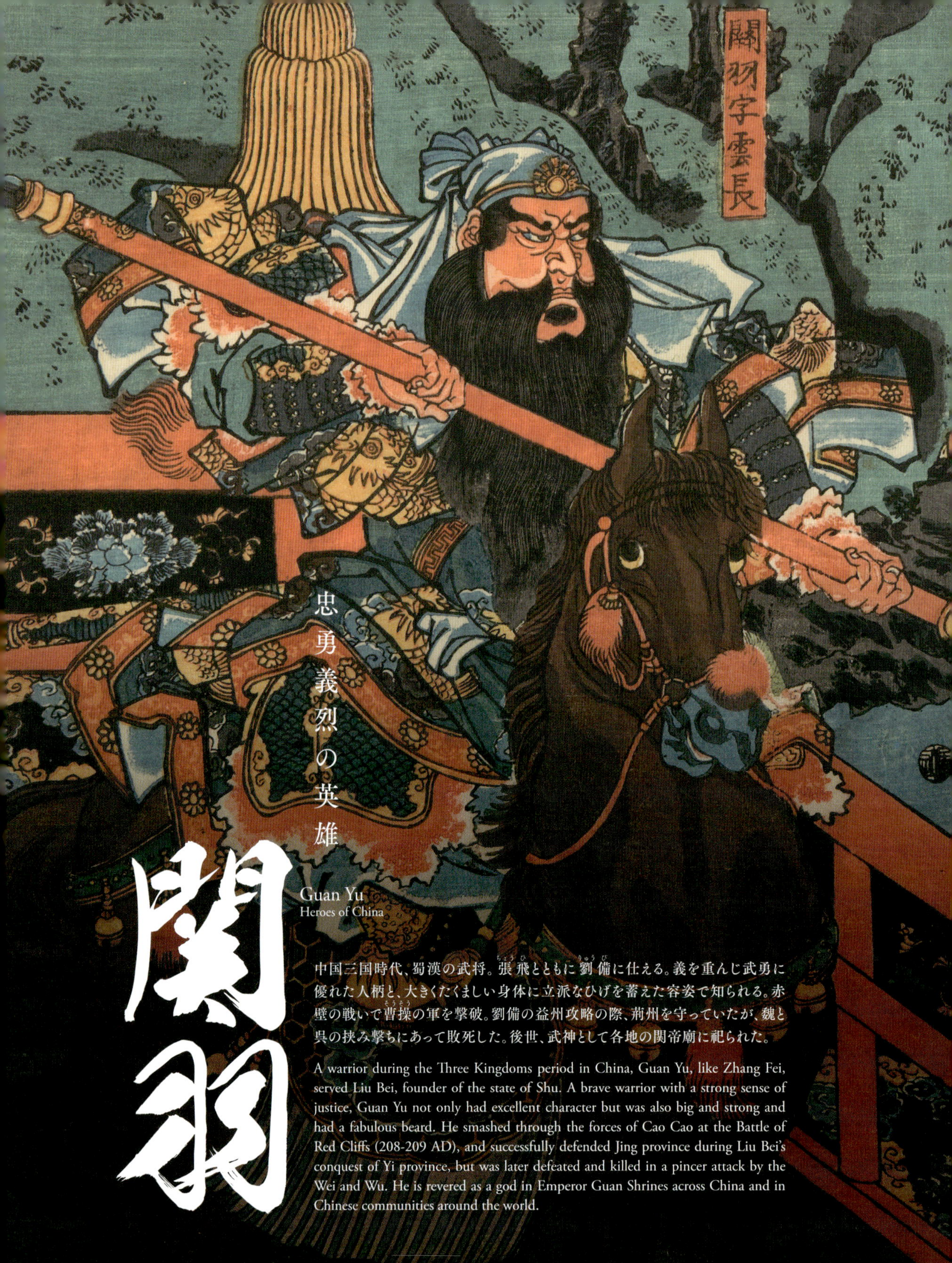

忠勇義烈の英雄

Guan Yu
Heroes of China

関羽

中国三国時代、蜀漢の武将。張飛とともに劉備に仕える。義を重んじ武勇に優れた人柄と、大きくたくましい身体に立派なひげを蓄えた容姿で知られる。赤壁の戦いで曹操の軍を撃破。劉備の益州攻略の際、荊州を守っていたが、魏と呉の挟み撃ちにあって敗死した。後世、武神として各地の関帝廟に祀られた。

A warrior during the Three Kingdoms period in China, Guan Yu, like Zhang Fei, served Liu Bei, founder of the state of Shu. A brave warrior with a strong sense of justice, Guan Yu not only had excellent character but was also big and strong and had a fabulous beard. He smashed through the forces of Cao Cao at the Battle of Red Cliffs (208-209 AD), and successfully defended Jing province during Liu Bei's conquest of Yi province, but was later defeated and killed in a pincer attack by the Wei and Wu. He is revered as a god in Emperor Guan Shrines across China and in Chinese communities around the world.

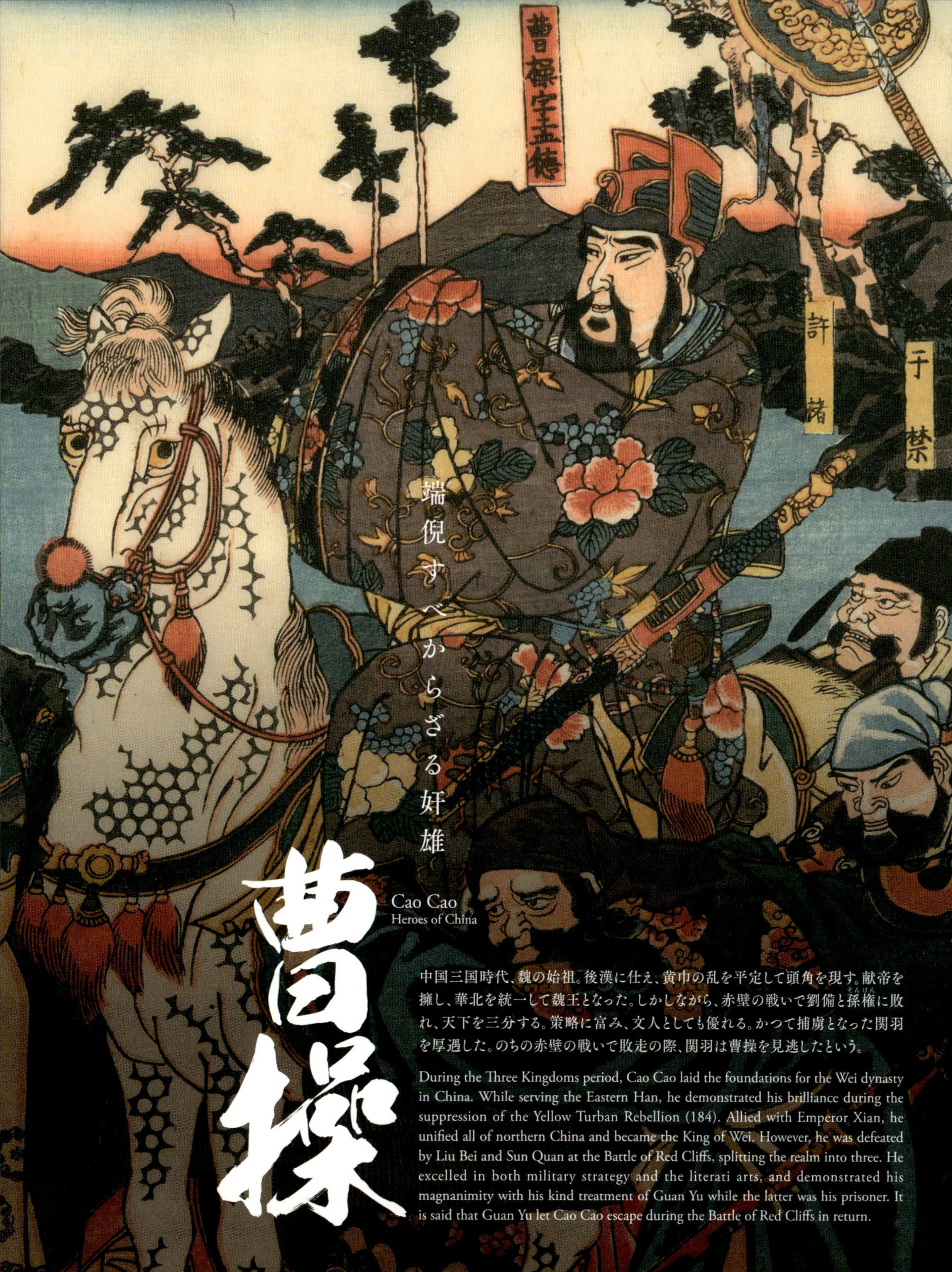

Cao Cao
Heroes of China

中国三国時代、魏の始祖。後漢に仕え、黄巾の乱を平定して頭角を現す。献帝を擁し、華北を統一して魏王となった。しかしながら、赤壁の戦いで劉備と孫権に敗れ、天下を三分する。策略に富み、文人としても優れる。かつて捕虜となった関羽を厚遇した。のちの赤壁の戦いで敗走の際、関羽は曹操を見逃したという。

During the Three Kingdoms period, Cao Cao laid the foundations for the Wei dynasty in China. While serving the Eastern Han, he demonstrated his brilliance during the suppression of the Yellow Turban Rebellion (184). Allied with Emperor Xian, he unified all of northern China and became the King of Wei. However, he was defeated by Liu Bei and Sun Quan at the Battle of Red Cliffs, splitting the realm into three. He excelled in both military strategy and the literati arts, and demonstrated his magnanimity with his kind treatment of Guan Yu while the latter was his prisoner. It is said that Guan Yu let Cao Cao escape during the Battle of Red Cliffs in return.

曹操

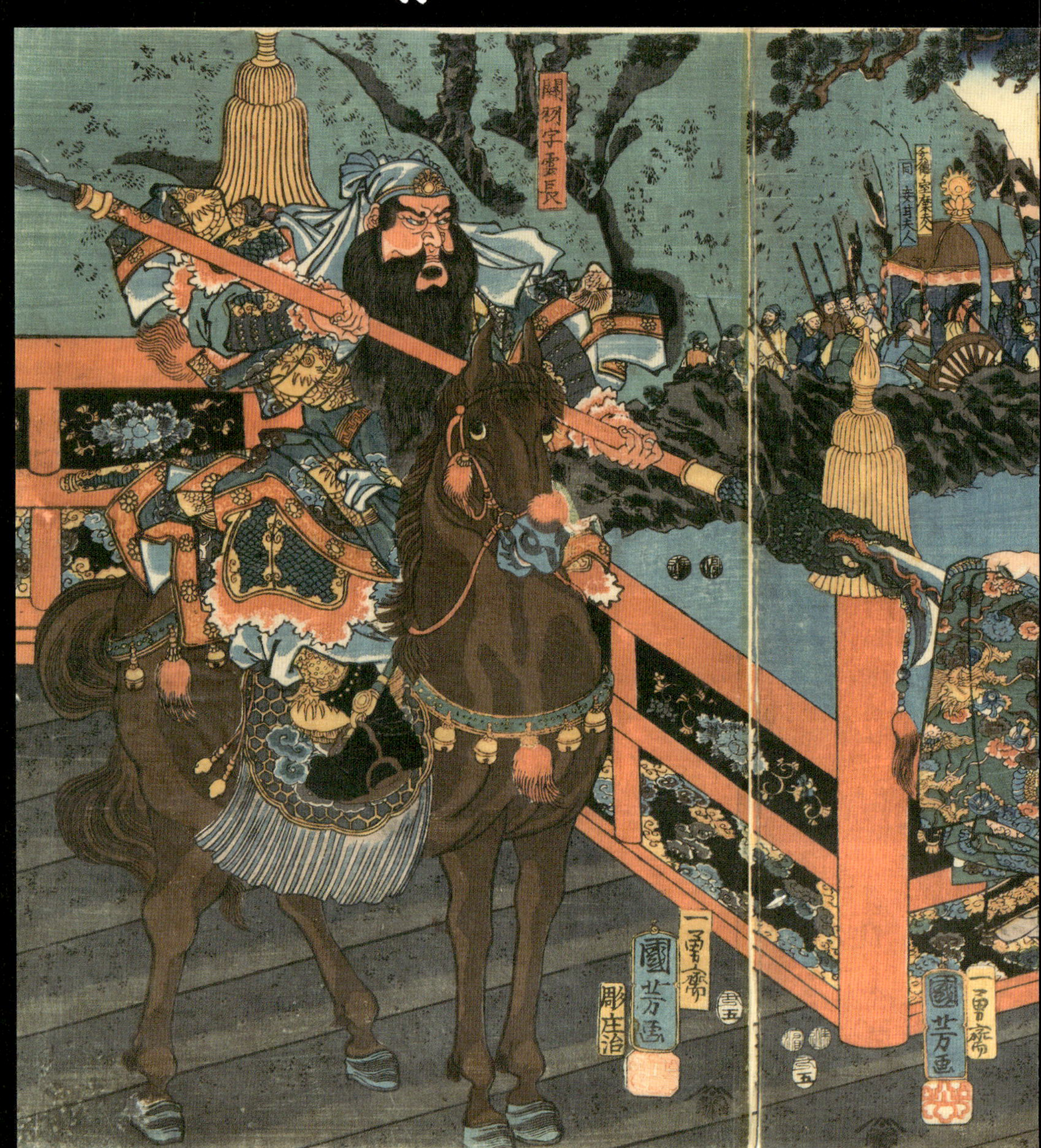

関羽字雲長

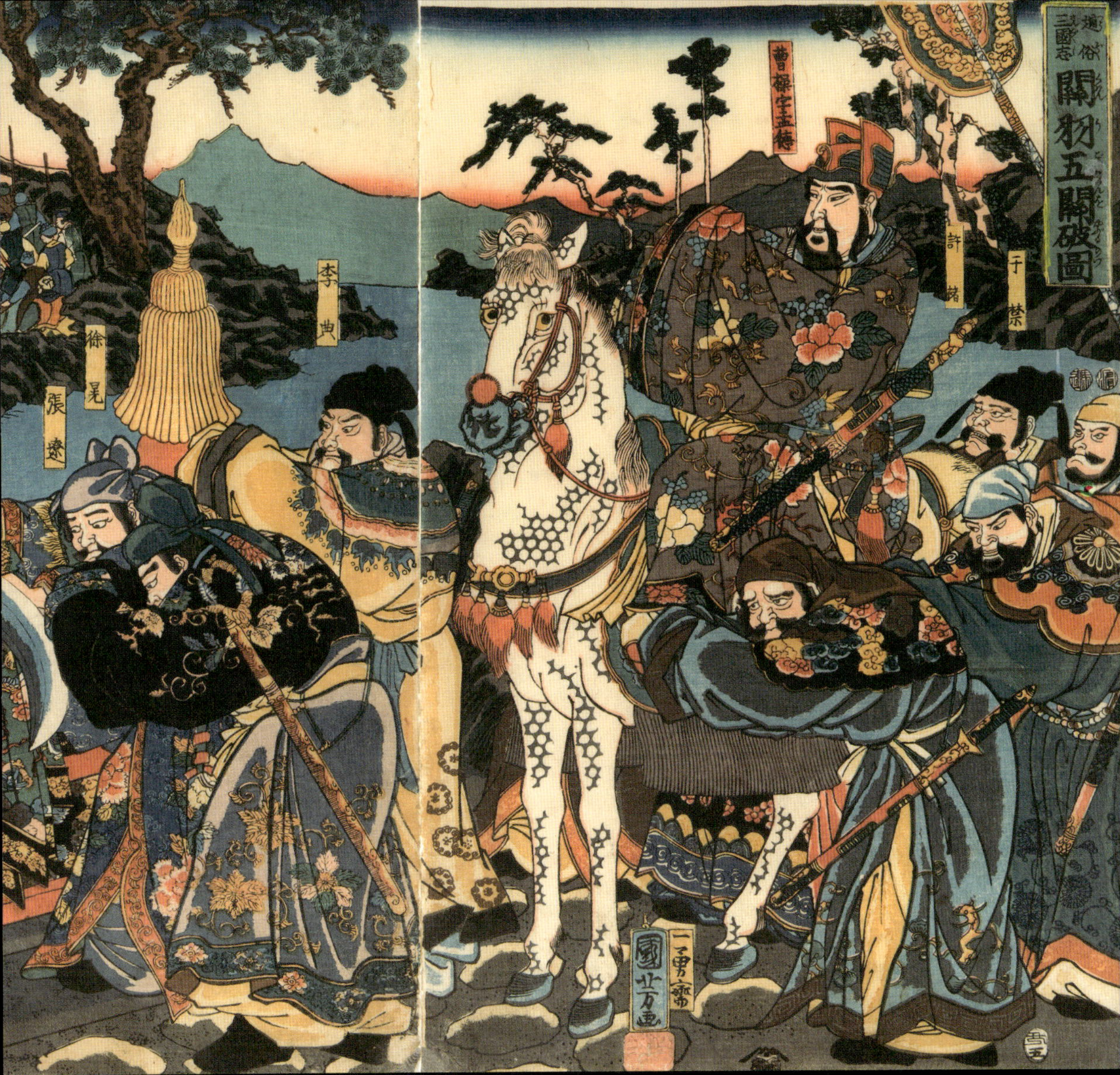
曹操
通俗三國志 關羽五關破圖
曹操字孟德
許褚
于禁
李典
徐晃
張遼
一勇齋國芳画

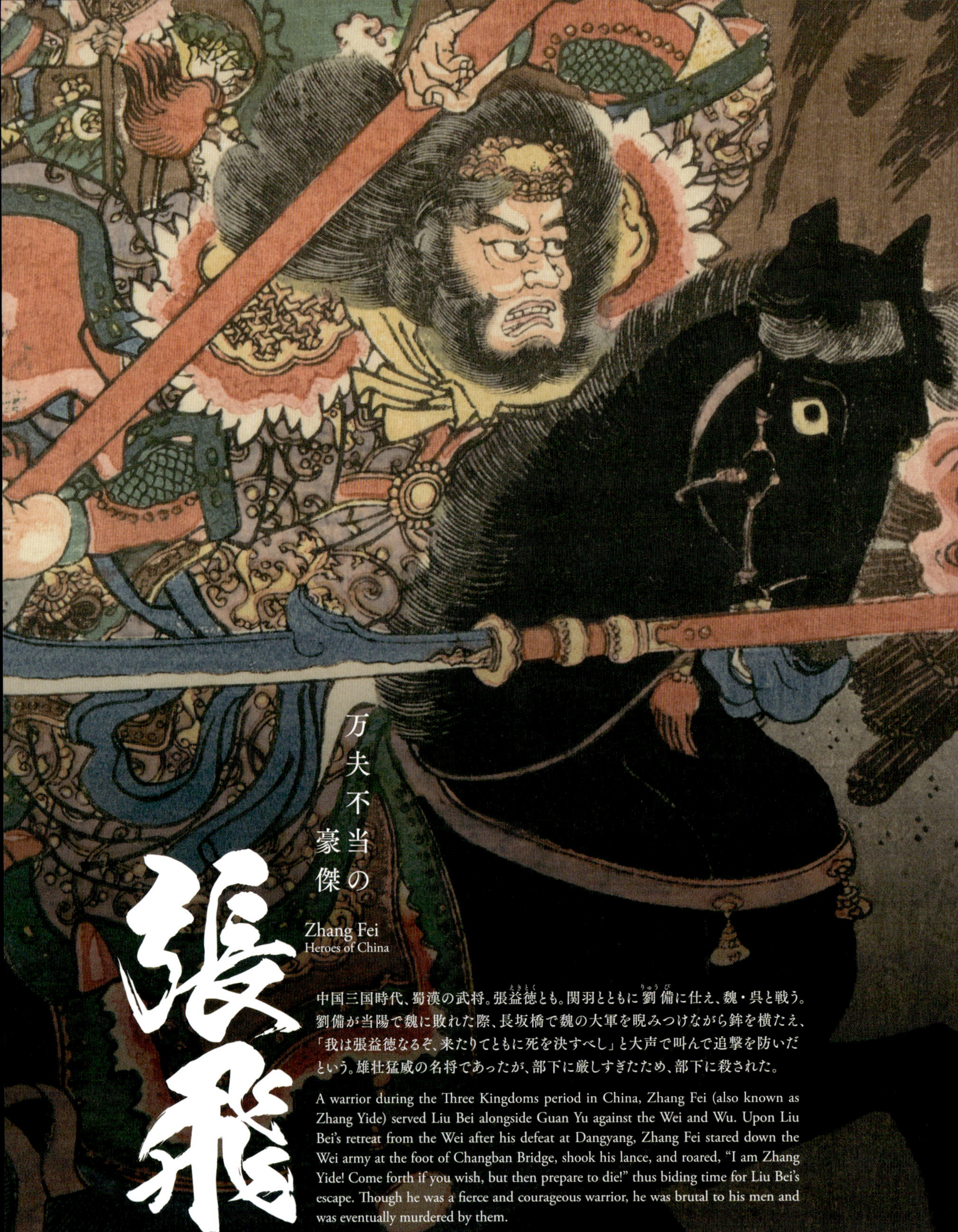

中国三国時代、蜀漢の武将。張益徳とも。関羽とともに劉備に仕え、魏・呉と戦う。劉備が当陽で魏に敗れた際、長坂橋で魏の大軍を睨みつけながら鉾を横たえ、「我は張益徳なるぞ、来たりてともに死を決すべし」と大声で叫んで追撃を防いだという。雄壮猛威の名将であったが、部下に厳しすぎたため、部下に殺された。

A warrior during the Three Kingdoms period in China, Zhang Fei (also known as Zhang Yide) served Liu Bei alongside Guan Yu against the Wei and Wu. Upon Liu Bei's retreat from the Wei after his defeat at Dangyang, Zhang Fei stared down the Wei army at the foot of Changban Bridge, shook his lance, and roared, "I am Zhang Yide! Come forth if you wish, but then prepare to die!" thus biding time for Liu Bei's escape. Though he was a fierce and courageous warrior, he was brutal to his men and was eventually murdered by them.

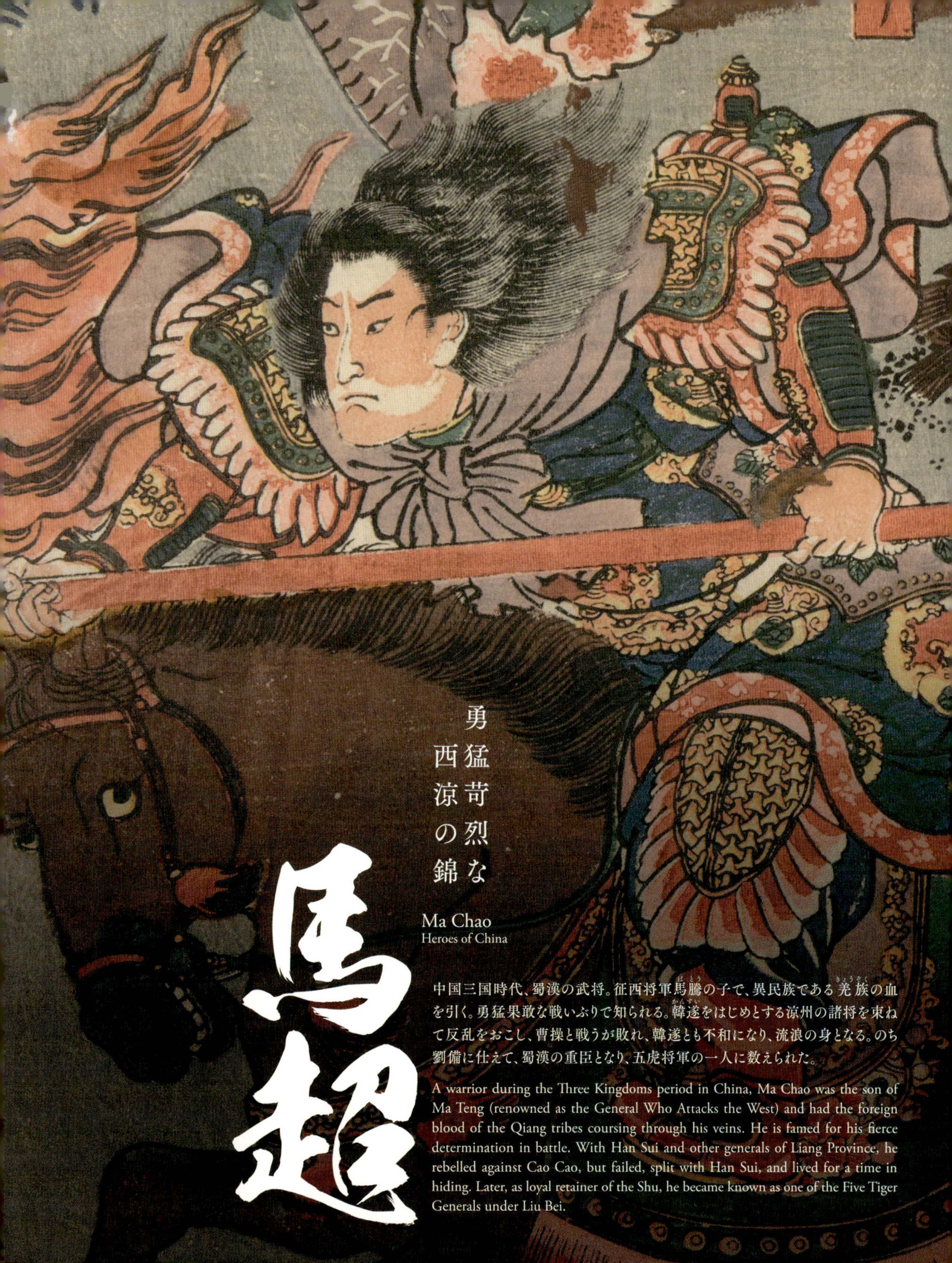

Ma Chao
Heroes of China

中国三国時代、蜀漢の武将。征西将軍馬騰の子で、異民族である羌族の血を引く。勇猛果敢な戦いぶりで知られる。韓遂をはじめとする涼州の諸将を束ねて反乱をおこし、曹操と戦うが敗れ、韓遂とも不和になり、流浪の身となる。のち劉備に仕えて、蜀漢の重臣となり、五虎将軍の一人に数えられた。

A warrior during the Three Kingdoms period in China, Ma Chao was the son of Ma Teng (renowned as the General Who Attacks the West) and had the foreign blood of the Qiang tribes coursing through his veins. He is famed for his fierce determination in battle. With Han Sui and other generals of Liang Province, he rebelled against Cao Cao, but failed, split with Han Sui, and lived for a time in hiding. Later, as loyal retainer of the Shu, he became known as one of the Five Tiger Generals under Liu Bei.

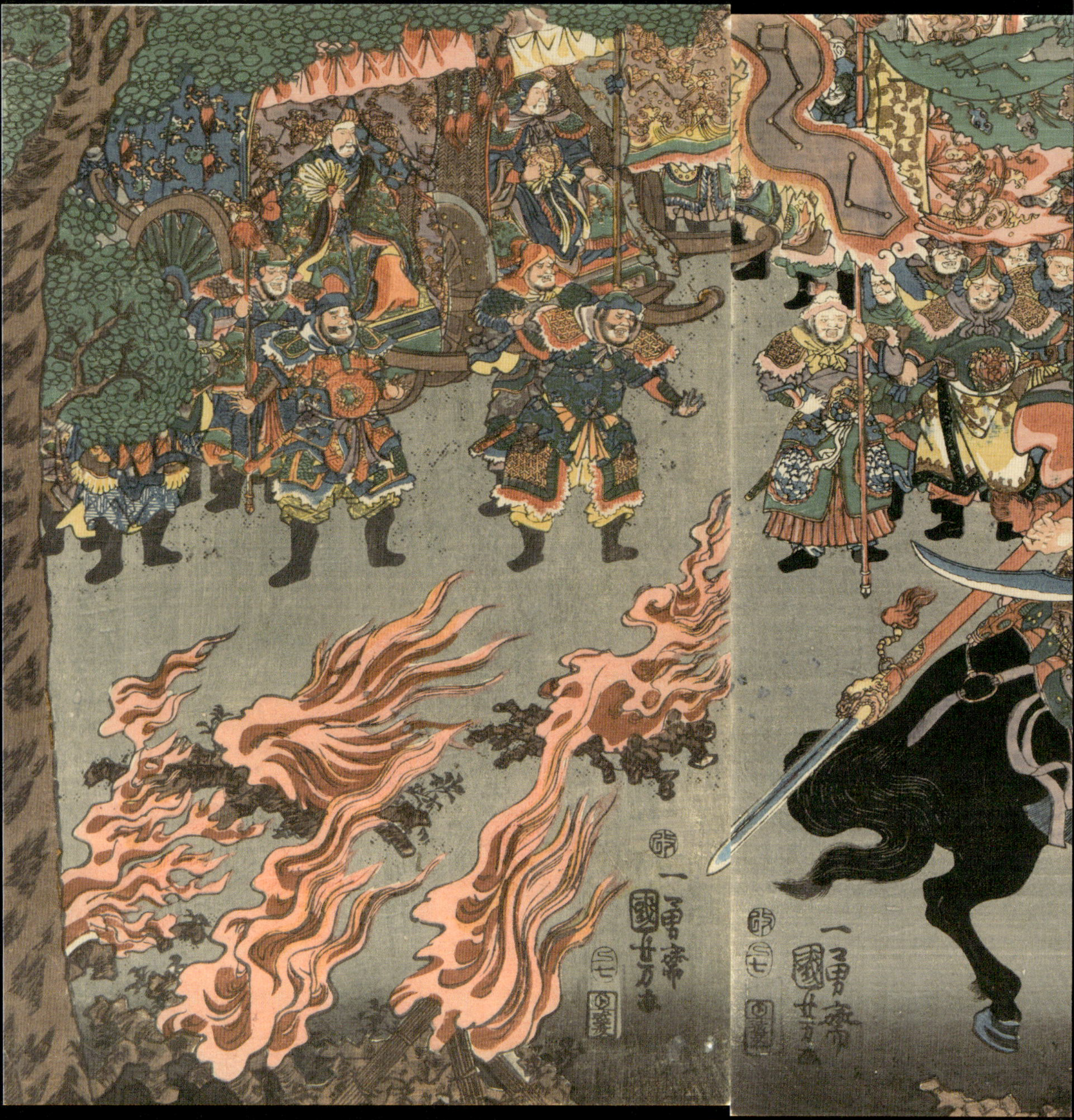

152

【三国志馬超張飛葭萌関戦】歌川国芳　安政4年（1857）
葭萌関に攻め込んだ馬超と、これを迎え撃つ張飛の一騎打ち。決着はつかなかったが、劉備は馬超を臣下に加える交渉を始める。

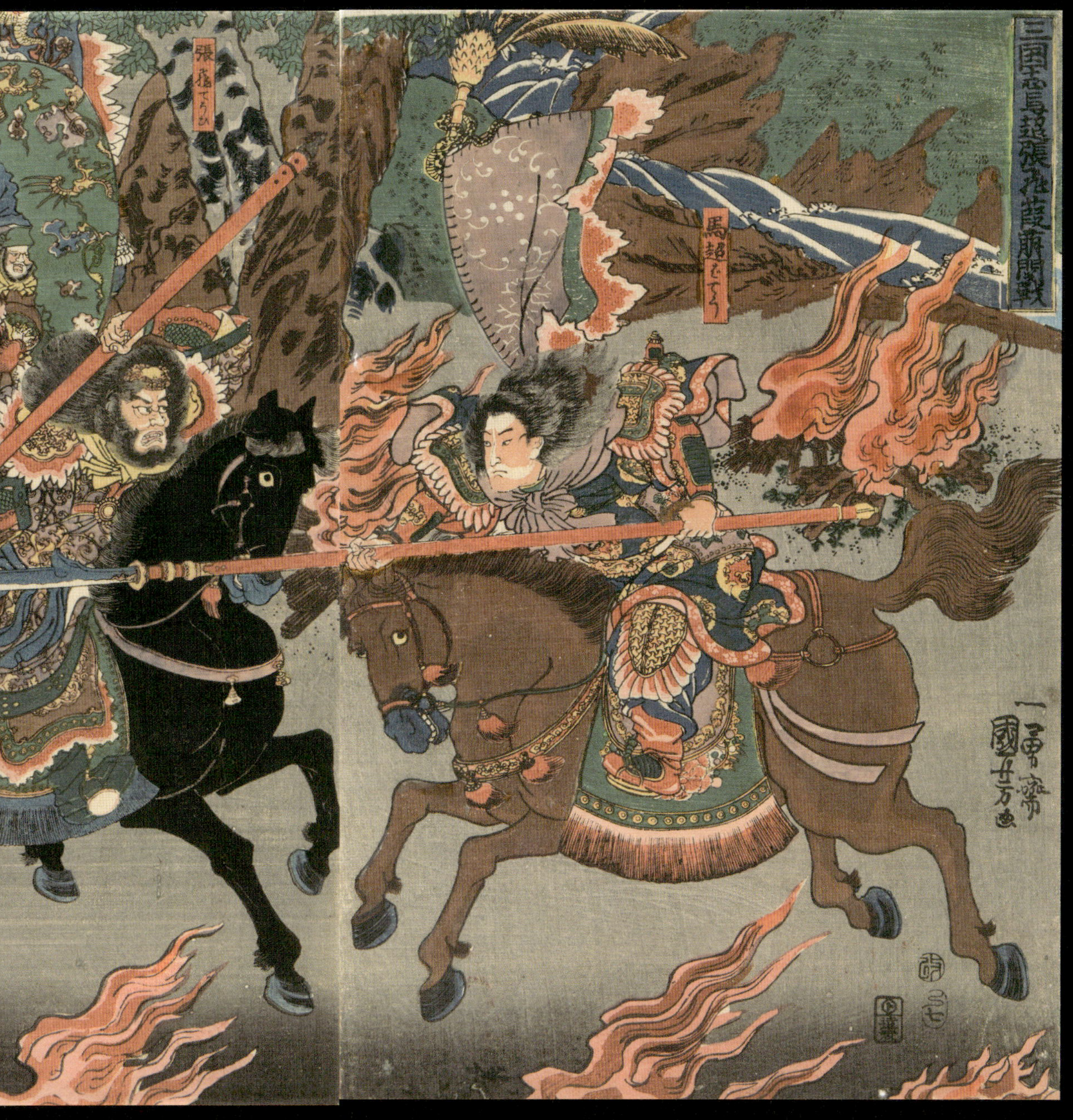

"Romance of the Three Kingdoms: Ma Chao versus Zhang Fei at the Battle of Jiameng Pass" by Utagawa Kuniyoshi

Mao Chao attacking and Zhang Fei defending at the Battle of Jiameng Pass.
Though the fight ended in a draw, it set in motion the process by which Ma Chao became a retainer of Liu Bei.

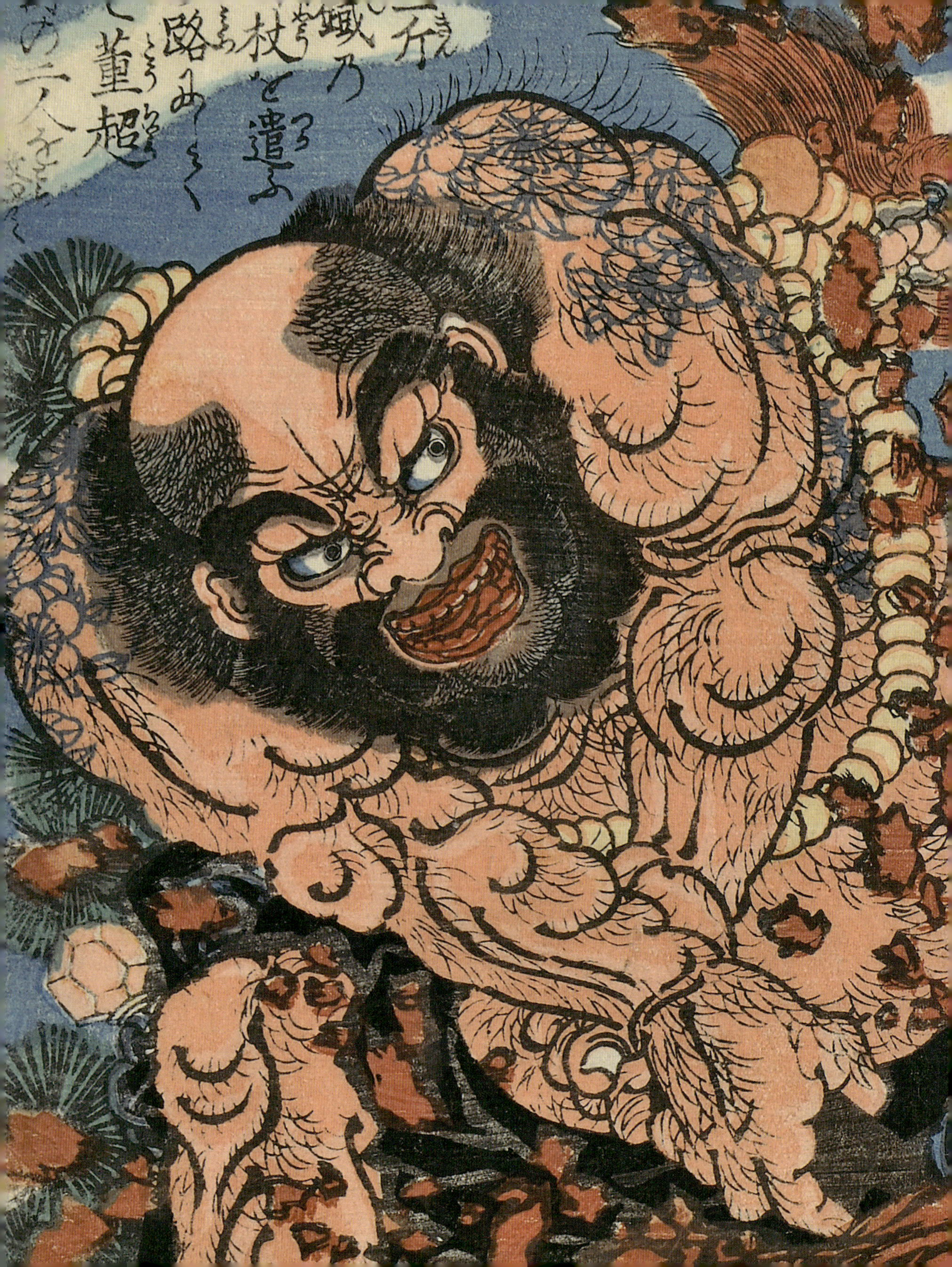
一丈
蠍乃
杖を遣ふ
略みつく
と董超

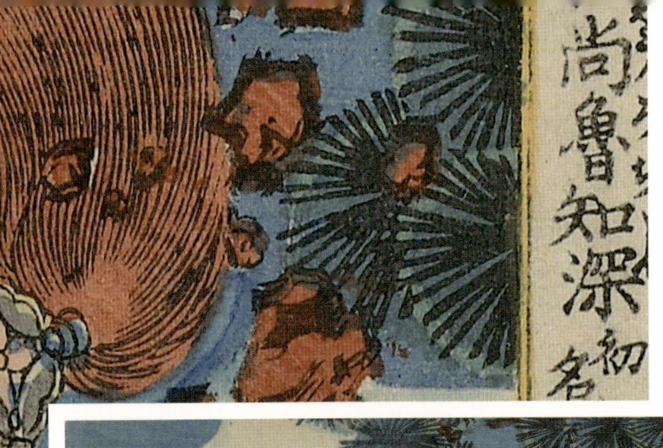

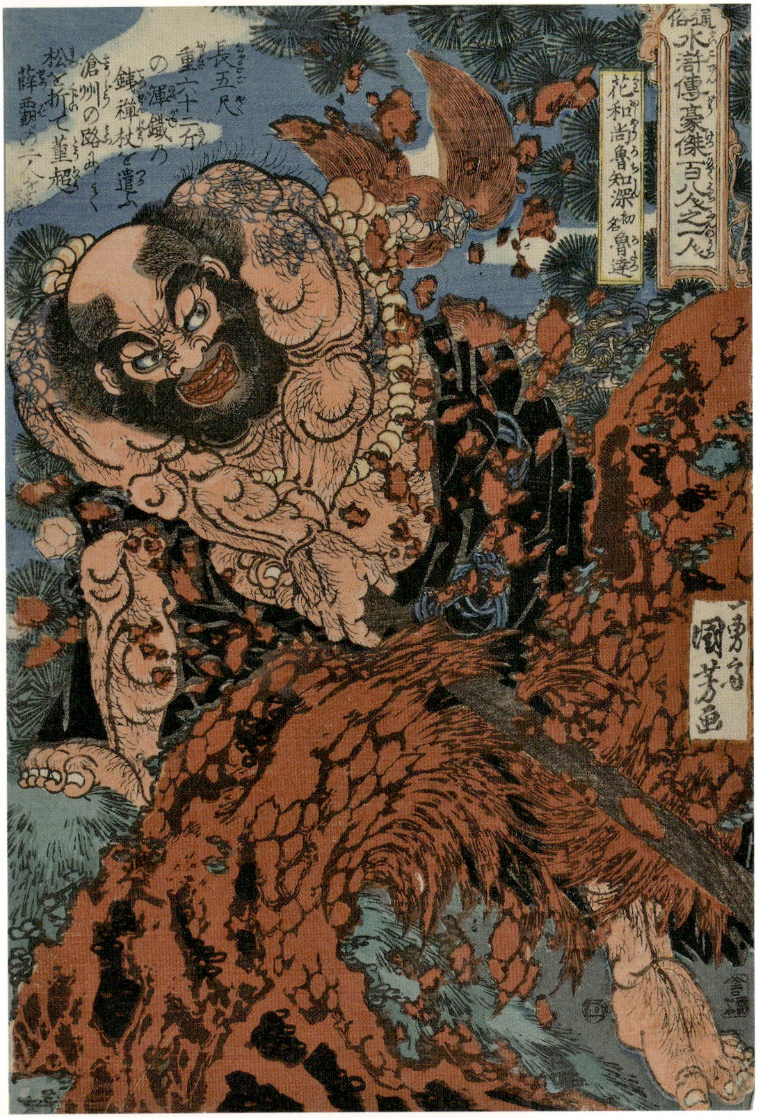

悪人を拳で黙らす破戒僧

魯智深

Lu Zhishen
Heroes of China

中国の通俗小説『水滸伝』の登場人物。元は武官で魯達と名乗ったが、人を殴り殺したので出家し、知深という法名を授かる。長さ五尺、重さ六十二斤の鉄の禅杖を武器とする。柳の木を腕で根こそぎ引っこ抜くほどの怪力の持ち主。戒を破って大酒を飲み、寺で大暴れしたために追放された。のち、冤罪で流刑となった義兄弟の林冲が、護送役人に殺されそうになったのを救出した。

A character from the Chinese epic *The Water Margin*, Lu Zhishen was originally a garrison major named Lu Da, but took the Buddhist name Zhishen (meaning "sagacious") after beating someone to death, fleeing home, and joining a monastery. As his weapon, he wielded an iron monk's staff measuring 1.5 meters and weighing almost 40 kg. He was so strong that he could yank out a willow at its roots with his bare hands. His love of alcohol and penchant for violence got him kicked out of the monastic community. When his blood brother Lin Chong was framed and exiled, Lu Zhishen saved him from being killed by his escort guards.

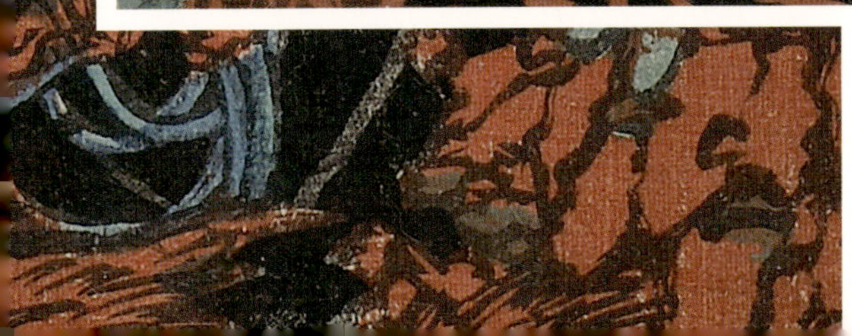

【通俗水滸伝豪傑百八人之一人 花和尚 魯知深 初名 魯達】
歌川国芳 文政10年（1827）頃
"108 Heroes of the Water Margin:
The Flowery Monk, Lu Zhishen" by Utagawa Kuniyoshi

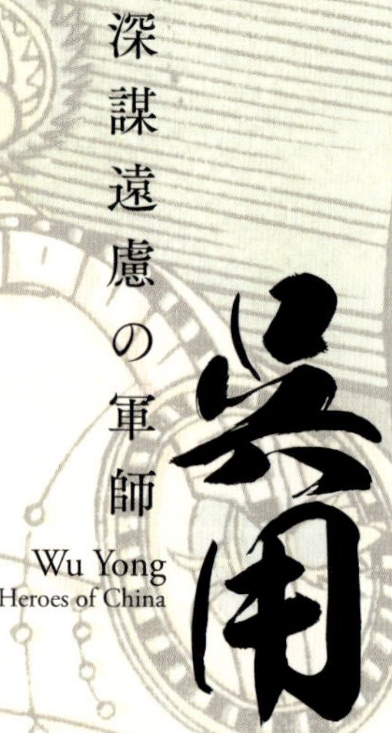

深謀遠慮の軍師

呉用

Wu Yong
Heroes of China

『水滸伝』の登場人物で、梁山泊の軍師。豪傑ぞろいのなか、随一の知性派。「観天望気」といって、星や大気を観測し天候を読むことで戦略をたてる。晁蓋（のちの梁山泊首領）が、不義の財を強奪する計画の相談をしに呉用を訪ね、北斗七星の瑞夢を見たと言うと、その数に合わせて七人の好漢を揃えよと助言した。

A character from *The Water Margin*, Wu Yong was a military strategist for the outlaws of Mount Liang. Among that congregation of gallant men, Wu Yong was the smartest. He based his strategies on the stars, the wind, and the weather. When Chao Gai (later leader of Mount Liang) hatched plans to steal ill-begotten imperial gifts, he consulted Wu Yong, who advised him to select seven trusted friends to carry out the deed, based on an auspicious dream he saw about the Big Dipper and its seven stars.

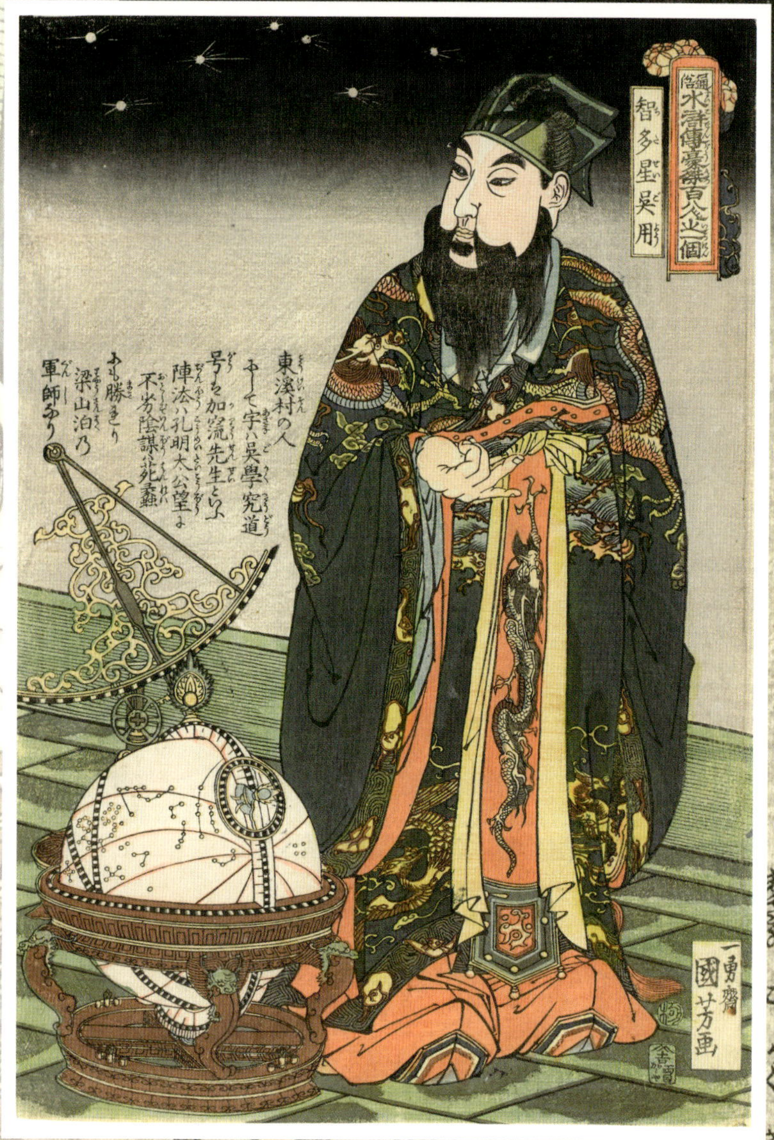

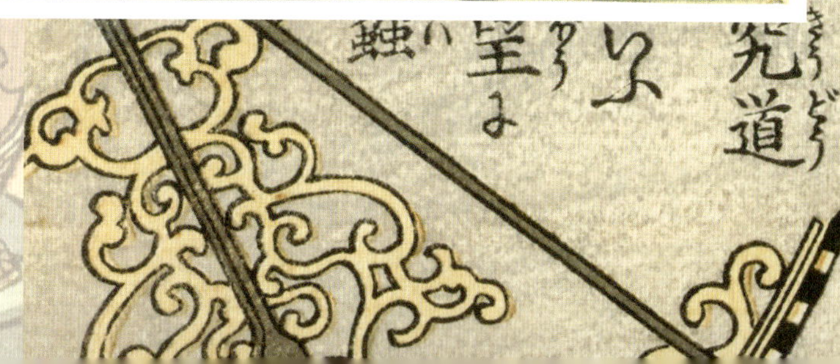

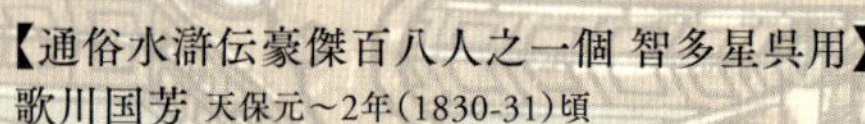

【通俗水滸伝豪傑百八人之一個 智多星呉用】
歌川国芳　天保元〜2年（1830-31）頃

"108 Heroes of the Water Margin:
The Knowledgeable Star, Wu Yong"
by Utagawa Kuniyoshi

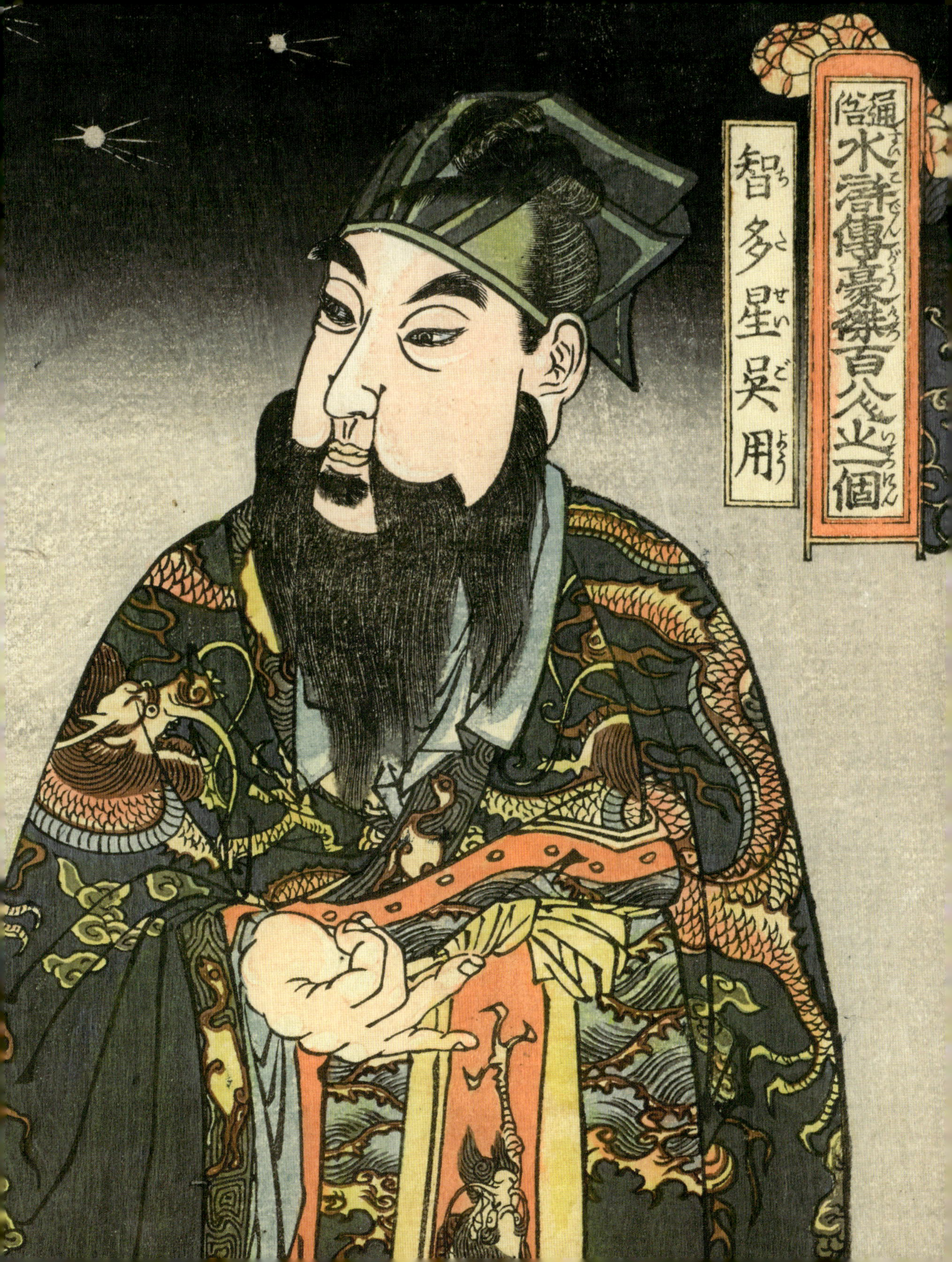
通俗水滸傳豪傑百八人之一個
智多星吳用

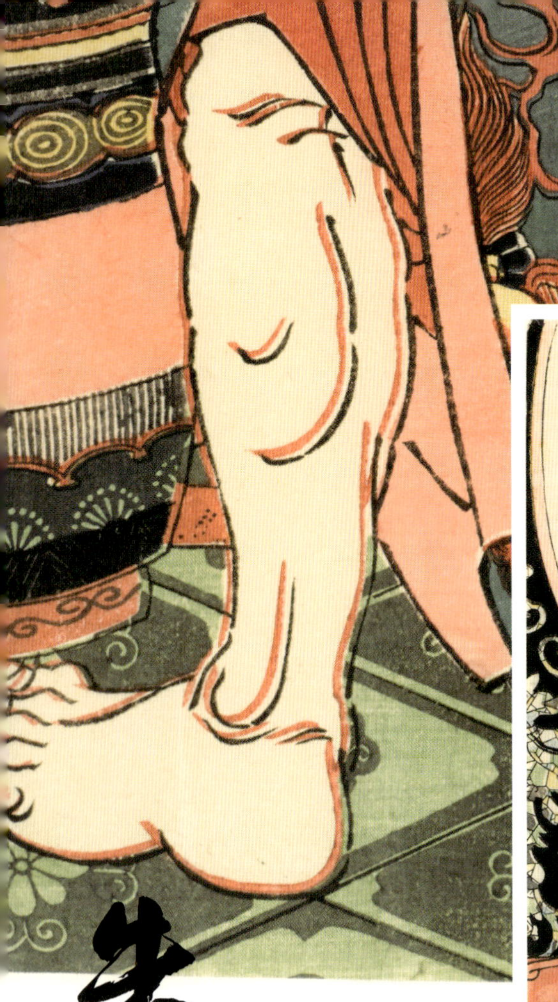

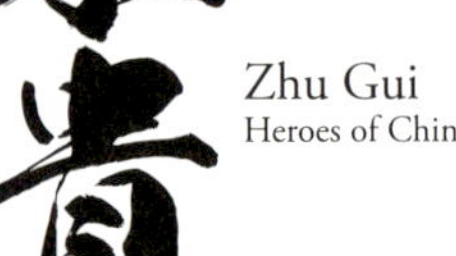

Zhu Gui
Heroes of China

『水滸伝』の登場人物。梁山泊の首領王倫に命じられ、ふもとの湖畔で居酒屋を営むかたわら、旅人から情報収集をしたり、金品を奪ったりしていた。梁山泊入りを希望する豪傑の手引きも行い、響箭を放って山中の砦に合図すると、舟がやってきて梁山泊へと乗せていく。

Under orders from Wang Lun, leader of the outlaws in *The Water Margin*, Zhu Gui ran a tavern beside Liangshan Marsh in order to gather intelligence and steal valuables from travelers. He was also responsible for arranging the entry of honored guests into the Mount Liang stronghold, which he did by firing a whistling arrow across the marsh, whereupon a boat would emerge from the reeds and take them across.

梁山泊の伊達男

【通俗水滸伝豪傑百八人之一個　旱地忽律朱貴】
歌川国芳　文政11〜12年（1828-29）頃
"108 Heroes of the Water Margin:
The Dry Land Alligator, Zhu Gui"
by Utagawa Kuniyoshi

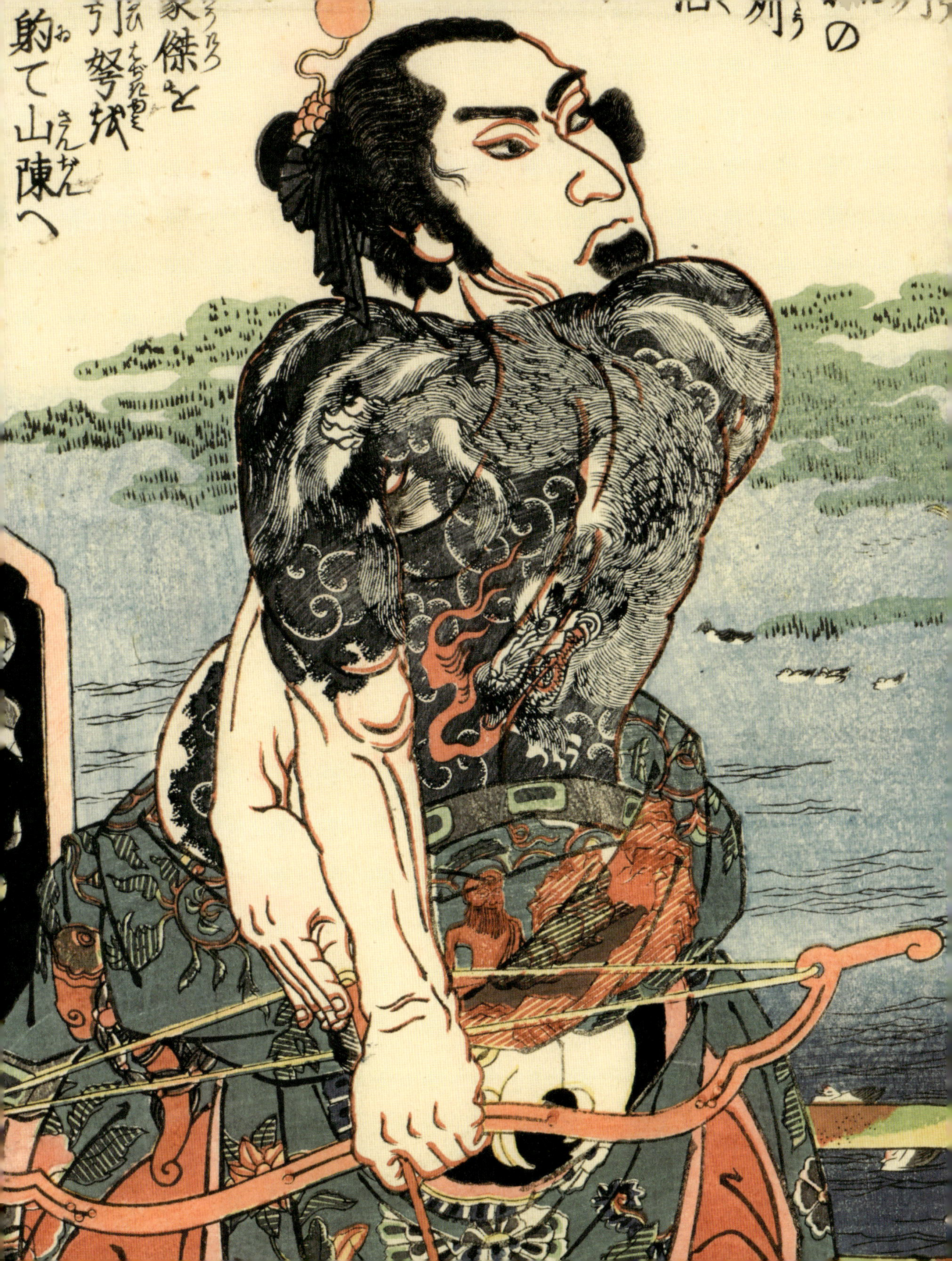

家傑を
引弩城
躬て山
陳へ

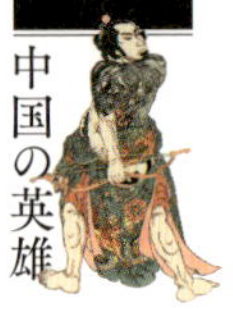

水中戦では負け知らず

張順

Zhang Shun
Heroes of China

160

『水滸伝』の登場人物。魚問屋の主人であったが、梁山泊入りし、水軍の頭領として活躍した。その肌は雪よりも白く、浪裏をひらりと跳ぶ魚のように泳ぎの達人であったという。敵軍が杭州城に立て籠もったため、水門を潜って敵陣に単独で侵入するが、そこには鉄格子が張られていた。最後は敵に見つかり無数の矢を浴びて、壮絶な死を迎える。

This former fishmonger served as the leader of marine forces after the joining the outlaws of Mount Liang in *The Water Margin*. His skin was whiter than snow, and he was able to leap from wave to wave while swimming like a fish. When enemy forces were holed up inside Hangzhou, Zhang Shun attempted to sneak alone beyond the city walls through a sluice gate, but finds it to be made of steel, whereupon he is spotted by his enemies and riddled with arrows.

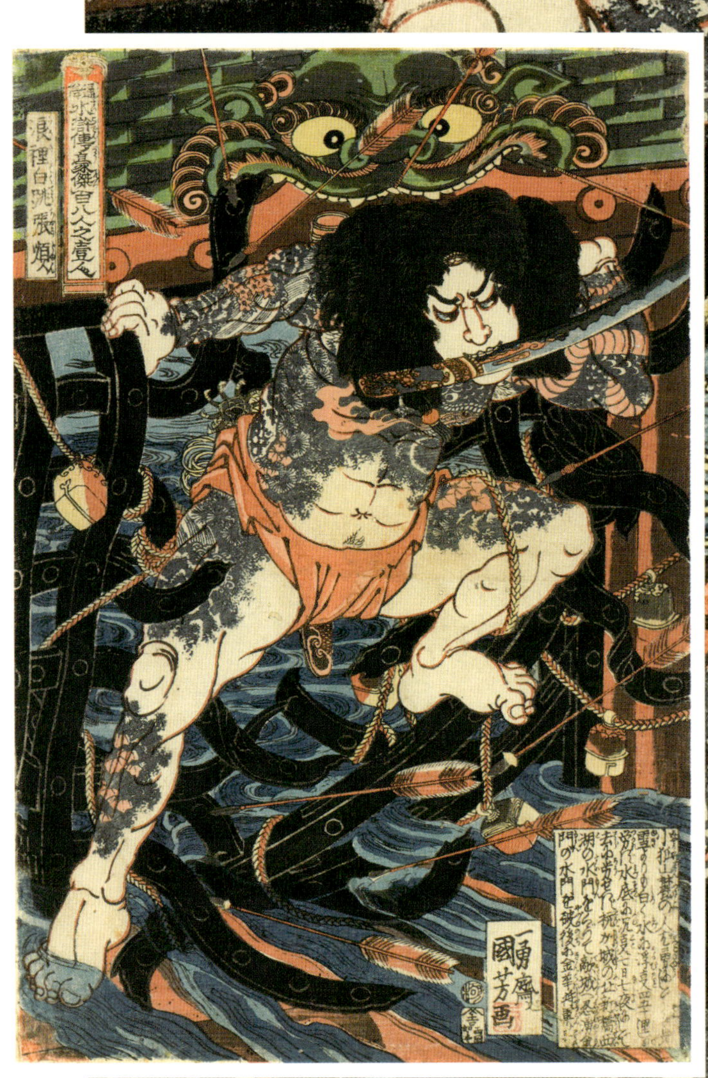

【通俗水滸伝豪傑百八人之壹人 浪裡白跳張順】
歌川国芳 文政11〜12年（1828-29）頃
"108 Heroes of the Water Margin:
The White Stripe in the Waves, Zhang Shun"
by Utagawa Kuniyoshi

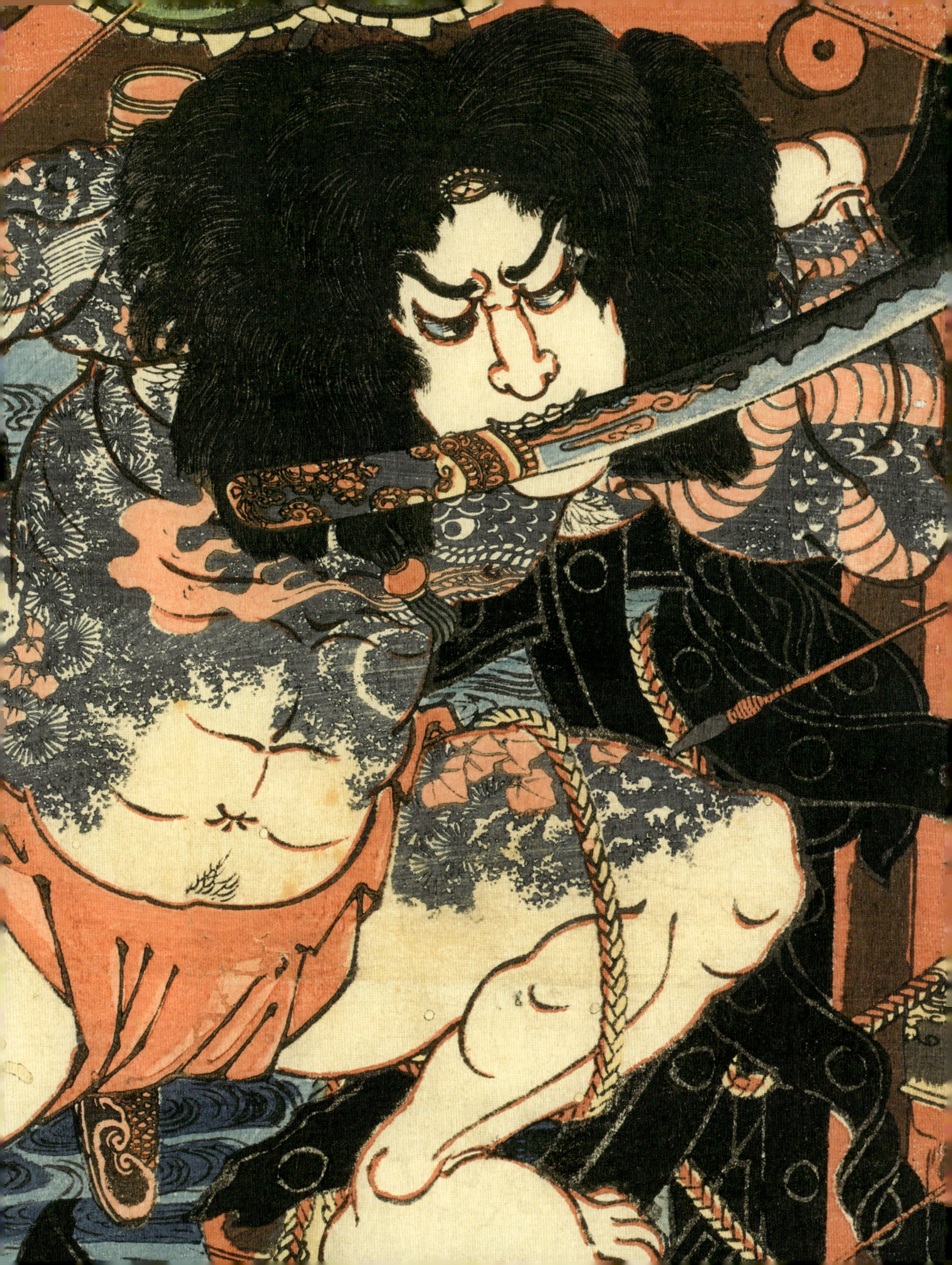

怪力自慢の黒旋風

李逵

Li Ku
Heroes of China

『水滸伝』の登場人物。二つの斧を振り回して敵をなぎ倒す荒くれ者。その威力は黒いつむじ風を起こすほどであることから、黒旋風と呼ばれた。獰猛な性格であるが、情に厚い。謀反の罪で捕らわれた兄貴分の宗江を救うため、刑場に乗り込み、役人、兵隊だけでなく、野次馬をも手当たり次第斬り倒していった。

This ruffian of a man, a character from *The Water Margin*, mowed down his enemies with a pair of axes. He gained the nickname Black Whirlwind from the fact that his fighting was so wild that it kicked up black dust devils. Though rough in temper, he was also warm-hearted toward his friends. When Song Jiang, leader of the outlaws, is imprisoned for treason, Li Kui sneaks into the prison where he is held and cuts down guards, soldiers, bystanders, and anyone else he can get his hands on.

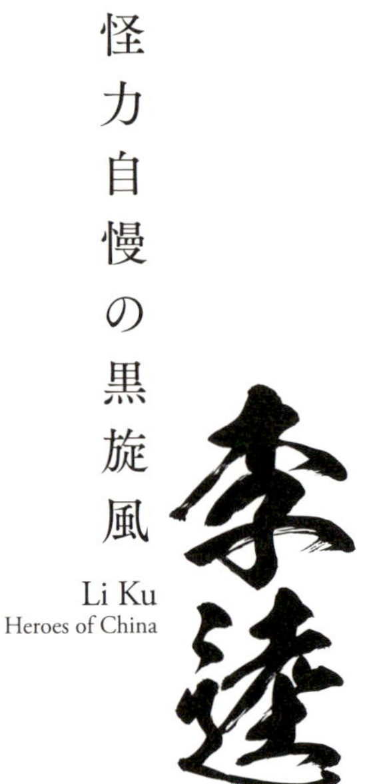

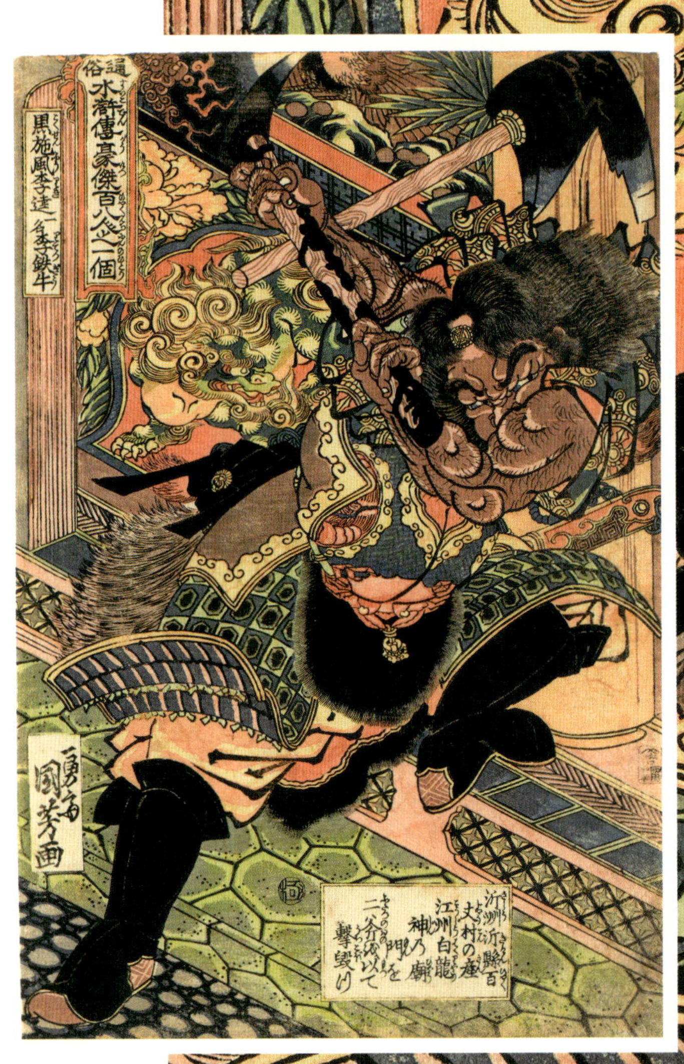

【通俗水滸伝豪傑百八人之一個
　黒旋風李逵 一名 李鉄牛】歌川国芳　文政10年（1827）頃

"108 Heroes of the Water Margin:
The Black Whirlwind, Li Kui, also known as the Iron Ox"
by Utagawa Kuniyoshi

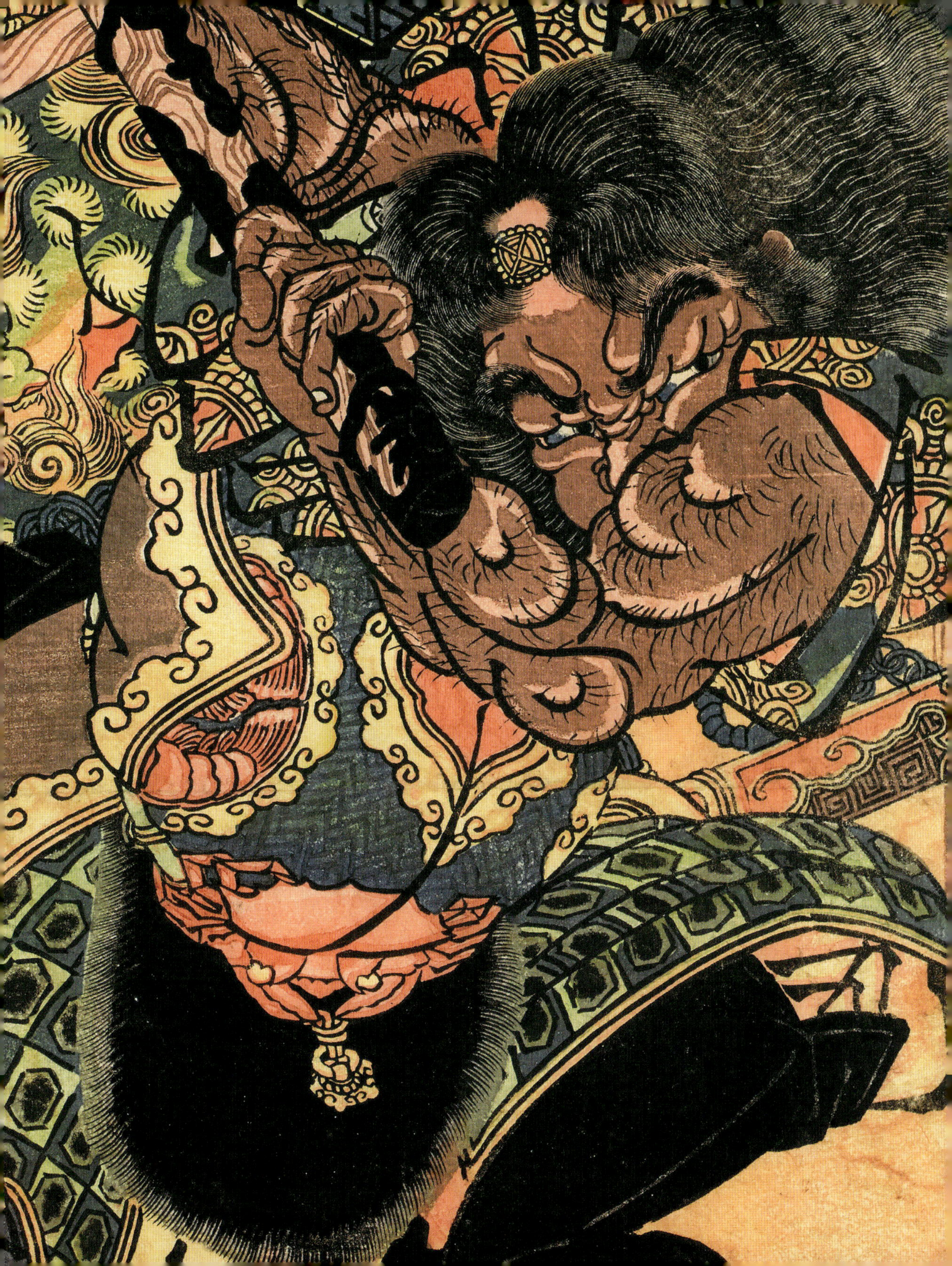

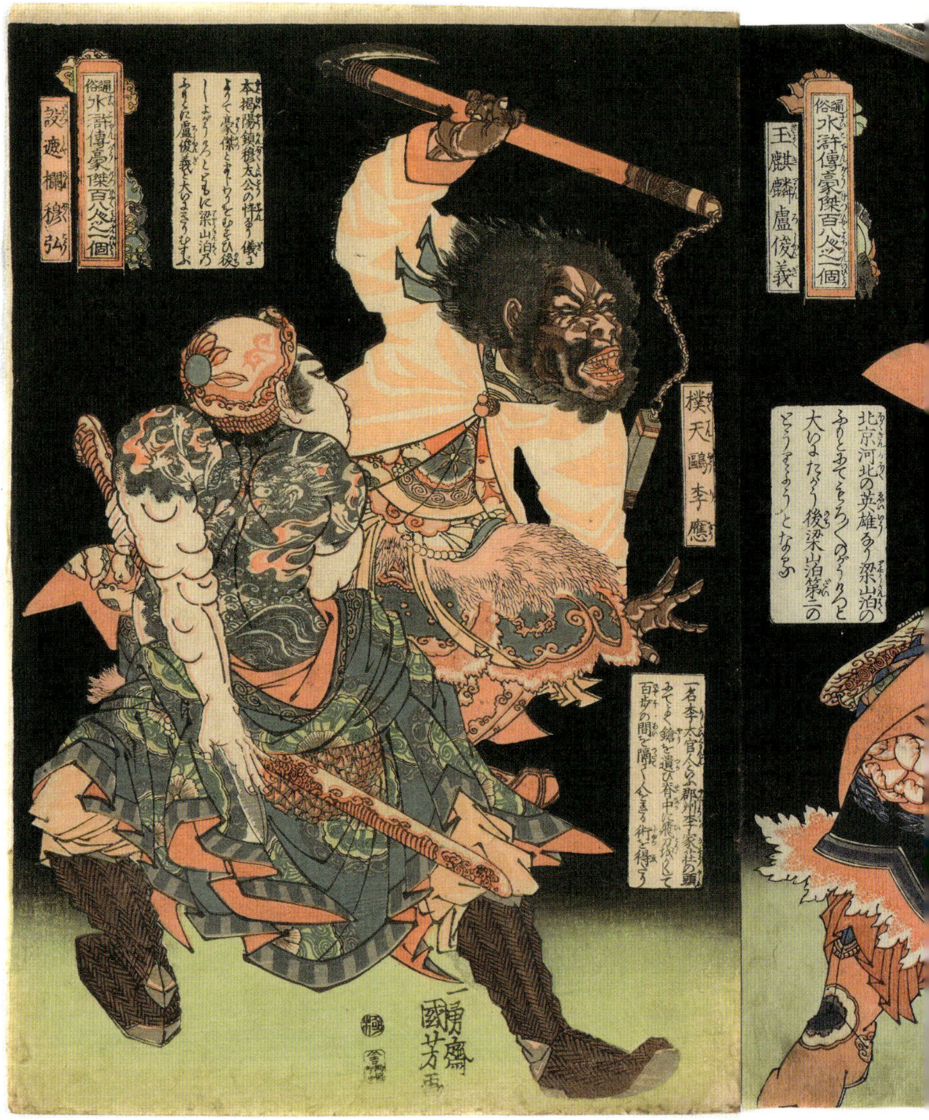

中国の英雄

梁山泊の好漢たち

李応
穆弘

Lu Junyi, Liu Tang, Li Ying, and Mu Hong
Heroes of China

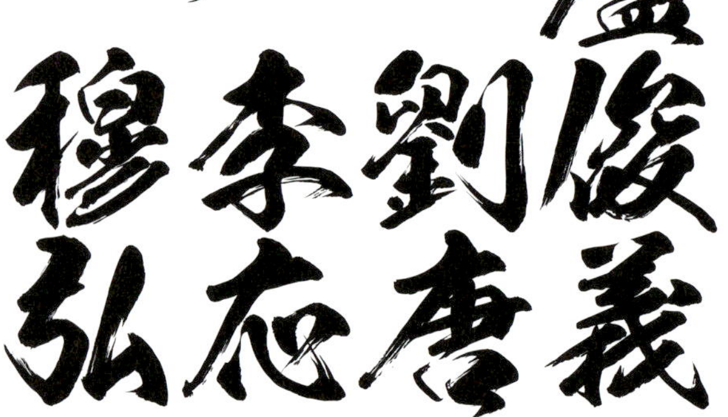

穆　李　劉　盧
弘　応　唐　俊
　　　　　　義

『水滸伝』の登場人物。武闘派の資産家盧俊義は、易者に変装した呉用に仕向けられ旅に出る。森の近くを盧俊義が通りかかったところ、梁山泊の豪傑たちが次々と襲ってきた。森の奥へと追いやられた盧俊義は、劉唐・李応・穆弘の三人に取り囲まれ、とうとう生け捕りにされた。実はこれは盧俊義を仲間に迎え入れるための計略であった。

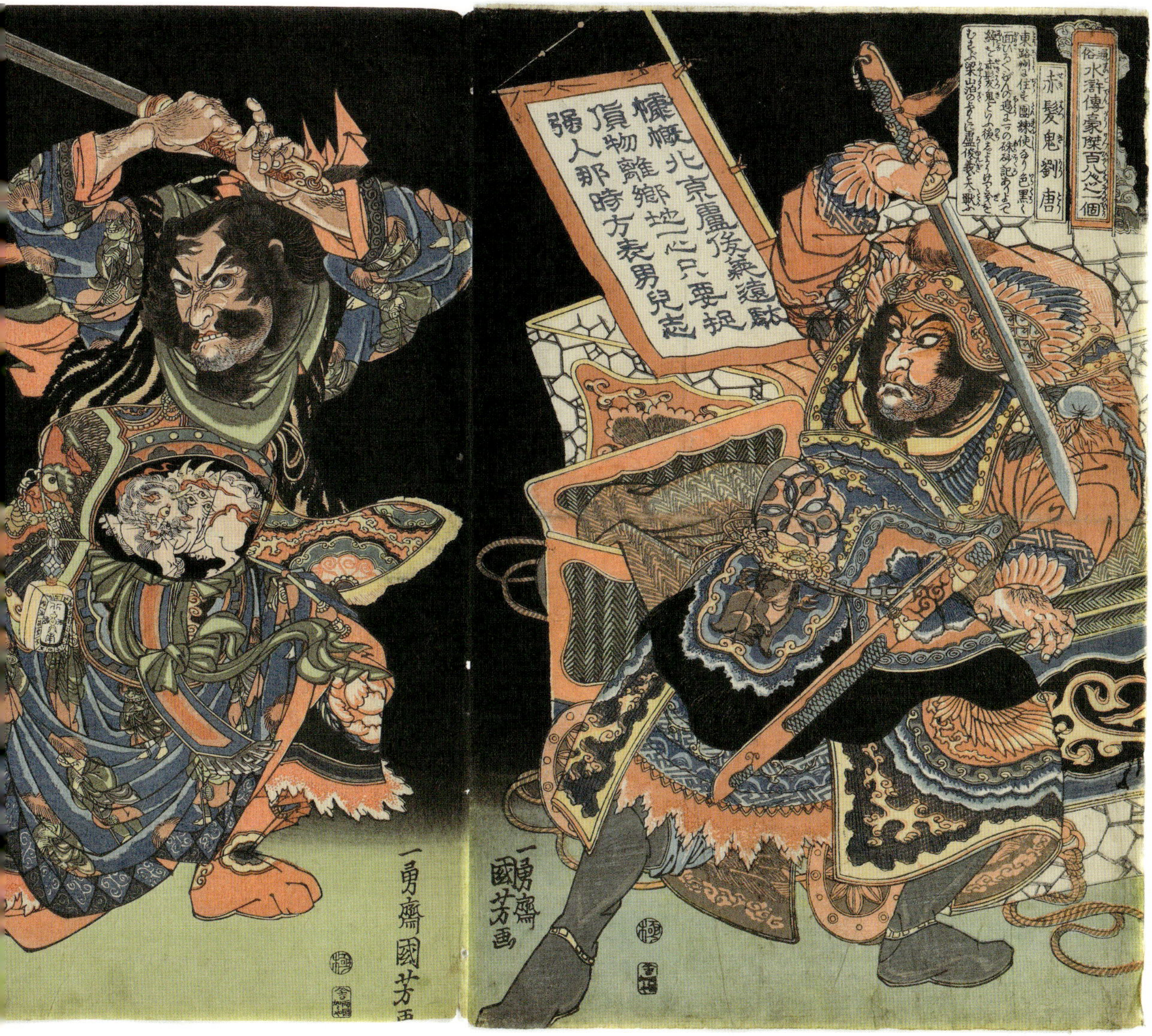

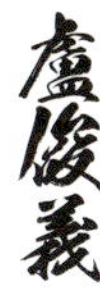

[左]【通俗水滸伝豪傑百八人之一個 設遮攔穆弘 撲天鵰李応】歌川国芳 文政11〜12年(1828-29)頃

"108 Heroes of the Water Margin: The Unrestrained, Mu Hong" by Utagawa Kuniyoshi

[中]【通俗水滸伝豪傑百八人之一個 玉麒麟盧俊義】歌川国芳 文政11〜12年(1828-29)頃

"108 Heroes of the Water Margin: The Jade Qilin, Lu Junyi" by Utagawa Kuniyoshi

[右]【通俗水滸伝豪傑百八人之一個 赤髪鬼劉唐】歌川国芳 文政11〜12年(1828-29)頃

"108 Heroes of the Water Margin: The Red-Haired Devil, Liu Tang" by Utagawa Kuniyoshi

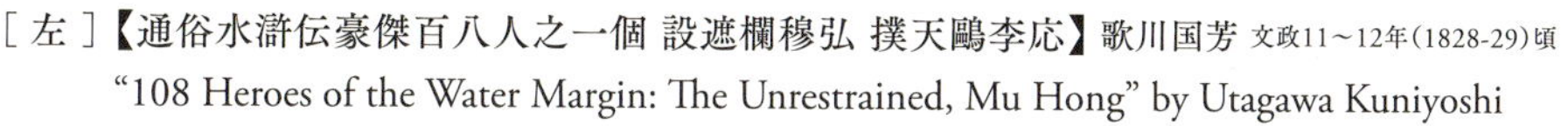
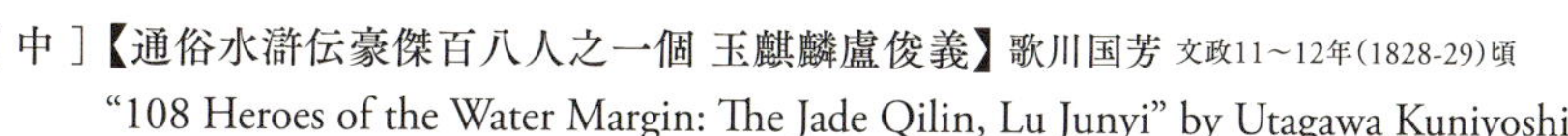
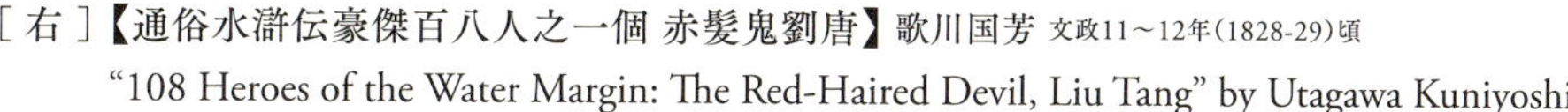

In *The Water Margin*, Lu Junyi is a wealthy squire who is adept at martial arts. Wu Yong disguises himself as a fortune teller and instructs Lu Junyi to go on a long trip, whereupon the latter is ambushed by the outlaws near Liangshan Marsh. Fleeing into the woods, Lu Junyi is surrounded and taken alive by Liu Tang, Li Ying, and Mu Hong – which is all just a ruse to get Lu Junyi to join the outlaws.

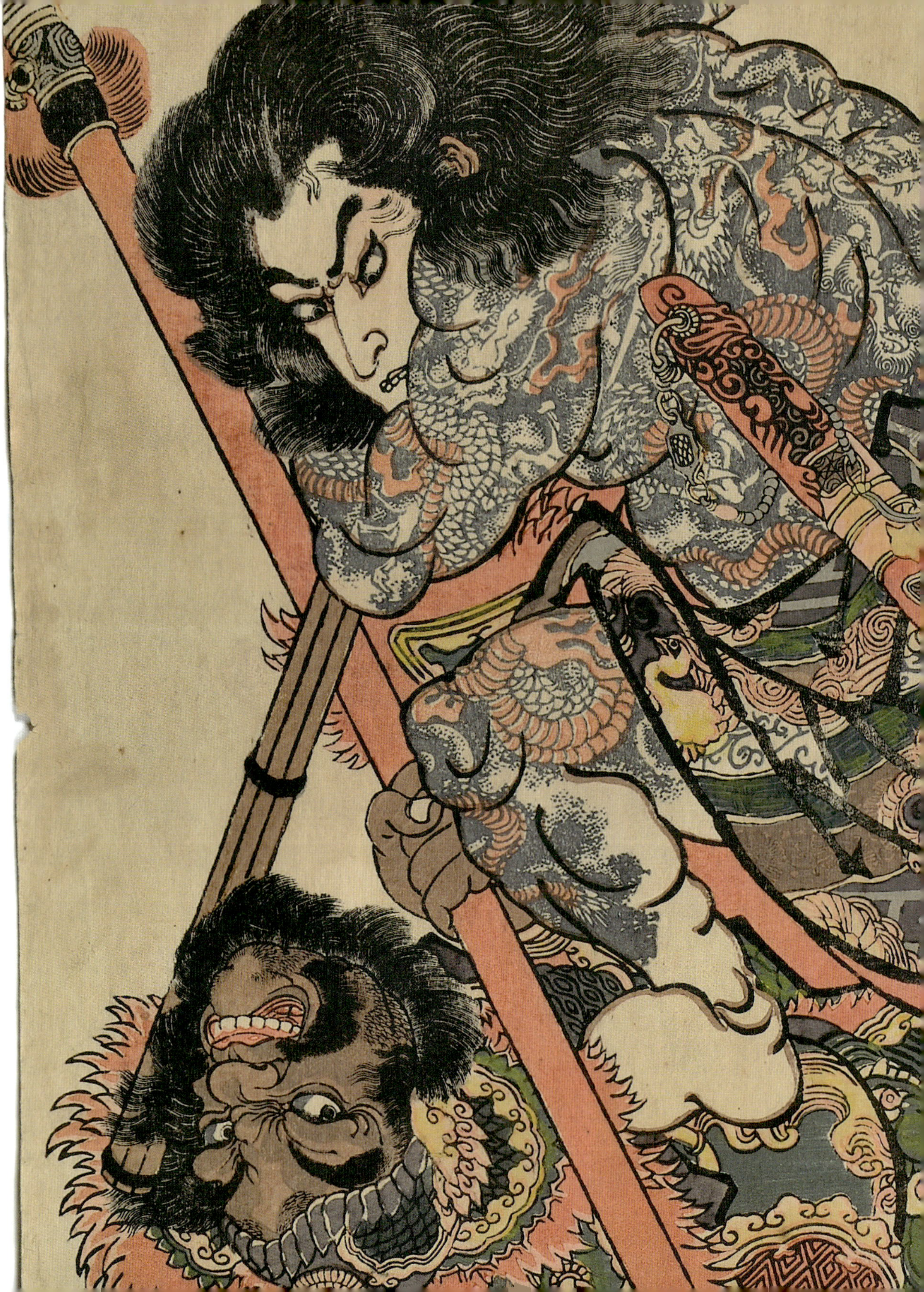

Shi Jin and Chen Da
Heroes of China

史進 陳達

167

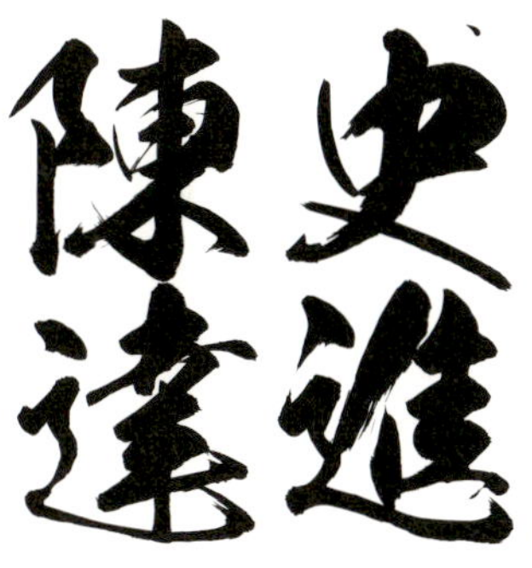

『水滸伝』の登場人物。史進は九龍の彫物があったことから、九紋龍と呼ばれる。大庄屋の子であったが、禁軍の王進に武芸を教わる。あるとき、少華山の山賊陳達と一騎打ちになり、これを打ち負かすが、以降、懇意になり史進は少華山の頭領となる。のち、華州で捕らえられていたところを梁山泊の呉用らに救われ、仲間入りした。

In *The Water Margin*, Shi Jin is known as the "Nine-Tattoo Dragon" because his torso is tattooed with nine different dragons. The son of a village headman, Shi Jin learns martial arts from the exiled Wang Jin. When Chen Da and the horseback bandits of Mount Shaohua attempt to ransack his village, Shi Jin defeats Chen Da, but subsequently becomes his friend and then leader of the bandits. Later, Shi Jin is captured in Huazhou, rescued by the Mount Liang outlaws, and joins their team.

【通俗水滸伝豪傑百八人之一個 九紋龍史進 跳澗虎陳達】
歌川国芳 文政10年（1827）頃
"108 Heroes of the Water Margin: The Nine-Tattoo Dragon, Shi Jin, and the Stream Leaping Tiger, Chen Da" by Utagawa Kuniyoshi

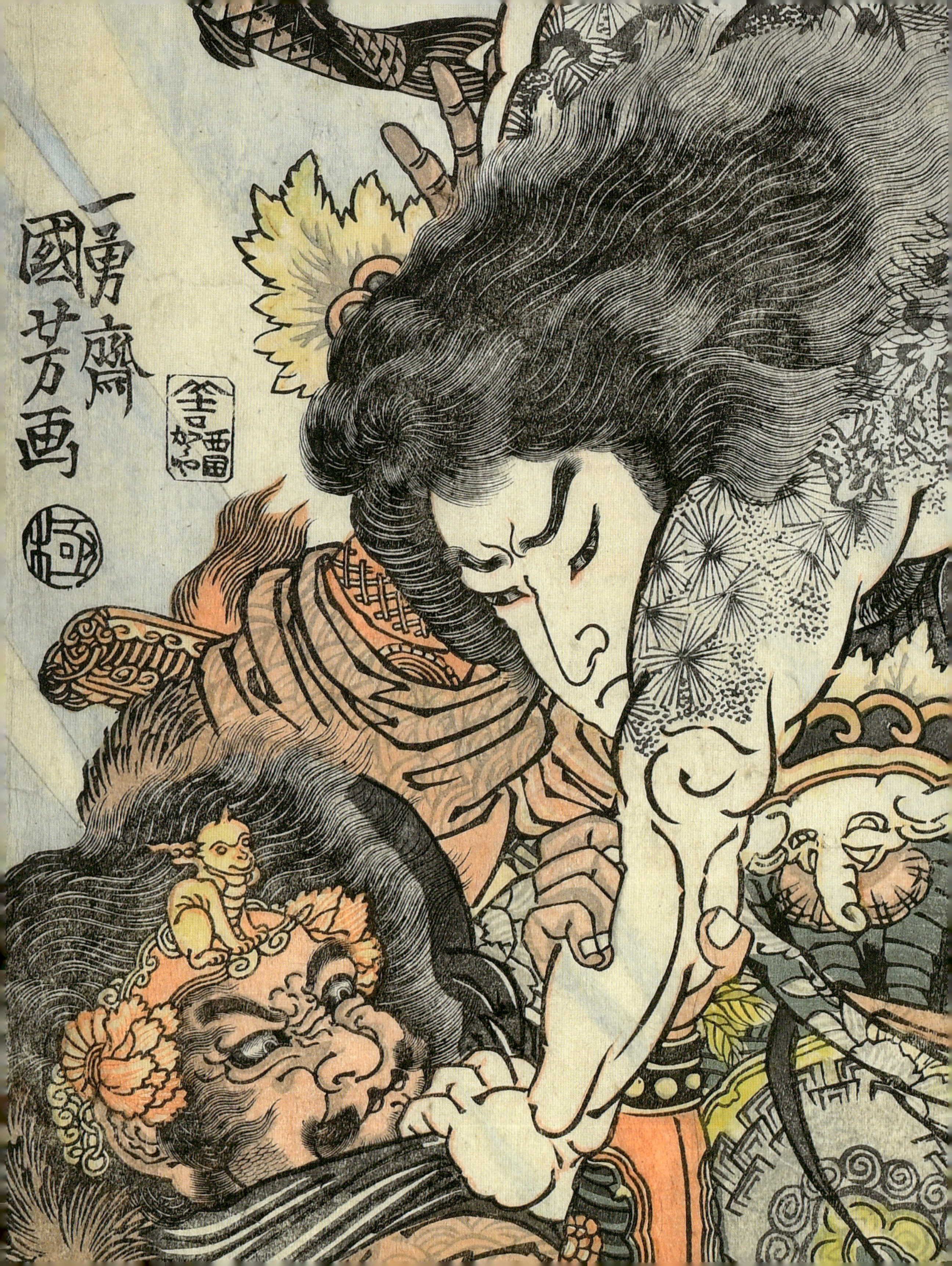

一勇齋
國芳画

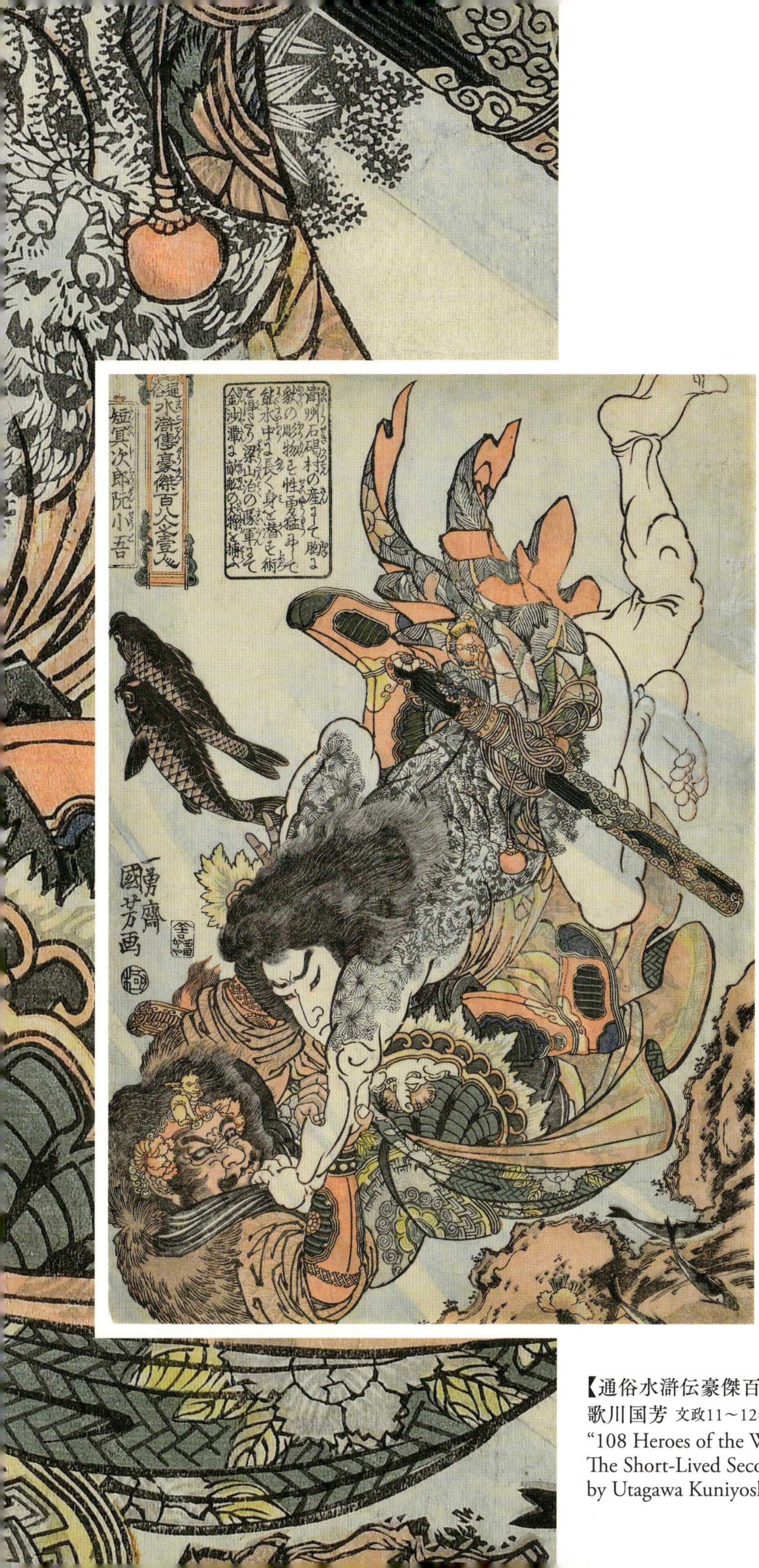

義俠心溢れる益荒男

阮小吾

Ruan Xiaowu
Heroes of China

『水滸伝』の登場人物。阮三兄弟の次男で、兄の阮小二、弟の阮小七とともに漁師をしていた。泳ぎに長じ、胸には豹の彫物がある。梁山泊に入って水軍の頭領として活躍し、出会った相手が短命となるため短命二郎と呼ばれた。済州の兵が船で梁山泊に攻め込んだ際、阮兄弟はそれぞれ船を操って敵船を金沙潭の入江に誘い込み、全滅させた。

Ruan Xiaowu is the second of the three Ruan Brothers in *The Water Margin*. Like his elder brother Xiaoer and his younger brother Xiaoqi, Xiaowu is a fisherman with amazing swimming skills. He has a leopard tattoo on his chest. As leader of the marine forces of the Mount Liang outlaws, he gains the name Short-Lived Second Son because any enemy who challenges him should expect a short life. When the Jizhou armies attempt to invade the Liangshan stronghold by ship, the Ruan Brothers each command a boat to lure their enemies to annihilation at Jinsha Lake.

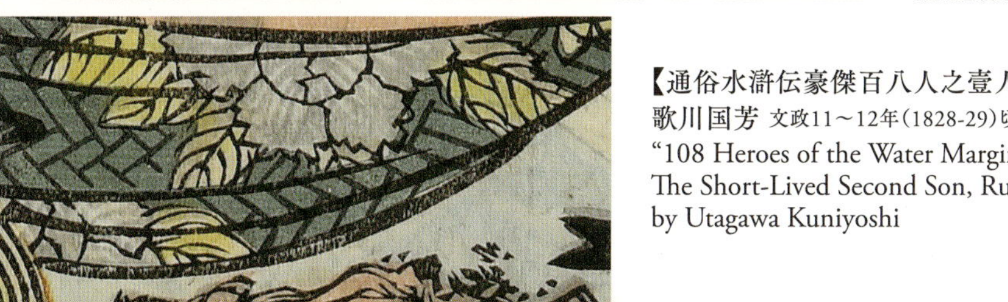

【通俗水滸伝豪傑百八人之壹人 短冥次郎阮小吾】
歌川国芳 文政11〜12年（1828-29）頃
"108 Heroes of the Water Margin:
The Short-Lived Second Son, Ruan Xiaowu"
by Utagawa Kuniyoshi

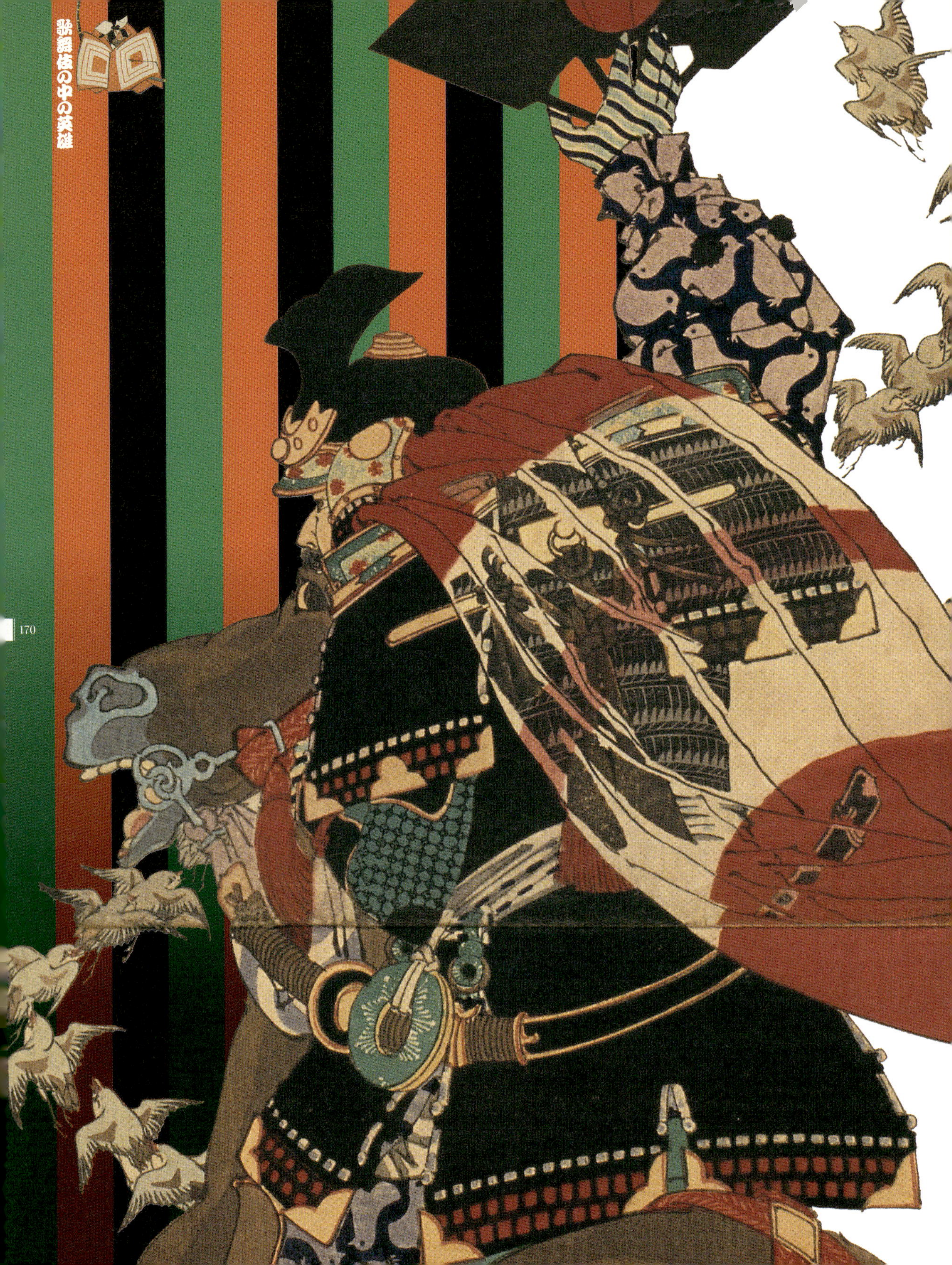

Kumagai Naozane
and Taira no Atsumori
lead character in the kabuki

熊谷直実 平敦盛

【歌舞伎ドラマの花形】
美しき若武者の最期

ともに平安時代末期の武将。熊谷直実ははじめ平氏に
仕えたが、のちに源氏に従った。一ノ谷の戦いで、奇襲
に敗れた平氏は海上に逃れるが、若武者平敦盛は逃げ
遅れてしまう。敵方の熊谷直実に呼び止められ、組合い
となり討たれた。笛の名手であった敦盛は、このとき祖父
が鳥羽院から賜った名笛「小枝」を身に携えていたとい
う。まだ16歳であった。これに無常を感じた直実は出家
し、敦盛の霊を弔った。

Both warriors of the late Heian period, Kumagai Naozane
originally served the Taira before joining the Minamato
clan. The Taira managed to escape to the sea after being
defeated at the Battle of Ichinotani, but left behind the
young Taira no Atsumori, who was killed by Naozane. It is
said that, at the time of his death, Atsumori, an exceptional
flutist, had on him a famous flute named Little Branch, a
gift from Retired Emperor Toba to his grandfather Taira no
Tadamori. Discovering this after killing Atsumori, who was
only sixteen at the time, Naozane quit military service and
prayed for Atsumori's soul.

【一之谷合戦】月岡芳年 明治18年（1885）

"The Battle of Ichinotani" (1885)
by Tsukioka Yoshitoshi

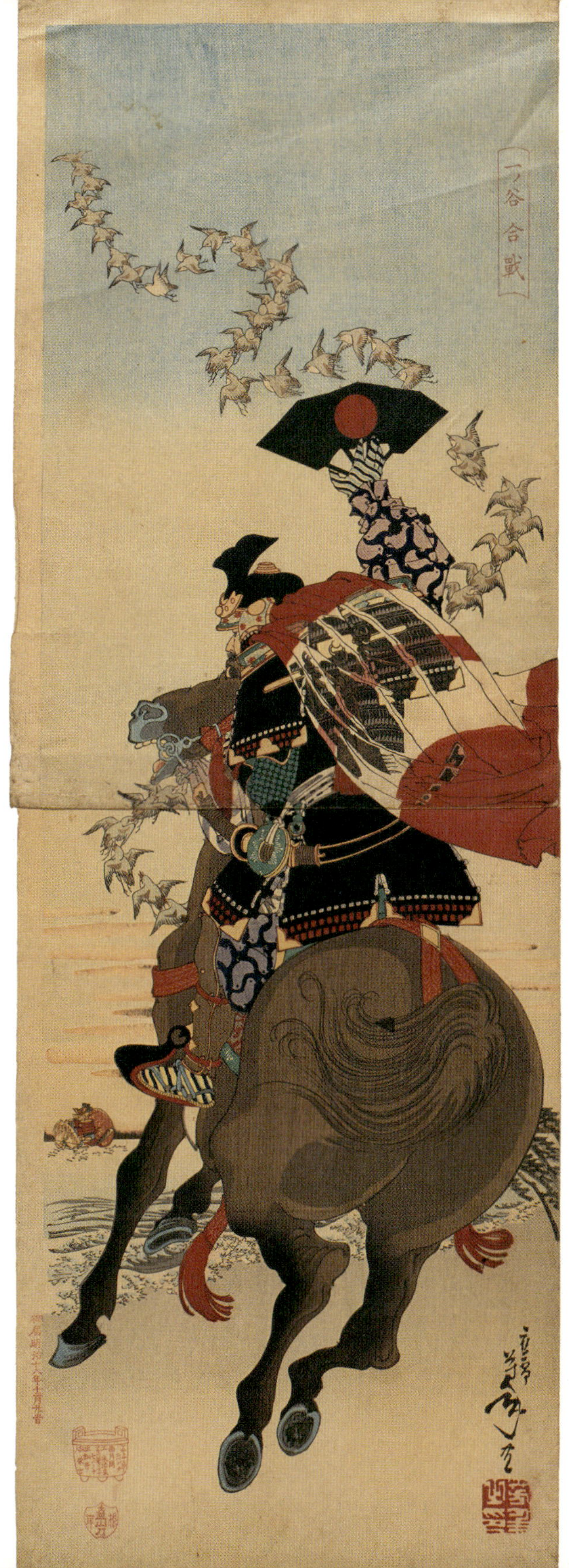

171

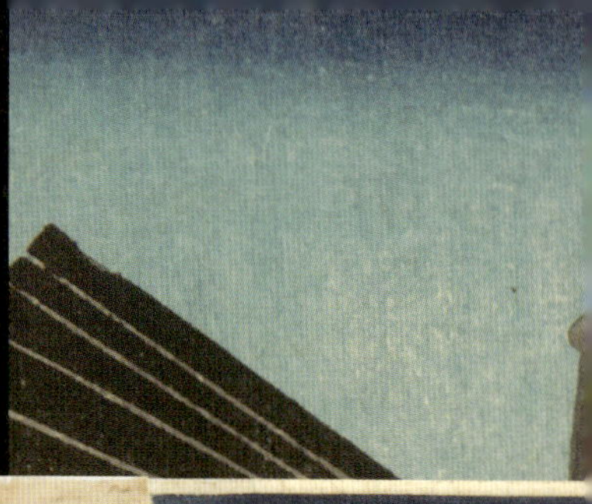

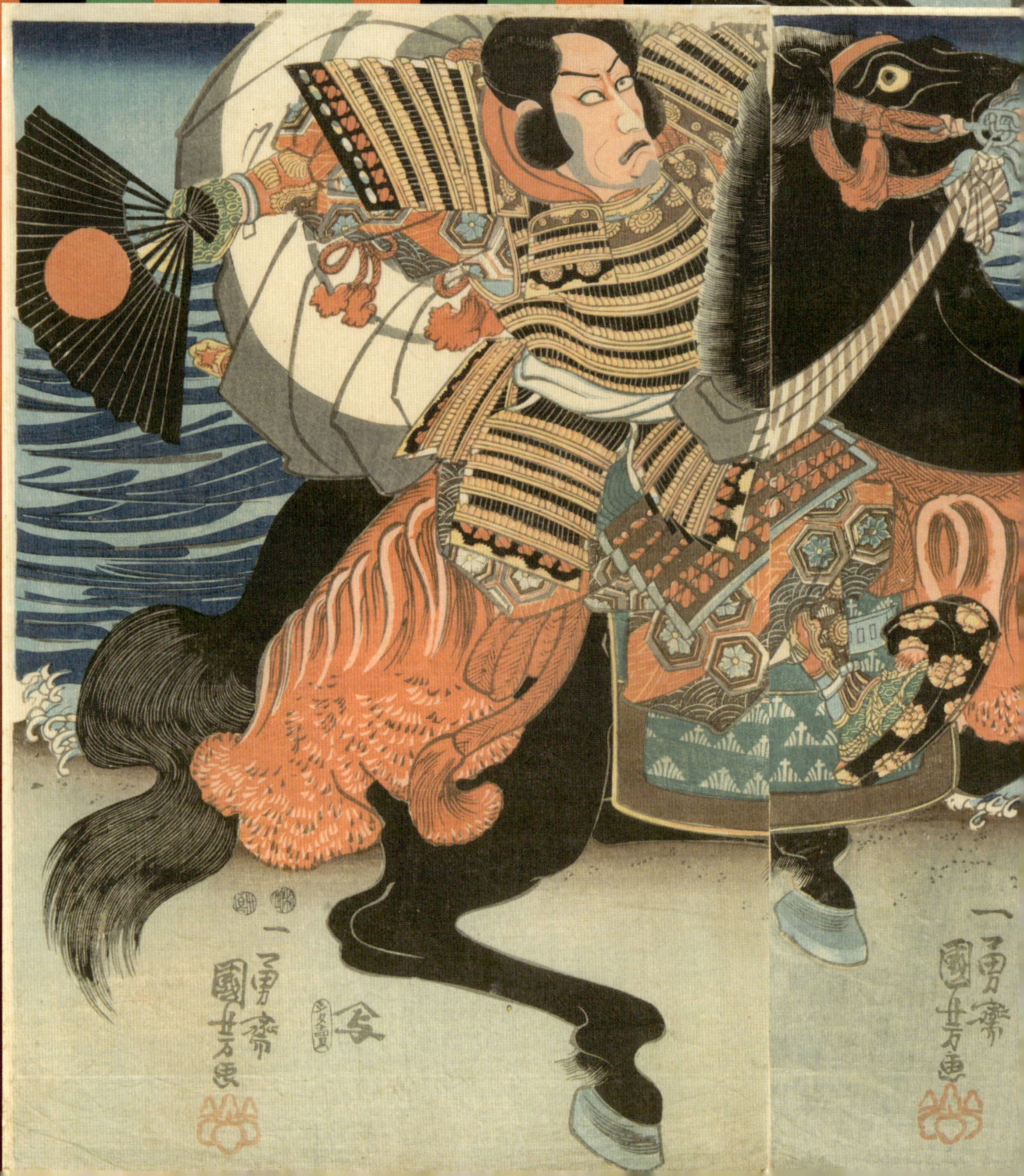

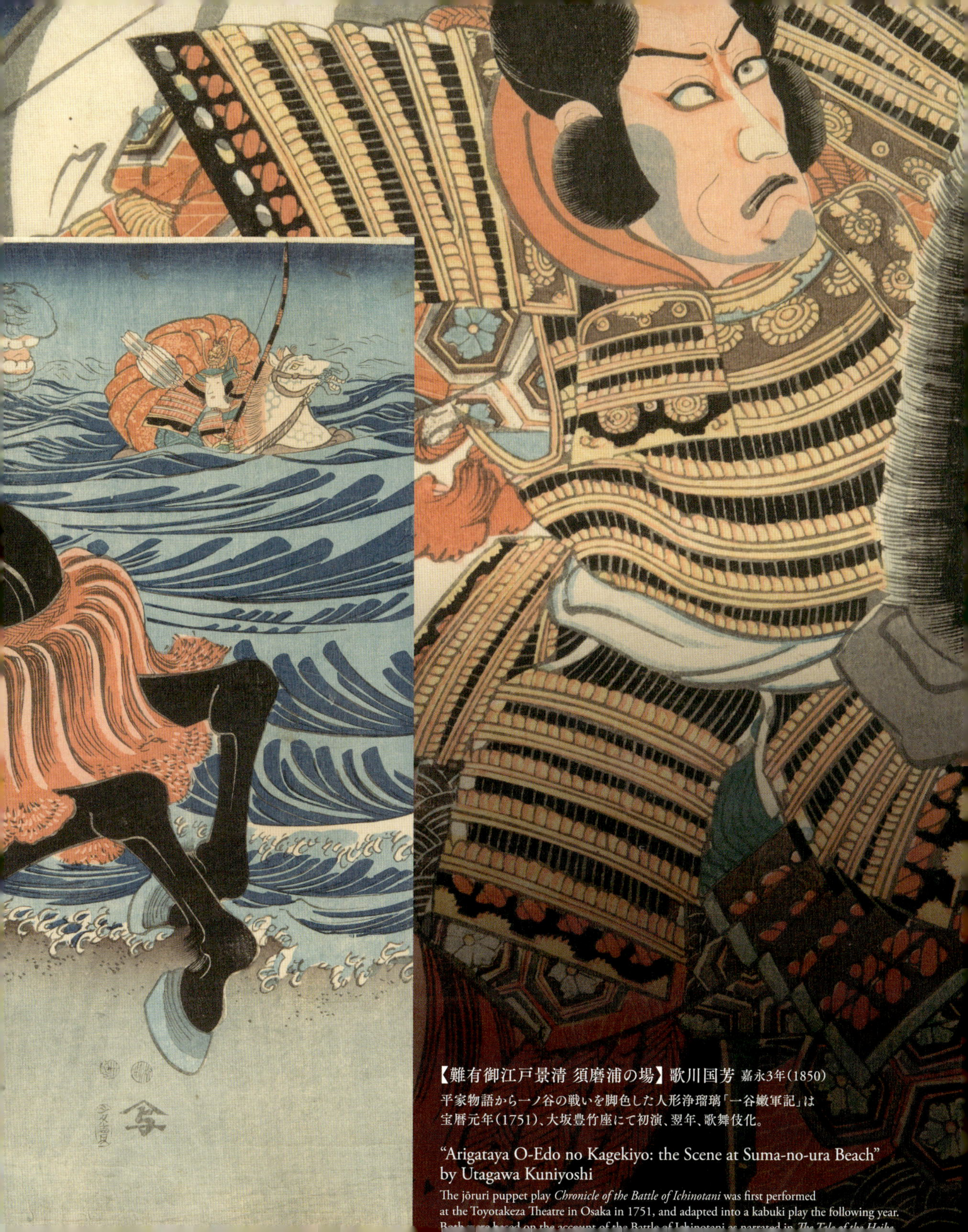

【難有御江戸景清 須磨浦の場】歌川国芳　嘉永3年（1850）
平家物語から一ノ谷の戦いを脚色した人形浄瑠璃「一谷嫩軍記」は
宝暦元年（1751）、大坂豊竹座にて初演、翌年、歌舞伎化。

"Arigataya O-Edo no Kagekiyo: the Scene at Suma-no-ura Beach"
by Utagawa Kuniyoshi

The jōruri puppet play *Chronicle of the Battle of Ichinotani* was first performed
at the Toyotakeza Theatre in Osaka in 1751, and adapted into a kabuki play the following year.
Both were based on the account of the Battle of Ichinotani as narrated in *The Tale of the Heike*.

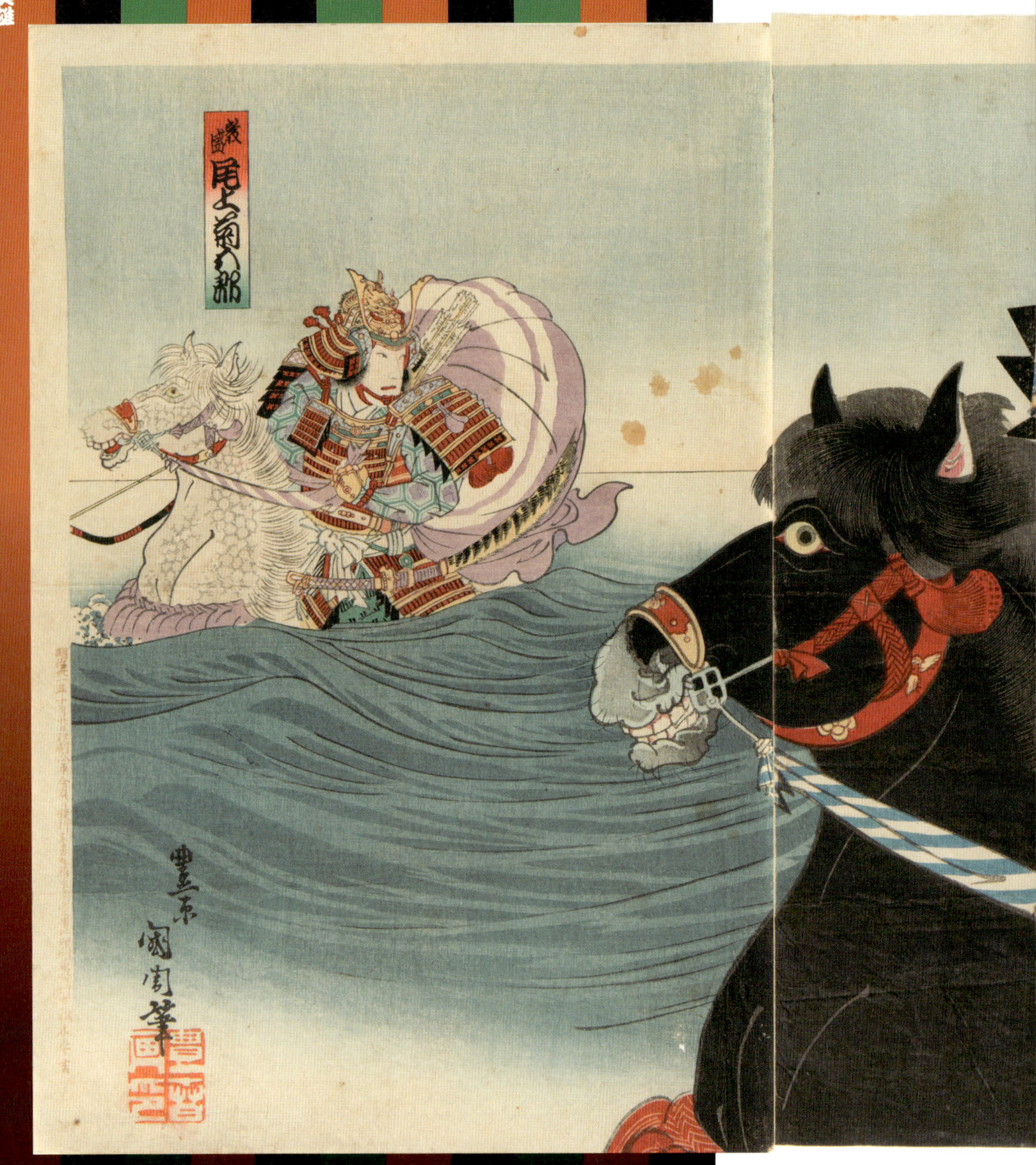

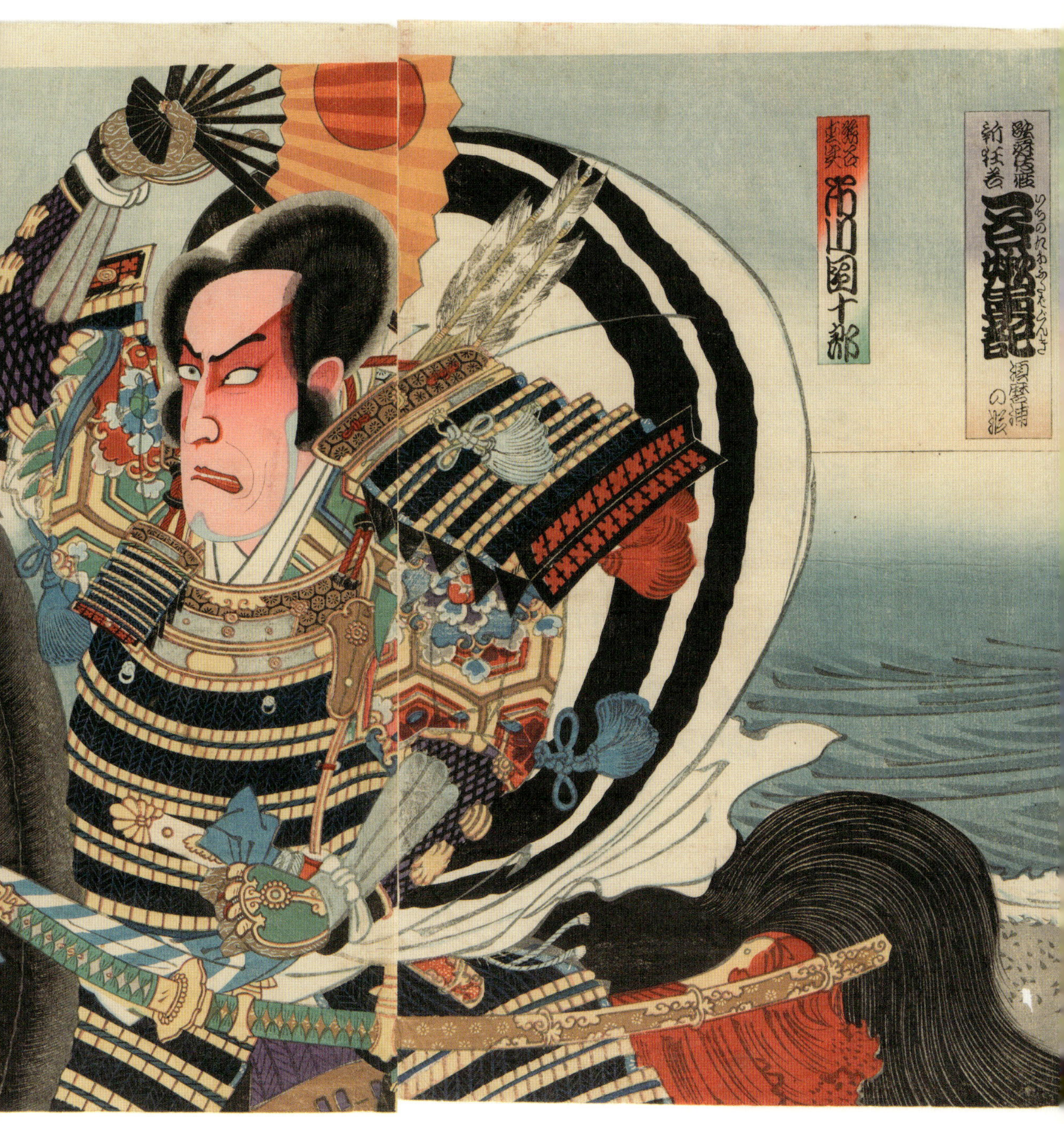

【歌舞伎座新狂言 一谷嫩軍記 須磨浦の段】豊原国周 明治31年（1898）
"New Kyōgen of the Kabuki Stage: Chronicle of the Battle of Ichinotani, Suma Beach" by Toyohara Kunichika

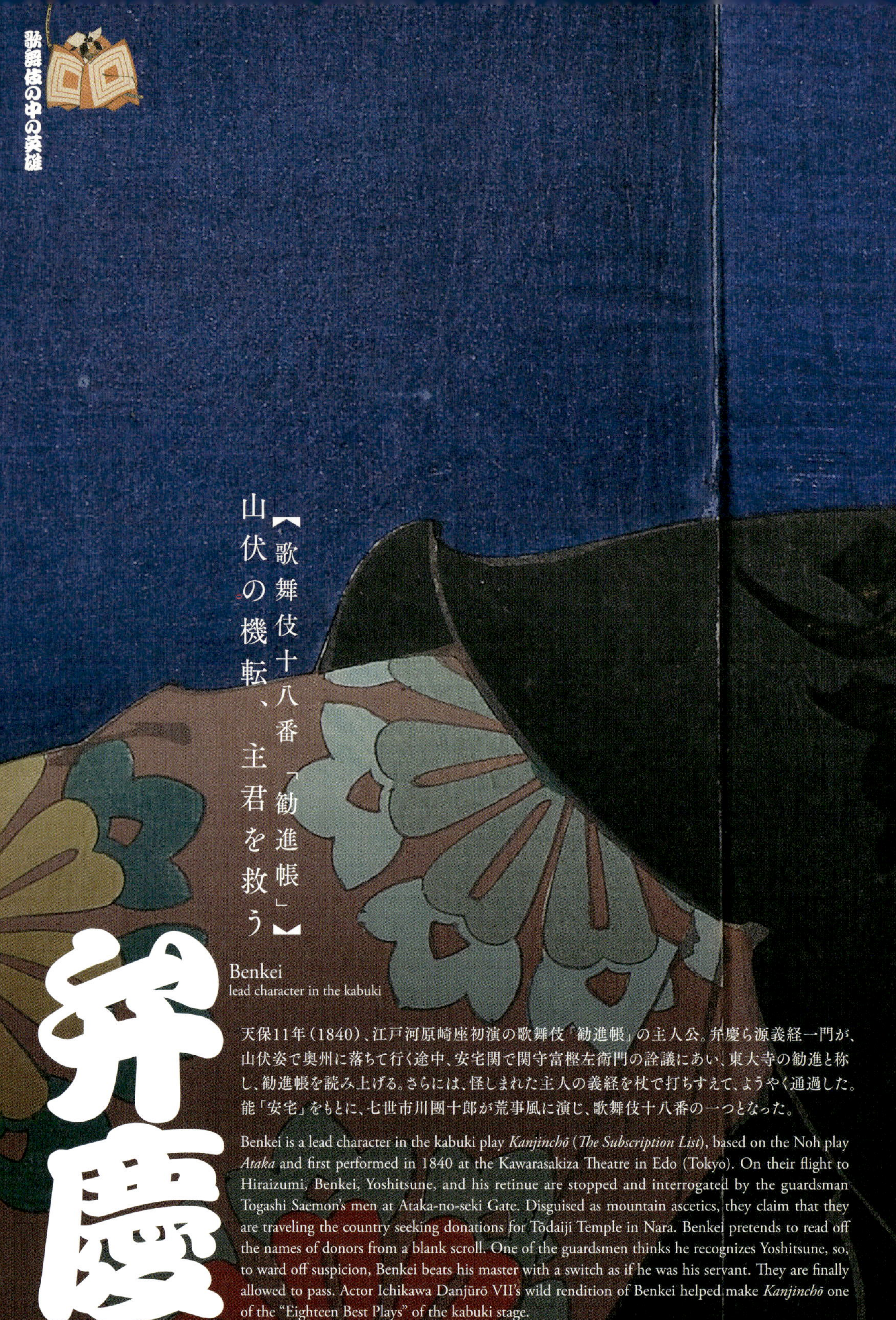

山伏の機転、主君を救う【歌舞伎十八番「勧進帳」】

Benkei
lead character in the kabuki

天保11年（1840）、江戸河原崎座初演の歌舞伎「勧進帳」の主人公。弁慶ら源義経一門が、山伏姿で奥州に落ちて行く途中、安宅関で関守富樫左衛門の詮議にあい、東大寺の勧進と称し、勧進帳を読み上げる。さらには、怪しまれた主人の義経を杖で打ちすえて、ようやく通過した。能「安宅」をもとに、七世市川團十郎が荒事風に演じ、歌舞伎十八番の一つとなった。

Benkei is a lead character in the kabuki play *Kanjinchō* (*The Subscription List*), based on the Noh play *Ataka* and first performed in 1840 at the Kawarasakiza Theatre in Edo (Tokyo). On their flight to Hiraizumi, Benkei, Yoshitsune, and his retinue are stopped and interrogated by the guardsman Togashi Saemon's men at Ataka-no-seki Gate. Disguised as mountain ascetics, they claim that they are traveling the country seeking donations for Tōdaiji Temple in Nara. Benkei pretends to read off the names of donors from a blank scroll. One of the guardsmen thinks he recognizes Yoshitsune, so, to ward off suspicion, Benkei beats his master with a switch as if he was his servant. They are finally allowed to pass. Actor Ichikawa Danjūrō VII's wild rendition of Benkei helped make *Kanjinchō* one of the "Eighteen Best Plays" of the kabuki stage.

弁慶

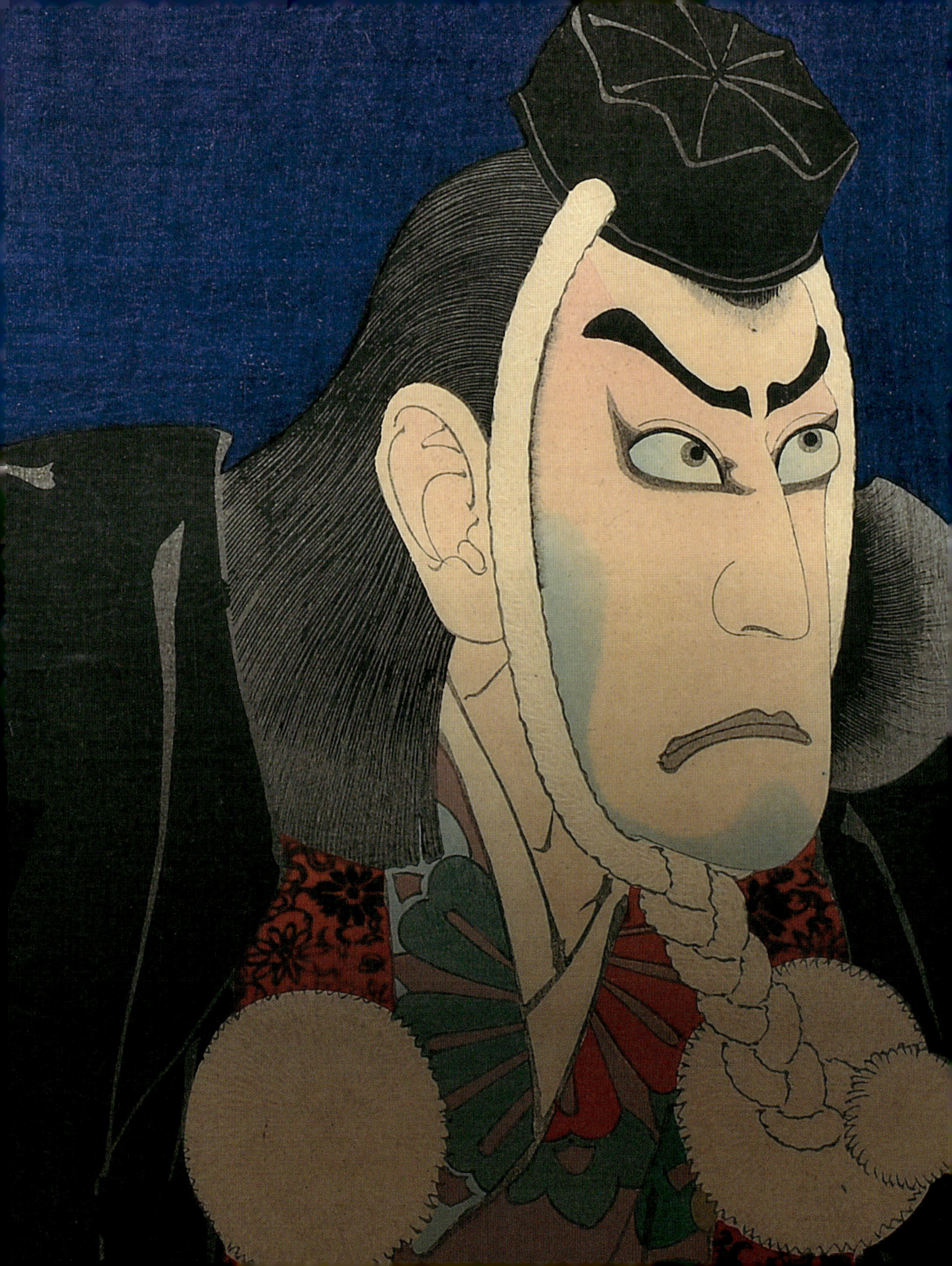

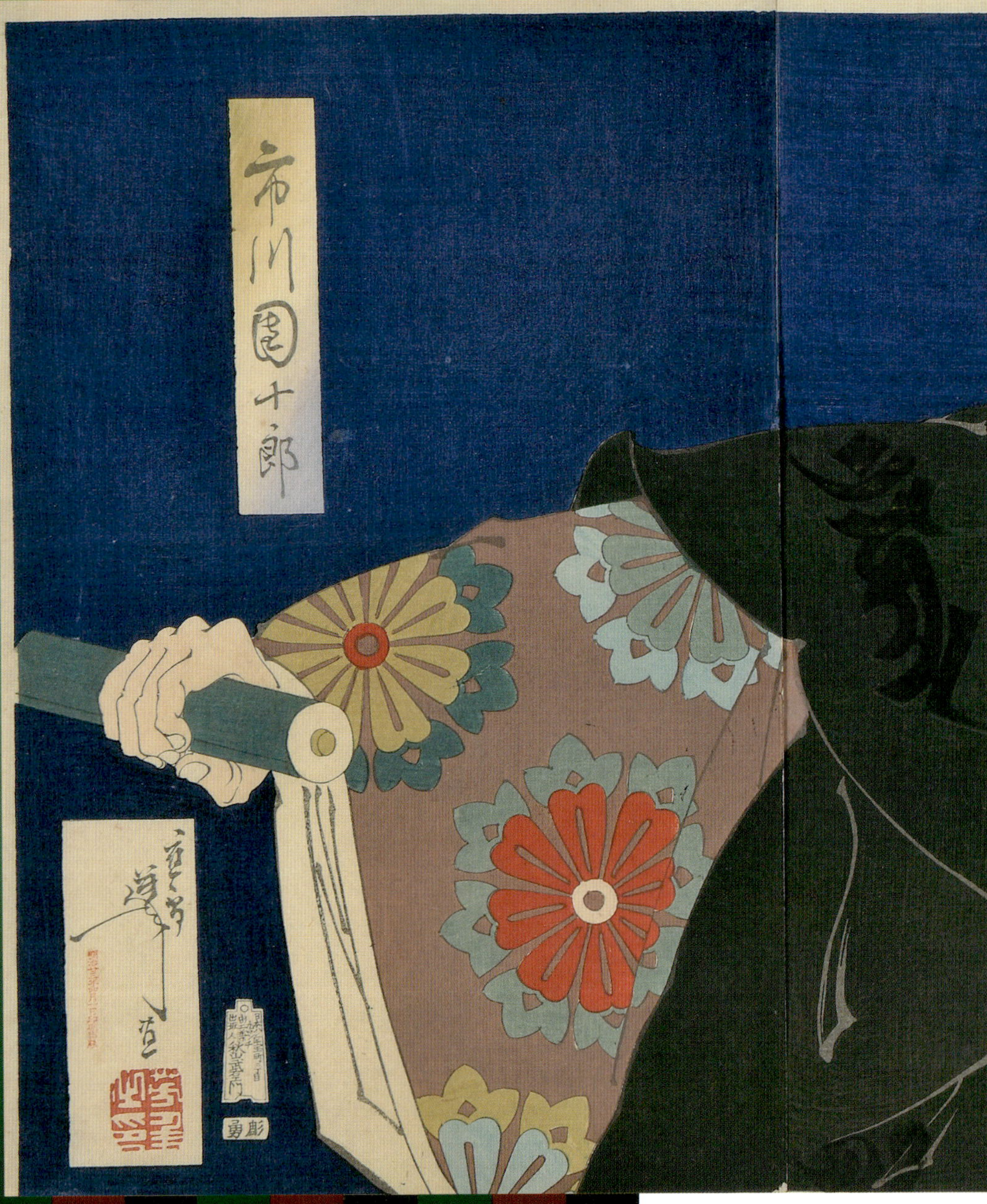
市川團十郎

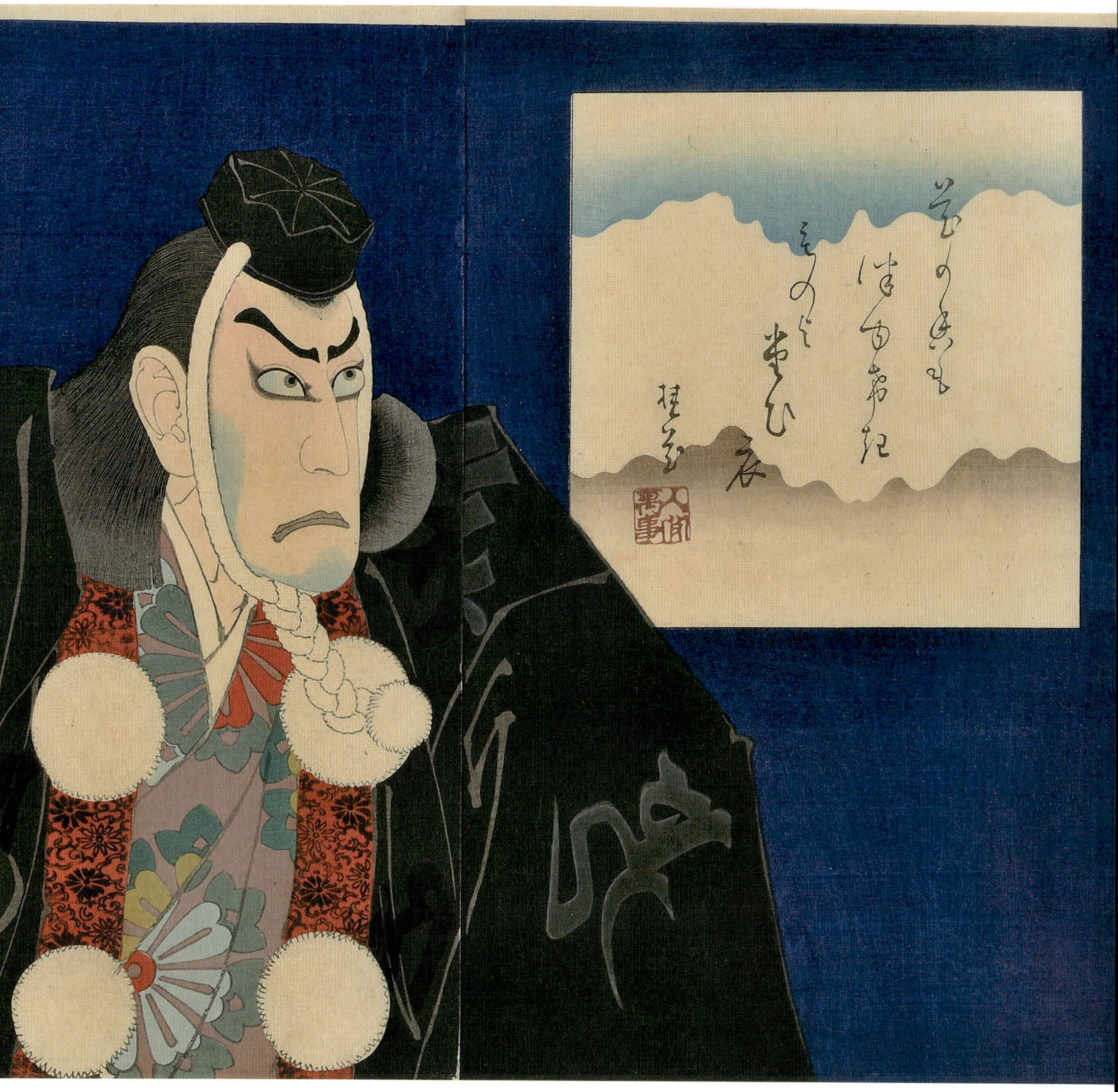

【弁慶 九代目市川團十郎】月岡芳年 明治23年（1890）
"Benkei, as played by Ichikawa Danjūrō IX" by Tsukioka Yoshitoshi

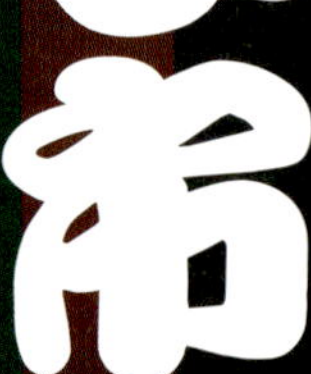

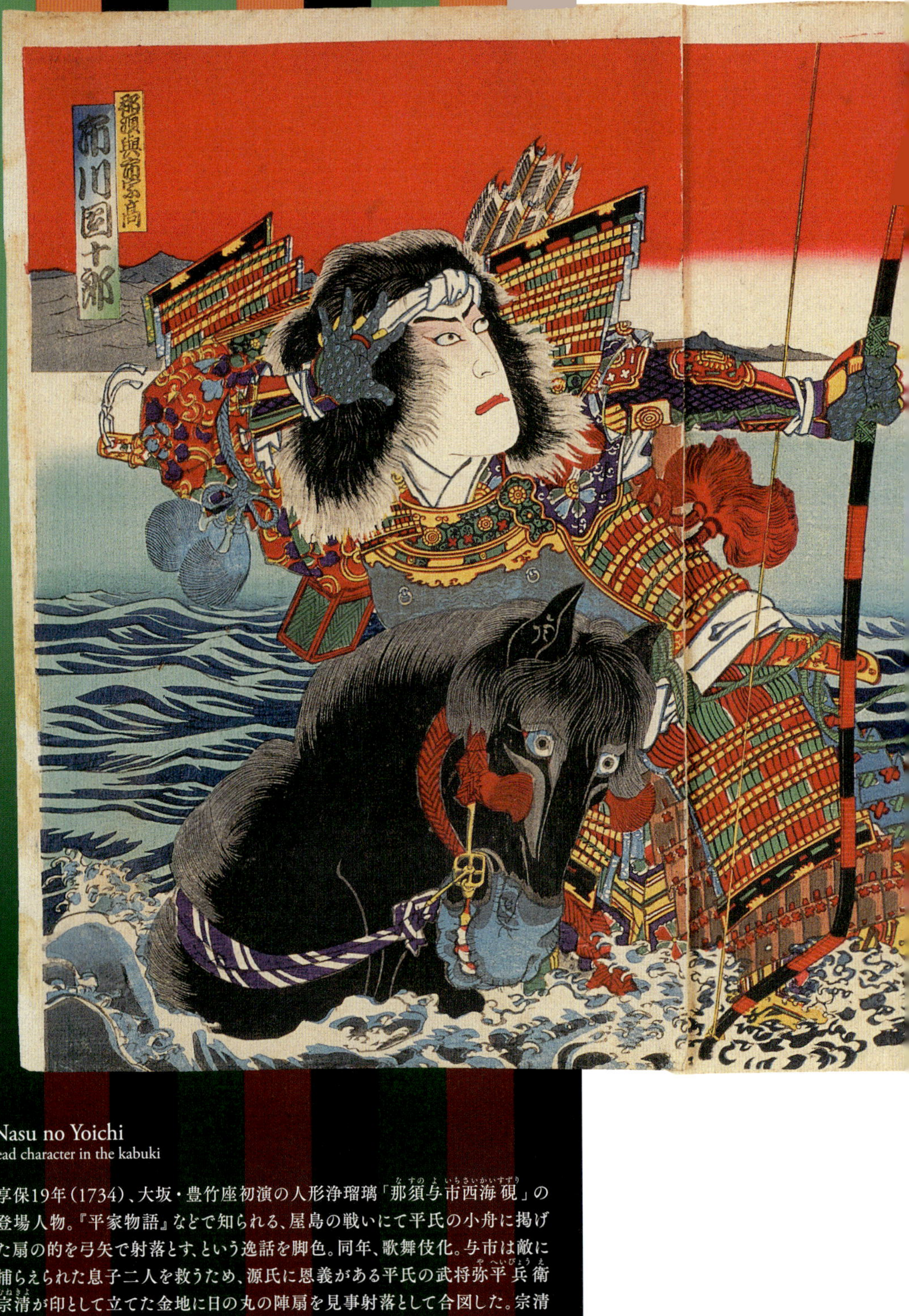

語り継がれる　神業の名場面

那須与市

Nasu no Yoichi
lead character in the kabuki

享保19年（1734）、大坂・豊竹座初演の人形浄瑠璃「那須与市西海硯」の登場人物。『平家物語』などで知られる、屋島の戦いにて平氏の小舟に掲げた扇の的を弓矢で射落とす、という逸話を脚色。同年、歌舞伎化。与市は敵に捕えられた息子二人を救うため、源氏に恩義がある平氏の武将弥平兵衛宗清が印として立てた金地に日の丸の陣扇を見事射落として合図した。宗清は兄弟を道連れに入水と見せかけ、二人を与市のもとに戻した。

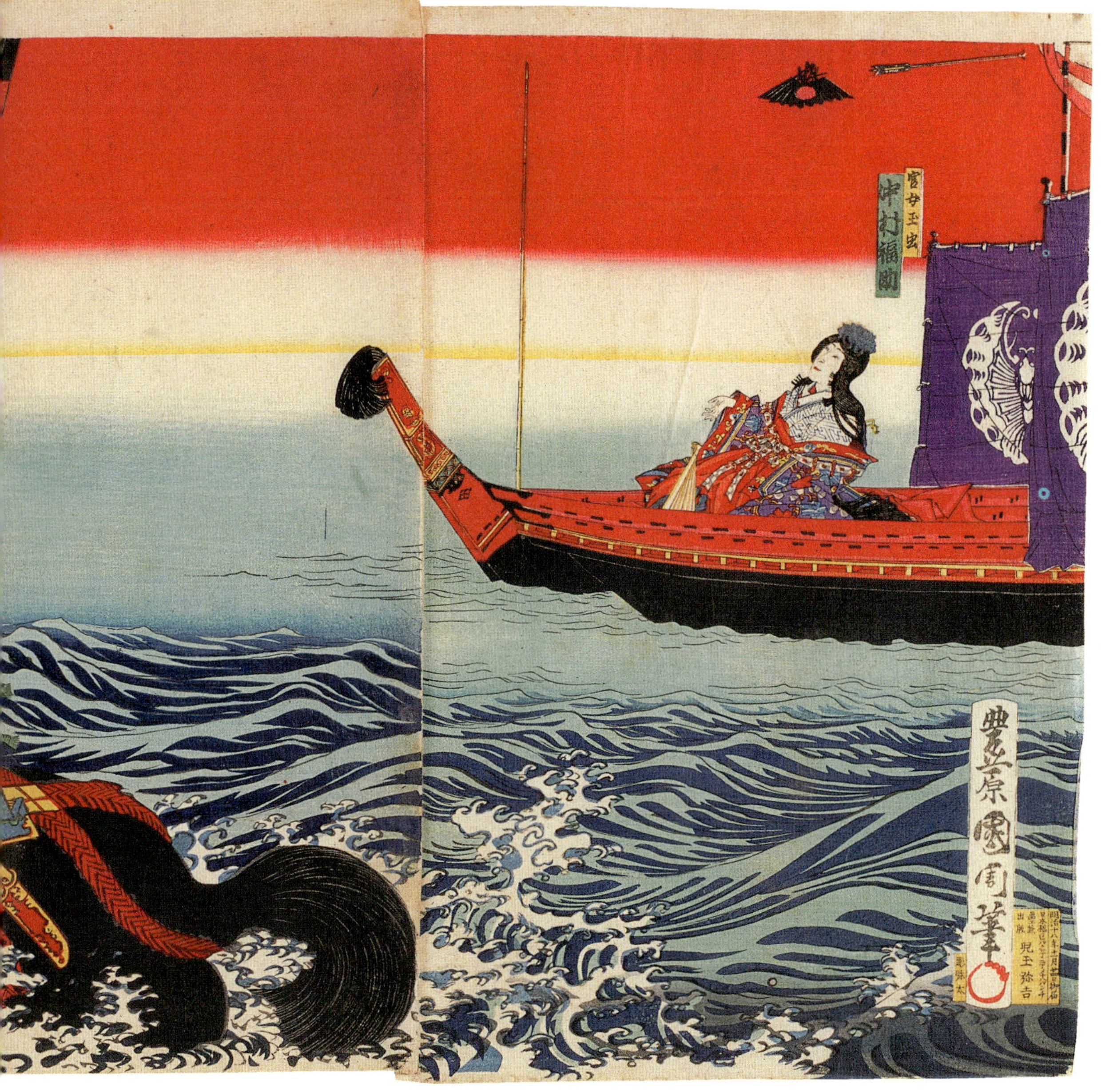

【那須与市扇的を射る】豊原国周 明治18年(1885)

"Nasu no Yoichi, as played by Ichikawa Danjūrō IX as" by Toyohara Kunichika

First performed at Osaka's Toyotakeza Theatre in 1734, the jōruri puppet play *Nasu no Yoichi on the Western Sea* is based on an episode in *The Tale of Heike* in which the great archer and Minamoto warrior Nasu no Yoichi shoots down a fan positioned on a rocking Taira boat. The story was turned into a kabuki play the same year. In a plan to return two abducted Minamoto brothers, the Taira warrior Yahei Munekiyo, who felt a sense of obligation to the Minamoto for past favors, arranges for Nasu no Yoichi to shoot down a fan featuring a rising sun on a gold background as a signal. After pretending that he drowns the children before his travel companion, Munekiyo then hands the brothers over to Yoichi.

野晒悟助

誰もが惚れる男伊達

Nozarashi Gosuke
lead character in the kabuki

慶応元年（1865）、江戸市村座初演、歌舞伎「鶴千歳曾我門松」の主人公。山東京伝の読本『本朝酔菩提全伝』を脚色し、男伊達の心意気を描いた。大坂の侠客野晒悟助は、住吉神社で土器売りの詫助を提婆組子分から救い、その娘お賤に惚れられる。その後、先の提婆組に囲まれ困っていた扇屋の娘小田井を助け、これまた惚れられる。仕返しに来た提婆の辱めに耐え、四天王寺の立ち回りで雪辱を晴らす。

First performed at the Ichimuraza Theatre in Edo (Tokyo) in 1840, the kabuki play *Tsuruchitose sogano kadomatsu* is based on Santō Kyōden's novel about chivalrous men, titled *A Complete Account of Drunken Enlightenment in Our Realm (Honchō suibodai zenden)*. When professional gambler Nozarashi Gosuke rescues pottery-seller Wabisuke from a gang at Sumiyoshi Shrine in Osaka, the latter's daughter falls in love with him. When a fan-seller's daughter is rescued from the same gang by Gosuke, she too falls in love with him. After being humiliated by the vengeful gang, Gosuke regains his honor in a final showdown at Shitennōji Temple.

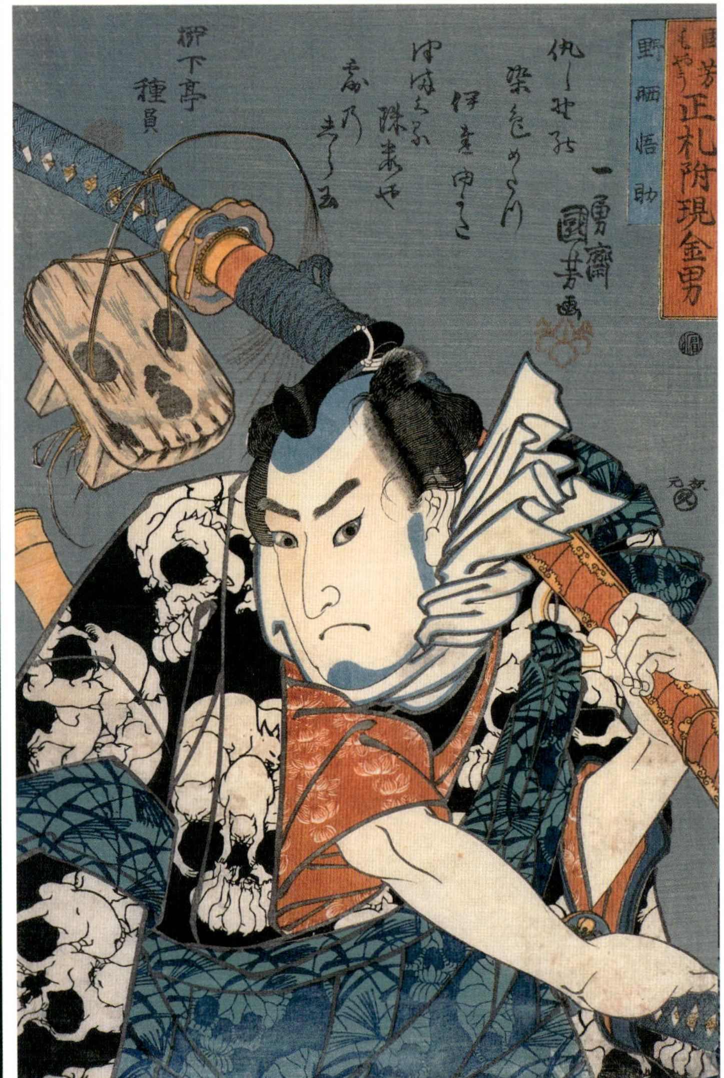

【国芳もやう正札附現金男 野晒悟助】歌川国芳 弘化2年（1845）頃

"Men of Ready Money with True Labels Attached: Nozarashi Gosuke" by Utagawa Kuniyoshi

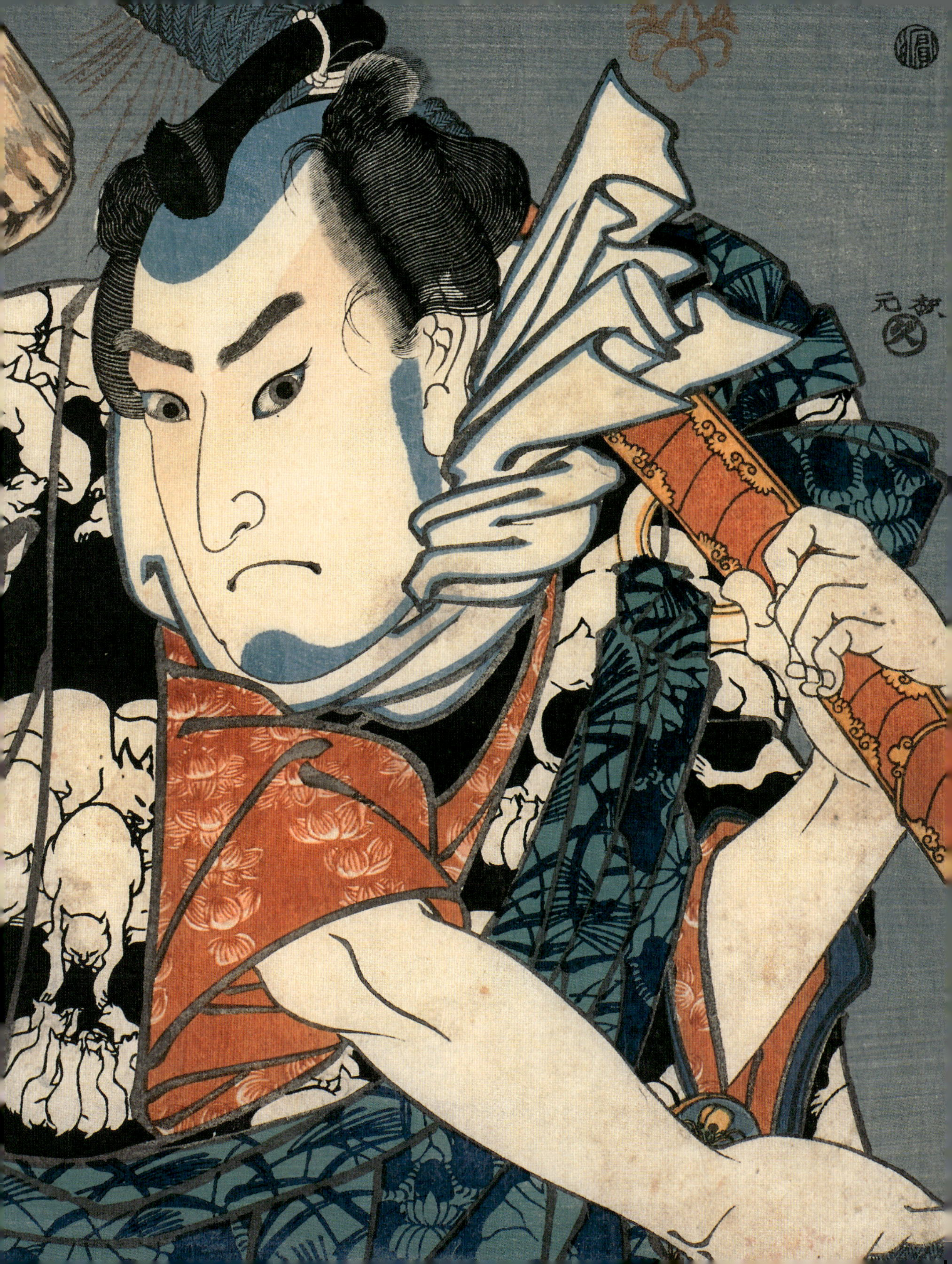

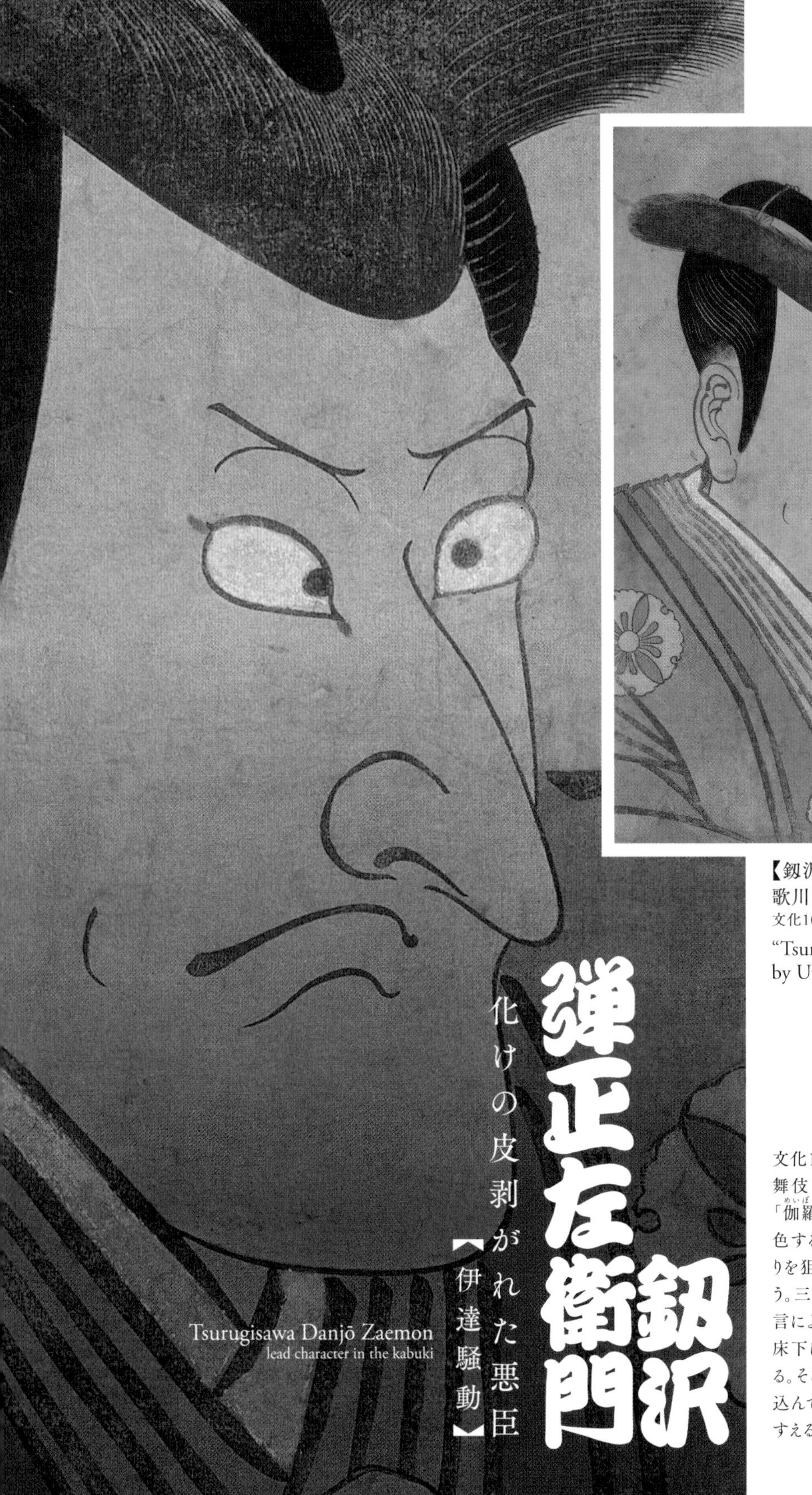

Tsurugisawa Danjō Zaemon
lead character in the kabuki

【釼沢弾正左衛門】
歌川国貞（三代豊国）
文化10年（1813）

"Tsurugisawa Danjō Zaemon"
by Utagawa Kunisada

釼沢弾正左衛門

化けの皮剥がれた悪臣

【伊達騒動】

文化10年（1813）、江戸森田座初演、歌舞伎「例燭曽我伊達染」の登場人物。「伽羅先代萩」の改作で、伊達騒動を脚色する。釼沢弾正左衛門は、お家乗っ取りを狙う足利家の悪臣で、鼠の妖術を使う。三浦荒男之助は足利家の忠臣で、讒言により謹慎させられているが、奥御殿の床下に潜んで、幼君鶴千代を警護している。そこへ巻物をくわえた怪しい鼠が飛び込んできたので、荒男之助が鉄扇で打ちすえると、弾正が現れた。

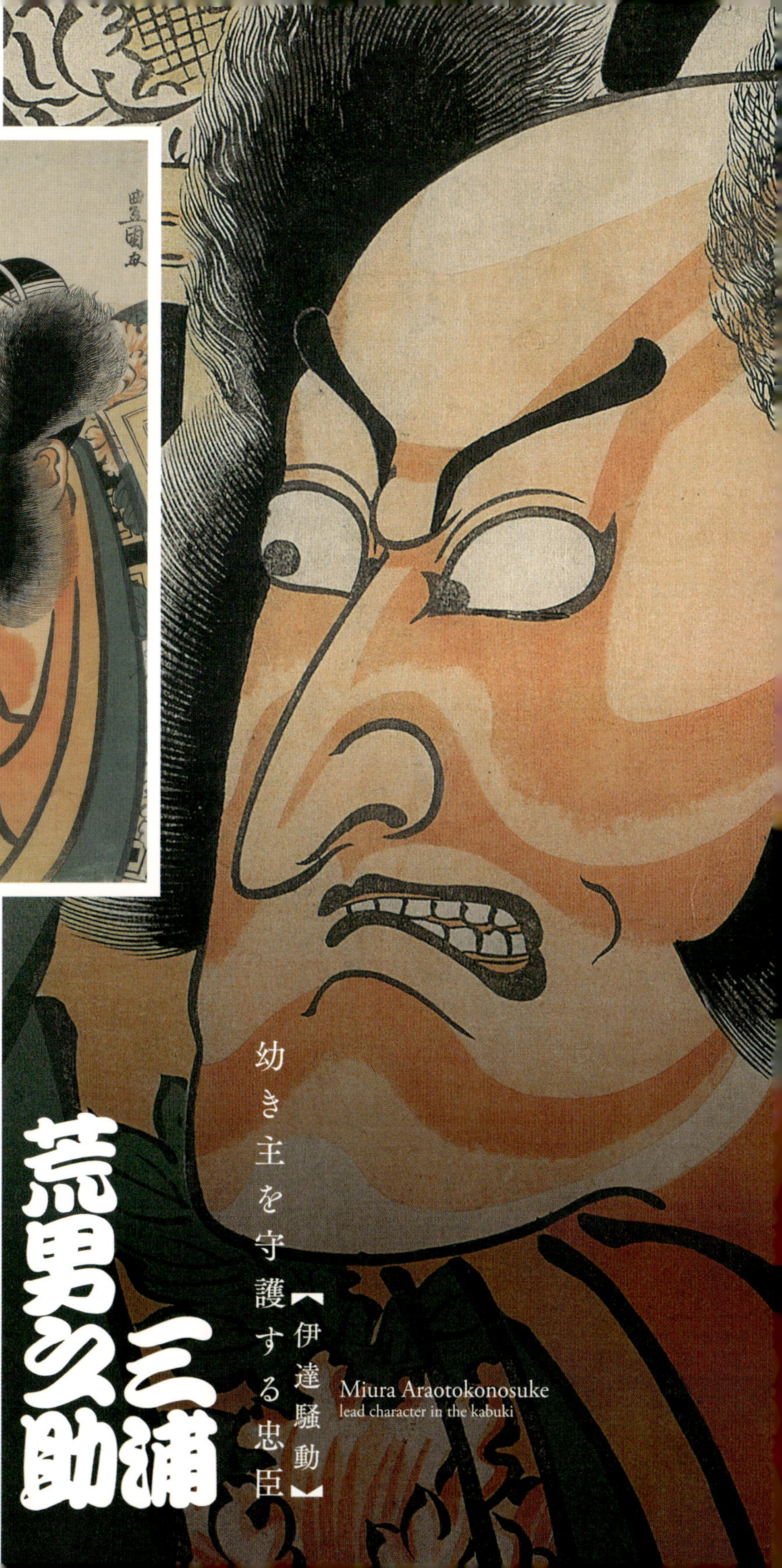

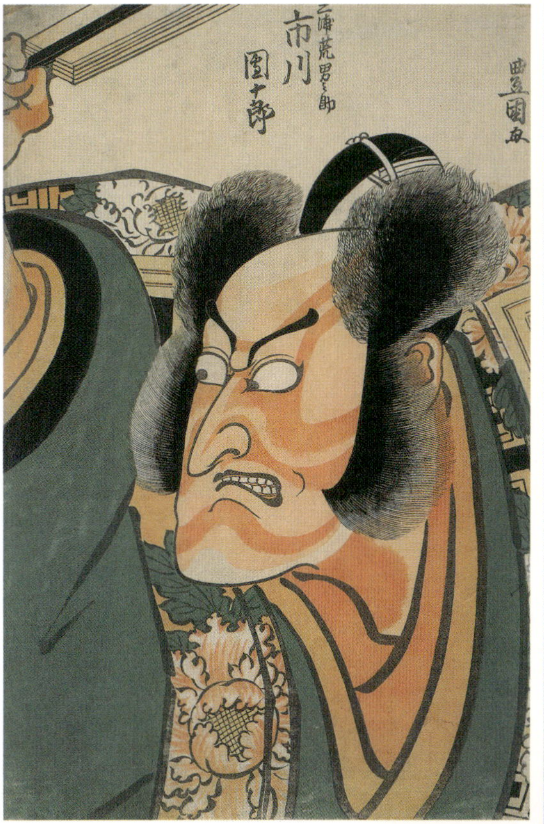

【三浦荒男之助】
歌川国貞（三代豊国）
文化10年（1813）

"Miura Araotokonosuke"
by Utagawa Kunisada

First performed at the Moritaza Theatre in Edo (Tokyo) in 1813, the kabuki play *Shikisemono Soga no Datezome* was based on the Noh play *The Disputed Succession* (*Meiboku sendai hagi*) and the events of the Date Disturbance. Tsurugisawa Danjō Zaemon is an evil retainer of the Ashikaga clan who plots to take over the domain using his powers of rat sorcery. Miura Araotokonosuke is a loyal retainer of the same Ashikaga clan. Cautious of slander, Araotokonosuke guards rightful heir Tsuruchiyo while hiding beneath the floorboards of the Ashikaga mansion, where suddenly appears a rat suspiciously holding a scroll in its mouth. Araotokonosuke strikes it with a metal fan, revealing the evil Danjō Zaemon.

Miura Araotokonosuke
lead character in the kabuki

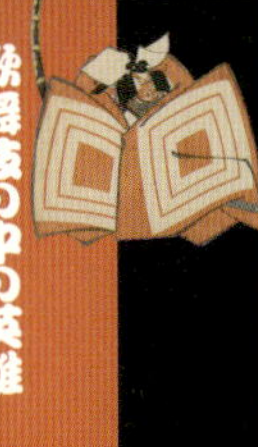

186

弱きを助け強きをくじく快男児

【歌舞伎十八番「暫」】

鎌倉景政

Kamakura Kagemasa
lead character in the kabuki

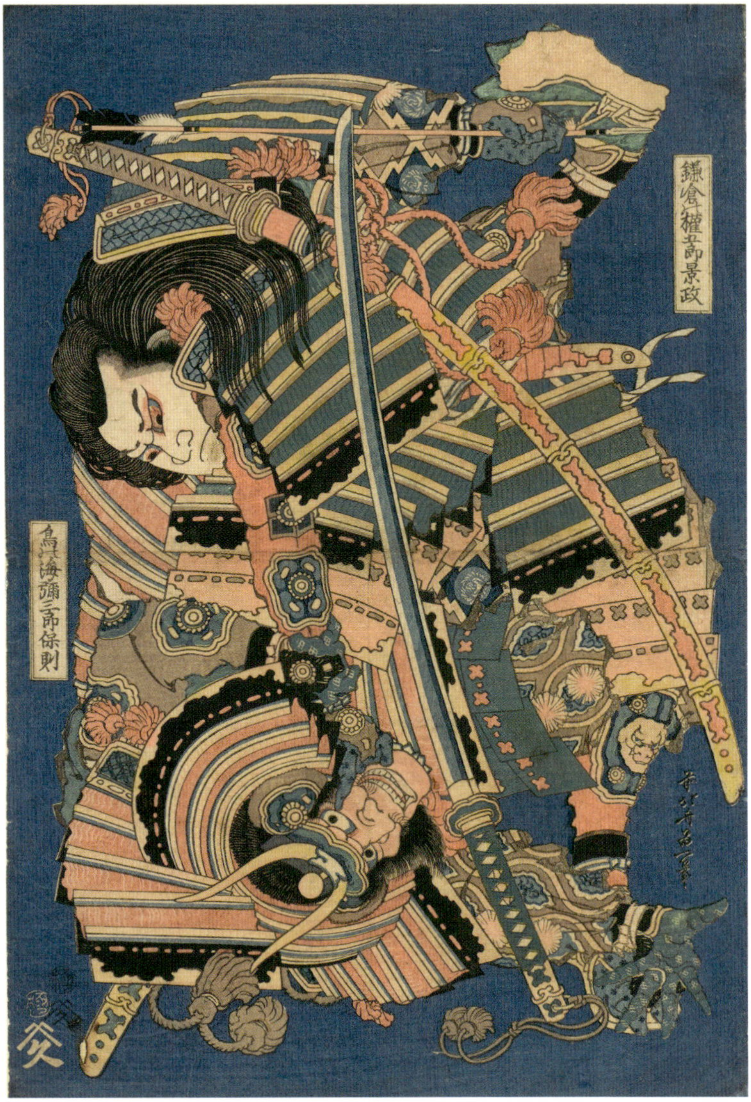

歌舞伎十八番の一つ「暫」の主人公。悪公卿が善良な人々を殺害しようとする瞬間、主人公が「暫」と声をかけて花道から登場し、悪人どもを懲らしめる。荒事の代表作で、毎年1月の顔見世狂言に市川家の俳優によって演じられたが、主人公の名はその年により異なった。今日では、鎌倉権五郎景政として上演されることが多い。景政は、平安後期、後三年の役で活躍した源義家の家臣。敵に右目を射られたが、これを追撃したという強者である。

As the hero of the famous kabuki play *Shibaraku (Just a Moment!)*, Kagemasa appears along the raised hanamichi runway that cuts through the audience at the play's climactic moment to declare "Just a moment!" just as the bad guys ready to kill the good people. This representative work of aragoto "wild style" kabuki has been performed each January as part of the annual all-star revue by one of the actors of the Ichikawa family. Though the name of the hero has changed over the years, today it is typically Kamakura Gongorō Kagemasa, a loyal retainer of Minamoto no Yoshiie during the Gosannen War of the late Heian period. So great was his strength that he is said to have kept fighting despite losing his right eye in battle during that war.

【鎌倉の権五郎景政
　鳥の海弥三郎保則】
葛飾北斎　天保（1830-44）前期

"Kamakura Gongorō Kagemasa
and Torinoumi Yasaburō Yasunori"
by Katsushika Hokusai

【歌舞伎十八番「暫」】
歌川国芳　天保8〜9年（1837-38）頃
ギャラリー紅屋収蔵

"The Eighteen Best Plays
of Kabuki: Shibaraku"
by Utagawa Kuniyoshi,
Gallery Beniya Collection

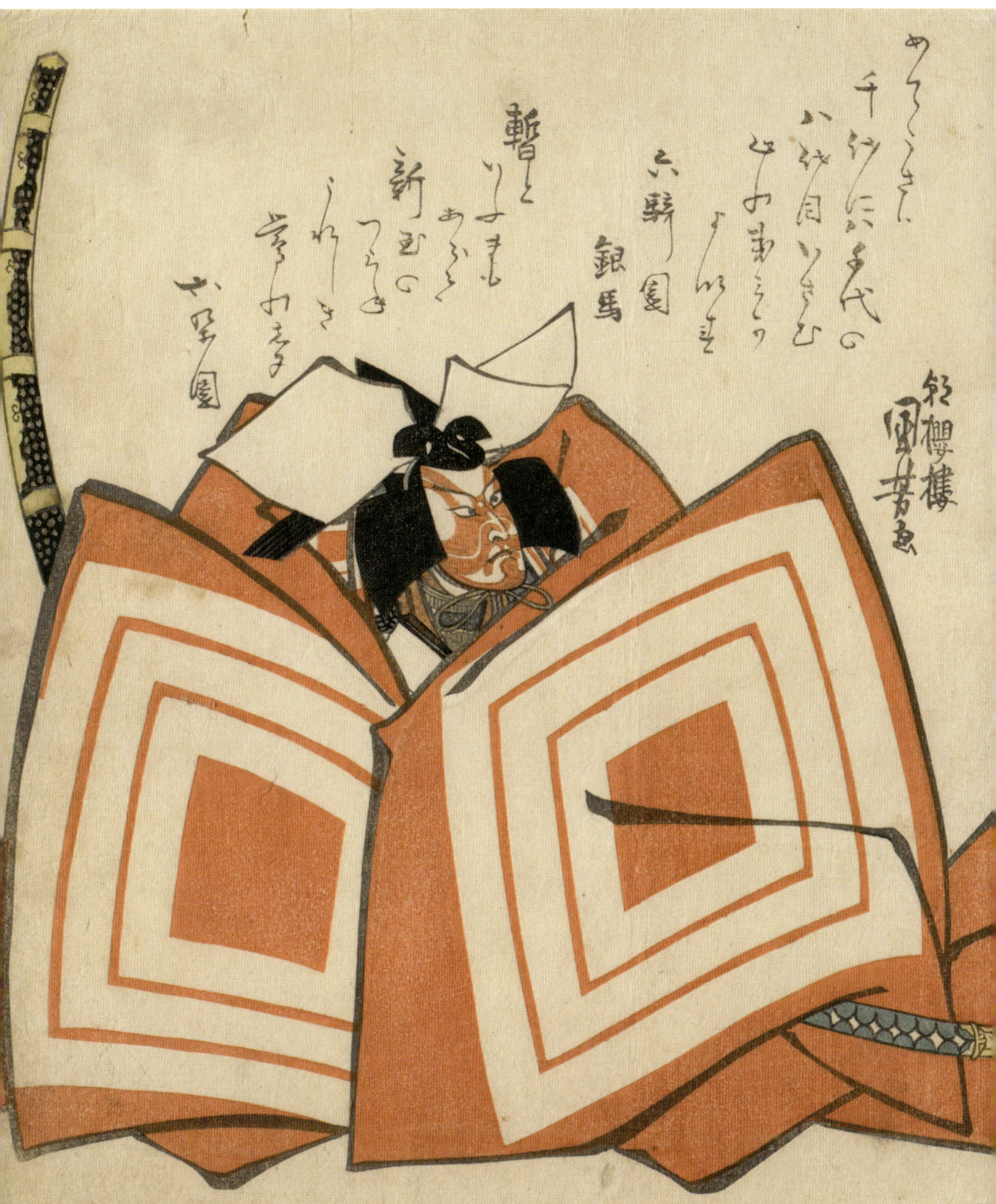

六輝圓　銀馬
紅櫻樓
國芳画

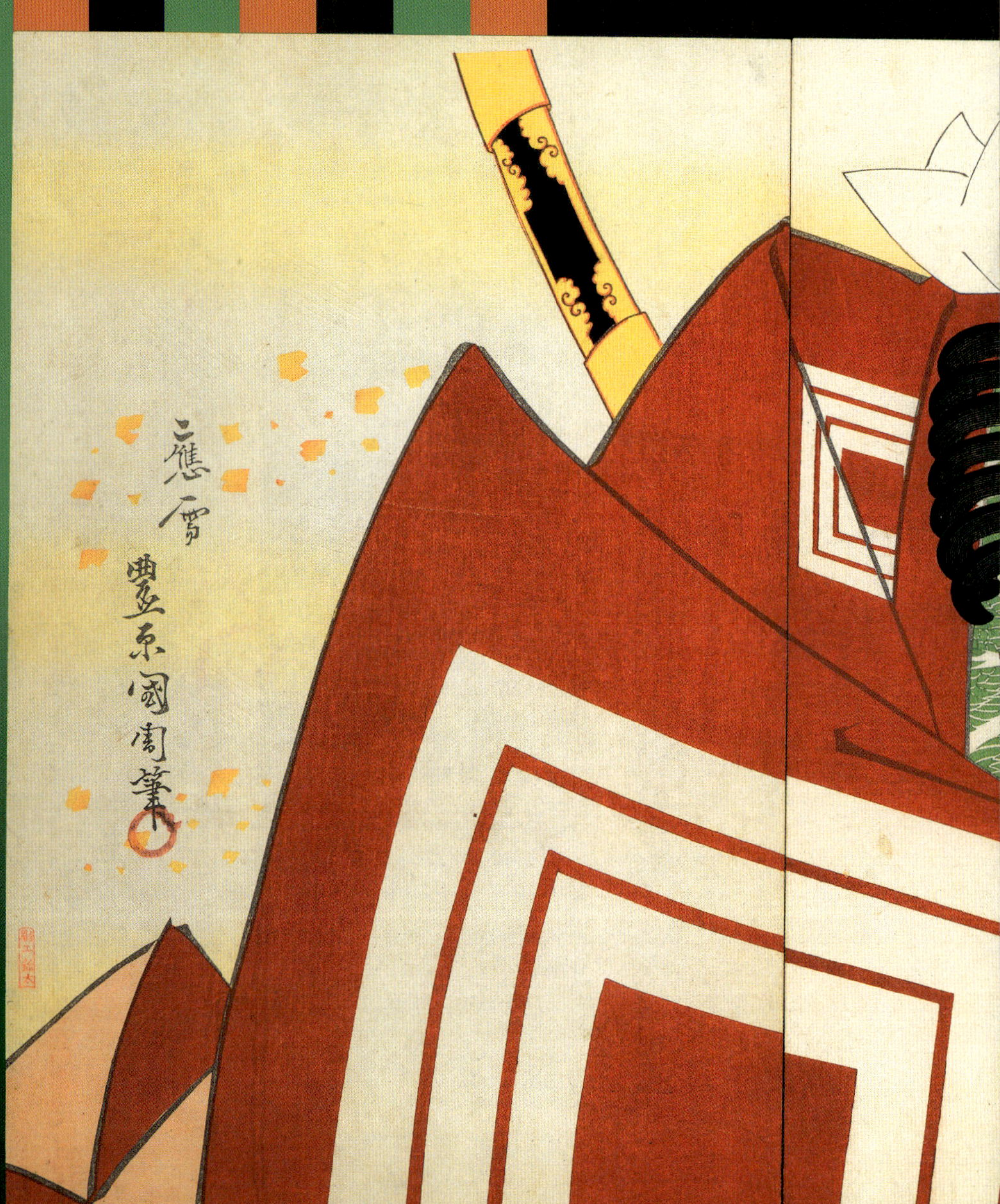
二應需
豊原國周筆

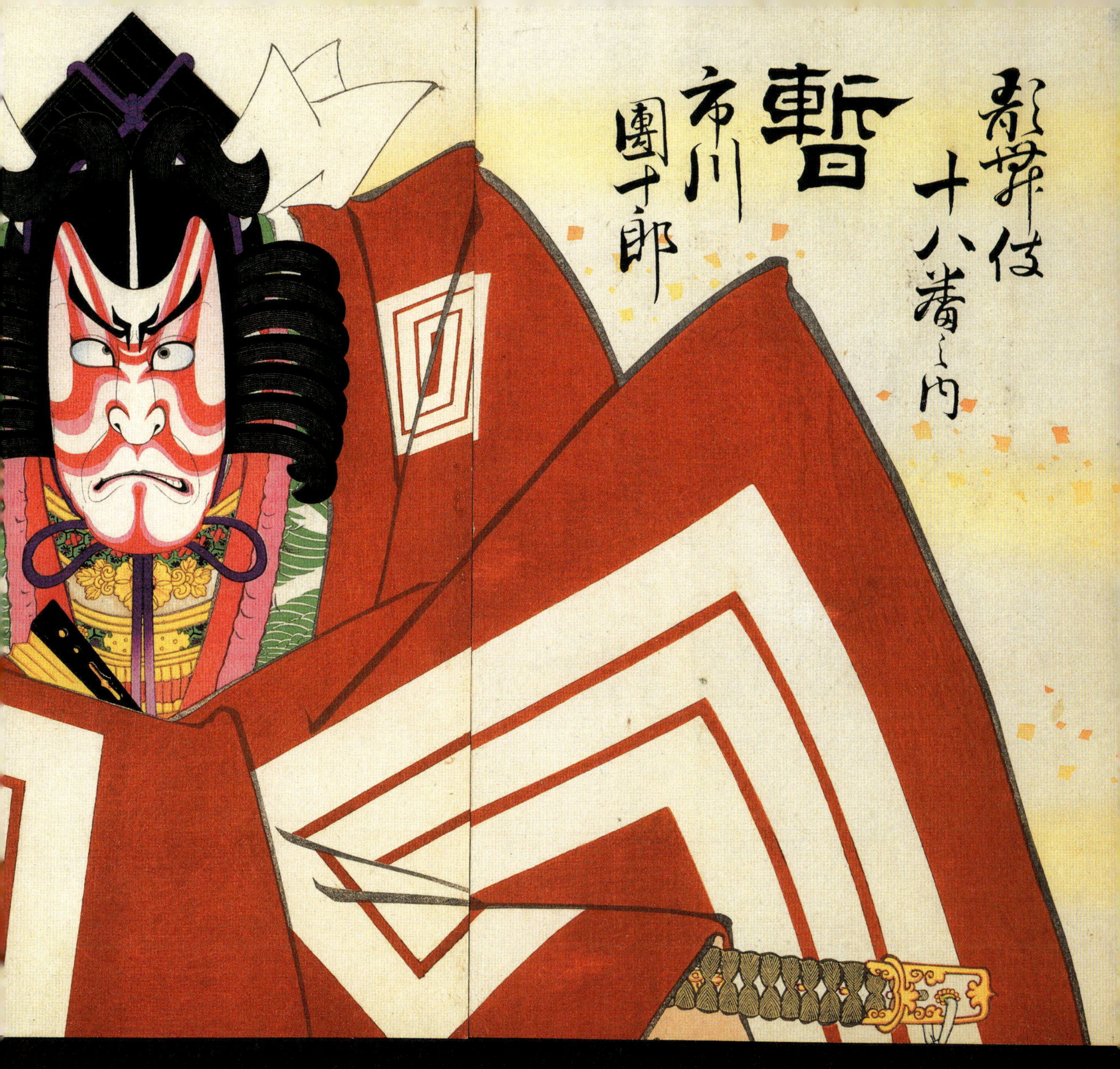

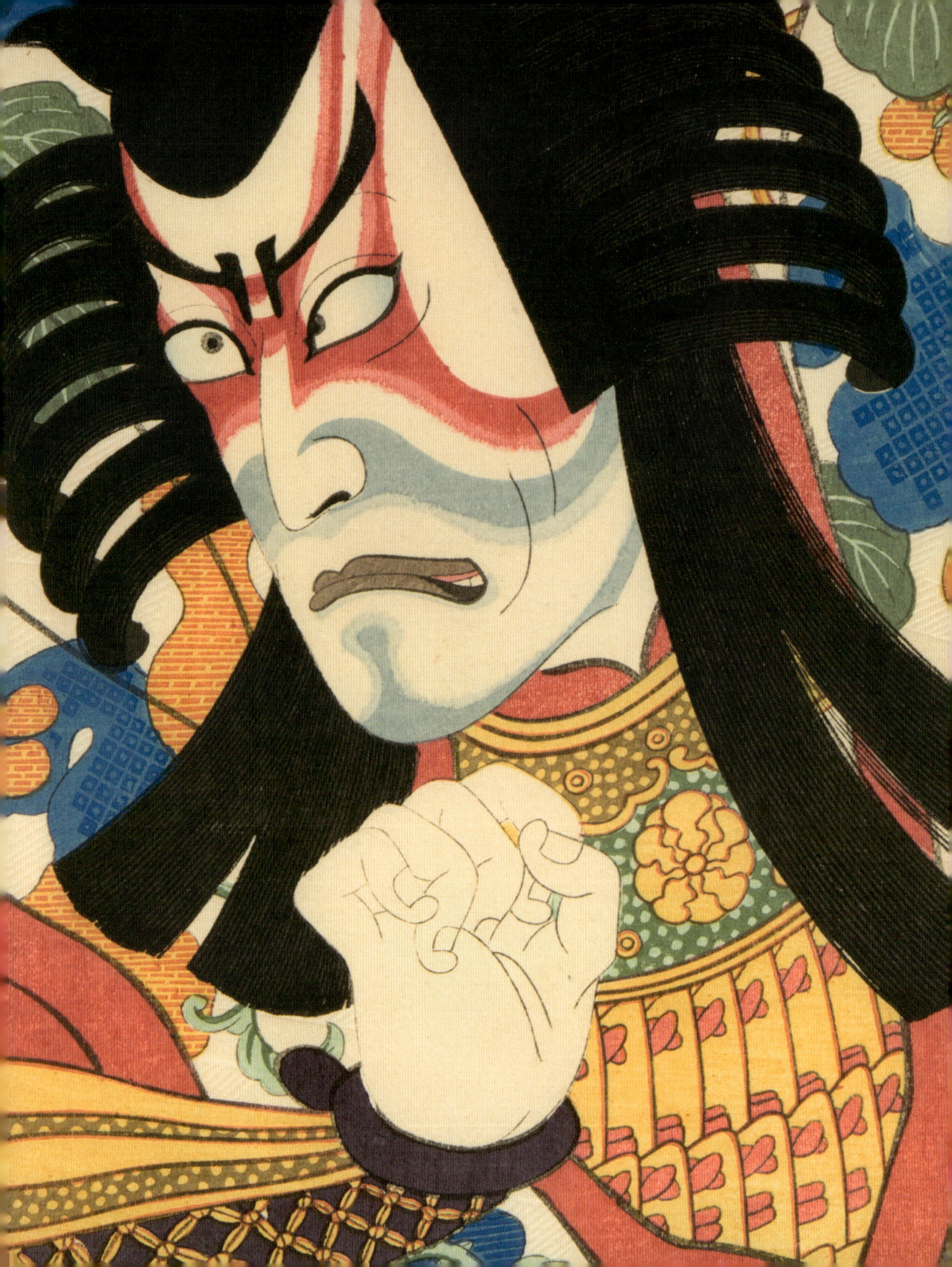

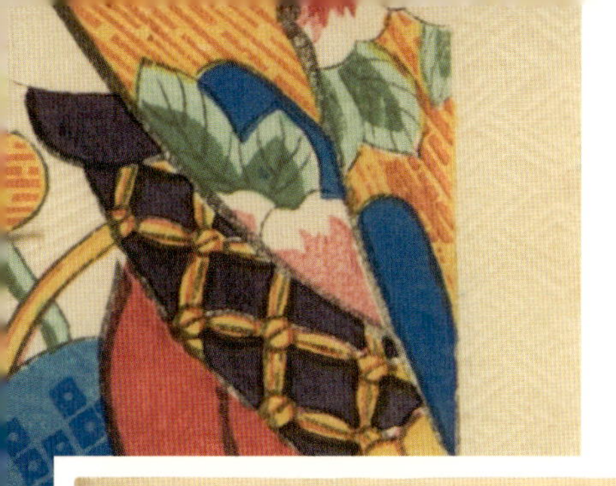

歌舞伎十八番「解脱」
怒髪天を衝き牢を破る

平景清

Taira no Kagekiyo
lead character in the kabuki

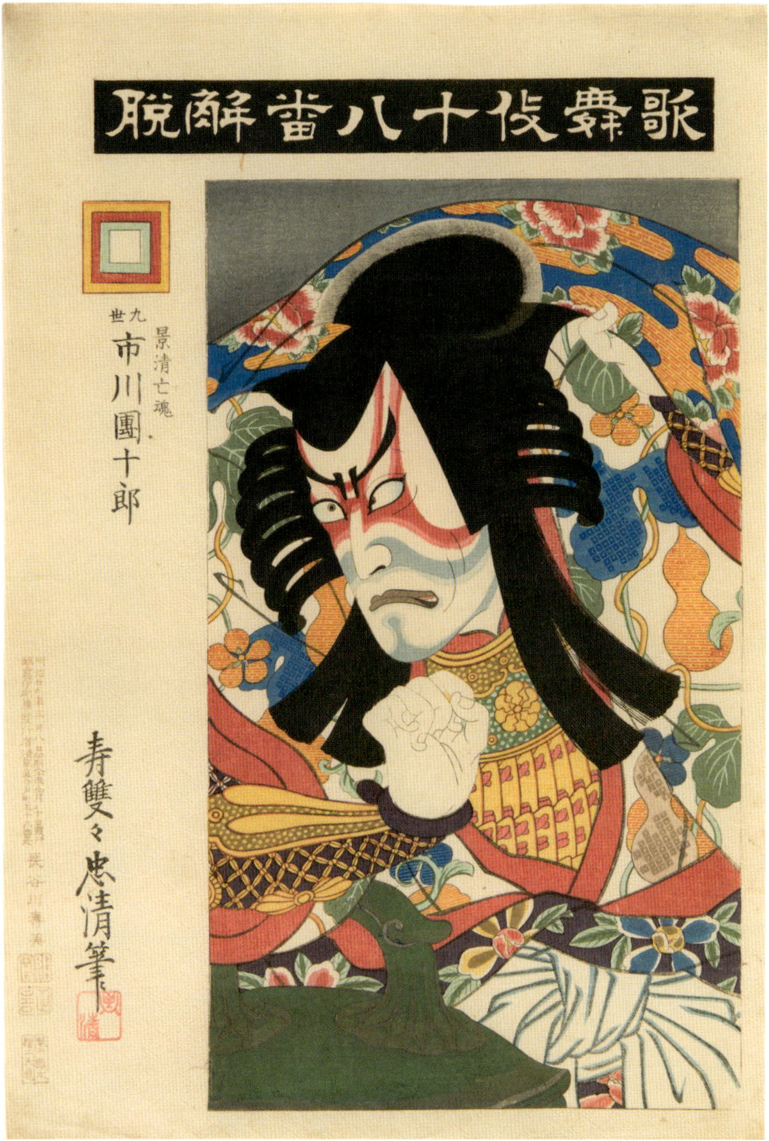

歌舞伎十八番の一つ「景清」の主人公。平氏の残党景清は、平氏滅亡後も頼朝を狙う。とうとう源氏方に捕まり、洞窟の牢屋に入れられる。源氏の武将が平家の宝のありかを聞き出そうとするも答えなかった。恋人の遊女阿古屋と娘の人丸を連れてきて責め立てたところ、景清は怒りを爆発させ、牢屋を破って大暴れした。また、同じく歌舞伎十八番の一つ「解脱」では、亡魂となった景清が迷い出て、荒事を見せたあと成仏するという筋が伝わる。

Kagekiyo is one of the official "Eighteen Best Plays" of kabuki. Though the Taira clan has been defeated, Kagekiyo continues to seek Minamoto no Yoritomo's death. He is finally captured by the Minamoto and imprisoned in a cave, where is interrogated about the location of the Taira's hidden treasure, but refuses to speak. To break him, the Minamoto torture his beloved courtesan Akoya and their daughter before his eyes, which only sends Kagekiyo into a wild rage. He rips off the prison cell's door and pummels his enemies. In another best-of-eighteen kabuki play, *Gedatsu* (*Deliverance*), a dead Kagekiyo appears as a violent wandering soul who is pacified only after the execution of extensive Buddhist rites.

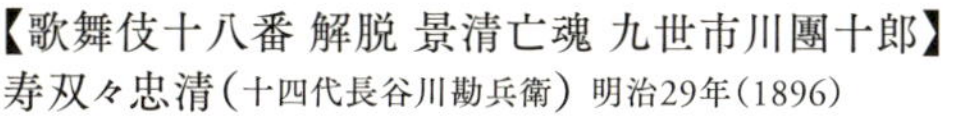

【歌舞伎十八番 解脱 景清亡魂 九世市川團十郎】
寿双々忠清（十四代長谷川勘兵衛）明治29年（1896）

"The Eighteen Best Plays of Kabuki: Gedatsu, the Ghost of Kagekiyo,
as played by Ichikawa Danjūrō IX" by Jusōsō Tadakiyo (Hasegawa Kanbee XIV)

三大仇討

曽我兄弟

神に誓った父の仇討ち

【三大仇討】

The Soga Brothers
Three Biggest Acts
of Revenge in Japan

ともに鎌倉時代の武士。伊豆の豪族河津祐
泰の子で、兄は祐成、弟は時致という。兄弟
が幼少のときに父を工藤祐経に殺され、仇討
ちを誓う。母の再婚により曽我氏を称す。建久
4年（1193）に源頼朝が催した富士の巻狩
の場で、祐経を討ち取った。祐成は仁田忠常
に討たれ、時致は女装した小舎人の御所五
郎丸によって捕らえられ、のちに処刑された。

Warriors of the Kamakura period, Sōga Sukenari
and his younger brother Tokimune were the
sons of the powerful Kawazu Sukeyasu of Izu,
who was murdered by another samurai named
Kudō Suketsune when they were still young.
Gaining the new family of Sōga upon their
mother's remarriage, the brothers avenged their
father in 1193, eighteen years after his death, by
killing his murderer upon hunting grounds
controlled by Minamoto no Yoritomo at the
foot of Mount Fuji. Sukenari was later cut down
by Minamoto retainer Nitta Tadatsune, while
Tokimune was captured by Yoritomo's page boy
Gosho Gorōmaru while the latter was in female
disguise, and then executed.

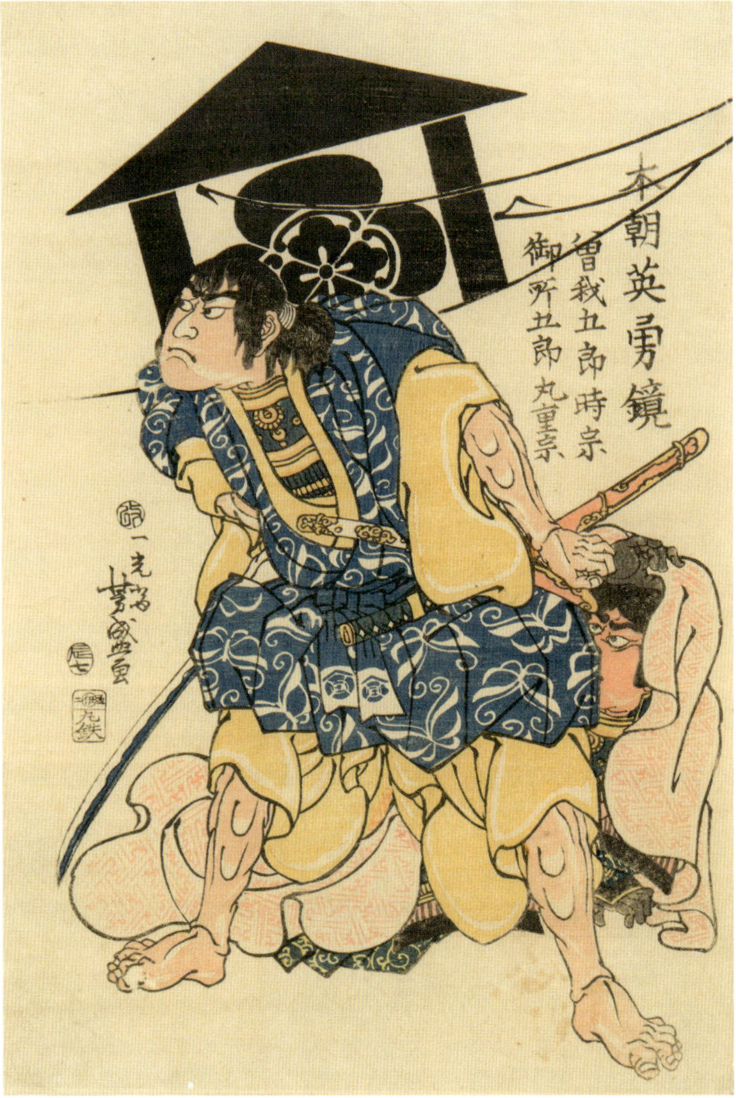

【本朝英勇鏡 曽我五郎時宗 御所五郎丸重宗】歌川芳盛 安政3年（1856）

"Heroes of Our Realm: Soga Gorō Tokimune and Gosho Gorōmaru Shigemune" by Utagawa Yoshimori

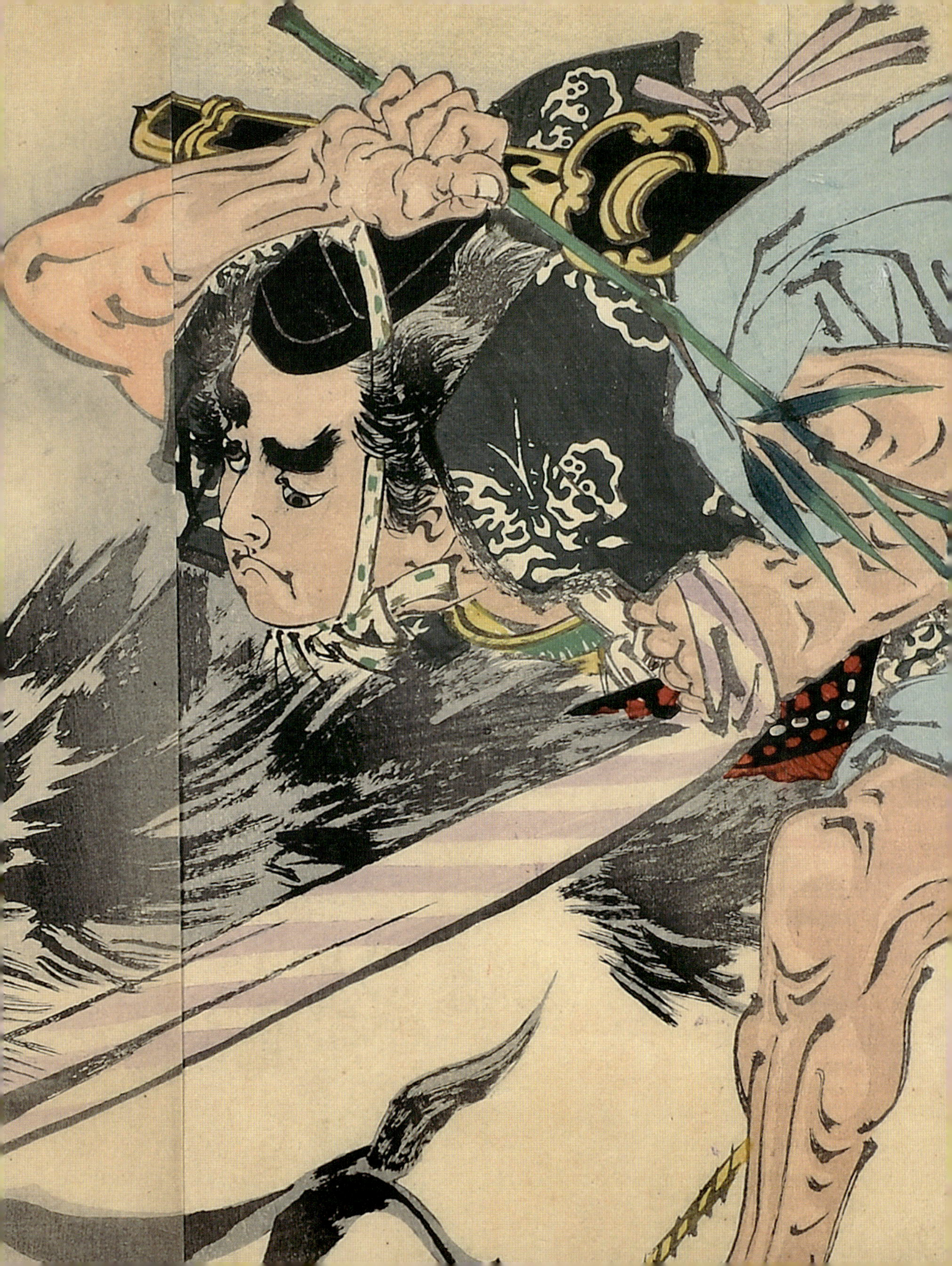

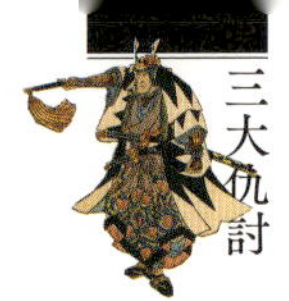

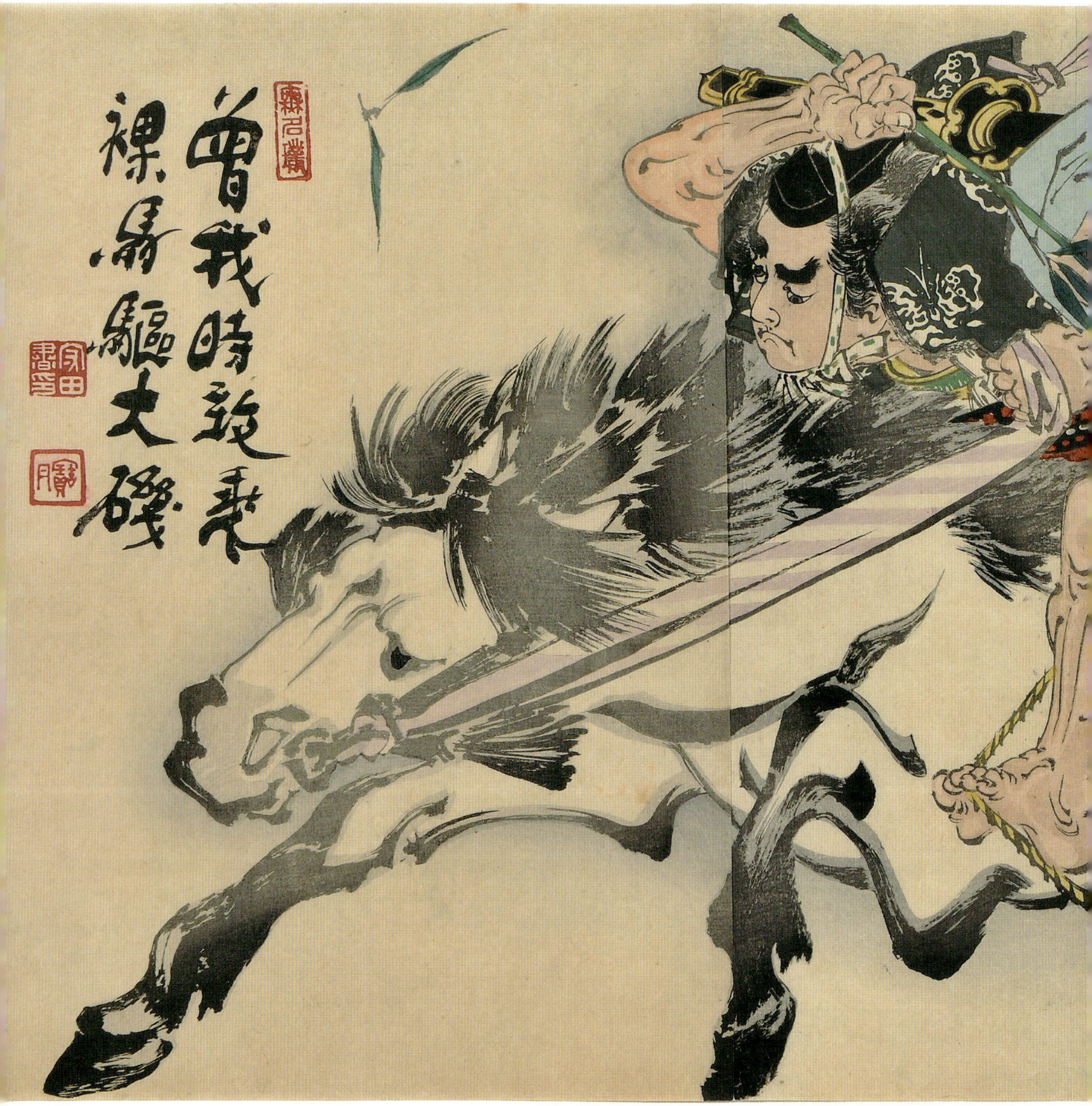

【曽我時致乗裸馬駆大磯】月岡芳年 明治18年(1885)
大磯付近を祐経が通ると聞きつけ、馬を走らせる時致。

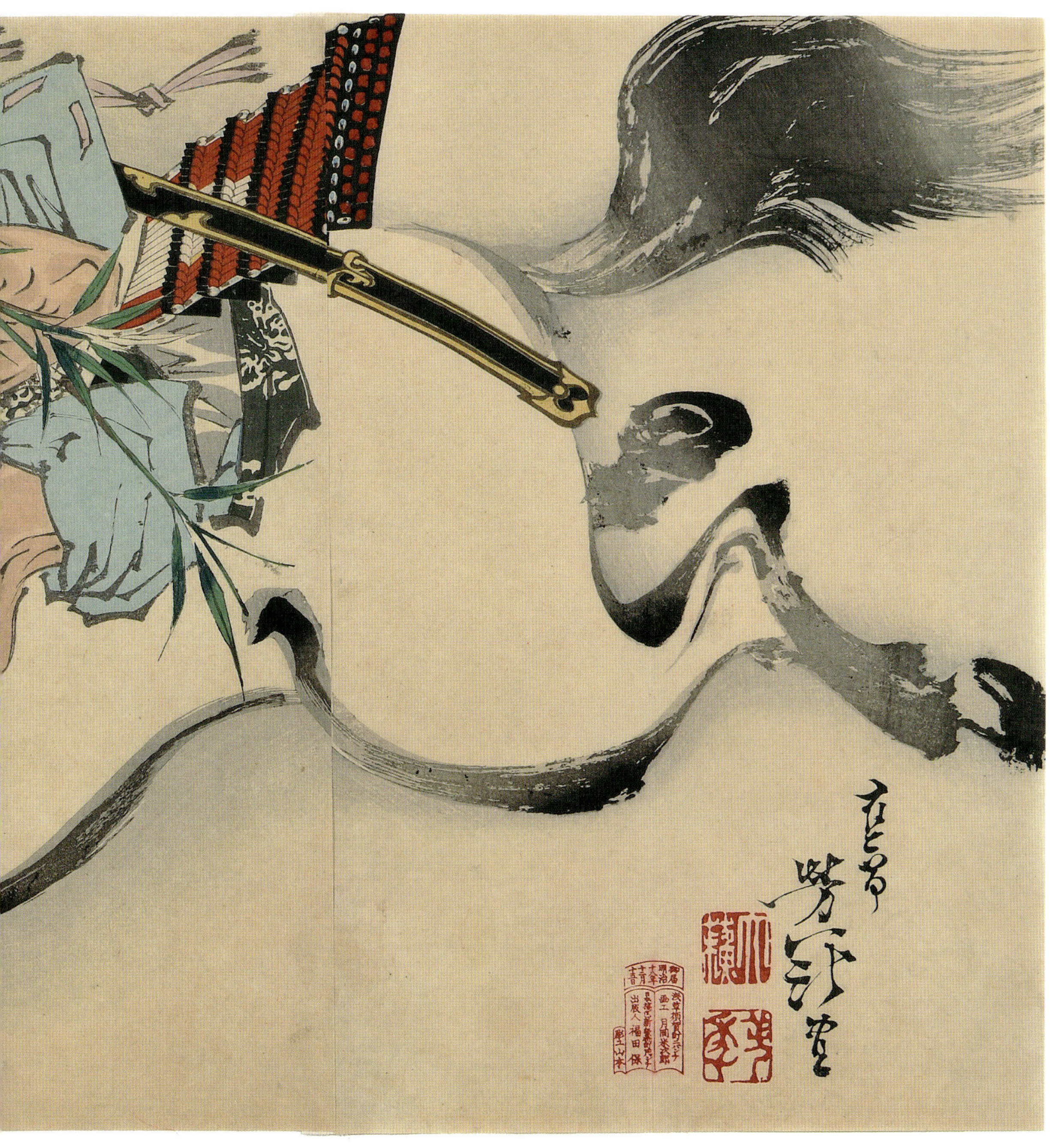

"Soga Tokimune Riding an Unsaddled Horse" by Tsukioka Yoshitoshi
Upon hearing that Kudō Suketsune will be passing nearby through Oiso, Tokimune rushes on horse to confront his father's murderer.

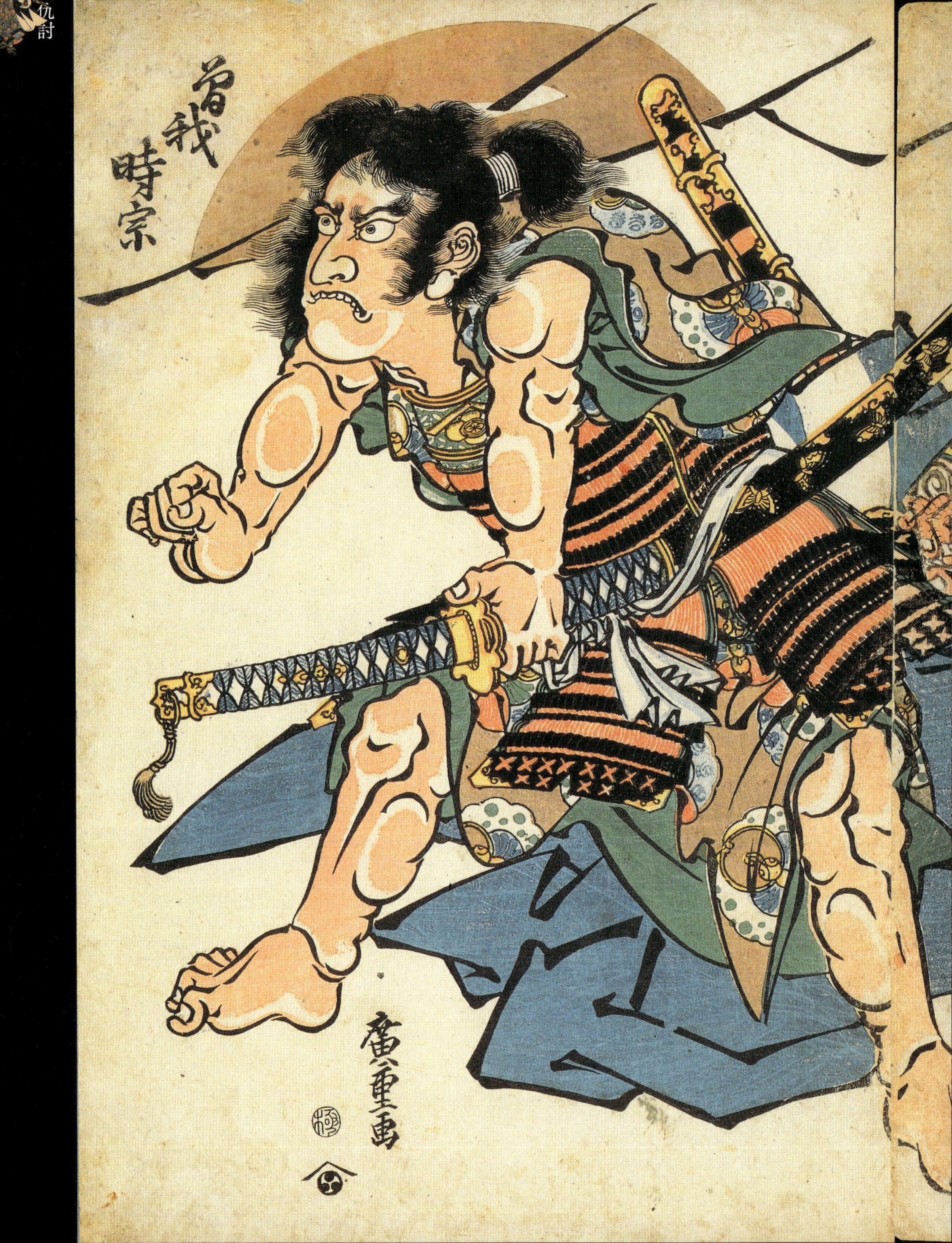
曽我
時宗
廣重画

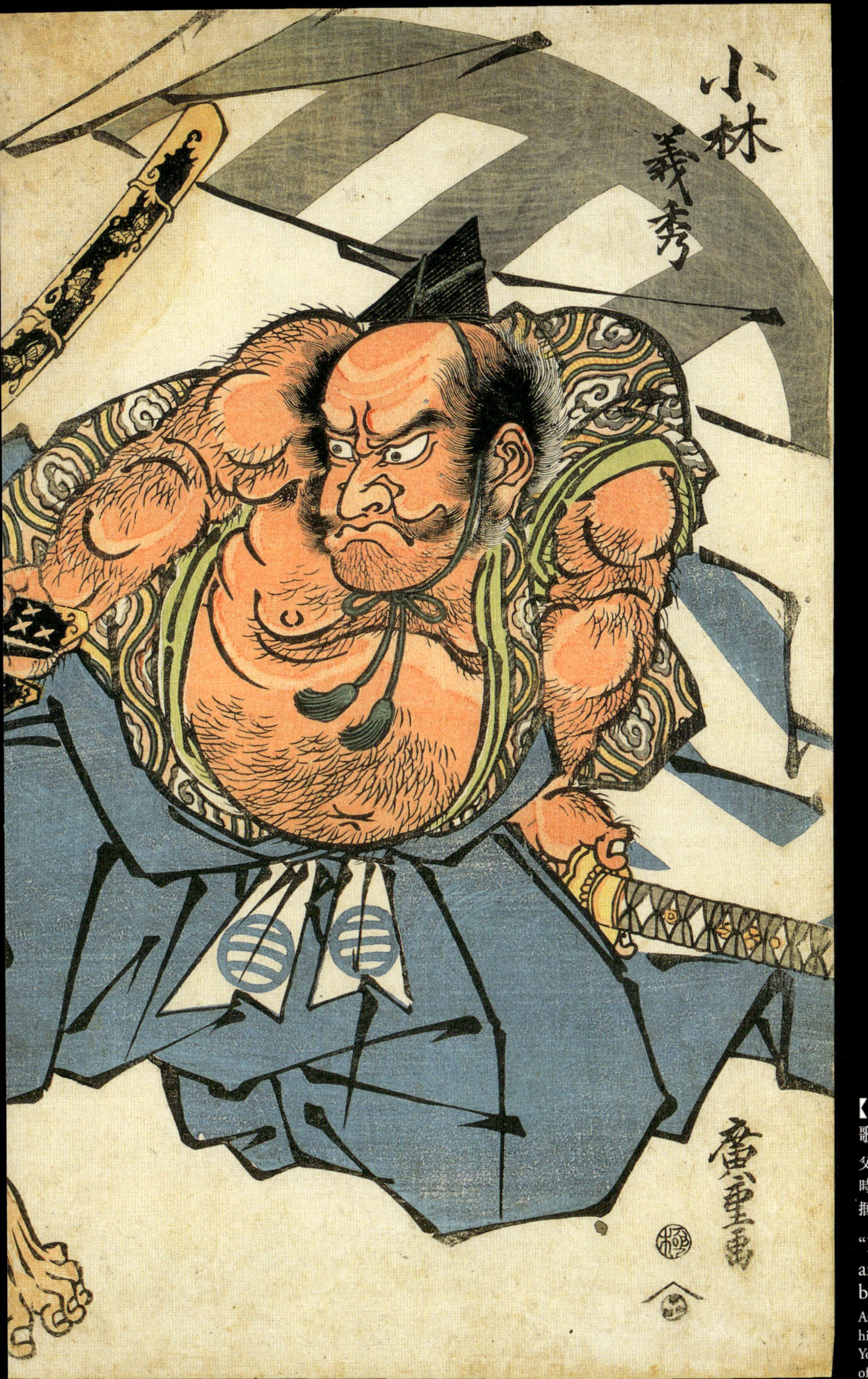

【小林義秀 曽我時宗】
歌川広重 文政（1818-30）後期

父の仇祐経に駆けつけようとする
時致を、小林義秀が鎧の草摺を
掴んで引き留める。

"Kobayashi Yoshihide
and Soga Tokimune"
by Utagawa Hiroshige

As Tokimune attempts to pursue
his father's murderer, Kobayashi
Yoshihide grabs the skirt plates
of his armor to hold him back.

【三大仇討】

卑怯許すまじ

荒木又右衛門　渡辺数馬

Watanabe Kazuma
and Araki Mataemon
Three Biggest Acts of Revenge in Japan

ともに江戸時代初期の武士。備前国岡山藩士の渡辺数馬は、姉の夫荒木又右衛門の助けを得て、弟（一説に父）の仇河合又五郎を伊賀上野城下の鍵屋の辻で討った。伊賀越の仇討ちで知られ、講談や歌舞伎に脚色された。決闘の際、又右衛門が36人斬りをした逸話が残るが、史実とは異なるという。

Samurai of the early Edo period, Watanabe Kazuma, Lord of Bizen Province in Okayama, seeks to avenge his younger brother's murder (or his father's, in some tellings) with the help of Araki Mataemon, his sister's husband. They do so near Iga Ueno Castle, cutting down Kawai Matagorō in a famed fight at Kagiya-no-tsuji crossroads. Also known as the Vendetta of Iga Pass, this episode was made famous through oral tales and kabuki plays. Mataemon is sometimes credited with felling thirty-six men at Kagiya-no-tsuji, though the historical record does not back this up.

【忠孝仇討図会 伊賀越】歌川広重　天保14～弘化3年（1843-46）頃
"Pictures of Loyalty and Vengeance: Vendetta at Iga Pass" Utagawa Hiroshige

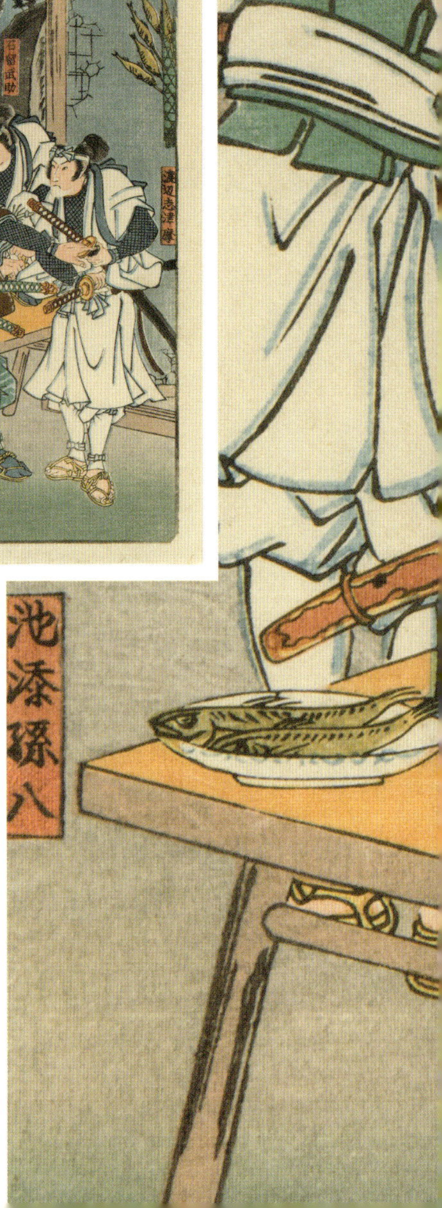

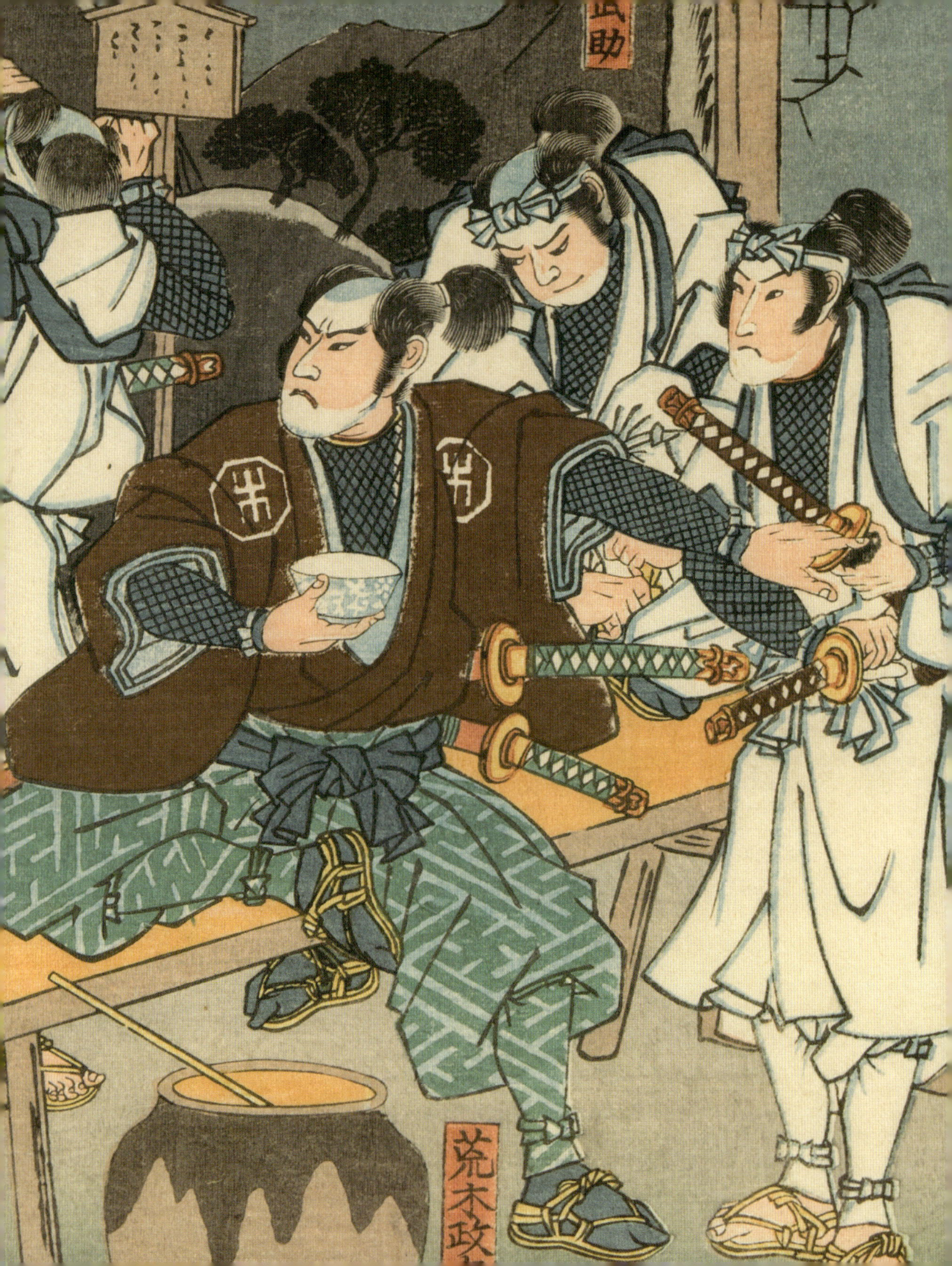
武助
荒木政

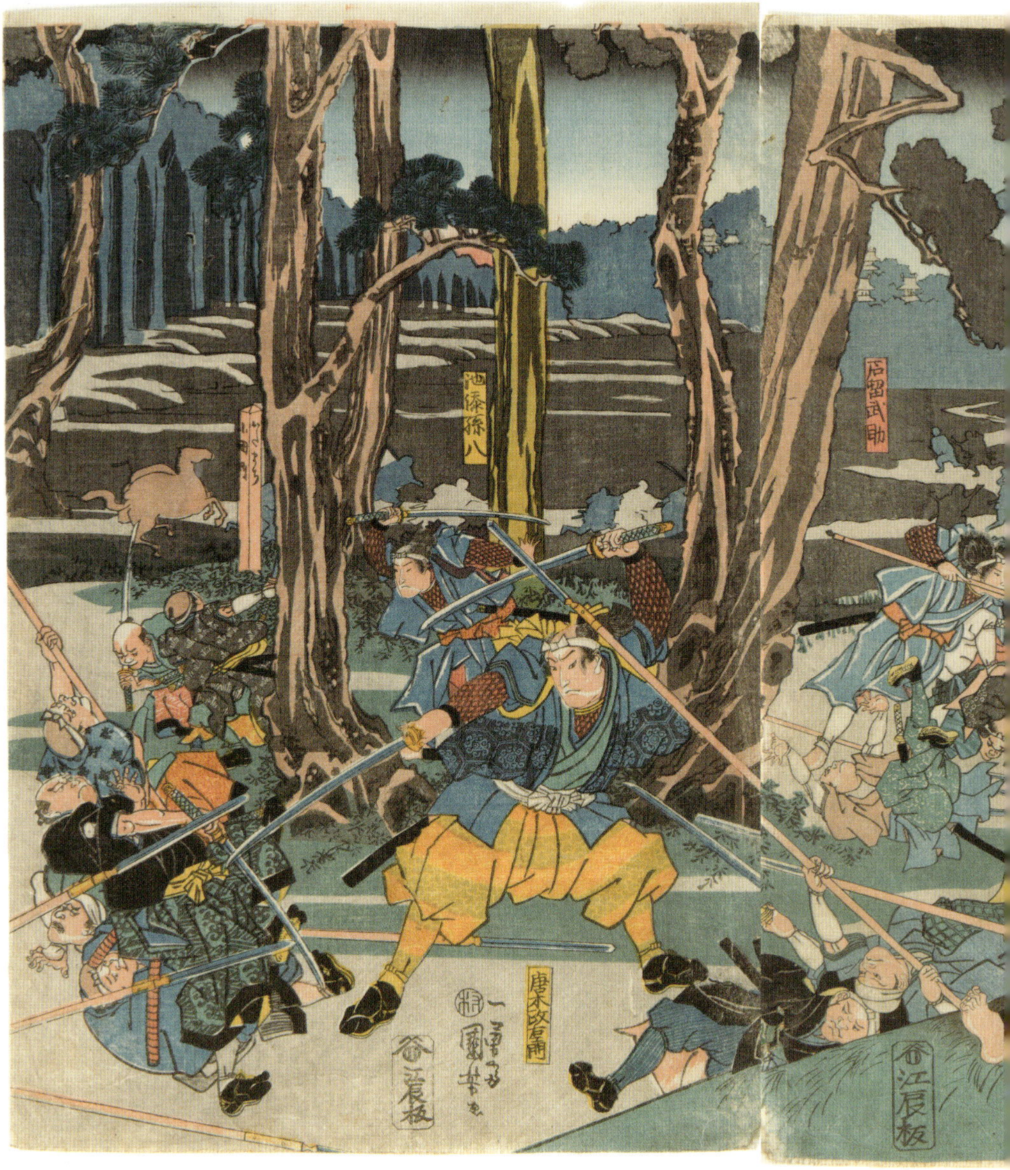

200

【伊賀上野敵討】歌川国芳　天保14〜弘化3年（1843-46）頃

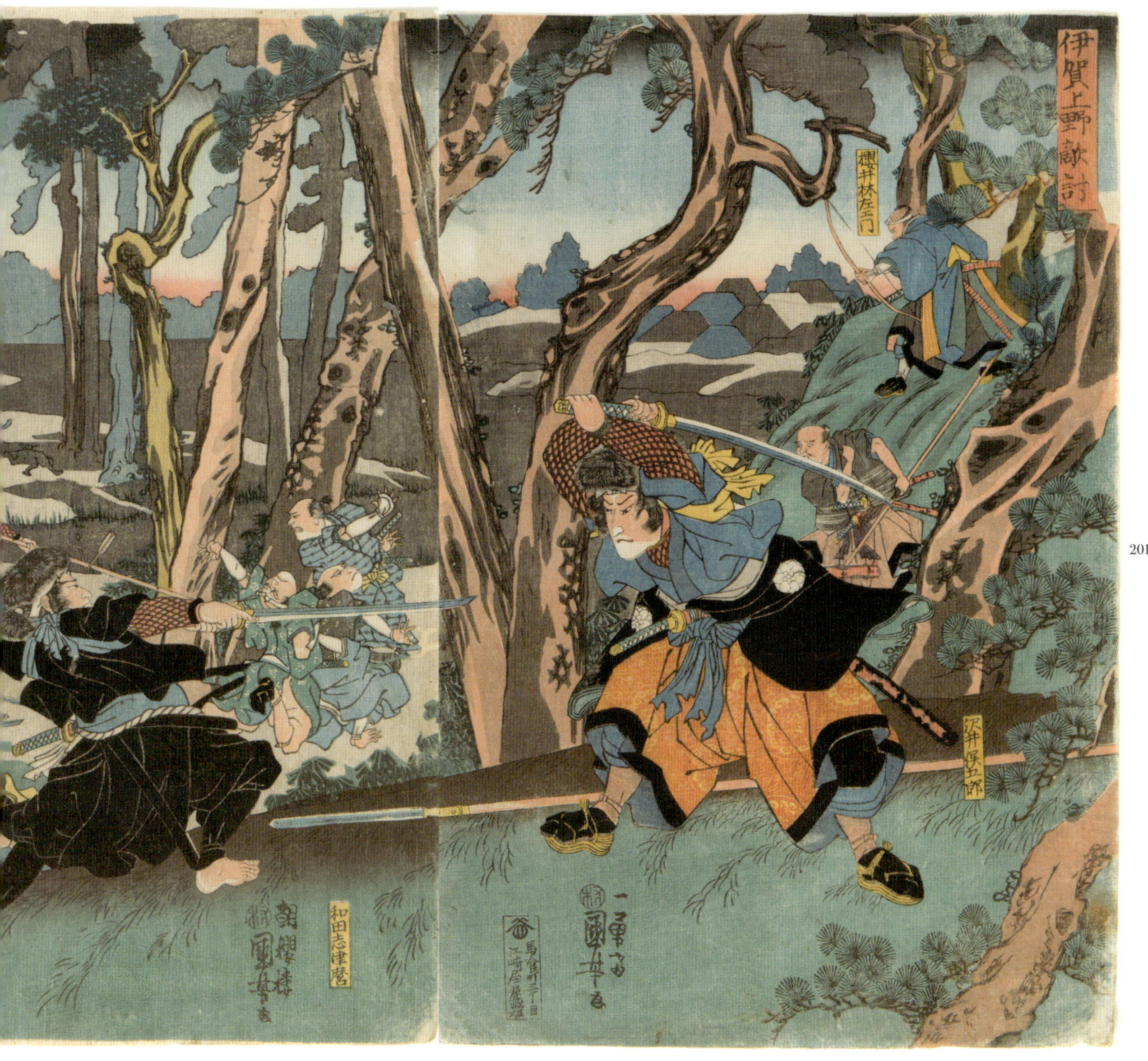

"Vengeance at Iga Ueno" by Utagawa Kuniyoshi

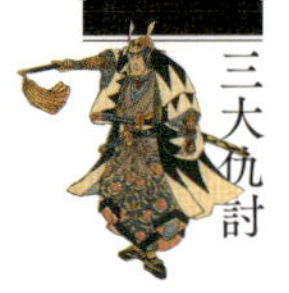

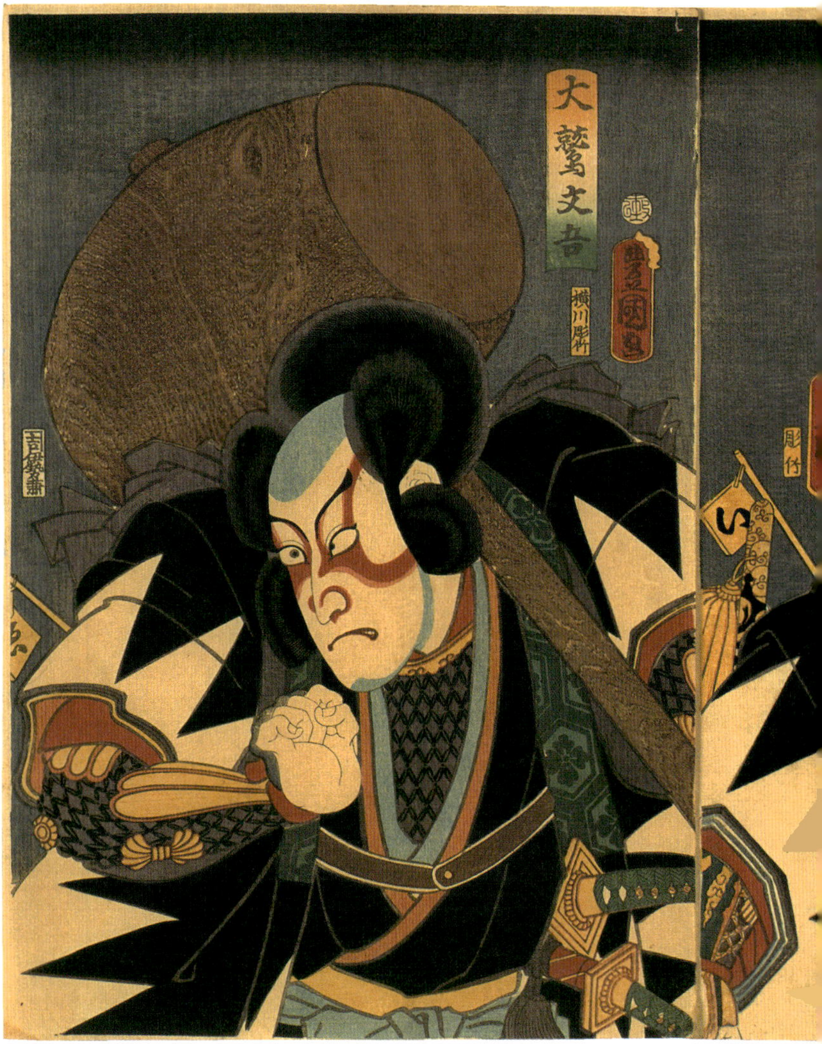

202

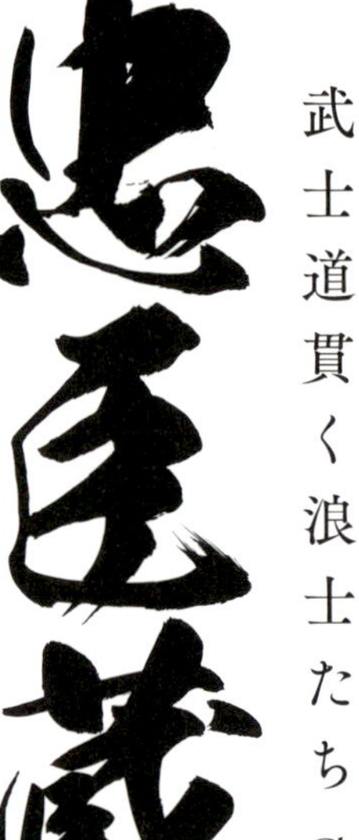

忠臣蔵

武士道貫く浪士たち【三大仇討】

Chūshingura, Forty-Seven Rōnin
Three Biggest Acts of Revenge in Japan

元禄14年（1701）、勅使走役の播磨赤穂藩主浅野内匠頭長矩が、指南役の吉良上野介義央に立腹して江戸城松之廊下で刃傷に及び、即日切腹・改易を命じられた。家老の大石内蔵助良雄をはじめとする赤穂浪士47人は、復讐を画策。翌年、吉良邸を襲撃して義央を討ち取り、主君の仇を討った。この事件はとりわけ民衆の人情に訴え、赤穂浪士は義士と称えられた。のちに「仮名手本忠臣蔵」など演劇・文学の題材となり、今もなお愛され続けている。

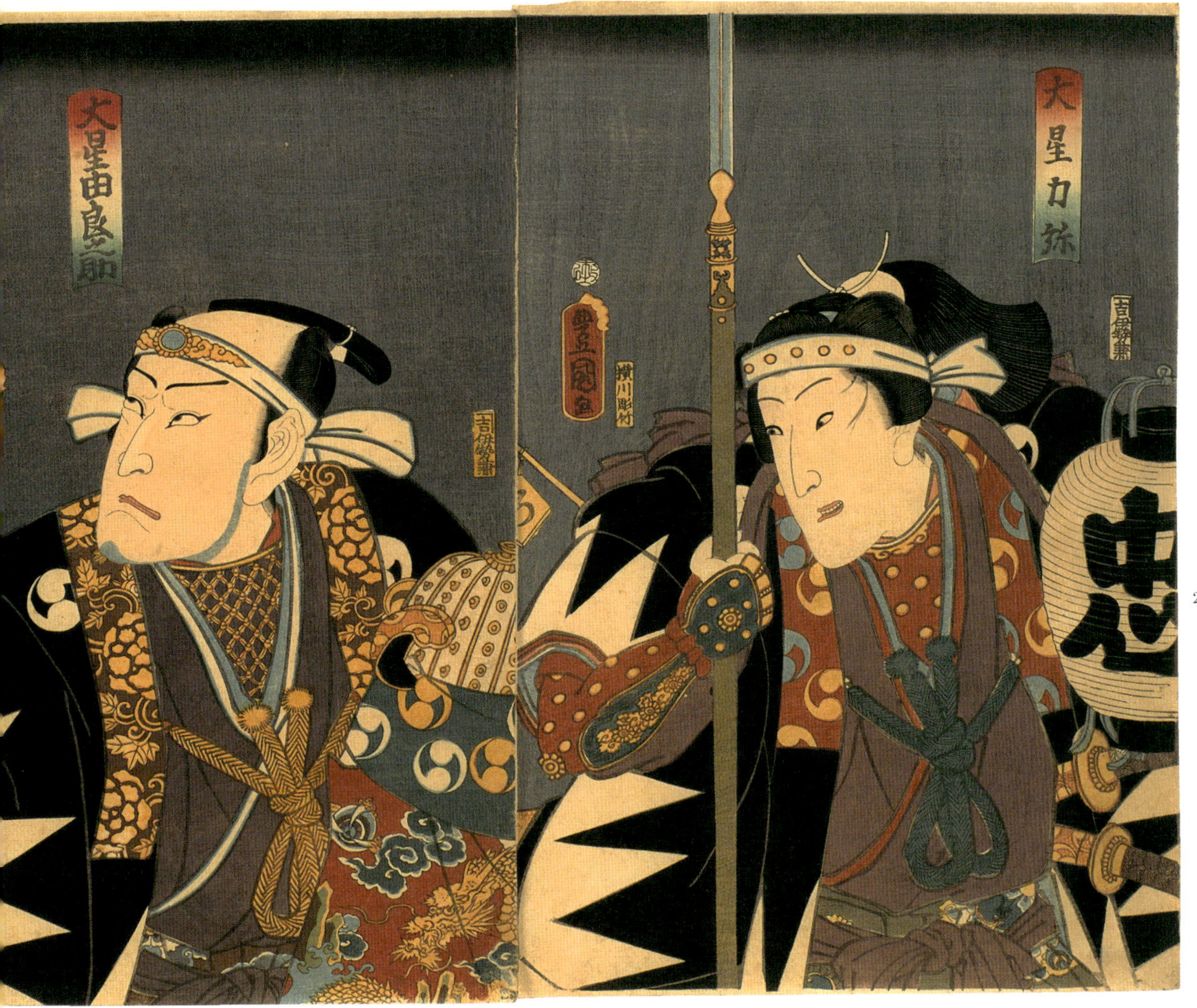

【大星力也 大星由良之助 大鷲文吾】歌川国貞（三代豊国）安政6年（1859）
"Ōboshi Rikiya, Ōboshi Yuranosuke, Ōwashi Bungo" by Utagawa Kunisada (Toyokuni III)

In 1701, Asano Naganori, Lord of Akō domain in Harima Province (Hyōgo), is ordered to commit seppuku after injuring court official Kira Yoshinaka in the halls of Edo Castle. The injustice of the punishment leads forty-seven Akō samurai, all now wandering rōnin due to the dissolution of the Akō domain, to plot revenge. Led by former Chamberlain Ōishi Kuranosuke, their dedication and loyalty made them heroes among the masses, especially as told in plays and literature as *Chūshingura* (commonly known in English as *The Forty-Seven Rōnin*), which is still beloved today.

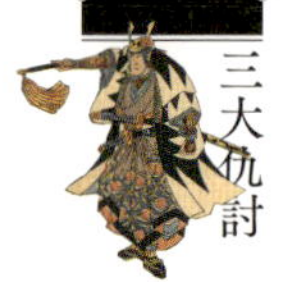

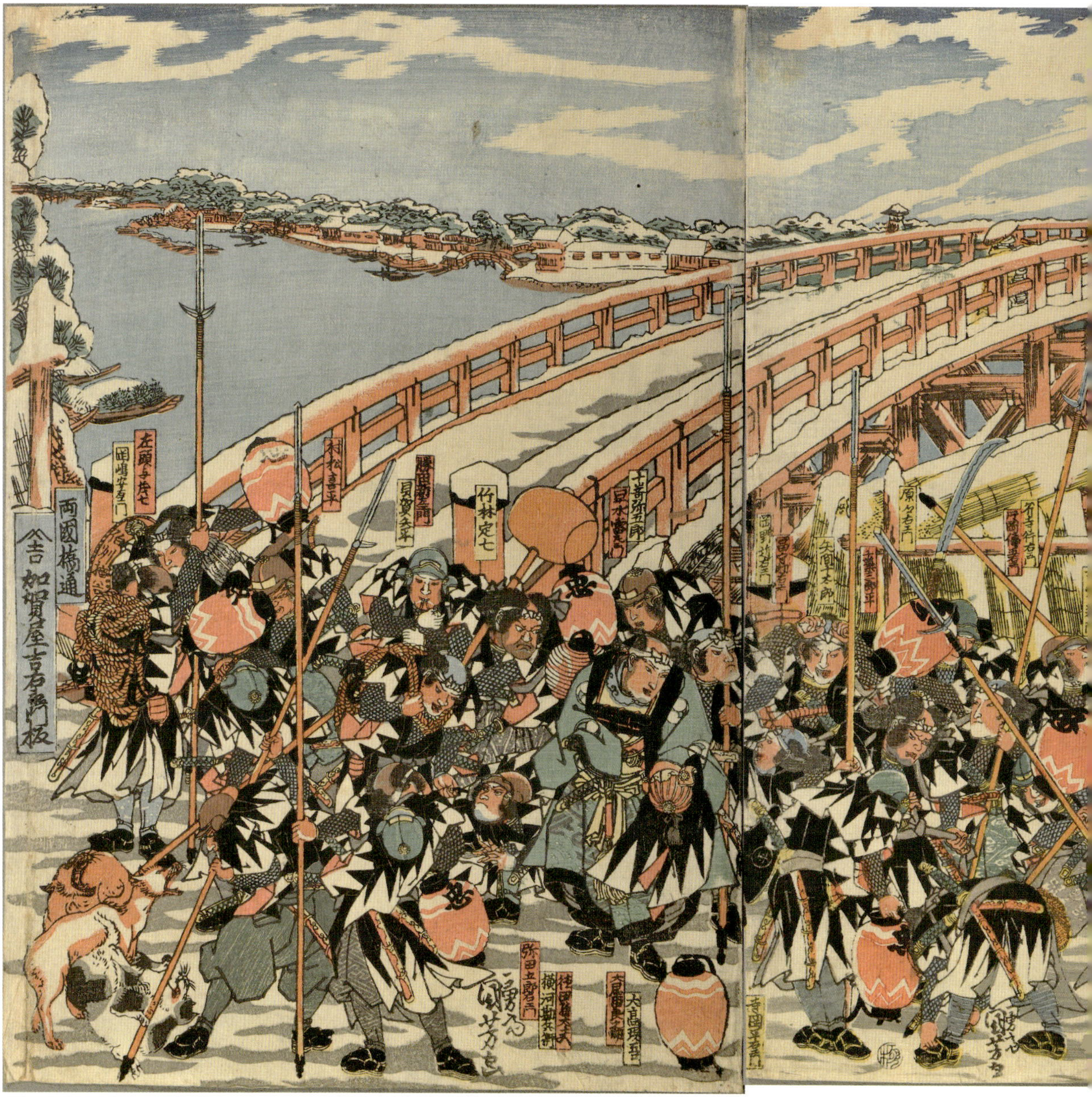

【忠臣蔵十一段目両国橋勢揃図】歌川国芳　文政10年（1827）頃

義士たちは討ち入りの夜、揃いの火事衣装を着て、江戸本所松坂町にある吉良邸近くの両国橋東詰に集結した。

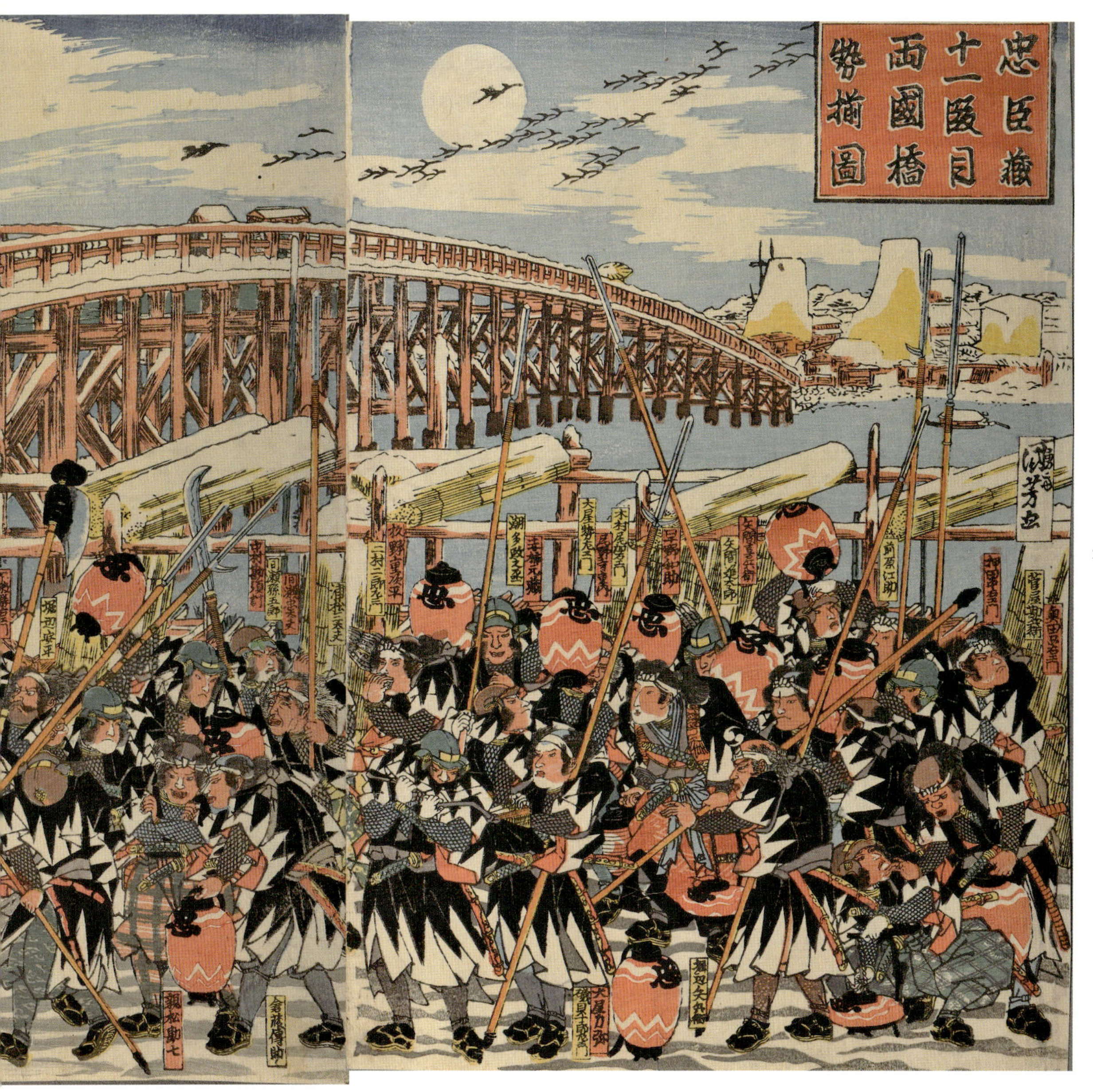

"The Forty-Seven Rōnin: Assembling at Ryōgoku Bridge" by Utagawa Kuniyoshi

The night before they are to exact their revenge, the loyal samurai of Akō assembled
at the eastern end of Ryōgoku Bridge, near Kira Yoshinaka's mansion in Edo, disguised as firemen.

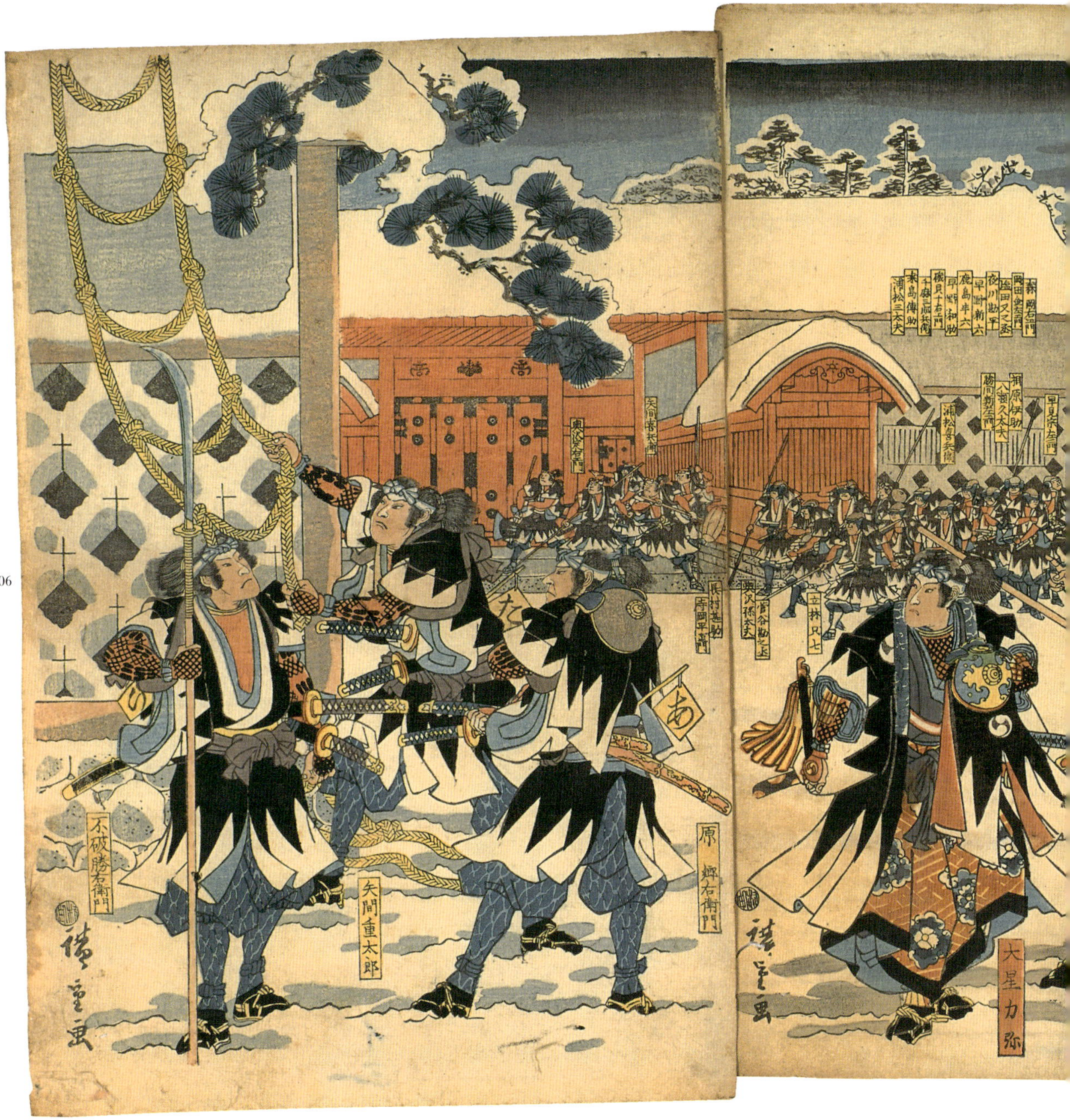

【義士仇討之図】歌川広重　弘化3年（1846）頃

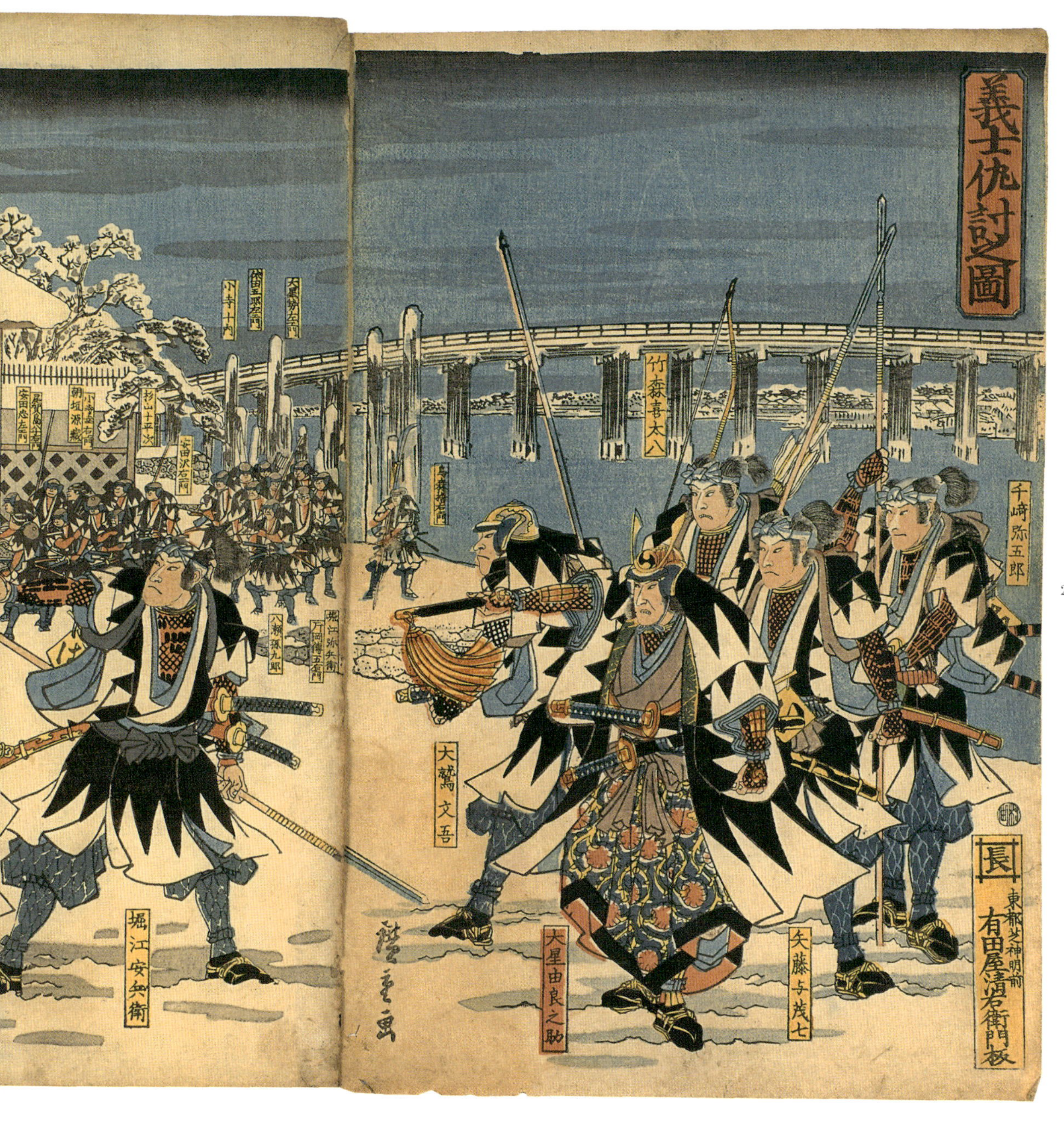

"The Loyal Retainers Execute Their Plans" by Utagawa Hiroshige

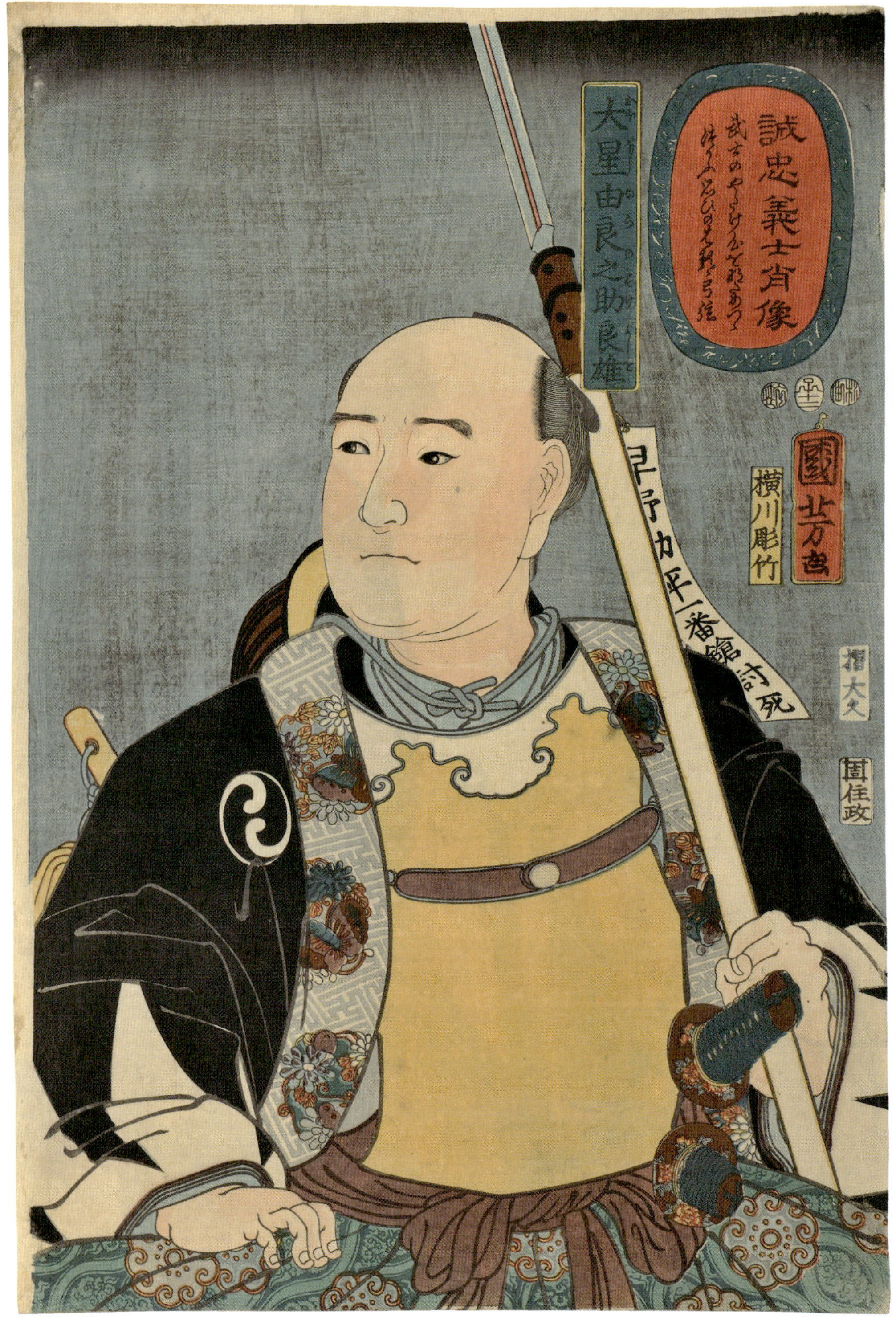

【誠忠義士肖像 大星由良之助良雄】歌川国芳 嘉永5年（1852）
"Ōboshi Yuranosuke Yoshio" by Utagawa Kuniyoshi

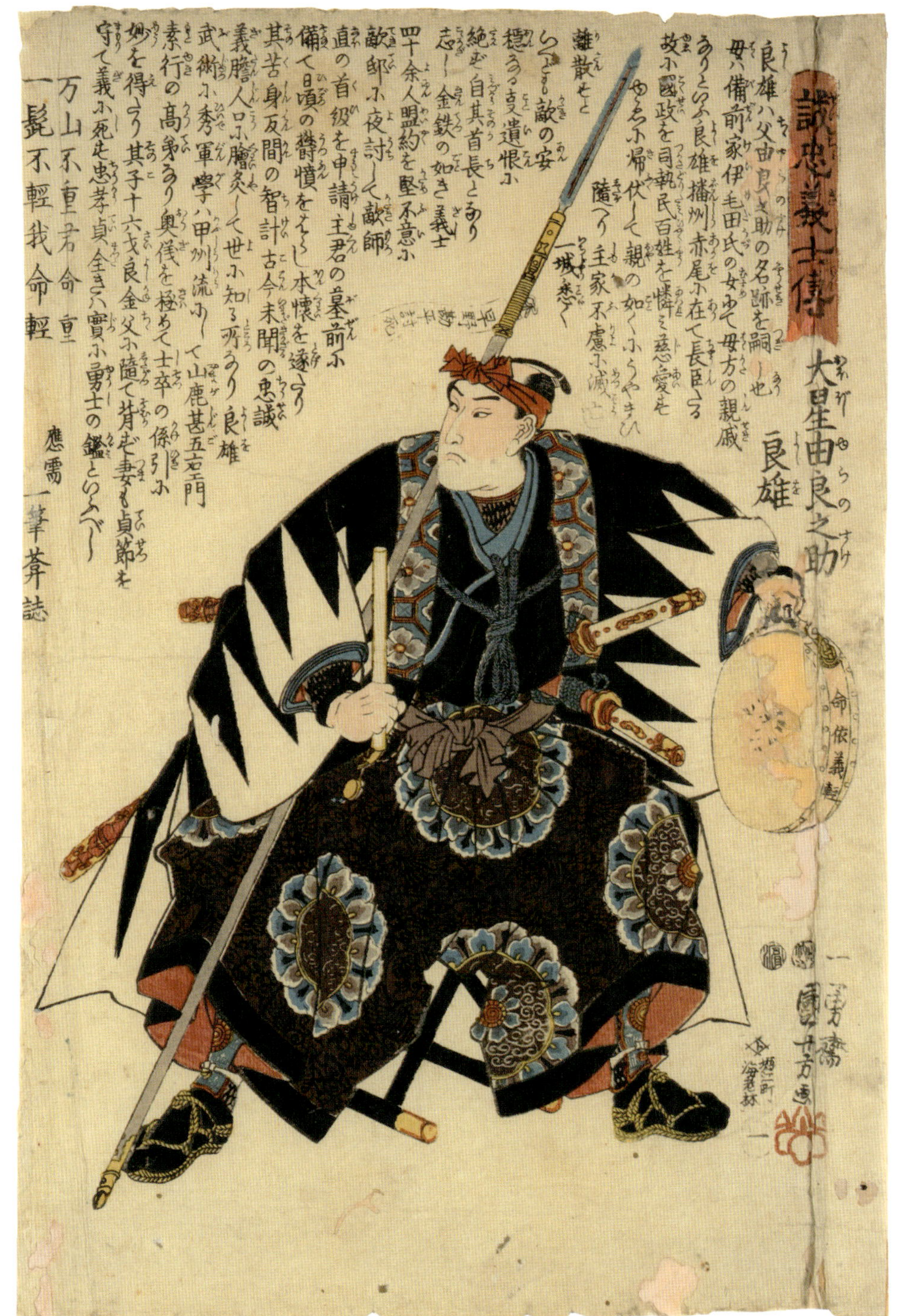

【誠忠義士伝 大星由良之助良雄】歌川国芳　弘化4年（1847）
大石内蔵助は浅野家の家老。刃傷事件後、主家の再興に尽力するも受け入れられず、赤穂義士の首領となって討ち入りを決行した。

"Ōboshi Yuranosuke Yoshio" by Utagawa Kuniyoshi

Ōishi Kuranosuke was Chamberlain of the Asano clan. After the fateful incident at Edo Castle,
he tried his best to restore the Akō domain's name, then became the head of loyal avengers once no other honorable paths were left open to them.

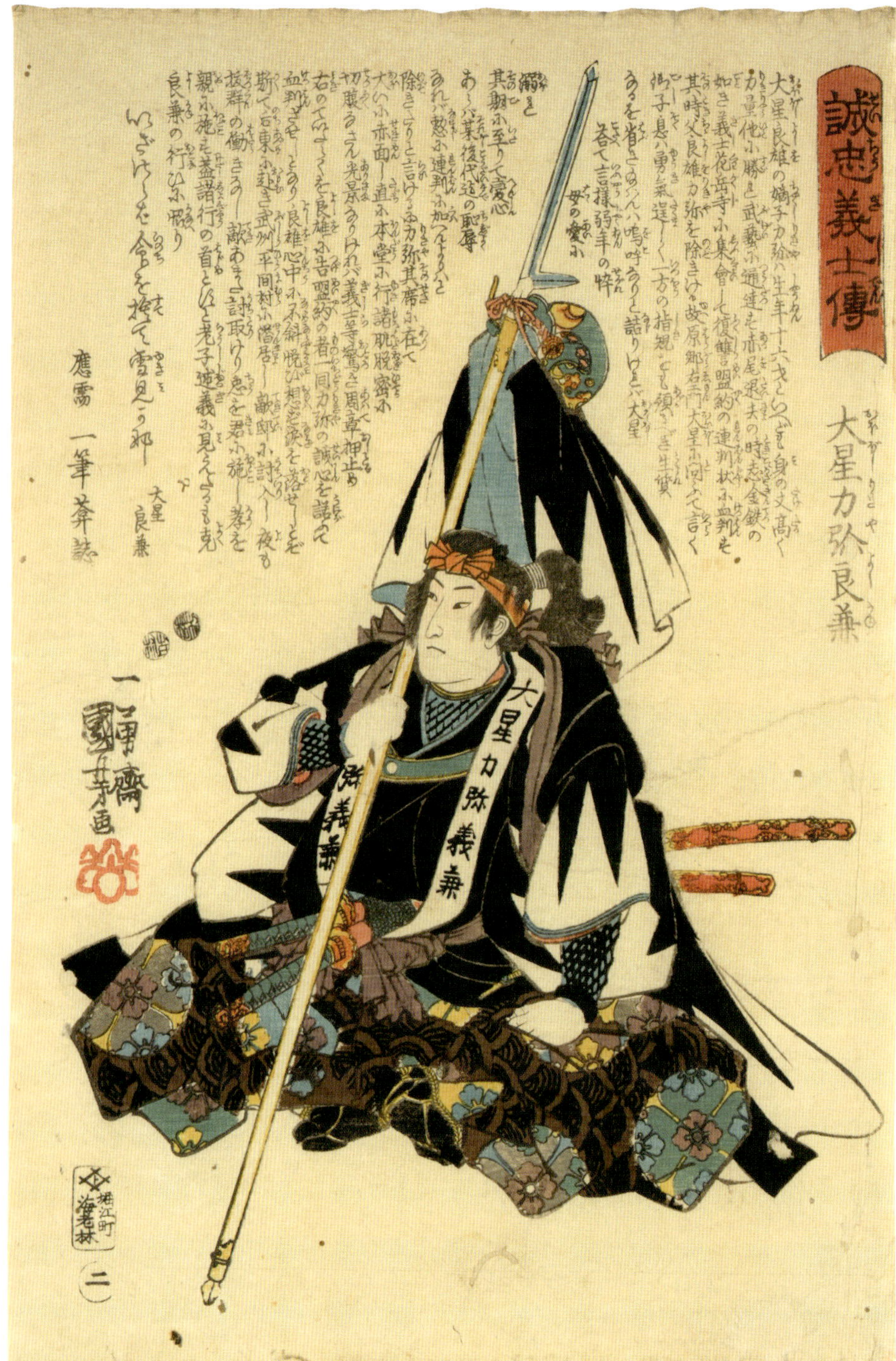

【誠忠義士伝 大星力也良兼】歌川国芳 弘化4年(1847)

大石主税は内蔵助の子で、赤穂義士最年少。討ち入り時には裏門隊の大将を務めた。

"Ōboshi Rikiya Yoshikane" by Utagawa Kuniyoshi

The son of Ōishi Kuranosuke, Ōishi Chikara (also known as Ōboshi Rikiya) was the youngest of the loyal Akō samurai.
During the raid on Kira Yoshinaka's mansion, he was put in charge of the group attacking from the rear gate.

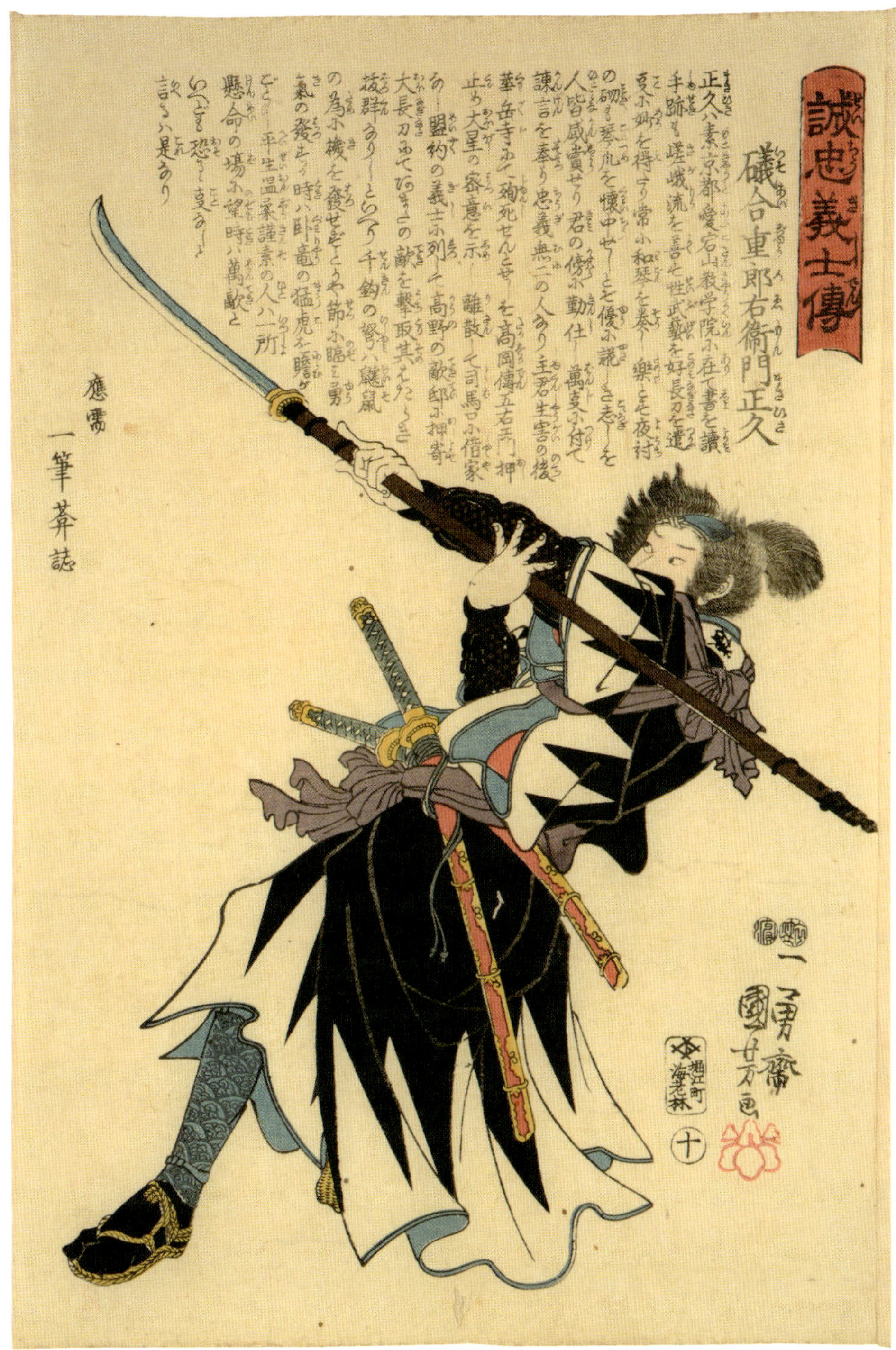

【誠忠義士伝 磯合重郎右衛門正久】歌川国芳 弘化4年（1847）

磯貝十郎左衛門は小姓として浅野内匠頭に仕え、のち、側用人にまで出世した。討ち入りの際には機転をきかせて、蝋燭を邸内に灯した。

"Isoai Jūrōemon Masahisa" by Utagawa Kuniyoshi

Isogai Jūrōzaemon became a page to a top minister in the Asano household before rising to secretary to the Shogun.
During the climatic raid, Isogai wisely thought to light up the interior of Kira's mansion with candles so that their prey could be more easily seen.

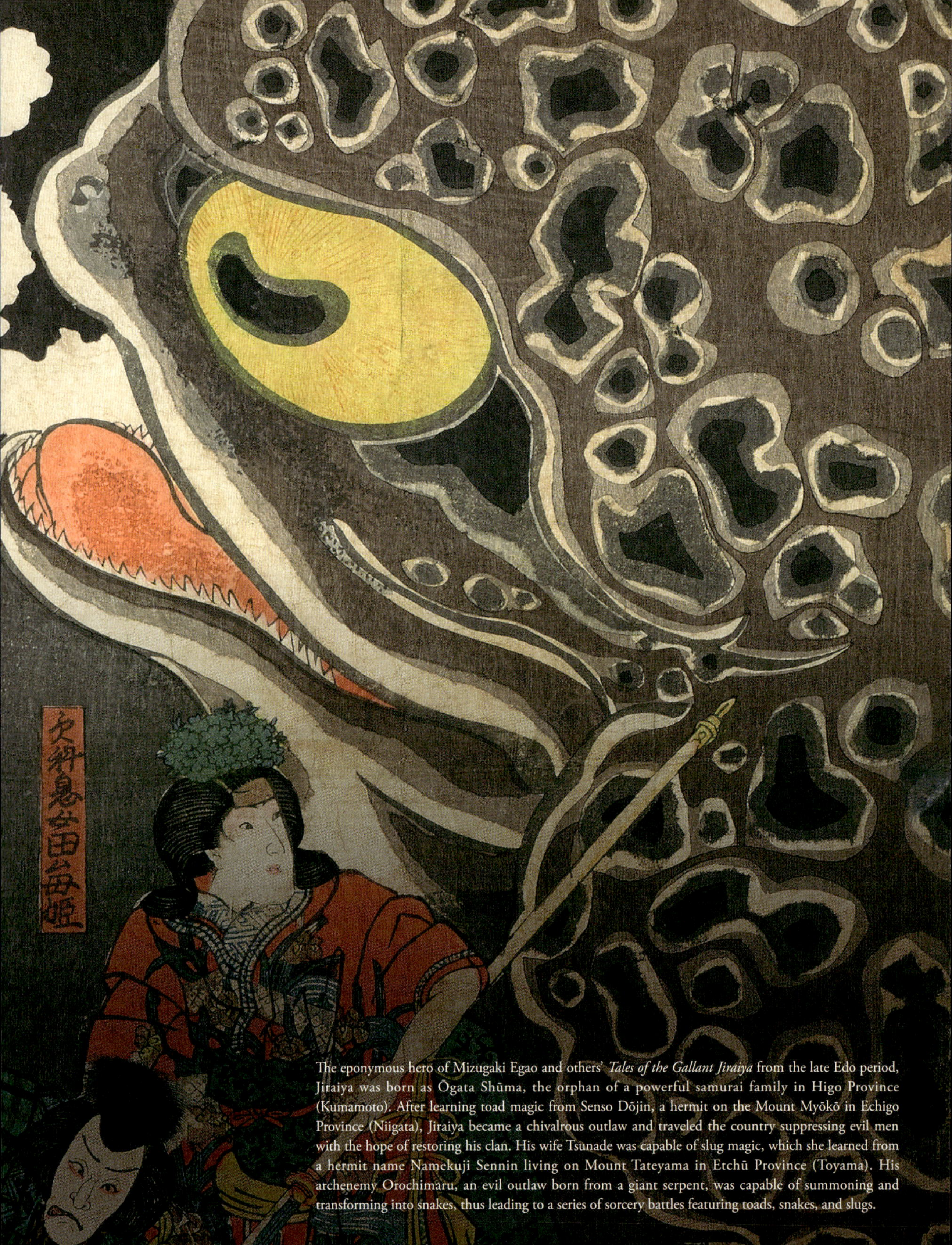

The eponymous hero of Mizugaki Egao and others' *Tales of the Gallant Jiraiya* from the late Edo period, Jiraiya was born as Ōgata Shūma, the orphan of a powerful samurai family in Higo Province (Kumamoto). After learning toad magic from Senso Dōjin, a hermit on the Mount Myōkō in Echigo Province (Niigata), Jiraiya became a chivalrous outlaw and traveled the country suppressing evil men with the hope of restoring his clan. His wife Tsunade was capable of slug magic, which she learned from a hermit name Namekuji Sennin living on Mount Tateyama in Etchū Province (Toyama). His archenemy Orochimaru, an evil outlaw born from a giant serpent, was capable of summoning and transforming into snakes, thus leading to a series of sorcery battles featuring toads, snakes, and slugs.

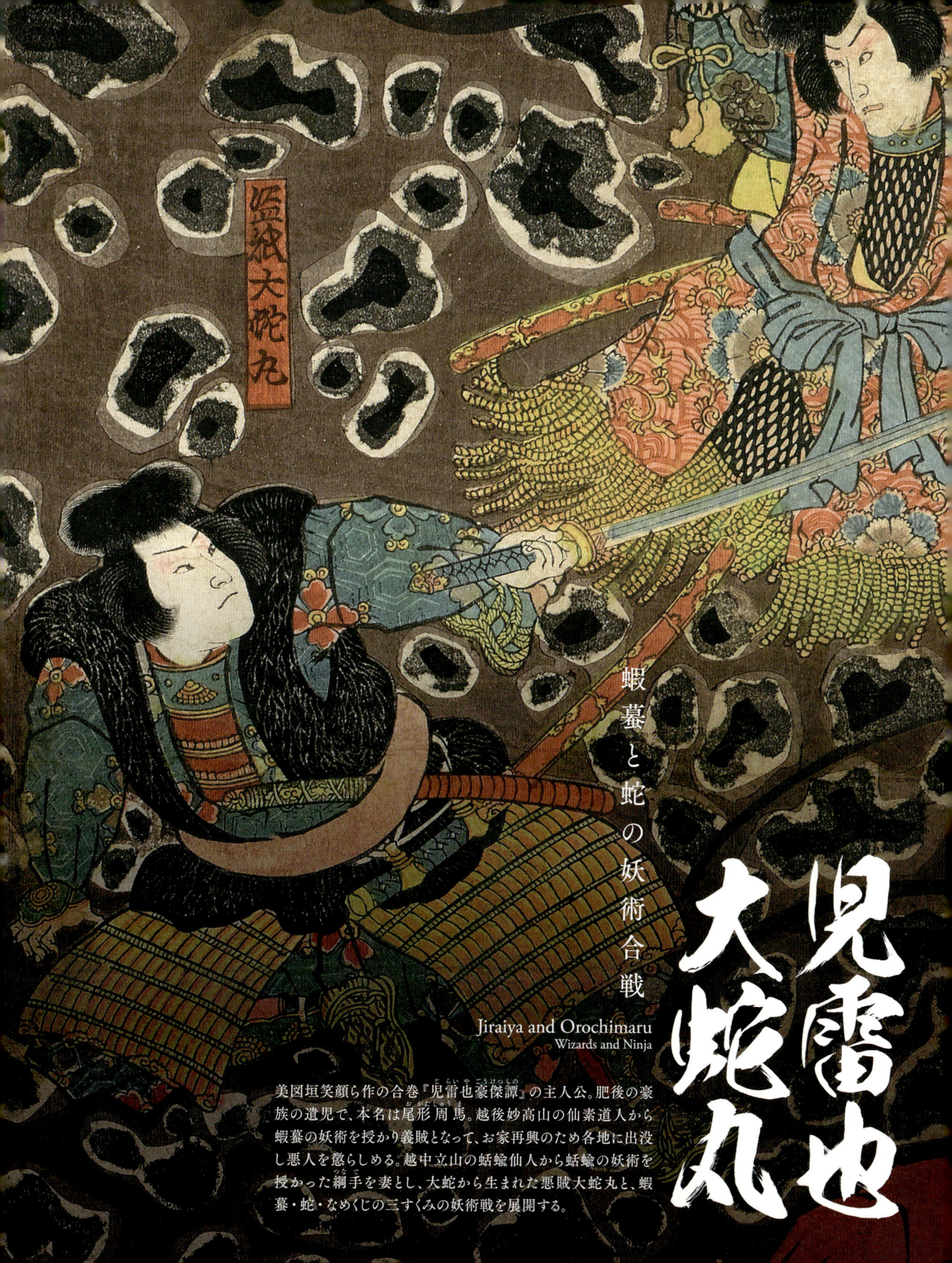

蝦蟇と蛇の妖術合戦

児雷也 大蛇丸

Jiraiya and Orochimaru
Wizards and Ninja

美図垣笑顔ら作の合巻『児雷也豪傑譚』の主人公。肥後の豪族の遺児で、本名は尾形周馬。越後妙高山の仙素道人から蝦蟇の妖術を授かり義賊となって、お家再興のため各地に出没し悪人を懲らしめる。越中立山の蛞蝓仙人から蛞蝓の妖術を授かった綱手を妻とし、大蛇から生まれた悪賊大蛇丸と、蝦蟇・蛇・なめくじの三すくみの妖術戦を展開する。

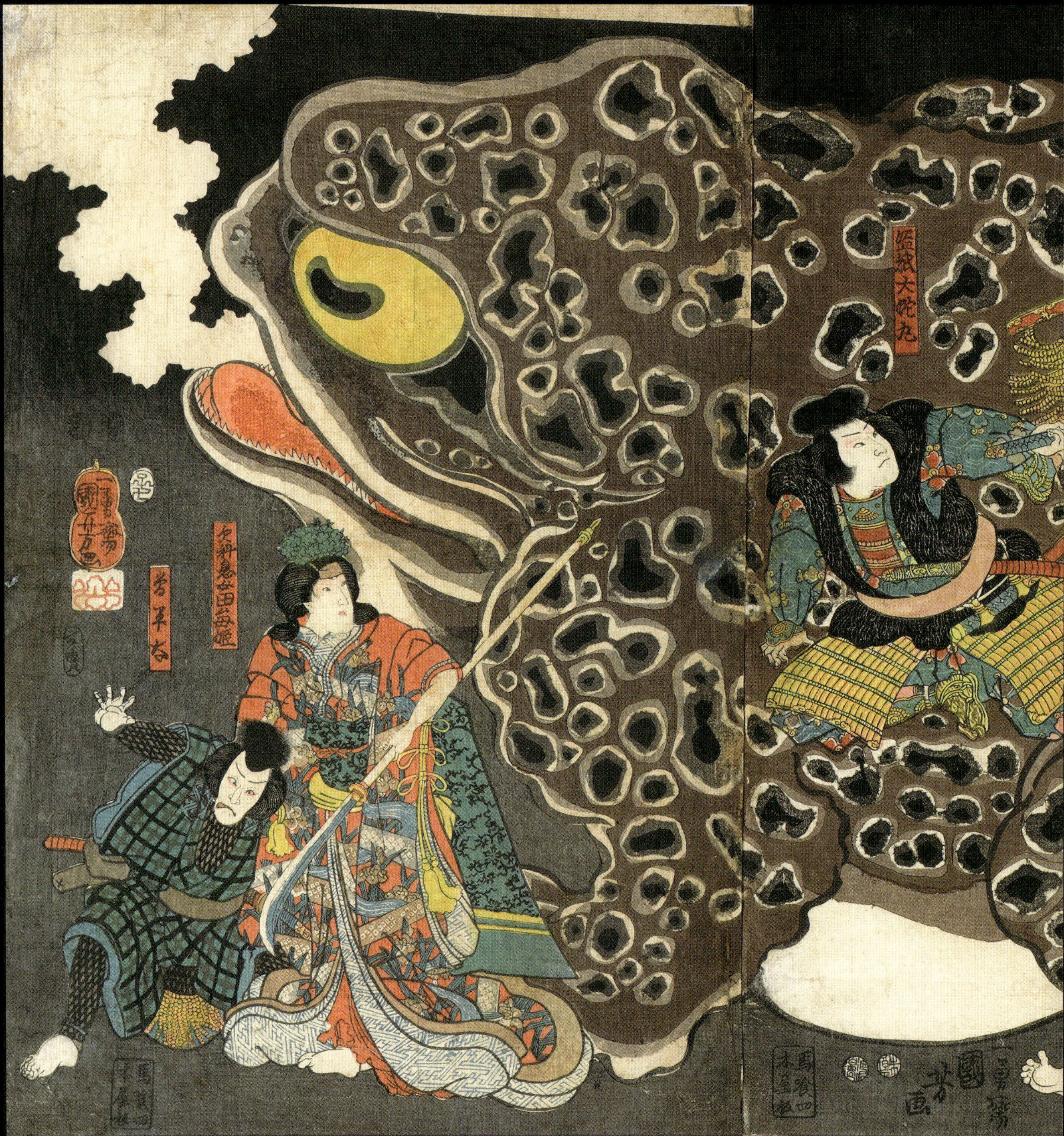

214

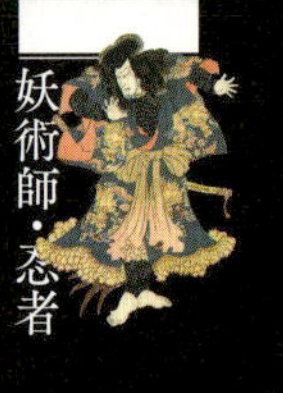

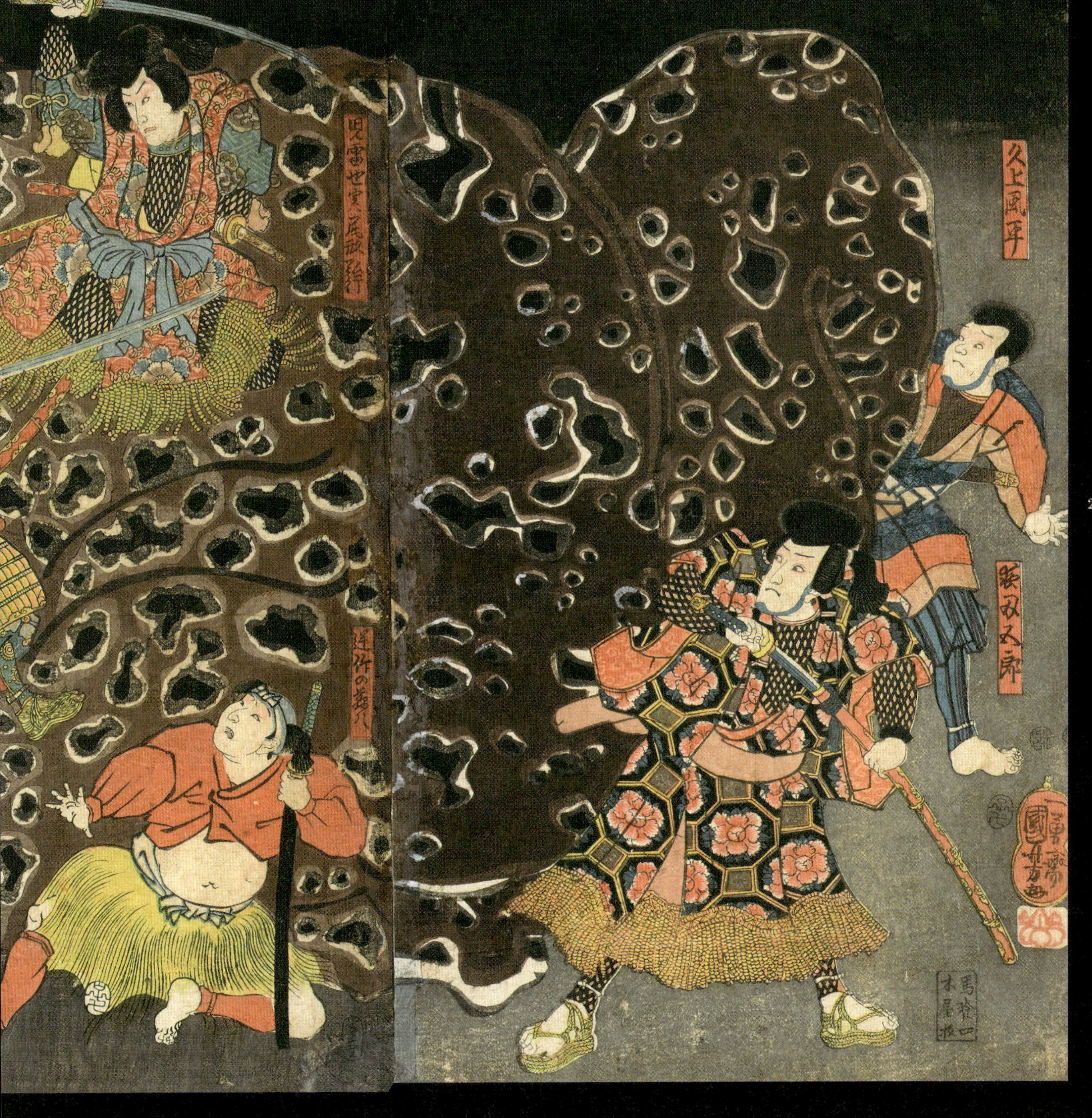

"Tales of the Gallant Jiraiya" by Utagawa Kuniyoshi
A battle between Jiraiya, master of summoning giant toads, and his archenemy Orochimaru,

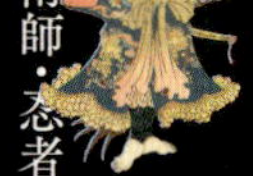

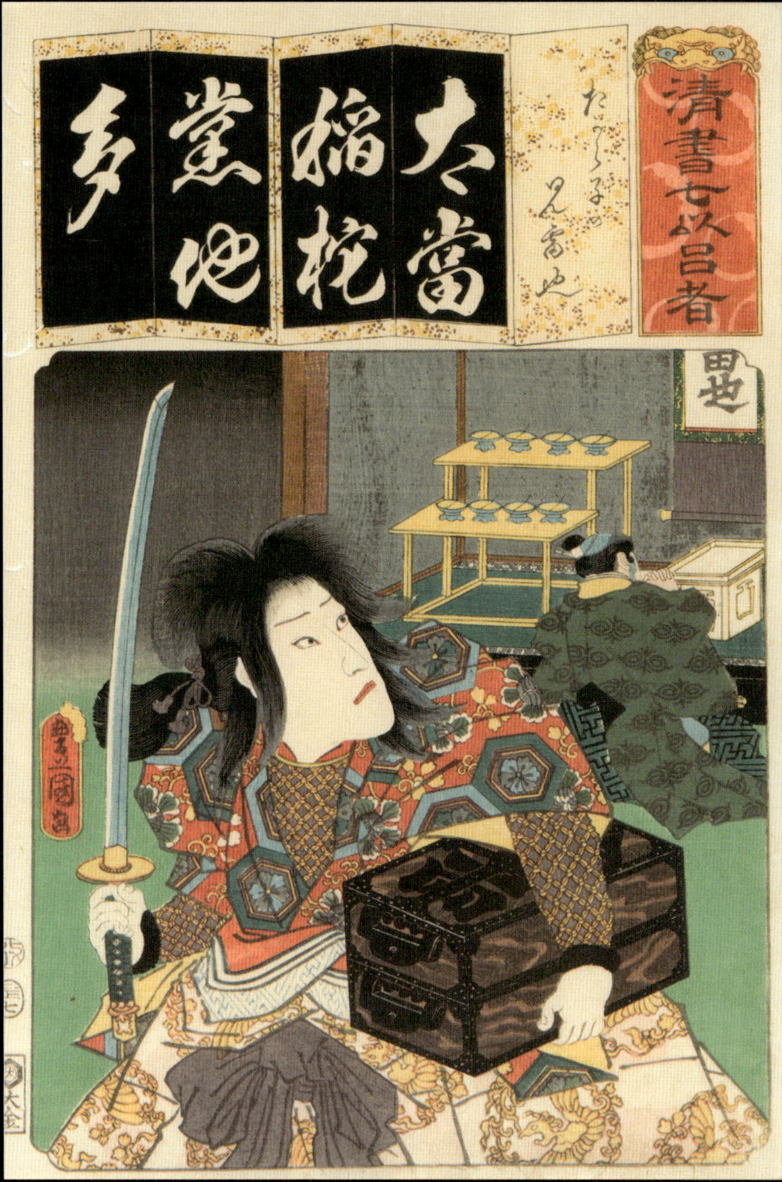

【清書七いろは たから子の児雷也】歌川国貞（三代豊国）安政3年（1856）

巫女の宝子に扮した児雷也は悪代官八鎌鹿六に、床の間に千両箱と灯明を飾って祈れば世界中の金が寄ってくると言って騙した。
児雷也が千両箱を奪って立ち去ると、掛軸の楊柳観音の絵は、「児雷也」の三文字に変わっていた。

"Seven Variations of the Iroha Alphabet: The Thief Jiraiya Impersonating Takarako" by Utagawa Kunisada (Toyokuni III)

Disguised as the female shrine attendant Takarako, Jiraiya tricks the evil magistrate Yakama Shikaroku into believing that,
if you place candles and a thousand gold pieces in a tokonoma alcove and pray to them, all the world's money will come your way.
As Jiraiya absconds with the gold, the hanging scroll in the alcove changes from a picture of the bodhisattava Yōryū Kannon to Jiraiya's name in kanji.

【本朝水滸伝豪傑八百人一個 尾形周馬寛行】歌川国芳 天保4〜6年（1833-35）頃

越後妙高山の蝦蟇の仙人を悩ませる隣国信濃黒姫山の大蛇の妖怪を、児雷也は大筒で砲撃して倒したという。

"Eight Hundred Heroes of Our Own Country's Water Margin: Ōgata Shūma Hiroyuki" by Utagawa Kuniyoshi

A giant serpent yōkai from Mount Kurohime in neighboring Shinano Province threatens Jiraiya's teacher,
the toad hermit of Mount Myōkō in Echigo. Jiraiya is shown here readying to blast the serpent with a giant cannon.

本朝水滸傳豪傑八百人一個
尾形周馬寛行

原三好ろ使へと浪人
より自來也きはり
越後國頸城郡
高田後姚
香山江信
濃乃岩
所ち住地国
績に来にて
蠶松ちる
中にる真
人のほげ
よって大炮
坡打かけく
蝌蚪を

一勇齋
國芳画

永遠の愛され童児

金太郎

Kintarō
Brave Heroes
and Gallant Men

頼光四天王の坂田金時の幼名。怪童丸とも
呼ばれる剛腕の持ち主で、相模国足柄山で熊
などの獣を友として育った。赤ら顔でよく太り、
腹掛けをかけ、まさかりを担いだ姿で表現され、
端午の節句には健康と出世を願って飾られる。

Kintarō is the boyhood name of Sakata Kintoki,
one of Yorimitsu's Four Guardian Kings. Due to
his brute strength, he was also called Kaidōmaru.
He was raised among bears and other wild
animals on Mount Ashigara in Sagami Province,
in present-day Hakone. He is usually depicted
chubby, red-faced, wearing a *harakake* apron, and
wielding a war axe, and features prominently in
Children's Day Festival decorations in Japan as a
symbol of personal effort and achievement

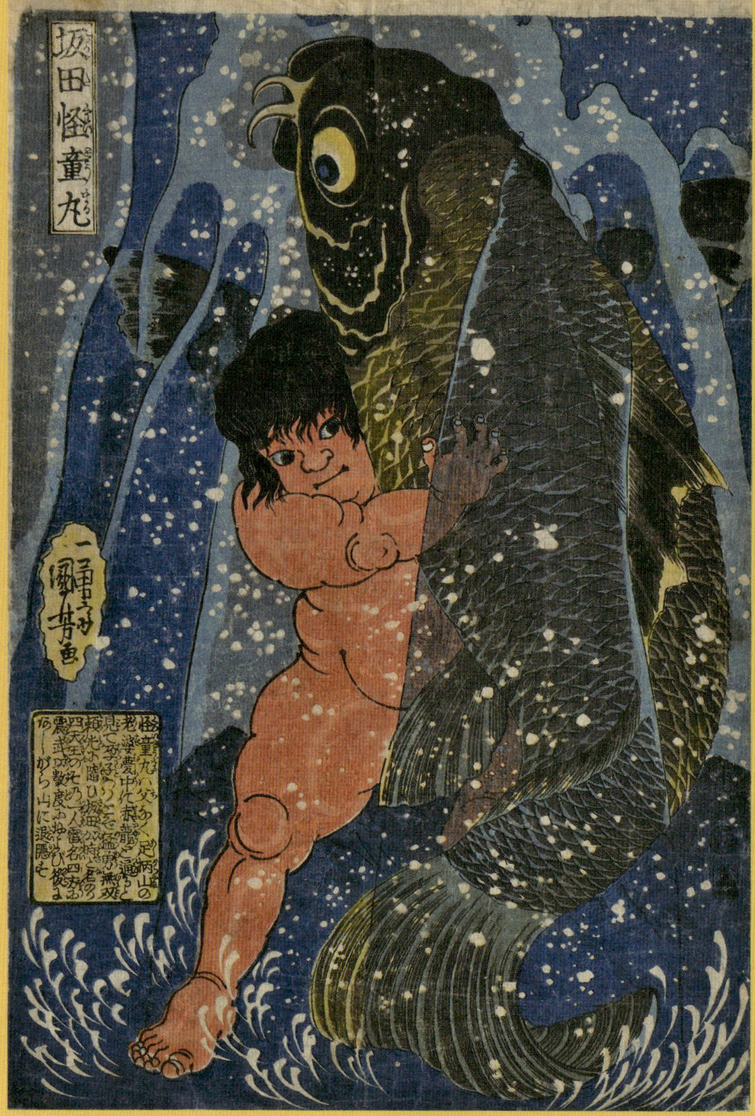

【坂田怪童丸】歌川国芳　天保7年（1836）頃
鯉の滝登りと金太郎はいずれも出世の象徴である。

"Sakata Kaidōmaru" by Utagawa Kuniyoshi

Like carp swimming upstream through a waterfall,
Kintarō is a symbol of going out and making something of yourself in the world.

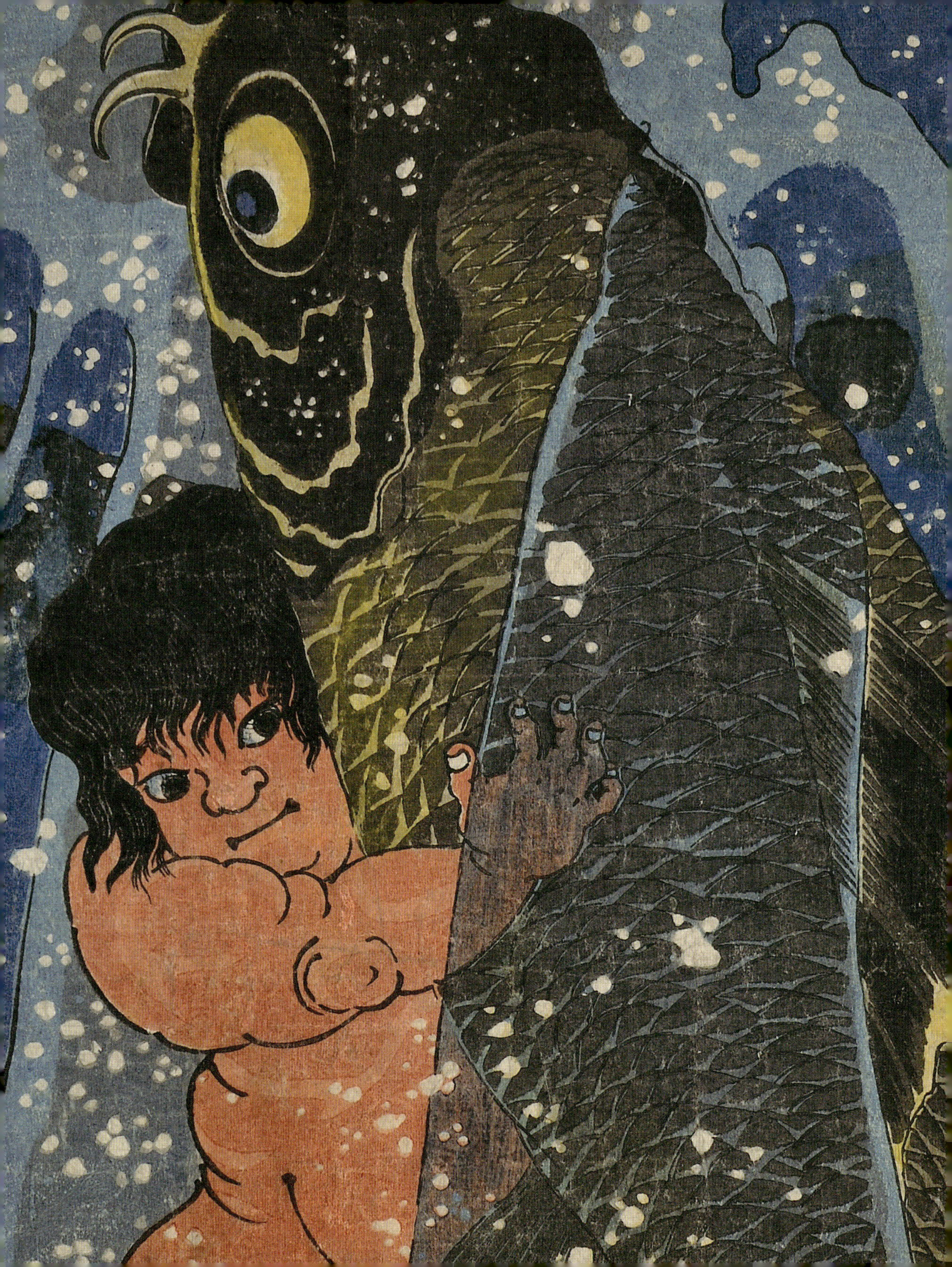

胸躍る勧善懲悪の冒険譚

桃太郎

Momotarō
Brave Heroes
and Gallant Men

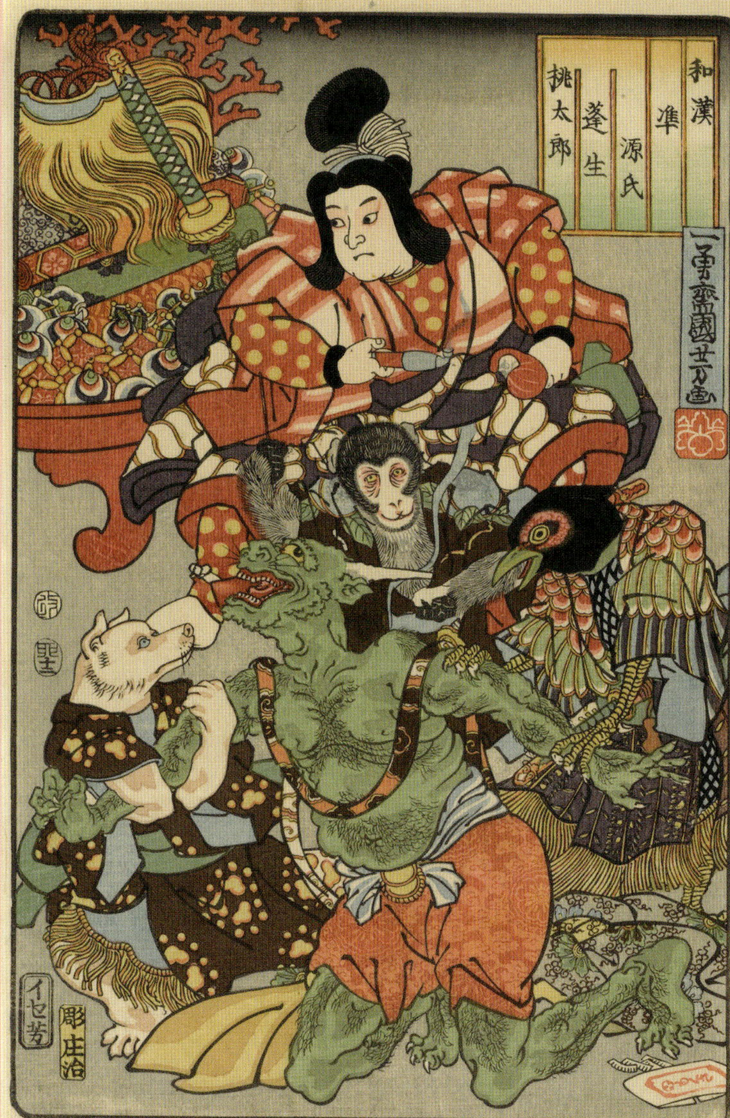

昔話の主人公。お婆さんが川で拾った桃の
中から生まれた男児で、桃太郎と名付けた。
成長し、鬼が島に鬼退治に出かけた途中で
犬、猿、雉に出会う。きび団子を与え家来とし、
ともに鬼を退治して財宝を持ち帰る。江戸時
代、赤本などで流布した。

A famous folktale hero, Momotarō (Peach Boy)
was so named because he was born from a giant
peach an old lady found floating down a stream.
Once older, Momotarō headed to Onigashima
Island to defeat the demons living there, on the
way befriending a dog, a monkey, and a
pheasant, who agree to be his retainers after
being given kibi-dango (millet dumplings)
made by his mother. Together they defeat the
demons and take their treasure. The story of
Momotarō has been popular in children's books
since the Edo period.

【和漢準源氏 蓬生 桃太郎】歌川国芳 安政2年（1855）ギャラリー紅屋収蔵
よもぎで作ったもぐさで鬼に灸をすえている。

"The Tale of Genji through Japanese and Chinese Allusions: The Wormwood Patch, Momotarō"
by Utagawa Kuniyoshi, Gallery Beniya Collection

Momotarō and his companions are shown here applying burning moxa made of wormwood
(an allusion to a chapter of *The Tale of Genji*) to a captured demon's back.

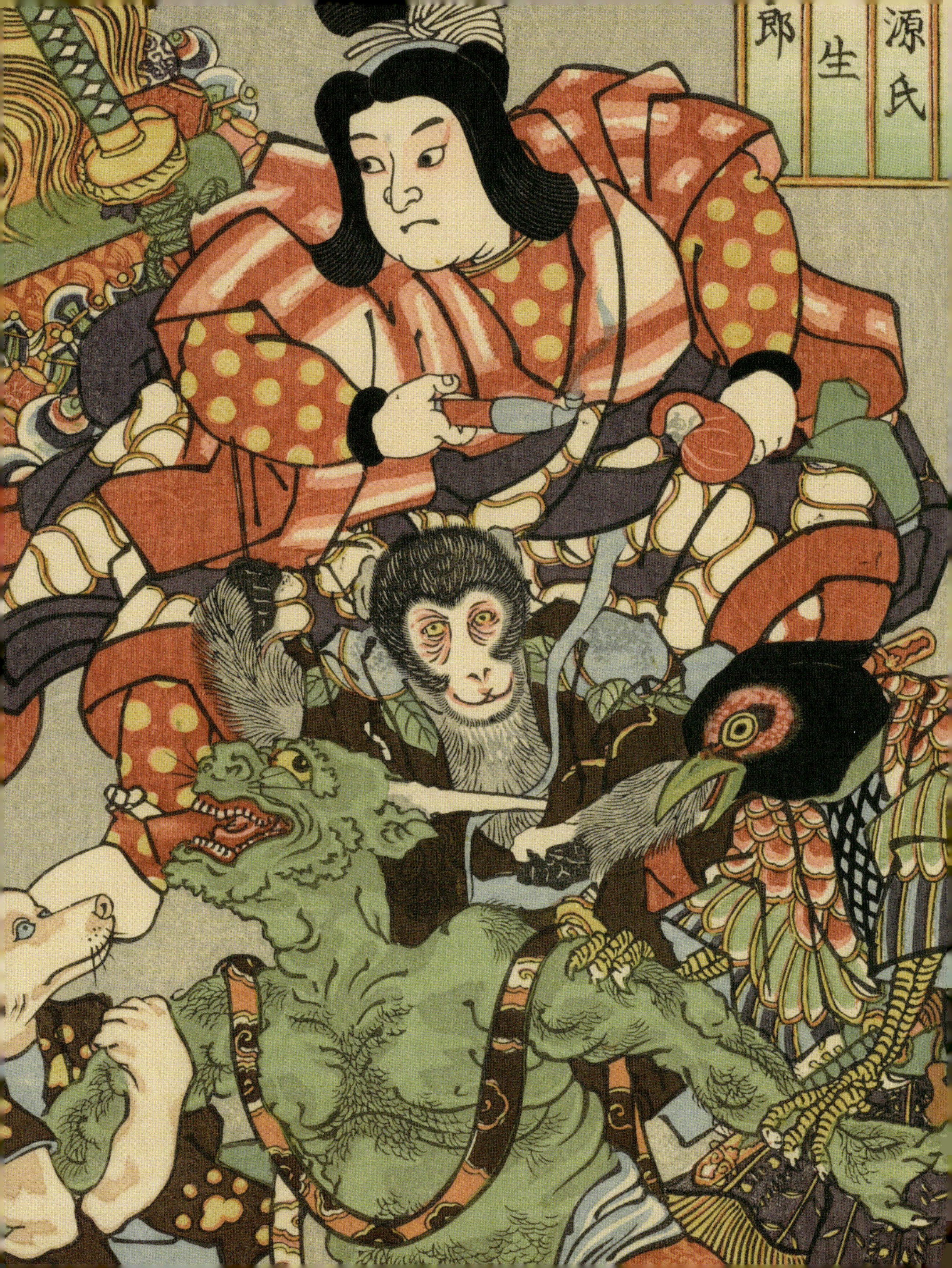

源氏
生
郎

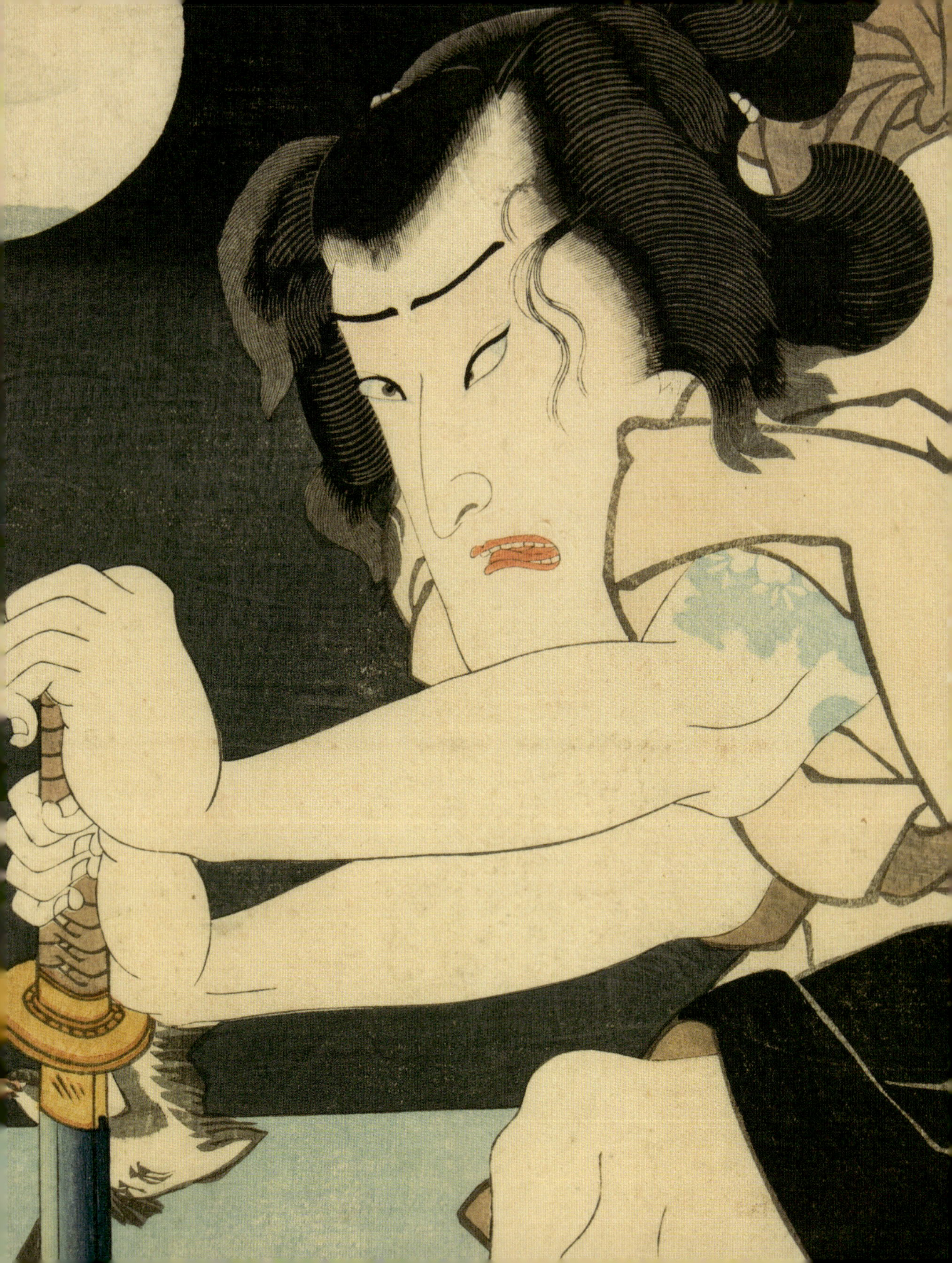

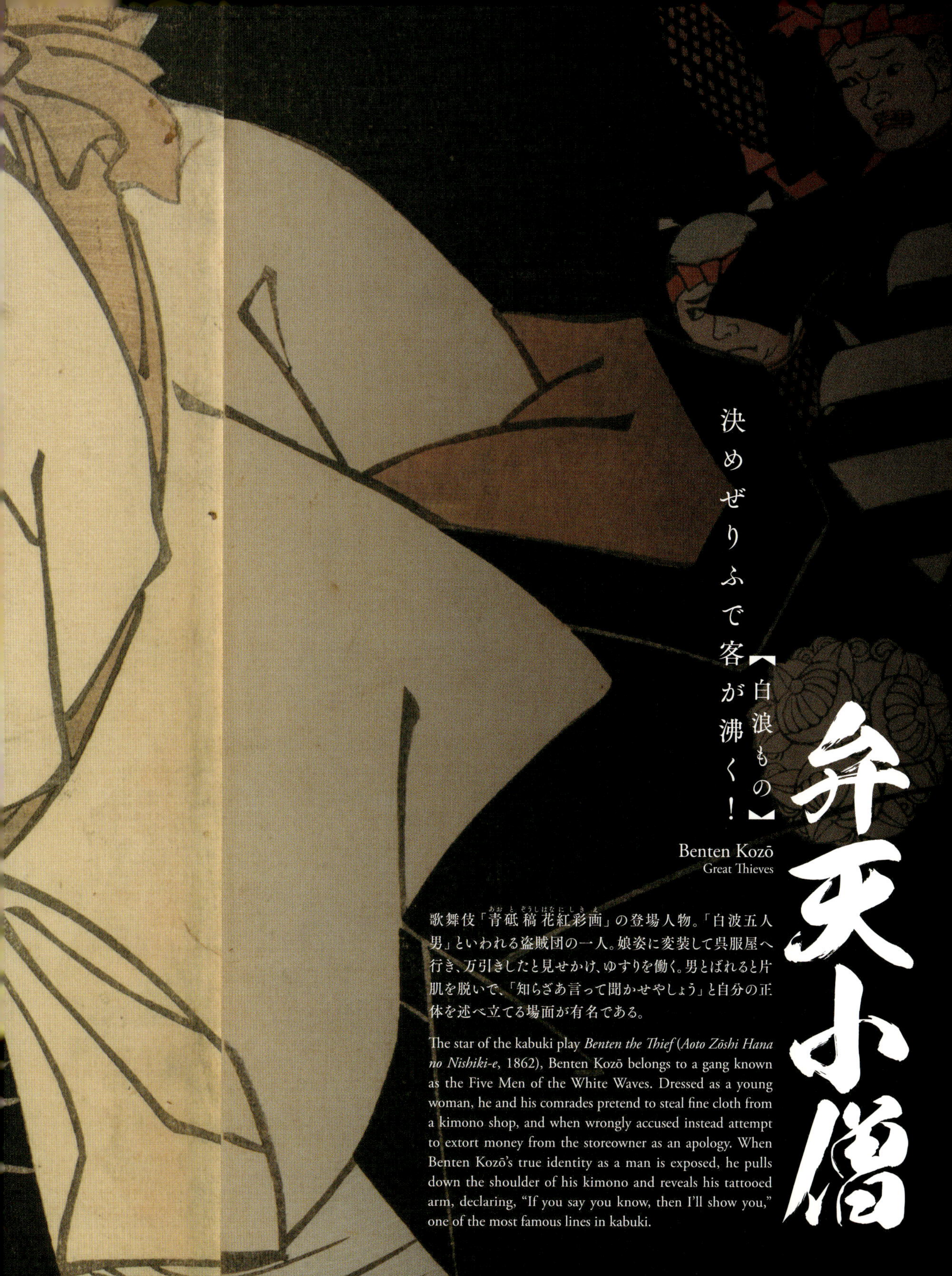

歌舞伎「青砥稿花紅彩画」の登場人物。「白波五人男」といわれる盗賊団の一人。娘姿に変装して呉服屋へ行き、万引きしたと見せかけ、ゆすりを働く。男とばれると片肌を脱いで、「知らざあ言って聞かせやしょう」と自分の正体を述べ立てる場面が有名である。

The star of the kabuki play *Benten the Thief* (*Aoto Zōshi Hana no Nishiki-e*, 1862), Benten Kozō belongs to a gang known as the Five Men of the White Waves. Dressed as a young woman, he and his comrades pretend to steal fine cloth from a kimono shop, and when wrongly accused instead attempt to extort money from the storeowner as an apology. When Benten Kozō's true identity as a man is exposed, he pulls down the shoulder of his kimono and reveals his tattooed arm, declaring, "If you say you know, then I'll show you," one of the most famous lines in kabuki.

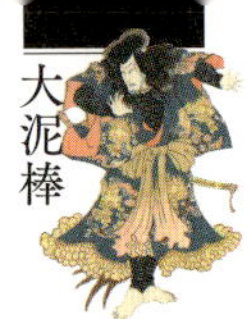

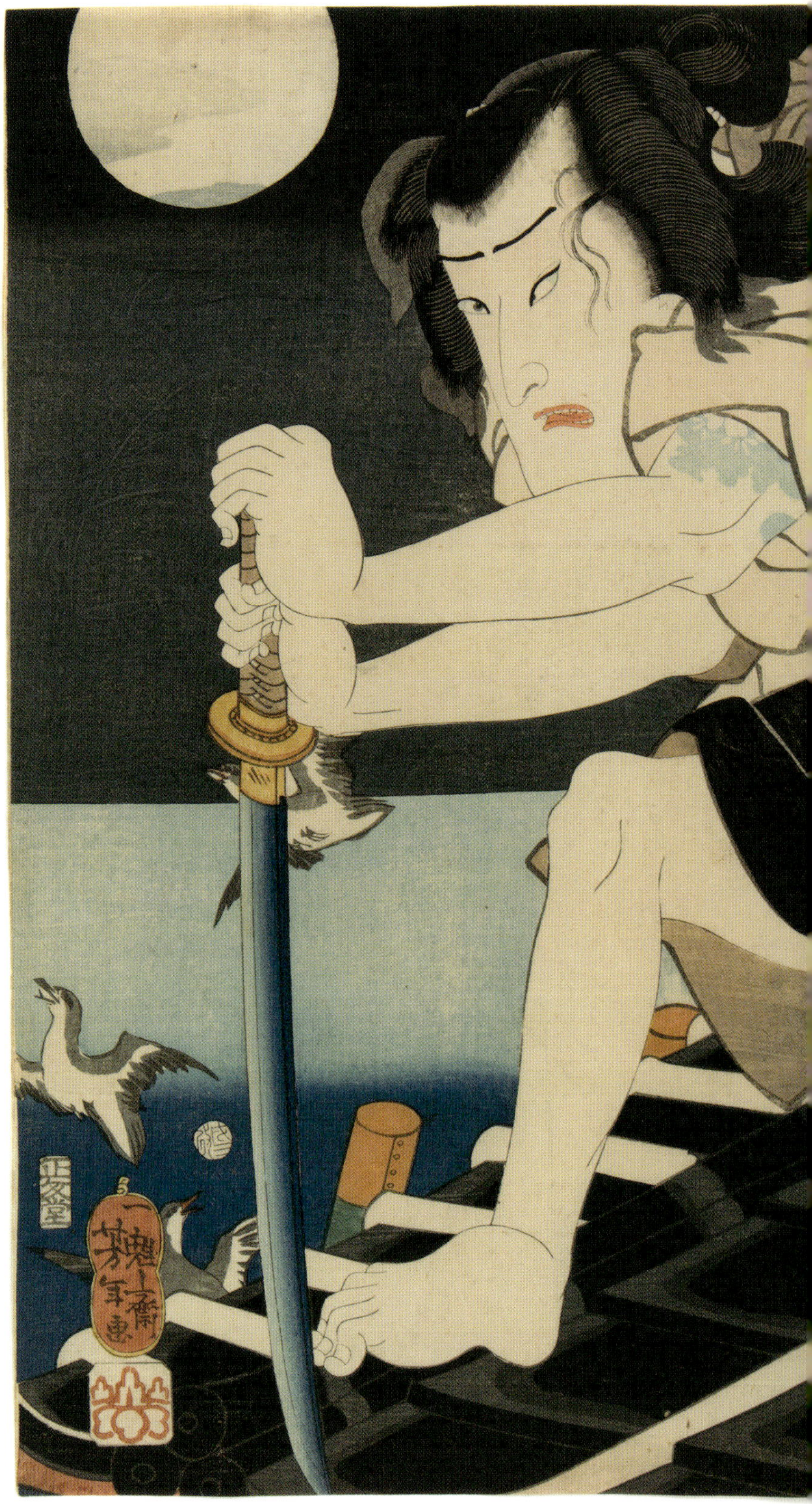

【弁天小僧菊之助 市村羽左衛門】
月岡芳年　文久2年（1862）
悪事の末、捕手に追われ、
極楽寺の屋根の上で腹を斬って自害する。

"Benten Kozō Kikunosuke,
as played by Ichimura Uzaemon"
by Tsukioka Yoshitoshi
Having committed a crime,
Benten Kozō is pursued by the police to
the roof of Gokurakuji Temple,
where he will commit suicide to atone for his crimes.

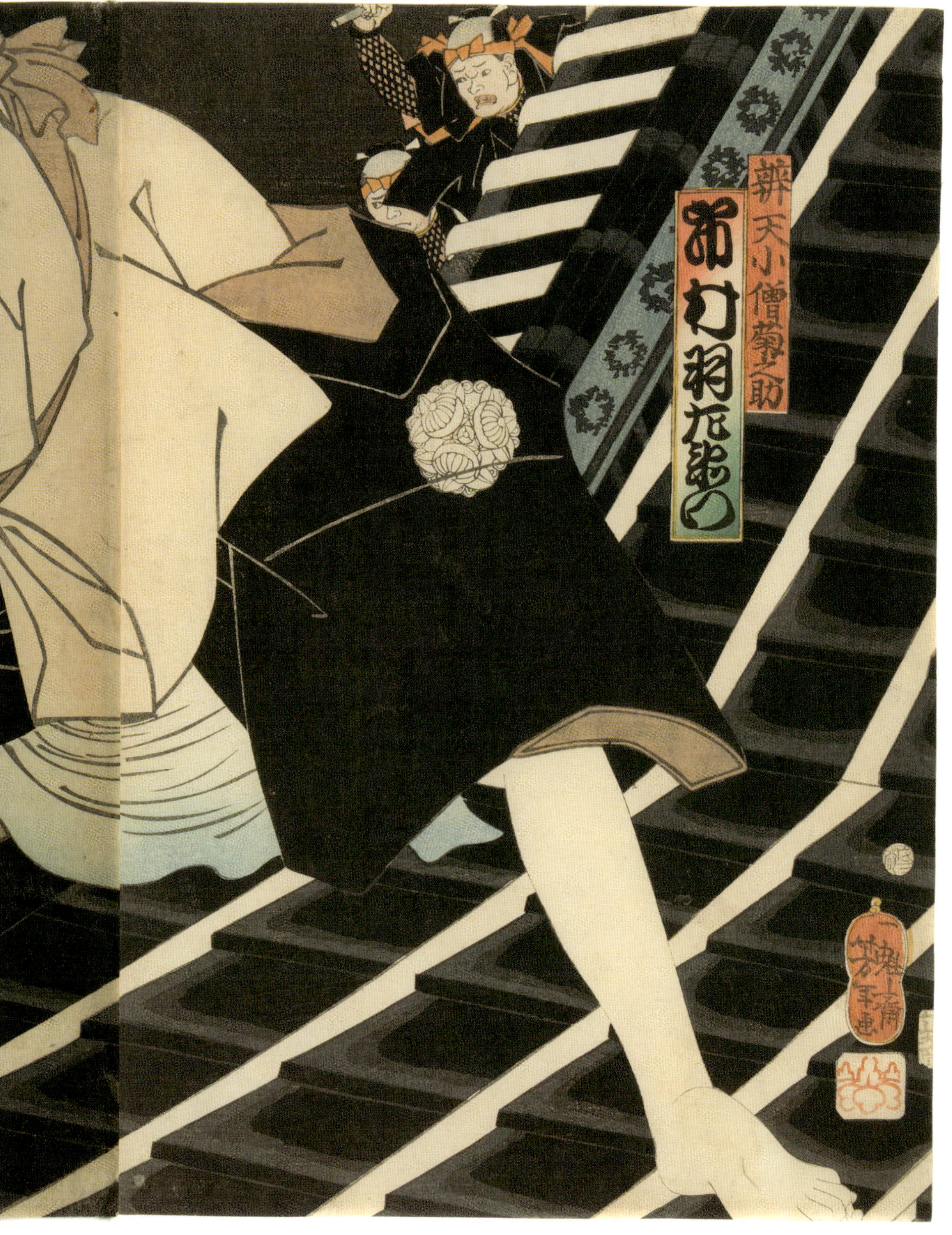

辧天小僧菊之助
市村羽左衛門

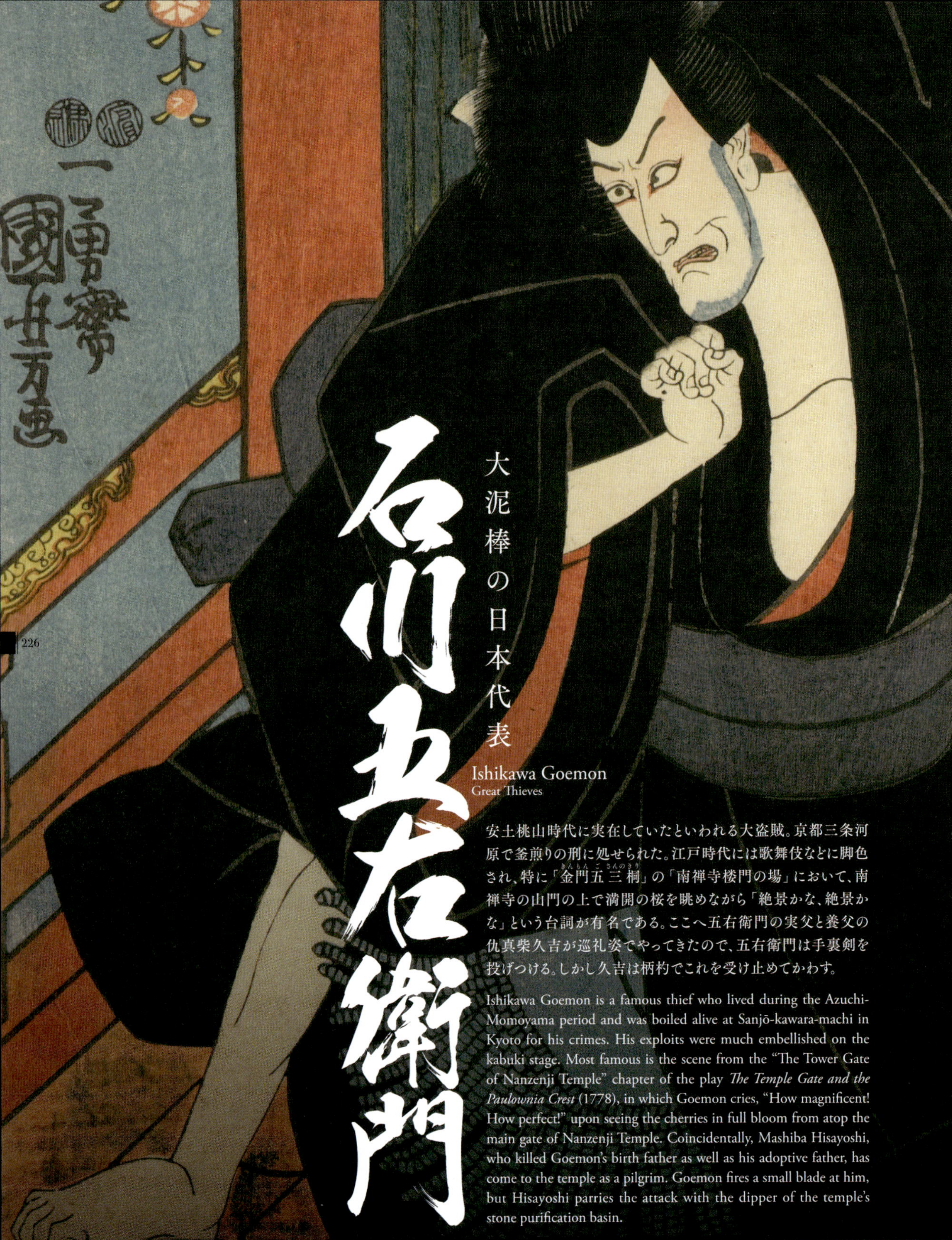

大泥棒の日本代表

石川五右衛門

Ishikawa Goemon
Great Thieves

安土桃山時代に実在していたといわれる大盗賊。京都三条河原で釜煎りの刑に処せられた。江戸時代には歌舞伎などに脚色され、特に「金門五三桐」の「南禅寺楼門の場」において、南禅寺の山門の上で満開の桜を眺めながら「絶景かな、絶景かな」という台詞が有名である。ここへ五右衛門の実父と養父の仇真柴久吉が巡礼姿でやってきたので、五右衛門は手裏剣を投げつける。しかし久吉は柄杓でこれを受け止めてかわす。

Ishikawa Goemon is a famous thief who lived during the Azuchi-Momoyama period and was boiled alive at Sanjō-kawara-machi in Kyoto for his crimes. His exploits were much embellished on the kabuki stage. Most famous is the scene from the "The Tower Gate of Nanzenji Temple" chapter of the play *The Temple Gate and the Paulownia Crest* (1778), in which Goemon cries, "How magnificent! How perfect!" upon seeing the cherries in full bloom from atop the main gate of Nanzenji Temple. Coincidentally, Mashiba Hisayoshi, who killed Goemon's birth father as well as his adoptive father, has come to the temple as a pilgrim. Goemon fires a small blade at him, but Hisayoshi parries the attack with the dipper of the temple's stone purification basin.

【浜真砂長久御摂 南禅寺山門の場】歌川国芳 嘉永4年（1851）
ギャラリー紅屋収蔵
"From the Main Gate at Nanzenji Temple" by Utagawa Kuniyoshi,
Gallery Beniya Collection

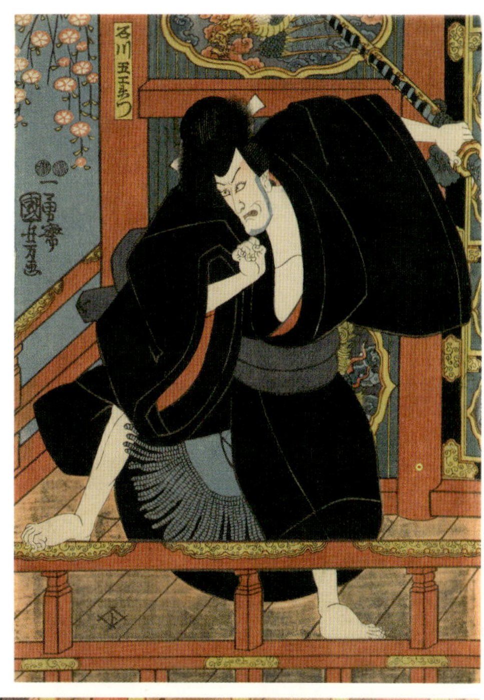

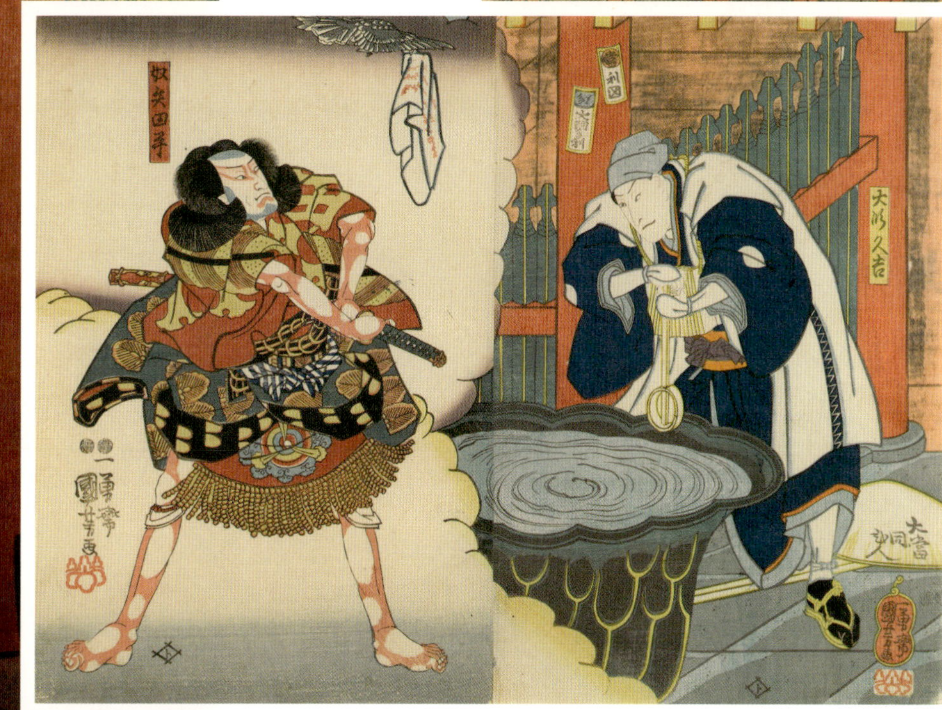

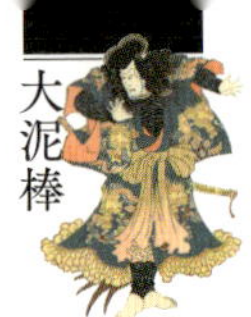

【清書七いろは ふたつともゑ 石川五右衛門】歌川国貞（三代豊国）安政3年（1856）

藤の森明神にて捕手を相手に立ち回りを繰り広げる。

"Seven Variations of the Iroha Alphabet: Ishikawa Goemon and the Double Tomoe"
by Utagawa Kunisada (Toyokuni III)

Goemon grappling with the police at Fujinomori Myōjin Shrine.

【石川五右衛門 中村芝翫】歌川国貞（三代豊国）文久2年（1862）

月代の伸びきった大百日鬘に、黒天鵞絨の褞袍といういでたちがトレードマーク。

"Ishikawa Goemon, as played by Nakamura Shikan" by Utagawa Kunisada (Toyokuni III)

A grown-out sakayaki hairdo (with the pate unshaven and the topknot wild) in the form of a shaggy ōbyakunichi wig,
along with a black velvet padded kimono, are the trademarks of Ishikawa Goemon's costume.

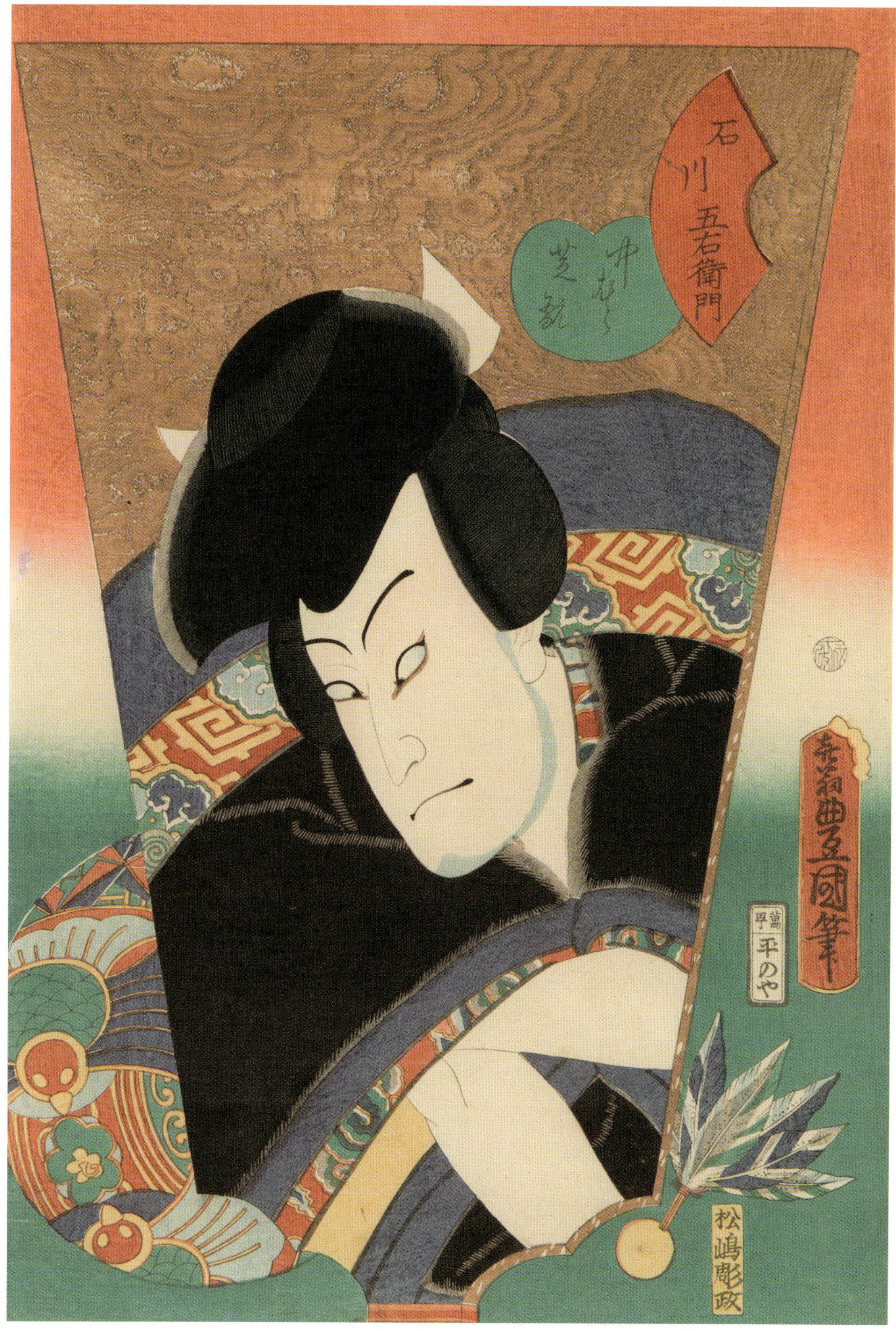

石川五右衛門
なかむら芝翫
昔話曲豆國筆
昔噺 平のや
松嶋彫政

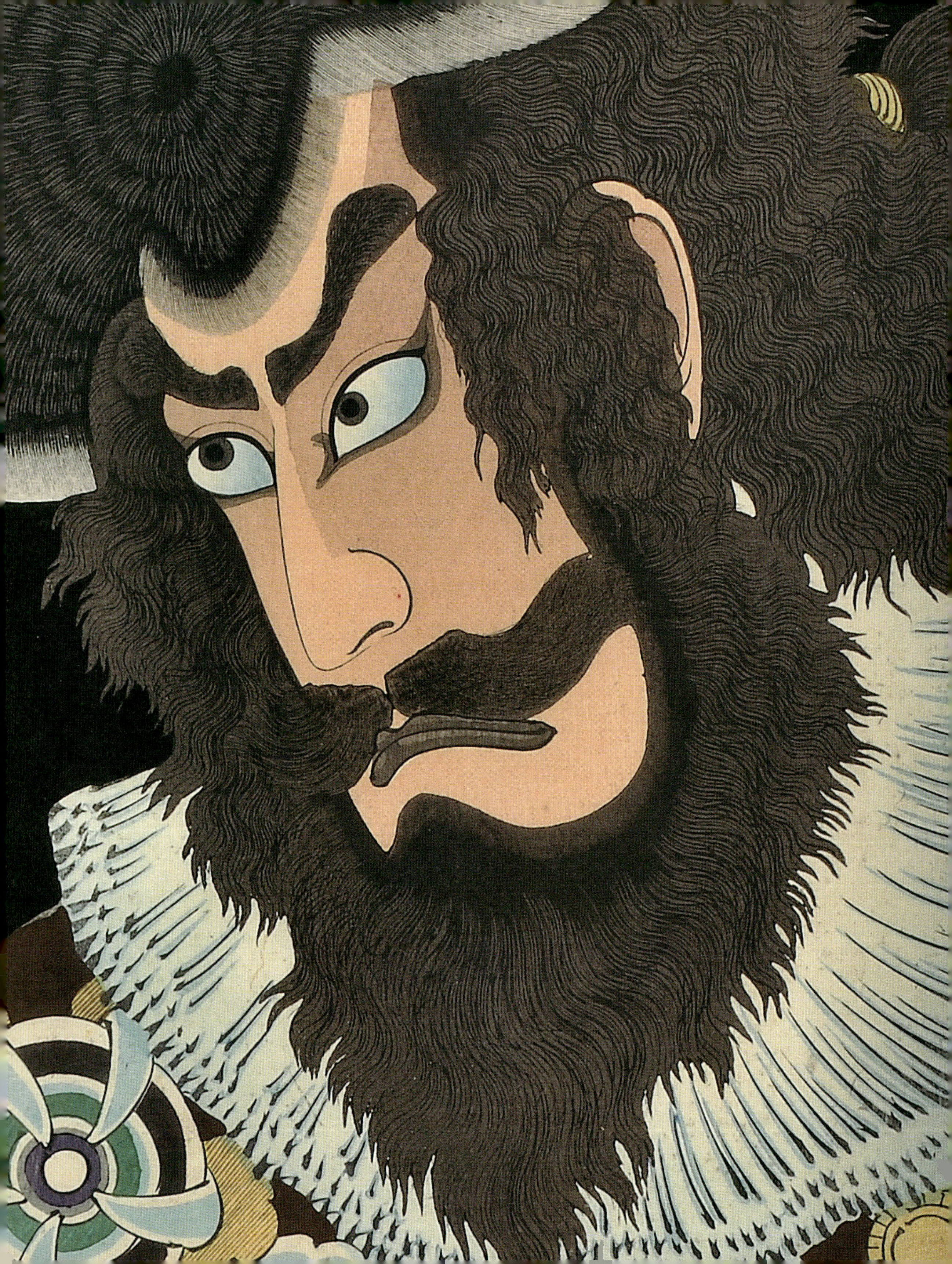

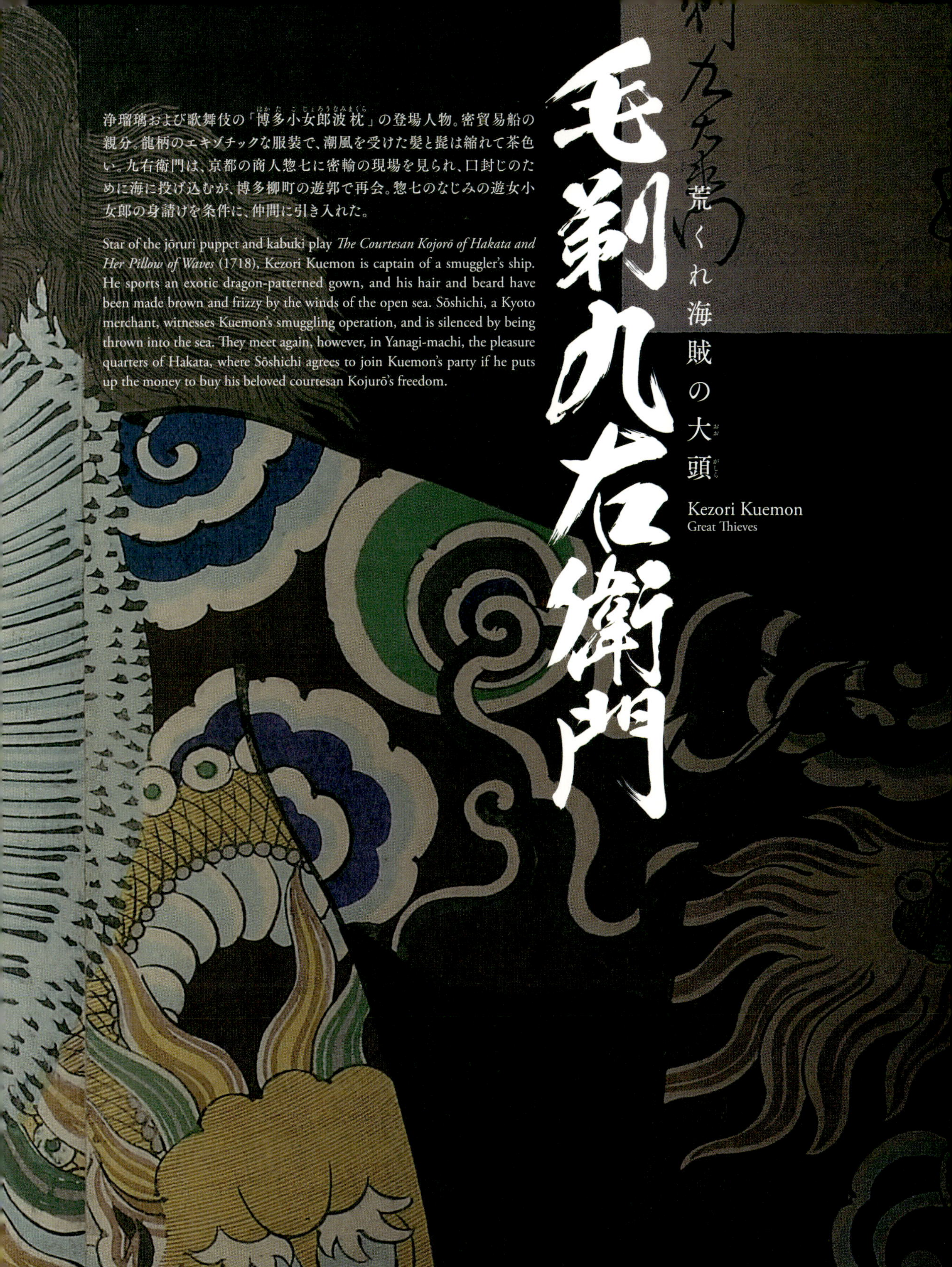

浄瑠璃および歌舞伎の「博多小女郎波枕」の登場人物。密貿易船の親分。龍柄のエキゾチックな服装で、潮風を受けた髪と髭は縮れて茶色い。九右衛門は、京都の商人惣七に密輸の現場を見られ、口封じのために海に投げ込むが、博多柳町の遊郭で再会。惣七のなじみの遊女小女郎の身請けを条件に、仲間に引き入れた。

Star of the jōruri puppet and kabuki play *The Courtesan Kojorō of Hakata and Her Pillow of Waves* (1718), Kezori Kuemon is captain of a smuggler's ship. He sports an exotic dragon-patterned gown, and his hair and beard have been made brown and frizzy by the winds of the open sea. Sōshichi, a Kyoto merchant, witnesses Kuemon's smuggling operation, and is silenced by being thrown into the sea. They meet again, however, in Yanagi-machi, the pleasure quarters of Hakata, where Sōshichi agrees to join Kuemon's party if he puts up the money to buy his beloved courtesan Kojurō's freedom.

荒くれ海賊 の大頭

毛剃九右衛門

Kezori Kuemon
Great Thieves

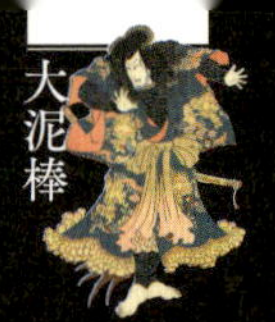

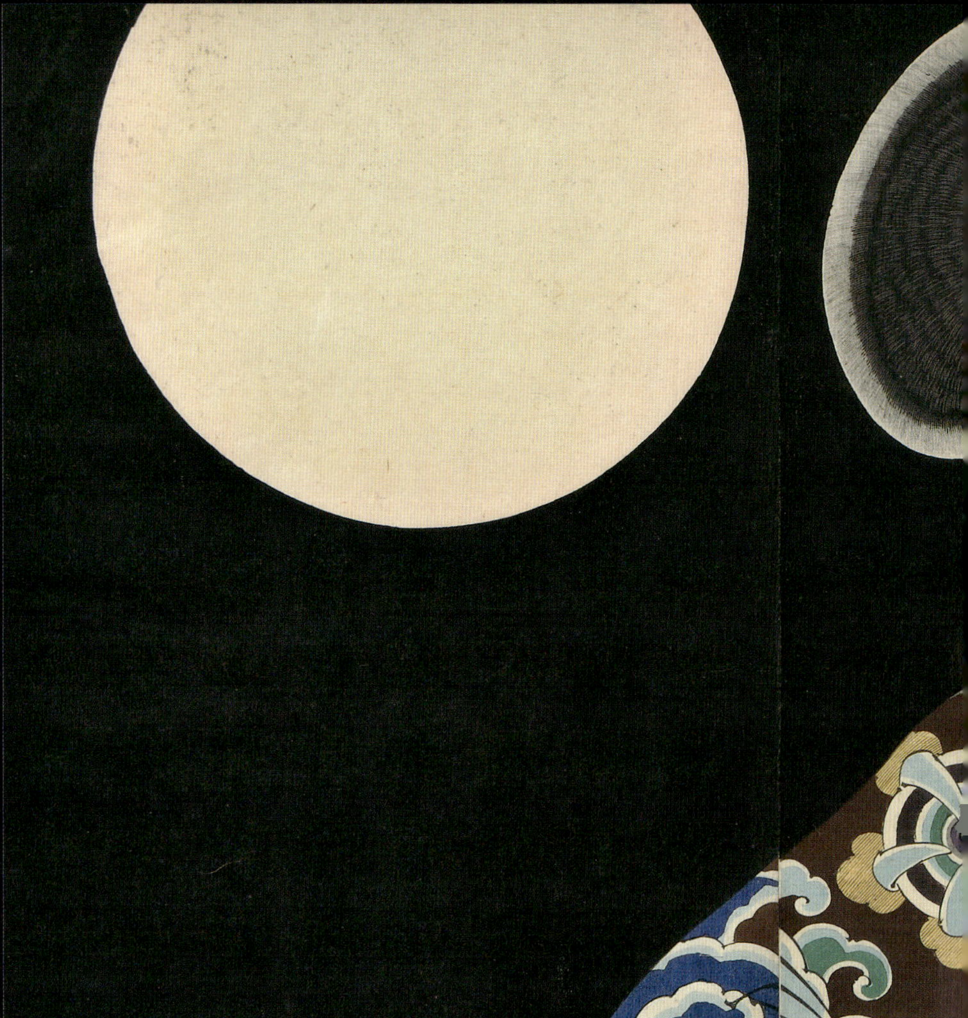

232

【雪月花の内 月 市川三升 毛剃九右衛門】月岡芳年 明治23年（1890）
満月の夜、文字ケ関の海上で汐の流れを見ようと、一人舳に仁王立ちする久右衛門。

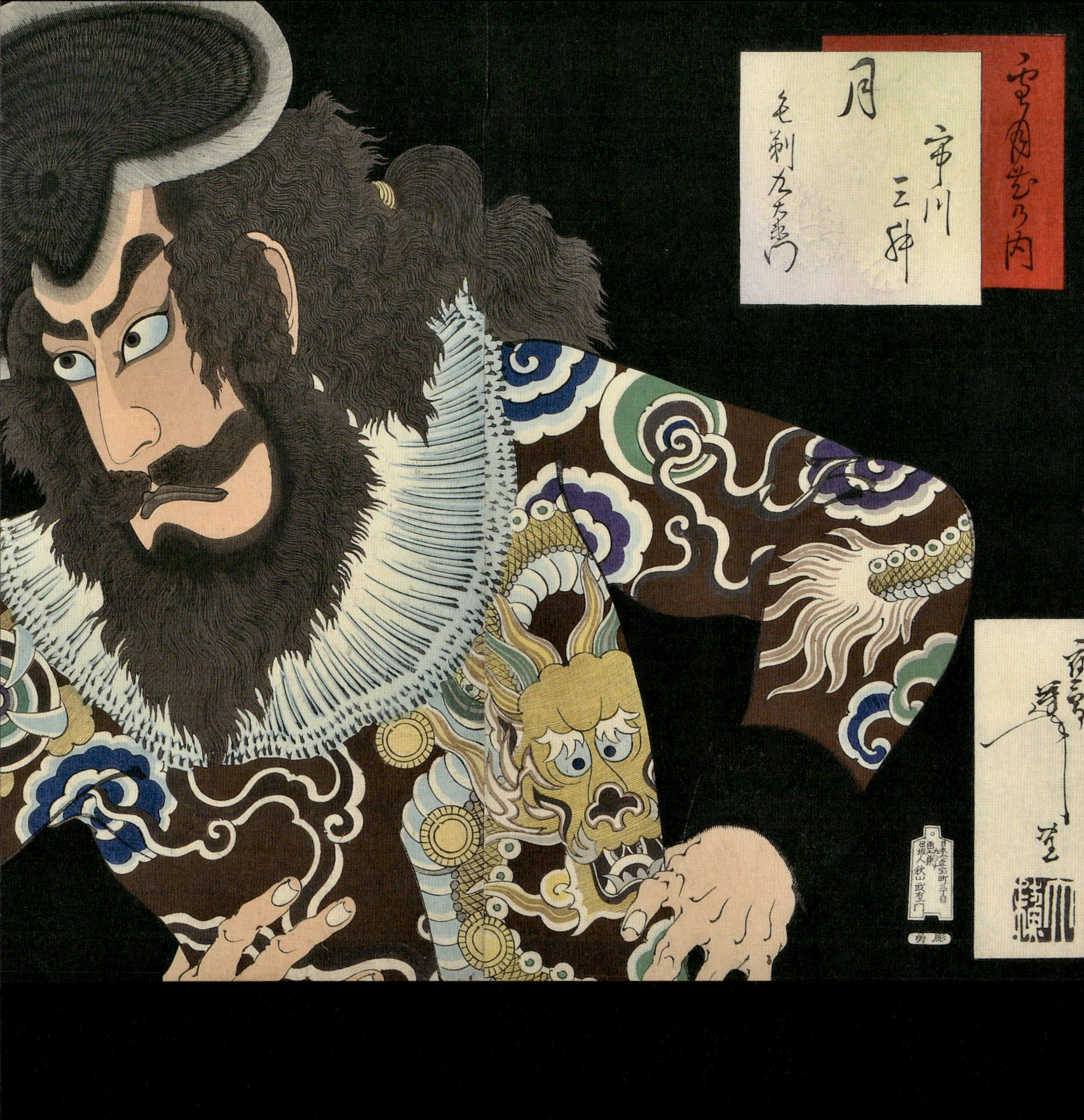

"Snow, Moon, and Flowers: Kezori Kuemon, as played by Ichikawa Sanshō" by Tsukioka Yoshitoshi

Standing boldly like a Buddhist guardian demon on the prow of his ship, Kuemon watches the tide of Shimonoseki Straits from Mojigaseki under the light of a full moon.

作品目録

Index

絵師解説

葛飾北斎

宝暦10年（1760）～嘉永2年（1849）。江戸後期の浮世絵師。
号は画狂人など。春章門人。名所絵など様々な分野で活躍。
代表作は「富嶽三十六景」。

勝川春亭

生年未詳～文政7年（1824）。江戸後期の浮世絵師。号は松高斎など。
春英門人。武者絵の礎を築く。

歌川国貞（三代豊国）

天明6年（1786）～元治元年（1864）。江戸後期の浮世絵師。号は五渡亭など。初代豊国
門人。のちに豊国を襲名。役者絵、美人画を得意とする。

歌川貞秀

文化4年（1807）～明治11、12年（1878、79）頃。
江戸後期～明治初期の浮世絵師。号は五雲亭など。国貞門人。
鳥瞰図による風景画を得意とする。

豊原国周

天保6年（1835）～明治33年（1900）。江戸末期～明治中期の浮世絵師。
号は一鴬斎など。長谷川派豊原周信、国貞（三代豊国）門人。役者絵、美人画を得意とする。

歌川広重

寛政9年（1797）～安政5年（1858）。江戸後期の浮世絵師。号は一立斎など。
豊広門人。名所絵の第一人者。代表作は「東海道五十三次之内」。

歌川国芳

寛政9年（1797）～文久元年（1861）。江戸後期の浮世絵師。号は一勇斎など。
初代豊国門人。武者絵の第一人者。

歌川芳艶

文政5年（1822）～慶応2年（1866）。江戸後期の浮世絵師。号は一英斎など。
国芳門人。武者絵を得意とする。

月岡芳年

天保10年（1839）～明治25年（1892）。江戸末期～明治前期の浮世絵師。
号は大蘇など。国芳門人。武者絵、歴史画を得意とする。

楊斎延一

明治5年（1872）～昭和19年（1944）。明治中後期の浮世絵師。
周延門人。美人画、歴史画、戦争画を得意とする。

歌川豊宣

安政6年（1859）～明治19年（1886）。
明治中期の浮世絵師。国貞（三代豊国）の孫。一陽斎を号す。武者絵を得意とする。

寿双々忠清（十四代長谷川勘兵衛）

弘化4年（1847）～昭和4年（1929）。
歌舞伎大道具師。舞台の仕掛けを工夫し、名人とうたわれた。また、役者絵を得意とする。

歌川芳盛

天保元年（1830）～明治18年（1885）。
江戸末期～明治中期の浮世絵師。号は一光斎など。武者絵を得意とする。

幸斎拱一

生没年不詳。北溪門人の溪里と同一人物か。

Notes on Artists

Katsushika Hokusai (1760-1849). *Ukiyo-e* artist of the late Edo period. One of the pseudonyms (*gō*) he used was Gakyōjin, the Madman of Art. Pupil of Shunshō. Active in various genres including landscapes (*meisho-e*). His best-known work is *Thirty-Six Views of Mount Fuji.*

Katsukawa Shuntei (-1824). *Ukiyo-e* artist of the late Edo period. One of the pseudonym (*gō*) he used was Shōkōsai. Pupil of Shun'ei. Pioneer of the warrior print genre (*musha-e*).

Utagawa Kunisada (also known as Utagawa Toyokuni III) (1786-1864). *Ukiyo-e* artist of the late Edo period. One of the pseudonyms (*gō*) he used was Gototei. Pupil of Toyokuni I. He later succeeded to the name Toyokuni. Specialized in kabuki actor prints (*yakusha-e*) and depictions of beautiful women (*bijin-ga*).

Utagawa Sadahide (1807-1878 or 1879). *Ukiyo-e* artist of the late Edo to early Meiji period. One of the pseudonyms (*gō*) he used was Gountei. Pupil of Kunisada. Specialized in landscape painting from a bird's eye view.

Toyohara Kunichika (1835-1900). *Ukiyo-e* artist from the end of the Edo to the mid-Meiji period. One of the pseudonyms (*gō*) he used was Ichiōsai. Pupil of Toyohara Chikanobu of the Hasegawa school, and Toyokuni III (Kunisada). Specialized in kabuki actor prints (*yakusha-e*) and depictions of beautiful women (*bijin-ga*).

Utagawa Hiroshige (1797-1859). *Ukiyo-e* artist of the late Edo period. One of the pseudonyms (*gō*) he used was Ichiryūsai. Pupil of Toyohiro. The foremost painter of *meisho-e* (pictures of famous places). His best-known work is the series *The Fifty-Three Stations of the Tōkaidō.*

Utagawa Kuniyoshi (1797-1861). *Ukiyo-e* artist of the late Edo period. One of the pseudonyms (*gō*) he used was Ichiyūsai. Pupil of Toyokuni I. The foremost painter of *musha-e* (pictures of warriors).

Utagawa Yoshitsuya (1822-1866). *Ukiyo-e* artist of the late Edo period. One of the pseudonyms (*gō*) he used was Ichieisai. Pupil of Kuniyoshi. Specialized in *musha-e* (pictures of warriors).

Tsukioka Yoshitoshi (1839-1892). *Ukiyo-e* artist of the late Edo to early Meiji period. One of the pseudonyms (*gō*) he used was Taiso. Pupil of Kuniyoshi. Specialized in *musha-e* (warrior prints) and *rekishi-ga* (depictions of famous historical scenes).

Yōsai Nobukazu (1872-1944). A printmaker of the mid Meiji period. A student of Yōshū Chikanobu, he specialized in images of beautiful women, historical themes, and contemporary wars.

Utagawa Toyonobu (1859-1886). A printmaker of the mid Meiji period. He was the grandson of Utagawa Kunisada (Toyokuni III) and also went by the name Ichiyōsai. He was famed for his warrior prints.

Jusōsō Tadakiyo (Hasegawa Kanbee XIV) (1839-1892). Professionally a set engineer for the kabuki theatre, known for his ingenious stage mechanisms, he also excelled at designing actor prints.

Utagawa Yoshimori (1830-1885). A printmaker from the late Edo to mid Meiji periods, among his other pennames was Ikkōsai. He is known for his warrior prints.

Kōsai Kyōichi (birth and death unknown). Some believe that he is the same person as Keiri, a student of Totoya Hokkei.

About *Ukiyo-e*

Three hundred and fifty odd years ago, in the early Edo period the art of *ukiyo-e* was born in Japan (Edo). *Ukiyo-e* referred to pictures (*e*) drawn of *ukiyo* (the "floating world"), or the lifestyle and scenes of the day. Unlike more upmarket works of art, *ukiyo-e* prints were readily available to the general population. *Ukiyo-e* were mostly woodblock prints, so it was possible to print the same picture as many times as desired, and they were a creative collaboration between the artist (*e-shi*) who drew the original picture, the engraver (*hori-shi)* who made the printing plate, the printer (*suri-shi*) who applied colour and rubbed to print, and the publisher who published them. There are also *ukiyo-e* painted by artists directly onto paper or silk, of which there is only one original in existence.

Even today many *ukiyo-e* artists are famous and popular, such as Utamaro, Hokusai, Sharaku, Toyokuni, Hiroshige, Kuniyoshi, and many more.

These artists provided entertainment through drawings of popular kabuki actors, scenes from the town, and the everyday life of ordinary people... what would now be called celebrity Instagrams, tourist guide books, and *manga* (comics). These days, it is easy to find out what is going on in the world through television and the internet, but back in those days, *ukiyo-e* played a major role as an important source of information on entertainment and fashions.

Once more unto the breach
Samurai Warriors and Heroes in *Ukiyo-e* Masterpieces

Supervisor:
Ei Nakau

Text:
Noriko Yamamoto

Translation:
Ryan Holmberg

Photo credits:
Nakau Collection, Gallery Beniya, Nishii Collection, Asahina Bunko, Toshihiko Isao

Editorial Design:
Minoru Mamata (rocka graphica)

Editor:
Yoshiyuki Oba

Editorial Assistant:
Rina Tanaka (Hiyoko-sha)

Special Thanks
Artone Co., Ltd.

PIE International Inc.
2-32-4 Minami-Otsuka, Toshima-ku, Tokyo 170-0005 JAPAN
international@pie.co.jp

©2019 Ei Nakau / PIE International
ISBN978-4-7562-5283-8
Printed in Japan

浮世絵とは

　今から350年ほど前の江戸時代初期、日本（江戸）で「浮世絵」は誕生しました。浮世絵とは、浮き世（今とき）の生活や風景を描いた絵のことです。多くが木版画で何枚も同じ絵柄を摺ることができ、元の絵を描く絵師と、版を作る彫師と、色を摺り上げる摺師と、それを出版する版元との共同作業で作られました。浮世絵版画は、高級な芸術品と違って、庶民が気軽に買うことができました。絵師（画家）が紙や絹に直接描いたこの世に1点しか存在しない肉筆画の浮世絵もあります。

　歌麿、北斎、写楽、豊国、広重、国芳など、今でも人気があり有名な浮世絵師がたくさん登場しました。

　彼らは、人気のある歌舞伎役者を描いたり、町の風景を描いたり、庶民の日常生活を描いたり…今で言う人気スターのブロマイド、観光ガイドブック、漫画として、人々に娯楽を提供していたのです。今はテレビやネットで世界中の情報を知ることができますが、当時は浮世絵がその手段として、お芝居や流行の情報を得る、貴重な情報源になっていました。

主要参考文献

三田村鳶魚校訂『仇討小説集』1929年、博文館

曲亭馬琴著・和田万吉校訂『椿説弓張月』上・中・下、1930-31年、岩波書店

井上和雄編『浮世絵師伝』1931年、渡邊版画店

施耐庵著・駒田信二訳『水滸伝』上・中・下、1967-68年、平凡社

原色浮世絵大百科事典編集委員会編『原色浮世絵大百科事典』2、1982年、大修館

藤元元著・板垣俊一校訂『前太平記』上・下、1988-89年、国書刊行会

高島俊夫著『水滸伝人物事典』1999年、講談社

馬淵和夫、国東文麿、稲垣泰一校注・訳『今昔物語集』3-4、2001-02年、小学館

曲亭馬琴著・濱田啓介校訂『南総里見八犬伝』2、2003年、新潮社

国際浮世絵学会編『浮世絵大事典』2008年、東京堂出版

岩切友里子監修『没後150年 歌川国芳展』2011年、日本経済新聞社

中右瑛監修『北斎 世界を魅了する浮世絵師と弟子たち』2013年、芸艸堂

【浮世絵でみる！英雄豪傑図鑑】

2019年11月16日　初版第1刷発行
2024年　1月16日　第2刷発行

監修　中右瑛

テキスト　山本野理子

資料協力　中右コレクション
　　　　　ギャラリー紅屋
　　　　　西井コレクション
　　　　　朝比奈文庫
　　　　　蒽俊彦

デザイン　眞々田 稔（ホンマチ組版）

協力　株式会社アートワン

編集　大場義行

編集協力　田中里奈（ヒヨコ舎）

発行人　三芳寛要

発行元　株式会社パイ インターナショナル
　　　　〒170-0005　東京都豊島区南大塚2−32−4
　　　　TEL. 03-3944-3981　FAX. 03-5395-4830
　　　　sales@pie.co.jp

印刷・製本　株式会社広済堂ネクスト

©2019 Ei Nakau / PIE International
ISBN978-4-7562-5266-1 C0071
Printed in Japan

本書の収録内容の無断転載・複写・複製等を禁じます。
ご注文、乱丁・落丁本の交換等に関するお問い合わせは、小社までご連絡ください。

［カバーイラスト］宮本武蔵の鯨退治　ギャラリー紅屋 収蔵